Pro Oracle Fusion Applications

Installation and Administration

Tushar Thakker

Apress®

Pro Oracle Fusion Applications

Tushar Thakker
Param Labs
Dubai, United Arab Emirates

ISBN-13 (pbk): 978-1-4842-0984-4   ISBN-13 (electronic): 978-1-4842-0983-7
DOI 10.1007/978-1-4842-0983-7

Library of Congress Control Number: 2015949704

Managing Editor: Welmoed Spahr
Lead Editor: Jonathan Gennick
Development Editor: Douglas Pundick
Technical Reviewer: Dhananjay Papde
Editorial Board: Steve Anglin, Mark Beckner, Gary Cornell, Louise Corrigan, Jim DeWolf, Jonathan Gennick, Robert Hutchinson, Michelle Lowman, James Markham, Susan McDermott, Matthew Moodie, Jeffrey Pepper, Douglas Pundick, Ben Renow-Clarke, Gwenan Spearing, Matt Wade, Steve Weiss
Coordinating Editor: Jill Balzano
Copy Editor: Kezia Endsley
Compositor: SPi Global
Indexer: SPi Global
Artist: SPi Global
Cover Designer: Anna Ishchenko

Distributed to the book trade worldwide by Springer Science+Business Media New York, 233 Spring Street, 6th Floor, New York, NY 10013. Phone 1-800-SPRINGER, fax (201) 348-4505, e-mail orders-ny@springer-sbm.com, or visit www.springeronline.com. Apress Media, LLC is a California LLC and the sole member (owner) is Springer Science + Business Media Finance Inc (SSBM Finance Inc). SSBM Finance Inc is a Delaware corporation.

For information on translations, please e-mail rights@apress.com, or visit www.apress.com.

Apress and friends of ED books may be purchased in bulk for academic, corporate, or promotional use. eBook versions and licenses are also available for most titles. For more information, reference our Special Bulk Sales–eBook Licensing web page at www.apress.com/bulk-sales.

Any source code or other supplementary material referenced by the author in this text is available to readers at www.apress.com. For detailed information about how to locate your book's source code, go to www.apress.com/source-code/.

Printed on acid-free paper

Dedicated to my parents, my beautiful wife Dipti and our beloved son Param.

About IOUG Press

*IOUG Press is a joint effort by the **Independent Oracle Users Group (the IOUG)** and **Apress** to deliver some of the highest-quality content possible on Oracle Database and related topics. The IOUG is the world's leading, independent organization for professional users of Oracle products. Apress is a leading, independent technical publisher known for developing high-quality, no-fluff content for serious technology professionals. The IOUG and Apress have joined forces in IOUG Press to provide the best content and publishing opportunities to working professionals who use Oracle products.*

Our shared goals include:

- Developing content with excellence
- Helping working professionals to succeed
- Providing authoring and reviewing opportunities
- Networking and raising the profiles of authors and readers

To learn more about Apress, visit our website at **www.apress.com**. Follow the link for IOUG Press to see the great content that is now available on a wide range of topics that matter to those in Oracle's technology sphere.

Visit **www.ioug.org** to learn more about the Independent Oracle Users Group and its mission. Consider joining if you haven't already. Review the many benefits at www.ioug.org/join. Become a member. Get involved with peers. Boost your career.

www.ioug.org/join

apress®

Contents at a Glance

Contents

About the Author

Tushar Thakker is a Senior Oracle Architect and an avid technology blogger. He is a Certified Oracle Apps DBA and Project Management Professional (PMP). He has more than 13 years of experience working on various Oracle products with some of the top technology giants, including Oracle and EMC as well as government organizations in India and UAE. Tushar is the founder of a technology startup called Param Labs and the well-known Oracle education blog OraTraining.com, where he writes a number of step-by-step guides for various Oracle products and their new releases. He also runs a free Oracle troubleshooting portal named OraSupport.com, where he resolves any Oracle-related issues faced by users. Tushar believes in spreading Oracle knowledge to as many people as possible, hence creating a larger Oracle user community.

About the Technical Reviewer

Dhananjay Papde has extensive IT experience on Oracle databases, the E-Business Suite, and BI. He is a lead specialist and Oracle Technical Architect at SITA in the UK. He is the author of *Oracle Enterprise Manager 12c Administration Cookbook* and was also the technical Reviewer of the book entitled *Pro Oracle Fusion Applications: Installation and Administration.* He is an Oracle ACE Associate and won the Oracle Fusion Middleware Innovation Award at Oracle Open World 2011. He has been a speaker at various events, including Oracle Open World 2013, 2014, UKOUG Annual Conferences in 2012, Tech13, Apps14 and SIG, and Oracle Data Innovation Forum in London and Dublin.

Acknowledgments

This book couldn't have been conceptualized without the overwhelming support from the users of my blog OraTraining.com, who recognized my efforts in bringing Oracle Fusion Applications knowledge to everyone at the time when there were limited online resources available. The feedback from my blog users, along with their success stories, encouraged me to spread the knowledge to a larger audience through this book.

I would like to thank my friend Anil Passi (founder of apps2fusion.com and author of several Oracle Applications books) for encouraging me to write this book. I sincerely thank the entire Apress Editorial team, especially Jonathan Gennick who gave me an opportunity to write this book, Douglas Pundick who guided me in every aspect of this project by providing best practices for authors, Jill Balzano who has been tremendously helpful throughout the book by answering all my queries in detail, and Dhanajay Papde who carefully reviewed all the chapters and provided accurate technical suggestions from an existing Oracle Applications Administrator's point of view. I must also thank all those who have helped directly or indirectly in my career to reach this stage, including but not limited to Raj Adigal, Palani Ramasamy, Banakar Basavaraj, Gautam Thakkar, Dr. Sabri Al Azazi, Jose Jayapal, and Rochak Puri.

Last but not the least, this book would not have been complete without exceptional support from my dear wife Dipti and our little son Param, who allowed me to spend countless days focusing on Oracle Fusion Applications when it was in its early stages as well as while writing this book despite the constant humming of the servers at home which hosted the Fusion Applications instance for this book. At the same time, the constant encouragement from my parents to learn from failure helped me stay strong through a number of challenges while installing initial versions of Fusion Applications on modest hardware.

Introduction

Oracle Fusion Applications is an evolving product and at present has matured enough for Oracle customers to start implementing it or plan their applications roadmap accordingly. Lately there have been many new projects kicking off and the curiosity toward Oracle Fusion Applications is constantly increasing. Since Oracle is investing heavily in Oracle Fusion Applications development and marketing, having this essential installation and administration book with practical tips will boost your confidence when building an on-premise implementation of Fusion Applications. This book will prove to be a must-have handbook for anyone planning an implementation of Oracle Fusion Applications.

How This Book Came About

I started working on Oracle Fusion Applications installation since its early releases and I can assure you that the installation process has evolved and improved a lot since then. After successfully completing the Fusion Applications installation on various releases, I noticed that a large number of users were facing difficulties in the provisioning process due to the complexity involved as well as because there was no step-by-step handbook available at that time. I started helping a large number of Fusion Applications aspirants through my blog and it was fulfilling to see a number of blog users successfully completing the tedious process of Fusion Applications installation using my step-by-step guides. Based on their success stories, I decided to share my experiences with a large number of readers using this comprehensive book.

Most of the examples in this book are from actual installations. I have been supporting a very large number of Fusion Applications aspirants during their Fusion Applications installation and helping them with various issues reported by them during provisioning process.

What You Will Learn

- Understand the Fusion Applications architecture and how it maps to your physical infrastructure

- Design network and storage topologies to support your installation

- Provision Identity Management to control and manage the applications access

- Provision an Oracle Fusion Applications environment

- Manage those environments on an ongoing basis

- Identify, diagnose, and resolve the day-to-day problems

- Understand types of Fusion Applications patches and various methods to apply them on a regular basis

Who This Book Is For

Oracle Fusion Applications is one of the most anticipated knowledge upgrades for most professionals in the Oracle Applications domain. *Pro Oracle Fusion Applications* is aimed at following the audience as well as all those who are involved in the technical aspects of standing up an on-premise installation of Oracle Fusion Applications. This includes:

- Oracle Database Administrators and Applications DBAs

- WebLogic Administrators

- Oracle Identity Management Administrators

- System Architects

- Technical consultants

- Application Implementers and Administrators

- Oracle Partners and System Integrators

- End-user clients planning to implement Oracle Fusion Applications

How This Book Is Structured

Pro Oracle Fusion Applications is organized into 16 chapters divided in four main sections. The book begins with an introduction to Oracle Fusion Applications followed by planning for the installation. Later it explains the end-to-end installation process followed by the day-to-day administration of the installed environment. In order to maintain the logical flow of the content, it is strongly recommended that you read the chapters in the given order.

Part I Introduction

Chapter 1: Introduction to Oracle Fusion Applications

We will begin with introducing Oracle Fusion Applications and the product families included in the suite along with their adoption options for new as well as existing Oracle customers. Later we will explain the Fusion Applications architecture along with explaining the key components or building blocks of the Fusion Applications instance, including the Oracle Identity Management infrastructure and how they interact. We will also look at the standard-based business process model and security model of Oracle Fusion Applications.

Part II Planning

Chapter 2: Planning an Installation

We begin this chapter with roles and responsibilities of various individuals involved in the entire process of planning, provisioning, and managing an Oracle Fusion Applications environment. We look at various possible topologies for Oracle Fusion Applications and learn how to choose the best suitable topology and required hardware for a specific installation. You also learn how to plan the required hardware, network, and storage configuration based on your business requirements. You also learn how to calculate the memory requirement for your installation based on the selected product configurations.

Chapter 3: Setting Up the Hosts for Provisioning

In this chapter, we first discuss the concepts of end-to-end Fusion Applications provisioning process. We will explore the role of each physical host of the selected topology and learn how to group them among Identity Management nodes and Fusion Applications nodes. We will discuss the steps involved in the provisioning process along with the dependencies among the steps. Later you will learn how to prepare the selected hosts for provisioning, including required operating system, network, and storage.

Part III Installation

Chapter 4: Creating Identity Management Database

This chapter deals with various options for preparing the Oracle Database to host Identity Management components. We look at installing the Identity Management database, applying required database patches, as well as creating the required schemas using the Repository Creation Utility for Identity Management.

Chapter 5: Preparing for Identity Management Provisioning

In this chapter, we discuss the structure of the Identity Management Provisioning framework and discuss how to install it on all Identity Management hosts of the selected topology. Later we look at the importance of the Identity Management provisioning response file and explore step-by-step instructions on creating them. We look at the importance of each of the parameters being stored while going through the relevant screens during the response file creation.

Chapter 6: Provisioning Identity Management Environment

This chapter provides a step-by-step guide on provisioning an Oracle Identity Management environment, which is a prerequisite for the Fusion Applications installation. We will explore the various graphical as well as command-line interfaces available to provision the Identity Management components. This chapter also explains how to deal with failed Identity Management installations and restart them manually.

Chapter 7: Post-Provisioning Configuration for Identity Management Nodes

This chapter concludes the Identity Management provisioning section by explaining how to validate the installed Identity Management components and perform the post-provisioning configuration for each of these components. These post-provisioning configuration steps prepare the Identity Management environment to be used with any fresh installation of Fusion Applications.

Chapter 8: Creating Fusion Applications Transaction Database

This chapter explains how to prepare the Fusion Applications Transaction database using the provisioning framework provided with the installation repository. We begin with learning how to install the Fusion Applications provisioning framework on the database nodes followed by how to use it to create a fresh transaction database with required patches and updates pre-installed. You also see how to run the Repository Creation Utility to prepare Fusion Applications-related schemas.

Chapter 9: Preparing for Fusion Applications Provisioning

This is a very important chapter before we look at the actual provisioning process since it deals with preparing the Fusion Applications provisioning response file. During the response file creation we explore all the important parameters required for setting up an Oracle Fusion Applications environment. We begin with understanding the directory structure and various options available with the provisioning framework. We prepare a response file based on the selected topology. We also have a look at updating an existing response file as well as creating one for extending an existing Applications environment.

Chapter 10: Provisioning Fusion Applications Environment

In this final chapter of the Fusion Applications installation, we look at the automated installation orchestration using the graphical wizard as well as the command-line interface. We look at the important input files used by the provisioning process as well as various output files, logs, and flags created during the installation which aids us while troubleshooting the installation issues. We also learn how to restart a failed or aborted installation using automated or manual cleanup/restore procedures.

Part IV Administration

Chapter 11: Understanding Fusion Applications Interface

After the installation is complete, we will have a bird's eye view of the applications interface. We learn how Fusion Applications differs from existing Applications Suites in Oracle as well as other vendors and how it provides the most efficient way to perform various tasks from a single consolidated interface. After reading this chapter, you will be able to identify and use many aspects of the interface, including dashboards, navigation icons, and personalization tools. You will also quickly look the Enterprise Scheduler, including learning how it maps with traditional applications suites and how to submit an example scheduled request.

Chapter 12: Getting Started with Administration

From this chapter onward, we begin looking at Fusion Applications administration. First we explore the various methods for starting up or stopping the complete Fusion Applications environment, including the Identity Management components. Later we look at Fusion Applications Functional Setup Manager and how it is one of the most important components for Administrators as well as Application Implementers.

Chapter 13: Managing Fusion Applications Security

Fusion Applications Security Setup is one of the first administration tasks you may need to perform before business users can start using the applications modules. We look at the role-based access control model of Fusion Applications along with various functional and data roles available. This chapter also explains how the roles are stored and synchronized between various Identity Management components. This chapter provides a step-by-step guide to setting up initial IT security-related roles and users.

Chapter 14: Monitoring Fusion Applications Environment

This chapter explains the importance of Oracle Enterprise Manager Cloud Control in managing a complete Fusion Applications environment, which replaces a number of individual Enterprise Managers and dashboards using a single consolidated interface. We look at the steps involved in installing Cloud Control software and it with all the components of Fusion Applications environment. We explore how we can leverage the consolidated interface of Cloud Control for monitoring every layer of Fusion Applications, including database, middleware and web tier. We also see how it compares to traditional monitoring interfaces used in earlier versions of Fusion Applications.

Chapter 15: Diagnosing and Troubleshooting

In this chapter, we discuss some of the most important Fusion Applications' administrative tasks, including diagnosing and troubleshooting various issues. Troubleshooting applications or database issues may involve liaising with multiple teams, including system administrators, network teams, core DBAs, and Identity Management specialists. We look at various steps involved in diagnosing and troubleshooting, including tracing the applications issues at the database level as well as troubleshooting them at the JVM level. This chapter also explains troubleshooting issues with Enterprise Scheduler jobs.

Chapter 16: Patching and Ongoing Administration

This chapters begins by explaining the various types of patches that are available for Fusion Applications environment, including applications and middleware artifacts. We look at the different patching mechanisms or each of these patch types including manual patching as well as patch automation utilities. Later we look at ongoing administration of Fusion Applications, including maintenance of the applications file system as well as database objects. We conclude the chapter by looking at the recommended practices for backing up and restoring the entire Fusion Applications environment.

Errata

Apress makes every effort to make sure that there are no errors in the text or the code. However, to err is human, and as such we recognize the need to keep you informed of any mistakes as they're discovered and corrected. Errata sheets are available for all our books at www.apress.com. If you find an error that hasn't already been reported, please let us know. The Apress web site acts as a focus for other information and support, including the code from all Apress books, sample chapters, previews of forthcoming titles, and articles on related topics.

Contacting the Author

If you have any questions regarding the book, please feel free to contact me directly at the following email address: tushar@paramlabs.com or at Twitter@tusharthakker.

PART I

Introduction

CHAPTER 1

■ ■ ■

Introduction to Oracle Fusion Applications

Oracle Fusion Applications is the next generation enterprise application suite from Oracle Corporation. It is not a new version or a release of Oracle's existing ERP products like E-Business Suite (EBS), PeopleSoft, JD Edwards, or Siebel. It's an entirely new suite of applications built from the ground up using *open standards* encompassing a large number of Oracle components as well as many third-party open source products. Oracle started developing Oracle Fusion Applications in early 2005 and the first release was generally available in late 2011. The adoption of Oracle Fusion Applications is steadily increasing, especially with recent releases. The current release as of the writing of this book is 11.1.9 (Oracle Fusion Applications 11g, Release 9).

There is considerable documentation available on Oracle's web site as well as a few blogs, but the purpose of this book is to provide a consolidated handbook for Oracle Fusion Applications enthusiasts using a simple step-by-step practical approach on the architecture, installation, and day-to-day administration. Since its architecture is fairly complex with a number of technology components involved, it is possible for someone new to Oracle Fusion Applications to feel overwhelmed during the course of learning. But rest assured that once you understand the basic foundation of Oracle Fusion Applications, you will feel confident about your role in implementing and managing Fusion Applications in your organization. The goal of this chapter is to make sure that you have a clear understanding of architectural components even though you may not be an expert in every aspect of the overall design of Fusion Applications.

Overview of Oracle Fusion Applications

It may be a natural question to ask why Oracle needed to build a completely new ERP applications suite from scratch when it already has proven ERP products like Oracle E-Business Suite, PeopleSoft, JD Edwards, Siebel, and so on. What has changed recently that created a need for an all-new set of enterprise applications products? The answer is simple; the technologies used in existing ERP products are becoming outdated and customers' requirements are becoming more and more business- and processes-centric instead of being confined to vendor-specific technologies. With the growth of heterogeneous systems there was a need for building an enterprise applications suite that's built on open standards and uses a service-oriented architecture to allow integration with a vast number of applications and systems.

With the acquisition of PeopleSoft and Siebel, Oracle had access to a large number of new customers. Oracle spent thousands of days working closely with customers and understanding what they needed from the next generation ERP system. Oracle Fusion Applications leverages the best functionalities and processes of E-Business Suite, PeopleSoft, JD Edwards, Siebel, and other Oracle products. The result is a 100% open standard-based applications suite that's future ready.

© Tushar Thakker 2015
T. Thakker, *Pro Oracle Fusion Applications*, DOI 10.1007/978-1-4842-0983-7_1

What's New in Oracle Fusion Applications?

Those who have already worked on other Applications suites, including the Oracle E-Business Suite, must have this common question. What's new in Oracle Fusion Applications and why should I migrate? In this section, we will look at the strategic features of Oracle Fusion Applications that make it unique and the right choice for the future. Oracle Fusion Applications can be distinguished by the following major new changes that it brings to existing application suites.

Deployment Options

Most of the traditional applications suites have on-premise deployment option only, while a few non-Oracle ERP or CRM products have cloud-only options available. Oracle Fusion Applications provides various deployment options based on customers' requirement and policies. Following are the deployment options available with Oracle Fusion Applications.

- *On-Premise*: So far this was the standard deployment strategy for current generation Oracle applications suites, including E-Business Suite, Siebel, and so on. The major differentiator here is the complexity and heavy footprint of the Oracle Fusion Applications environment. Depending on the availability of hardware and resources, this strategy provides maximum control over infrastructure and security. The standard licensing terms apply in this option.

- *Private Cloud*: Provides an intermediate solution between complete control and security of an on-premise setup and the flexibility of a public cloud. Organizations that are not yet prepared to move their transaction data outside their firewall but would like to leverage the benefits of the cloud can opt for private cloud setup, which can be managed by their own team or by a third party. Since the applications are specific to the organization, the customer needs to procure licenses instead of using a user-based subscription.

- *Public Cloud/SaaS*: Oracle has introduced Fusion Applications in a cloud or SaaS (Software as a Service) model on a subscription basis. The complete application infrastructure is managed by the Oracle or SaaS provider and the customer has only its data on a shared infrastructure. This provides a faster go live option but with less control over the infrastructure.

- *Hybrid*: Some organizations opt for a mix of these options for different application families and gradually plan to migrate to either deployment option depending on their confidence level with a particular deployment option.

Take a look at which factors influence the selection of a particular deployment strategy. Figure 1-1 provides the basic idea of the decision-making process. There may be other factors also, but these are primary ones.

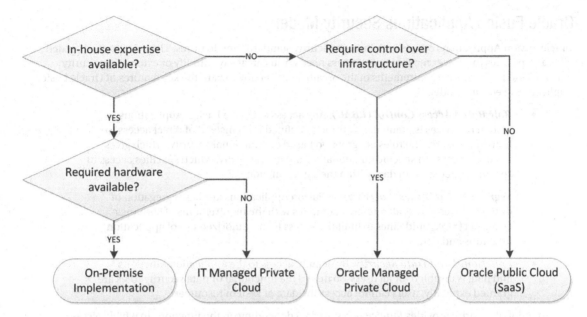

Figure 1-1. *Decision-making process for Oracle Fusion Applications deployment strategy*

Standard-Based Architecture

Enterprises can no longer afford to be tied up with proprietary standards of application suites built more than a decade ago. Oracle Fusion Applications has been built using open standards and service-oriented architecture to make sure that it integrates seamlessly with existing business applications. It also facilitates the migration to Oracle Fusion Applications or coexistence along with existing application modules.

Oracle Fusion Applications has Oracle Fusion Middleware at its foundation. We will discuss the components of Oracle Fusion Middleware later in this chapter. The reason behind opting for open standards is not surprising. With an increasing number of applications products, organizations need a number of resources to manage proprietary methods. Having open standards such as Java, XML (Extensible Markup Language), BPEL (Business Process Execution Language), and service-oriented architectures makes it easy to find talent for UI, metadata, workflows, and web services development. This also reduces the integration cost and time to implement or extend the features.

Business Process Model

Oracle has reengineered the design of the application suite by focusing on the Business Process Model. Oracle has consolidated the best practices from E-Business Suite, Siebel, PeopleSoft, and JD Edwards applications and from customers' processes into the design of Oracle Fusion Applications. The Business Process Model classifies each task into five levels. The last level in the hierarchy defines the actual function or task while the remaining four levels map to the Business Process or activity.

- Level 0 (L0): Industry
- Level 1 (L1): Business Process Area
- Level 2 (L2): Business Process
- Level 3 (L3): Activity
- Level 4 (L4): Task

Oracle Fusion Applications Security Model

Oracle Fusion Applications comes with built-in security standards and features. There are several seeded roles and policies that cover most of the business needs. You can always modify or extend the security policies based on security requirements of the organization. Following are the key features of Oracle Fusion Applications Security Model.

- *Role Based Access Control (RBAC)*: Any access to Oracle Fusion Applications system resources is granted only through defined roles instead of direct access to individual users. The roles are grouped based on functional security, which gives the users access to specific functionality, and data security, which specifies access to specific dimensions of data within the same function.

- *Segregation of Duties (SoD)*: Oracle Fusion Applications applies segregation of duties policies across all roles and complies with the requirements of Sarbanes-Oxley Act (SOX) guidelines to limit the access to unauthorized use of application functions and data.

- *Functional and Data Security*: By default, access to the application functions and data is disabled for all users. So unless the functional or data security roles are granted explicitly, users cannot access the data or system resources.

Functional security provides *implicit access* to data depending on the functions to which access is granted. It is mainly achieved through the following roles.

- *Duty Roles*: Duty roles are the groups of tasks or functions that are duties of a particular job. Duty Roles are assigned to Job Roles or Abstract Roles instead of directly to users to make sure that minimum effort is needed to extend or change duties of a particular job within an organization.

- *Job Roles*: Job Roles are collections of related Duty Roles. These roles are assigned to the users based on their job profiles and access to only those functions will be available to the grantee.

- *Abstract Roles*: Abstract Roles are used to group users based on non-functional grouping, for example, employees, managers, approvers, and so on. Abstract Roles are also directly assigned to users, similar to Job Roles.

Data security provides *explicit access* to data. It is achieved through **data roles**, which provide access to specific subset of data within the given functional role.

Adoption Options

Oracle provides several adoption models for Oracle Fusion Applications.

- *Migrate to Oracle Fusion Applications*: It may be much easier for new ERP adopters to move directly to Oracle Fusion Applications, as it may not involve migration risks. For organizations with existing applications suites, if all the current modules are covered in Oracle Fusion Applications suite, they can plan moving to the next generation applications, as the confidence around Oracle Fusion Applications is increasing steadily.

- *Coexistence with existing applications*: Due to its *service-oriented architecture*, we can implement some Oracle Fusion Applications modules along with existing applications modules and expose the new functionalities through web services and business events. There are also many coexistence modules readily available as part of Oracle Fusion Applications in HCM, Financials, Supply Chain, and CRM product families. They can be used out-of-the-box without need for manually creating integrations.

- *Upgrade existing applications to the latest releases to prepare for future adoption*: If the other two options are not viable at the moment, it is important that you upgrade existing E-Business Suites or other applications to their latest releases. Oracle is moving its E-Business Suite Applications toward Oracle Fusion Middleware foundation since release 12.2. In the future, the architecture would be very similar to Oracle Fusion Applications, which may also provide simpler migration in the future.

Oracle Fusion Applications Product Families

Oracle Fusion Applications includes more than 100 individual modules or products that are grouped into product offerings based on their functionalities and features. At the time of planning for licensing, you need to select the required product offerings that need to be licensed.

Oracle Fusion Applications 11g Release 9 includes the following product families.

- Oracle Fusion Financials

- Oracle Fusion Human Capital Management

- Oracle Fusion Customer Relationship Management

- Oracle Fusion Procurement

- Oracle Fusion Project Portfolio Management

- Oracle Fusion Supply Chain Management

- Oracle Fusion Setup

- Oracle Fusion Governance, Risk and Compliance

■ **Note**   Although Oracle Fusion Governance, Risk and Compliance is part of the Oracle Fusion Applications suite, it is not included in an Oracle Fusion Applications standard installation. You can download the "Oracle Governance, Risk and Compliance" product from Oracle's software delivery cloud.

The Oracle Fusion Setup family is installed and configured by default regardless of which product family or product offering was selected. Oracle Fusion Setup contains the common functionalities of Oracle Fusion Applications, including the user dashboard, Help pages, and the Oracle Fusion Functional Setup Manager. We will discuss the Oracle Fusion Functional Setup Manager in detail in later chapters.

Figure 1-2 provides summary information on the available product offerings within each product family.

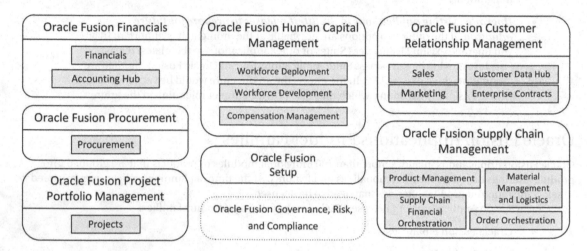

Figure 1-2. *Oracle Fusion Applications product families and product offerings*

Fusion Applications Architecture

Oracle Fusion Applications has a very complex architecture involving a large number of technology components hosted on each node. Because of this, it requires members from various teams to be involved in the implementation and management of an Oracle Fusion Applications environment. Figure 1-3 shows a high-level look at the major components involved in an Oracle Fusion Applications *logical architecture*. We will discuss these components in detail later in this chapter.

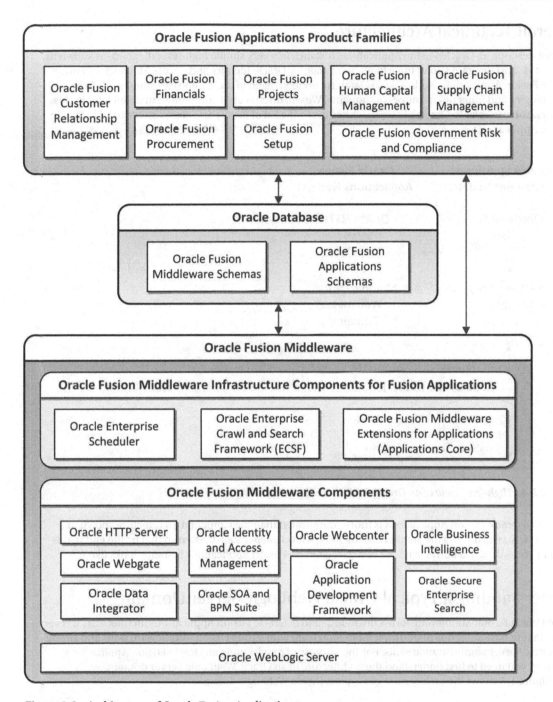

Figure 1-3. *Architecture of Oracle Fusion Applications*

Before going into the details of every component of the complete environment, let's consider a high-level overview of an Oracle Fusion Applications instance. We will start with a macro-level diagram and then look at each high-level component along with the sub-components and technologies involved.

Overall Technical Architecture

We can describe an Oracle Fusion Applications instance in a very simple high-level diagram, as shown in Figure 1-4. This diagram shows three major tiers, namely Oracle Identity and Access Management node(s), Oracle Fusion Applications node(s), and Database node(s). Each of these tiers uses standard Oracle technologies and other open source components. We will discuss each component in detail later in this chapter. You can refer to Oracle's licensing notes to see the list of third-party components used in Oracle Fusion Applications.

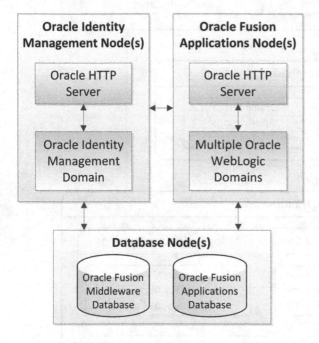

Figure 1-4. *High-level view of an Oracle Fusion Applications instance*

Since Oracle Fusion Applications is more complicated than the simplified architecture shown in Figure 1-4, we will discuss the architecture by going a level deeper step-by-step so that by the end of this chapter you will have a fairly clear idea of what an Oracle Fusion Applications instance looks like.

Understanding a Typical Oracle WebLogic Server Domain

Since Oracle Fusion Middleware forms the foundation of Oracle Fusion Applications architecture, it is very important to have someone in the implementation team with strong Fusion Middleware skills and strong WebLogic Server administration skills. For the purpose of provisioning an Oracle Fusion Applications instance, you need to first understand the architecture of an Oracle WebLogic Server domain.

Figure 1-5 shows the architecture of a typical Oracle WebLogic domain.

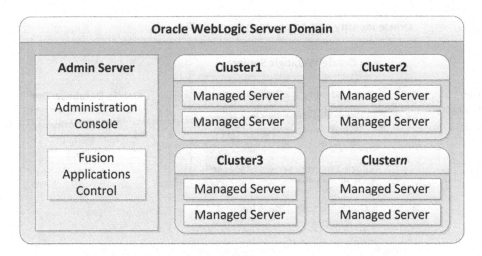

Figure 1-5. *Components of a typical Oracle Fusion Applications WebLogic domain*

Each WebLogic domain has one active administration server regardless of the number of hosts used in the Oracle WebLogic domain. There are several Oracle managed servers in an Oracle WebLogic Sever domain. The actual application functionality is generally deployed in the form of EAR (Enterprise ARchive) files to one of the managed servers. If more than one server hosts the same functionality then you can host multiple instances of the same managed servers in a WebLogic Server cluster. Each cluster hosts multiple instances of the same managed server to provide high availability and scalability for the required functionality.

The role of administration server is to configure and manage the WebLogic managed servers in the domain. The status of administration server does not impact the actual functionality of the managed server; however, it allows centralized control and management of all WebLogic Servers in the domain across multiple nodes. The Oracle WebLogic environment also includes a component called *Node Manager,* which monitors and controls the status of all WebLogic servers, including the administration server as well as WebLogic managed servers.

Oracle WebLogic server provides management interfaces in the form of Administration Console and Oracle Fusion Middleware Enterprise Control. In the case of Oracle Fusion Applications, each product family domain can be managed by the Oracle Enterprise Manager Fusion Applications Control (commonly referred as the Oracle Fusion Applications Control). You can also install and configure Oracle Enterprise Manager Cloud Control to manage every component in your Oracle Fusion Applications infrastructure. In fact, Cloud Control is the recommended interface to manage Fusion Applications instances. More details on these components will follow in later chapters, where we will discuss Oracle Fusion Applications administration.

Oracle Identity Management Infrastructure

Now coming back to the Oracle Fusion Applications architecture, let's further drill down the components in each of the tiers shown earlier in Figure 1-4. Let's take a look at Oracle Identity and Access Management infrastructure first. Oracle Fusion Applications requires Oracle Identity Management components to provide authentication and authorization as well as Single Sign-On (SSO) functionality. It uses the Oracle Internet Directory (OID) as identity and policy stores.

Let's look at the major components that constitute the Oracle Identity Management infrastructure, as shown in Figure 1-6.

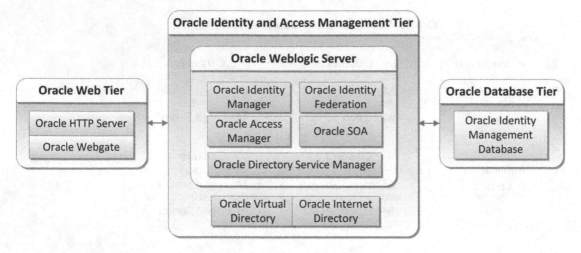

Figure 1-6. *Components of the Oracle Identity Management tier*

We can see the major components of Oracle Identity Management infrastructure in three different tiers adhering to Enterprise Deployment Architecture.

- ***Oracle Identity Management Web Tier***: Oracle Identity Management Web Tier includes the Oracle HTTP server, which provides a web listener to handle all web requests to Oracle Identity Management infrastructure. This tier also includes WebGate, which intercepts the HTTP requests and forwards the requests for protected URLs to Oracle Access Manager for authentication and authorization. Earlier versions of Oracle Fusion Applications (prior to 11.1.7) required manual installation of the Oracle HTTP server for Identity Management, but with Oracle Fusion Applications release 11.1.7 onward, it is automatically installed and configured as part of the Identity Management provisioning process. We will look at this process in detail in Chapter 3.

- ***Oracle Identity and Access Management Application Tier***: Components of Oracle Identity Management tier are hosted on one or more servers. Following are the components of Oracle Identity Management. We will discuss each of these components in the following sections.

  - Oracle Identity Manager (OIM)

  - Oracle Access Manager (OAM)

  - Oracle Directory Services Manager (ODSM)

  - Oracle Virtual Directory (OVD)

  - Oracle Internet Directory (OID)

  - Oracle SOA Suite (SOA)

  - Oracle Identity Federation (OIF) (optional)

The components OIM, OAM, ODSM, and so on, are installed and configured as part of the Oracle Identity Management (IDM) WebLogic domain. This tier also has Oracle Internet Directory and optionally Oracle Virtual Directory, which provide identity and policy stores for the Oracle Identity Management and Oracle Fusion Applications. We will look at these components in the next section, where we discuss all technical components involved in a complete Oracle Fusion Applications environment.

- ***Oracle Identity Management Database Tier***: Oracle Identity Management database schemas are stored in the IDM database. The database schemas are seeded using the Oracle Identity Management Repository Creation utility. This is covered in Chapter 4.

Oracle Fusion Applications Infrastructure

After having a look at the Oracle Identity Management infrastructure, you'll now see how an instance of Oracle Fusion Applications looks once it's installed and configured. Once again we consider a multi-tier enterprise deployment to understand which technical components are located on which tier.

Figure 1-7 shows some of the major components you will see in an installed Oracle Fusion Applications instance and you may need to focus on managing these services while administering an Oracle Fusion Applications instance.

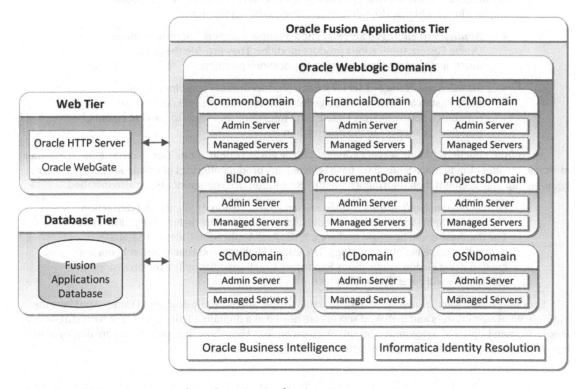

Figure 1-7. *Major components of Oracle Fusion Applications tier*

In an enterprise deployment of Oracle Fusion Applications, we can divide the major components of Oracle Fusion Applications infrastructure in three different tiers, similar to those of the Oracle Identity Management infrastructure. We have already discussed the product families, product offerings, and individual Oracle Fusion Applications products in an earlier section. In this section, we will discuss the common technical components in each tier of Oracle Fusion Applications and how the modules are deployed in the product WebLogic domains.

- *Oracle Fusion Applications Web Tier*: Similar to Oracle Identity Management, Oracle Fusion Applications Web Tier also includes an instance of Oracle HTTP Server and WebGate, which forward the HTTP requests for any protected resources to OAM. Since the first release of Oracle Fusion Applications provisioning framework includes the Oracle Fusion Applications Web Tier, it automatically is installed and configured during the Oracle Fusion Applications provisioning process. Depending on the topology selected, the Web Tier could be hosted internally or in DMZ. We will discuss multiple topology options in the next chapter.

- *Oracle Fusion Applications Tier*: Oracle Fusion Applications Tier mainly consists of individual Oracle WebLogic domains for each product family. Each domain has a dedicated admin server and a set of Oracle WebLogic clusters. Each cluster hosts a WebLogic managed server where the Oracle Fusion Applications products are deployed. There are two types of managed servers hosted in Oracle Fusion Applications WebLogic domains, depending on the deployments.

  - *Application Managed Servers*: These managed servers host one or more Oracle Fusion Applications product modules. They provide the actual functionality of the Oracle Fusion Applications products.

  - *Middleware Managed Servers*: Each product domain contains one or more Fusion Middleware managed servers, for example SOA, Enterprise Scheduler, Secure Search, Oracle Data Integrator, and so on to provide essential middleware services to the product family.

Apart from Oracle WebLogic Server Domains, Oracle Fusion Applications Tier also contains an instance of Oracle Business Intelligence Suite. If we have selected any product offerings of Oracle Fusion Customer Relationship Management then Informatica Identity Resolution (IIR) components are also installed.

- *Oracle Fusion Applications Database Tier*: Oracle Fusion Applications Transaction Database Schemas are stored in a dedicated database for Oracle Fusion Applications. The database could be single node or a RAC (Real Application Clusters) database, depending on selection of topology. The initial database tablespaces and schema are created using Fusion Applications Repository Creation utility before the provisioning process. We will cover this in Chapter 8.

Let's now have a look at an example Oracle Fusion Applications family domain to understand how the multiple WebLogic clusters and managed servers are hosted in a domain. Figure 1-8 uses HCMDomain (Oracle Fusion Human Capital Management domain) as an example to show how the applications are deployed in a typical Oracle Fusion Applications WebLogic domain.

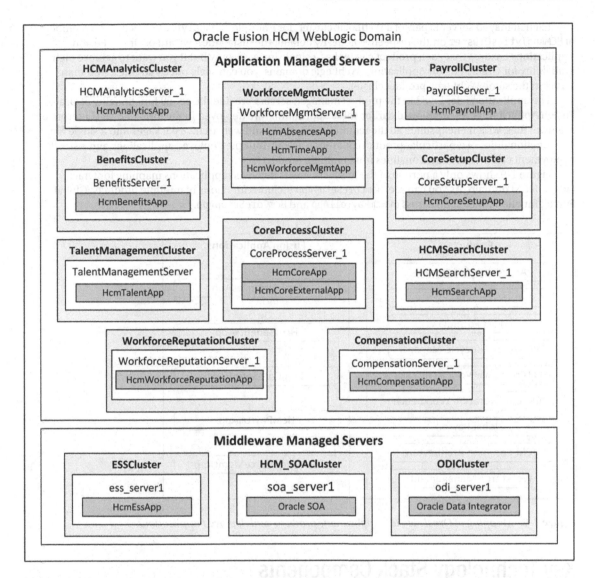

Figure 1-8. *Oracle WebLogic domain for Oracle Fusion HCM product family*

You may notice that each managed server has at least one primary application deployed in it, which will allow the managed server to serve that specific product functionality related requests. Many applications have their functionalities covered by more than one managed server, but for the purpose of clarity, the diagram in Figure 1-8 shows only the primary application deployed on each managed server.

As you can see in the diagram in Figure 1-8, there are a number of managed servers in HCMDomain in addition to the administration server. The managed servers are classified as Application Managed Servers and Middleware Managed Servers. The administration server is not shown in this diagram, but each product domain has an exclusive administration server as well. For each node of Oracle Fusion Applications, you can also see a Node Manager component. It is not shown in Figure 1-8 since it is common across multiple product domains.

Each managed server is part of a WebLogic cluster; for example HCMAnalyticsServer_1 is a member of HCMAnalyticsCluster on the respective node. By default, the installation wizard of Oracle Fusion Applications ensures that each product cluster has a single instance only but if you want to achieve high availability for Oracle Fusion Applications WebLogic domains, you can scale out by adding a new managed server in the same WebLogic product cluster.

The applications deployed in the product managed servers provide the actual functionality of Oracle Fusion Applications. As mentioned earlier, these applications are deployed in the form of EAR (Enterprise ARchive) files, which encapsulate all the required J2EE, XML, and web archive packages into a single file. The functionalities of a particular product could span across multiple deployed applications and a single deployment can include functionalities from multiple products.

Figure 1-9 shows only a portion of the products versus deployed applications mapping for Oracle Fusion HCM domain. As you can see, HcmCoreSetupApp includes functions of multiple products. Global Payroll functionalities span across in HcmPayrollApp and HcmCoreSetupApp.

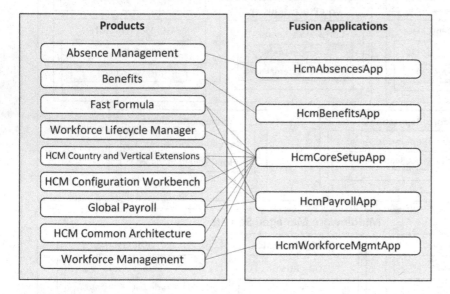

Figure 1-9. *Mapping of Oracle Fusion Applications products and deployed applications*

Key Technology Stack Components

As mentioned earlier, an Oracle Fusion Applications instance contains a variety of Oracle and third-party products, all of which are based on open standards. In order to understand the key technical components involved in Oracle Fusion Applications, let's go back and have a look at Figure 1-3. We have already discussed Oracle Fusion Applications product families in a previous section. These product families use Oracle Fusion Middleware infrastructure and framework components for Oracle Fusion Applications.

Oracle Fusion Middleware Components

We have discussed the Fusion Middleware infrastructure components used in Oracle Fusion Applications Product domains. Now let's look at the common Oracle Fusion Middleware components that make up the Oracle Fusion Applications infrastructure.

Oracle Identity and Access Management

Oracle Fusion Applications uses Oracle Identity and Access Management components for user authentication and authorization policies. These components are prerequisites for Oracle Fusion Applications provisioning, so they must be installed and configured prior to installing Oracle Fusion Applications.

- *Oracle Internet Directory (OID)*: The identity and policy repository for the Oracle Fusion Applications environment. Although Oracle Fusion Applications supports other LDAP directories for identity store, this is the only supported directory for policy store. So OID must be installed as a prerequisite.

- *Oracle Virtual Directory (OVD)*: An optional component of Oracle Identity Management that can handle LDAP requests for multiple directory sources and provide a single view of directories. Although it is an optional component in standard Oracle Identity Management installation, the IDM provisioning wizard included from Oracle Fusion Applications 11g Release 7 (11.1.7) onward configures and enables OVD by default.

- *Oracle Identity Manager (OIM)*: Provides the self-service management interface to manage user accounts and roles. It periodically runs reconcile jobs to retrieve the latest changes from OID.

- *Oracle Access Manager (OAM)*: Responsible for managing Authentication and Authorization policies. It provides Single Sign-On functionality based on the seeded policies and created through self-service user interface.

- *Oracle Identity Federation (OIF)*: Another optional component that can provide Single Sign-On functionality in a multiple-directory environment. It is installed by the Oracle Identity Management provisioning process but remains disabled by default. It can be enabled and configured if required.

- *Oracle Directory Service Manager (ODSM)*: Provides a graphical interface to manage any OID or OVD instances. This eliminates the need to use command-line tools for various operations.

Oracle SOA Suite

Since Oracle Fusion Applications is built on service-oriented architecture, the Oracle SOA suite plays a crucial role and is at the heart of Oracle Fusion Applications. The SOA suite provides infrastructure components required for orchestrating, deploying, and managing services into SOA composite applications and business processes.

Oracle WebLogic Server

Oracle WebLogic Server is the application server used in Oracle Fusion Applications and Oracle Identity Management. It is based on Java Enterprise Edition, and it's secure and scalable, based on enterprise requirements.

Oracle HTTP Server

Oracle HTTP Server is based on Apache HTTP server technology with more features. It provides the web listener to the deployed applications. It can host web pages locally as well as provide redirection to WebLogic server handlers based on user-defined rules.

WegGate

WebGate is a web server plugin that acts between the HTTP server and Oracle Access Manager. It intercepts user requests received by the HTTP server and checks with OAM for access validation.

Oracle Application Development Framework (ADF)

ADF is the next-generation framework based on Java Enterprise Edition and open source technologies. It allows rapid application development based on metadata, design patterns, and graphical tools to create service-oriented applications.

Oracle Business Intelligence

Oracle Business Intelligence is the default reporting and analytics solution integrated into Oracle Fusion Applications. It replaces earlier traditional methods of manually reporting by giving complete control of the analytics to users right in the application dashboard.

Oracle WebCenter

The Oracle WebCenter suite is the integrated suite of Oracle Fusion Middleware to create web sites, dynamic pages, and portals using service-oriented architecture. Even Oracle E-Business Suite R12.2 uses Oracle Fusion Middleware for applications deployment certified with WebCenter. Oracle WebCenter is staged to replace Oracle Portal so we can see the technological synergy between EBS and Oracle Fusion Applications.

Oracle Data Integrator (ODI)

Oracle Data Integrator facilitates high-performance data load, data extract, batch processing, and SOA data events for Oracle Fusion Applications product families.

Oracle Fusion Middleware Infrastructure Components

Each Oracle Fusion Applications product family uses the following core components to provide core UI functionality, scheduling services, and Enterprise search functionality.

Middleware Extensions for Applications (Applications Core)

These components mainly include the following extensions.

- *UI Shells*: Provide the common user interface to all Oracle Fusion Applications products. Page templates include consistent common layouts that support tasks and user-based screen elements. We will discuss common user interfaces in Chapter 11.

- *Flexfields*: Provide extensibility features by allowing you to create dynamic custom attributes on the UI.

- *Trees*: Allow you to create a multi-level hierarchy to organize the content in tree-based menus. Business rules control the tree structure and application performance can be improved by using collapsible and expandable roll-up queries to display data faster due to row-based or column-based flattening.

- *Attachments*: Provide a mechanism for adding a file, text, or URL to be added to UI pages.

Oracle Enterprise Scheduler

Those familiar with Oracle E-Business Suite can understand Oracle Enterprise Scheduler as a replacement of Concurrent Manager but with more features. The role of Oracle Enterprise Scheduler is to define, schedule, run, and monitor different type of jobs, business intelligence reports, and programs. Similar to Concurrent Manager in E-Business suite, it can run a program on demand or on a predefined schedule and control the complete lifecycle of a job. Having the Enterprise Scheduler Service (ESS) with every product family allows you to give dedicated control of related jobs to the same product family.

Oracle Enterprise Crawl and Search Framework

Oracle Enterprise Crawl and Search Framework (ECSF) is a metadata-driven component that provides foundation to Oracle Secure Enterprise Search (SES). It allows seamless search functionality in every Oracle Fusion Applications product with full transactional search.

Oracle Database

Oracle Database must be installed and configured before installing Oracle Identity Management or Oracle Fusion Applications. Oracle Fusion Applications does not support any other database. The databases for Identity Management and Fusion Applications contain database schemas for Oracle Identity Management and Oracle Fusion Applications, respectively. The initial database repository is created using the repository creation utility prior to installing Oracle Fusion Applications.

Fusion Applications Interaction with Identity Management

As we know now, Oracle Identity Management provides the infrastructure for Single Sign-On and manages the user identity and policy information for authentication and authorization. In this section, we will see how these components fit together in real-world scenarios.

Figure 1-10 provides a bird's eye view of the interaction between Fusion Applications and Identity Management components. Please note that this is only a subset of the integration to give you an idea how the components talk to each other.

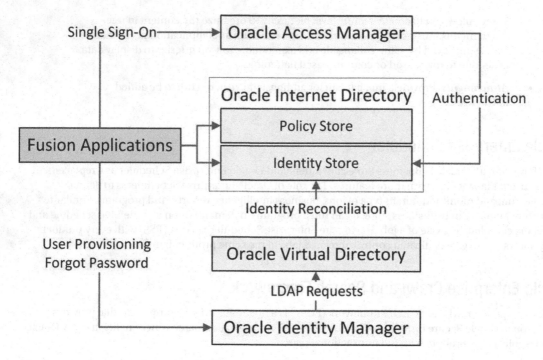

Figure 1-10. *Interaction example betweeen Fusion Applications and Identity Management*

Oracle Fusion Applications contacts Oracle Access Manager for any SSO requests that further access Oracle Internet Directory for user authentication. Similarly, the Fusion Applications user provisioning or self-service functions such as Forgot Password interact with Oracle Identity Manager, which uses the Oracle virtual directory to communicate with OID and to reconcile users/roles.

Figure 1-11 shows a typical flow of events when a page request is made from a user through an Oracle Fusion Applications interface. You can see that it involves multiple technology components in Oracle Identity Management and Fusion Applications hosts.

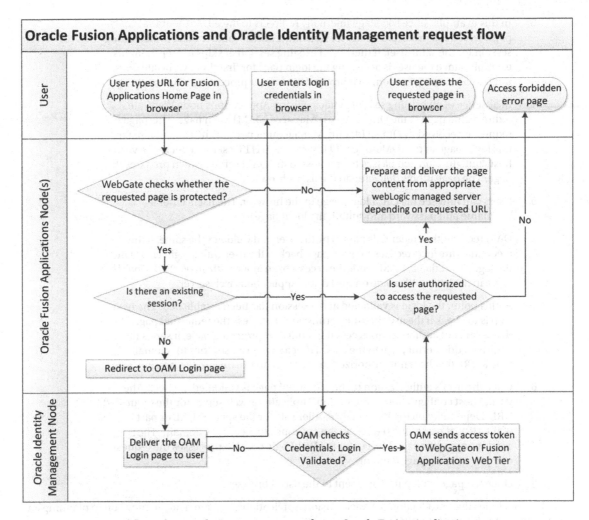

Figure 1-11. *Typical flow of events during a user request for an Oracle Fusion Applications page*

1. The user types a URL in the browser. Consider an example of a login page. The format of the homepage URL is as follows:

   `https://<Web_Server_or_Load_Balancer>:<port>/homePage`

For example, `https://fahost.paramlabs.com:10634/homePage`.

2. The request is received by the Oracle Fusion Applications Web Tier and the WebGate checks with OAM as to whether the requested page is protected. If the page is not protected as per OAM policy, it redirects the request to the corresponding WebLogic domain based on the HTTP virtual host configuration of the WebLogic handler. The respective managed server prepares the page and serves it back to the user. If the requested page is a protected resource as per OAM policy, it proceeds to further processing as follows.

3. In this example, since homePage internally redirects to the adfAuthentication page, which is a protected resource, WebGate checks whether there is an existing session for the same user. If there is an existing session, it skips to Step 7. In this example, since the user is accessing the login page for first time, WebGate does not find an existing session, so it proceeds to further processing as follows.

4. In absence of an existing session, Oracle Fusion Applications node WebGate redirects the page to the Oracle Access Manager (OAM) login page. This page request is received by Oracle Identity Management node WebGate and it passes this login page to the IDM node HTTP server. The HTTP server checks the virtual host configuration and passes the request to the OAM server, which prepares the page. The page is now delivered to the user's browser.

5. Users can now see the OAM login page in the browser. The users enter a username and password and submit the login page.

6. OAM receives the credentials passed by the user and validates the same. If the credentials are incorrect, it sends the page back to the user with a login error. Once the login is validated, OAM sends the access token along with an OAMAuthnCookie value in the URL to WebGate on the Fusion Applications web server.

7. At this point, the login is validated and a session has been established. The next step is to check if the user has the permissions to access the requested page. If the user is not authorized to access the requested protected page, it sends the page forbidden error page to the user. This can when a user tries to manually type a URL that he is not authorized to access in an existing or new session.

8. Once the user's authorization to the requested page is validated, it checks the virtual host configuration of the Fusion Applications web server for the requested URL. Depending on the WebLogic handler rule for the specific URL or part of the URL, it passes the request to the appropriate WebLogic domain. The corresponding managed server for the WebLogic domain processes the request and prepares the page content.

9. Once the page is prepared, it is sent to the user's browser.

This concludes the introduction of Oracle Fusion Applications. You are ready to move on to planning an Oracle Fusion Applications installation.

Summary

By now you should have a fair understanding of what an Oracle Fusion Applications environment looks like along with the architectural components involved. We know the synergy between Oracle Fusion Applications and existing applications suites and how Oracle Fusion Applications utilizes the best processes and practices from existing application suites using a service-oriented architecture.

The next chapter looks at how to plan for an optimal installation of Oracle Fusion Applications. We will look at various topology options and discuss how to choose the best option. We will also look at individual roles and responsibilities in the planning and implementation processes.

PART II

Planning

CHAPTER 2

■ ■ ■

Planning an Installation

This chapter is very important for enterprises and individuals planning for an Oracle Fusion Applications on-premise installation. While provisioning Fusion Applications, you must decide on the product offerings in advance since the current architecture of Fusion Applications does not allow you to add new product offerings of the same release in an already provisioned instance. With Oracle E-Business Suite, you can select a few products at the time of installation and then select/license more products later. This isn't possible in Oracle Fusion Applications due to major architectural differences. In later sections of this chapter, we will discuss this limitation and an exception condition to this. It is very critical to set clear expectations early since having more or less than the required modules may affect the functionality or performance due to the large hardware footprint of Fusion Applications.

Individual Roles and Responsibilities

You may wonder whether you need to know everything about all of the components of Oracle Fusion Applications during an implementation. The answer is not really. Implementation of an Oracle Fusion Applications environment requires various skillsets from one or more technical and functional resources. Depending on your organization's size and structure, you may have multiple people involved during the lifecycle of Oracle Fusion Applications. Following are some of the roles required during the lifecycle of Oracle Fusion Applications and the roles may overlap across people based on availability of the resources and their expertise. A person might have multiple responsibilities or a group of people could assume the same role and work in parallel. You may see yourself in one or more of these duties during the course of reading this book.

- *Oracle Database Administrator (DBA)*: The Oracle Database Administrator is responsible for making sure the database servers are prepared as per the minimum requirements and are able to host Oracle Identity Management and Oracle Fusion Applications schemas. The DBA is also responsible for day-to-day administration, maintenance, and monitoring and tuning the Oracle databases and grid infrastructure (in the case of a RAC database).

- *Oracle Fusion Middleware specialist*: The role of Oracle Fusion Middleware specialist is pivotal in the implementation and management of an Oracle Fusion Applications instance, as Fusion Middleware is the foundation of Fusion Applications. Knowledge of various components of it is key to a successful implementation. An Oracle Applications DBA, Oracle Identity Management Administrator, or Oracle WebLogic Administrator can also develop skills to manage this role if it's not defined in the organization structure.

© Tushar Thakker 2015

T. Thakker, *Pro Oracle Fusion Applications*, DOI 10.1007/978-1-4842-0983-7_2

- ***Network Administrator***: Although the role of Network Administrator, Network Engineer, or Network Security Administrator is more crucial in the initial phase of Oracle Fusion Applications installation and implementation, there would be continual involvement of Network/Security Administrator for troubleshooting the network, load-balancer, and proxy- and firewall-related issues. Since Oracle Fusion Applications is generally hosted on multiple servers located in multiple tiers with different network VLANs, the Network Administrator's role is to ensure reliable connectivity across the servers, load-balancer, reverse proxy, web proxy, and so on.

- ***System Administrator***: Depending on the operating system and hardware selection, you may need help of a System Administrator or UNIX/Windows Administrator who can provision, install, and manage the operating system and OS clusters and servers as per the finalized architecture for Oracle Fusion Applications installation. Since the hardware requirements for System Administrator are high, it is responsibility of the System Administrator is to make sure that the Fusion Applications instance is operating optimally during the normal operation or peak activity periods.

- ***Storage Administrator***: Depending on the topology selection and organization policy, you may need a Storage Administrator whose role is to provide reliable shared storage infrastructure and sometimes work along with System Administrator to provide robust backup/recovery solutions.

- ***Oracle Fusion Functional specialist***: The role of the Oracle Functional specialist comes into play mainly in the initial requirements gathering, during post-install steps and then during the course of implementation. Since Oracle Fusion Applications can't add new product families in an already provisioned instance of same release, it is important that the Oracle Fusion Functional Specialist or lead gather the business requirements precisely and prepare the list of products required to be provisioned.

- ***Oracle Identity Management Security specialist***: Since Oracle Fusion Applications uses Oracle Identity Management as the foundation of Application security, Oracle Identity Management Security specialist plays a key role in provisioning and troubleshooting issues with Application users, roles, policies, and integration with existing Identity Management components.

- ***Oracle Business Intelligence specialist***: Business Intelligence specialist role mainly comes into play after the installation and implementation of Oracle Fusion Applications is complete and Oracle Fusion Applications is in operations mode. The Oracle Business Intelligence specialist works closely with business users to make full use of enterprise reporting capabilities of Oracle Fusion Applications.

- ***Enterprise Architect***: Enterprise Architect has an important role during the decision-making process of Oracle Fusion Applications topology, especially for on-premise implementations. Enterprise Architect translates the business requirements to implementation of the Oracle Fusion Applications infrastructure.

- ***Oracle Fusion Applications Developer***: Similar to Oracle Business Intelligence specialist, the Oracle Fusion Application Developer's actual role begins after initial provisioning of Oracle Fusion Applications. The role of Application Developer in extension or customization of Oracle Fusion Applications is beyond the scope of this book.

Fusion Applications Topologies

Since the Oracle Fusion Applications architecture is fairly complex and involves a large number of technology stack components, we need to carefully select the topology for the new on-premise installation. The same theory applies even while implementing on a private cloud, if it is managed by your own team on-site or remotely depending on the location of private cloud servers. Note that selecting a simpler or more complex topology will not drastically reduce the minimum hardware requirement for an Oracle Fusion Applications installation, so you will need reasonably good servers for preparing an instance of Fusion Applications. We are going to discuss the minimum hardware requirements later in this chapter after we have discussed various topologies and how to select one for your environment.

Let's first look at some *basic rules* for selecting the Oracle Fusion Applications topology. Note that theoretically it is possible to break these rules, but it's not recommended and you will see the good reasons for the rules once you start the provisioning process.

- *Do not install Oracle Identity Management (IDM) and Oracle Fusion Applications (FA) DB schemas on the same database.* They can be on same server but must be on separate databases. This guideline was not specifically mentioned in the initial releases of Fusion Applications but recent releases suggest that both databases be on a different node.

- *Do not install Oracle Identity Management (IDM) and Oracle Fusion Applications (FA) Middleware components on the same node.*

The following components will be installed regardless of the selection of topology, so let's look at the major components that we will consider while selecting a topology.

- **Oracle Identity Management**

  - Web Server: Includes Oracle HTTP Server

  - Application Server: Includes Oracle WebLogic domain

  - Directory Server: Includes Oracle Internet directory

  - Database Server: Includes Oracle database

- **Oracle Fusion Applications**

  - Web Server: Includes Oracle HTTP Server

  - Application Server: Includes a number of Oracle WebLogic Server domains, depending on the selection of product offerings

  - Database Server: Includes Oracle database

Now let's look at some of the possible topologies for an Oracle Fusion Applications installation. We will look at various single-tier, two-tier, and three-tier topologies with the number of nodes ranging from 2 to 8 for non-high availability architecture or more nodes for high-availability architecture.

Single-Tier Topology

Any application architecture with single-tier topology utilizes one physical server for all three logical layers of an application, namely web, application, and database. This is a suitable topology for *non-production* and *demo instances* where data security policy is not strictly imposed. There is only one supported topology for single-tier implementation of Oracle Fusion Applications, where we can use two servers for Identity

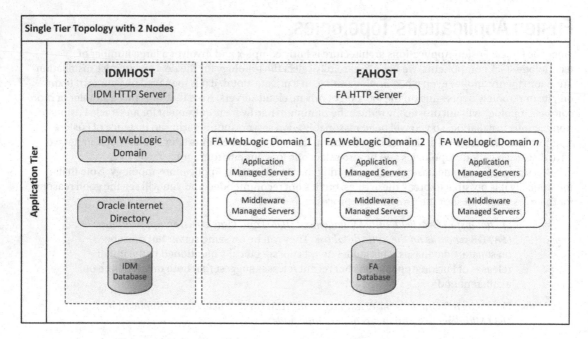

Figure 2-1. *Single-tier topology with two nodes*

Management and Fusion Applications installation, one for each. Figure 2-1 shows the only possible supported single-tier topology.

Note that the chapter section uses these acronyms for better readability:

- *IDM*: Oracle Identity Management

- *FA*: Oracle Fusion Applications

The physical servers/hosts are represented using dotted lines in the diagrams.

■ **Caution** You may want to install all the components on a single server for a proof-of-concept installation, but it is not a supported or recommended topology. In theory, it is possible with some tweaks.

Single-tier topology with two nodes is the simplest of all possible topologies and also requires a minimum configuration of nodes for an Oracle Fusion Applications on-premise installation. It has only one server each for the Oracle Identity Management and Oracle Fusion Applications components. The first node's hardware requirements are modest compared to the second node, which hosts the bulk of Oracle WebLogic Server domains. As mentioned earlier, we will discuss the specific hardware requirements of each of these servers in next section. The following components are hosted on each node in this topology:

- *Node 1 (IDMHOST)*: IDM Web Server, IDM Application Server, IDM Directory Server, and IDM Database

- *Node 2 (FAHOST)*: FA Web Server, FA Application Server, and FA Database

Two-Tier Topologies

Any application architecture utilizing this topology uses two distinct servers for the database and application/web tiers. Let's look at some of the architecture choices for two-tier implementation of an Oracle Fusion Applications instance. Figure 2-2 shows an example of a two-tier topology with three nodes.

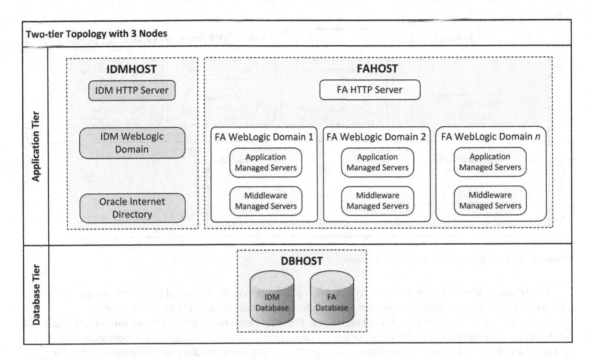

Figure 2-2. *Two-tier topology with three nodes*

The topology shown in Figure 2-2 isolates databases into different tiers, which is the ideal way of implementing any enterprise application. The remaining components are the same as in the previous topology. In this example, we have hosted IDM and FA databases a on single physical server. In this case, the database host must have a sufficient hardware configuration in order to provide optimal database performance for the IDM and FA databases.

The following components are hosted on each node:

- *Node 1 (IDMHOST)*: IDM Web Server, IDM Application Server, and IDM Directory Server

- *Node 2 (FAHOST)*: FA Web Server and FA Application Server

- *Node 3 (DBHOST)*: IDM Database and FA Database

Next we will look at an example of a two-tier topology with four nodes, as shown in Figure 2-3.

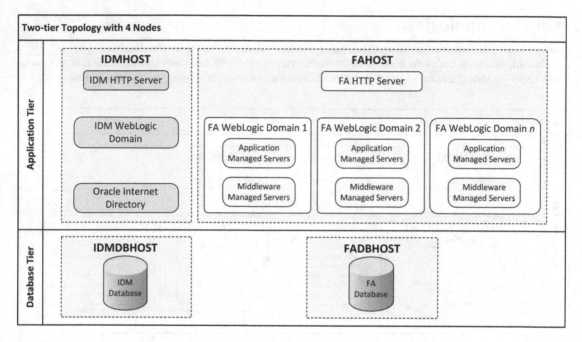

Figure 2-3. *Two-tier topology with four nodes*

The topology shown in Figure 2-3 is an extension of the previously discussed topology, but in this case the IDM and FA databases are hosted on different physical hosts. This eliminates the performance bottleneck during peak-load situations. This also helps when you have two moderately sized database servers instead of a single high-configuration database server. This topology is best suited for non-production setups among those discussed so far. If your organization does not have strict policy for three-tier architecture then this topology allows rapid provisioning and simpler management of an Oracle Fusion Applications instance.

The following components are hosted on each node:

- *Node 1 (IDMHOST)*: IDM Web Server, IDM Application Server, and IDM Directory Server

- *Node 2 (FAHOST)*: FA Web Server and FA Application Server

- *Node 3 (IDMDBHOST)*: IDM Database

- *Node 4 (FADBHOST)*: FA Database

Three-Tier or Enterprise Topologies

Three-tier topology is also referred to as an enterprise topology. It is the recommended topology as per most security standards adopted by large enterprises. This section discusses three-tier topologies that are generally used in deploying any standard enterprise applications, including a production installation. Let's look at some of the supported installation options in this topology. We will begin with an example of a three-tier topology with four nodes, as shown in Figure 2-4.

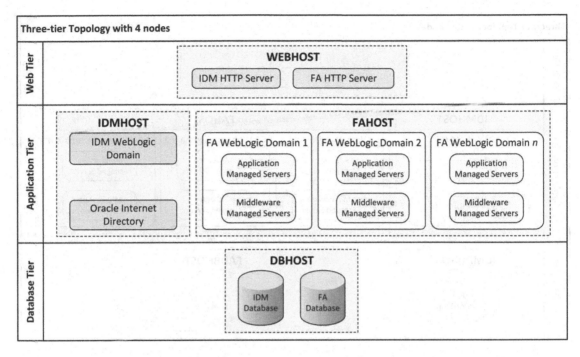

Figure 2-4. *Three-tier topology with four nodes*

The topology shown in Figure 2-4 is one of the simplest forms of the three-tier architecture, showing the minimum required four hosts. The major difference here is the isolation of the web host. This allows you to keep the application and database servers in more secure networks while the users can access only the web host or network load balancers in the web or DMZ tiers. We will discuss network load balancers and DMZ in next sections and chapters. The following components are installed on each of the physical hosts:

- *Node 1 (WEBHOST)*: IDM Web Server and FA Web Server

- *Node 2 (IDMHOST)*: IDM Application Server and IDM Directory Server

- *Node 3 (FAHOST)*: FA Application Server

- *Node 4 (DBHOST)*: IDM Database and FA Database

Next we will see an extension of the previous topology, which is a three-tier topology with five nodes, as shown in Figure 2-5.

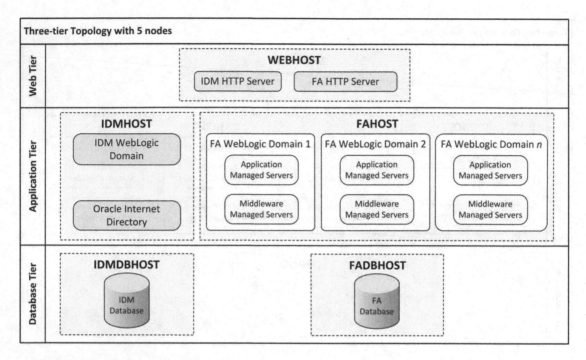

Figure 2-5. *Three-tier topology with five nodes*

In Figure 2-5 you can see that both databases have been moved to dedicated hosts. This topology requires five servers. The WEBHOST, IDMHOST, IDMDBHOST, and FADBHOST servers require mid-range server configuration. The maximum load remains on FAHOST, which contains all products WebLogic domains, hence it requires high server configuration. The actual amount of memory required will be discussed in following section. Here are the components on each node:

- *Node 1 (WEBHOST)*: IDM Web Server and FA Web Server
- *Node 2 (IDMHOST)*: IDM Application Server and IDM Directory Server
- *Node 3 (FAHOST)*: FA Application Server
- *Node 4 (IDMDBHOST)*: IDM Database
- *Node 5 (FADBHOST)*: FA Database

This topology still does not have dedicated hosts for IDM as well as FA on each tier. Take a look at an example of a three-tier topology with six nodes, shown in Figure 2-6. This is the first topology with a dedicated host at each tier for IDM as well as with FA components.

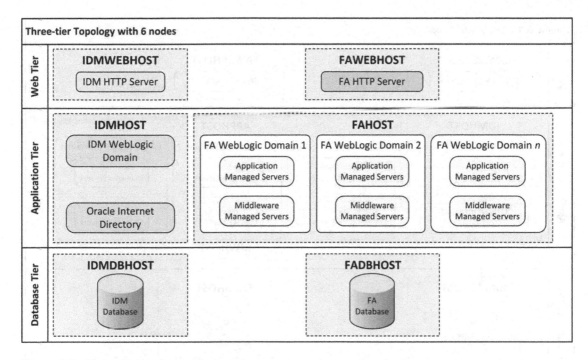

Figure 2-6. *Three-tier topology with six nodes*

As shown in Figure 2-6, the three-tier topology with six nodes represents a clear three-tier architecture for both IDM and FA. It includes three individual nodes for IDM components and three nodes for FA components.

■ **Note**   It's also possible to have *n*-tier topology for IDM components and *n+1*-tier topology for FA components or vice versa. To keep the explanation simple, we are not discussing those here, but it is absolutely fine to do that as long as your organization's policy does not prohibit it.

In this configuration, the maximum load remains on FAHOST due to the large number of technology components and application deployments. As you can see, the dedicated web nodes are have the lightest load so you should be able to use an entry-level server for this tier. Let's look at the components on each of these nodes in this topology:

- *Node 1 (IDMWEBHOST)*: IDM Web Server

- *Node 2 (FAWEBHOST)*: FA Web Server

- *Node 3 (IDMHOST)*: IDM Application Server and IDM Directory Server

- *Node 4 (FAHOST)*: FA Application Server

- *Node 5 (IDMDBHOST)*: IDM Database

- *Node 6 (FADBHOST)*: FA Database

Now we will discuss two more non-high available three-tier topologies with further distribution of load across multiple nodes. We will start with an example of a three-tier topology with seven nodes, as shown in Figure 2-7.

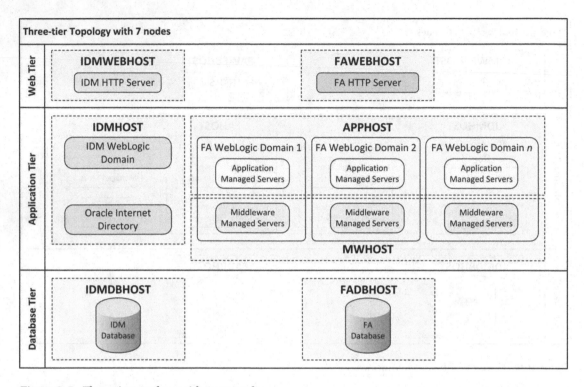

Figure 2-7. *Three-tier topology with seven nodes*

The topology shown in Figure 2-7 is an extension of the true three-tier architecture with two hosts used to accommodate Fusion Applications middle-tier components on dedicated nodes. The advantage of this strategy is that you can reduce the load on a single FA Application node. This is achieved by manually selecting the application managed servers to be deployed on one node (APPHOST), while keeping the middleware managed servers on a second node (MWHOST). You will see this in Chapter 9 during provisioning response file creation and you will notice that it is not mandatory to segregate the managed servers in Application and Middleware managed servers. Instead, you can manually pick which managed server should be hosted on which node. On the other hand, the provisioning process becomes a bit complex since each installation phase needs to finish on all FA nodes before moving to next phase. Let's look at the components installed on each host in this topology:

- *Node 1 (IDMWEBHOST)*: IDM Web Server

- *Node 2 (FAWEBHOST)*: FA Web Server

- *Node 3 (IDMHOST)*: IDM Application Server and IDM Directory Server

- *Node 4 (APPPHOST)*: FA WebLogic Administration Servers and Application WebLogic Managed Servers

- *Node 5 (MWHOST)*: Middleware WebLogic Managed Servers

- *Node 6 (IDMDBHOST)*: IDM Database

- *Node 7 (FADBHOST)*: FA Database

Now let's look at another supported option for true three-tier topology with *non-high availability*. Figure 2-8 shows an example of a three-tier topology with five+*n* nodes, where *n* depends on the amount of load distribution required. It can be any number from 1 to the total number of WebLogic domains, depending on offerings selected for provisioning.

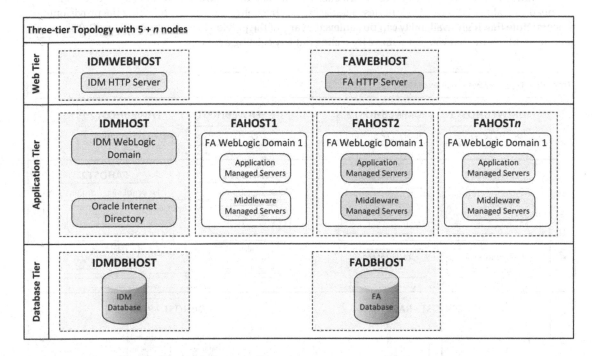

Figure 2-8. *Three-tier topology with five+n nodes*

Figure 2-8 shows the last type of non-high available topology we will discuss here. We can view this topology as a true three-tier architecture from an individual Oracle WebLogic domain point of view. Each domain has components hosted in three different tiers on three different hosts. The FA WebLogic domains are hosted on individual dedicated nodes. The prime benefit of this topology is that you can reuse the organization's existing mid-range servers for each host instead of going for very high hardware configuration servers. In case of ad hoc performance issues with one server, it will not impact other product domains' performance.

We will look at this selection screen in Chapter 9, where we will be allowed to select specific physical nodes for one or more WebLogic domains. Depending on the number of nodes selected in this screen, this topology will have five+*n* nodes. Let's look at the components installed on each of the nodes in this topology:

- *Node 1 (IDMWEBHOST)*: IDM Web Server

- *Node 2 (FAWEBHOST)*: FA Web Server

- *Node 3 (IDMHOST)*: IDM Application Server and IDM Directory Server

- *Node 4 (IDMDBHOST)*: IDM Database

- *Node 5 (FADBHOST)*: FA Database

- *Node 6 (FAHOST1)*: One or more Product WebLogic domains

- *Node n (FAHOSTn)*: One or more Product WebLogic domains

High-Availability Topologies

We will discuss high-availability topologies in general only since by default the Oracle Fusion Applications installation does not have an out-of-the-box option for selecting true high-availability during the provisioning process. The provisioning wizard allows each WebLogic domain to be hosted on one node, so you need to scale out the WebLogic nodes, databases, or other components after finishing the provisioning process. Note that high-availability can be achieved in any of the previous architectures. Figure 2-9 shows a generic architecture that you can achieve by scaling out any existing topology.

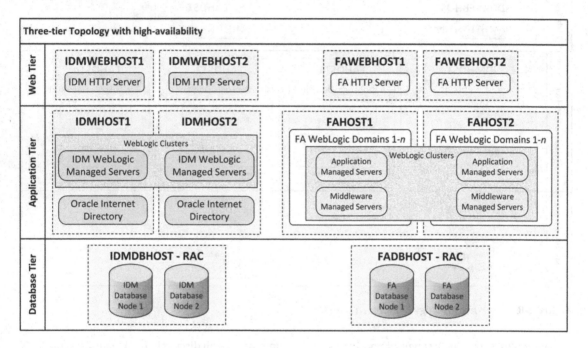

Figure 2-9. Three-tier topology with high-availability

Fusion Applications Directory Structure

In this section we will look at the directory structure of the Oracle Identity Management instance and the Oracle Fusion Applications instance once they are installed. By default the product directories are shared across servers, but we can also select Local Configuration for certain directories during the provisioning. We will discuss this in the installation chapters.

For non-enterprise topologies, you don't have to keep local directories as each WebLogic server is installed and configured for single node itself. Those directories are not used by other servers despite the fact that they are hosted on a shared disk. If you are using an enterprise topology, you might want to store the local configuration on a non-shared disk to control and tune both cluster servers independently.

Oracle Identity Management Directory Structure

Let's begin with understanding the directory structure of Identity Management nodes. Figure 2-10 shows some of the important directories on the IDM node after the Identity Management components are installed and configured.

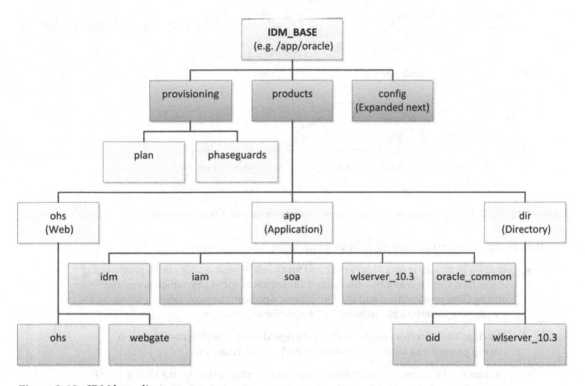

Figure 2-10. *IDM base directory structure*

The root directory for the installation (for example, /app/oracle) is called IDM_BASE and it contains the following major subdirectories.

- provisioning: This directory is created and used during IDM provisioning. It contains the provisioning plan and the status information for each provisioning phase for every server in the topology.

- products: This directory contains the Identity Management product suites and the related home directories for WebLogic Server, OAM, OIM, OID, SOA, and so on.

- config: This directory contains instance-specific configuration for middleware components. We will discuss the contents of this directory separately in the following section.

In Figure 2-10, you can also see another directory called config, which contains the shared configuration for the IDM instances including but not limited to WebLogic domains, Oracle HTTP Server configurations, and Oracle Internet directory configurations. Let's look at the contents of the config directory, shown in Figure 2-11.

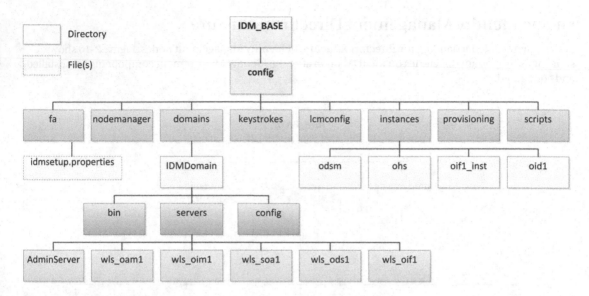

Figure 2-11. *IDM Config directory structure (components specific to a Fusion Applications installation)*

The config directory contains the following important subdirectories:

- fa: This directory is specifically required for Oracle Fusion Applications provisioning in the next step. It contains a file named idmsetup.properties, which is created during IDM provisioning and used for Fusion Applications provisioning response file creation to automatically populate IDM-specific information.

- domains: This directory contains the WebLogic domain specific configuration, startup parameters for managed servers, and log information.

- instances: This directory contains the instance configuration for the Oracle HTTP Server, Oracle Internet Directory instances, and optional Identity Federation instance configuration.

If you enable Local Configuration during the installation, you can see the following two directories in the local non-shared location. These directories include local node-specific instance configuration. This allows you to tune the local node independently to troubleshoot issues specific to node. The location of the local directory should be outside the shared IDM_BASE directory. For example, /app/local.

- domains

- instance

Oracle Fusion Applications Directory Structure

We have seen the Oracle Identity Management directory structure, which mainly focuses on a single WebLogic domain that hosts all the Identity Management components. Oracle Fusion Applications node's directory structure is more complex compared to IDM nodes. We will look at the major directories in an installed Oracle Fusion Applications instance, which are essential for you to know. This will help you better understand the installation process as well as manage the instance efficiently.

Let's first look at the main applications base directory, which acts as a root directory for a complete Fusion Applications installation, as shown in Figure 2-12.

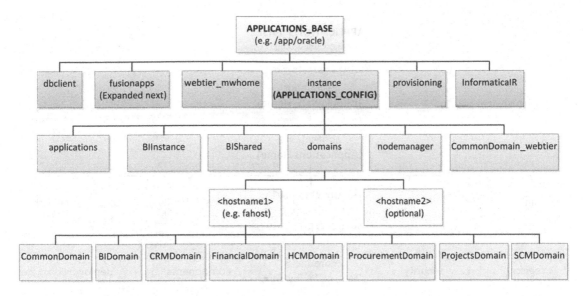

Figure 2-12. *Fusion Applications base directory structure*

You can see a shared configuration directory named `instance` under the application base, similar to what you have seen in the IDM node. This directory is referred to as `APPLICATIONS_CONFIG`. The major difference here is that we have more than one WebLogic domain and they can span across multiple servers. You may see the host-specific directory under the `domains` subdirectory to identify the domains hosted on that particular node. Let's look at the major directories of importance in the Fusion Applications base.

- `instance`: This directory contains individual instance-specific configurations for Web Server (`CommonDomain_webtier`) and Business Intelligence (`BIInstance`) in addition to applications-specific configurations. It also contains the node manager configuration, which is required for monitoring and controlling of provisioned WebLogic managed servers. It also contains configuration for each product WebLogic domain under the directory specific to the node that hosts that product domain.

- `dbclient`: Contains Oracle client software.

- `webtier_mwhome`: Web Server home directory.

- `InformaticaIR`: Optional Informatica Identity Resolution component that's installed and configured along with any CRM products.

- `provisioning`: Contains status and restart information for all phases on each node during an Oracle Fusion Applications provisioning process.

You can see a directory named `fusionapps` in Figure 2-12. This is the main middleware home directory that contains all middleware and applications components. Figure 2-13 shows major subdirectories of importance in this directory.

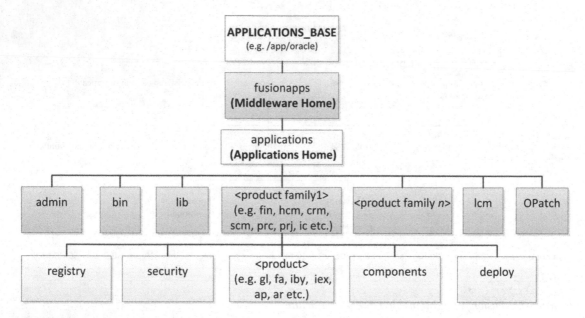

Figure 2-13. *Fusion Applications home directory structure*

Figure 2-13 focuses on the Fusion Applications Home directory, which is called `applications` under `Middleware Home`. It contains the top-level directories for each product family, including `fin`, `hcm`, `crm`, `scm`, `prc`, `prj`, and so on. These directories in turn contain individual products directories included in that family. The organization is similar to E-Business Suites, except here we have a hierarchy based on the product family and the individual products. Those who are familiar with E-Business Suite administration will know the other directories like `admin` (contains patch logs and administration files), `bin` (scheduler specific binaries), `lib` (library files), and `OPatch`. In addition to this, we can see the `lcm` directory for Oracle Fusion Applications Lifecycle Management components. It also contains AD directory, which is similar to E-Business Suite, but contains a new patching framework and startup/shutdown scripts. We will discuss this directory in detail in the Oracle Fusion Applications administration chapters.

If you select Enable Local Applications Configuration during the provisioning response file creation (explained in Chapter 9), the installer will make a local copy of the following directories on each node where the respective product domain will be installed. The root directory for this local configuration can be any directory that resides outside the shared configuration location, such as `/oracle/local`.

- `domains/<local hostname>`
- `BIInstance`

Planning an Installation Topology

Deciding on an Oracle Fusion Applications installation topology not only requires you to decide on the number of servers or tiers to be used, but also requires you to finalize other details, including the product offering selection, memory and storage sizing, and planning for network components. We will discuss each of these in the following sections.

Deciding the Product Offerings To Be Provisioned

We discussed the relationship between a product family and a product offering in Chapter 1. Before you choose the products to be installed, you need to understand the concept of provisioning configurations. There are predefined provisioning configurations during Oracle Fusion Applications installation that allow you to select from the following major group of product offerings.

- Oracle Fusion Customer Relationship Management
  - Marketing
  - Sales
- Oracle Fusion Financials
  - Financials
  - Procurement
  - Projects
- Oracle Fusion Human Capital Management
  - Workforce Deployment
  - Workforce Development
  - Compensation Management
- Oracle Fusion Supply Chain management
  - Product Management
  - Order Orchestration
  - Material Management and Logistics
  - Supply Chain Financial Orchestration
- Oracle Fusion Accounting Hub
- Customer Data Hub
- Enterprise Contracts
- Oracle Fusion Incentive Compensation

It is important to note that regardless of which specific product offerings are selected for provisioning, the installer will provision, configure, and deploy all the product offerings within the configuration. But it will enable only the required WebLogic managed servers for automatic startup. However, we can enable the product offerings from Oracle Fusion Functional setup screen later as well. This will help us reduce the number of managed servers started and hence the amount of memory required for the instance. We can always enable the features within same configuration whenever required.

Based on your business requirements, you may select a combination of provisioning configurations and a selection of individual product offerings within a configuration (except configurations with standalone product offerings, which do not have further selections).

■ **Caution**   Note that the current architecture of Oracle Fusion Applications does not allow you to add product offerings that are not already provisioned in an existing environment. So be very careful when selecting the product offerings to be provisioned. The only way to provision new products in an existing environment is while upgrading to new release.

Deciding the Installation Topology

Although we have seen example topologies with a combination of Oracle Identity Management and Oracle Fusion Applications nodes, you can also decide their topologies independently. Since Oracle Identity Management doesn't consume a lot of resources, you can decide to consolidate multiple tiers as well unless the Organization Policy restricts you only to use a three-tier topology.

Note that even if you are planning to host the database on a shared DB host or the same host as application server, we recommend you use a different hostname for DB by adding an alias to the same IP in DNS or hosts files in order to enable migrating the database to dedicated servers in the future if required. This will be explained in detail in Chapter 3 when you learn to prepare the servers for provisioning. For the purposes of this book, we are going to keep a two-tier topology as follows.

- *Node 1*: Oracle Identity Management Web Server and Oracle Identity Management Application Sever

- *Node 2*: Oracle Identity Management Database

As discussed in an earlier section, the Oracle Fusion Applications nodes can be deployed in single-tier, two-tier, or three-tier topologies. Except for the high-availability architecture, the total memory and disk sizing will remain more or less same for all these topologies. This is because each component takes its own required memory and disk size so it does not really matter where the component is installed. So the trade-off here is that if you go for a single-tier topology, you will need a single high-configuration server. For multi-tier topologies, you can utilize multiple medium configuration servers at each tier.

For the purpose of this book, we are going to select a two-tier topology for Fusion Applications nodes, similar to what we selected for the Oracle Identity Management Server.

- *Node 1*: Fusion Applications Web Server, all Products WebLogic domains

- *Node 2*: Fusion Applications Database

Memory Sizing for the Servers

The first question that most Enterprise architects ask is, "Why does Oracle Fusion Applications require such a large amount of memory (RAM)?" You may need to justify to management why you need all that memory in order to get the hardware procurement or allocation approved. This section explains how to calculate the amount of memory required for an Oracle Fusion Applications installation.

■ **Caution**   It may be tempting for some Fusion middleware administrators to tweak these memory requirements by tuning JVM configurations for proof-of-concept installations, but it is strongly recommended to leave the JVM parameters untouched to avoid any performance issues with the Oracle Fusion Applications instance. We will discuss these JVM parameters in the following sections.

Here, we discuss recommended and minimum memory requirements. Recommended memory requirements suggest the amount of memory that will allow your Oracle Fusion Applications instance to perform optimally, while minimum memory requirements suggest the minimum prerequisite memory size that the installer will check for and throw a warning message if the requirements are not met.

■ **Note**   Every node must have a minimum swap space size of 10% of the installed physical memory. Depending on the installation topology and usage, a larger swap space could be required. We suggest that if you are hosting product managed servers on a single physical node, the swap space size be at least 30% of the installed memory size.

Recommended Memory Requirement for DB Instances

The default Oracle Fusion Applications provisioning XML files contain values for a single node database instance for non-production or starter databases. Table 2-1 lists the memory requirements for starter and production databases. Although it is possible to modify the default memory parameters for the database instances, it's better to keep the minimum default values for optimum performance.

Table 2-1. *Recommended Memory Requirements for Fusion Applications Database Instance (Single Node)*

Component	Instance Type	Memory Required
SGA	Starter/Non-Production	9 GB
	Production	18 GB
PGA	Starter/Non-Production	4 GB
	Production	8 GB

In the chapters covering Fusion Applications installation, you will see the XML files that contain the default values and learn how they impact the installation when the minimum recommended values do not match. You'll also learn about possible workarounds.

Recommended Memory for Identity Management Nodes

The minimum recommended memory for Oracle Identity Management is 16 GB (installed memory), with an additional 8 GB swap space if the database is hosted outside the given node. This includes 2 GB for each WebLogic managed server and memory required for the operating system itself. Note that the initial startup memory for IDM components might be less but during the normal operation the memory requirement may vary.

Recommended Memory for Fusion Applications Nodes

Let's now look at the recommended memory suggested by Oracle for the optimal performance of an Oracle Fusion Applications instance. You can calculate the total recommended memory requirements for the Oracle Fusion Applications tier node using Table 2-2.

Table 2-2. *Recommended Memory Requirement for Oracle Fusion Applications WebLogic Domains*

WebLogic Server Type	Product Family Selected for Provisioning	Required Memory
Admin Sever	Yes	2048 MB
	No	1024 MB
Managed Server	Yes	2048 MB
	No	2048 MB
Oracle Business Intelligence Instance	N/A (Always installed)	6144 MB

Now you may wonder how to determine how many managed servers are going to be provisioned during a fresh installation of Oracle Fusion Applications. For that, you may want to refer to configuration selection page in Chapter 9 during the Oracle Fusion Applications provisioning response file creation steps. In the same screen, you can click the Details button, which will show a pop-up window with the list of Oracle WebLogic domains that will be provisioned along with the list of WebLogic managed servers. This list can be handy while calculating the memory requirement for the servers. We have prepared a sample list of all managed servers for Oracle Fusion Applications Release 8 provisioning. For later versions you can prepare the response file on a demo machine to get the list of managed servers for each configuration. We will use these numbers in the next section to calculate the memory sizing for individual nodes.

According to this table, the enterprise architect (or anyone responsible for planning the topology) needs to prepare a spreadsheet with the number of managed servers multiplied by 2 GB, the number of administration servers for the product domains selected for provisioning by 2 GB, and the number of administration servers for the product domains not selected for provisioning but will be installed due to product dependencies by 1 GB. In addition to this, 6 GB is recommended for the BI Instance along with Oracle Essbase. You must also have at least 4 GB of additional memory for the node operating system. Of course, other than this recommended memory, the more memory you have on the server, the better it is for the performance of an Oracle Fusion Applications instance.

Calculating Memory Requirements for an Installation

Note that the final number might not exactly match the one that the installer checks during prerequisite check phase. You might wonder how the installer comes up with the minimum memory requirements and why that number does not match the recommended memory requirements.

The recommended memory size assumes a standard 2 GB memory for all managed servers to keep some free memory after the components are started. The absolute bare minimum memory required is based on the actual JVM size specified for each WebLogic server to be provisioned. Table 2-3 shows an example table prepared from the Oracle Fusion Applications 11g, Release 9. A similar table can be prepared for all other releases as well. This table shows the exact amount of JVM memory required for each administration server, managed server, or cluster to be provisioned for each product family WebLogic domain. The Main column shows values for JVM if the managed server belongs to the product selected for provisioning. The Non-Main column shows values for JVM if the managed server belongs to a product domain being installed due to dependency only.

Table 2-3. *The Minimum Memory Requirements for Oracle Fusion Applications WebLogic Domains*

Domain	WebLogic Cluster	Main	Non-Main
Default	Default	2048m	1024m
CommonDomain	AdminServer	2048m	
	ESSCluster	1024m	
	FS_SOACluster	2048m	
	FunctionalSetupCluster	2048m	
	GrcCoreCluster	1200m	
	HelpPortalCluster	2560m	
	HomePageCluster	2048m	
	IPMCluster	1024m	
	WLCSCluster	1024m	
	WLCSSIPCluster	1024m	
	SESCluster	1024m	
	UCMCluster	1024m	
	EDQCluster	8192m	
	FS_SPACESCluster	1024m	
	FS_SERVICESCluster	1024m	
CRMDomain	AdminServer	2048m	1024m
	ContractManagementCluster	2048m	1024m
	CRMAnalyticsCluster	1024m	2048m
	CRMCommonCluster	2048m	1500m
	ESSCluster	2048m	1024m
	ODICluster	2048m	1024m
	CRMPerformanceCluster	2048m	
	CRMSearchCluster	2048m	
	CRM_SOACluster	2048m	1500m
	CustomerCluster	2048m	
	EmailMarketingCluster	1500m	
	MarketingCluster	2048m	
	OrderCaptureCluster	2048m	
	SalesCluster	2048m	
FinancialDomain	AdminServer	2048m	1024m
	FinancialAnalyticsCluster	2048m	1024m
	FinancialCommonCluster	2048m	1024m
	ESSCluster	2048m	1024m
	FinancialSearchCluster	2048m	1024m
	FIN_SOACluster	2048m	1024m
	GeneralLedgerCluster	2048m	1024m
	PayableCluster	2048m	1024m
	ReceivableCluster	2048m	1024m

(continued)

45

Table 2-3. (continued)

Domain	WebLogic Cluster	Main	Non-Main
SCMDomain	AdminServer	2048m	1024m
	AdvancedPlanningCluster	2048m	1500m
	CostManagementCluster	2048m	1500m
	LogisticsCluster	2048m	1500m
	OrderOrchestrationCluster	2048m	1024m
	OrchestrationInfrastructureCluster	1200m	1200m
	ProductManagementCluster	2048m	1024m
	SCMCommonCluster	2048m	1024m
	ESSCluster	2048m	1024m
	ODICluster	2048m	1024m
	SCM_SOACluster	2048m	1500m
	ConfiguratorCluster	1200m	1200m
	FinancialOrchestrationCluster	1200m	1200m
HCMDomain	AdminServer	2048m	1024m
	BenefitsCluster	2048m	
	CompensationCluster	2048m	
	CoreProcessesCluster	2048m	1024m
	CoreSetupCluster	2048m	1500m
	HCMAnalyticsCluster	2048m	1024m
	ESSCluster	2048m	1024m
	ODICluster	2048m	1024m
	HCM_SOACluster	2048m	1500m
	PayrollCluster	2048m	
	HCMSearchCluster	2048m	
	TalentManagementCluster	2048m	1024m
	WorkforceMgmtCluster	2048m	1200m
	WorkforceReputationCluster	2048m	1024m
ProjectsDomain	AdminServer	2048m	1024m
	ESSCluster	2048m	1024m
	ProjectsFinancialsCluster	2048m	1024m
	ProjectsManagementCluster	2048m	1024m
	PRJ_SOACluster	2048m	1024m
ProcurementDomain	AdminServer	2048m	1024m
	ESSCluster	2048m	1024m
	ProcurementCluster	2048m	1024m
	PRC_SOACluster	2048m	
	SupplierPortalCluster	2048m	

(continued)

Table 2-3. (*continued*)

Domain	WebLogic Cluster	Main	Non-Main
ICDomain	AdminServer	2048m	1024m
	ESSCluster	2048m	1024m
	ODICluster	2048m	1024m
	IncentiveCompensationCluster	2048m	1200m
	IC_SOACluster	2048m	1024m
BIDomain	AdminServer	1024m	
	bi_cluster	6144m	
	obi	2048m	
OSNDomain	AdminServer	512m	
	OSNCluster	512m	

If you cannot find a value for a specific managed server in the Main or Non-Main category, you can use the default value specified in the first line. When you calculate the memory requirement based on this table, you may get the exact number that the provisioning wizard prerequisite check function yields. The memory size calculated with this may be enough for starting an Oracle Fusion Applications instance, but it may not run with optimal performance. If you are running short of hardware resources or the particular installation is for demo purposes only, you can go ahead with this memory size.

■ **Tip** Due to an incorrect value in the provisioning framework shipped with Fusion Applications 11g Release 8, the Workforce Management Cluster in Fusion HCM used to be configured with 1200 MB instead of the required 2048 MB. This issue has been fixed in Fusion Applications 11.1.9. Table 2-3 reflects the correct values. Similarly, BI Cluster of the BI domain has been enhanced from 2048 MB to 6144 MB in Release 9.

Let's consider an example to understand the memory sizing calculation. We will select the Oracle Fusion Human Capital Management configuration with all three available product offerings, namely Workforce Deployment, Workforce Development, and Compensation Management. For more details, you can refer to the "Provisioning Response File Creation" section in Chapter 9. Figure 2-14 shows a screenshot of the configuration selection. Note that this is only an example and the actual selection and values for the selected release at the time of your installation may vary.

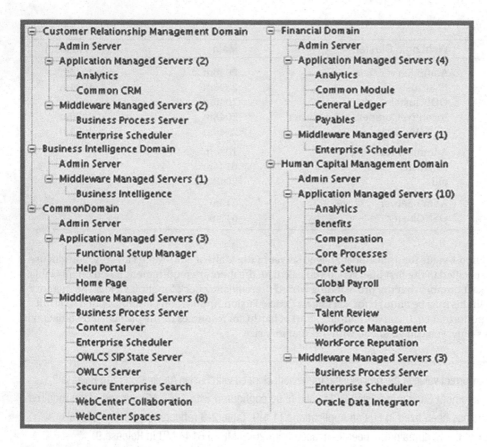

Figure 2-14. *List of WebLogic managed servers selected for Fusion HCM provisioning*

You will see that this configuration selects five Admin Servers, 19 application managed servers, and 15 middleware managed servers. Since `CommonDomain` and `BIDomain` are configured regardless of product selection, the recommended memory size can be calculated as follows:

Admin servers: 3 x 2 GB + 2 x 1 GB = 8 GB

Managed servers: 34 x 2 GB = 68 GB

OS free memory: 4 GB

Web server: Approx. 2 GB

Total: 82 GB

If you want to calculate bare minimum memory required to match the installer's requirements, you can calculate as per the numbers mentioned in Table 2-3.

Admin servers: 2 x 2 GB + 3 x 1 GB = 7 GB

Managed servers: 61,880 MB (Approx. 61 GB)

Total (excluding OS free and web server) = 68 GB

So the installer will only check for 68 GB, despite the fact that the recommended memory is 82 GB. This is the bare minimum required memory for Fusion HCM instance alone (assuming the database instance is on a different node). In addition to this, a minimum of 8 GB is required for Oracle Identity Management node. You also have similar memory requirements for both Oracle Database instances, as discussed earlier.

Planning Network and Storage

A successful Fusion Applications installation depends on sound planning of the infrastructure components, which includes network, storage, and security devices. We will look at network as well as storage requirements in this section.

Planning Internal and External Firewall

The networking requirements for Fusion Applications installation vary depending on the topology selected. For single node topology, both nodes will essentially be on the same network subnet so there is no additional network firewall required between servers. For two-tier and three-tier architecture, depending on the organization policy, you may have a network security firewall between web and application servers as well as application and database servers. If the firewalls are in deny all mode, then all required network ports should be opened in order to allow the hosts to communicate with each other. The users network might be in a different subnet or VLAN so all the required ports from the user network to web servers or network load balancer need to be opened in the firewall.

Planning Load-Balancer or Reverse Proxy

If you selected Load Balancing Enabled during provisioning response file creation (explained in Chapter 9) with aliases for internal and external URLs, you may need to have a load balancer that accepts the requests on different IPs and forwards them to the appropriate servers on a specified port. A reverse proxy solution can also be used in absence of a hardware load balancer to forward external requests to internal IPs. Load balancers can act as entry points even in a high-availability setup. Reverse proxy may be suitable when you have single web node for Fusion Applications. A network load balancer also reduces the number of ports to be opened. We will discuss this more in the installation chapter.

Understanding SSL Certificates Requirements

If you are using a network load balancer you may wish to offload SSL to the load balancer while keeping hosts listening on non-SSL ports. In that case your servers will be listening on non-SSL port while your external URLs are using HTTPS to connect to the applications. Also if you are using load balancer then you may need to install SSL certificate. Otherwise, an SSL certificate needs to be installed at the host if the users are directly accessing the web server.

■ **Note** By default, Fusion Applications web servers are configured in SSL mode and a dummy certificate is configured automatically during installation. If a valid SSL certificate is not installed on either load balancer or web host, users might get a certificate error upon accessing the login page. This can be ignored on demo systems but for production instance you must install the certificate.

DMZ Tier Requirements

If your organization requires hosting external facing web listeners in the DMZ, then either you can use a load balancer in the DMZ, which can forward the requests to internal web servers or you can host the web servers in the DMZ itself. For the latter approach you may need to have a local directory structure for storing DMZ artifacts since DMZ directories should not be shared with internal hosts for security reasons.

Web Proxy Requirements

If you need any external integration (web services hosted on servers outside your internal network) from within Fusion Applications, you may need to configure Web Proxy to allow external requests from Fusion Applications Servers. The internal and external firewalls also need to allow such traffic from Application Servers to external hosts.

Let's look at a couple of sample network architecture diagrams with load balancer and DMZ with high-availability, as shown in Figure 2-15.

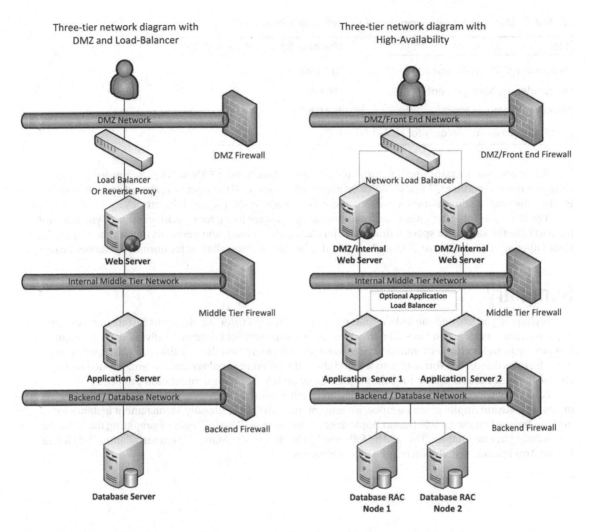

Figure 2-15. *Sample network architecture diagrams for a Fusion Applications instance*

Recommended Storage Space

Table 2-4 lists the disk space requirement for the installation. It is very important to allocate at least double the disk space as compared to the initial installation requirement for operational space growth and diagnostic logs. For example, if the IDM node space requirement is 100 GB, you should allocate 200 GB for storage (shared or local depending on topology) for the server. This also allows for future scaling and upgrades.

Table 2-4. *Disk Space Requirements Fusion Applications Installation*

Host	Minimum Space for Installation
Web Server Node (IDM and FA)	50 GB each
Oracle Identity Management Node	100 GB
Fusion Applications Node	300 GB
/mnt/hwrrepo directory (only for HCM)	1 TB

A storage administrator needs to provision this space directly on a SAN or NAS storage device if the storage is directly connected to a server or on a network file server if the storage is shared on a file server. Further, the system administrator needs to mount the storage on the required directories.

The details in Table 2-4 consider shared storage so if you are using more than one server, you may not need to have the same disk space requirement for each node. In total, you need this much space for the bare installation. An equal amount of space is required to be free after installation for normal operational usage.

Summary

In this chapter, you learned the tasks required to plan an Oracle Fusion Applications installation and the required infrastructure. You have seen the roles and responsibilities of different individuals in the complete installation as well as implementation cycle. You have likely identified the role that you will be assuming from the roles discussed. You have also learned about the different topology options and learned how to choose the best suitable option for your on-premise or private cloud implementation project.

Now we will move on to the installation of an Oracle Fusion Applications environment. Before we provision a Fusion Applications instance, we must prepare an Oracle Identity Management instance in order to be used for the Oracle Fusion Applications environment. We will begin by preparing the hosts for provisioning in next chapter. This will be followed by Oracle Identity Management installation and Oracle Fusion Applications installation in subsequent chapters.

CHAPTER 3

■ ■ ■

Preparing the Hosts for Provisioning

Oracle Fusion Applications installation has so far been one of the biggest hurdles for many Fusion Apps enthusiasts from learning this new generation of applications. This is true mainly for two reasons—high configuration of the required hardware and the complex installation process. As far as the hardware is concerned, you can purchase your own hardware or lease remotely hosted servers from various cloud server providers like Amazon, Oracle IaaS, Rackspacc, and others. Once the hardware is in place, rest assured that if you follow these few chapters of Oracle Fusion Applications installation, you will be able to host your own instance of Oracle Fusion Applications for learning, evaluation, and later, for a production environment. Avoid skipping any of these sections, since the tasks mentioned here are the minimum list of activities required for a successful installation. Although these steps are tailored for Oracle Fusion Applications 11g Release 7, 8, and 9, there will be only a few differences. I will mention important differences in the installation between various releases at each appropriate step.

Introduction to the Provisioning Process

Oracle Fusion Applications installation consists of a number of subtasks, but we can mainly classify these tasks into two major groups. The installation media used for both of the following sections is the same, as it contains all the required software for the overall provisioning process.

- Oracle Identity Management provisioning
- Fusion Applications provisioning

We will always start with Identity Management provisioning followed by Fusion Applications provisioning since the latter requires the presence of Identity Management infrastructure to seed identity data and policies. The Fusion Applications provisioning process has evolved a lot in recent releases. The earlier releases involved a lot of manual tasks that have been automated in the recent releases. In the recent versions of Oracle Fusion Applications, we can see a lot of similarities between the Identity Management and Fusion Applications provisioning processes. Before starting the installation, let's first discuss the concepts of the provisioning process and the overall installation orchestration.

Understanding Installation Orchestration

Oracle Fusion Applications provisioning uses the Apache ANT foundation to orchestrate the installation process instead of using the traditional make utility used in other application suites installation. Apache ANT is a modern automation tool that uses various XML build files for controlled execution of any set of tasks.

The advantage of ANT is that it's based on a selection of products and topology the installer will utilize various build files and control codes to smoothly provision the IDM or FA environment. Another major advantage of using Apache ANT-based orchestration is that it understands dependencies between phases, actions, and action groups. The XMLs provide verbose information on activities being performed, which simplifies troubleshooting issues with the installation. ANT does not pose any technology limitation and supports building of Java or non-Java applications.

The main orchestration build XML file contains the overall flow of the installation while every phase of installation will utilize specific XML files for particular stages or products like Common, Business Intelligence, and so on. Each XML file contains a set of execution targets. Each target contains a set of actions to be completed with parameters, including timeout, error condition actions, and so on. Actions can include a range of tasks including file system commands, Java executions, compilations, and custom code execution (including C, C++, and validations), among many other possible tasks. The installation utilizes status and restart files in case it needs to be restarted for any reason.

Once we go through the actual provisioning phases and installation troubleshooting sections, you will have a clearer idea of how the installation progresses at each phase.

Classification of Hosts for an Installation

You can classify the hosts in any selected topology in following categories. With the exception of the DMZ host, all these host roles are available in any topology including a single-tier topology. A host can have one or more of these roles based on the selected topology. For example, in the single-tier architecture, the IDM and FA hosts will have each of these three roles, namely primordial host, primary host, and secondary host.

Regardless of the number of nodes in the architecture, the installation will run the appropriate phases on each of these three hosts. Don't be surprised if you see the Configure Secondary Nodes phase being run during the provisioning phase even on a single-tier topology. This is because certain generic actions are performed only during this phase in order to make sure that all nodes in topology have already been configured. Each phase will run the appropriate set of actions on the same host, so there will not be an overlap of actions. Let's now review the classification of the hosts in various topologies:

- *Primordial host*: In any selected topology there will be only one primordial host regardless of the total number of nodes in the architecture. In the case of Fusion Applications provisioning, the server that hosts the administration server of the common domain will be considered the primordial host. For Identity Management provisioning, the node that runs the installer and shares the disk with other hosts is considered the primordial host. Even in high-availability architecture there will be only one primary administration server host that will act as the primordial host. The concept of the primordial host in Fusion Applications is similar to the administration/patching node in the E-Business Suite.

■ **Tip** The installer assumes that the host on which response file is being created is the primordial host, so make sure to create/modify the response file only from the primordial host.

- *Primary host*: There will one primary host for each WebLogic domain. There could be multiple primary hosts in a selected topology if the domains are installed on multiple nodes. In this case, the host that contains the administration server for a product family domain will act as the primary host for that particular domain.

- *Secondary host*: There can be one or more secondary hosts for each domain depending on the number of servers where the managed servers of a particular domain are configured. In most topologies, there will be none or one secondary host. If the managed servers of a particular domain span across multiple hosts, secondary host will always be distinct from the primary host even if the primary host also contains some managed servers.

- *DMZ host (optional)*: If the selected topology has web servers in the DMZ (the demilitarized zone) then this server will host the Oracle HTTP server on non-shared disks. This server will be in a restricted zone behind a firewall.

Figure 3-1 shows how example hosts act as primordial, primary, secondary hosts, or a combination of them.

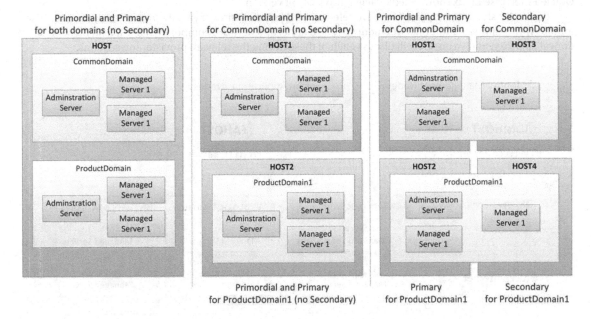

Figure 3-1. *Examples of primordial, primary, and secondary hosts in various topologies*

Supported Component Versions

Table 3-1 shows the supported minimum component versions for Oracle Fusion Applications installation as of Oracle Fusion Applications 11.1.9 release. Refer to Oracle's certification matrix when new releases become available in the future.

Table 3-1. *Minimum Required Component Versions for Fusion Applications*

Component	Fusion Applications Release 8	Fusion Applications Release 9+
Oracle Database	11.2.0.4.0 / 11.2.0.3.0	11.2.0.4.0
Oracle Real Application Clusters	11.2.0.4.0 / 11.2.0.3.0	11.2.0.4.0
Oracle WebLogic Server	10.3.6.0.0	10.3.6.0.0
Oracle Identity Management	11.1.1.7.0	11.1.1.7.0

Let's begin with the example topology that we will use for this installation. Depending on the topology you selected, some minor steps can vary but we will make sure to include all possible differences while explaining each step. You may notice some tips or cautions. Pay special attention to those tips to simplify your installation and reduce the number of errors encountered.

Selected Topology for the Installation

For the purpose of the guided installation in this book, we are going to use a two-tier topology with four nodes since the web is a light component and does not require a dedicated server for the demo installation. The Identity Management instance will use two nodes—IDMHOST and IDMDBHOST—while the Fusion Applications instance will use two nodes—FAHOST and FADBHOST. The operating system on the nodes is Oracle Enterprise Linux (now called Oracle Linux), 64-bit version.

Figure 3-2 shows the topology we have selected for this installation. If you are provisioning an enterprise topology, you may see additional web nodes, a DMZ node, and network components like a load balancer, a firewall, a proxy, and so on. We will discuss each of these during the relevant provisioning sections.

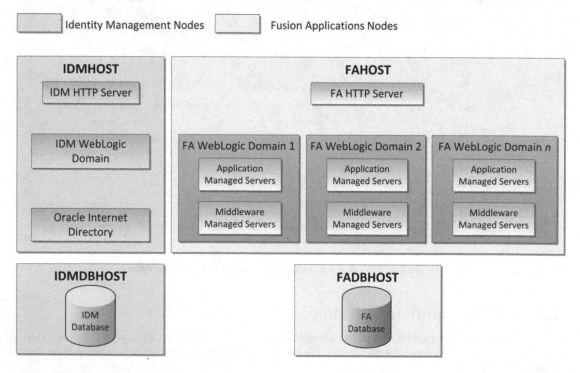

Figure 3-2. *Fusion Applications environment topology selected for this installation*

Let's look at the components that we are going to provision on each of these nodes. Table 3-2 shows the technical components to be installed and configured on each of the four nodes during this installation.

Table 3-2. Hosts in the Selected Topology

Host	Role	Components
IDMHOST	Identity Management Application Node	IDM Oracle HTTP Server instance Oracle Internet Directory instance Oracle Virtual Directory instance IDM WebLogic Domain IDM Administration Server Oracle Access Manager Oracle Identity Manager Oracle Directory Service Manager Oracle Identity Federation IDM SOA Server
IDMDBHOST	Identity Management Database Node	IDM Oracle Database
FAHOST	Fusion Applications Application Node	FA Oracle HTTP Server instance Common (Setup) Domain BI Domain All Product families WebLogic Domains Standalone components like IIR (for CRM)
FADBHOST	Fusion Applications Database Node	FA Oracle Database

Note that even after IDMHOST and IDMDBHOST are installed and configured, we will always need them up and running during the Fusion Applications nodes installation. The FA provisioning process will seed identity and policy data in OID and related database tables. During the FA nodes provisioning, make sure to monitor the performance of IDM related nodes as well. You may see a spike in IDM nodes' CPU usage, especially during the configure or postconfigure phases of FA provisioning, which load seed data in identity and policy stores. A performance issue in IDM nodes can result in errors during FA nodes provisioning due to timeout and related events.

Also note that network connectivity between IDM and FA nodes is not interrupted during any point in time during Fusion Applications provisioning, since it may result in failure of respective provisioning phase on FA nodes. However, if the IDM nodes are not reachable or slow for some reason and the FA provisioning fails, the framework provides reliable cleanup and restore methods to restart the failed phase. We will look at this mechanism in the relevant sections.

Fusion Applications Provisioning Steps

In this section we will look at the steps required for provisioning Identity Management and Fusion Applications components. Since we are categorizing the large number of steps in two major groups, we will first look at the steps involved in Identity Management provisioning followed by the Fusion Applications counterpart. Later we will look at the dependencies between these steps and will see how we can save time by combining independent tasks.

Provisioning Steps for Identity Management Components

Oracle has been constantly improving the Fusion Applications provisioning experience since the first release and those who have been working on it from earlier releases would know that the current provisioning processes is much more seamless compared to earlier versions. As far as Identity Management provisioning is concerned, the major shift in the installation process came after Fusion Applications 11g, release 7 along with Oracle Identity Management version 11.1.1.7. Until then the Identity Management installation included a manual process of installing, configuring, patching, and integrating IDM components in order to prepare the infrastructure for the Oracle Fusion Applications installation. From Fusion Applications Release 7 onward, Oracle provides the IDM provisioning framework or the IDM Lifecycle Management Tools (IDM LCM) to transparently provision Identity Management without going through the tedious manual process, which was prone to errors. We will briefly discuss the installers included with pre-11.1.7 Fusion Applications releases and then will focus on the current provisioning process through the Provisioning wizard.

IDM Provisioning Steps for Earlier Versions of Fusion Applications

Since all new releases of Oracle Fusion Applications now include the IDM provisioning framework and that is the recommended process of IDM provisioning, we will only quickly overview the manual process. This method was followed for Fusion Applications release 11.1.6 and earlier, which included Identity Management version up to 11.1.1.6. For new releases of Oracle Fusion Applications, you need to skip to the next section. Reading this section will help you understand what goes on behind the scenes and better understand the provisioning process phases. Also if your organization has specific requirements for earlier releases, these steps may give you an overview of the tasks involved.

1. **Install the Oracle database for the Oracle Identity Management infrastructure**

   Installing an Oracle database is a prerequisite to provisioning the Identity Management components. In older releases there is no installer included specifically for the Identity Management database so we need to manually create a database before proceeding to the next step.

2. **Run Repository Creation Utility (RCU) for the Oracle Identity Management components**

   Once the database is created we need to create an Oracle Identity Management repository in the database. This step is required to create required tablespaces, schemas, and packages in the blank database. It also loads seed data related to the Identity Management components once the schema objects are created.

3. **Install the Oracle Identity and Access Management Components**

   Once the Oracle Identity Management database is installed and the repository is created, we will go ahead and install the Identity and Access Management components on the IDM primary host. This includes the following steps:

   a. Install JDK.

   b. Install Oracle HTTP Server.

   c. Patch Oracle HTTP Server (for Fusion Applications Release 11.1.4 or earlier).

   d. Install Oracle WebLogic Server.

   e. Install Oracle Identity Management (Oracle Internet Directory, Oracle Virtual Directory, Oracle Directory Integration Platform, Oracle Identity Federation, and so on).

   f. Patch Oracle Identity Management (for Fusion Applications Release 11.1.4 or earlier).

   g. Install SOA suite.

   h. Install Oracle Identity and Access Manager.

4. **Apply mandatory patches.**

We need to apply additional mandatory patches as part of this step. The required patches at the time of release are included in the installation repository. But there might be additional patches to be downloaded and applied at the time of installation based on latest release notes.

  a.   Apply database PSU 11.2.0.3.4 if not already applied.

  b.   Apply WebLogic Server patches using Smart Update.

  c.   Apply Identity Management patches.

  d.   Patch Common Oracle home.

  e.   Apply IAM (Identity and Access Management) patches.

  f.   Apply SOA patches.

  g.   Apply Oracle HTTP Server patches.

5. **Configure the Oracle Identity and Access Management components.**

Next we need to create a new WebLogic domain for Identity Management (IDMDomain) and then extend the same to include OIM, OAM, SOA, ODSM, and so on, and optionally configure the Oracle Virtual Directory. The configure stage includes the following activities:

  a.   Provision the OIM login modules to the WebLogic Server library and create wlfullclient.jar file.

  b.   Configure web tier.

  c.   Create WebLogic domain for Identity Management (IDMDomain).

  d.   Extend the domain to include Oracle Internet Directory.

  e.   Prepare identity and policy stores.

  f.   Extend the domain to include the Oracle Directory Service Manager.

  g.   Extend the domain to include the Oracle Virtual Directory (optional).

  h.   Configure Oracle Access Manager.

  i.   Configure Oracle Identity Manager and SOA.

  j.   Configure HTTP aliases for OAM, OIM, SOA, and ODSM.

  k.   Prepare OIM to reconcile from ID store.

  l.   Post-configure tasks.

6. **Integrate Oracle Identity Manager (OIM) and Oracle Access Manager (OAM).**

At this stage we need to install and configure WebGate for the access manager and integrate the components to communicate with each other. Later, we need to configure the components with Oracle HTTP server using aliases to redirect the HTTP requests to the appropriate managed server.

  a.   Update existing LDAP users with the required object classes.

  b.   Integrate Oracle Access Manager with Oracle Identity Manager.

  c.   Assign Administrator Groups and Roles.

  d.   Add Admin role to the OAMAdministrators group.

    e.   Update WebLogic servers boot.properties files to include encrypted usernames and passwords.

    f.   Install WebGate.

    g.   Deploy WebGate to Oracle HTTP Server.

    h.   Apply WebGate patches.

IDM Provisioning Steps for Fusion Applications 11.1.7 or Later

As mentioned earlier, beginning from Fusion Applications 11.1.7, the installer includes IDM provisioning framework or IDM lifecycle tools, which eliminate the need for most of the manual steps for IDM provisioning. The previous steps give you a fair idea about what to expect as a result of the provisioning wizard. Let's now look at the list of IDM provisioning steps for Fusion Applications 11, Release 7 (11.1.7) or later.

1.   Prepare the host operating system on all nodes in the topology.

2.   Install the Oracle 11g database (Identity Management database).

3.   Run the Repository Creation Utility (RCU) for Oracle Identity Management.

4.   Install the Identity Management Provisioning wizard.

5.   Create the IDM provisioning response file.

6.   Provision Identity Management.

7.   Perform post-provisioning configuration.

    Figure 3-3 shows the steps mentioned previously along with the dependencies. We will discuss each of these steps in detail in Chapters 4-7.

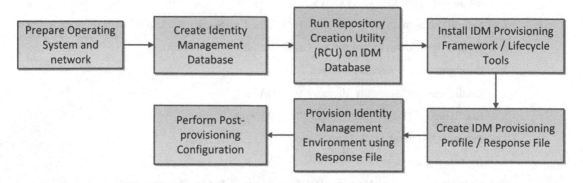

Figure 3-3. *Oracle Identity Management provisioning steps*

■ **Tip**   We can also run some steps of FA installation in parallel to IDM installation, which are independent of each other. Refer to next section for the list of steps, which can be run in parallel to save installation time.

Provisioning Steps for Fusion Applications Components

Unlike Identity Management provisioning, the Fusion Applications provisioning process has remained nearly same since the initial releases, but the overall process has matured a lot over last few releases. The overall provisioning experience is better and the provisioning success rate is much better as well. For example, the failure recovery has improved a lot in recent releases and the false errors have reduced. We will mention every important change compared to earlier releases in every applicable sections. The following is the list of steps required for provisioning Fusion Applications components.

1.   Prepare the host operating system on all nodes in the topology.

2.   Install the Fusion Applications provisioning framework on all nodes in the selected topology.

3.   Prepare the Fusion Applications database.

4.   Install the Oracle 11g database (Fusion Applications DB).

5.   Run the Fusion Applications Repository Creation Utility.

6.   Create the Fusion Applications provisioning response file.

7.   Provision the Fusion Applications environment.

Figure 3-4 shows the dependency diagram with the sequence of the provisioning steps, which suggests that each of these steps must be done serially, only after the previous step completes.

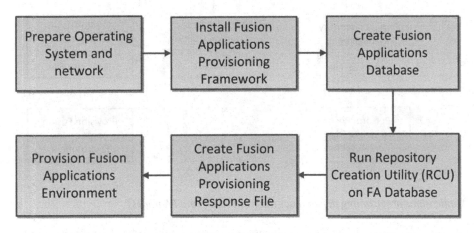

Figure 3-4. *Fusion Applications provisioning steps*

■ **Note**   The Fusion Applications provisioning response file was called the provisioning plan in earlier releases of Fusion Applications before Oracle Fusion Applications 11g, Release 4. The term "provisioning plan" is no longer used. All command-line parameters related to provisioning plan are now deprecated.

Dependencies Between IDM and FA Provisioning Steps

If you look at the overall provisioning process, including the Identity Management and Fusion Applications nodes, the complete picture looks as shown in Figure 3-5. This figure allows you to understand the overall dependency for end-to-end major steps of the provisioning process.

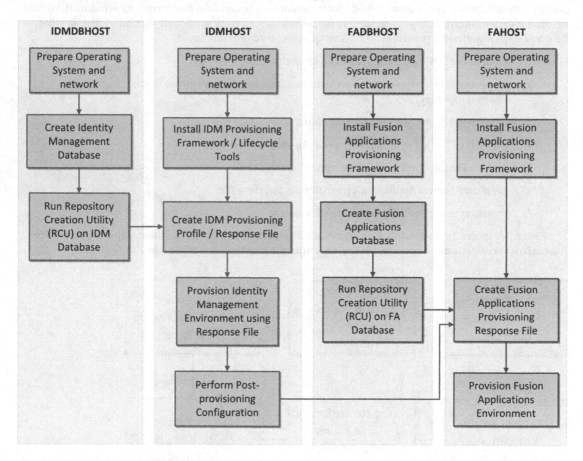

Figure 3-5. *Fusion Applications provisioning dependency diagram (IDM and FA nodes)*

Figure 3-5 shows a very interesting aspect of Fusion Applications provisioning. You may think that Oracle Fusion Applications provisioning is a serial process and all the steps must be done one at a time. Do we need to wait for all previous steps to complete before proceeding to the next step? The answer is, not always. Each step in the provisioning process is dependent on one or more steps. But we are performing provisioning on two distinct node categories, namely IDM and FA. So there are some steps that do not require all previous tasks to be completed on other nodes. This gives you an opportunity to parallelize a lot of tasks. This makes the overall provisioning process a mix of serial and parallel activities.

Consider this important tip to speed up the overall Fusion Applications installation process. Refer to Figure 3-5 and you will see the dependent tasks for each step are shown by connecting an arrow between the dependent tasks. Some steps—for example, Prepare Operating System and Network—are not dependent on any other tasks. So we can perform this operation on all nodes at same time. There are two advantages to this. You will save a lot of time by skipping all previous steps between these tasks and you will be doing similar tasks on each node, so you can maintain the flow and reduces the chances of error.

Similarly, you can prepare the IDM and FA databases in parallel as these steps are not dependent on each other. This applies to database installation and to running the Repository Creation Utilities. Since the Fusion Applications database RCU takes longer, you can start these processes and let them run in parallel. This will save a lot of time in the overall provisioning process.

An important point to note about the parallel activities is that all the other steps must be complete before you can proceed with Fusion Applications Response File creation and the provisioning the Fusion Applications nodes. So when you are about to start the Fusion Applications Response File creation, you must have a fully configured Identity Management instance and Fusion Applications Database with repository loaded already. Although we say that Fusion Applications provisioning is dependent on Identity Management infrastructure, the actual dependency starts from Response File creation step and all previous steps on FA nodes can be completed independently of the IDM nodes.

Creating the Installation Repository

Oracle Fusion Applications installation media includes all the required software installers, including Oracle database, Identity Management, and Fusion Applications components. The installation files can be downloaded from Oracle Software delivery cloud for the supported platforms.

■ **Note**   We are using Oracle Enterprise Linux (now called Oracle Linux) 64-bit as the operating system for all the examples in this book, including the installation steps. Download the installation media for your selected platform only.

The installation media comes in several ZIP files. You will need an unzip program installed in the host from where you create the installation repository. The repository should be created on a shared location so that all the nodes, including database, IDM, and FA can access it during the course of installation. The repository can be safely removed after the installation is complete. The repository location will be referred to as REPOSITORY_LOCATION in the installation steps. For example, we have created a directory named /stage on a network file server where we will unzip the media files. The same directory will be mounted on all nodes as /stage for the purpose of this installation demonstration.

■ **Tip**   Keep the repository location name short, especially with Windows hosts. The installer repository has deep levels of subdirectories and files that sometimes cross the 255 character limit on Windows hosts. There are at least two files in the installer media that have a path length very close to 255 characters. Ignoring this will result in failure of the provisioning process and it is difficult to locate the installation error. The error message is not clear enough to mention the specific missing file. It's best to use a short path like /stage instead of something like /fusion/apps/1119/stage.

Directory Structure of the Installation Repository

Once the installer repository is created, you can mount the same installer root directory to each node and each provisioning process will use certain subdirectories. In order to better understand the directory structure of Installation Repository, let's divide the subdirectories into two main groups. The first group is related to Identity Management provisioning while second is related to Fusion Applications provisioning. This will help you understand the role of each important directory within the installation repository. We will see them one by one in the following section.

Identity Management-Specific Directories

Figure 3-6 shows some of the important directories used during provisioning of Identity Management nodes. We will show similar directory structures for the important directories required for Fusion Applications nodes in next section.

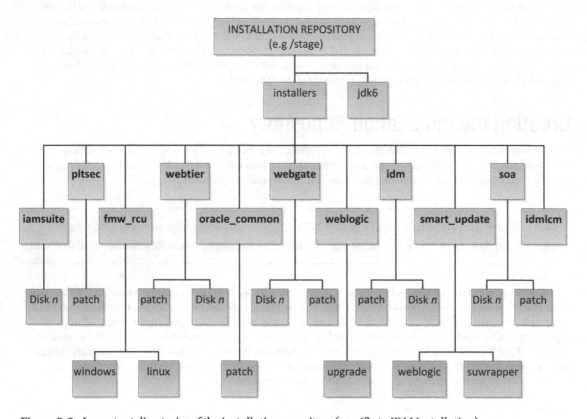

Figure 3-6. *Important directories of the installation repository (specific to IDM installation)*

Let's start with the top-level directories mentioned in Figure 3-6 and their importance in overall provisioning of Oracle Fusion Applications.

- Installers: This is the base directory for all the component's setup files. While creating a provisioning response file or at the time of the actual provisioning, the wizard checks for the presence of this directory under the repository location. If this directory is not present directly under the staging location, the installer will throw an error.

- jdk6: This directory contains the required version of JDK software that can be used as a temporary JAVA_HOME directory until JDK is installed on the host. There is another directory named jdk under the main installers directory as well (not shown in the diagram) and it contains the JDK software in ZIP format. You can unzip the installers/jdk/jdk6.zip directory to your host to create a permanent JAVA_HOME for your instance.

Let's look at the important subdirectories under `installers`, which are related to the Identity Management installation.

- `idm`: Contains the Oracle Identity Management installer for creating the IDM home, which contains Oracle Internet Directory, Oracle Virtual Directory, Oracle Directory Integration Services and so on. These components are created and configured during the Identity Management provisioning process.

- `iamsuite`: Contains the Oracle Identity and Access Management installer to create OIM home, which contains the Oracle Identity Manager and Oracle Access Manager.

- `soa`: Contains the Oracle SOA Suite installation files. SOA provides components required for orchestrating, deploying, and managing services into SOA composite applications and business processes.

- `webtier`: Contains the Oracle HTTP Server installation files. Oracle HTTP Server constitutes the web tier of the Oracle Identity Management environment.

- `webgate`: Contains Oracle WebGate installation files. The WebGate plugin accepts requests from the Oracle HTTP server and forwards them to Oracle Access Manager for protected pages authorization.

- `oracle_common`: Contains the Oracle Common home-related patches. The patches are applied on `oracle_common` home under Fusion middleware home directory. With earlier versions of Identity Management installers, we had to apply these patches manually but now these are automatically applied as part of the Identity Management Provisioning wizard.

- `weblogic`: Contains the Oracle WebLogic Server installation files. WebLogic is the Application Server of Oracle Fusion middleware used in Identity Management.

- `smart_update`: Contains Oracle WebLogic Server patches and patching utility. The Fusion Applications provisioning process automatically applies all required patches so you need not manually invoke the patching utility for the WebLogic servers.

- `pltsec`: Contains patches related to Oracle Internet Directory (OID), Oracle Virtual Directory (OVD), and OID Tools. These are also applied automatically while provisioning through Identity Management lifecycle tools.

- `idmlcm`: Contains Identity Management lifecycle tool installation files.

- `fmw_rcu`: Contains the Repository Creation utility for Identity Management database and related dump files. This must be installed prior to starting the Identity Management provisioning process.

Fusion Applications-Specific Directories

In this section we will look at the important directories of the common installation repository from Fusion Applications provisioning point of view. Since you will be using the same installation repository root directory for both IDM and FA provisioning, even after Identity Management provisioning is complete, you should not remove the Identity Management-related directories from the repository. This is because there are a lot of files that are used by both installations. If you are not using shared location for installation repository between IDM and FA nodes then make sure to follow the same guidelines for creating the repository on Fusion Applications nodes, including the maximum character length for the base directory name.

Figure 3-7 shows the important directories with respect to Fusion Applications provisioning.

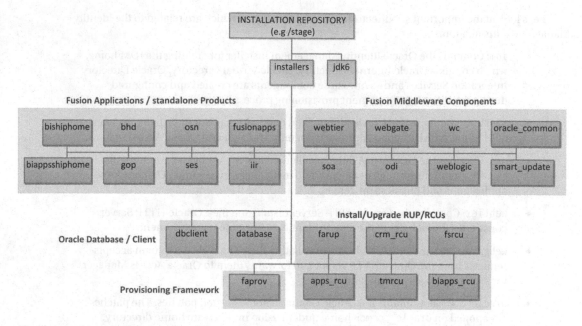

Figure 3-7. Important directories of the installation repository (specific to Fusion Applications)

We have already seen the top-level directories `installers` and `jdk6` in the previous section. Now we will look at the important subdirectories under the `installers` directory, which are specific to Fusion Applications provisioning. I will classify them under four main categories based on their role in the installation.

1. **Fusion Applications product-related directories.**

   - `fusionapps`: Contains the Fusion Applications Product Families. The products are installed under the `applications` subdirectory within the `fusionapps` directory. It contains the EAR files that are deployed on the respective WebLogic managed servers of the product domains.

   - `bishiphome`: Contains Fusion Middleware Oracle Business Intelligence installation files. Oracle BI provides integrated reporting and analytics functionality to Oracle Fusion Applications. Oracle BI acts as the default reporting server for Fusion Applications, replacing all report servers of the E-Business Suite.

   - `biappsshiphome`: Contains Fusion Middleware Oracle Business Intelligence Applications installation files. Note that OBIA software is copied only to the Oracle BI home directory as `biapps` during Fusion Applications provisioning but it is not configured. In order to use and license Oracle Business Intelligence applications, you must manually install and configure time after Fusion Applications provisioning has completed.

   - `iir`: Contains Informatica Identity Resolution product installation files. IIR gets configured only when you are provisioning any products from the Oracle CRM family. IIR is the data quality engine for Fusion CRM, which allows you to match and search identity data and duplicate records. It also provides data-cleansing features.

- osn: Contains Oracle Social Network installation files. OSN provides context-based real-time communication and sharing capabilities to Oracle Fusion Applications. OSNDomain is created and configured only when the Oracle Social Network is installed.

- ses: Contains Secure Enterprise Search installation files. SES is installed and configured on all Fusion product domains and provides a secure search functionality across all the applications.

- bhd: Contains Bounce Handling Daemon installation files for the Fusion Customer Relationship Management (CRM) email marketing server. BHD keeps track of the email messages sent through email marketing server, which cannot be delivered by parsing the returned emails and records the reason for email bounce.

- gop: Contains Global Order Promising installation files for the Fusion Supply Chain Management (SCM). This allows the organization to accurately promise the quick delivery of orders considering all the constraints in the distributed global supply chain.

2. **Oracle Fusion middleware related directories.**

- webtier: Contains the Oracle HTTP Server installation files. Oracle HTTP Server constitutes the web tier of the Oracle Fusion Applications environment. The Oracle HTTP server is based on the Apache HTTP Server with enhancements to facilitate load balancing and provides better integration with WebLogic and other products.

- webgate: Contains Oracle WebGate installation files. The WebGate plugin accepts requests from Oracle HTTP server and forwards them to Oracle Access Manager for protected pages authorization.

- wc: Contains the Oracle WebCenter installation files. WebCenter replaces traditional Oracle Portal pages and provides a service-oriented dashboard to Oracle Fusion Applications users. The WebCenter Spaces component also allows users and groups to collaborate with each other.

- weblogic: Contains the Oracle WebLogic Server installation files. WebLogic is the Application Server of Oracle Fusion middleware used in Fusion Applications and replaces any earlier versions of Oracle Applications Servers used in EBS. The product families have their dedicated WebLogic domains to effectively manage, control, and utilize WebLogic server capabilities for each of the Fusion Applications products.

- smart_update: Contains the Oracle WebLogic Server patches and patching utility. The Fusion Applications provisioning process automatically applies all required patches so you don't have to manually invoke the patching utility for WebLogic servers.

- soa: Contains the Oracle SOA Suite installation files. SOA provides components required for orchestrating, deploying, and managing services into SOA composite applications and business processes.

- odi: Contains the Oracle Data Integrator installation files. ODI is used for high-performance data loads, data extracts, and batch processing for Oracle Fusion Applications.

- oracle_common: Contains patches for Common Oracle home under the Fusion Applications home directory. The Provisioning wizard automatically applies the required patches from this directory during installation.

3. **Oracle database-related directories.**

   - database: Contains the Oracle Database software installation files along with the templates for the blank Fusion Applications starter database. It also contains the patches and PSUs required for upgrading the database to supported release for Fusion Applications. All the patches are applied along with database installation through Fusion Applications provisioning framework.

   - dbclient: Contains Oracle Client release 11gR1 (11.1.0.7 until recent releases) specifically for Oracle Fusion middleware components. Since the database version is higher, the 11gR1 client software is installed separately with this release under Applications Base Directory.

4. **RCUs and RUPs related to installation or upgrade.**

   - apps_rcu: Contains the Repository Creation Utility for Fusion Applications database and related dump files for repository creation. This is required to be installed prior to starting the provisioning process. It is also used during upgrade process on non-Linux environments to manually load schemas related to new or modified products from previous releases.

   - crm_rcu: Contains the Oracle CRM Sales Predictor Repository Creation utility (RCU). It creates sales predictor-related data warehouse database objects provided OBIA is already configured.

   - biapps_rcu: Contains the Business Intelligence Applications Suite Repository Creation Utility (RCU). This is used to create the Business Analytics Warehouse and BI applications components schemas.

   - fsrcu: Contains the Repository Creation Utility (RCU) for the Functional Setup Manager component. This is also required during the upgrade process on non-Linux environments to manually load the FS repository in the database.

   - tmrcu: Contains the Repository Creation Utility (RCU) for the Topology Manager component. This is also required during the upgrade process on non-Linux environments to manually load the topology manager repository in the database.

   - farup: Contains the upgrade orchestrator utility for upgrading Oracle Fusion Applications from previous releases to the current release. The invocation of the upgrade process has changed in recent releases. Now it contains a subdirectory called orchestration under the upgrade directory. This directory contains the orchestration.zip file that contains the Fusion Applications upgrade utility.

Preparing the Hosts Operating System

Before we begin the installation, we need to make sure that a supported operating system is installed and the required system parameters are set. We will discuss a few important settings here but refer to the latest Fusion Applications Release Notes as well as the Certification Matrix to see the list of supported operating systems and parameters.

■ **Note** It is recommended to use physical nodes for database servers. Application and web servers can be on supported virtualization platforms.

We are going to use Oracle Enterprise Linux (OEL) 5, 64-bit as the base operating system for this installation. OEL 6 is also supported but at this moment the IDM Provisioning wizard has some issues with specific versions of OEL 6. This examples uses OEL 5. Follow these steps on all nodes in the selected topology, including IDM host, IDM DB host, FA host, and FA DB host to keep the operating system parameters in sync for ease of troubleshooting.

■ **Tip**   If you have enabled firewall or SE Linux during the Linux operating system installation, make sure to allow all required ports and applications manually before starting the installation.

Preparing Network and Name Resolution

If you are using DNS in your environment then you must make sure that all servers have proper the DNS client setup completed and the hosts can resolve names. Make sure to add entries in your internal DNS server for all the nodes in the selected topology, in this case idmhost, idmdbhost, fahost, and fadbhost.

In addition to hostnames, if you are planning to use Network Load Balancer (NLB) or Virtual IPs (VIP) for your installation (you will see the list of VIPs that can be configured during installation) then you must register those in your internal DNS as well as external DNS (if the URLs are going to be accessed from external IPs). The load balancer also needs to be configured to receive inbound connections on specific ports and forwarded to appropriate servers on the same or different ports. The session persistence policy also needs to be set accordingly on the load balancer.

If you are *not* using DNS to resolve hostnames then make sure all your nodes /etc/hosts file includes entries for idmhost and fahost as well as database hosts idmdbhost and fadbhost. In the /etc/hosts file you must keep the Fully Qualified Hostname first followed by the regular hostname. Keeping the fully qualified name after the regular hostname will cause issues during the provisioning process. Java-based installation wizards initiated from clients will not be able to display the progress log on the screen due to a known bug. Hence it is very important to have the host entry in the following syntax.

```
<IP address>   <Fully Qualified hostname>   <hostname>
```

A typical /etc/hosts file in this environment will look like this. It includes all four nodes and IP addresses so they can communicate with each other.

```
[root@idmhost ~]# more /etc/hosts
127.0.0.1 localhost.localdomain localhost
#::1 localhost6.localdomain6 localhost6
10.26.12.141 idmhost.paramlabs.com idmhost
10.26.12.151 idmdbhost.paramlabs.com idmdbhost
10.26.12.161 fahost.paramlabs.com fahost
10.26.12.171 fadbhost.paramlabs.com fadbhost
```

■ **Tip**   Even if you are using a single-tier topology and hosting database and middleware on same node, we recommend you have two extra entries in the hosts file for the same IPs. In the future, if you want to move the database to a different server, you can easily do it since the installed configuration uses a dedicated DB hostname and never uses IP.

If you are not using DNS resolution, comment out following entries in the /etc/resolve.conf file to speed up name resolution directly through the hosts file. If this is not done then you may apparently find slowness in the SSH login screen where it will wait longer before prompting for credentials. Ignore this step if DNS is being used in your environment. Let's look at this file after the change is done.

```
[root@idmhost ~]# cat /etc/resolv.conf
#search paramlabs.com
```

Preparing Storage

Make sure to configure the disk and swap space on each node as per the requirements specified in the previous chapter. Make sure the shared file system is mounted on each node except DMZ. You can either prepare the installation repository locally on the /stage directory or if you have prepared it on another machine then you can mount the directory on your local server as follows.

```
[root@idmhost ~]# mkdir /stage
[root@idmhost ~]# mount -t nfs <fileserver>:stage /stage
```

Make sure you can see the installer directories.

```
[root@idmhost ~]# ls -l /stage
drwxrwxrwx 1 root root 8192 Oct 24 03:02 installers
drwxrwxrwx 1 root root 4096 Oct 24 03:03 jdk6
```

For Database hosts, make sure tmpfs size is more than the size you want to keep for the database SGA and PGA. We can check the current size of tmpfs using the df -h command. To make any changes to tmpfs size, you need to add/modify the same in the /etc/fstab file.

```
[root@idmdbhost ~]# cp -p /etc/fstab /etc/fstab.bak
[root@idmdbhost ~]# vi /etc/fstab
```

Change the values as follows (only if it is less than SGA and PGA size or the memory_target value). You need to restart the host in order for these parameters to come into effect.

```
[root@idmhost ~]# grep tmpfs /etc/fstab
tmpfs /dev/shm tmpfs size=8G 0 0
```

Similarly for FADBHOST (Fusion Applications Database Host), keep the tmpfs size to a much higher value.

■ **Note** If this size is less than memory_target then you will get the following error:

```
ORA-00845: MEMORY_TARGET not supported on this system
```

Installing Required Operating System Packages

Depending on your operating system, the installer may require a specific list of packages to be installed as a prerequisite. You can either refer to latest release notes or simply go ahead with the installation wizard, which will prompt you to install the missing packages. You can save time by preparing the list of missing packages in advance by manually running the prerequisite check from the installer repository. The following is the command-line syntax for checking the prerequisites before installing the provisioning framework.

For the database host:

<REPOSITORY_LOCATION>/installer/database/Disk1/runInstaller -executePrereqs -silent

This will generate output at <home>/oraInventory/logs/installActions<timestamp>.log.
For the application host:

**<REPOSITORY_LOCATION>/installer/<product>/Disk1/runInstaller -sv -jreLoc **
<REPOSITORY_LOCATION>/jdk6

This will generate the output at <home>/oraInventory/logs/install<timestamp>.log. Review the relevant log and look for the section with "Check Name: Packages". It will look as follows.

```
Check Name:Packages
Check Description:This is a prerequisite condition to test whether the packages recommended
for installing the product are available on the system.
Checking for binutils-2.17.50.0.6; found binutils-2.17.50.0.6-20.el5_8.3-x86_64.
Passed
Checking for compat-libstdc++-33-3.2.3-x86_64; found compat-libstdc++-33-3.2.3-61-x86_64.
Passed
Checking for compat-libstdc++-33-3.2.3-i386; found compat-libstdc++-33-3.2.3-61-i386.
Passed
Checking for elfutils-libelf-0.125; found elfutils-libelf-0.137-3.el5-x86_64.    Passed
Checking for elfutils-libelf-devel-0.125; found elfutils-libelf-devel-0.137-3.el5-x86_64.
Passed
Checking for gcc-4.1.1; found gcc-4.1.2-54.el5-x86_64.                          Passed
Checking for gcc-c++-4.1.1; found gcc-c++-4.1.2-54.el5-x86_64.                  Passed
Checking for glibc-2.5-12-x86_64; found glibc-2.5-107-x86_64.                   Passed
Checking for glibc-2.5-12-i686; found glibc-2.5-107-i686.                       Passed
Checking for glibc-common-2.5; found glibc-common-2.5-107-x86_64.              Passed
Checking for glibc-devel-2.5-x86_64; found glibc-devel-2.5-107-x86_64.          Passed
Checking for glibc-devel-2.5-12-i386; found glibc-devel-2.5-107-i386.           Passed
Checking for libaio-0.3.106-x86_64; found libaio-0.3.106-5-x86_64.              Passed
Checking for libaio-0.3.106-i386; found libaio-0.3.106-5-i386.                  Passed
Checking for libaio-devel-0.3.106; found libaio-devel-0.3.106-5-i386.           Passed
Checking for libgcc-4.1.1-x86_64; found libgcc-4.1.2-54.el5-x86_64.             Passed
Checking for libgcc-4.1.1-i386; found libgcc-4.1.2-54.el5-i386.                 Passed
Checking for libstdc++-4.1.1-x86_64; found libstdc++-4.1.2-54.el5-x86_64.       Passed
Checking for libstdc++-4.1.1-i386; found libstdc++-4.1.2-54.el5-i386.           Passed
Checking for libstdc++-devel-4.1.1; found libstdc++-devel-4.1.2-54.el5-i386.    Passed
Checking for make-3.81; found make-1:3.81-3.el5-x86_64.                         Passed
Checking for sysstat-7.0.0; found sysstat-7.0.2-12.0.1.el5-x86_64.              Passed
Check complete. The overall result of this check is:                           Passed
```

If any package is missing, you may find these lines:

```
Checking for glibc-devel-2.5-12-i386; Not found. Failed <<<<
```

Compile a list of all such failed checks and then manually install these packages/RPMs from the operating system installer media.

■ **Tip** If you are using Oracle Enterprise Linux, it is recommended to install `oracle-validated-<version>` `.el5.<platform>` for OEL 5 and `oracle-rdbms-server-<version>-preinstall` RPM packages to automatically set the required kernel configuration, OS groups, and so on. During the Linux installation you may use the Customize Now option followed by selecting the Servers on left panel and System Administration tools on the right side. Select the Oracle Validated or Oracle Pre-installation RPM packages. If you have already installed Linux, you can manually install the RPM with from the OEL media.

Creating Operating System Users and Groups

Let's create a Fusion installation owner user. Oracle validated setup RPM has already created dba and oinstall groups along with default oracle user. Here we will create a new user named fusion, which will be the owner of the Fusion Applications software directories. We are keeping the same name for all nodes here for ease of understanding. Using the same username also helps to access files from shared disk on different nodes. Let's create OS groups called dba and oinstall first if they are not already created.

```
[root@idmhost ~]# groupadd dba
[root@idmhost ~]# groupadd oinstall
```

Now let's create the fusion software owner user. This user needs to be member of the dba and oinstall OS groups.

```
[root@idmhost ~]# useradd fusion -g dba -G oinstall
```

Create a password for the fusion user.

```
[root@idmhost ~]# passwd fusion
Changing password for user fusion.
New UNIX password:
Retype new UNIX password:
passwd: all authentication tokens updated successfully.
```

Configuring Required Kernel Parameters

This section discusses some important kernel parameters and their minimum required values. Note that these parameters can have higher values depending on your tuning exercises. Use root user to make any kernel parameter changes.

Although we have installed Oracle-validated RPM packages, the username we have used is different than what Oracle creates as part of the package. Hence we need to add following lines in the /etc/security/ limits.conf file for the new user. Make a backup of the /etc/security/limits.conf file first.

```
[root@idmhost ~]# cp -p /etc/security/limits.conf /etc/security/limits.conf.bak
```

Add the following the values in the file /etc/security/limits.conf as follows:

```
fusion soft nofile 327679
fusion hard nofile 327679
```

Also make sure UsePAM is set to Yes in the /etc/ssh/sshd_config file. If not, back up the file and change it. In our case it is already set so there is no need to modify anything.

Edit /proc/sys/fs/file-max and set it to 6553600. The change will become effective immediately but will not persist after a reboot. So we need to add the set fs.file-max = 6553600 in /etc/sysctl.conf file to make the change permanent. In our case this value is already higher than the required, so no action is necessary.

Now we need to make sure that the max user process is set to at least 16384. Let's check the current value first.

```
[root@idmhost ~]# ulimit -u
24064
```

The output should be 16384 or more so in this case there is no further action is necessary. If the number is less than the required, we need to change the max user processes. If required, modify the /etc/security/limits.conf file as follows:

```
fusion soft nproc 16384
fusion hard nproc 16384
```

Because in this case the value is already more than 16384, we will leave it unchanged.

Now make sure that the ip_local_port_range value is 32768 to 61000. First check the existing value.

```
[root@idmhost ~]# cat /proc/sys/net/ipv4/ip_local_port_range
9000 65500
```

Now let's change as per the requirement.

```
[root@idmhost ~]# echo "32768 61000" > /proc/sys/net/ipv4/ip_local_port_range
```

To confirm the change, run the following command.

```
[root@idmhost ~]# cat /proc/sys/net/ipv4/ip_local_port_range
32768 61000
```

To make this change persistent across reboots, change the value of net.ipv4.ip_local_port_range in /etc/sysctl.conf to the previous values. Let's check the values after modification.

```
[root@idmhost ~]# grep 61000 /etc/sysctl.conf
net.ipv4.ip_local_port_range = 32768 61000
```

Before you install the Oracle database using the Provisioning wizard, ensure that the value of the kernel parameter shmmax on the database host is greater than the value of the SGA's (System Global Area) memory size.

If you used the Fusion Applications provisioning framework to create a starter database for the IDM database as well, the value of SGA memory (sga_target) is 9 GB in the default Database Configuration Assistant (DBCA) template for the starter database. For manual installation, you would have already set the value of SGA as per your requirement. Ensure that shmmax > (shmall * shmmni) > SGA memory, where shmmax, shmall, and shmmni are the kernel parameters.

For example, to retrieve the values of these kernel parameters on Linux, use the following command:

```
[root@idmhost ~]# /sbin/sysctl -a | grep shm
kernel.shmmax = 4398046511104
kernel.shmall = 1073741824
kernel.shmmni = 4096
vm.hugetlb_shm_group = 0
```

Use the following command to set the value of a kernel parameter.

```
[root@idmhost ~]# /sbin/sysctl -w sys.kernel.shmmax=value
```

Finally, make sure that the Linux host has sufficient entropy values (more than 1000). To check the current value, execute the following command.

```
[root@idmhost ~]# cat /proc/sys/kernel/random/entropy_avail
```

If the output is less than 1000 then run following command as the root user to increase the value.

```
[root@idmhost ~]# rngd -r /dev/urandom -o /dev/random
```

■ **Note**   For the Solaris operating system, you must set memory limits for each user in the /etc/project file to higher value. Otherwise, the user processes throw out-of-memory errors despite the fact that the memory is not fully utilized. This is the default behavior of the Solaris operating system, so make sure to allocate a high-memory limit for the fusion user in the /etc/project file.

Preparing Operating System for the Remaining Nodes

Remember to repeat the complete process for all the other nodes in the selected topology. Since the operating system related parameters are the same (except a few differences mentioned earlier), I will not repeat the same information again. This section serves as a reminder for setting up the remaining nodes operating system, network and storage only.

At the end of this section you should be able to reach each of the nodes in the topology from every other node. This includes network reachability as well as opening firewall ports if your environment utilizes firewall across the web, application, and database tiers. Note all the ports during the installation process and make sure to work with the network security team to open each of the required firewall ports between the nodes.

Make sure that you do the same steps on both databases as well as the application nodes. This concludes our operating system configuration for all nodes.

Summary

This chapter provides an overview of the Fusion Applications provisioning process. You should now understand the concepts of the orchestration process and the role of each node during the provisioning process. You've seen how the provisioning steps are grouped between Identity Management and Fusion Applications components. You have also seen the dependencies between the IDM and FA provisioning steps.

We learned about the topology selected for this example installation and also the components that will be installed and configured on each of the nodes in the selected topology. We have also seen how to prepare the operating system, network, and storage for each of the nodes. You now also know how to create an installation staging directory and the structure of Fusion Applications installation repository. In Chapters 4-7, you will learn how to prepare an Identity Management environment required for a Fusion Applications instance. Chapters 8-10 will demonstrate the Fusion Applications components provisioning processes.

PART III

Installation

CHAPTER 4

∎ ∎ ∎

Preparing the Identity Management Database

As you saw in previous chapter, you can run multiple installation tasks in parallel. For the purposes of clarity, we will run through the Fusion Applications installation in sequence by completing the Identity Management related tasks first followed by the Fusion Applications related tasks. In Chapters 5-7, we will go through the Oracle Identity Management provisioning process using an example installation. In order to provision an Identity Management environment, you must already have a database in place with all the required schemas created as a prerequisite. In this chapter, we will look at creating a new blank database for Identity Management and then we will see how to create an Identity Management repository in this newly created database.

Installing the Database for IDM

As you saw in Chapter 3, you must create an Oracle database for Identity Management before starting the IDM provisioning process. The current version of the Identity Management provisioning framework does not support creating a new Identity Management database as of Oracle Fusion Applications Release 9. However, future releases of the IDM provisioning framework may support installation of a new IDM database right from the same wizard. Note that the Fusion Applications provisioning wizard already supports creating a new applications transactional database directly, so the following steps are specific to the Identity Management database only.

Overall, you have three options to create a blank Identity Management database.

1. IDM provisioning wizard: Once we look at the Identity Management provisioning framework, you will notice that the option to create a database for IDM is currently disabled in the current releases. However, it will be enabled in future releases so then we should be able to use IDM Provisioning wizard to create a new Identity Management Database. This option will take care of all required patches and other prerequisites automatically and will create a blank database with certified versions and patches. Once it's available, you should use only this option for creating an Identity Management database.

2. Manual installation: Manually install an Oracle 11g version (11.2.0.3 or 11.2.0.4 or later based on the selected release requirement) on a single database node or RAC. In this case, you will need to manually apply Patch Set Updates (PSU) and other patches to bring the database to the supported level. Be careful while selecting this option since you may need to make sure that all required parameters and patches are in place to avoid any issues related to known bugs during installation or normal operation.

© Tushar Thakker 2015
T. Thakker, *Pro Oracle Fusion Applications*, DOI 10.1007/978-1-4842-0983-7_4

3. Use the Fusion Applications provisioning wizard as a workaround: You may want to use the Fusion Applications provisioning wizard as a workaround and create a blank single node database on Identity Management database node. This step relieves you from having to manually apply patches, PSUs, and so on, since the installer automatically applies all recommended patches and configuration. This method saves time but it is not recommended for production installation since this option is specifically tailored to an application transactional database. For demo systems this may serve the purpose. In order to use this option you may need to temporarily install the Fusion Application provisioning framework on a database node as well.

Option 1 is not yet available. Option 3 is simple but not suggested by Oracle so we will skip it in this section, but you can refer to Chapter 8 to learn about this option and, if necessary, use it as a workaround on IDM node. In this example, we will use option 2, which is the manual installation of the Oracle 11g Database.

We will prepare the Identity Management database with the recommended patches in the following four steps.

1. Install a blank database using the media provided in the Fusion Applications installation repository.

2. Apply the *PSU (Patch Set Update)* manually (if included along with the installation media) to bring the database to the supported version.

3. Apply all recommended patches included along with the installation media.

4. Set the recommended parameters that are specific to the Identity Management database.

Although you most likely how to install an Oracle 11gR2 database from standard installer, we will quickly go through the screens for the sake of completeness. Start the database installer from the media located at <INSTALLATION_REPOSITORY>/installers/database/Disk1:

```
[fusion@idmdbhost ~]$ cd /stage/installers/database/Disk1/
[fusion@idmdbhost Disk1]$ ./runInstaller&
```

Figure 4-1 shows an optional screen for most Oracle products. We will look at some common screens like this once and then skip to the next chapters in order to avoid any repetitions.

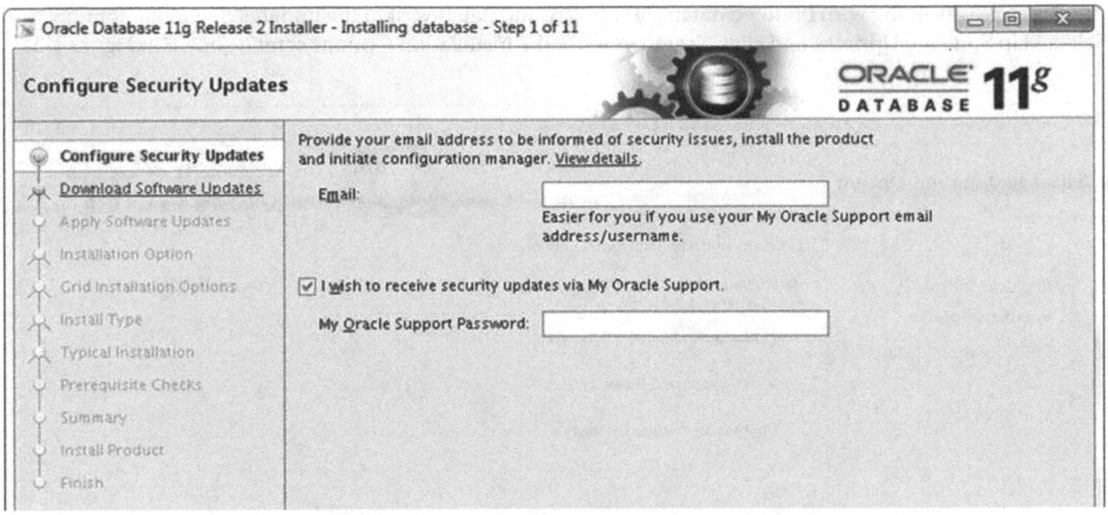

Figure 4-1. *Configure Security Updates email configuration screen*

If you wish to receive an email update about the Oracle product being installed, you can enter an email in the field. If you want to receive security updates directly in your existing Oracle support account then you may enter the credentials in the next field. Otherwise uncheck the checkbox. Click *Next* to continue with the installer. It may prompt you for confirmation if you have not entered any information in this screen. Now you will be taken to the Download Software Updates screen shown in Figure 4-2.

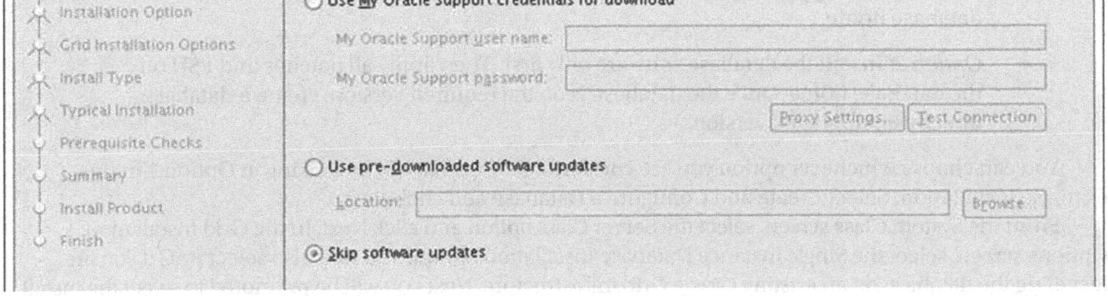

Figure 4-2. *Download Software Updates screen*

Since we are going with bundled database software and patches, skip the updates download for now. Select Skip Software Updates and click Next to move to the Installation Options screen shown in Figure 4-3.

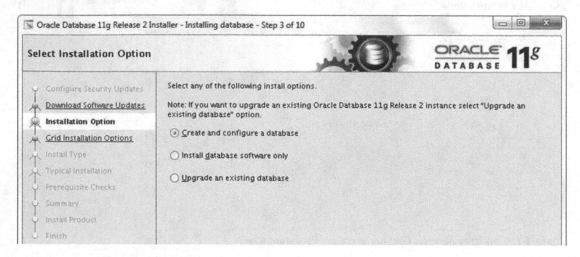

Figure 4-3. *Select Installation Option screen*

■ **Note**   Note that the server must have an Internet proxy configured in order to send the information to Oracle in both of these screens. If there is no outside connectivity, skip both screens. It may prompt you to confirm before you can skip.

You can create a database now or later since we need to later apply recommended patches in order to bring to supported level with Fusion Applications. Following are the available options shown in Figure 4-3. The Upgrade Database option is not applicable since this is fresh installation.

- *Option 1*: Create and configure the database in a single step and then apply the patches and PSU (Patch Set Update) on the database home. You will need to manually run upgrade scripts on the database later to bring it to same level as the database home.

- *Option 2*: Install the database software only first. Then apply all patches and PSU on the database home. Once the database is on the required version, create a database directly on upgraded version.

You can choose whichever option you are comfortable with. We will be looking at Option 1 in this example installation. Select Create and Configure a Database and click Next.

From the System Class screen, select the Server Class option and click Next. In the Grid Installation Options screen, select the Single Instance Database Installation option. You may also select RAC if you are installing the database on an existing Oracle Grid infrastructure. Next you will be promoted to select the install type. You may select Advanced Install to edit detailed parameters related to memory, database files, locations, passwords, and so on. In this example we are only looking at basic database installation, so we use the Typical option. Let's skip to installation parameters screen for Typical Installation type, as shown in Figure 4-4.

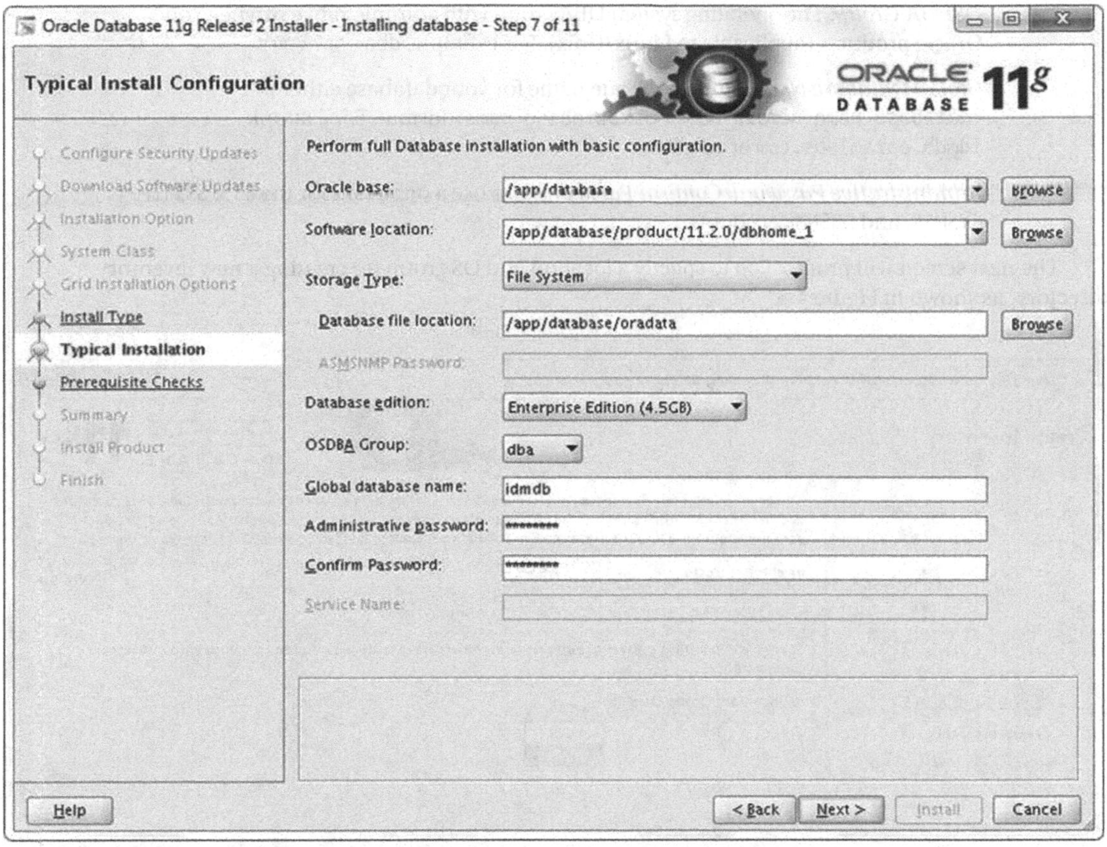

Figure 4-4. Installation location and configuration details screen

At this point the installer prompts you to provide the installation location and the following details.

- *Oracle Base*: The ORACLE_BASE location value. It will be the base location for various Oracle products and components. Select /app/database here. If the /app directory does not exist, then installer will not be able to create this path, so create the directory as the root user and change the owner to database installer user.

```
[root@idmdbhost ~]# mkdir /app
[root@idmdbhost ~]# chown fusion:dba /app
```

- *Software Location*: The ORACLE_HOME location for the database. This value will be automatically populated based on ORACLE_BASE value. Typically it will be <ORACLE_BASE>/product/11.2.0/dbhome_1. Change it if required.

- *Storage Type*: File system or Automatic Storage Management. We have selected File System in this example.

- *Database File Location*: The location where the database files will be created. For example, /app/database/oradata.

- *Database Edition*: You must select Enterprise Edition only here.

- *OSDBA Group*: The operating system DBA group with administrative privilege on Oracle products (applicable to Linux/Unix). For example, dba.

- *Global Database Name*: Enter a unique name for your database either in `<database_name.domain_name>` or `<database_name>` format. For example, `idmdb.paramlabs.com` or `idmdb`.

- *Administrative Password/Confirm Password*: Choose a password for the SYS, SYSTEM, SYSMAN, and DBSNMP accounts.

The next screen will prompt you to specify a location and OS group for creating a new inventory directory, as shown in Figure 4-5.

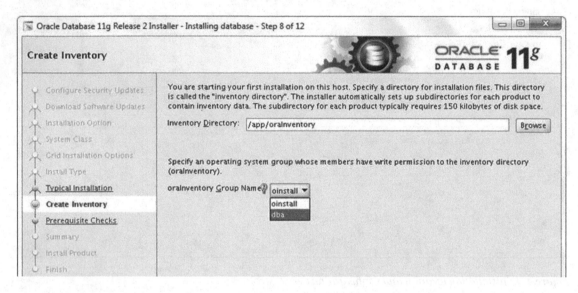

Figure 4-5. *Oracle Inventory details screen*

Specify the location of the inventory directory. This is already filled in, as shown in Figure 4-5, so change it if required. Select the oraInventory group name. Any users in this group will be able to create a new inventory entry in this directory. Typically, you can select from the dba and oinstall groups, depending on the default group of your Oracle-related users. Click *Next* to continue.

The installer now checks for various prerequisites, including operating system version, kernel parameters, disk space, memory, and so on. Once it's complete, it will automatically move to the Summary screen shown in Figure 4-6.

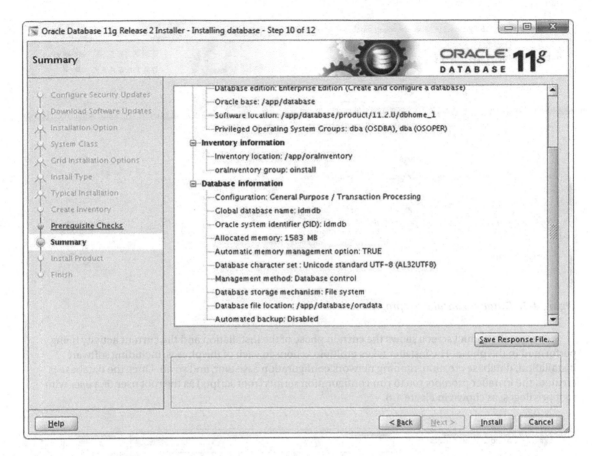

Figure 4-6. Pre-install summary screem

The pre-install summary screen will show the responses you entered. Review the values and click Back if you want to modify anything. Click Save Response File if you want to install the software later or for documentation purposes. Once you review and confirm everything, click Install to start the database installation process. The wizard will now proceed to the Install Product screen, as shown in Figure 4-7.

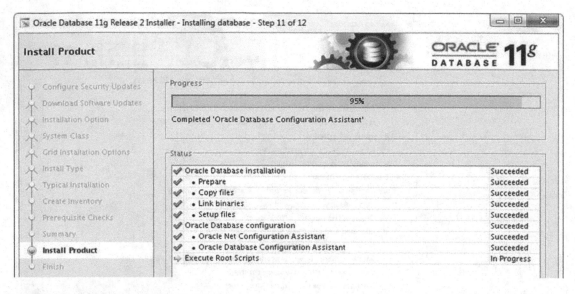

Figure 4-7. *Database installation progress screen*

The Install Product screen shows the current phase of the installation and the current activity being performed in the phase. The installer takes multiple actions in each of the phases, including software installation, database creation, running network configuration assistant, and so on. Once the database is created, the installer prompts you to run configuration scripts (root scripts) as the root user or a user with root privileges, as shown in Figure 4-8.

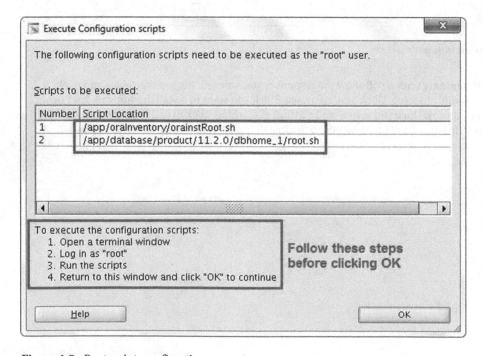

Figure 4-8. *Root scripts confimation prompt*

As you can see in Figure 4-8, the installer prompts you to run two scripts on the database node as the root user. If you run the scripts you'll see the output shown in Figure 4-9.

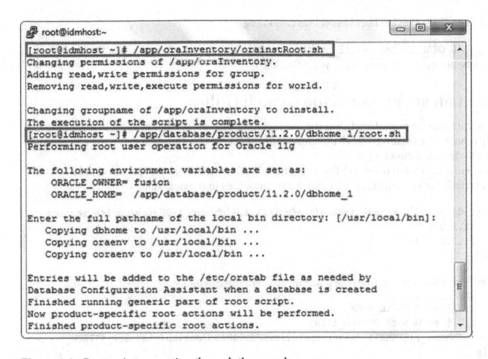

Figure 4-9. Root scripts execution through the console

The first script creates the `oraInventory` directory and a pointer file for the inventory. The second script creates env files with environment variables set in the local `bin` directory. The database entry is also added to the `/etc/oratab` file with the database's hostname and auto startup details. Once you click OK, you will see a confirmation screen with post installation information, as shown in Figure 4-10.

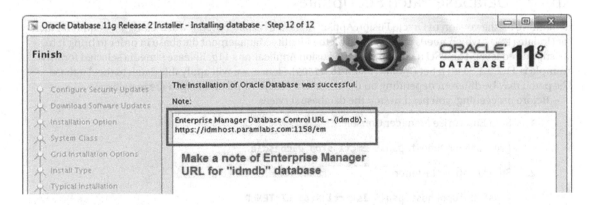

Figure 4-10. Installation completion screen

The final completion screen shows the URL of the configured Enterprise Manager. Save this URL for future reference. You can always get this URL by running the emctl status dbconsole command on the OS prompt. You can find the log of this install session at the following location:

<Inventory_Location>/logs/installActions<timestamp>.log

Set the ORACLE_SID, ORACLE_HOME, ORACLE_UNQNAME, and PATH variables in your shell profile file so that the parameters will be always set automatically when you log in.

Installing the Latest Version of the OPatch Utility

You can download the latest version of OPatch or the one included with the media. In order to install the new version of OPatch, rename the existing OPatch directory under ORACLE_HOME and then unzip the contents of the bundled patch to the same directory.

Let's check the current version of OPatch first using the $ORACLE_HOME/OPatch/opatch version command. We will check the version again after copying the new files in the next step.

```
[fusion@idmdbhost database]$ /app/database/product/11.2.0/dbhome_1/OPatch/opatch version
Invoking OPatch 11.2.0.1.7
OPatch Version: 11.2.0.1.7
OPatch succeeded.
```

Now will install the latest version from the patch included in the media.

```
[fusion@idmdbhost ~]$ cd $ORACLE_HOME
[fusion@idmdbhost ~]$ mv OPatch OPatch_11201
[fusion@idmdbhost dbhome_1]$ unzip /stage/installers/database/opatch/p6880880_112000_
Linux-x86-64.zip
```

Let's make sure the version of OPatch is updated.

```
[fusion@idmdbhost dbhome_1]$ /app/database/product/11.2.0/dbhome_1/OPatch/opatch version
OPatch Version: 11.2.0.3.4
OPatch succeeded.
```

Apply a Database Patch Set Update

Depending on the version of Oracle Fusion Applications, the installer media will include the required Patch Set Update (PSU), which needs to be applied on the Identity Management database in order to bring it to the supported level. The PSU included with the Fusion Applications 11g, Release 9 media selected for this example is 11.2.0.4.3 Patch Set Update (Patch 18522509). Hence, we will apply this patch to the database. The patch may be different depending on the version of Fusion Applications you are installing.

Before proceeding, you need to stop the database services.

1. Stop Enterprise Manager Console.

    ```
    [fusion@idmdbhost psu]$ emctl stop dbconsole
    ```

2. Stop Database Listener.

    ```
    [fusion@idmdbhost psu]$ lsnrctl stop LISTENER
    ```

3. Shut down the database.

    ```
    SQL> shutdown immediate;
    ```

Let's apply the PSU and related patches. Change the directory to <Installation_Repository>/installers/database/psu:

```
[fusion@idmdbhost ~]$ cd /stage/installers/database/psu/
```

Run OPatch for patch number 18522509:

```
[fusion@idmdbhost psu]$ $ORACLE_HOME/OPatch/opatch apply 18522509
...
Verifying environment and performing prerequisite checks...
OPatch continues with these patches:   17478514  18031668  18522509

Do you want to proceed? [y|n]
y
...
Please shutdown Oracle instances running out of this ORACLE_HOME on the local system.
(Oracle Home = '/app/database/product/11.2.0/dbhome_1')

Is the local system ready for patching? [y|n]
y
...
OPatch completed with warnings.
```

We have now upgraded the Oracle home binaries, but since we already have a database configured, we must run catbundle.sql to update the metadata and load modified SQLs in the existing database. The script is located at $ORACLE_HOME/rdbms/admin.

```
[fusion@idmdbhost ~]$ cd $ORACLE_HOME/rdbms/admin
```

Start the database now.

```
[fusion@idmdbhost admin]$ sqlplus / as sysdba
Connected to an idle instance.
SQL> startup
```

Run the catbundle.sql script as follows.

```
SQL> @catbundle.sql psu apply
Check the following log file for errors:
/app/database/product/11.2.0/dbhome_1/cfgtoollogs/catbundle/catbundle_PSU_IDMDB_
APPLY_2015Feb21_00_54_12.log
```

Let's make sure that the database software version is as expected.

```
SQL> select * from v$version;

BANNER
--------------------------------------------------------------------------------
Oracle Database 11g Enterprise Edition Release 11.2.0.4.0 - 64bit Production
PL/SQL Release 11.2.0.4.0 - Production
CORE    11.2.0.4.0      Production
TNS for Linux: Version 11.2.0.4.0 - Production
NLSRTL Version 11.2.0.4.0 - Production
```

Apply Database Patches

Once the PSU is applied, you can apply other mandatory patches for the Oracle database. The patches are included in the `<Installation_Repository>/installers/database/patch` directory.

```
[fusion@idmdbhost Disk1]$ cd /stage/installllers/database/patch/
[fusion@idmdbhost patch]$ ls -ltr
total 8
drwxrwxrwx 1 root root    0 Dec 18  2013 17357979
drwxrwxrwx 1 root root    0 Dec 19  2013 17036973
drwxrwxrwx 1 root root    0 Dec 20  2013 17209410
drwxrwxrwx 1 root root    0 Jan 10  2014 17775506
drwxrwxrwx 1 root root    0 Jan 12  2014 11733603
... and more
```

Let's apply all these patches in one go. Invoke opatch with the napply option to apply all of them together.

```
[fusion@idmdbhost patch]$ /app/database/product/11.2.0/dbhome_1/OPatch/opatch napply
Oracle Interim Patch Installer version 11.2.0.3.4
...
Verifying environment and performing prerequisite checks...
OPatch continues with these patches:   17357979  17036973  17209410  17775506  11733603
14084247  18154779  18135678  13073613  13498243  17982555  16980342  16907774  12716670
17811789  18700740  14285317  18418934  18966843  16524926  19194799  18767554  19238601
19249319

Do you want to proceed? [y|n]
y
...
Please shutdown Oracle instances running out of this ORACLE_HOME on the local system.
(Oracle Home = '/app/database/product/11.2.0/dbhome_1')

Is the local system ready for patching? [y|n]
y
...
Patches 17357979,17036973,17209410,17775506,11733603,14084247,18154779,18135678,13073613,
13498243,17982555,16980342,16907774,12716670,17811789,18700740,14285317,18418934,18966843,
16524926,19194799,18767554,19238601,19249319 successfully applied.
OPatch Session completed with warnings.
...
OPatch completed with warnings.
```

The typical option in the Oracle Database installation configures the listener on default port 1521. It is optional but recommended to change the default listener port to a new value as part of database security best practices. We will change the default port in this example to 1531.

- Change the default listener name and port in `listener.ora`.

- Update listener port and listener entry in `tnsnames.ora`.

- Change the `LOCAL_LISTENER` parameter in the `SPFILE` database to point to the new listener.

- Restart the database and listener.

Now the TNS entry for the Identity Management database looks as follows.

```
IDMDB =
  (DESCRIPTION =
    (ADDRESS = (PROTOCOL = TCP)(HOST = idmdbhost.paramlabs.com)(PORT = 1531))
    (CONNECT_DATA =
      (SERVER = DEDICATED)
      (SERVICE_NAME = idmdb)
    )
  )
```

Edit Recommended Database Parameters

IDM must have an open_cursors parameter set to 800. If you installed a new database using Fusion Applications provisioning framework then the value would be set at 500; otherwise, the current default value will be 300. In both cases we need to set it to 800. Make sure to use the scope=both option in order to retain the change after the database restarts.

```
SQL> show parameter open_cursors
NAME                                 TYPE        VALUE
------------------------------------ ----------- --------
open_cursors                         integer     300
SQL> alter system set open_cursors=800 scope=both sid='*';
System altered.
```

We need to set the processes parameter to at least 500. Change that as well in SPFILE.

```
SQL> show parameter processes
NAME                                 TYPE        VALUE
------------------------------------ ----------- -----------------------------
processes                            integer     150
SQL> alter system set processes=500 scope=spfile;
System altered.
```

■ **Tip**   If you created the Identity Management database using Fusion Applications provisioning framework then you may want to reduce the database memory target. The default SGA target is set to 9 GB through the Fusion Applications provisioning framework database creation scripts. You can leave it unchanged if you have enough memory on Identity Management database server to accommodate it.

Restart database to bring the parameters in effect from SPFILE.

Create XA Views as Prerequisites of the Repository Creation Utility

OIM requires Oracle XA related views in order to allow distributed transaction processing. However, by default these required views are not created in a fresh database. To avoid an expected error related to the XA view in RCU, we need to create the required XA views v$xatrans$ and v$pending_xatrans$ first using the xaview.sql script located in the RDBMS admin directory.

```
[fusion@idmdbhost bin]$ cd $ORACLE_HOME/rdbms/admin/
[fusion@idmdbhost admin]$ sqlplus / as sysdba
SQL> @xaview.sql
DROP VIEW v$xatrans$
*
ERROR at line 1:
ORA-00942: table or view does not exist

DROP VIEW v$pending_xatrans$
*
ERROR at line 1:
ORA-00942: table or view does not exist
View created.
View created.
```

Running the IDM Repository Creation Utility

The Repository Creation Utility (RCU) for the Oracle Identity Management components is only available for Linux and Windows platforms. Earlier versions of Fusion Applications installer media used to ship with Linux RCU only for Identity Management components but recent versions have both Linux and Windows versions included in the installation media.

If you are using Windows-based RCU then the Windows machine should be able to communicate with the database host. The required database ports need to be opened from the network firewall. We will use Linux RCU in this step since the database host includes the Linux operating system.

Before starting the RCU, you need to install JDK on the host from the ZIP file provided in the media. This will create a folder named /app/oracle/jdk6 and this will be our JAVA_HOME, which will be used for RCU and other Java-based installers.

```
[fusion@idmdbhost ~]$ mkdir /app/oracle
[fusion@idmdbhost ~]$ cd /app/oracle/
[fusion@idmdbhost oracle]$ unzip /stage/installers/jdk/jdk6.zip
```

Let's create a directory to extract the RCU files.

```
[fusion@idmdbhost ~]$ mkdir -p /app/oracle/provisioning/fmw_rcu
[fusion@idmdbhost ~]$ cd /app/oracle/provisioning/fmw_rcu
```

Unzip the RCU that ships with the installation.

```
[fusion@idmdbhost fmw_rcu]$ unzip /stage/installers/fmw_rcu/linux/rcuHome.zip
```

Let's launch the Repository Creation Utility now.

```
[fusion@idmdbhost ~]$ cd /app/oracle/provisioning/fmw_rcu/bin
[fusion@idmdbhost bin]$ ./rcu&
```

The *Welcome screen* is informative only and provides information on the purpose of this utility. No action is necessary on this screen. Click *Next* to continue with the wizard. Next you will be prompted to select the RCU option, as shown in Figure 4-11.

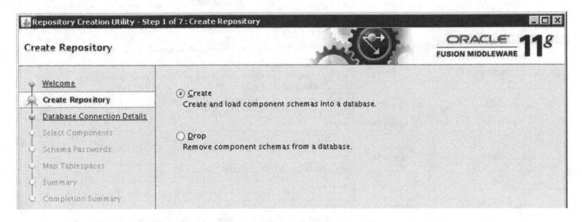

Figure 4-11. *Create or drop a repository from this selection screen*

This screen of Identity Management RCU provides two options to choose from.

- *Create*: This is the default option for the RCU. This option is used to create the necessary database objects and seed the repository data, which is the sole purpose of the utility.

- *Drop*: This option should be selected if you faced any issues with the RCU or the latter part of IDM provisioning. Since the current release of IDM provisioning wizard does not support automatic cleanup and restore, we may need to use this option to bring the database back to its original state and restart the complete provisioning process if it encountered any issues.

    Once you have dropped the existing repository, you need to launch the same screen again with the Create option in order to recreate the repository.

Since we are running RCU for the first time, select Create and the click Next to proceed to the Database Connection Details screen, as shown in Figure 4-12.

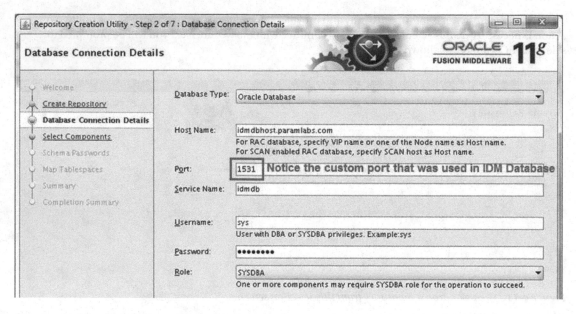

Figure 4-12. *Database Connection Details screen*

This screen prompts for the connection details for the database in which the repository needs to be created. The following information must be entered.

- *Database Type*: Identity Management RCU is a common utility for all Fusion Middleware components and since some of these components support non-Oracle databases like Microsoft SQL Server, IBM DB2, MySQL, and so on, you may see them in the drop-down menu. However, we must select Oracle Database since most of our selected components support Oracle Database only.

- *Host Name*: For single node databases, enter the name of the host where you installed the blank Identity Management database. For RAC, enter the name of SCAN hostname. In this case, it is single node database so we will enter idmdbhost.paramlabs.com.

- *Port*: The default value for the port is 1521. If you are using non-default port for your Identity Management database, then enter the value that you have configured. In this case, we are using port 1531.

- *Service Name*: In the case of the RAC database, enter Service Name while in case of Single Node database, enter SID value here. In this case, it is idmdb.

- *Username and Password*: Enter the credentials of SYSDBA privilege. We will enter SYS user here.

- *Role*: We must select the SYSDBA role here for the SYS user.

Enter these details and then click *Next* to proceed to the Prerequisites Check screen, as shown in Figure 4-13.

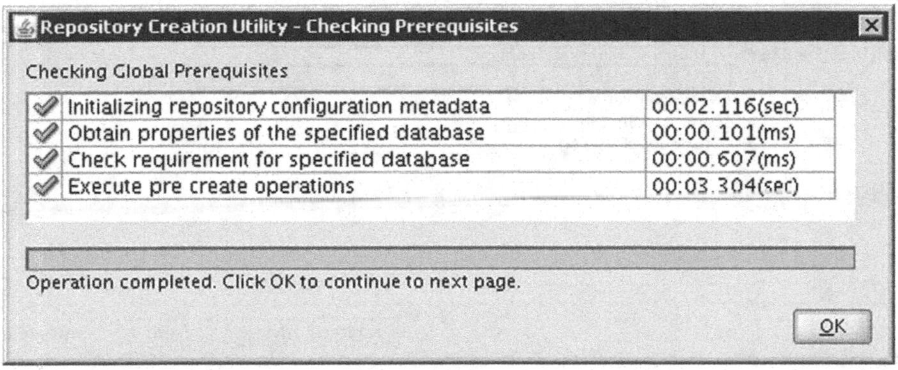

Figure 4-13. Prerequisites check pop-up screen

You will now see a pop-up screen that shows the prerequisites results for the Repository Creation Utility. If there are any errors in the previous screen where you provided database connection details, you may see failure in the validation here.

Once the prerequisites check completes, click OK to proceed. The next screen allows you to select the components for which you want to create the repository, including required the tablespaces and schema shown in Figures 4-14 and 4-15.

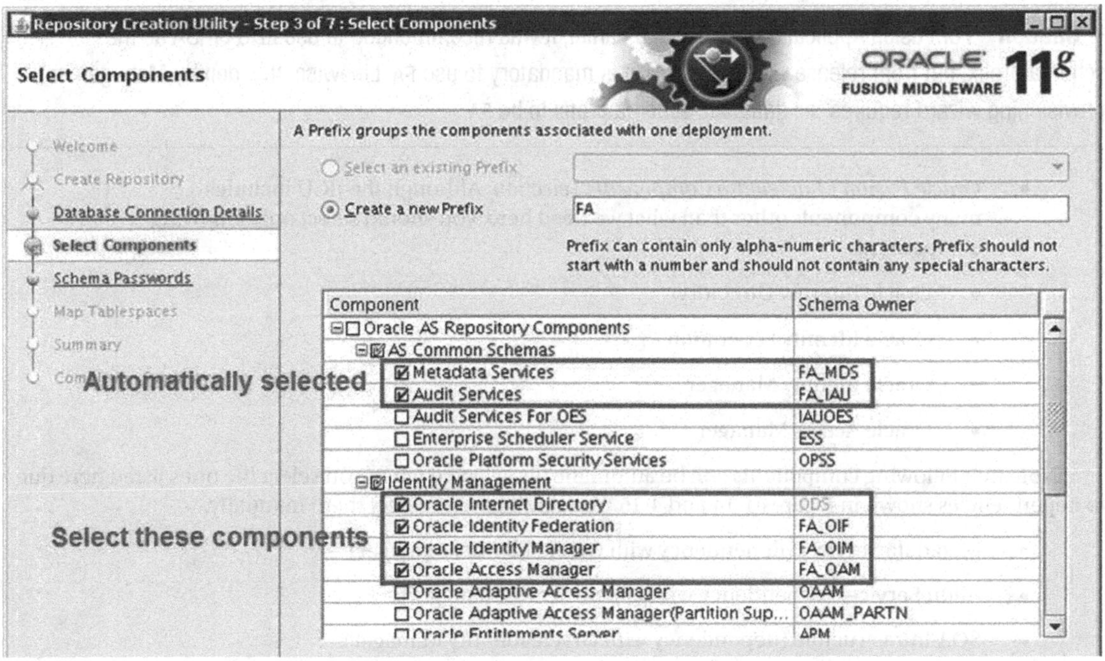

Figure 4-14. Repository components selection screen for creating new schemas

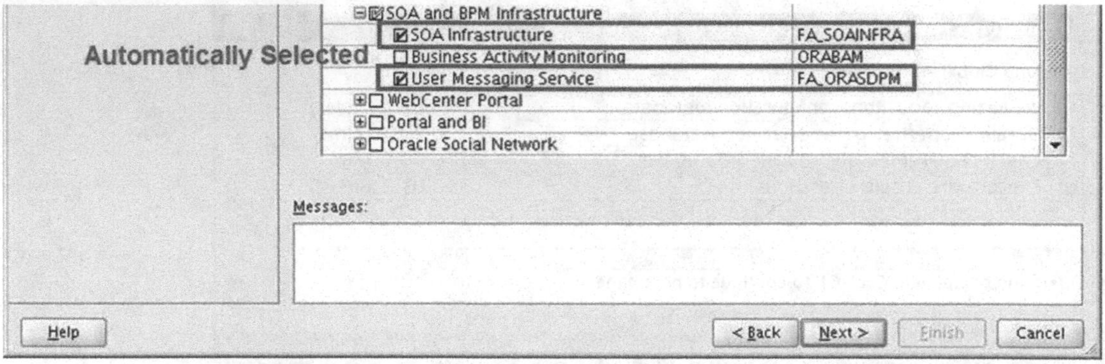

Figure 4-15. *Repository components selection screen for creating new schemas (continued)*

This screen prompts for the following values:

- *Create a New Prefix*: This is the Schema Prefix for the new schemas to be created except for the Oracle Internet Directory. As of now, OID does not support a prefix so any database can host only a single instance of OID. The schema name for OID is ODS by default and this cannot be changed. All the remaining schema names have the mandatory prefix of FA.

■ **Caution**   For Fusion Applications 11.1.6 and earlier, it was recommended to use EDG or ISA as the schema prefix, but from release 11.1.7 onward, it is mandatory to use FA. Likewise, the Identity Management provisioning wizard requires the database schema prefix to be FA.

- *Oracle Fusion Middleware Components Selection*: Although the RCU includes many components other than what we need here, you should select only following components.

  - Oracle Internet Directory

  - Oracle Identity Federation

  - Oracle Identity Manager

  - Oracle Access Manager

Note that following components will be automatically selected when you select the ones listed here due to dependencies shown in Figures 4-14 and 4-15. You don't have to select them manually.

- Metadata Services (dependency with Oracle Identity Manager)

- Audit Services (dependency with Oracle Access Manager)

- SOA Infrastructure (dependency with Oracle Identity Manager)

- User Messaging Service (dependency with Oracle Identity Manager)

Make the appropriate selections shown here and then click Next to continue with the wizard. Now you may again see a prerequisite check screen based on the previous selection, as shown in Figure 4-16.

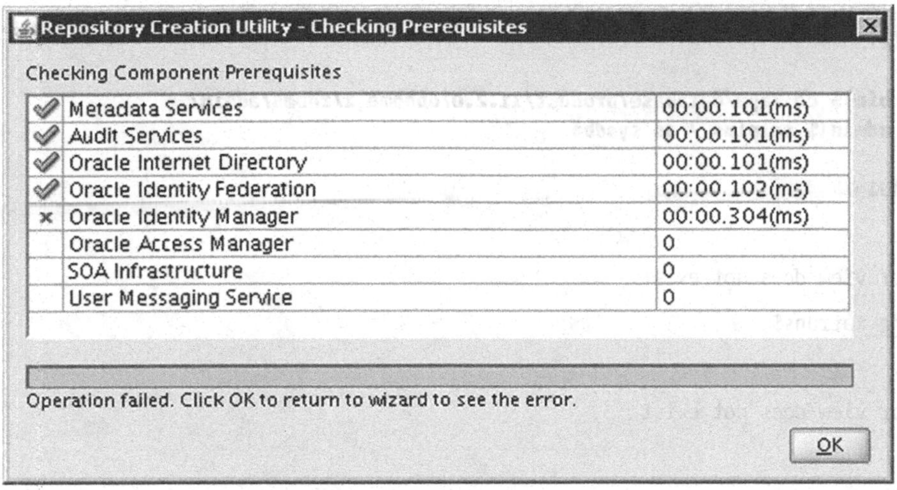

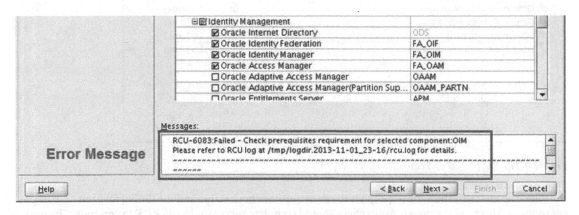

Figure 4-16. *Example of a failed prerequisites check*

This screen shows the validation status and duration for each of the components selected. The prerequisite checks might fail if you have not followed the database-creation steps mentioned in previous section properly. Figure 4-16 shows an example of a failed prerequisites check screen for reference. In this case, the prerequisites check for Oracle Identity Manager failed.

Click OK to see the error message details, which will take you back to the previous screen, as shown in Figure 4-17.

Figure 4-17. *Example error message screen after failed prerequisite checks*

The error message will appear in the previous screen under the Messages textbox after the pop-up is closed. The error message in this case is the following.

```
Error: XATRANS Views are not installed on this Database. This is required by the OIM Schema
Action: Install view XAVIEWS as SYS user on this Database.
Refer to the Oracle Database Release Documentation for installation details.
RCU-6092:Component Selection validation failed.
```

To fix this error, run the following SQL to create XA views if they were missed during the database-preparation step earlier.

```
[fusion@idmdbhost bin]$ cd /app/database/product/11.2.0/dbhome_1/rdbms/admin/
[fusion@idmdbhost admin]$ sqlplus / as sysdba
SQL> @xaview.sql
DROP VIEW v$xatrans$
*
ERROR at line 1:
ORA-00942: table or view does not exist

DROP VIEW v$pending_xatrans$
*
ERROR at line 1:
ORA-00942: table or view does not exist
View created.
View created.
```

Once the view creation is complete, click Next to rerun the prerequisites check, as shown in Figure 4-18.

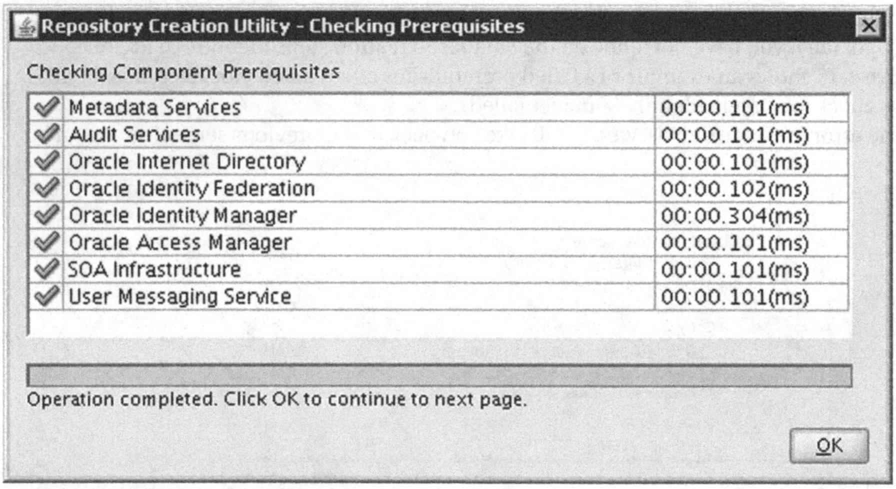

Figure 4-18. *Successful prerequisites check screen*

Once again it will show the pop-up for the prerequisites check status and the timing for each component. This time the prerequisites check should complete successfully. Click OK to continue. The next screen prompts you to select a password for each repository schema to be created, as shown in Figure 4-19.

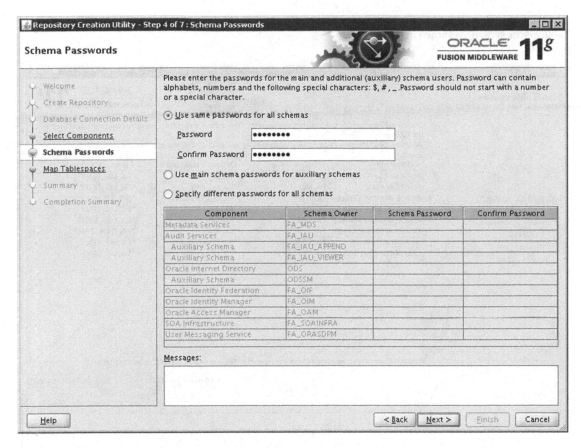

Figure 4-19. Schema Passwords selection screen

As you can see, the wizard creates main schemas based on the selection and creates corresponding AUXILIÇARY schemas for certain components. It provides three options for password selection. The passwords must contain at least eight characters with a combination of alphabetical, numerical, and/or special characters.

- *Same Password for All Schemas*: This option assigns the same password to all the main and auxiliary schemas.

- *Use Main Schema Passwords for Auxiliary Schemas*: This option allows you to select passwords for main schemas and the related auxiliary schemas will be assigned the same password as the main schema.

- *Specify Different Passwords for All Schemas*: This option enables all password textboxes and you can assign individual passwords for each schema as long as they confirm to the password complexity requirement.

■ **Caution** Identity Management provisioning framework suggests you have the same password for all schema passwords during provisioning. You can change the passwords later, but until IDM provisioning is complete, it is recommended you keep the schema passwords the same.

We have selected to have the same password for all schemas. Click Next to continue to the Map Tablespaces screen, as shown in Figure 4-20.

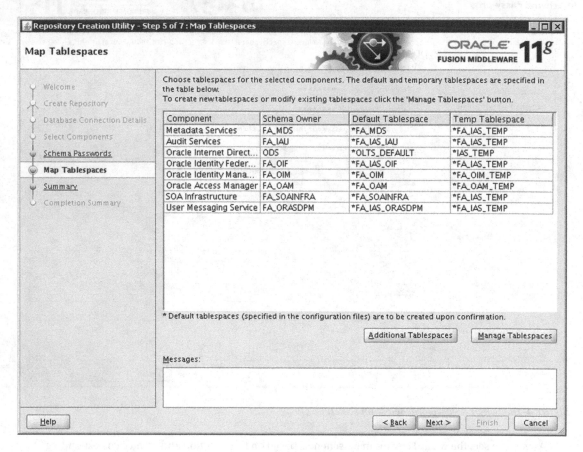

Figure 4-20. Map Tablespaces screen

There are other options—such as Additional Tablespaces and Manage Tablespaces—that allow you to select different names and types, or add or modify data filenames and sizes, as well as other tablespace-related operations.

Once you click Manage Tablespaces, the screen shown in Figure 4-21 comes up. This screen collects the information about the tablespaces, while the actual operation is performed in the next screen.

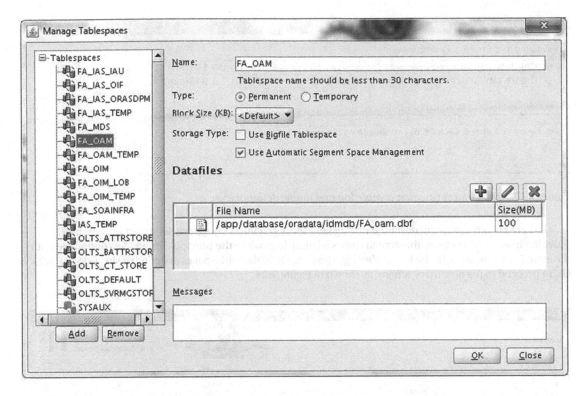

Figure 4-21. The Manage Tablespaces screen

Review this screen and modify the values if required. Click OK to close the window and you'll be returned to the previous screen. Now click Next to proceed with the tablespaces creation. The wizard prompts for confirmation to create the tablespaces, as shown in Figure 4-22.

Figure 4-22. Confirmation message screen for creating new tablespaces

If you are ready to proceed, click OK to confirm the tablespace creation. Once confirmed, the screen shown in Figure 4-23 appears. It shows the status of the tablespaces creation activity along with the timing information.

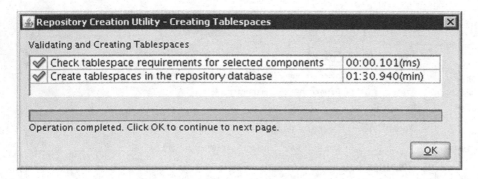

Figure 4-23. *Tablespaces Creation completion and timing details screen*

If there are any errors encountered during tablespaces creation due to any incorrect information provided in an earlier screen, this screen shows a failure icon while the previous screen gets populated with the actual error message in the lower Messages textbox. Once the tablespaces are created successfully, click *OK* to proceed to the Summary screen, as shown in Figure 4-24.

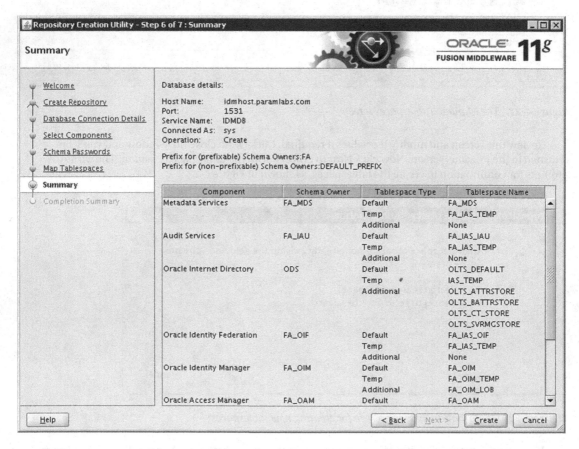

Figure 4-24. *Summary information of schemas to be created along with tablespace mapping*

This screen provides the overall summary of the selected RCU configuration before actually creating repository, including database connection details, schema prefix selected, and the list of components selected along with the schema name as well as its default and temporary tablespaces.

Review the information. If you find something that needs correction then click the Back button to modify the values provided earlier. If everything looks fine then click Create to start creating the repository schemas. Now you can see a pop-up screen shown in Figure 4-25 with the status of the repository creation progress for each component selected along with its timing information.

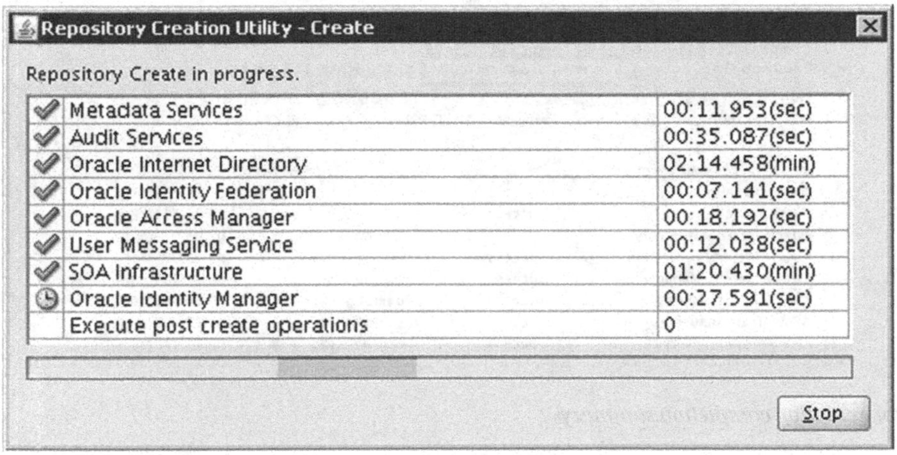

Figure 4-25. *Repository Creation progress and timing information*

Depending on the specification of database host, it may take a few minutes to complete. The screen will close automatically once the repository is created. Once RCU completes its tasks, you will see the Completion Summary screen shown in Figure 4-26. It provides the status summary along with timing information for each component selected, as well as overall execution time. It also provides the location and name of the log files. You can review the logs to understand what happens behind the scenes during repository creation.

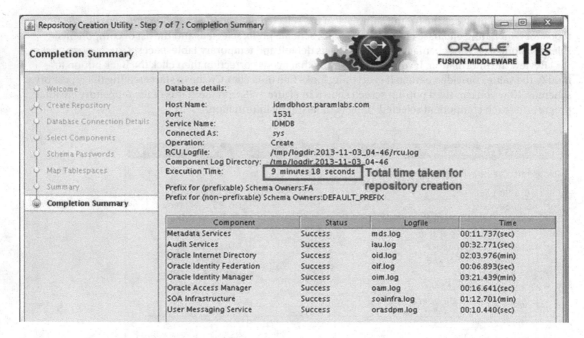

Figure 4-26. *Repository creation completion summary*

Review the summary and click Close. Once the RCU is complete, you can log in to the database and check the newly created schemas, tablespaces, and so on. Table 4-1 shows summary information about all the new schemas and tablespaces created after RCU completion.

Table 4-1. *Summary Table of Fusion Middlleware Components and Schemas After RCU*

Component	Schema	Default Tablespace	Temporary Tablespace
Oracle Internet Directory	ODS	OLTS_DEFAULT	TEMP
	ODSSM	OLTS_SVRMGSTORE	TEMP
Oracle Identity Management	FA_IAU	FA_IAS_IAU	FA_IAS_TEMP
	FA_IAU_APPEND	FA_IAS_IAU	FA_IAS_TEMP
	FA_IAU_VIEWER	FA_IAS_IAU	FA_IAS_TEMP
	FA_MDS	FA_MDS	FA_IAS_TEMP
	FA_OAM	FA_OAM	FA_OAM_TEMP
	FA_OIF	FA_IAS_OIF	FA_IAS_TEMP
	FA_OIM	FA_OIM	FA_OIM_TEMP
	FA_ORASDPM	FA_IAS_ORASDPM	FA_IAS_TEMP
	FA_SOAINFRA	FA_SOAINFRA	FA_IAS_TEMP

Summary

In this chapter, you learned about various options available to prepare the Identity Management Database as of Fusion Applications 11g, Release 9 and the expected options to be available in future releases. You also looked at the Repository Creation Utility for Identity Management. At this point you should be able to log in to the Identity Management database and check that the related schemas have been created in the database. You can monitor and manage the Identity Management database using the Oracle Database Enterprise Manager console or using Enterprise Manager Cloud Control if it is configured in your environment. We will look at configuring Cloud Control for the Fusion Applications environment in Chapter 14.

In the next chapter, we will have a look at the tasks required for creating an Identity Management Provisioning response file before proceeding with the actual provisioning process.

■ ■ ■

## CHAPTER 5

Prepare for Identity Management Provisioning

At this stage we have Identity Management database ready with the required repository schemas in place. The next step in the provisioning process is to create a Provisioning response file or Provisioning Profile. In order to do this, we must install the provisioning framework on the Identity Management Application node. The Identity Management provisioning framework is part of the Identity Management lifecycle tools, which include the Provisioning wizard as well as other command-line tools. Note that if your selected topology has multiple application nodes for Identity Management then you must install the provisioning framework on all the application nodes. Once we have the framework installed, we will use the Provisioning wizard on the primordial host to create the response file. This file will be used in the next chapter to provision the actual Identity Management environment.

Installing the IDM Provisioning Framework

Fusion Applications 11g, Releases 7, 8, and 9 include Oracle Identity and Access Management version 11.1.1.7, while earlier versions use version 11.1.1.6. If you are installing Oracle Fusion Applications 11g, Release 6 or earlier, you need to install the Identity Management components manually, as discussed in Chapter 3.

From Oracle Fusion Applications 11g, Release 7 onward, Oracle bundles the Provisioning wizard for Identity Management along with the installer media. This saves us time and the complexity of the manual installation, configuration, and integration. This greatly decreases the chances of errors during manual configuration. Before we can provision Identity Management we must first install the Identity Management provisioning framework or wizard, which is included as part of the Identity Management lifecycle tools. In this section, we will have a look at how to install the IDM lifecycle tools.

If your application host is different than the database host (two- or three-tier topology) then you need to install JDK on the host from the ZIP file provided in the media.

```
[fusion@idmhost ~]$ mkdir /app/oracle
[fusion@idmhost ~]$ cd /app/oracle/
[fusion@idmhost oracle]$ unzip /stage/installers/jdk/jdk6.zip
```

This will create a folder named /app/oracle/jdk6 and this will be our JAVA_HOME for all further installation steps. Now let's install the Provisioning wizard using the Identity Management lifecycle management tools installer (ldmlcm).

```
[fusion@idmhost admin]$ cd /stage/installers/idmlcm/idmlcm/Disk1/
[fusion@idmhost Disk1]$ ./runInstaller -jreLoc /app/oracle/jdk6
```

© Tushar Thakker 2015
T. Thakker, *Pro Oracle Fusion Applications*, DOI 10.1007/978-1-4842-0983-7_5

If this is the first Oracle product being installed on this machine, then you may see the inventory location screen shown in Figure 5-1.

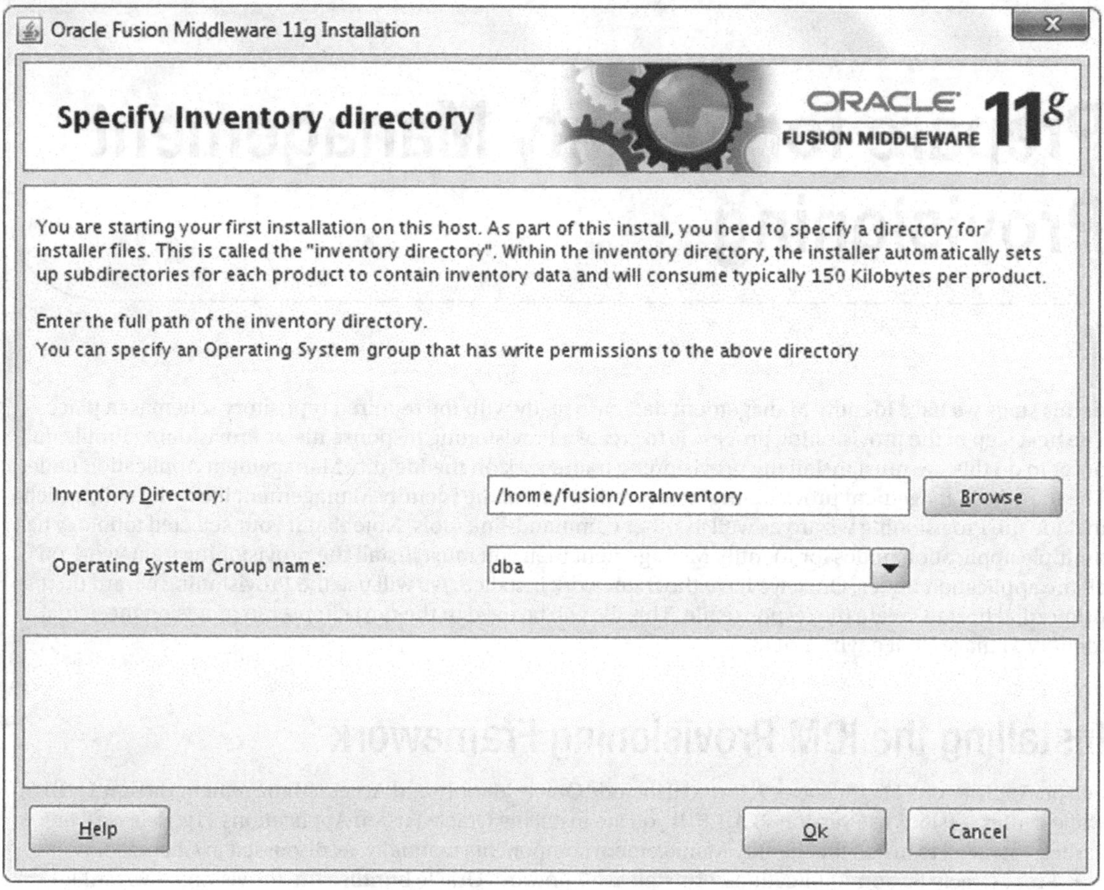

Figure 5-1. *Specify new inventory directory location*

In this screen you specify a location for the inventory directory. If in the next screen you confirm this inventory as the central inventory on the host, this becomes the central inventory in the system configuration files and other Oracle products will be installed here by default.

You also need to specify the operating system group for this directory. This will enable all other Oracle software installation users who are part of same group to read the central inventory directory. In this case, we will specify the dba group, which is already installed. You could also select oinstall but then you must make sure that all future Oracle product installations on this node have the same default group for the user. If you know that this is not the first Oracle product being installed on this host and you already have an inventory, make sure that the /etc/oraInst.loc file has read permission to the fusion installation user.

Once you click OK, the installer will prompt for the executing inventory registration scripts, as shown in Figure 5-2.

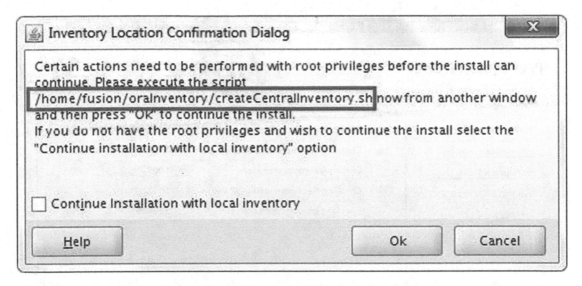

Figure 5-2. Central inventory registration scripts prompt

This screen prompts you to run the <Inventory_location>/createCentralInvetory.sh script as the root user. If you have root access then open a new terminal window and run the script as the root user. This script will assign the directory location as the central inventory for the host in the /etc/oraInst.loc file, which is used by all Oracle Software installations.

```
[root@idmhost ~]# /home/fusion/oraInventory/createCentralInventory.sh
Setting the inventory to /home/fusion/oraInventory
Setting the group name to dba
Creating the Oracle inventory pointer file (/etc/oraInst.loc)
Changing permissions of /home/fusion/oraInventory to 770.
Changing groupname of /home/fusion/oraInventory to dba.
The execution of the script is complete
```

If you do not have root privileges or you do not want to register IDMLCM in the central inventory then you select the Continue Installation with Local Inventory checkbox. In this case, the installer will create an inventory but will not assign it as the central inventory in the /etc/oraInst.loc file.

Click OK once you have executed the script or selected the checkbox to proceed with IDM lifecycle tools installation. The Welcome screen provides information about the purpose of this installer. No action is necessary on this screen. Click Next to proceed to the Prerequisite Checks screen, as shown in Figure 5-3.

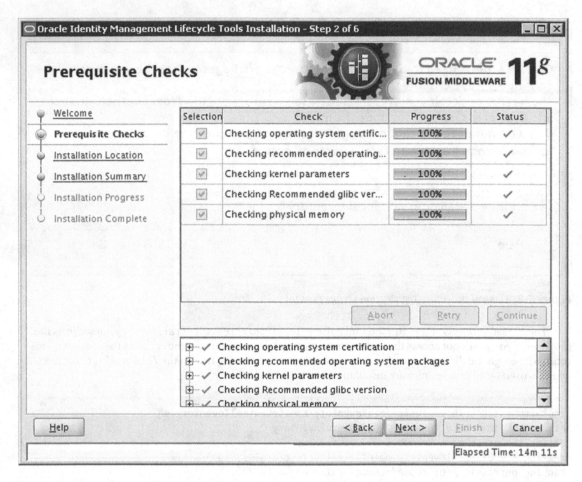

Figure 5-3. *Prerequisite Checks status screen*

This step checks the following required operating system prerequisites for Oracle Identity Management lifecycle tools installation.

- *Operating System Certification*: Some very old or very recent versions of operating systems are not supported, so make sure that you have the supported operating system and it is not the lowest version supported for future support sustainability and to avoid OS upgrades in the near future. You can check the list of compatible OSs for a current version using Oracle Certification Matrix in the Oracle support portal.

- *Operating System Packages*: Although we have already installed the recommended packages/RPMs for the operating system, this wizard will confirm it.

- *Kernel Parameters*: It will check all required kernel parameters for required minimum values. Note that kernel parameters values will be checked for the current session only, so make sure that you have also added the values in the relevant system files permanently.

- *Recommended glibc Version*: Although the mandatory packages would have already taken care of this, it specifically checks for the glibc version as well.

- *Physical Memory*: It will check the total amount of the installed memory on the host.

Once the prerequisites check is successful, click Next to continue to the installation location screen, as shown in Figure 5-4.

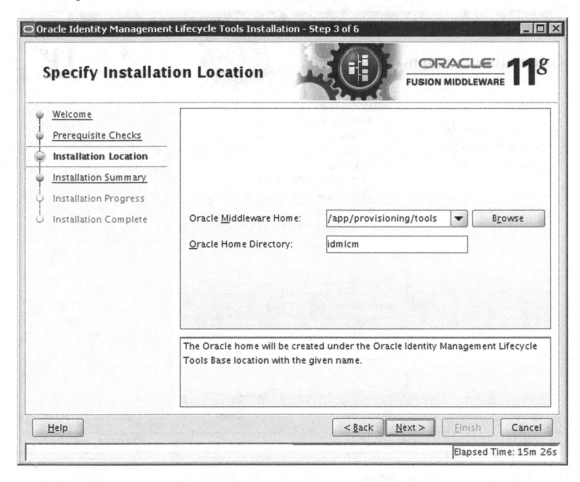

Figure 5-4. *Installation Location selection screen*

The Installation Location screen prompts for the following details:

- *Oracle Middleware Home*: It is important not to get confused by the Oracle Fusion Middleware Home directory under which we will install all the IDM components. This is a parent directory only for the IDM lifecycle tools and will not be used after the provisioning is complete. This should be on a shared location if you are installing IDM components on multiple nodes. In this case, we will use /app/provisioning/ tools. Make sure that there is a writable /app directory available. If there isn't one, use the following command to create it:

  ```
  [root@idmhost ~]# mkdir /app
  [root@idmhost ~]# chown fusion:dba /app
  ```

- *Oracle Home Directory*: The home directory of the IDM lifecycle tools. It recommended that you name it idmlcm. The tools and related utilities will be installed under this directory.

Click Next to proceed to the Installation Summary screen, as shown in Figure 5-5.

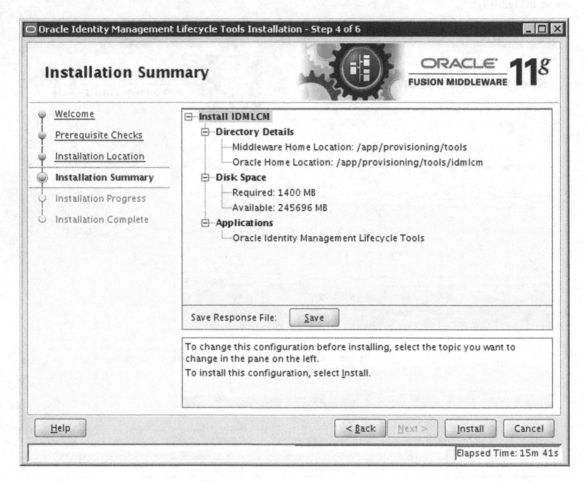

Figure 5-5. *Installation Summary screen*

The installation summary summarizes the directory locations selected, verifies the amount of disk space available, and confirms the component being installed. Click Save to save the entered information in a file. This will help if you want to start the installation at a later stage or restart it after any errors. It can also help in doing multiple identical installations. Review the Summary screen and click Install to start the installation process, as shown in Figure 5-6.

Figure 5-6. IDM lifecycle tools Installation Progress screen

The installation screen shows the progress of the overall installation and the installation log file's location and name. It also shows the status message of the current activity being performed. Any errors or warnings will be displayed here. The overall installation time is shown at the bottom of the screen. In case of any errors, refer to the log file created at <Inventory_location>/logs/install<timestamp>.log.

Once the installation is complete, click Next to proceed to the installation summary, as shown in Figure 5-7.

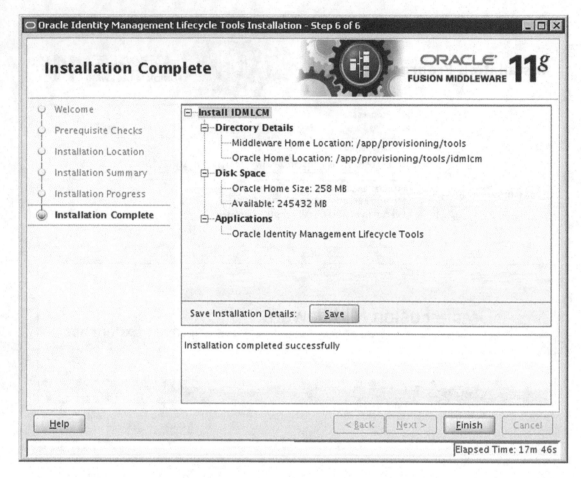

Figure 5-7. *Installation summary screen*

Review the installation summary and save the same for project documentation purposes.

Understanding the Directory Structure

Now we have the Identity Management lifecycle tools installed, which can be used to provision an Identity Management instance for Fusion Applications. Let's first look at the directory structure. Note that the IDM provisioning framework is evolving, so you may find some directories empty but they will be used in future versions of the framework. Certain functionalities are disabled in the framework that are included in the media of Oracle Fusion Applications 11g, Releases 7, 8, and 9. Figure 5-8 shows some of the important directories of interest in the IDM lifecycle management tools home.

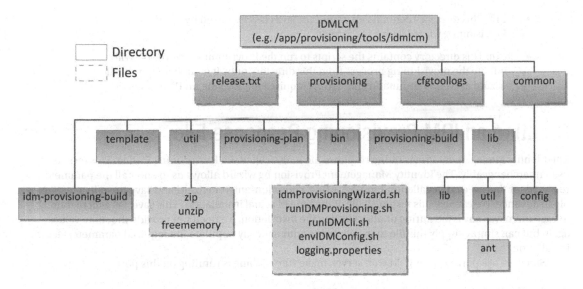

Figure 5-8. Important directories of the IDM provisioning framework (IDM lifecycle tools)

Let's explore the important directories and files shown in Figure 5-8 one by one.

- common: This directory contains important libraries and utilities like apache ANT.

- cfgtoollogs: This directory contains the logs for the IDM lifecycle tools installation. The log files in this directories are available in <oraInventory>/logs as well. Note that this directory does not contain the logs for the IDM provisioning phases, but contains the installation logs for the lifecycle tools only.

- release.txt: This file contains the version details for the IDM lifecycle tools for the purpose of troubleshooting and informing Oracle support while reporting any issues with the installer.

- provisioning: This directory contains the IDM provisioning framework. It has following important subdirectories.

  - util: This directory contains various common utilities like zip, unzip, freememory, and so on, which are used by the tools during provisioning

  - provisioning-build: This directory is identical to the one included in Fusion Applications provisioning framework .It mainly contains XML build files that are not currently required by IDM Provisioning wizard but are only FA provisioning.

  - idm-provisioning-build: This directory contains all the XML build files that are required for the IDM provisioning orchestration process. You may find all provisioning targets and actions performed during the actual provisioning process.

  - provisioning-plan and template: Similar to the provisioning-build directory, these directories are identical to one used by Fusion Applications provisioning framework and are placeholders in this release of IDM provisioning framework.

- lib: This directory contains all important Java class files used by the IDM Provisioning wizard in the jar format.

- bin: This directory contains the scripts to run the Provisioning wizard. We will initiate the provisioning process from this directory only. It contains a graphical wizard as well as command-line scripts required to provision an IDM instance.

Creating an IDM Provisioning Response File

The Identity Management Provisioning response file is also called the Provisioning Profile. This term is used interchangeably. The Identity Management Provisioning wizard allows us to enter all the parameters required for the selected installation topology using a question-answer wizard and save them in a response file in advance. We can use this response file at the time of actual installation. This saves us a lot of time in case there was any issue during or after starting the installation, we need not provide the same values again but can simply supply this file to the wizard to automatically populate the required parameters for the installation.

Since we use port 7777 for IDM web server, make sure nothing is running on this port.

```
[fusion@idmhost ~]$ netstat -an | grep 7777
```

■ **Note** Until Fusion Applications 11.1.7, Apache ANT utility was missing from the repository so if you are installing Identity Management from the 11.1.7 media, the solution is to either install the Fusion Applications provisioning framework on this node as well, which includes ANT, or manually download ANT (version 1.7.1 or higher) from http://ant.apache.org/ for your platform.

From Fusion Applications 11.1.8 onward, Apache ANT is included in the IDM lifecycle tools common utilities directory.

Launch the IDM Provisioning wizard to create a new response file.

```
[fusion@idmhost ~]$ export JAVA_HOME=/app/oracle/jdk6
[fusion@idmhost ~]$ cd /app/provisioning/tools/idmlcm/provisioning/bin/
[fusion@idmhost bin]$ ./idmProvisioningWizard.sh
```

The Welcome screen, as shown in Figure 5-9, is an informal screen that cautions the user to ensure that the prerequisites are already performed before proceeding.

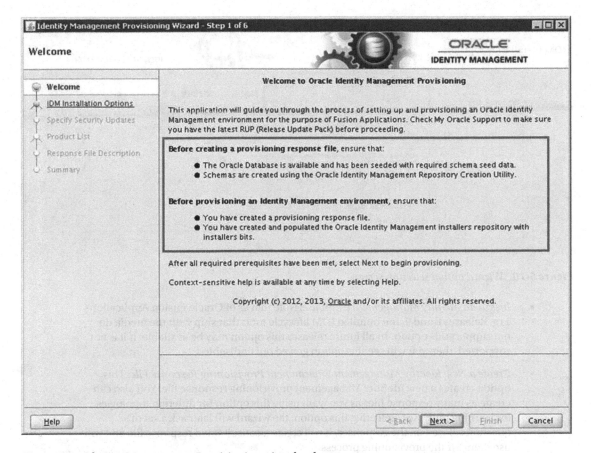

Figure 5-9. *Identity Management Provisioning wizard welcome screen*

When you create a provisioning response file, you need to ensure that an exclusive Oracle database has been created for hosting Identity Management components and also the required repository has been created using Oracle Identity Management RCU. Make sure to bring up the database and listener on the database host (idmdbhost in this case) since the wizard verifies the connection details later. Once this is ensured, click Next to proceed.

This screen provides four different options of activities that can be performed by the IDM Provisioning wizard, as shown in Figure 5-10.

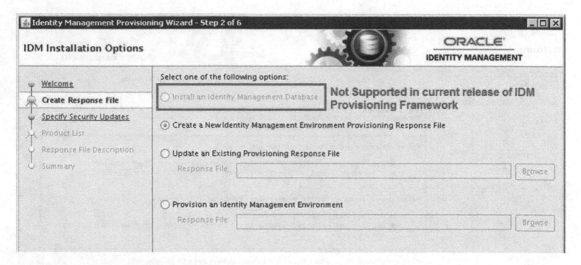

Figure 5-10. *Wizard option selection screen*

- *Install an Identity Management Database*: Note that as of Oracle Fusion Applications 11g, Releases 8 and 9, the bundled IDM lifecycle tools that ship with the media do not support this option. In all future releases this option may be available. If it is not supported, then you will see this option grayed out or disabled.

- *Create a New Identity Management Environment Provisioning Response File*: This option creates a new Identity Management provisioning response file. You also can create as many response files as you want using this option for different topologies for learning purposes. Selecting this option, the wizard will later ask a set of questions. Based on the responses, it will create a consolidated response file and will use them for the provisioning process.

- *Update an Existing Provisioning Response File*: This option should be used if you find that there was any mistake in providing the details while creating the response file earlier or if there is any change in some parameters. Instead of creating a new response file all over again, you can use this option to modify the changed values and resave.

- *Provision an Identity Management Environment*: We will use this option later to install and configure an Oracle Identity Management environment using an already created provisioning response file. It will also provide an option to review certain sections before proceeding with the installation process. We will look at this section later.

■ **Caution**   Although the IDM Provisioning wizard enables you to update the existing response file, it is not yet fully supported in the build supplied with Fusion Applications 11g, Release 8. So it is recommended not to use this option in this release.

Select Create a New Identity Management Environment Provisioning Response File and click Next to proceed. Now you will see a common Oracle installer screen that prompts for an email address, where you want to be notified in case there are any important security issues and updates. Provide the details as requested or else just leave this empty and click Next to proceed to the Products List screen, as shown in Figure 5-11.

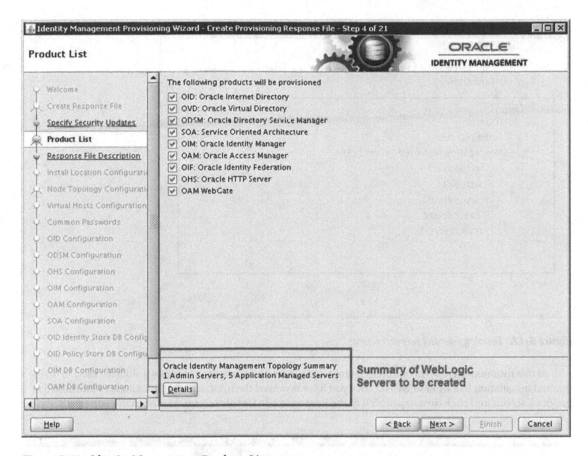

Figure 5-11. *Identity Management Products List screen*

This screen allows you to select which Identity Management Products you want to provision. Since this wizard can be used for non-Fusion applications environment as well, it provides an option to check or uncheck the individual products. But for the Identity Management infrastructure to be used with Oracle Fusion applications, you need to select *all* the products as shown in Figure 5-11. By default, all products are selected. Leave the selection unchanged.

■ **Note**   From Oracle Fusion Applications 11g, Release 9 onward the bundled IDM provisioning framework has the products selection screen *grayed out* so that you do not deselect any product by mistake.

The lower panel of this screen provides a summary information of the Oracle Identity Management topology. It displays the number of WebLogic servers that will be configured, including Administration Servers Application Managed Servers. Click on the Details button to launch a pop-up screen with the list of WebLogic servers that will be created during provisioning, as shown in Figure 5-12.

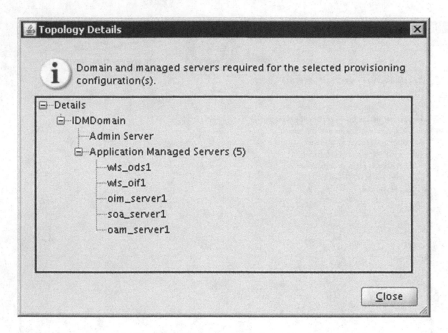

Figure 5-12. *Topology details pop-up screen*

At this moment there is no option to change the names of the managed servers unlike we used to do in manual installation in earlier releases. Once you have reviewed the information, click Close to return to the previous screen and click Next to proceed to the Response File Details screen, as shown in Figure 5-13.

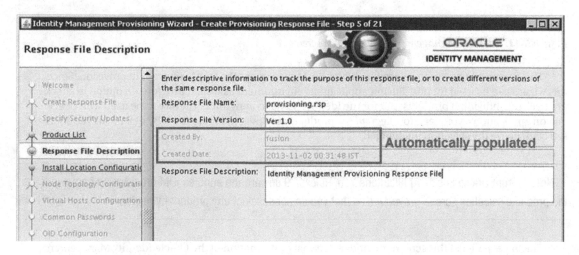

Figure 5-13. *Response File Description screen*

This screen will prompt for the following provisioning response file details.

- *Response File Name*: The default name is provisioning.rsp. You can change it to any name so that you can recognize the response file by name itself if you have created multiple response files for different topologies.

- *Response File Version*: You can manually maintain the version numbers of the response file if you have made any changes since last time.

- *Created By*: Automatically populated by the wizard. Defaults to the operating system user who started the wizard. This value cannot be changed. In this case its value is fusion.

- *Created Date*: Automatically populated by the wizard. This is the time when the response file was *first* created and this does not change even if you modify the response file later. This field cannot be changed as well.

- *Response File Description*: You can specify any arbitrary description for your response file. You can read the response file and summary files using any text editors later.

Enter the response filename provisioning.rsp and click *Next* to proceed to the Installation Location details screen, as shown in Figure 5-14.

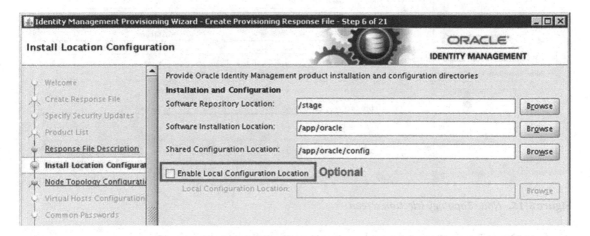

Figure 5-14. *Install Location Configuration screen*

The Provisioning wizard now prompts for the following location parameters. Make sure to have these directories on a shared disk if you are using multiple nodes topology for IDM.

- *Software Repository Location*: Provide the location where you have created the installer repository. The wizard checks for the availability of installers directory within this location provided. In this case it is /stage so provide that here.

- *Software Installation Location*: This is the location where the middleware homes for the WebLogic server, HTTP server, and directory servers will be installed. Make sure that the base directory is on a writable location. We already have an /app directory owned by the fusion user. Enter the value as /app/oracle or any desirable path under 45 characters length.

- *Shared Configuration Location*: This value will be populated automatically once you have provided the value of the software installation location. Make sure that this folder is on a shared disk if you are using multi-node architecture since this directory contains the instance and domain configuration files, startup scripts, logs, and so on.

- *Enable Local Configuration*: This should be selected only if you are using an Enterprise topology to isolate the configuration files for each tier. This is also required if you are going to use high-availability architecture and want to keep configuration settings for each node separate to allow tuning the nodes separately. Once you check this checkbox then the next field becomes active where you can select a location for local configuration directory. This directory has to be on a local disk that's not shared with other nodes. For example, /app/local/oracle.

Once the details are entered, click Next to proceed to the topology selection, as shown in Figure 5-15.

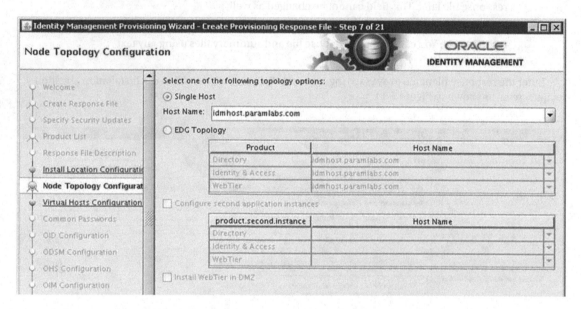

Figure 5-15. *Node Topology selection screen*

In the Node Topology selection, we have two top-level options to choose from.

- *Single Host*: When you select this option, all IDM components will be installed on the same host. In this case, it is idmhost.paramlabs.com.

- *EDG Topology*: Use this option for three-tier Enterprise topology. Since initial releases of Oracle Identity Management 11g, Oracle uses the term EDG for Enterprise Deployment Guide, but now it is called Enterprise Topology only. It allows us to change the hostname for Directory Server, Web Server, and Application Server (Identity and Access Management) with three different hostnames.

If you have selected EDG topology, the checkbox selection for Configure second application instances will be enabled. This option allows you to enable high availability for all products of Oracle Identity Management. If you select this checkbox then it will prompt you to select a secondary host for the Directory server, Web server, and IAM server. This will allow you to use up to six hosts for the selected topology.

Note that the wizard will not allow you to keep any value blank. You can use the same hostname again but do not leave it blank. The last checkbox is for Install Web Tier in DMZ. Select this option only if you have selected EDG topology and you have DMZ set up in your environment.

Note that once you select EDG topology and/or second instances and specify any values in the hostnames, if you want to change back to the Single Host selection, you must make sure to remove each values from Second instance hostnames first before unchecking it and change each hostname value in EDG topology fields to same hostname before switching to Single Host. Due to some bug, if the field values contain different hostnames the installer may fail.

■ **Caution**   Be very careful while making selections in this screen, as changing the topology will alter some values in further screens as well, for example port values, hostnames, and so on. Even if you change the values back to originals, the other screen's value does not change back to the original unless you start the response file creation from scratch. This can cause the actual provisioning process to fail at install or configure phases.

Table 5-1 shows the different topology combinations available in this screen and the impact of the selected topology on other components selection. Note that this table excludes DMZ node.

Table 5-1. *Toplogy Options Available in the IDM Provisioning Wizard*

Select Option	High Availability	Load Balancer Required?	Number of Hosts	Identity Store	Policy Store
Single Host	No	No	1	OID	OID
EDG Topology	No	Yes	up to 3	OVD	OID
EDG Topology + Configure Second instances	Yes	Yes	up to 6	OVD	OID

In this example, we will select idmhost.paramlabs.com for the single hostname and click Next to proceed to the Virtual Hosts Configuration screen, as shown in Figure 5-16.

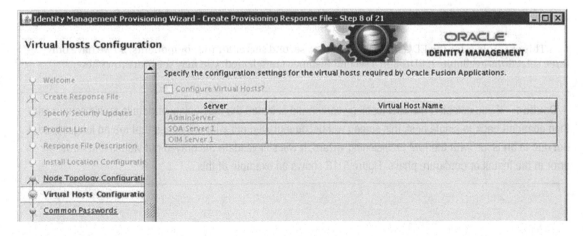

Figure 5-16. *Virtual Hosts Configuration settings screen*

The options in the Virtual Hosts Configuration screen will be grayed out if you have selected Single Host option in the previous screen since there is no other node for the Virtual IP to fail over or migrate. This option is available for the EDG topology even if you have not selected second instances. This is an optional selection so you might not want to select a virtual hostname in the EDG topology as well. You have the option to select the virtual hostname for each server in the topology, including second instances. Each virtual hostname should be different. You also need to register these hostnames in DNS so that the other hosts and load balancer can reach these servers.

■ **Note**   Note that virtual hostname should not be mistaken with the network load balancer name. The load balancer will forward requests received at a single IP or name to multiple servers, while the virtual hostname is used here only to give a different alias than the actual hostname. That way, if you want to failover or migrate to another host, you need not reconfigure the application.

Figure 5-17 shows an example of this screen with the Configure Virtual Hosts option selected.

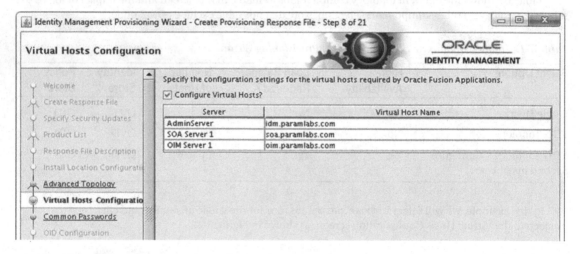

Figure 5-17. *Virtual Hosts Configuration settings screen*

This example is for the EDG topology without a second server for the components. So we have only three selections available. If EDG and a second instance are selected, you may see more rows here.

■ **Caution**   If you selected the EDG topology earlier and selected the load balancer details in this screen and then changed back to single host, this screen will become grayed out with old values that are no longer valid. But due to an issue with the IDM Provisioning wizard, it will still validate the grayed out values and throw an error in the install or configure phase. Figure 5-18 shows an example of this.

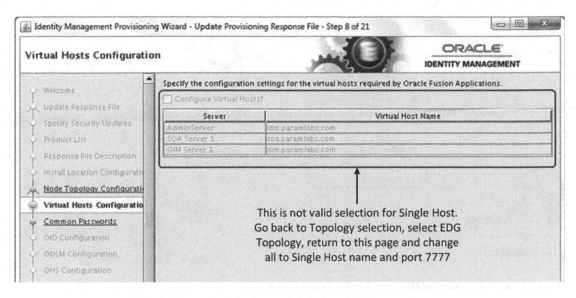

Figure 5-18. *Incorrect virtual hostname selection screen for the Single Host topology*

Once you have made suitable selection and entered the virtual hostnames, click Next to continue to the Common Passwords screen, as shown in Figure 5-19.

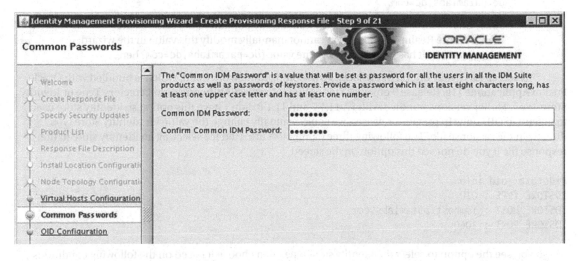

Figure 5-19. *IDM Common Passwords screen*

You will be prompted to enter a common IDM password and the same password will be set for all users in the IDM suite products as well as the keystores. The password policy is similar to what you've seen earlier but the difference here is that it requires at least one uppercase letter in addition to policy of eight characters maximum, with alphabetical and numerical requirements.

Enter a common IDM password in both fields and click Next to proceed to OID configuration, as shown in Figure 5-20.

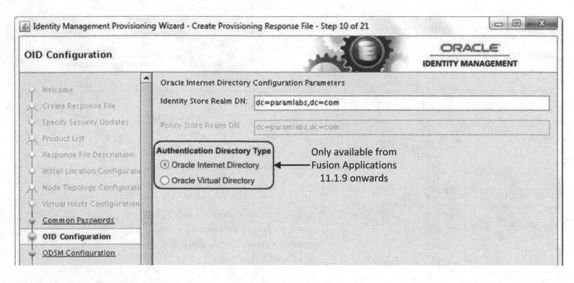

Figure 5-20. *Oracle Internet Directory Configuration screen*

In OID Configuration page prompts for the following values:

- *Identity Store Realm DN*: Enter the Identity Store Realm Distinguished name (DN). The format is generally similar to dc=domain,dc=com. In this case, we will use dc=paramlabs,dc=com.

- *Policy Store Realm DN*: This value is automatically populated the same as the Identity Store Realm DN value. You cannot manually modify this value in the wizard. As you can see, it has populated the same value (dc=paramlabs,dc=com) here.

This screen has a new option in the latest Provisioning framework build, which is bundled with Oracle Fusion Applications 11g, Release 9 onward. This option is to select Authentication Directory Type or Identity Store Type. Earlier versions bundled with FA 11.1.7 and 11.1.8 didn't have this option so identity store used to default to OID only. In previous releases, we could manually change the value for Identity Store type directly in the response file. The following three parameters are used for selecting an identity store in the response file if you do not see this option on the screen.

```
#idstore -oid info
IDSTORE_TYPE : OID
IDSTORE_HOST : idmhost.paramlabs.com
IDSTORE_PORT : 3060
```

If you see the option to select the identity store type, then choose it based on the following conditions.

- Oracle Internet Directory (OID): Use this for a single IDM host topology

- Oracle Virtual Directory (OVD): Use this option for the EDG Topology with or without a second instances host

Click Next to proceed to the ODSM port configuration, as shown in Figure 5-21.

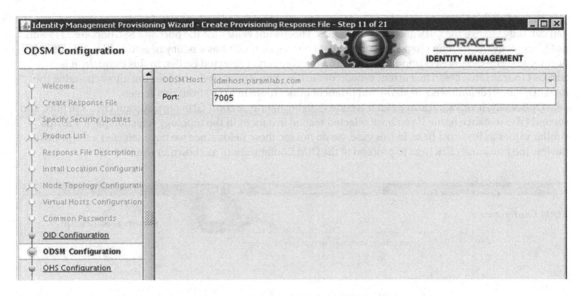

Figure 5-21. Oracle Directory Service Manager Configuration screen

In the ODSM configuration page, the hostname will be automatically populated based on the values entered in the Topology Configuration page. If you have selected the EDG topology with second instances then you will see entries for the second host as well. The default port for ODSM is 7005. You may change it if your security policy does not allow default ports to be used or if you have any port conflicts on the host. Click Next to proceed to OHS Configuration, as shown in Figure 5-22.

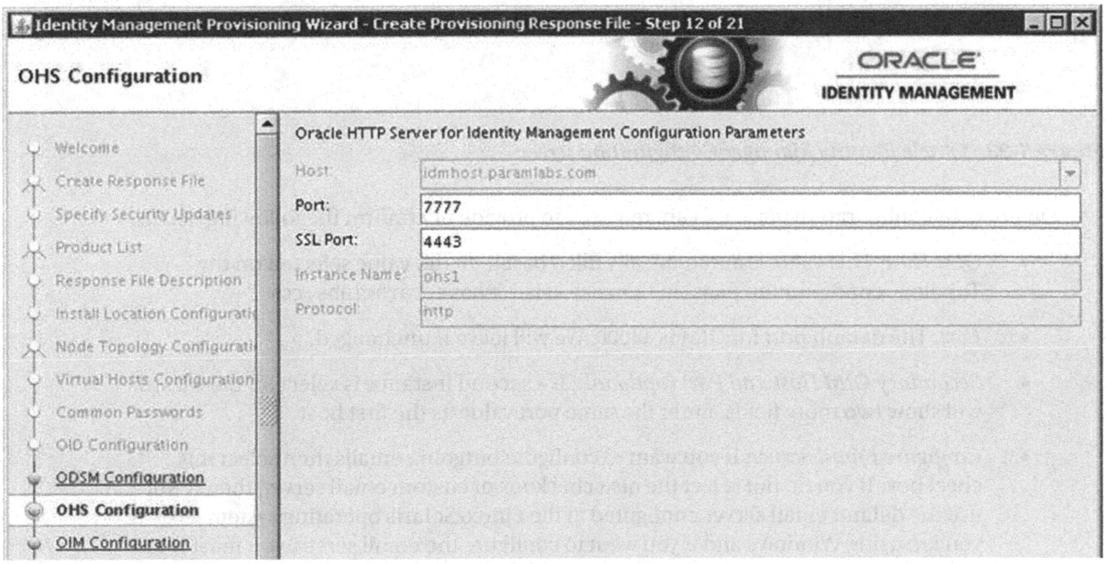

Figure 5-22. Oracle HTTP Server Configuration screen

In the Oracle HTTP Server (OHS) Configuration page, the default values are already populated and you can only change the OHS and SSL port values. The default values for the port and SSL port are 7777 and 4443, respectively. You can change these values if your organization has a policy of setting non-default port values. The OHS host is populated based on the Web server selected earlier. In this example, it is idmhost.paramlabs.com. The current version of the IDM Provisioning wizard does not allow changing the instance name (default ohs1 or ohsn) and protocol values (default http) from this screen.

Optionally, it will also prompt for a second OHS hostname, second OHS port, second OHS SSL port, and second OHS instance name if you have selected second instances in the topology selection page. Provide similar values as first host here. In this case, we do not see these fields since we have selected a single host. Review the ports and click Next to proceed to the OIM Configuration, as shown in Figure 5-23.

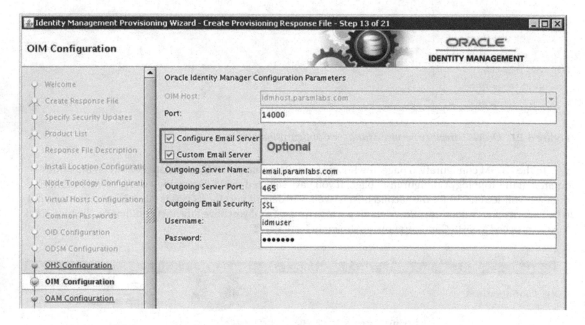

Figure 5-23. *Oracle Identity Manager Configuration screen*

On the OIM configuration page, you are required to provide or confirm the following details.

- *OIM Host*: This value is automatically filled based on the value selected on the Topology configuration page. In this case, it is idmhost.paramlabs.com.

- *Port*: The default port for OIM is 14000. We will leave it unchanged.

- *Secondary OIM Host and Port (optional)*: If a second instance is selected, the wizard will show two more fields. Enter the same port value as the first host.

- *Configure Email Server*: If you want to configure outgoing emails then select this checkbox. If you do not select the next checkbox of custom email server, then it will use the default email server configured at the Linux/Solaris operating system level. If you are using Windows and if you want to configure the email server, you must select the custom server settings as well.

- *Custom Email Server*: This option is used to manually set outgoing the email server settings if no default email server is set at host or if you want to use different email server.

  - *Outgoing Server Name*: Provide a name or IP of an outgoing email server.

  - *Outgoing Server Port*: The default SSL port is 465 and non-SSL port is 25. Enter a value according to the outgoing server security.

  - *Outgoing Server Security*: Enter None (insecure), TLS, or SSL.

  - *Username and Password*: If your outgoing email server requires authentication then enter the username and password here.

Enter and verify all of this information and click Next to proceed to OAM Configuration, as shown in Figure 5-24.

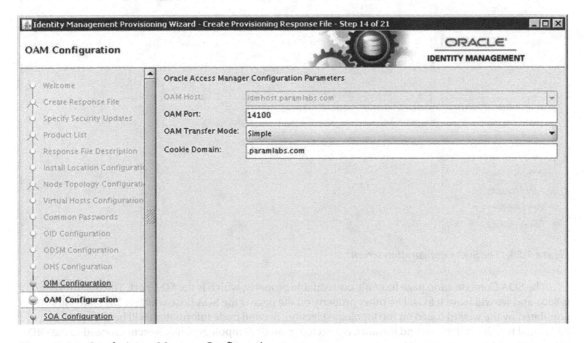

Figure 5-24. *Oracle Access Manager Configuration screen*

The OAM configuration page requires the following information:

- *OAM Host*: The hostname is automatically filled based on the topology configuration and is not editable.

- *OAM Port*: The default OAM port is 14100. Change it only if required.

- *OAM Transfer Mode*: There are two options, Simple and Open. For Linux platform, we must select it as Simple.

- *Cookie Domain*: Enter a value for setting the cookie domain. In our case, we entered .paramlabs.com. Make sure to put a dot (.) before the domain name.

■ **Note**   Until 11.1.6 we were allowed to use Open Transfer mode. But from 11.1.7 onward, we must use Open for AIX OS only and for all other OS, we must specify Simple.

Enter the required values and click Next to proceed to the SOA configuration, as Figure 5-25.

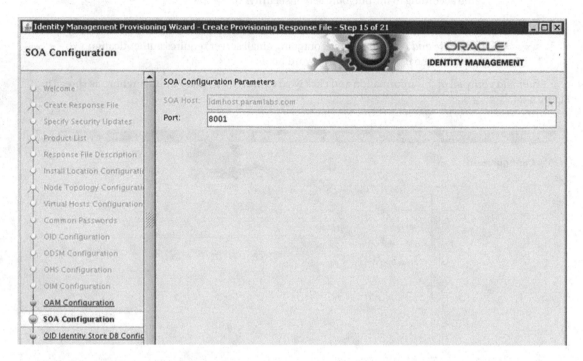

Figure 5-25. *The SOA Configuration screen*

The SOA Configuration page has only one editable property, which is the SOA port. The default value is 8001 and we will leave it as is. The other property on the page is the SOA host, which is automatically populated by the wizard based on the topology selection. Second node information will be requested as additional two fields if the second instance is selected in an EDG topology. Click Next to proceed to the OID Identity Store database information screen, as shown in Figure 5-26.

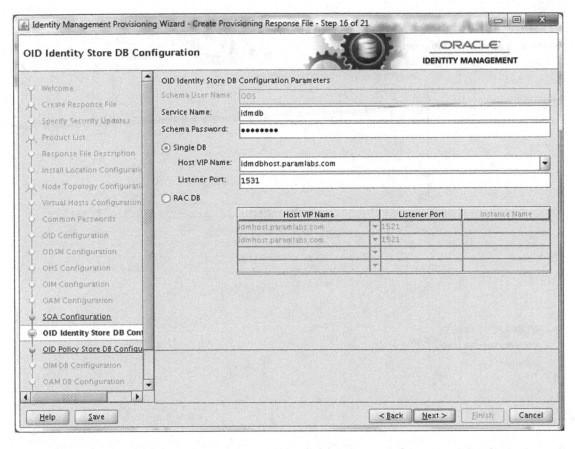

Figure 5-26. *OID Identity Store DB Connection parameters screen*

IDM Provisioning allows us to have a different database of directory services and another database for IDM components. This screen prompts for the following database connection details of the OID Identity Store database.

- *Schema User Name*: The username cannot be changed and it remains ODS only. This username does not have the schema prefix that was selected during RCU. This field is not editable.

- *Service Name*: This is a Database Service Name in the case of the RAC database and SID in the case of Single Node database. We will enter idmdb here.

- *Schema Password*: Enter the password for the ODS schema.

- *Single DB/RAC DB*: Select the appropriate option to select single or RAC database. Provide connection details such as hostname and listen port for single or RAC nodes. We will select single node DB with idmdbhost.paramlabs.com as the hostname and custom listener port 1531, which we selected during IDM database creation.

Enter the database details and click Next to proceed to the OID Policy Store Database Configuration screen, as shown in Figure 5-27.

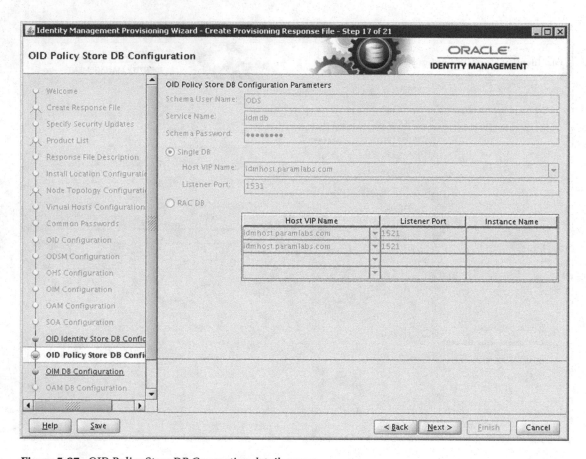

Figure 5-27. *OID Policy Store DB Connection details screen*

Since the OID policy store resides on the same database as the Identity Store, we will see that the screen is grayed out and the values are uneditable. All the information will remain same as provided in the OID Identity Store DB Configuration page.

■ **Tip** At any point in time during the response file creation, click Back to go back to any previous screen and review or update the values. Once you modify a value in the previous screens and return to where you left, you need not reenter the details again. The values are saved during the session until you cancel or finish the response file creation.

Review the information and click Next to proceed to the OIM Database Configuration screen, as shown in Figure 5-28.

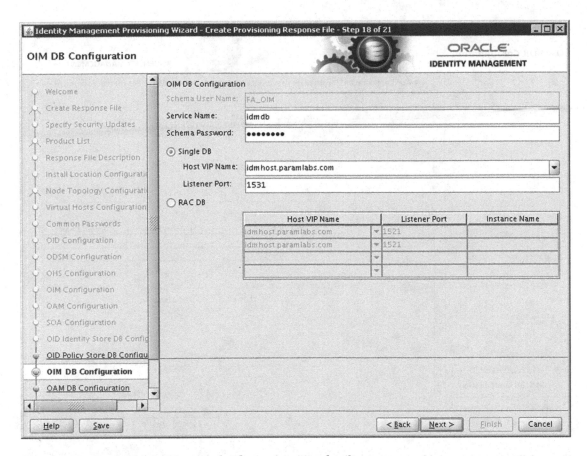

Figure 5-28. *Oracle Identity Manager database connection details screen*

This screen prompts for the database connection details of database containing OIM specific schemas. As mentioned earlier, IDM Provisioning allows us to one database for Directory Services and another database for IDM components. You can either enter the same database details (which is the case in our installation) or if you have provisioned IDM schemas in different database then enter that database details here. Note that the Schema username cannot be changed and it remains FA_OIM as created while running RCU. Once the connection details are entered or verified, click Next to proceed to the OAM Database configuration screen, as shown in Figure 5-29.

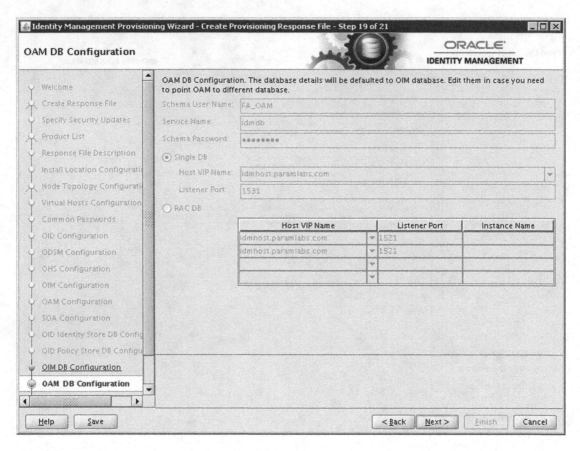

Figure 5-29. Oracle Access Manager database connection details screen

This screen shows the connection details for the database containing Oracle Access Manager schema (FA_OAM), which is invariably the same as OIM DB. Hence the fields on this screen remain disabled. Review the information and click Next to proceed to the Load Balancer Configuration, as shown in Figure 5-30.

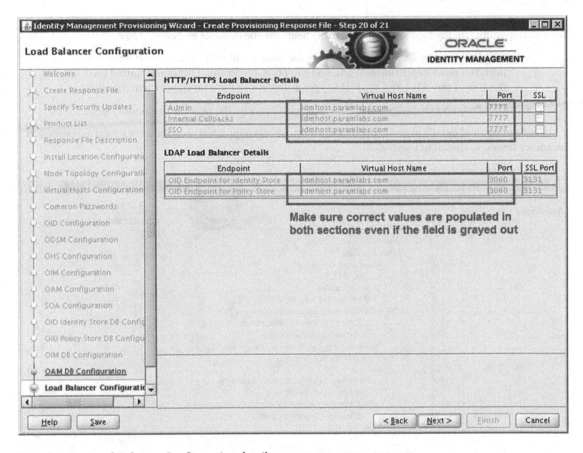

Figure 5-30. Load Balancer Configuration detail screen

If you have selected a single host for the IDM components in the topology selection page, then the Load Balancer Configuration screen will be completely grayed out, as shown in Figure 5-30. If you have selected EDG topology with or without a second instance then you should use Network Load Balancer (NLB) or virtual hostname. The role of load balancer in a single Web server would be just to forward the requests or act as an alias. In the case of multiple hosts the load balancer will accept the requests on the same or a different port and forward them to internal servers on the OHS port configured earlier.

You have to provide a virtual hostname and an NLB port for following three endpoints. You also need to specify whether you want to use SSL for the virtual host or not. This screen is slightly different in recent releases of IDM lifecycle tools (Fusion Applications 11.1.9 onward). As cautioned earlier in Figure 5-18, be careful to make sure that there is no incorrect virtual hostname grayed out for a single host topology.

- *Admin*: This will be the virtual hostname for administration activities.

- *Internal Callbacks*: This will be the virtual hostname for Identity Management internal callbacks across components.

- *SSO*: This will be the single sign-on page virtual host. Generally you should select SSL (HTTPS) for this page since this will be the URL that users see when they launch the Fusion Applications Login screens.

On the same screen, we also can select Load Balancer for LDAP or Directory Server components as follows. Depending on the topology selected, these fields may be editable or non-editable.

- *OID Endpoint for Identity Store*: Provide the value for Identity Store virtual host and port. You need to provide non-SSL and SSL ports. By default, OID is configured on the 3060 (non-SSL) and 3131 (SSL) ports unless you have modified them manually.

- *OID Endpoint for Policy Store*: This value will always be the same as the identity store.

Provide required details or verify the details automatically populated on screen click *Next* to proceed to Summary screen as shown in Figure 5-31.

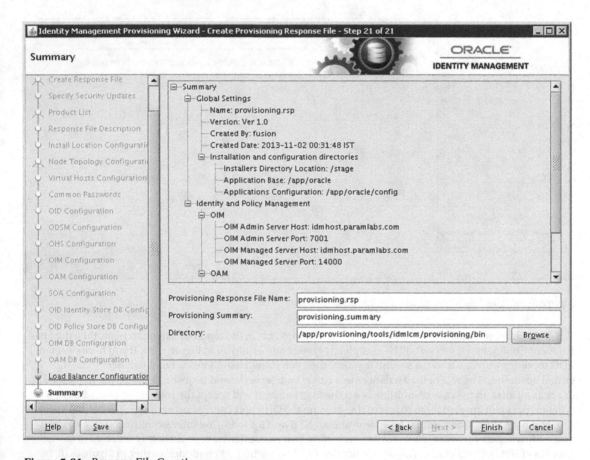

Figure 5-31. *Respone File Creation summary screen*

Review the installation summary carefully since it shows consolidated information to be stored in the response file. If you find something is not correct, you can go back to the desired page and change the values.

This page prompts for the following three details. The values are automatically populated so it is optional to change them.

- *Provisioning Response File Name*: Same as what you mentioned in the response file description earlier. Change it if required.

- *Provisioning Summary*: Name of the provisioning summary file with the same name as the response file and with a .summary extension. Although the installer doesn't use this file, it contains the summary information in the file for later review and documentation purposes.

- *Directory*: The location where the Identity Management Provisioning response file and summary will be created. You can change it to another location if required. The default location is <IDMLCM_HOME>/provisioning/bin or the same location from where the provisioning scripts were invoked.

Review the summary and click Finish to complete the response file creation and then close the window. Once this is done, you will see these two files created under the previously mentioned directory. Make sure to check the timestamp to confirm these are the files created by the wizard if you already have existing response files in this location.

Modify the IDM Provisioning Response File for Fusion Applications

Since the IDM provisioning is generic, we must change the following values in order to meet the requirements for the Fusion Applications provisioning. Change the following values manually in the provisioning.rsp file (or the name you specified).

```
#IDStore UserNames Configuration
IDSTORE_OAMADMINUSER=oamadmin
IDSTORE_OAMSOFTWAREUSER=oamLDAP
IDSTORE_OIMADMINUSER=oimLDAP
```

Go to the provisioning response file directory and back up the existing response file for precaution.

```
[fusion@idmhost ~]$ cd /app/provisioning/tools/idmlcm/provisioning/bin/
[fusion@idmhost bin]$ cp -p provisioning.rsp provisioning.rsp.bak
```

Edit the response file and change the values of IDSTORE_OAMADMINUSER, IDSTORE_OAMSOFTWAREUSER and IDSTORE_OIMADMINUSER as mentioned.

```
[fusion@idmhost bin]$ vi provisioning.rsp
```

Let's make sure that the correct lines were changed and compare them with the original file.

```
[fusion@idmhost bin]$ diff provisioning.rsp provisioning.rsp.bak
355,357c355,357
< IDSTORE_OAMADMINUSER=oamadmin
< IDSTORE_OAMSOFTWAREUSER=oamLDAP
< IDSTORE_OIMADMINUSER=oimLDAP
—
> IDSTORE_OAMADMINUSER=oamAdminUser
> IDSTORE_OAMSOFTWAREUSER=oamSoftwareUser
> IDSTORE_OIMADMINUSER=oimAdminUser
```

Copy Credentials Wallet File to DMZ Hosts (Optional)

If you are using DMZ hosts in your topology, you must copy certain files to the DMZ nodes since they are not on the shared location. In this case, you will see another directory named `<provisioning_filename>_data` under the same location where the IDM Provisioning response files have been created. You will see a file named `cwallet.sso`, which contains the credentials information for encryption and decryption purposes. Copy the response file as well as this folder to the same location on DMZ hosts or any hosts that do not have shared disks visible.

Summary

In this chapter, you have seen the structure of the Identity Management provisioning framework and the steps for installing it. Later you learned about the process of creating the Identity Management provisioning profile or response file. At this stage, we created the Provisioning response file, which will be used later as the source profile for creating an Identity Management environment. The wizard allows you to create many response files for different topologies. If you copy the file to another server, you should be able to provision an Identity Management environment using the same file in plain text with different variables and their respective values. At the end of this chapter, you read about the importance of various screens of the response file and learned which values you should choose.

CHAPTER 6

■ ■ ■

Provision Identity Management Environment

After creating the IDM provisioning response file, we will now proceed to installing the Identity Management environment for Fusion Applications. So far no component from the selected topology except the database has been installed and all our installation-related responses were stored in a plain-text response file. The provisioning process will use this response file to fetch the required installation-related parameters. In the beginning of this chapter, we will look at various interfaces available for Identity Management provisioning, followed by understanding individual phases of the IDM provisioning process. Later we will see proceed to an example installation process using both interface options.

Identity Management Provisioning Interfaces

We have two interface options for provisioning an Identity Management environment. We can use either of these options to yield the same provisioned environment, installation log files, status information, and so on. Note that we have similar options for Oracle Fusion Applications as well, so the same concept will apply in case of the Fusion Applications provisioning.

- *GUI-based wizard*: This is essentially same response-based wizard that we have used for creating or updating a response file earlier. This is only to be used for the primordial host. Once each phase is completed on the primordial host, you need to wait until it is completed on the other hosts using the command-line interface. For a single H-host topology, it is recommended you use the GUI-based wizard for provisioning. For a single host, you need to run it only on one node. As soon as the phase is complete, you can move on to the next phase.

- *Command-line interface (CLI)*: This is the recommended method of provisioning for a multi-host installation. Although you can use this interface for all nodes, including the primordial host, the ability to understand the progress of the phase in a non-graphical interface will be limited. So it is possible to use GUI-based provisioning on the primordial host and CLI-based provisioning for other hosts, including the primary, secondary, and DMZ hosts once the respective phase on the primordial host is complete. In addition to this, in case of manual cleanup and restore, you also need to use the command-line interface.

© Tushar Thakker 2015

T. Thakker, *Pro Oracle Fusion Applications*, DOI 10.1007/978-1-4842-0983-7_6

■ **Tip** Although the GUI-based installer gives you much more visibility and monitoring capability, the CLI (the command-line interface) always completes without any issues. When using GUI for older releases of Fusion Applications, you might need to download the patch 16708003 from the Oracle Support portal and apply it immediately after the Install phase has completed to fix an issue that it may encounter in the Configure phase. However, for recent releases of Identity Management provisioning frameworks, this is not required.

Identity Management Provisioning Phases

The Identity Management provisioning process includes the same following phases that we will see during the Fusion Applications provisioning, but the actions you take during these phase are different depending on the products being provisioned. We will discuss each of these phases and which actions are performed during each in detail when we look at the screens for specific phases during the installation.

- *Preverify*: Checks whether required the operating system, databases, and other prerequisites are fulfilled.

- *Install*: Installs Oracle Fusion Applications Binaries.

- *Preconfigure*: Creates the WebLogic domain and configures the directory servers and Web server.

- *Configure*: Performs the Oracle Identity Manager configuration.

- *Configure Secondary*: Performs the Oracle Identity Manager and Oracle Access Manager integration.

- *Postconfigure*: Configures WebGate identity federation. Performs tuning, OIM reconciliation, and SSL configuration.

- *Startup*: Starts all services that are in the enabled state.

- *Validate*: Validates all component services and verifies service URLs for all components.

Figure 6-1 shows the Identity Management provisioning phases and their order of execution, along with the failure or success actions.

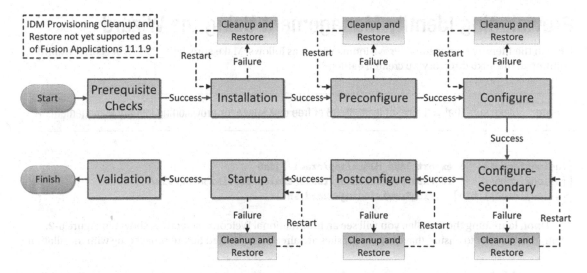

Figure 6-1. Identity Management provisioning phases

Possible States of an IDM Provisioning Phase

Each provisioning phase that has already been initiated has the following possible states.

- STARTED: This means the phase is currently running.

- COMPLETED: This means the phase has completed doing its actions and performing post-completion actions.

- ENDED: This means the phase has finished and is ready to move on to the next phase on this host. For IDM provisioning, COMPLETED and ENDED are AT nearly the same time, but for Fusion Applications provisioning, these two phases have distinct meanings. You will understand the difference between COMPLETED and ENDED more during Fusion Applications provisioning.

- FAILED: This means the entire phase or part of it has failed. For example, the entire phase except OIM-related activities have failed. In both cases the phaseguard file for the phase will have FAILED status.

- ABORTSIGNALED: This means that the user pressed Cancel during the provisioning process and the phase was aborted. The status first becomes ABORTSIGNALED and once the provisioning processes have existed completely, it changes to FAILED.

Note that all of these phases must run in the given sequence. Only if the predecessor phase is successful can the next phase start. Provisioning framework controls this by a directory named phaseguards. Accordingly, the installer will create a file named **<phase>-<hostname>-<status>.grd** in the <INSTALLATION_BASE>/provisioning/phaseguards directory. Upon restarting the provisioning process, the installer detects the current status of each phase based on the phaseguards and proceeds accordingly.

■ **Tip**   Before you begin Identity Management provisioning, back up the database since at the moment automatic cleanup and restore of IDM provisioning is not supported. Although this is not mandatory, it will help you reduce the time needed to restart the installation in case of failure.

Provisioning Identity Management Using the Wizard

Launch the Identity Management Provisioning wizard as follows. Make sure JAVA_HOME is set correctly and pointing to the jdk6 directory we created earlier.

■ **Note**   Make sure that you have at least 35 GB of free disk space for provisioning Identity Management.

```
[fusion@idmhost ~]$ export JAVA_HOME=/app/oracle/jdk6
[fusion@idmhost ~]$ cd /app/provisioning/tools/idmlcm/provisioning/bin/
[fusion@idmhost bin]$ ./idmProvisioningWizard.sh
```

Upon launching the installer, you will see an informational Welcome screen, as shown in Figure 6-2. It cautions the user to ensure that the prerequisites are already performed before proceeding with installation.

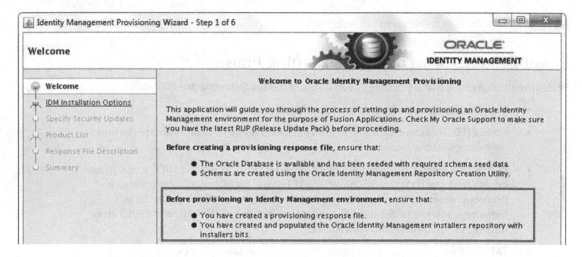

Figure 6-2. *Identity Management Provisioning wizard welcome screen*

Since you are provisioning the Identity Management environment, ensure that a provisioning response file has already been created. Also make sure that the installation media has been extracted to the installation repository location and is available on all hosts. If you have restarted the database servers in between, make sure that the IDM database and listener have been started.

Once you check these settings, click Next to proceed to the wizard option selection screen, as shown in Figure 6-3.

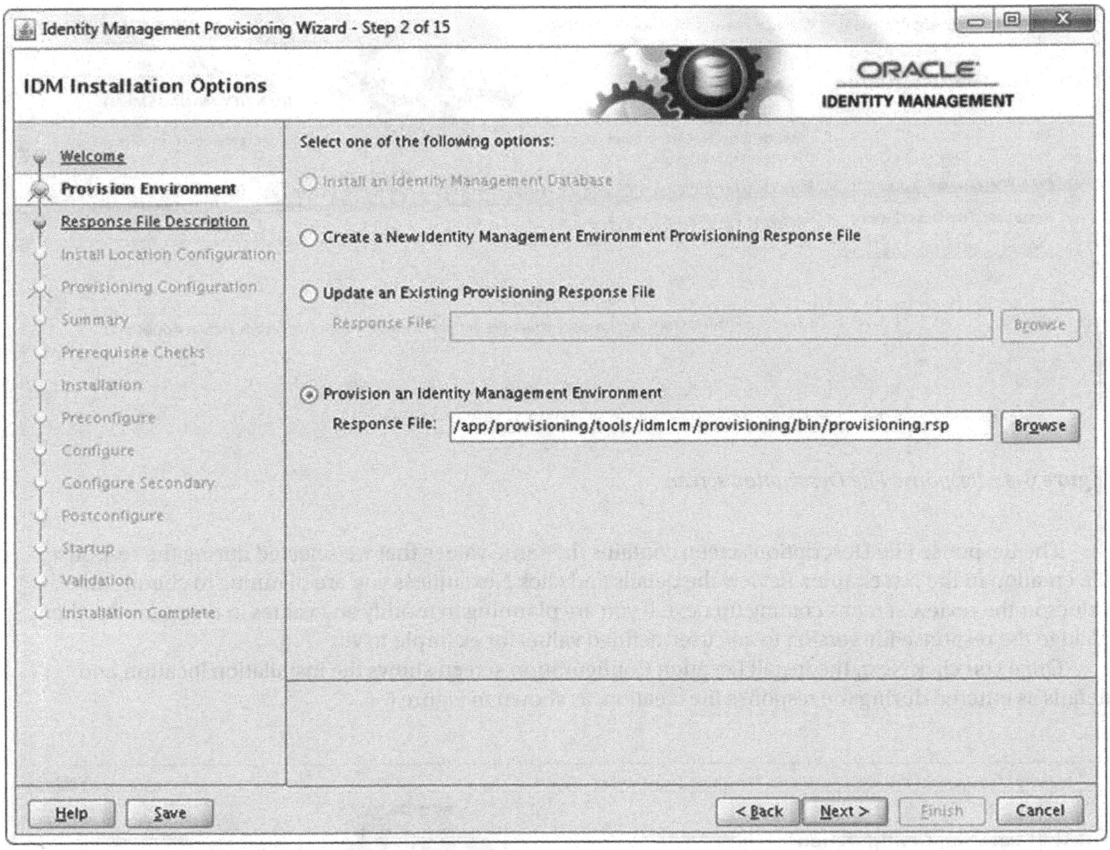

Figure 6-3. *Identity Management Provisioning option selection screen*

You have seen the screen in Figure 6-3 earlier when creating a new Identity Management environment provisioning response file. The first option is related to the IDM database (disabled for the current release), while options 2 and 3 are related to the provisioning response file creation and update. In this case we will select option 4, which is to provision an Identity Management environment.

The wizard asks you to enter the response file name with the full path. Enter the path of the response file created in the previous step. Alternatively, you can click on Browse to locate the file in the directory tree. Make sure to select the file with the .rsp extension, not with .summary.

Once the response file's name has been provided, click Next to proceed to the Response File Description screen, as shown in Figure 6-4.

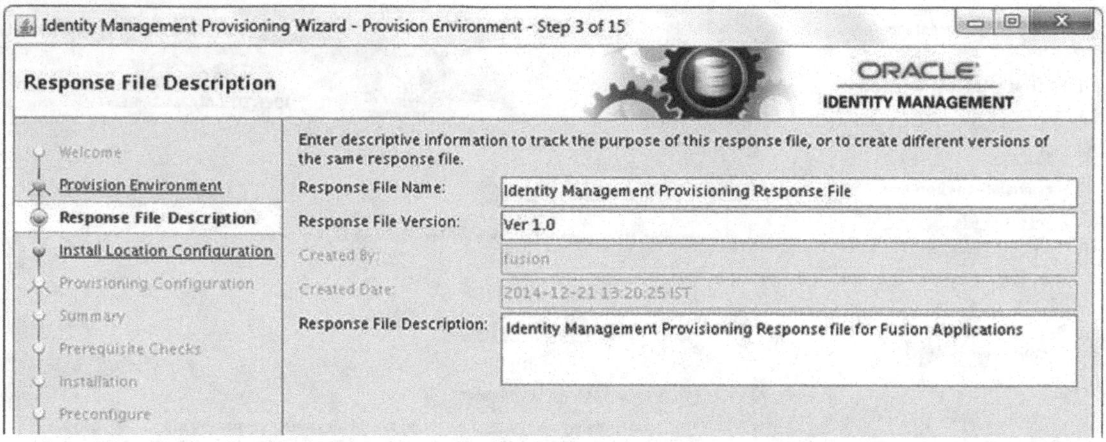

Figure 6-4. *Response File Description screen*

The Response File Description screen contains the same values that we selected during the response file creation in the last chapter. Review the details and click Next unless you are planning to change any values in the review screens coming up next. If you are planning to modify any values in next screens, then change the response file version to any user-defined value, for example to Ver 2.0.

Once you click Next, the Install Location Configuration screen shows the installation location and details as entered during the response file creation, as shown in Figure 6-5.

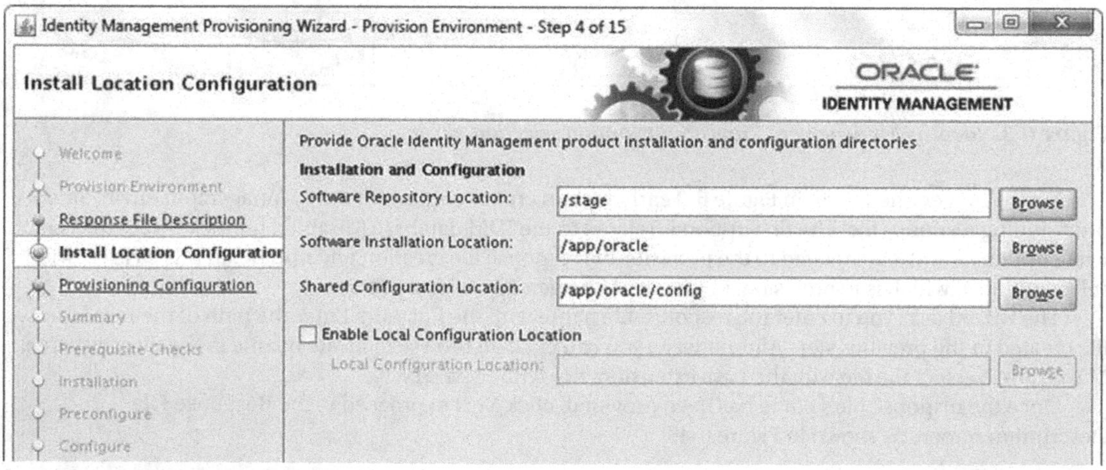

Figure 6-5. *Installation Location Configuration screen*

If you want to change any of these location parameters, you need not recreate or modify the response file manually. Instead the installer enables you to select it right from this screen and the installer will use the updated parameters. We have already gone through details of the following fields in the last chapter while creating response file, so you already know the importance of them.

Review the information provided and update it if required. Click Next to continue to the Configuration Review screen, as shown in Figure 6-6.

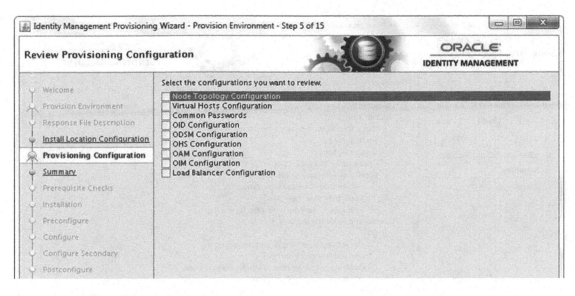

Figure 6-6. *Configuration Review screen*

The Review Provisioning Configuration screen allows you to review any of the following configurations and modify them if necessary in the subsequent screens.

- Node topology configuration

- Virtual hosts configuration

- Common passwords

- OID configuration

- ODSM configuration

- OHS configuration

- OAM configuration

- OIM configuration

- Load balancer configuration

■ **Tip**   Although reviewing these configurations is optional, it may be wise to do so if you are having the slightest doubt about any of the section details. Any incorrect detail may lead to installation failure.

If you have selected any of these checkboxes, the wizard will launch the response file update screens related to the selected configuration. Otherwise, click Next to continue to the Installation Summary screen, as shown in Figure 6-7.

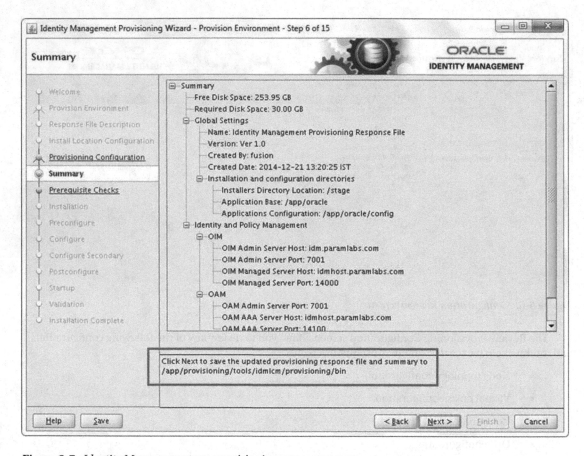

Figure 6-7. *Identity Management pre-provisioning summary screen*

Review the pre-provisioning summary before starting the actual provisioning process. Any changes you made before this step will be updated automatically in the response and summary files. These changes are also reflected in the Summary shown in Figure 6-7, which makes it easier for you to review in single-tree view. Click Next to save the changes (if any) in the response file and proceed with the prerequisite checks.

Before we look at each of these phases, it is important to understand the common layout of the Provisioning wizard so that you can better understand the further screens and any errors encountered during the installation.

IDM Provisioning Wizard Layout During the Provisioning Phases

From this phase onward, the installation screen layout will look similar until the end of the installation. So it is necessary to understand the layout. The screen is mainly divided into the following three panels:

- *Left panel*: Shows the list of steps required during the installation. It highlights the current step and shows the recently completed step along with next step in the queue.

- *Top panel*: Shows the following information.

- *Host*: The name of the host where the phase is running.

- *Status*: Current status of the phase. It can be Starting, Restarting, Completed, Failed, or Aborted.

- *Log*: You can click on the log icon to open the log file for this phase (not only product but the overall phase).

- *Domains*: The list of domains on which this phase has to run. For IDM provisioning, it will be only the IDMDomain.

- *Bottom panel*: The following are important elements in the bottom panel of the screen.

  - *Retry Button*: Remains disabled until any phase has failed.

  - *Back Button*: Active only until the Prerequisite Checks screen. From the next screen onward, this button is always disabled and the only way to go back is to cancel the installation and start from beginning after cleanup.

  - *Next Button*: Active only after the phase has successfully completed. All other times it remains disabled.

  - *Cancel Button*: You can click this button at any time during the installation to abort the phase. The status of the phase will become ABORTED and the Retry button will be activated if you want to restart the installation.

  - *Messages Text Area*: This textbox is not visible until you select any action item in the screen. This textbox will contain any errors or warnings encountered in the particular activity. If you want to see all the errors or warnings during the phase, you should select the top menu item, called Build Messages for Orchestration Product Family.

Now let's proceed to the Prerequisites Check step shown in Figure 6-8.

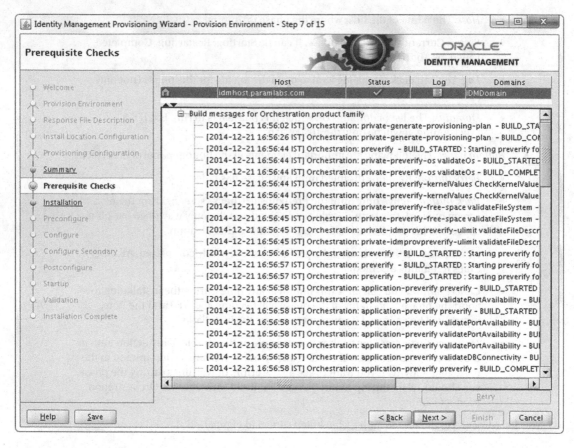

Figure 6-8. *Prerequisite Checks screen*

The Prerequisites Checks or Preverify phase checks for all the prerequisites required for the installation, including disk space, operating system version, OS parameters and utilities, port availability, database reachability, required memory size, and so on. It validates these parameters based on the topology selected, so you may see same parameters with different values being checked.

Depending on how critical the parameter being checked is, it will either show a warning or an error message. The installer will show errors and warnings in the bottom pane. If there are any errors or warnings, resolve the issues and click Retry to restart the Prerequisites Check phase. You can find the installation logs at <CONFIG_DIR>/provisioning/logs; for example, /app/oracle/config/provisioning/logs/idmhost.paramlabs.com.

The following log files correspond to this phase. Review these files for detailed error logs.

```
runIDMProvisioning-preverify.out
runIDMProvisioning-preverify.log
```

You can see following phaseguard files at <IDM_BASE>/provisioning/phaseguards the end of the installation.

```
preverify-idmhost.paramlabs.com-STARTED.grd
preverify-idmhost.paramlabs.com-COMPLETED.grd
preverify-idmhost.paramlabs.com-ENDED.grd
```

148

Once the prerequisites check is successful, click Next to proceed with the install phase, as shown in Figure 6-9. Remember that the Back button is no longer available after this phase.

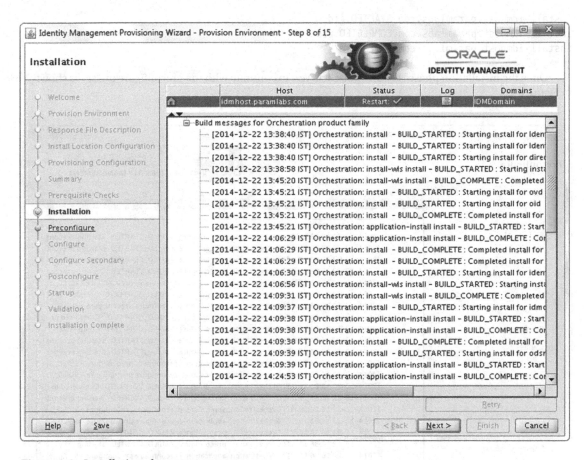

Figure 6-9. *Installation phase status screen*

The Installation phase installs all the required software, including the Oracle Fusion middleware binaries. Once the required software binaries are installed, it will apply all the available patches in the installer media for the Oracle Fusion middleware components, including Oracle HTTP Server, the IDM suite, and the WebLogic patches. It invokes OPatch or the WebLogic smart update, depending on the component being patched.

The log files generated at the <CONFIG_DIR>/provisioning/logs directory are as follows. Review these log files in case there are any errors or warnings.

runIDMProvisioning-install-logstatus.log
runIDMProvisioning-install.log
runIDMProvisioning-install.out

The phaseguard files for this phase generated at the `<IDM_BASE>/provisioning/phaseguards` directory are as follows.

```
install-idmhost.paramlabs.com-STARTED.grd
install-idmhost.paramlabs.com-COMPLETED.grd
install-idmhost.paramlabs.com-ENDED.grd
```

Once the installation phase is successful, click *Next* to continue with the preconfigure phase, as shown in Figure 6-10.

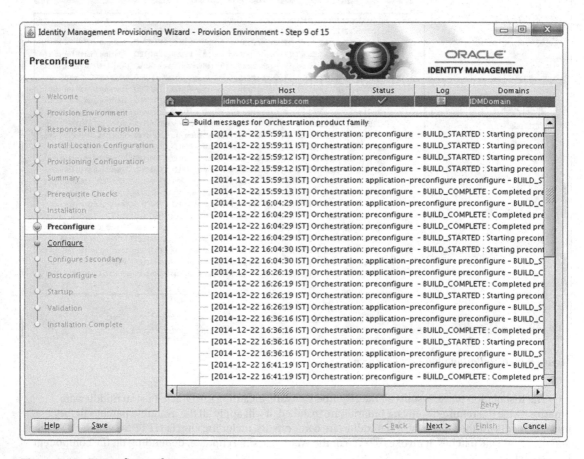

Figure 6-10. *Preconfigure phase status screen*

The Preconfigure phase performs the following activities.

- Configure the Oracle Internet Directory (OID) and Oracle Virtual Directory (OVD)

- Prepare the identity store by seeding OID with the required users/groups

- Create the Oracle WebLogic domain

- Create the Oracle HTTP Server (OHS) instance

- Extend the domain to configure Oracle Directory Service Manager (ODSM)

The following log files are generated at <CONFIG_DIR>/provisioning/logs during this phase.

runIDMProvisioning-preconfigure.log
runIDMProvisioning-preconfigure-logstatus.log
runIDMProvisioning-preconfigure.out

The following phaseguard files are generated at <IDM_BASE>/provisioning/phaseguards during this phase.

preconfigure-idmhost.paramlabs.com-STARTED.grd
application-<component>-preconfigure-COMPLETED.grd
preconfigure-idmhost.paramlabs.com-COMPLETED.grd
preconfigure-idmhost.paramlabs.com-ENDED.grd

Once the Preconfigure phase is successful, the Next button will be activated again. Click *Next* to proceed with the configure phase, as shown in Figure 6-11.

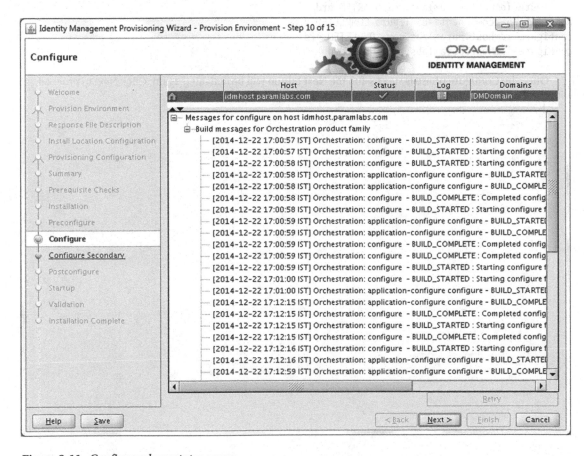

Figure 6-11. *Configure phase status screen*

The following activities are performed during the configure phase.

- Configure Oracle Access Manager
- Configure Oracle Identity Manager and SOA
- Associate Policy Store with Identity Store (OID)
- Associate Oracle Access Manager with OID

The following are the important log files for this phase in same location.

```
runIDMProvisioning-configure.log
runIDMProvisioning-configure-logstatus.log
runIDMProvisioning-configure.out
```

The phaseguard files for this phase (after successful completion) are as follows.

```
configure-idmhost.paramlabs.com-STARTED.grd
application-<component>-configure-COMPLETED.grd
configure-idmhost.paramlabs.com-COMPLETED.grd
configure-idmhost.paramlabs.com-ENDED.grd
```

Once the Configure phase is successful, the Next button will be activated again. Click Next to proceed with the Configure Secondary phase, as shown in Figure 6-12.

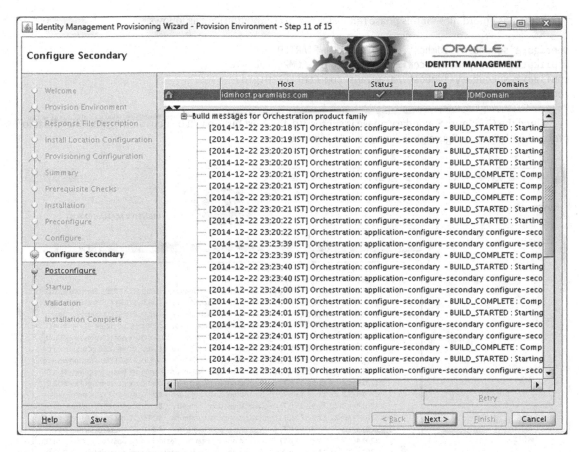

Figure 6-12. *Configure Secondary phase status screen*

Once the Configure phase is completed, the wizard will proceed to the Configure Secondary phase regardless of whether you have selected single-host or EDG topology. During the Configure Secondary phase, the installer mainly performs the following actions. The reason why these actions are kept in the Configure Secondary phase is that if there are any secondary servers then the configure stage should have completed on all nodes before the following actions can be performed. In this case, there are no second node-specific actions performed.

- Integrate WebLogic domain with Oracle HTTP Server instance by creating aliases for OAM, OIM, SOA, and ODSM

- Perform integration of Oracle Access Manager and Oracle Identity Manager

The following are the important log files to look at for this phase in the same location.

```
runIDMProvisioning-configure-secondary.log
runIDMProvisioning-configure-secondary-logstatus.log
runIDMProvisioning-configure-secondary.out
```

The phaseguard files for this phase (after successful completion) are as follows.

```
configure-secondary-idmhost.paramlabs.com-STARTED.grd
application-<component>-configure-secondary-COMPLETED.grd
configure-secondary-idmhost.paramlabs.com-COMPLETED.grd
configure-secondary-idmhost.paramlabs.com-ENDED.grd
```

Once the Configure Secondary phase is successful, the Next button will be activated again. Click Next to proceed with Postconfigure phase, as shown in Figure 6-13.

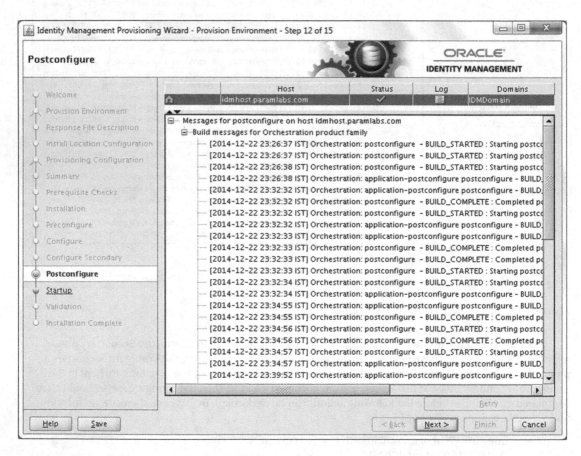

Figure 6-13. *Postconfigure phase status screen*

At this stage, we have the base infrastructure of the Identity Management component ready and the installer will move on to perform post-configuration tasks that include but not limited to the following major actions.

- Configure WebGate and integrate it with the HTTP server

- Register OID with WebLogic domain IDMDomain

- Tune and configure SSL for OID

- Configure OIF (it remains disabled after configuration)

- Configure and run reconciliation of OIM from the ID store

The following important log files are generated at <CONFIG_DIR>/ provisioning/logs for this phase. Review the log files for detailed execution information as well as for error messages.

```
runIDMProvisioning-postconfigure.log
runIDMProvisioning-postconfigure-logstatus.log
runIDMProvisioning-postconfigure.out
```

The phaseguard files for this phase (after successful completion) are as follows.

```
postconfigure-idmhost.paramlabs.com-STARTED.grd
application-<component>-postconfigure-COMPLETED.grd
postconfigure-idmhost.paramlabs.com-COMPLETED.grd
postconfigure-idmhost.paramlabs.com-ENDED.grd
```

Once the Postconfigure phase is completed successfully, click Next to proceed to the Startup phase, as shown in Figure 6-14.

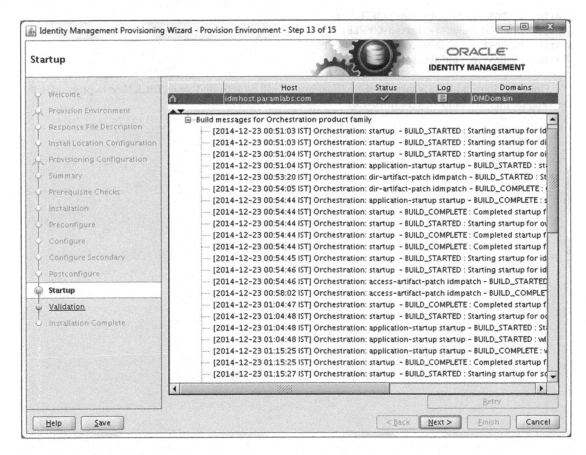

Figure 6-14. Startup phase status screen

■ **Note**   At the end of Postconfigure phase, all the components are already started. The next phase will gracefully bounce them one by one.

The Startup phase attempts to cleanly shut down and restart all services that are enabled for startup. By default, except Oracle Identity Federation (OIF), all services are enabled for startup in this release of the IDM Provisioning wizard. The wizard monitors the state file of each WebLogic managed server being started and once it shows a RUNNING state, it moves to the next component's startup.

The following are the important log files for this phase, found at `<CONFIG_DIR>/ provisioning/logs`.

```
runIDMProvisioning-startup.log
runIDMProvisioning-startup-logstatus.log
runIDMProvisioning-startup.out
```

The phaseguard files for this phase (after successful completion) are as follows.

```
startup-idmhost.paramlabs.com-STARTED.grd
application-<component>-startup-COMPLETED.grd
startup-idmhost.paramlabs.com-COMPLETED.grd
startup-idmhost.paramlabs.com-ENDED.grd
```

Once the Startup phase is successful, the Next button will be activated again. Click Next to proceed with the Validate phase, as shown in Figure 6-15.

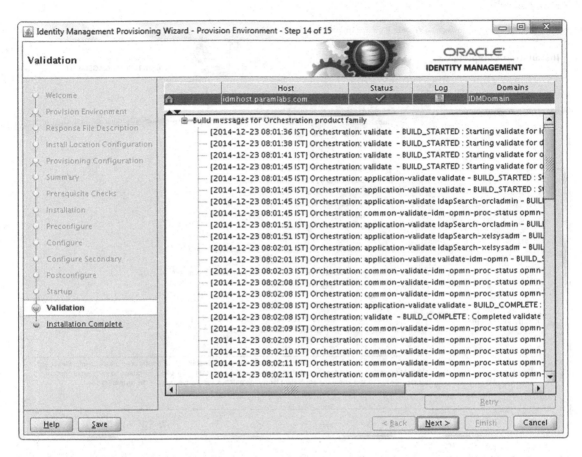

Figure 6-15. *Validation phase status screen*

The last phase in Identity Management provisioning is Validate. This phase checks for online status and connectivity for all managed servers and instances, invokes test URLs to make sure the desired response is received, and performs other validations. Any validation error or warning will be displayed in the lower panel. However, in this phase, cleanup is not supported and upon retry all startup-related actions will be performed again.

The following are the important log files for this phase at the same common log location.

```
runIDMProvisioning-validate.log
runIDMProvisioning-validate-logstatus.log
runIDMProvisioning-validate.out
```

The phaseguard files for this phase (after successful completion) are as follows.

```
validate-idmhost.paramlabs.com-STARTED.grd
validate-idmhost.paramlabs.com-COMPLETED.grd
validate-idmhost.paramlabs.com-ENDED.grd
```

Once the Validate phase completes, the Next button will be activated. Click Next to go to the Post-Installation Summary page, as shown in Figure 6-16.

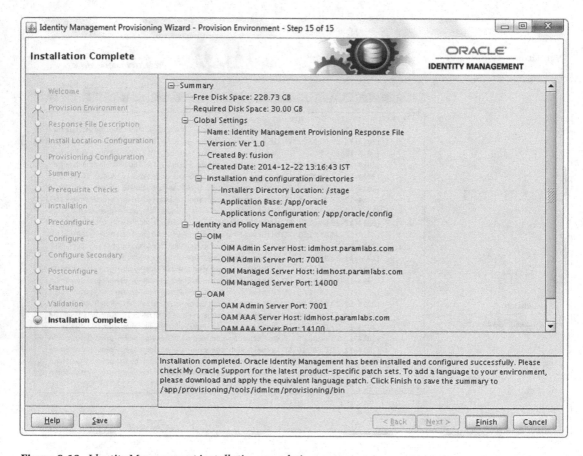

Figure 6-16. Identity Management installation completion summary

Review the post-installation summary details, as shown in Figure 6-16. This page includes all the installed Oracle Fusion Applications products with the configured ports and URLs. The same summary is saved to the default location of <IDMLCM_HOME>/provisioning/bin directory in readable text format. Keep the summary file with your earlier summary files for project documentation.

Click Finish to save the summary and exit the installation wizard.

Provisioning Using the Command-Line Interface (CLI)

As explained earlier, in case of multi-host environments or when the GUI-based installer is not working on specific operating system versions, you may want to provision Identity Management using the command-line interface. The process is essentially the same except here you will initiate each phase manually after completing the previous phase.

Similar to when using the graphical wizard, you will need the already created response file. In this example, the response file generated in an earlier step is located at /app/provisioning/tools/idmlcm/provisioning/bin/provisioning.rsp. We will need to supply this response file at each phase of provisioning. The syntax for the command-line provisioning is as follows.

For the Unix Platform
IDMLCM_HOME/provisioning/bin/runIDMProvisioning.sh -responseFile <filename> -target <phase>
For the Windows Platform
IDMLCM_HOME\provisioning\bin\runIDMProvisioning.bat -responseFile <filename> -target <phase>

Run Preverify Phase

Let's begin with the Preverify phase. This is the same as the Prerequisites Checks phase, as seen in the Graphical Provisioning wizard. Make sure to finish this phase on all nodes in the topology before starting the next phase. Here is an example of the Preverify phase on a Linux host.

```
[fusion@idmhost ]$ cd /app/provisioning/tools/idmlcm/provisioning/bin
[fusion@idmhost bin]$ ./runIDMProvisioning.sh -responseFile /app/provisioning/tools/idmlcm/
provisioning/bin/provisioning.rsp -target preverify
*** Checking java and fusion repository setting...
*** Using fusion repository at /stage
*** Valid java version. Using JAVA_HOME environment at /app/oracle/jdk6
*** Using local ant setting at /app/fusion/provisioning/ant

...
2013-11-03 05:35:31.842 TRACE
BUILD SUCCESSFUL
Total time: 20 seconds

Successfully finished preverify.
Proceed with install.
```

Run Install Phase

Once the Preverify has completed on all nodes, start the Install phase on the primordial node. The syntax for running the Install phase on the Linux operating system is as follows.

```
[fusion@idmhost bin]$ ./runIDMProvisioning.sh -responseFile
/app/provisioning/tools/idmlcm/provisioning/bin/provisioning.rsp -target install
...
*** Checking java and fusion repository setting...
*** Using fusion repository at /stage
*** Valid java version. Using JAVA_HOME environment at /app/oracle/jdk6
*** Using local ant setting at /app/fusion/provisioning/ant

...
2013-11-03 08:32:33.621 TRACE
BUILD SUCCESSFUL
Total time: 150 minutes 24 seconds

Successfully finished install.
Proceed with preconfigure.
```

Run Preconfigure Phase

Once the Install Phase has completed on all nodes, start the Preconfigure phase on the primordial node. Here is an example of running the Preconfigure phase using the command-line interface on the Linux operating system.

```
[fusion@idmhost bin]$ ./runIDMProvisioning.sh -responseFile
/app/provisioning/tools/idmlcm/provisioning/bin/provisioning.rsp -target preconfigure
fusionRepository from rsp file: /stage
*** Checking java and fusion repository setting...
*** Using fusion repository at /stage
*** Valid java version. Using JAVA_HOME environment at /app/oracle/jdk6
*** Using local ant setting at /app/fusion/provisioning/ant
...
2013-11-03 13:17:42.263 TRACE
BUILD SUCCESSFUL
Total time: 30 minutes 15 seconds

Successfully finished preconfigure.
Proceed with configure.
```

Run Configure Phase

Once the Preconfigure phase has completed on all nodes, start the Configure phase on the primordial node. The syntax for running the Configure phase on the Linux operating system is as follows.

```
[fusion@idmhost bin]$ ./runIDMProvisioning.sh -responseFile
/app/provisioning/tools/idmlcm/provisioning/bin/provisioning.rsp -target configure
fusionRepository from rsp file: /stage
*** Checking java and fusion repository setting...
*** Using fusion repository at /stage
*** Valid java version. Using JAVA_HOME environment at /app/oracle/jdk6
*** Using local ant setting at /app/fusion/provisioning/ant
...
2013-11-03 13:56:06.366 TRACE
BUILD SUCCESSFUL
Total time: 30 minutes 19 seconds

Successfully finished configure.
Proceed with configure-secondary.
```

Run Configure Secondary Phase

When Configure phase has completed on all nodes, you can run the Configure Secondary phase on the primordial node. Here is the syntax for our example installation.

```
[fusion@idmhost bin]$ ./runIDMProvisioning.sh -responseFile
/app/provisioning/tools/idmlcm/provisioning/bin/provisioning.rsp -target configure-secondary
fusionRepository from rsp file: /stage
*** Checking java and fusion repository setting...
*** Using fusion repository at /stage
```

```
*** Valid java version. Using JAVA_HOME environment at /app/oracle/jdk6
*** Using local ant setting at /app/fusion/provisioning/ant
...
2013-11-03 14:13:07.792 TRACE
BUILD SUCCESSFUL
Total time: 5 minutes 50 seconds

Successfully finished configure-secondary.
Proceed with postconfigure.
```

Run Post Configure Phase

Once the Configure Secondary phase has completed on all nodes, start the Post Configure phase on the primordial node. The syntax for running the Post Configure phase using the command-line interface on the Linux operating system is as follows.

```
[fusion@idmhost bin]$ ./runIDMProvisioning.sh -responseFile
/app/provisioning/tools/idmlcm/provisioning/bin/provisioning.rsp -target postconfigure
fusionRepository from rsp file: /stage
*** Checking java and fusion repository setting...
*** Using fusion repository at /stage
*** Valid java version. Using JAVA_HOME environment at /app/oracle/jdk6
*** Using local ant setting at /app/fusion/provisioning/ant
...
2013-11-03 15:03:24.987 TRACE
BUILD SUCCESSFUL
Total time: 40 minutes 39 seconds

Successfully finished postconfigure.
Proceed with startup.
```

Run Startup Phase

After the Post Configure phase has finished on all nodes, move on to the Startup phase to bring up all components on all nodes in the topology. The syntax for running the Startup phase using the command-line interface is as follows.

```
[fusion@idmhost bin]$ ./runIDMProvisioning.sh -responseFile
/app/provisioning/tools/idmlcm/provisioning/bin/provisioning.rsp -target startup
...
*** Checking java and fusion repository setting...
*** Using fusion repository at /stage
*** Valid java version. Using JAVA_HOME environment at /app/oracle/jdk6
*** Using local ant setting at /app/fusion/provisioning/ant
...
2013-11-03 16:02:01.282 TRACE
BUILD SUCCESSFUL
Total time: 28 minutes 34 seconds

Successfully finished startup.
Proceed with validate.
```

Run Validate Phase

Once the Startup phase has completed, we will go ahead with the final phase of IDM provisioning, which is the Validate phase. Here is an example of running the Validate phase using the command-line interface on the Linux operating system.

```
[fusion@idmhost bin]$ ./runIDMProvisioning.sh -responseFile
/app/provisioning/tools/idmlcm/provisioning/bin/provisioning.rsp -target validate
fusionRepository from rsp file: /stage
*** Checking java and fusion repository setting...
*** Using fusion repository at /stage
*** Valid java version. Using JAVA_HOME environment at /app/oracle/jdk6
*** Using local ant setting at /app/fusion/provisioning/ant
...
2013-11-03 16:30:29.582 TRACE
BUILD SUCCESSFUL
Total time: 2 minutes 56 seconds

Successfully finished validate.
```

Restarting After a Failed Installation

The Identity Management provisioning framework has option to initiate a cleanup and restore if a phase fails for any reason. But as of the installer bundled with Fusion Applications release 11.1.9, this feature is not supported. It will be supported in future releases.

Once a phase fails while performing any action, the status of the phase changes to FAILED and the installer pauses with the Retry button activated. Once you click the Retry button, it should initiate a cleanup operation followed by a restore to previous phase auto-backup. Since the IDM cleanup and restore options are not yet supported, you will see a message in Figure 6-17 on your screen.

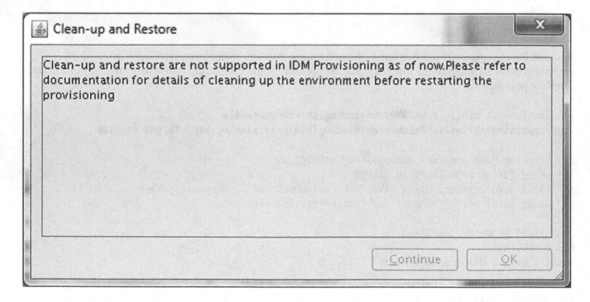

Figure 6-17. Cleanup and Restore message box as of Fusion Applications 11.1.9

Once IDM cleanup and restore is supported, you can run cleanup and restore using the command-line interface as well, as follows.

```
./runIDMProvisioning.sh -responseFile <filename> -target cleanup-<phase>
./runIDMProvisioning.sh -responseFile <filename> -target restore-<phase>
```

For example, to clean up and restore after failed Configure phase, you use the following:

```
./runIDMProvisioning.sh -responseFile <filename> -target cleanup-configure
./runIDMProvisioning.sh -responseFile <filename> -target restore-configure
```

Since you need to do a manual cleanup instead, you have two options when you need to restart the IDM provisioning, as shown in Figure 6-18.

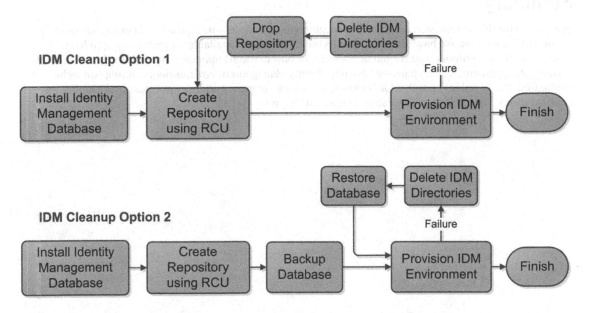

Figure 6-18. *Options for IDM manual cleanup and restore*

It's important to understand that steps involved in manual cleanup and restore until the feature is enabled in the IDM provisioning framework.

- *Option 1*: If you do not make a full database backup before beginning IDM provisioning then this is the preferred method of IDM provisioning cleanup. This includes the following steps.

  a. IDM processes might be running, depending on at which phase the provisioning has failed. Kill all the IDM related processes, if any.

  b. Delete all IDM-related directories created by the wizard under IDM_TOP. For example, /app/oracle/products and /app/oracle/config, and so on.

    c.   Start the Repository Creation Utility and select the Drop Repository option to drop the existing repository schemas from the database.

    d.   Recreate the repository using RCU's Create Repository option.

- *Option 2*: If you have taken a full (preferably cold) backup of the database before the provisioning was initiated, this is the fastest way to clean up the failed installation. This includes the following steps.

    a.   Kill all the IDM related processes if any.

    b.   Delete all IDM related directories created by the wizard under IDM_TOP. For example, /app/oracle/products and /app/oracle/config, and so on.

    c.   Restore or replace the full/cold backup of the database.

Summary

You should be able to provision an Identity Management environment using the provisioning response file created in last chapter. We have also seen various interface options available for provisioning an Identity Management environment. You should now also know how to restart manually after a failed installation of Identity Management. At this stage, we have our Identity Management environment running and technically configured. But in order to use this for Fusion Applications, we must perform some post-provisioning configurations. We will look at those steps in the next chapter.

CHAPTER 7

■ ■ ■

Post-Provisioning IDM Configuration

In the previous chapter, we learned about the steps required to provision an Identity Management environment using the provisioning framework bundled with the Fusion Applications installation repository. At this stage we already have an installed and running instance of Oracle Identity Management. At the beginning of this chapter we will see how to manually validate each Identity Management component. Later, we will look at the post-provisioning actions required to tune the default parameters in order to use the Identity Management instance for Fusion Applications. We will also look at some post-steps required to fix some issues related to earlier versions of the Identity Management installer. By the end of this chapter, your Identity and Access Management infrastructure will ready to be used with Oracle Fusion Applications.

Validating the Oracle Identity Management Installation

Once Oracle Identity Management provisioning is complete, we will make sure that all the components are configured and running as expected before going ahead with post-provisioning configurations.

Validating the OID and OVD

Let's confirm that OID is running fine. We will see the status of the processes first. Log in as the Fusion Software owner user (in this example, fusion) and run the following command.

```
[fusion@idmhost ~]$ /app/oracle/config/instances/oid1/bin/opmnctl status
Processes in Instance: oid1
--------------+--------------+-------+-------
ias-component | process-type | pid   | status
--------------+--------------+-------+-------
ovd1          | OVD          | 14778 | Alive
oid1          | oidldapd     | 15011 | Alive
oid1          | oidldapd     | 14999 | Alive
oid1          | oidldapd     | 14910 | Alive
oid1          | oidmon       | 14780 | Alive
EMAGENT       | EMAGENT      | 14777 | Alive
```

© Tushar Thakker 2015
T. Thakker, *Pro Oracle Fusion Applications*, DOI 10.1007/978-1-4842-0983-7_7

In this output, you may see a number of OID processes (depending on configuration) and an OVD process. Make sure that both the SSL and non-SSL ports are accepting LDAP requests. The syntax used is as follows.

```
ldapbind -h <OID/OVD host> -p <OVD/OID non-SSL port> -D "cn=orcladmin" -q
ldapbind -h <OID/OVD host> -p <OVD/OID SSL port> -D "cn=orcladmin" -q -U 1
```

These commands will prompt you for the directory administrator user that you entered during the IDM provisioning response file creation. Let's validate OVD first using both SSL and non-SSL ports.

```
[fusion@idmhost bin]$ ldapbind -h idmhost.paramlabs.com -p 6501 -D "cn=orcladmin" -q
Please enter bind password:
bind successful

[fusion@idmhost bin]$ ldapbind -h idmhost.paramlabs.com -p 7501 -D "cn=orcladmin" -q -U 1
Please enter bind password:
bind successful

Next we will validate OID using both SSL and non-SSL ports.
[fusion@idmhost bin]$ ldapbind -h idmhost.paramlabs.com -p 3060 -D "cn=orcladmin" -q
Please enter bind password:
bind successful

[fusion@idmhost bin]$ ldapbind -h idmhost.paramlabs.com -p 3131 -D "cn=orcladmin" -q -U 1
Please enter bind password:
bind successful
```

Validating the Oracle HTTP Server

Let's make sure that the HTTP processes are running and accepting incoming requests. Invoke the opmnctl script from the <INSTANCE_TOP>/ohs1/bin directory.

```
[fusion@idmhost ~]$ /app/oracle/config/instances/ohs1/bin/opmnctl status
Processes in Instance: ohs1
--------------+--------------+-------+-------
ias-component | process-type | pid   | status
--------------+--------------+-------+-------
ohs1          | OHS          | 16798 | Alive
```

Now let's launch the OHS base URL http://<OHS Host>:<OHS port> to see the static homepage of Oracle Fusion Middleware 11g. For example, http://idmhost.paramlabs.com:7777.

You should be able to see a screen like the one shown in Figure 7-1. This validates the Oracle HTTP Server installation.

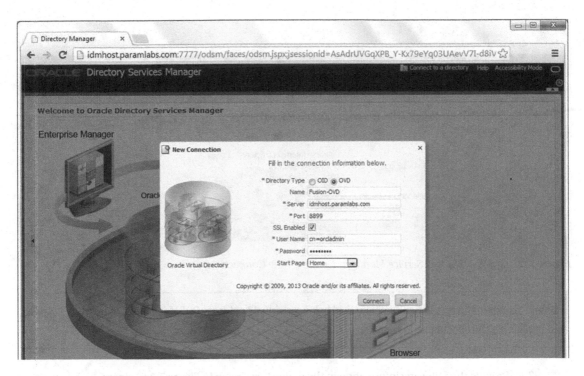

Figure 7-1. Oracle HTTP Server homepage

Validating the Oracle Directory Service Manager

Although in the next section, we will make sure through the WebLogic Administration console that the wls_ods1 managed server is in the RUNNING state, we need to manually create directory connections to OID and OVD in order to make sure that we are able to connect to them using the Oracle Directory Service Manager (ODSM).

Creating ODSM Connections to the Oracle Virtual Directory

Before you can manage the Oracle virtual directory, you must create connections from ODSM to the Oracle virtual directory instance. To do this, proceed as follows:

1. Access ODSM using http://<OVD HOST>:<OHS port>/odsm.

    For example, http://idmhost.paramlabs.com:7777/odsm.

2. To create connections to the Oracle virtual directory, click on Connect to a Directory. Since there is no saved connection information yet, click on Create a New Connection, as shown in Figure 7-2.

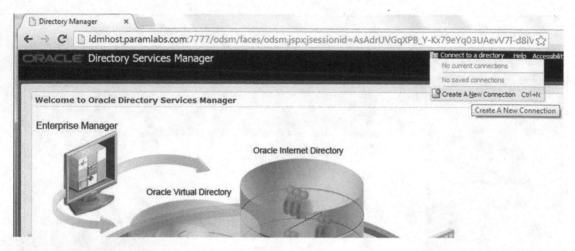

Figure 7-2. Oracle Directory Service Manager: Create a New Connection

---

■ **Note**   Use of the Oracle Virtual Directory load balancer virtual host from ODSM is not yet supported, so you must provide an OVD hostname to connect.

---

    3.   Provide the following information in the dialog box shown in Figure 7-3 to create a direct connection to OVD. It will save the information in ODSM.

        Host: idmhost.paramlabs.com
        Port: 8899 (The Oracle Virtual Directory proxy port, OVD_ADMIN_PORT)
        It is recommended to *Enable* the SSL option.
        User: cn=orcladmin
        Password: <password that was provided during response file creation>

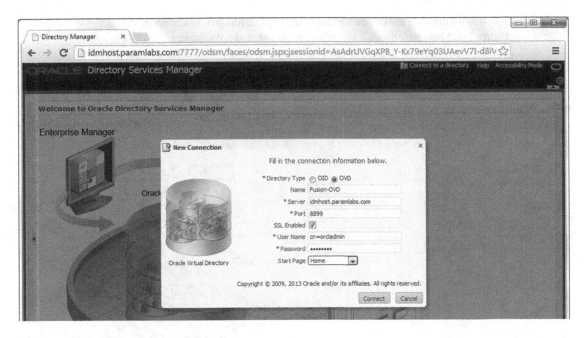

Figure 7-3. New Connection details screen

4.   Click Connect to save the connection information in ODSM and connect to the
     Oracle virtual directory.

5.   Since we have selected SSL, if you do not have a valid SSL certificate installed
     for the selected domain, then you may see the Certificate Trust Validation screen
     shown in Figure 7-4. Click Always if you do not want to manually validate trust
     every time you connect to the Oracle Virtual directory. Select This Session Only if
     you want to manually validate the certificate trust on each connection from ODSM.

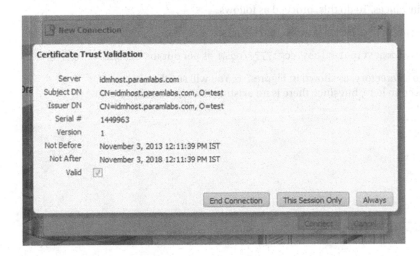

Figure 7-4. Certificate Trust Validation

6. You should now see the Oracle Virtual Directory Dashboard, as shown in Figure 7-5. Make sure that all adapters and listeners are available.

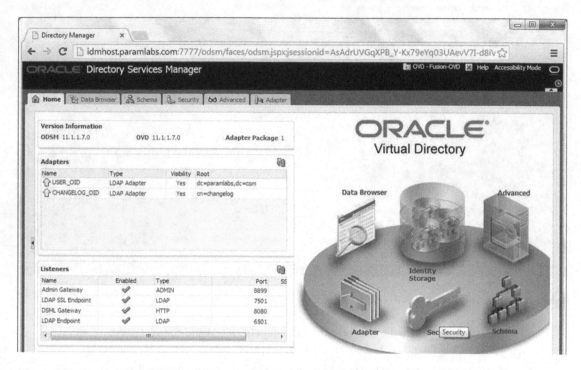

Figure 7-5. *Oracle Virtual Directory homepage*

Creating ODSM Connections to the Oracle Internet Directory

Before you can manage the Oracle Internet directory, you must create connections from ODSM to each of your Oracle Internet directory instances. To do this, proceed as follows.

1. Access ODSM using `http://<OID Host>:<OHS port>/odsm`.

    For example, `http://idmhost.paramlabs.com:7777/odsm`, as per our installation.

2. Click on Connect to a Directory, as shown in Figure 7-6. You will see the already created OVD connection here, but since there is no existing OID connection, we will create one here.

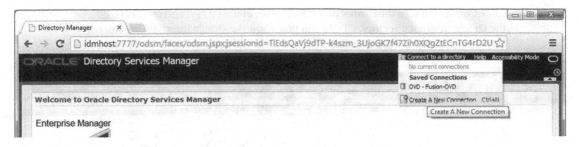

Figure 7-6. Oracle Directory Service Manager: Create a New OID Connection

3.   Click on Create a New Connection. Enter the information in the pop-up screen shown in Figure 7-7 to connect to OID and save the information in ODSM for future reference (except the password).

```
Host: OID hostname (For example idmhost.paramlabs.com)
Port: OID non-SSL port (3060)
Deselect the SSL option.
User: cn=orcladmin
Password: <password that was specified during response file creation>
```

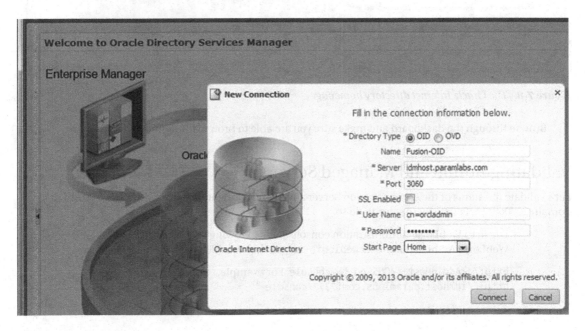

Figure 7-7. New Connection details screen

4. Click Connect to save the connection information in the ODSM and connect to the Oracle Internet directory. ODSM will now show the Oracle Internet Directory Dashboard, as shown in Figure 7-8.

Figure 7-8. *The Oracle Internet directory homepage*

Browse through the dashboard and make sure you are able to browse through the identity store.

Validating Admin and Managed Servers

Let's validate the status of the Administration Server and all the configured managed servers in WebLogic domain IDMDomain. Follow these steps to do so.

1. Log in to WebLogic Administration console at the following URL using the WebLogic Administrator user weblogic_idm, as shown in Figure 7-9.

    http://<AdminHost>:<OHS port>/console. For example,
    http://idmhost.paramlabs.com:7777/console

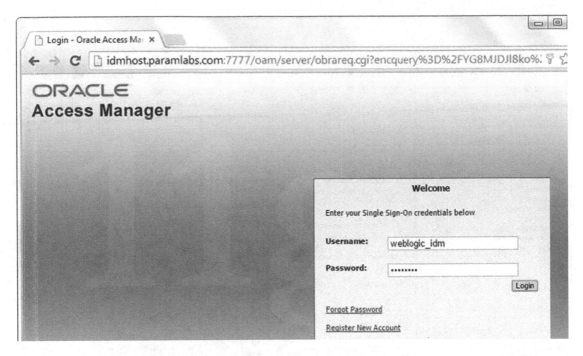

Figure 7-9. OAM credentials collector page (redirected from the WebLogic Administration console URL)

2. You will now see the Admin server homepage, as shown in Figure 7-10. Click on Servers.

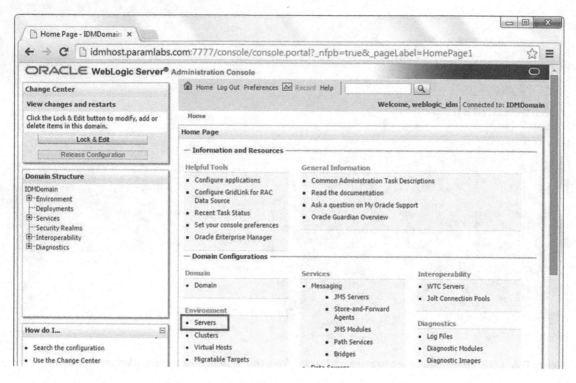

Figure 7-10. *Oracle WebLogic Server Administration console homepage*

3. You can see that all servers except OIF are running, as shown in Figure 7-11. This is the default configuration after IDM provisioning since Oracle Identity Federation (OIF) is optional for this setup and we will not start it unless we are going to use it. Oracle Identity Federation is required only when you are going to use directories across multiple domains. That allows Identity Management to communicate with multiple external identity providers.

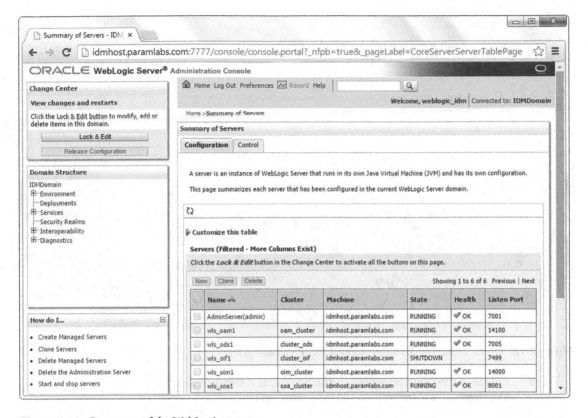

Figure 7-11. *Summary of the WebLogic servers*

4. Now log in to the Oracle Enterprise Manager Fusion Middleware Control at http://<Admin Host>:<OHS port>/em using the weblogic_idm user. For example, http://idmhost.paramlabs.com:7777/em.

5. You will see the Accessibility Features screen, as shown in Figure 7-12 if you are connecting to the Enterprise Manager for the first time. This preference can be changed later as well. We will look at accessibility options, including Screen Reader mode, in Chapter 11 when we look at the applications interface.

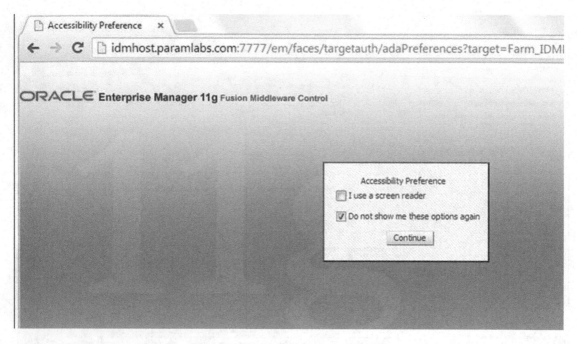

Figure 7-12. *Oracle Enterprise Manager Accessibility Preference screen*

6. You can see the Enterprise Manager homepage, as shown in Figure 7-13. All components except OIF should have running status.

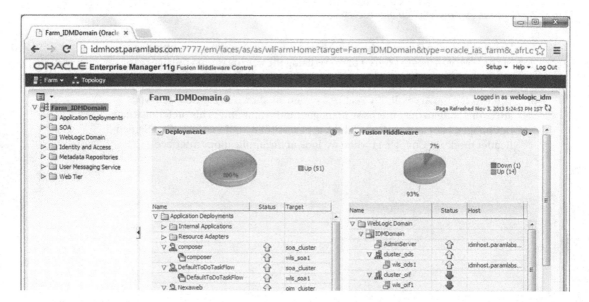

Figure 7-13. *Oracle Enterprise Manager (Fusion middleware control) homepage*

Browse through the Enterprise Manager interface to see the configuration of the WebLogic domain and other components, including OID, OHS, and so on.

Validating the Oracle Identity Manager

The next component to be validated is the Oracle Identity Manager (OIM). You can validate the OIM as follows.

1. Log in to http://<OIM Host>:<OHS port>/oim using the OIM administrator user xelsysadm.

   For example, http://idmhost.paramlabs.com:7777/oim.

2. You can now see Oracle Identity Manager dashboard, as shown in Figure 7-14.

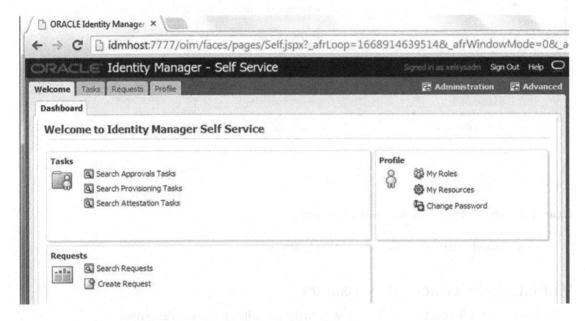

Figure 7-14. *Oracle Identity Manager Self Service dashboard*

Browse through the interface to see the various features.

Validating the Oracle Access Manager

Now validate the Oracle Access Manager (OAM) by logging into the OAM console as follows.

1. Log in to the Oracle Access Manager console as the Oracle Access Manager administration user oamadmin at the following URL.

   http://<OAM Host>:<OHS port>/oamconsole

   For example, http://idmhost.paramlabs.com:7777/oamconsole.

2. You should now be able to see the Oracle Access Manager 11g homepage, shown in Figure 7-15.

177

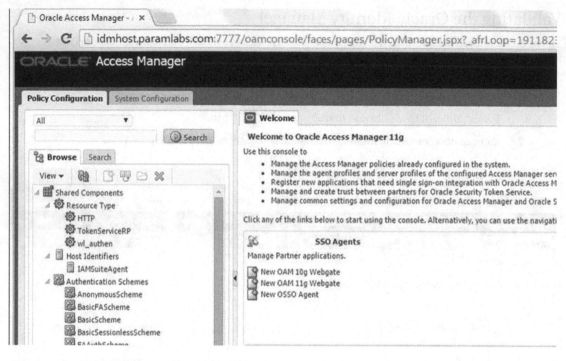

Figure 7-15. *Oracle Access Manager console homepage*

Browse through the interface to review the configuration.

Validating the Oracle SOA Instance

Let's launch the Oracle SOA Platform homepage to make sure it lists the available services.

1. To launch the SOA homepage, open the URL `http://<IDM Host>:<OHS port>/`
    `soa-infra`.

    For example, `http://idmhost.paramlabs.com:7777/soa-infra`.

2. It will prompt for authentication via a pop-up dialog box, as shown in Figure 7-16.
    Enter the WebLogic Administration user `weblogic_idm` credentials here.

Figure 7-16. Oracle SOA login screen

    3.   You should see the Oracle SOA Platform homepage, as shown in Figure 7-17.

Figure 7-17. Oracle SOA homepage

Performing the Post-Provisioning Configuration

We need to make a few changes to the Identity Management environment to fix certain issues with the earlier versions of installer and to tune some Identity Management component settings so they are suitable for use with Fusion Applications.

Correcting the Data Source Configuration

Due to a bug in an earlier version of Identity Management provisioning, you need to make changes to the following data sources through the WebLogic Administration console.

```
EDNLocalTxDataSource
mds-oim
mds-owsm
mds-soa
oamDS
oimJMSStoreDS
OraSDPMDataSource
SOALocalTxDataSource
```

■ **Note**   This is applicable only for the installer bundled with Fusion Applications 11.1.7. The installer has been fixed in later versions. If you are installing the latest version of Fusion Applications, you can skip this section.

To make these required changes, proceed as follows.

1. Log in to WebLogic Administration console at http://<hostname>:7777/ console. For example, http://idmhost.paramlabs.com:7777/console.

2. Now log in with the username weblogic_idm and the password that you provided before provisioning.

3. Click Lock & Edit.

4. Navigate to Services ➤ Data Sources, as shown in Figure 7-18.

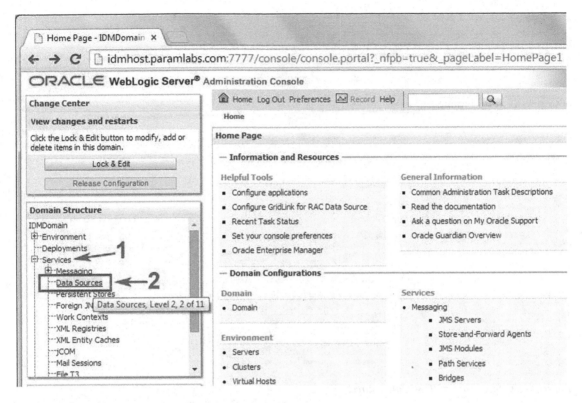

Figure 7-18. *Oracle WebLogic Administration console*

5. Click on the data source from the list of data sources to be updated, as shown in Figure 7-19. For example, EDNLocalTxDataSource.

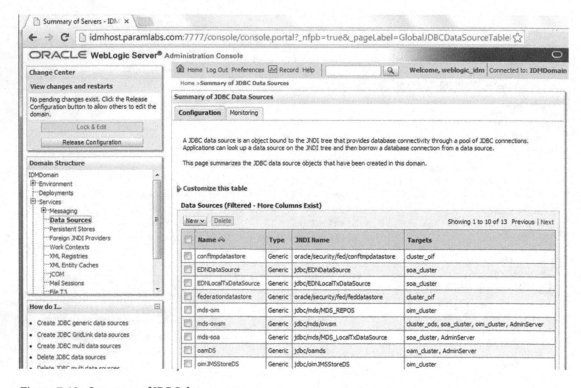

Figure 7-19. *Summary of JDBC data sources*

6. Click on the Transaction tab, as shown in Figure 7-20.

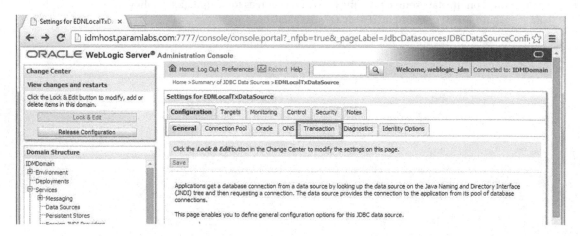

Figure 7-20. *Example Data Source Configuration screen*

7. Deselect Supports Global Transactions, as shown in Figure 7-21. If it is already deselected, no action is necessary.

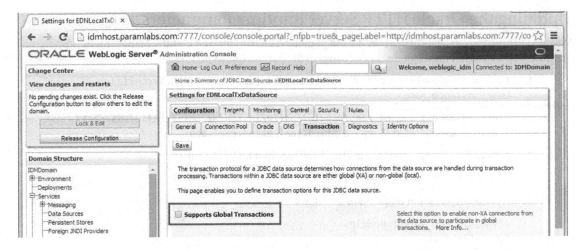

Figure 7-21. *Example Data Source Transaction tab*

8. Click Save.

9. Repeat Steps 4-7 for all the listed data sources in the beginning.

■ **Note** We had to change the checkbox only for oamDS in this example. It was already deselected for all other data sources.

---

10. Click Activate Changes. You will see the confirmation message shown in Figure 7-22.

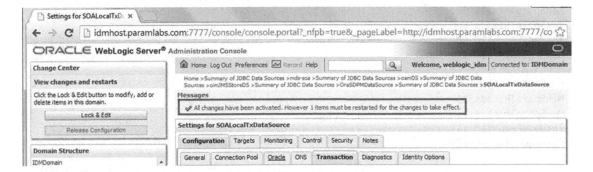

Figure 7-22. *Post-activation confirmation message*

11. Restart all the WebLogic managed servers.

Updating the Oracle HTTP Server Runtime Parameters

We need to tune the Oracle HTTP Server default parameters to support the Identity Management environment for Fusion Applications. Let's change at the parameters as follows.

1. First, back up the httpd.conf file, which is located at <OHS_INSTANCE>/config/OHS/<instance_name>/.

   [fusion@idmhost ~]$ **cd /app/oracle/config/instances/ohs1/config/OHS/ohs1/**
   [fusion@idmhost ohs1]$ **cp -p httpd.conf httpd.conf.bak**

2. Now edit the httpd.conf file and find an entry that looks like this:

   <IfModule mpm_worker_module>

3. Update the values in this section as follows:

   ```
   <IfModule mpm_worker_module>
   ServerLimit 20
   MaxClients 1000
   MinSpareThreads 200
   MaxSpareThreads 800
   ThreadsPerChild 50
   MaxRequestsPerChild 10000
   AcceptMutex fcntl
   </IfModule>
   ```

4. Leave all remaining values unchanged. Save the file.

   Let's verify the changes by comparing them with original file.

```
[fusion@idmhost ohs1]$ diff httpd.conf httpd.conf.bak
164,169c164,168
< ServerLimit 20
< MaxClients 1000
< MinSpareThreads 200
< MaxSpareThreads 800
< ThreadsPerChild 50
< MaxRequestsPerChild 10000
—
> MaxClients 150
> MinSpareThreads 25
> MaxSpareThreads 75
> ThreadsPerChild 25
> MaxRequestsPerChild 0
```

Backing Up the IDM Configuration File

Upon completion of Identity Management provisioning, it creates a specialized property file named idmsetup.properties that contains all the IDM configuration parameters at <CONFIG_DIR>/fa. Back up this file using the –p option to preserve the file timestamp. Optionally, you can also move to the Fusion

Applications primordial host if it is already available. Or you can move the file while creating Fusion Applications provisioning response file.

```
[fusion@idmhost ~]$ cd /app/oracle/config/fa/
[fusion@idmhost fa]$ ls -ltr idmsetup.properties
-rw-r-r- 1 fusion dba 3548 Dec 22 13:16 idmsetup.properties
[fusion@idmhost fa]$ cp -p idmsetup.properties idmsetup.properties.backup
```

Post-Provisioning Steps for the Oracle Identity Manager

You need to perform the following task so that the Oracle Identity Manager (OIM) works correctly after provisioning due to a bug in the IDM provisioning framework.

Adding an Oracle Identity Manager Property

We must add an Oracle Identity Manager property. Let us have a look at the steps involved in the same.

1. Log in to the WebLogic console at http://<idmhost>:<OHS port>/console.

2. Navigate to Environment ➤ Servers. You will see the Summary of Servers screen, as shown in Figure 7-23.

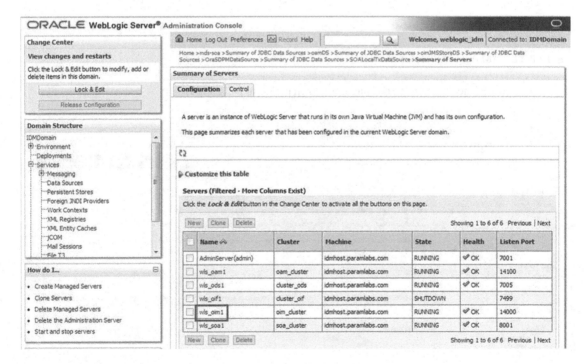

Figure 7-23. WebLogic Managed Servers Summary screen

3. Click the Lock & Edit button.

4. Click on the wls_oim1 server in the Servers Summary table.

5. Click on the Server Start tab, as shown in Figure 7-24.

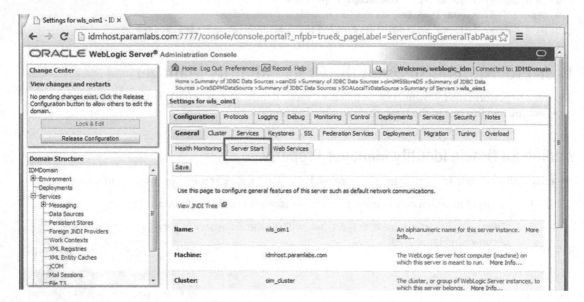

Figure 7-24. *OIM managed server settings*

6. You will see the Server Start page, as shown in Figure 7-25.

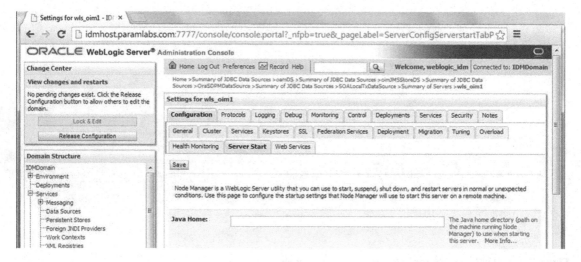

Figure 7-25. *OIM Settings - Server Start tab*

7. Append the following to the Arguments field at the end, as shown in Figure 7-26.

```
-Djava.net.preferIPv4Stack=true
```

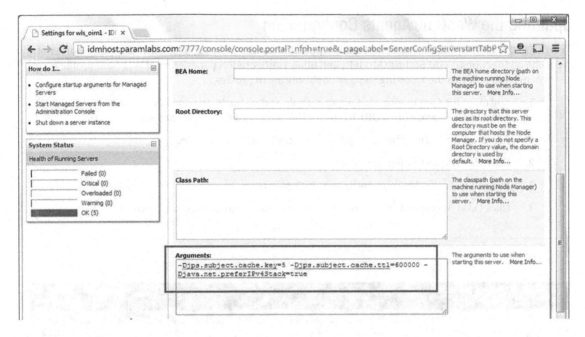

Figure 7-26. *Edit OIM Server Start arguments*

8. Click Save and then click Activate Changes button. You will see a confirmation message, as shown in Figure 7-27, that suggests that you restart the managed server.

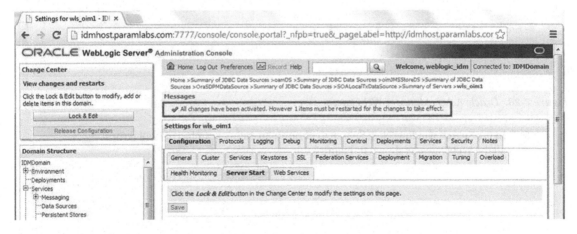

Figure 7-27. *Post-activation confirmation message*

9. Restart the wls_oim1 managed server through the administration console.

Post-Provisioning Steps for Oracle Access Manager

Now let's look at the required post-provisioning steps for the Oracle Access Manager (OAM).

Updating the WebGate Agents Configuration

In order to use Identity Management for Fusion Applications, we need to update the maximum number of WebGate connections, OAM Security Models, and other configuration parameters of WebGate profiles.

We need to perform the following steps on WebGate agent profiles.

1. Log on to the Oracle access manager console as the Oracle Access Manager admin user (oamadmin) at URL http://<IDM host>:<OHS port>/oamconsole.

    For example, http://idmhost.paramlabs.com:7777/oamconsole.

2. Click the System Configuration tab.

3. Expand to Access Manager Settings ➤ SSO Agents.

4. Click OAM Agents and select Open from the Actions menu, as shown in Figure 7-28.

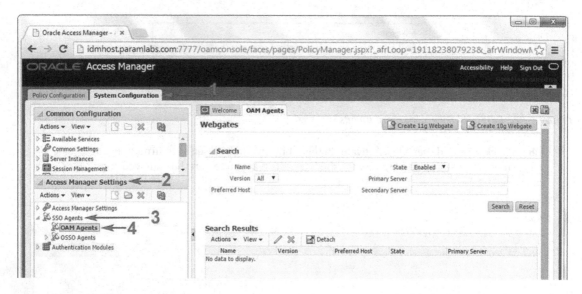

Figure 7-28. *Oracle Access Manager WebGates screen*

5. In the Search window, click Search to perform an empty search. This will return all the WebGates, as shown in Figure 7-29.

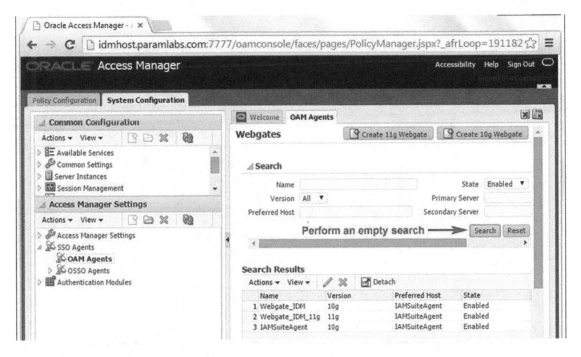

Figure 7-29. *OAM Agents list*

6. Click IAMSuiteAgent.

7. Set the security value to the security model in the OAM Configuration screen
    of the Identity Management provisioning wizard, as shown in Figure 7-30. In
    this case, it is Simple. Note that this should already be set for Webgate_IDM and
    Webgate_IDM_11g, so we will do this only for the remaining profiles.

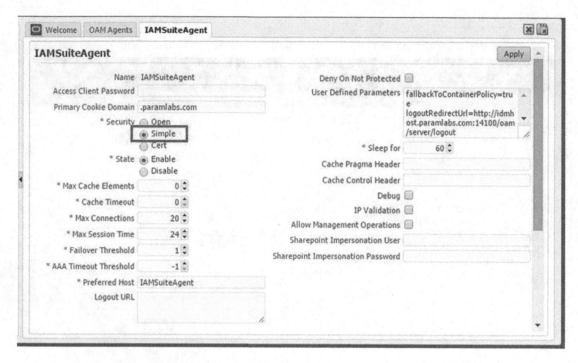

Figure 7-30. IAMSuiteAgent Properties screen

8. Go back to the OAM Agents screen by clicking on its tab.

9. Select a WebGate agent. For example, `Webgate_IDM`.

10. Set Maximum Number of Connections to 20 for a two OIM instances topology and 10 for a single OIM instance topology.

11. Set the AAA Timeout Threshold to 5.

12. In the User Defined Parameters box, set `client_request_retry_attempts` to 11.

13. If the following logout URLs are not listed, add them.

    ```
    /oamsso/logout.html
    /console/jsp/common/logout.jsp
    /em/targetauth/emaslogout.jsp
    ```

14. Click Apply to save the changes.

15. Repeat Steps 9-14 for each WebGate. Figures 7-31 and 7-32 show the changes required for both WebGates.

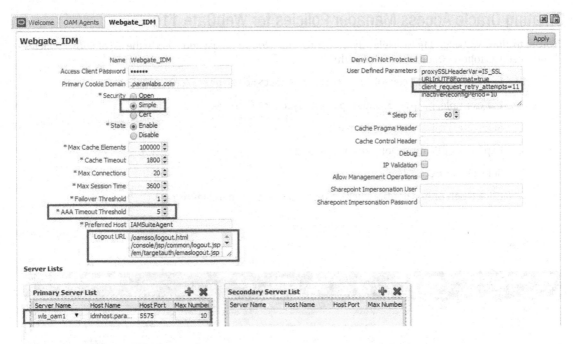

Figure 7-31. Webgate_IDM Properties screen

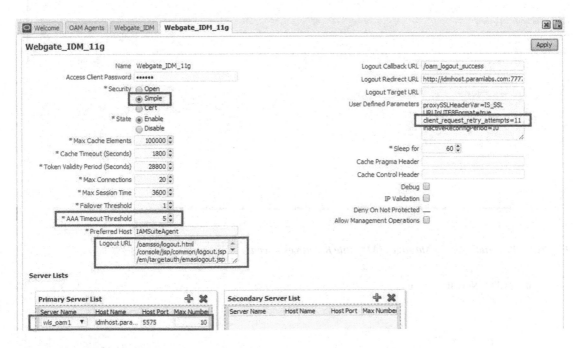

Figure 7-32. Webgate_IDM_11g Properties screen

16. Restart the managed server called `wls_oam1` from the WebLogic Administration console.

Creating Oracle Access Manager Policies for WebGate 11g

In order to allow WebGate 11g to display the credential collector, you must add /oam to the list of public policies. Proceed as follows in order to achieve this.

1. Log in to the OAM console at http://<IDM Host>:<OHS port>/oamconsole.

    For example, http://idmhost.paramlabs.com:7777/oamconsole.

2. Select the Policy Configuration tab.

3. Expand Application Domains ➤ IAM Suite.

4. Select Resources.

5. Click Open or just double-click on resources, as shown in Figure 7-33.

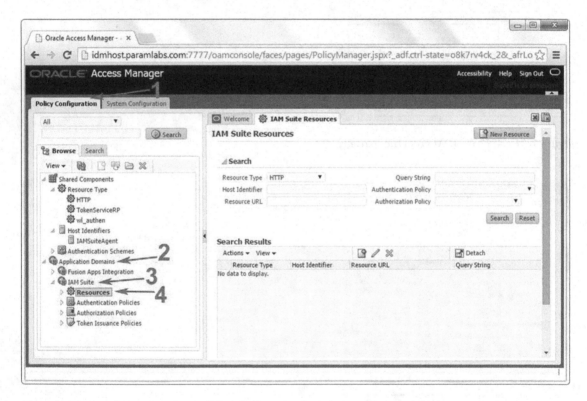

Figure 7-33. Oracle Access Manager IAM Suite Resources screen

6. Click New Resource.

7. Provide the following values as shown in Figure 7-34. Leave all other fields at
    their default values.

    ```
    Type: HTTP
    Description: OAM Credential Collector
    Host Identifier: IAMSuiteAgent
    Resource URL: /oam
    Protection Level: Unprotected
    Authentication Policy: Public Policy
    ```

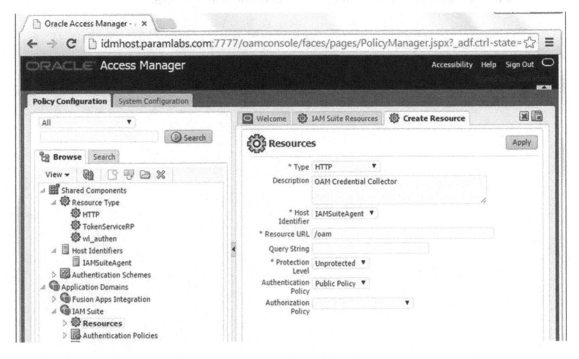

Figure 7-34. *Create New Resource screen*

8. Click Apply.

■ **Note**   If you are planning to use Oracle Identity Federation (OIF), which is optional in Identity Management
for Fusion Applications, you should do it at this stage.

This concludes the IDM host-related setup. At this stage, we have an Identity Management instance
running independently that can be integrated into a new instance of Fusion Applications. We will now move
on to Fusion Applications host setup in the next chapter.

Summary

This chapter you learned how to validate all components of an Identity Management environment after the completion of the provisioning process. Later you learned about the post-provisioning configuration required for each Identity Management component in order to use this environment for Fusion Applications. Note that this environment can be used only for any new installation of Fusion Applications. However, once the Fusion Applications environment has been provisioned, it will contain identity and policy information of Fusion Applications. Afterward, it can only be used for that instance of Fusion Applications.

This chapter concludes the Identity Management installation and configuration. In the next three chapters, we will look at the provisioning process of the Fusion Applications nodes.

CHAPTER 8

■ ■ ■

Creating Fusion Applications Transaction Database

In previous chapters, you learned the basics of the provisioning process followed by a step-by-step illustration of Identity Management provisioning. This builds the foundation of the Fusion Applications identity layer, which is mandatory in order to begin using the provisioning process of the Fusion Applications components. From this chapter onward, you will see a step-by-step installation of the Fusion Applications components with an example topology and a specific selection of products. By the end of the Fusion Applications provisioning-related chapters, you should feel confident about preparing a complete on-premise or private cloud-based Fusion Applications environment.

It's best to not skip any of the steps mentioned during the provisioning process, since doing so may result in failure at the final provisioning step. Fusion Applications provisioning is a time-consuming process and may not be complete in one day, so be patient and make sure that experts from the respective teams are available to prepare systems, network, storage, and so on, and to troubleshoot any issues during provisioning.

Current Status of Provisioning

Let's look at the nodes that are already provisioned and the components that we are going to provision now. Table 8-1 shows the technical components installed and configured on each of the four nodes during the installation. You may notice the components already configured in last chapter for IDMHOST and IDMDBHOST. In this and upcoming chapters, we will configure FAHOST and FADBHOST.

© Tushar Thakker 2015
T. Thakker, *Pro Oracle Fusion Applications*, DOI 10.1007/978-1-4842-0983-7_8

Table 8-1. *Provisioning Status of Components*

Host	Components	Component Name	Provisioning Status
IDMHOST	IDM Oracle HTTP Server instance	ohs1	Complete
	Oracle Internet Directory instance	oid1	
	Oracle Virtual Directory instance	ovd1	
	IDM WebLogic Domain	IDMDomain	
	IDM Administration Server	AdminServer	
	Oracle Access Manager	wls_oam1	
	Oracle Identity Manager	wls_oim1	
	Oracle Directory Service Manager	wls_ods1	
	Oracle Identity Federation	wls_oif1	
	IDM SOA Server	wls_soa1	
IDMDBHOST	IDM Oracle Database	idmdb	Complete
FAHOST	FA Oracle HTTP Server instance	ohs1	Pending
	Oracle Fusion Common (Setup) Domain	CommonDomain	
	BI WebLogic Domain	BIDomain	
	All selected Product families WebLogic Domains	<HCMDomain	
	Standalone components like IIR (for CRM)	FinancialDomain	
		CRMDomain etc.>	
FADBHOST	FA Oracle Database	fusiondb	Pending

Figure 8-1 shows the already provisioned and yet to be provisioned nodes in our selected topology. In this chapter, we will focus on installing and configuring components on FADBHOST (the Fusion Applications Database Host).

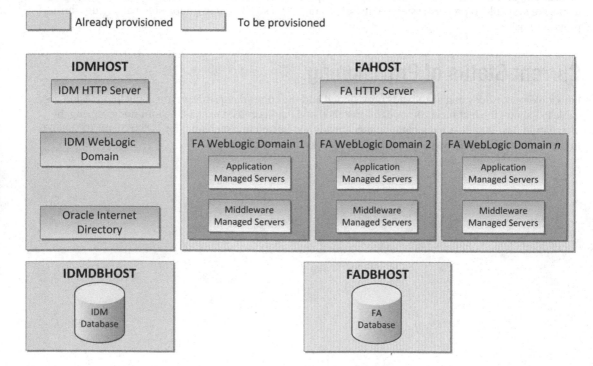

Figure 8-1. Fusion Applications environment topology selected for this installation

In order to create an Identity Management database, you need to perform the following tasks in the given order. We will discuss each of these in detail in the following sections.

- **Install the Oracle Fusion provisioning framework on a database node.**

    This step is required to install the Wizard that allows us to create a single-node, blank Oracle 11g Transaction database for Fusion Applications. This same wizard can also be used for other tasks, such as creating a provisioning response file for Fusion Applications, updating an existing response file, or provisioning a Fusion Applications environment using an existing response file. But on the database node the sole purpose of this framework is to install a blank transactional database for Fusion Applications. The Fusion Applications provisioning framework must be installed regardless of whether you are using the wizard to create the database or using a manual installation of single-node or Oracle RAC database since the provisioning framework contains a blank template for the Fusion Applications database. You will see this in detail in the next section.

- **Install the Oracle 11g database for Fusion Applications.**

    Once the provisioning framework is installed, we will use the wizard, which is included in the framework, to create a blank single-node Fusion Applications Transaction database automatically using the included template. The wizard also takes care of installing any required technology patches and updates. You can also create a single node or Oracle RAC database manually but you must make sure to install all the required patches, including the patch set update to bring the database to the supported version for the specific release of Fusion Applications.

- **Run the Repository Creation Utility (RCU) for Fusion Applications.**

    Similar to Identity Management RCU, Fusion Applications RCU also creates empty tablespaces for Fusion Middleware and Fusion Applications schemas followed by creation of the required database schemas. At the end it seeds the default data from the dump files along with RCU using Oracle Data Pump. It also creates the resource plan for controlling the database CPU usage based on queries triggered from different functional groups defined for Fusion Applications.

We will now look at each of these tasks one by one in the following sections. During the course of these sections, we will create a Transaction database for Fusion Applications for demonstration purposes.

Install Fusion Applications Provisioning Framework

Fusion Applications provisioning framework contains the GUI wizard and command-line utilities. The provisioning framework helps us create a new Fusion Applications Transaction database, create or update a Fusion Applications provisioning response file, and provision a Fusion Applications environment using an existing response file. Since on the database node we are going to use this wizard to create a single-node, blank Fusion Applications Transaction database for small demo systems, we will need to first install the provisioning framework followed by the database creation.

Note that you will need to install the same provisioning framework on database node as well as on Fusion Applications nodes. If you are using the single-tier topology and hosting the database and application on the same physical host, you need not install the provisioning framework multiple times as the same framework can be used for the database as well as for applications provisioning.

The Fusion Applications provisioning framework installer is available in the installer repository, under the directory named faprov. Recall that you saw the Fusion Applications installer repository directory structure in Figure 3-7 of Chapter 3. We grouped this directory separately in that diagram since this is the only directory required for provisioning framework installation on a database as well as on any application nodes.

Let's start the installation of Fusion Applications provisioning framework from the <REPOSITORY_LOCATION>/installers/faprov/Disk1 directory. For example:

```
[fusion@idmhost ~]$ cd /stage/installers/faprov/Disk1/
[fusion@idmhost Disk1]$ ./runInstaller
...
Please specify JRE/JDK location ( Ex. /home/jre ), <location>/bin/java should exist : /stage/jdk6
```

■ **Note**   Make sure not to use an ampersand (&) to start the installer since this will prompt for a Java directory if the JAVA_HOME is not set. Enter <REPOSITORY_LOCATION>/jdk6 to set the JAVA_HOME temporarily to the staging JDK directory.

If this is the first Oracle software on this machine using this user, it will prompt for the inventory directory location as you have seen this screen during Identity Management provisioning. But since this is different host, you may see the screen here as well.

If you know that it is not the first Oracle product being installed on this host and you already have an inventory on this host, make sure that the /etc/oraInst.loc file has read permission for the fusion installation user. Once you click OK, the installer will prompt you to run the root script named <Inventory_location>/createCentralInvetory.sh as the root user. If you have root access, open a new terminal window and run the script as the root user. This script will point to the previous directory location as the central inventory for the host in the /etc/oraInst.loc file, which is used by all Oracle Software installations.

```
[root@fadbhost ~]# /home/fusion/oraInventory/createCentralInventory.sh
Setting the inventory to /home/fusion/oraInventory
Setting the group name to dba
Creating the Oracle inventory pointer file (/etc/oraInst.loc)
Changing permissions of /home/fusion/oraInventory to 770.
Changing groupname of /home/fusion/oraInventory to dba.
The execution of the script is complete
```

Once the script executes successfully, click OK to proceed. Now you will see the informal Welcome screen, which provides details about the purpose of this installer. No action is necessary on this screen. Click Next to continue to the prerequisite checks, as shown in Figure 8-2.

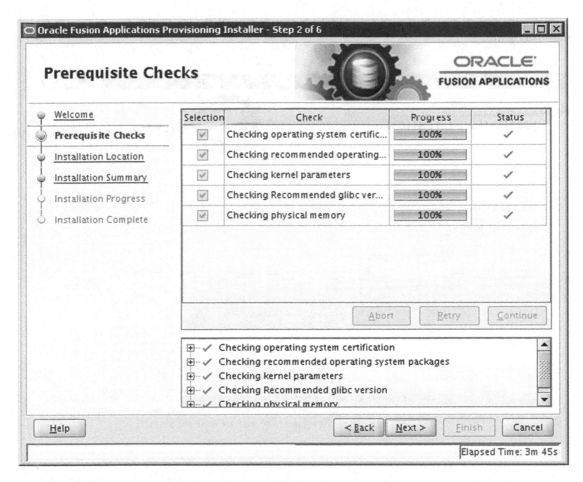

Figure 8-2. *Prerequisite Checks status screen*

This step checks the following required operating system prerequisites for the Oracle Fusion Applications Provisioning Framework installation.

- *Operating System Certification*: Makes sure that you have the supported operating system and it is not the lowest version supported as per Oracle Certification matrix for future support sustainability and to avoid OS upgrade in near future.

- *Operating System Packages*: Checks for the recommended packages/RPMs for the selected operating system.

- *Kernel Parameters*: Checks all required kernel parameters and their minimum values. Please note that for some kernel parameters the wizard will only check the values for the current session, so make sure that you have also added the values in the relevant system files permanently.

- *Recommended glibc Version*: Although the mandatory packages would have already taken care of this, it specifically checks for the glibc version as well.

- *Physical Memory*: Checks the total amount of installed memory on the host.

199

Once the prerequisite check is completed, click Next to proceed to the Installation Location screen, as shown in Figure 8-3.

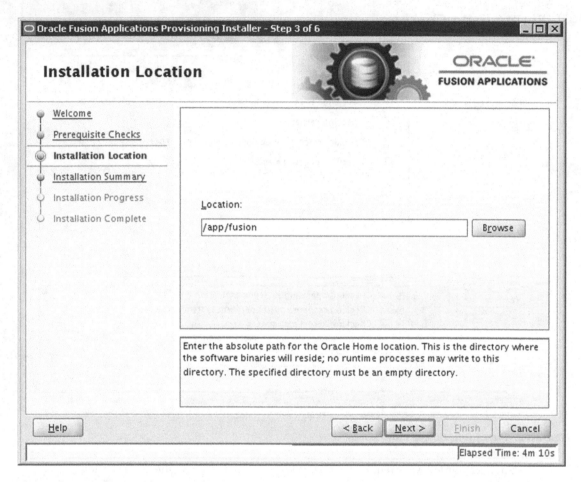

Figure 8-3. *Installation Location screen*

The Installation Location screen prompts you for the location where the provisioning framework needs to be installed. A directory named provisioning will be created under this location at the end of the installation. We will enter /app/fusion for the location of the provisioning installer.

Meanwhile, create the root directory for the installation directories as follows.

```
[root@fadbhost ~]# mkdir /app
[root@fadbhost ~]# chown fusion:dba /app
```

Note that if the directory is not already created or if the installation user (fusion in our case) does not have the required permissions to write in the parent directory, you may see error similar to one in Figure 8-4.

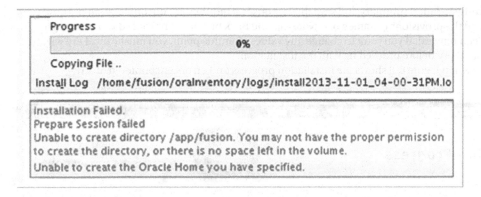

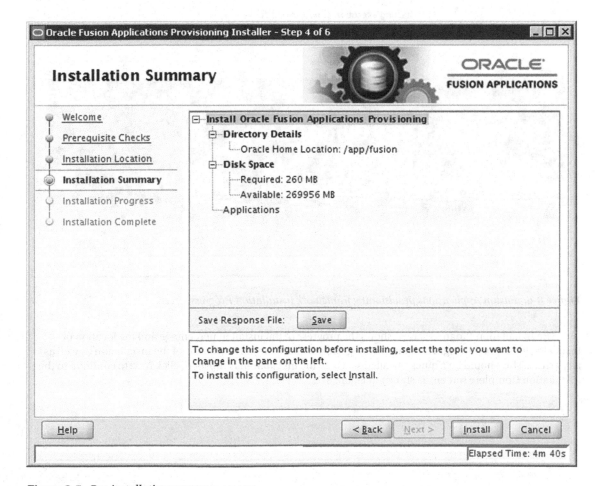

Figure 8-4. Installation error example

Once the base directory is created, click Next to proceed to the pre-installation summary shown in Figure 8-5.

Figure 8-5. Pre-installation summary screen

Review the pre-installation summary and save the responses if required for documentation purposes. Click Install to install the provisioning framework. Note that the Back button is enabled so you cannot go back from next screen onward. If you want to change any values after this point, you must cancel the wizard and clean up the directory before proceeding with the installation.

The screen shown in Figure 8-6 shows the installation progress and errors encountered, if any.

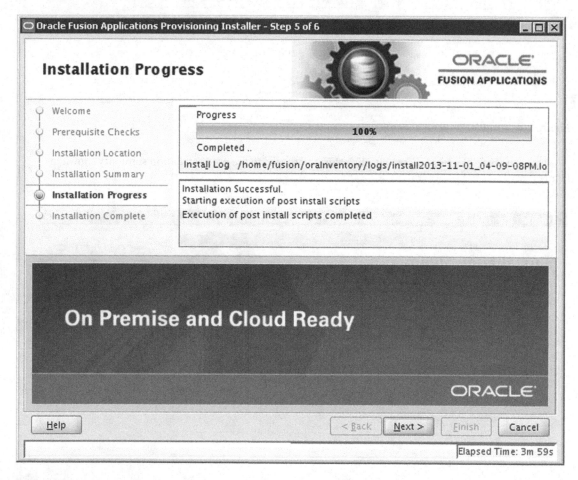

Figure 8-6. *Fusion Applications provisioning framework Installation Progress screen*

The Installation Progress screen shows the progress of the install in percentage and the location of install log file for reviewing. The status message box displays the current status of the installation as well as any errors. This should be a quick installation. Once the installation is finished, click *Next* to continue to the Installation Complete screen, as shown in Figure 8-7.

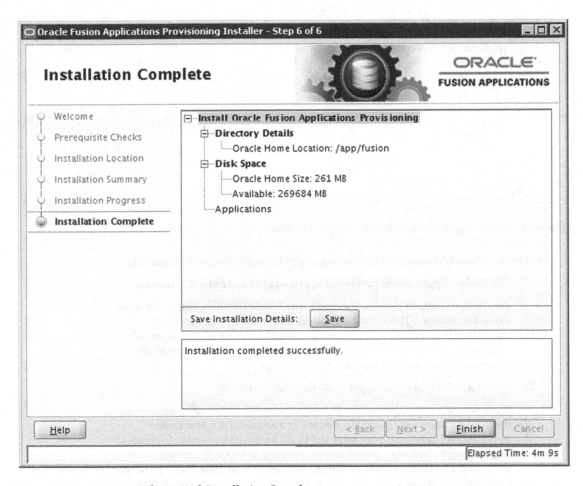

Figure 8-7. Provisioning framework Installation Complete screen

The Installation Complete screen shows the location of the installation where the provisioning framework has been installed with the directory named provisioning. Review the summary and save it if required for project documentation purposes. Click Finish to close the wizard and complete the installation of the Oracle Fusion Applications provisioning framework.

Preparing Fusion Applications Database

Now we have Fusion Applications provisioning wizard installed so we can go ahead and create the Fusion Applications Transaction database using the wizard. If you want a production-scale or high-available RAC database, you must install the database manually. Even if you are installing the database manually, you must use the template provided under the provisioning framework templates directory. Figure 8-8 shows the location and names of the available templates for creating a starter Fusion Applications Transaction database. These template files contain the database structure and features and not seeded data files, so these generic templates can be used across any platforms.

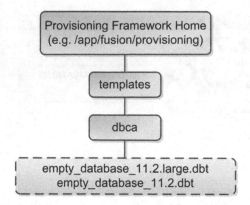

Figure 8-8. *Fusion Applications Database templates location*

Let's look at the available options for creating an Applications Transaction database.

1. **Use Fusion Applications Provisioning Framework to create a database**.

   This option creates a blank, single node, small-scale database that suites most demo installations. This is the best advisable option for most single-node databases since it creates the required version of database after applying all mandatory patches and PSU automatically and sets the required database parameters. We will use this option in our example.

2. **Install production-scale single-node database manually.**

   If you want to create a production-scale database with advanced options selection, then you can install an Oracle 11g, Release 2 database (11.2.0.3 for Fusion Applications 11g Release 8 or earlier and 11.2.0.4 onward for Fusion Applications 11g, Release 9 and above). You must use the database template provided along with Fusion Applications provisioning framework. For example, you can use the template named empty_database_11.2.large.dbt for creating a production-scale database. Make sure to copy the template to the installer templates directory before starting the installation. Once the database installation is done, it will be still at base release and you must upgrade to the required database release. Apply the PSU for your selected platform in order to upgrade the database. Once the database is upgraded, make sure to apply all mandatory patches required for your platform based on the Fusion Applications release notes.

3. **Install Oracle RAC (Real Application Clusters) database manually.**

   Similar to option 2, for Oracle RAC database you must use the template to create a blank starter database with production-scale memory parameters followed by applying PSU and other mandatory patches. Make sure to check the required database parameters for the current release and set the values accordingly in order to run the production application on this database.

■ **Tip**   If you are not planning to create a RAC database at this stage, we suggest you use the provisioning wizard and then tune the required parameters later. This will save you a lot of time since all the patches and PSU are applied automatically.

Install JDK

Since Fusion middleware is based on Java, all the installers included in the media require JDK to be installed on the host machine. Although we have seen in previous step of Installing Fusion Applications provisioning wizard that we can also use the JDK directory included in the installation repository, we must have a permanent Java home location on the host. Since the JDK version included with current release of Fusion Applications is JDK 6, we will install it there.

Although we can get the JDK installer from the Oracle web site as well, in this case we only need to unzip the JDK ZIP file to any desired location. The compressed JDK 6 file (jdk6.zip) is included at <REPOSITORY_LOCATION>/installers/jdk. In this example, we will unzip it to our provisioning installer root directory /app/fusion, but you can select any location.

```
[fusion@fadbhost ~]$ cd /app/fusion/
[fusion@fadbhost fusion]$ unzip /stage/installers/jdk/jdk6.zip
```

This will create a directory named jdk6 at the selected location. In this example, it will be /app/fusion/jdk6. We will specify this directory as Java home in any further installations on this host. Most of the installers can detect the Java home if it is created in the Oracle Base directory.

Installing Fusion Applications Transaction Database

Since we are going with option 1 of the database installation options mentioned previously, we will invoke the Fusion Applications provisioning wizard in order to install the Oracle Database. To install the Applications Transactional database, we need to run Oracle Fusion Applications provisioning wizard from <framework_location>/provisioning/bin.

<framework_location> refers to the location where we installed the Fusion Applications provisioning framework in previous step; for example, /app/fusion.

```
[fusion@fadbhost ~]$ cd /app/fusion/provisioning/bin/
[fusion@fadbhost bin]$ export JAVA_HOME=/app/fusion/jdk6
[fusion@fadbhost bin]$ ./provisioningWizard.sh &
```

The Welcome screen is an informal screen that suggests you check the following two prerequisites.

- The Fusion Applications installation repository (installation stage directory) has been created. We have already done this as part of the earlier steps.

- The installation repository has been populated with the Oracle database installer and required patches. This is also taken care of since we have extracted all required ZIP files into the installation repository, which also includes the database related directories. This is required because the database-creation option will internally invoke the installer from the database directory of the installation repository.

Once you have confirmed that the required prerequisite steps are complete, click Next to proceed to the wizard option selection screen shown in Figure 8-9.

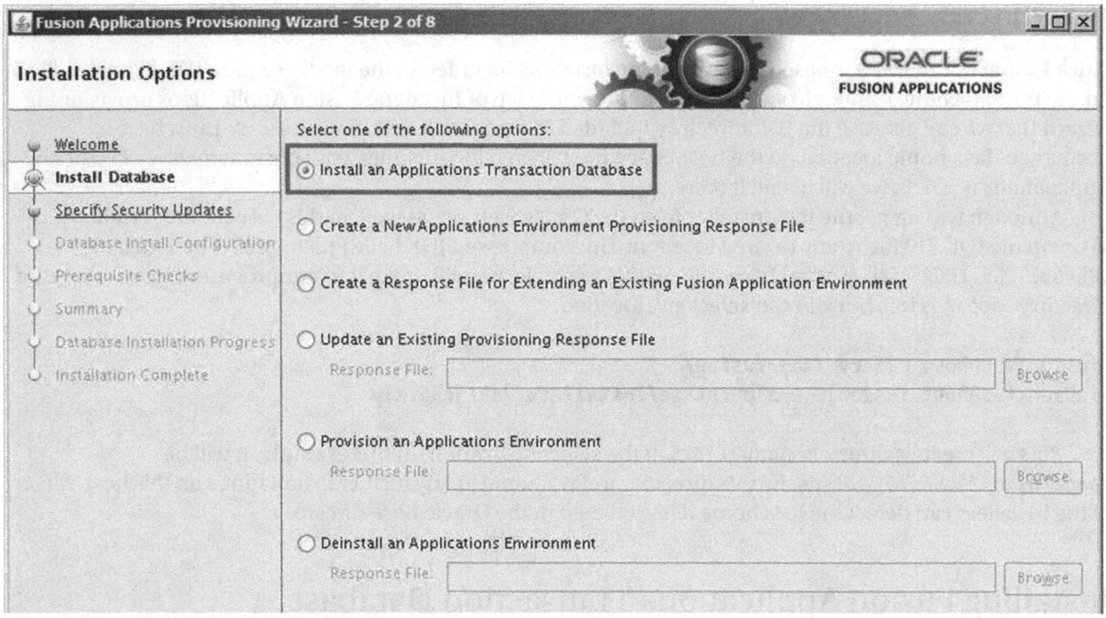

Figure 8-9. *Wizard option selection screen*

The provisioning option selection screen provides six provisioning-related options.

1. Install an Applications Transaction database.

2. Create a New Applications Environment provisioning response file.

3. Create a response file for extending an existing Fusion Applications environment (available on Fusion Applications 11.1.9 onward).

4. Update an existing Provisioning response file.

5. Provision an Applications environment.

6. Uninstall an Applications environment.

Out of these, only the first option is related to the database, while the other five options are specific to Applications provisioning. We will discuss about the remaining options in next chapter. This option will initiate a short questionnaire for database installation details only. Since most of the database parameters are preselected in the template, they will not be prompted during this wizard.

Select Install an Applications Transactional Database and click Next to proceed to the Security Updates screen. We have already seen this screen where you can optionally enter your email address or Oracle Support credentials to receive updates related to the selected product. Enter the email address or leave the field empty and click Next to proceed to the Database Install Configuration screen, as shown in Figure 8-10.

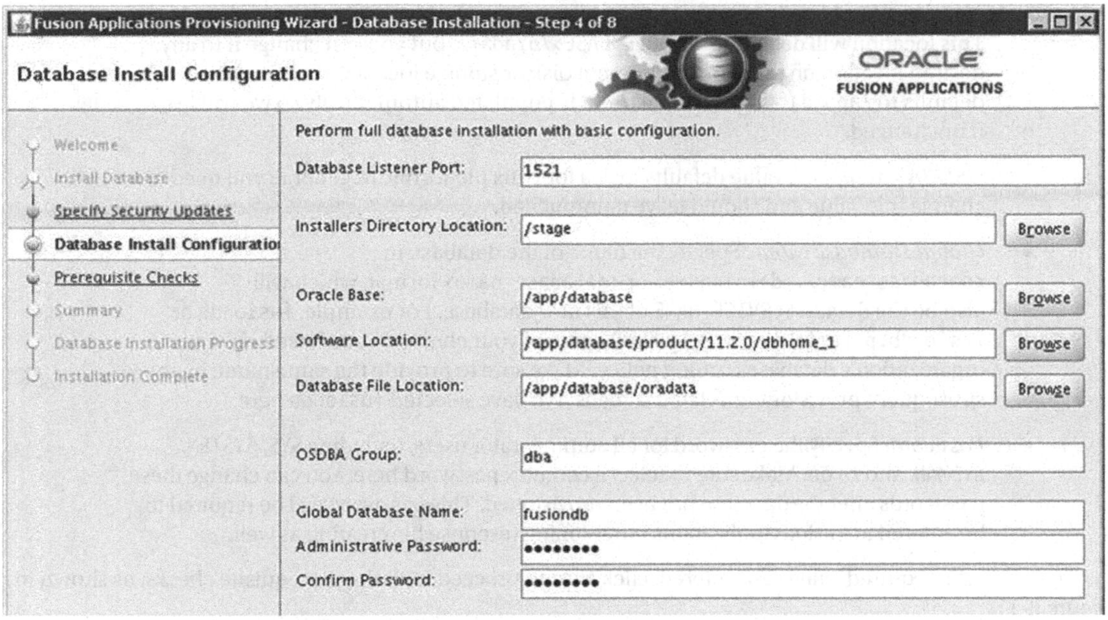

Figure 8-10. *Fusion Applications Database Install Configuration screen*

Note that the screen shown in Figure 8-10 is the only screen with database installation related questionnaire unlike a typical database installation. So except for the following details, everything else remains as per the seeded template and is not modifiable at this stage. This screen prompts for the following values to be entered.

- *Database Listener Port*: The default value is 1521 and we can change it to any preferred value. We had changed the listener port to 1531 for the Identity Management database. In this example, we will keep it to 1521 in order to easily distinguish the databases in provisioning screens. Remember the value specified and enter the same value in the provisioning response file in the next steps.

- *Installer's Directory Location*: Enter the location of the Fusion Applications installation repository here. Note that this is not the location of the database installation subdirectory, but the main installation staging directory. The installer will look for a subdirectory named installers in the specified directory. If the installers directory is not found in this location then an error will be displayed on the screen. In this case the directory is /stage.

- *Oracle Base*: Specify the directory that you want to create as the Oracle Software Base. The subsequent database directories including Oracle home will be created under this directory. You can specify any location that's writable for the installation user. In this case, we have specified /app/database as the Oracle Base.

- *Software Location*: Specify the software location that will be same as the Oracle home directory. Once you have specified the Oracle Base value, this field will be automatically populated as <ORACLE_BASE>/product/11.2.0/dbhome_1. For example, /app/database/product/11.2.0/dbhome_1.

207

- *Database File Location*: Specify the location for the database files or data files. This location will default to <ORACLE_BASE>/oradata, but you can change it to any desired location on the same or different disk or storage location. In this case, it defaults to /app/database/oradata and is populated automatically so we will leave it unchanged.

- *OSDBA group*: This value defaults to dba for Unix platforms. In general, you need not change this value and should leave it untouched.

- *Global Database Name*: Specify the name of the database in <database_name>.<domainname> or <database_name> format, which will also be the default SERVICE_NAME of this new database. For example, fusiondb or fusiondb.paramlabs.com. Select any name of your choice or one based on your organization's database naming policy. Make sure to provide the same name in any subsequent provisioning-related screens. We have selected fusiondb here.

- *Password*: Specify the password for all administrator users, including SYS, SYSTEM, SYSMAN, and so on. Make sure to select a complex password here. You can change these passwords after the database has been provisioned. This password will be required to be entered in Fusion Applications Provisioning response file creation as well.

Once all the required values are entered, click Next to proceed with the prerequisite checks, as shown in Figure 8-11.

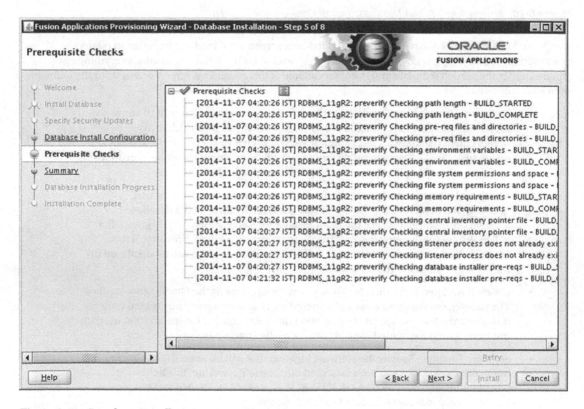

Figure 8-11. *Database installation prerequisite checks status*

This screen will run all the required prerequisites, including hardware, operating system, and network, as well as determine the existence of inventory, inventory pointer files, and listener processes. The status of all the prerequisite checks, including any error or warning messages, will be displayed on the same screen between the BUILD_STARTED and BUILD_COMPLETE messages along with the warning or error symbol.

■ **Caution** If the screen remains blank and you do not see any messages on the screen but instead see a success, error, or warning mark at the top, do not proceed. This means that the installer is not able to forward the standard output content to the screen. This is a Java-specific issue and is caused when the host's entry in the /etc/hosts file is in the <IP Address> <hostname> <hostname.domainname> format instead of <IP Address> <hostname.domaname> <hostname>. Fix the host file entry and restart the installation.

The Retry button is deactivated by default. If there are any errors in the prerequisites check, the Retry button will be activated. In case of warnings, the Retry button will not be activated but if you want to fix the warnings also then you can always click Back to run it again. In case of errors, you can fix the issues in a separate window and then click on the Retry button to rerun the prerequisite checks. Although warnings will not prevent you from continuing the installation, it is always advisable to make sure that there are no errors or warnings in this screen.

■ **Tip** You might see some warnings related to memory if you are using less than 26 GB of memory for this host. If you are doing a demo installation and planning to reduce the SGA/PGA values afterward, you can ignore the warning for now.

Once the prerequisites check is successful, click Next to proceed to the pre-installation summary screen, as shown in Figure 8-12.

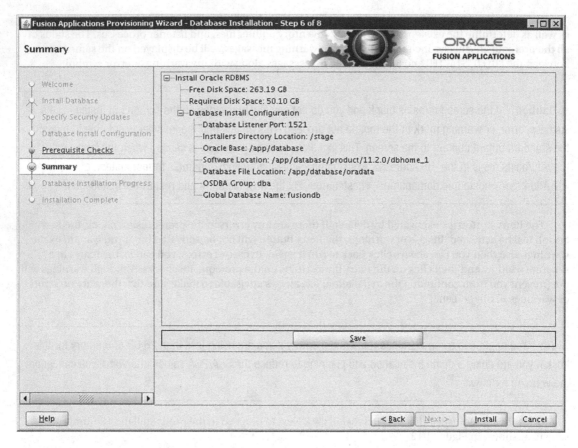

Figure 8-12. *Database pre-installation summary*

Since this is the last screen before you start the database installation, make sure you check the summary details, including the installation path, global database name, listener port, and so on. If you want to modify any details then use the Back button to go back to previous screens. The Back button will be disabled after this screen. Save the pre-installation summary if required and then click Install to begin the database software installation along with the database instance creation.

Once database installation portion completes (at approximately 20% of the overall progress), the provisioning wizard will prompt you to execute the root configuration scripts as shown in Figure 8-13.

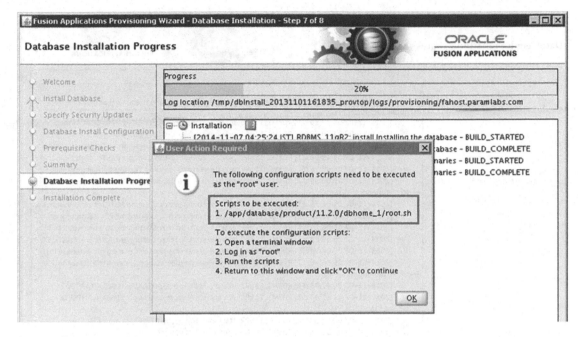

Figure 8-13. *Root scripts execution prompt*

This script will add the required entry in /etc/oratab and other configuration files. Open a new terminal window and run the script <ORACLE_HOME>/root.sh as the root user. The following is example output of the script execution.

```
[root@fadbhost ]# /app/database/product/11.2.0/dbhome_1/root.sh
Check /app/database/product/11.2.0/dbhome_1/install/root_fadbhost.paramlabs.com_2013-11-
01_16-43-36.log for the output of root script
[root@fadbhost ]# more/app/database/product/11.2.0/dbhome_1/install/root_fadbhost.paramlabs.
com_2013-11-01_16-43-36.log
Performing root user operation for Oracle 11g
The following environment variables are set as:
ORACLE_OWNER= fusion
ORACLE_HOME= /app/database/product/11.2.0/dbhome_1
Creating /etc/oratab file...
Entries will be added to the /etc/oratab file as needed by
Database Configuration Assistant when a database is created
Finished running generic part of root script.
Now product-specific root actions will be performed.
Finished product-specific root actions.
Click OK
```

Once the script is executed, click OK to continue with the next phases of the overall database installation, as shown in Figure 8-14.

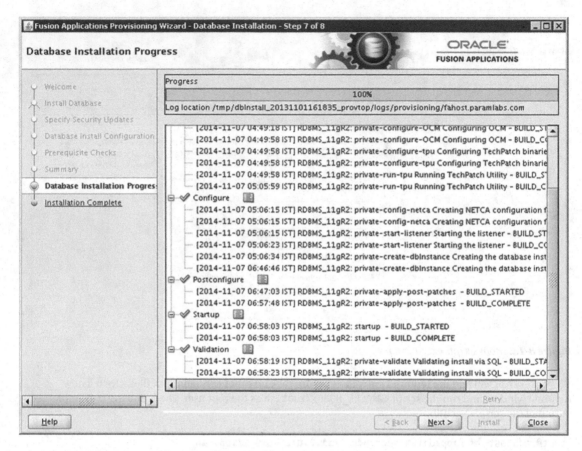

Figure 8-14. *Database installation and configuration progress*

The Database Installation Progress screen shows the following phases for this task.

- *Install*: During this phase the database software gets installed with the base release only. The database or instance is not yet created and the database patches or PSU are not applied yet.

- *Preconfigure*: During the Preconfigure phase the Tech Patch Utility (TPU) and Oracle Configuration Manager (OCM, which is used to upload configuration details to Oracle Support) are configured. All the patches and PSU located in <REPOSITORY_ LOCATION>/installers/database/psu and <REPOSITORY_LOCATION>/installers/ database/patch are applied to the database home as well. At this moment the database is not created so a database metadata upgrade is not required at this stage.

- *Configure*: During this phase the database instance, service, and listener are created and configured. It creates the database using a seeded template and sets the necessary parameters. The network configuration files are also created at this stage.

- *PostConfigure*: At this stage any necessary post patch steps and post-configuration steps are performed. The database is technically installed and ready at this stage.

- *Startup*: Although the required services are already started by now, this stage makes sure that any components that are not yet started should be started now.

- *Validation*: This phase performs the database validation for completeness of the installation and runs the validation SQL for checking connectivity and integrity of the database.

After collapsing the status tree, the screen will look like the one shown in Figure 8-15. Its shows a short summary of your overall progress. You may see tick mark (√), an error sign(x), a warning sign (!), or a clock icon (for an ongoing phase), depending on the status of the activity. Once installation until validation is complete, click Next to proceed to the installation summary, as shown in Figure 8-16.

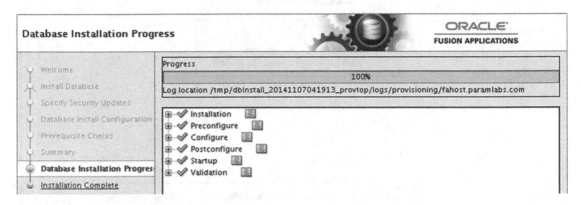

Figure 8-15. Successful completion of each phase

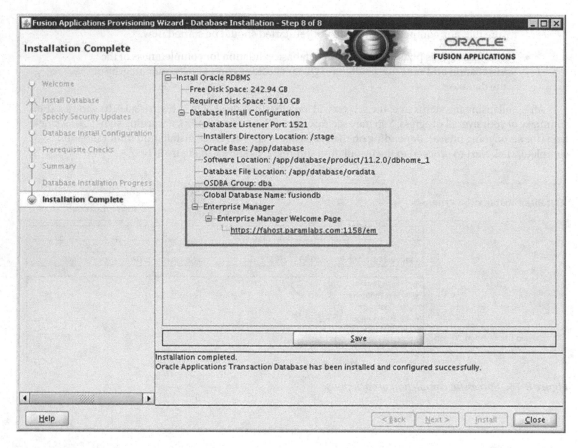

Figure 8-16. *Fusion Applications Transaction database post-installation summary*

In the summary screen you can see the URL of the configured Fusion Applications Database Enterprise Manager. Make a note of this URL or save the summary for documentation purposes. Click Close to complete the installation and close the wizard.

Validate the Database Installation

Whether you have installed the Fusion Applications database manually or used the provisioning wizard, it is necessary to make sure that the database is installed correctly and with correct component version. Depending on the release of Fusion Applications the minimum required version of the database will be different. For example, if you installed the Applications Transaction database for Fusion Applications 11g, Release 8 (11.1.8) then you should have the database version as 11.2.0.3. For Fusion Applications 11g Release 9, the required database version is 11.2.0.4.

Execute the following SQLs to validate the database and components version after installation.

```
SQL> column PRODUCT format A40
SQL> column VERSION format A15
SQL> column STATUS format A20
SQL> select * from PRODUCT_COMPONENT_VERSION;
```

```
PRODUCT                                 VERSION          STATUS
--------------------------------------- ---------------- --------------------
NLSRTL                                  11.2.0.4.0       Production
Oracle Database 11g Enterprise Edition  11.2.0.4.0       64bit Production
PL/SQL                                  11.2.0.4.0       Production
TNS for Linux:                          11.2.0.4.0       Production
```

```
SQL> column COMP_NAME format A40
SQL> select COMP_NAME, VERSION, STATUS from dba_registry;
COMP_NAME                               VERSION          STATUS
--------------------------------------- ---------------- --------------------
Oracle Enterprise Search                11.2.0.4.0       VALID
Oracle Enterprise Manager               11.2.0.4.0       VALID
Spatial                                 11.2.0.4.0       VALID
Oracle Multimedia                       11.2.0.4.0       VALID
Oracle XML Database                     11.2.0.4.0       VALID
Oracle Text                             11.2.0.4.0       VALID
Oracle Expression Filter                11.2.0.4.0       VALID
Oracle Rules Manager                    11.2.0.4.0       VALID
Oracle Workspace Manager                11.2.0.4.0       VALID
Oracle Database Catalog Views           11.2.0.4.0       VALID
Oracle Database Packages and Types      11.2.0.4.0       VALID
JServer JAVA Virtual Machine            11.2.0.4.0       VALID
Oracle XDK                              11.2.0.4.0       VALID
Oracle Database Java Packages           11.2.0.4.0       VALID

14 rows selected.
```

In addition to this, if you have installed the database manually, make sure to have following options enabled in your database.

- Oracle Partitioning
- Oracle Data Mining

Adjust the Memory Size of the Database

By default the Fusion Applications Transaction database created through the provisioning framework will have 9 GB SGA and 4 GB PGA set for a non-production database. For a production database, the memory should be changed to 18 GB SGA and 8 GB PGA. If you are only doing a proof-of-concept (POC) installation, you can even reduce the SGA and PGA to a lesser value (not recommended by Oracle) to reduce the memory usage on the host. Make sure you adjust the tmpfs and swap sizes according to the memory allotted to the Oracle instance on Linux OS.

Let's first set the ORACLE_HOME, PATH, and ORACLE_SID variables in order to connect to the database. Make sure you add these lines in the user profile so that you need not set it every time you want to connect to or manage the database.

```
[fusion@fadbhost ]$ ORACLE_HOME=/app/database/product/11.2.0/dbhome_1; export ORACLE_HOME
[fusion@fadbhost ]$ PATH=$PATH:$ORACLE_HOME/bin; export PATH
[fusion@fadbhost ]$ ORACLE_SID=fusiondb; export ORACLE_SID
[fusion@fadbhost bin]$ sqlplus / as sysdba

SQL> show parameter pga
```

```
NAME                TYPE VALUE
------------ ---- ----------
pga_aggregate_target big integer 4G

SQL> show parameter sga
NAME                TYPE VALUE
------------ ---- ----------
lock_sga boolean FALSE
pre_page_sga boolean FALSE
sga_max_size big integer 9G
sga_target big integer 9G

SQL> create pfile from spfile;
File Created.

SQL> shut immediate;
```

Now modify the SGA and PGA values in the initfusiondb.ora file as per the requirements. Once it is done, recreate SPFILE using this PFILE and then start up the database.

```
[fusion@fadbhost dbs]$ sqlplus / as sysdba
SQL> create spfile from pfile;
File created.

SQL> startup
```

Non-Default Parameters for the Fusion Applications Database

If you created the Fusion Applications transaction database using the Provisioning wizard, you need not look at this section since all these parameters are set for you automatically as part of the database template. If you have created the Fusion Applications database (single node or Oracle RAC) manually, you must set the following parameters in order to tune the database parameters for use with Fusion Applications Environment.

Table 8-2 shows the list of parameters with non-default values. Since many of these parameters cannot be modified while the database is running, you may need to set all these values in SPFILE and restart the database.

Table 8-2. *Summary Table of Fusion Applications-Related Schemas after RCU*

Parameter Name	Default Value	Fusion Applications Specific Value
_ACTIVE_SESSION_LEGACY_BEHAVIOR	FALSE	TRUE
_b_tree_bitmap_plans	TRUE	FALSE
_fix_control	5483301:ON,6708183:OFF	5483301:OFF,6708183:ON
audit_trail	DB	NONE
db_securefile	PERMITTED	ALWAYS
nls_sort	Varies	BINARY
open_cursors	50	500
pga_aggregate_target	0	4GB (Development) 8GB (Production)
session_cached_cursors	50	500
sga_target	0	9GB (Development) 18GB (Production)
plsql_code_type	INTERPRETED	NATIVE
processes	100	5000

Change the default values for these parameters before provisioning the Fusion Applications environment. The following example shows you how to change the value for the open_cursors parameter from the current value of 50 to the recommended value of 500. Do the same for all the other parameters as well.

```
SQL> show parameter open_cursors
NAME            TYPE     VALUE
------------ ------- -------
open_cursors integer 50

SQL> alter system set open_cursors=500 scope=both sid='*';
System altered.

SQL> show parameter open_cursors
NAME            TYPE     VALUE
------------ ------- -------
open_cursors integer 500
```

Running Fusion Applications Repository Creation Utility

After the blank database has been installed, you must create the repository for Fusion Applications components in this database. The RCU performs the following actions on the database.

1. Create empty tablespaces for the Fusion Applications components and schemas.

2. Create required schema owners and populate the required database objects, including tables, views, and so on. Fusion Applications RCU includes both Fusion middleware components as well as Fusion Applications Runtime schema owners.

3. Import the seed data for BI and Fusion Applications schemas using the Oracle Data pump export files included in the RCU.

Fusion Applications installer comes with RCU included in the media. Note that Fusion Applications RCU is available only for Windows and Linux platforms with 64-bit architecture. So if you are hosting your database on Windows 64-bit or Linux x86-64 then you can run the RCU from the database host. But if you have selected a non-Windows and a non-Linux host, you need a remote Windows or Linux machine that can connect to this database from where you can run the RCU and seed the data into the Fusion Applications database. Make sure you have consistent connectivity to the Fusion Applications database from the remote host throughout the RCU process. You may need to open the database port in a firewall if you are running the remote machine from a different network VLAN.

Figure 8-17 shows the two options available to run the RCU—one for Windows/Linux hosts and the later for database hosts with other operating systems. As you can see in the first option, you simply need to unzip the RCU from installation repository to the database host and run it locally. With the second option, we have introduced another host to run the RCU remotely.

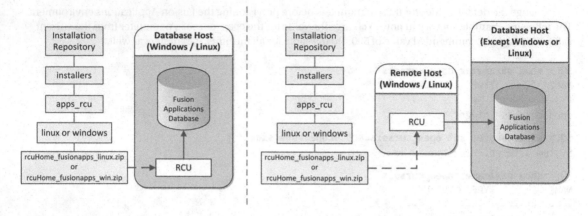

Figure 8-17. *RCU host and DB host for Windows/Linux versus other operating systems*

As you can see, there are two RCU ZIP files available along with Fusion Applications installation repository, under the folder names windows and linux. Since we have selected 64-bit Oracle Linux host for database, we will go ahead with Linux RCU here.

For Linux, the RCU is located at <REPOSITORY_LOCATION>/installers/apps_rcu/linux with the rcuHome_fusionapps_linux.zip filename. We need to unzip this directory in any local location on database server or the remote machine from where we are going to run the RCU. Let's create a directory on the database server's local disk. For example, /app/fusion/provisioning/apps_rcu.

```
[fusion@fadbhost dbs]$ mkdir /app/fusion/provisioning/apps_rcu
```

The reason we have created the apps_rcu directory under the existing provisioning directory is just to keep the installation-related directories in one location. We will call this location APPS_RCU_HOME.

Now we will extract the compressed RCU file to this location. This will create the Repository Creation Utilities as well as the dump files that the utilities will import to the database. Let's unzip the file <REPOSITORY_LOCATION>/installers/apps_rcu/linux/rcuHome_fusionapps_linux.zip to APPS_RCU_HOME directory. All dependent components that the Fusion Applications RCU requires are included in this ZIP file.

```
[fusion@fadbhost dbs]$ cd /app/fusion/provisioning/apps_rcu
[fusion@fadbhost apps_rcu]$ unzip /stage/installers/apps_rcu/linux/rcuHome_fusionapps_linux.zip
```

Create a temporary directory on the database server. We will extract the data pump export dump files in this directory. Note that regardless of whether you are running RCU from a database host or remote machine, this directory must be created on a database host only since data pump always reads from and writes to the database host itself. Make a note of the location as we will need to enter this location in the next screen when we are required to specify a value for FUSIONAPPS_DBINSTALL_DP_DIR.

```
[fusion@fadbhost apps_rcu]$ mkdir /app/fusion/provisioning/apps_rcu/dp_dir
```

The required data pump dump files are located in the newly created RCU directory under location APPS_RCU_HOME/rcu/integration/fusionapps/export_fusionapps_dbinstall.zip. We will extract the contents of this ZIP file to the temporary directory we just created (FUSIONAPPS_DBINSTALL_DP_DIR).

```
[fusion@fadbhost apps_rcu]$ cd /app/fusion/provisioning/apps_rcu/dp_dir
[fusion@fadbhost dp_dir]$ unzip \ /app/fusion/provisioning/apps_rcu/rcu/integration/
fusionapps/export_fusionapps_dbinstall.zip
```

```
Archive: /app/fusion/provisioning/apps_rcu/rcu/integration/fusionapps/export_fusionapps_
dbinstall.zip
inflating: fusionapps_dbinstall_latest_06.dmp
inflating: fusionapps_dbinstall_latest_02.dmp
inflating: fusionapps_dbinstall_latest_07.dmp
inflating: fusionapps_dbinstall_latest_04.dmp
inflating: fusionapps_dbinstall_latest_03.dmp
inflating: fusionapps_dbinstall_latest_01.dmp
inflating: fusionapps_dbinstall_latest_05.dmp
inflating: fusionapps_dbinstall_latest_08.dmp
```

There is another export dump file named otbi.dmp at APPS_RCU_HOME/rcu/integration/biapps/ schema location. In order to keep all the export dump files in one location, we will copy this file to the temporary data pump dump directory called FUSIONAPPS_DBINSTALL_DP_DIR.

```
[fusion@fadbhost ]$ cd /app/fusion/provisioning/apps_rcu/dp_dir
[fusion@fadbhost dp_dir]$ cp -p \ /app/fusion/provisioning/apps_rcu/rcu/integration/biapps/
schema/otbi.dmp .
```

Now since we have all the required data pump export dump files available locally, we can launch the Repository Creation Utility, which is located at the APPS_RCU_HOME/bin directory with a script name of rcu.

```
[fusion@fadbhost dp_dir]$ cd /app/fusion/provisioning/apps_rcu/bin
[fusion@fadbhost bin]$ ./rcu
```

The Welcome screen is informative only and provides information on the purpose of this utility. No action is necessary on this screen. Click Next to see repository creation options, as shown in Figure 8-18.

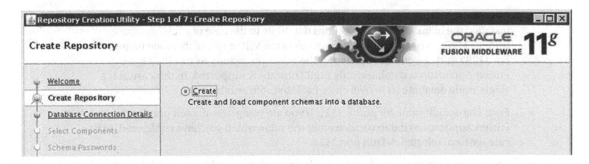

Figure 8-18. *Currently available options in Fusion Applications RCU*

As of the current release, Fusion Applications RCU provides only a Create option for the repository, unlike Identity Management RCU, which provides both Create and Drop options. This option allows us to create necessary database tablespaces, schemas, and objects, and then to seed default data in them.

Make sure that the database for which this RCU is being run does not have any of the existing components installed. You must run this RCU against a newly created blank Fusion Applications Transaction database only. Click Next to proceed to the DB Connection Details screen shown in Figure 8-19.

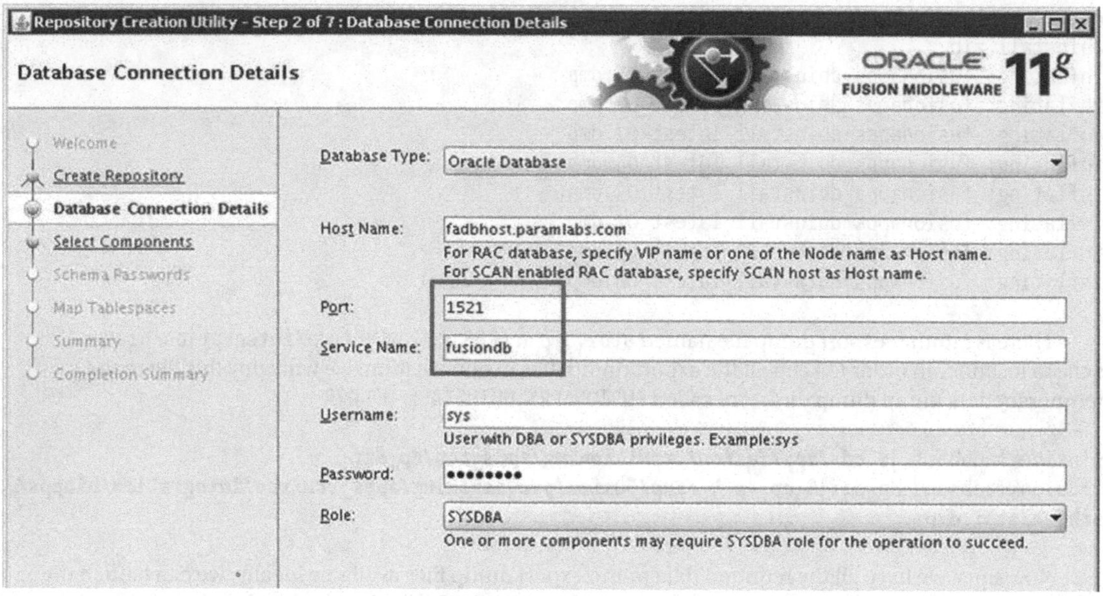

Figure 8-19. Fusion Applications Transaction Database Connection Details screen

This screen prompts for connection details for the database in which the repository needs to be created. The following information is required to be entered.

- *Database Type*: We must select Oracle Database here. Although RCU for some non-Applications components supports non-Oracle databases, our required components support Oracle Database only.

- *Host Name*: For a single-node database, enter the name of the host where we have installed the blank Fusion Applications database. In the case of a RAC database prior to 11gR2, we need to enter the names of the VIP or one of the node names. For 11gR2 and newer databases, enter the SCAN hostname. As this RCU is for Fusion Applications database, only 11gR2 onward is supported. In this case, it is a single-node database so we will enter fadbhost.paramlabs.com.

- *Port*: The default value for port is 1521. If you are using non-default port for the Fusion Applications database then enter the value which you have configured. In this case we have selected default port 1521.

- *Service Name*: In the case of a RAC database, enter the service name, while in the case of a single-node database, enter the SID value here. In this case, it is fusiondb.

- *Username*: Enter a username with SYSDBA privilege. We will enter SYS here.

- *Password*: Enter the password for the selected user.

- *Role*: We must select the SYSDBA role here for the SYS user.

Enter the appropriate details of the Fusion Apps database created in the previous step. Click Next to proceed to the prerequisites check, as shown in Figure 8-20.

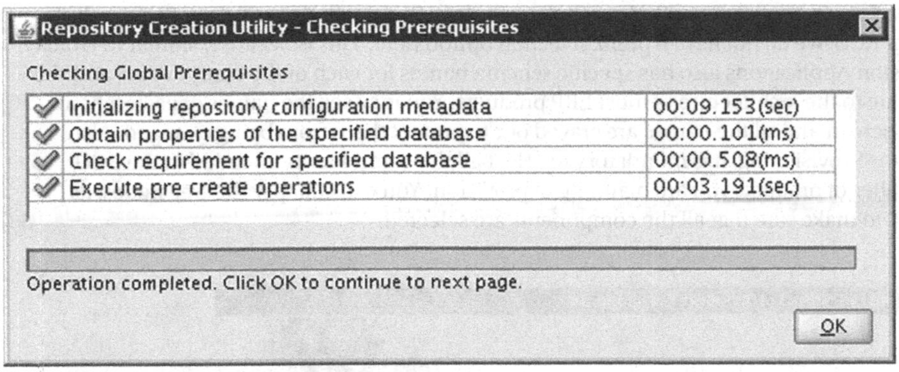

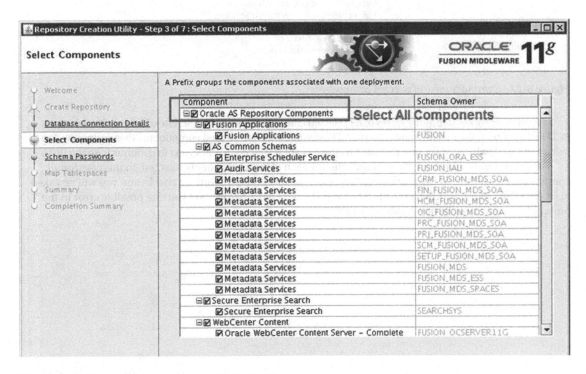

Figure 8-20. RCU Prerequisites check status

You will now see a pop-up dialog box that shows the status of various prerequisites checks that will run against the database using the connection parameters specified in previous screen. If there were any errors in the previous screen while providing database connection details, you may see failure in validation here. Any errors in these checks will abort the prerequisites check and show the error details in the messages panel of main screen. Once the prerequisite check completes successfully, click OK to proceed to the Components Selection screen, as shown in Figure 8-21.

Figure 8-21. Repository components selection screen

Now you will see Fusion Applications RCU components selection screen. You will notice that unlike Identity Management RCU, we do not have a prefix selection option here. This is because, similar to Oracle E-Business Suite, Fusion Applications also has specific schema names for each of the components and this cannot be changed due to the architecture of most ERP products. You may see the names of each schema being created on the screen and all the names are grayed out to protect them from being changed. Also for Fusion Applications Provisioning, it is mandatory to select all the components included in the RCU regardless of the number of products you are planning to provision. You can collapse the tree nodes, as shown in Figure 8-22, to make sure that all the components are selected.

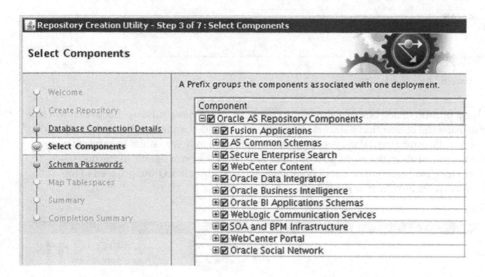

Figure 8-22. *Summary view of selected components*

Figure 8-22 shows a summary view of all selected components for your reference. You can see that the RCU includes both the Fusion Applications and Fusion middleware-related components that are required to be loaded in this database. Make sure that all components are selected and click Next to continue with the RCU.

Now the wizard will check the prerequisites for each of the components selected, in this case for all components since everything is selected. Any error will abort the prerequisite checks and you will be asked to fix the error before rerunning the prerequisites checks. Figure 8-23 shows you one possible error in the prerequisites check for Fusion Applications RCU.

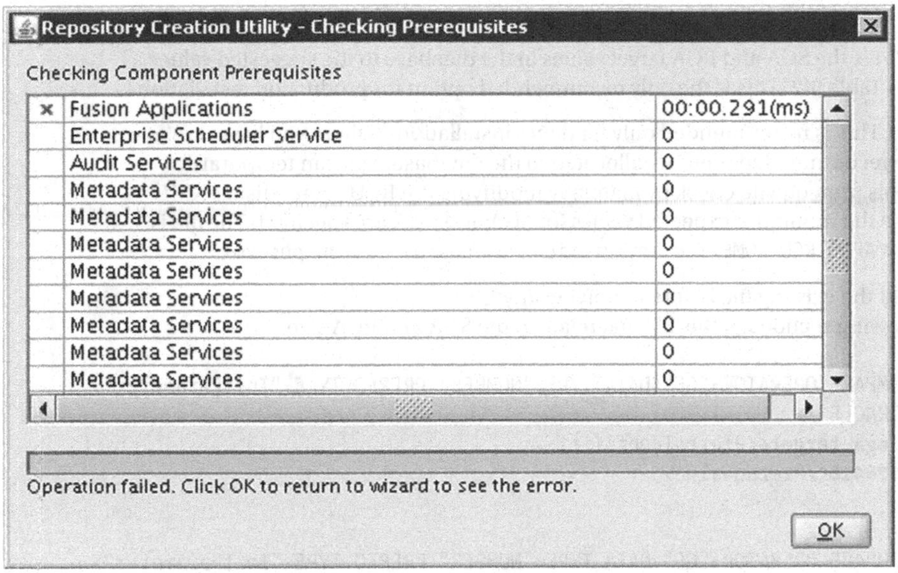

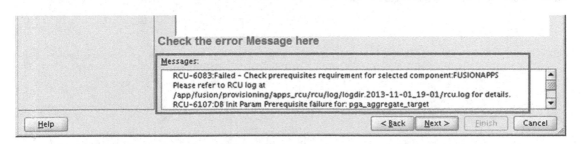

Figure 8-23. *Example failure condition in prerequisites check*

As you can see, you do not see any error messages but only a checkmark in front of the component's name. The message at the bottom suggests that an error has occurred. Once you click OK, you will be taken back to the previous screen. Now here you will see the actual error in the Messages panel at the bottom. Now in this particular example we are seeing following error, as shown in Figure 8-24.

```
RCU-6107:DB Init Param Prerequisite failure for: pga_aggregate_target
Current Value is 0. It should be greater than or equal to 4294967296.
RCU-6107:DB Init Param Prerequisite failure for: sga_target
Current Value is 0. It should be greater than or equal to 9663676416.
```

Figure 8-24. *Prerequisites check error message*

This specific error appears only if you had reduced SGA/PGA/memory size after the database installation to reduce the amount of memory required on a demo or proof-of-concept host. Or if you manually set the MEMORY_TARGET value instead of the SGA and PGA target values.

We have two ways to fix this issue.

- *Option 1*: Fix the SGA and PGA target values in the database to the suggested values as shown in Table 8-2. This is the only recommended option for production installations.

- *Option 2*: This is recommended only for demo installations, where you have don't have the recommended memory allocated to the database. You can temporarily bypass this prerequisite check by manually modifying the RCU prerequisites XML file where the minimum expected values for SGA and PGA are specified. The file is located at APPS_RCU_HOME/rcu/integration/fusionapps/fusionapps.xml.

Make a backup of the existing file before modifying anything.
You can see following sections in this file that relate to the SGA and PGA size.

```
<DBPrerequisite COMPARE_OPERATOR="GE" DATA_TYPE="NUMBER" PREREQ_TYPE="InitParameter">
<ValidIf DBTYPE="ORACLE"/>
<PrereqIdentifier>sga_target</PrereqIdentifier>
<PrereqValue>9663676416</PrereqValue>
</DBPrerequisite>
...
<DBPrerequisite COMPARE_OPERATOR="GE" DATA_TYPE="NUMBER" PREREQ_TYPE="InitParameter">
<ValidIf DBTYPE="ORACLE"/>
<PrereqIdentifier>pga_aggregate_target</PrereqIdentifier>
<PrereqValue>4294967296</PrereqValue>
</DBPrerequisite>
```

Change the values to match with your existing setup. If you used MEMORY_TARGET and kept SGA/PGA values to 0 then you can set these minimum values to 0 as well to avoid prerequisites check error. Once again we want to remind you that this is not recommended option and should be used only if you have no other option to increase the memory size on the database.

Due to a bug in the current version of RCU, you may need to click Back twice and click Next in order to see the prerequisite checks with new values.

You may see each component prerequisites check status and timing information on the screen, as shown in Figure 8-25. Once the prerequisites check is successful, click OK to proceed to the Schema Passwords screen, as shown in Figure 8-26.

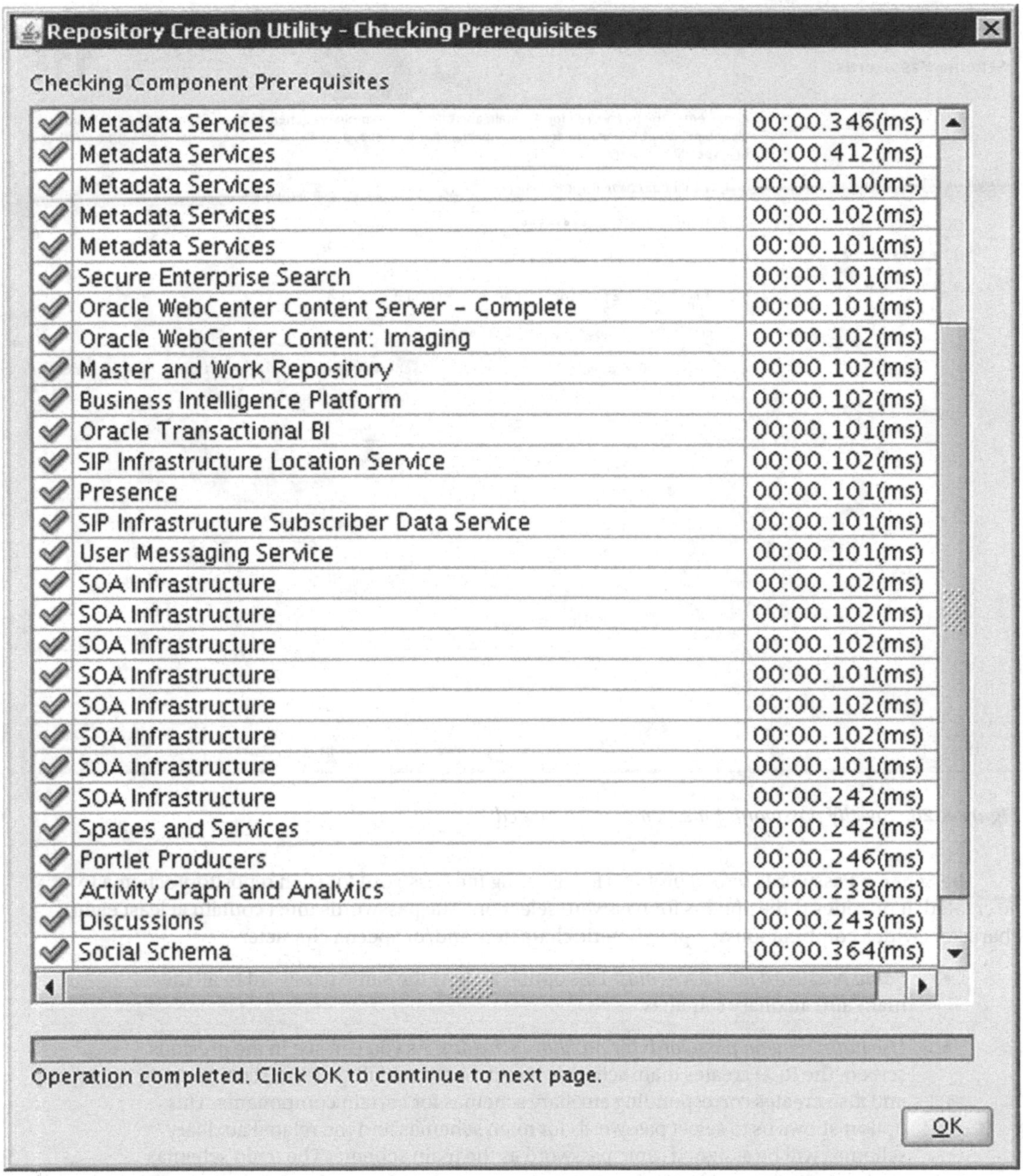

Repository Creation Utility - Checking Prerequisites   ☒

Checking Component Prerequisites

✔	Metadata Services	00:00.346(ms)
✔	Metadata Services	00:00.412(ms)
✔	Metadata Services	00:00.110(ms)
✔	Metadata Services	00:00.102(ms)
✔	Metadata Services	00:00.101(ms)
✔	Secure Enterprise Search	00:00.101(ms)
✔	Oracle WebCenter Content Server - Complete	00:00.101(ms)
✔	Oracle WebCenter Content: Imaging	00:00.102(ms)
✔	Master and Work Repository	00:00.102(ms)
✔	Business Intelligence Platform	00:00.102(ms)
✔	Oracle Transactional BI	00:00.101(ms)
✔	SIP Infrastructure Location Service	00:00.102(ms)
✔	Presence	00:00.101(ms)
✔	SIP Infrastructure Subscriber Data Service	00:00.101(ms)
✔	User Messaging Service	00:00.101(ms)
✔	SOA Infrastructure	00:00.102(ms)
✔	SOA Infrastructure	00:00.102(ms)
✔	SOA Infrastructure	00:00.102(ms)
✔	SOA Infrastructure	00:00.101(ms)
✔	SOA Infrastructure	00:00.102(ms)
✔	SOA Infrastructure	00:00.102(ms)
✔	SOA Infrastructure	00:00.101(ms)
✔	SOA Infrastructure	00:00.242(ms)
✔	Spaces and Services	00:00.242(ms)
✔	Portlet Producers	00:00.246(ms)
✔	Activity Graph and Analytics	00:00.238(ms)
✔	Discussions	00:00.243(ms)
✔	Social Schema	00:00.364(ms)

Operation completed. Click OK to continue to next page.

OK

Figure 8-25. *Successful prerequisites check*

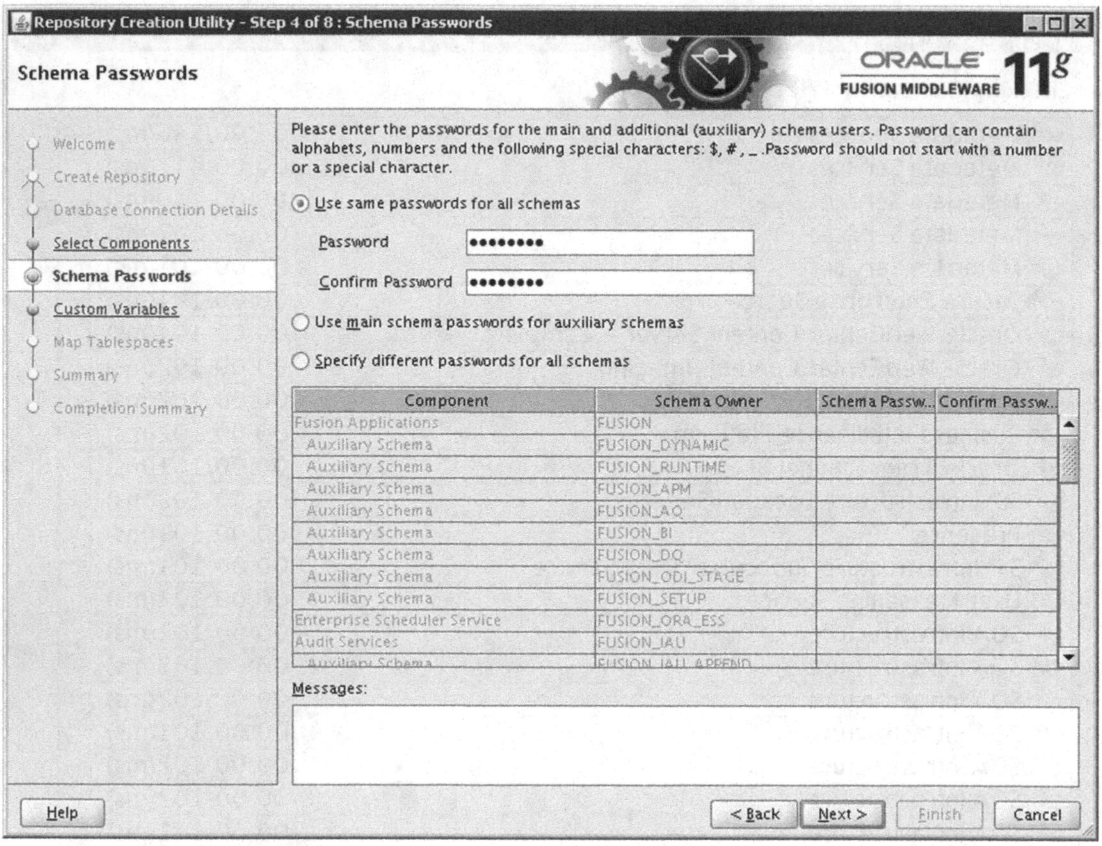

Figure 8-26. *Specify passwords for schemas to be created*

The Schema Passwords screen prompts for selecting the password for each repository schema to be created. It provides three options for password selection. The passwords must contain at least eight characters with a combination of alphanumeric characters and/or special characters.

- *Same password for all schemas*: This option assigns the same password to all the main and auxiliary schemas.

- *Use main schema passwords for Auxiliary schemas*: As you can see in the previous screen, the RCU creates main schemas based on the initially selected components and also creates corresponding auxiliary schemas for certain components. This option allows us to select passwords for main schemas and the related auxiliary schemas will be assigned same password as the main schema. The main schemas textbox remains enabled in this option,

- *Specify different passwords for all schemas*: This option enables all password textboxes and you can assign individual password for each schema as long as it confirms to the password complexity requirement.

For this example, I have selected the first option of selecting the same password for all schemas. Enter and confirm the password. Click Next to proceed to the Custom Variables screen, as shown in Figure 8-27.

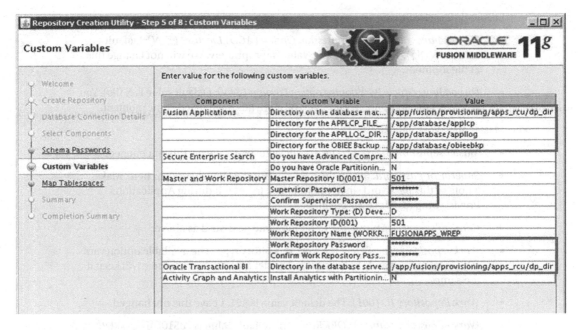

Figure 8-27. *Fusion Applications RCU Custom Variables screen*

Before you enter the values in next screen, you may need to create certain directories which you will need to provide during the RCU and later. Open a new terminal window and create the following directories for custom environment variables.

```
[fusion@fadbhost ~]$ mkdir /app/database/applcp
[fusion@fadbhost ~]$ mkdir /app/database/appllog
[fusion@fadbhost ~]$ mkdir /app/database/obieebkp
```

The Custom Variables screen requires you to input the following values. You need to click on the Value cell and paste or type in the required values. Note that due to the data grid size limitation, the text field may not show the complete value entered, but you can resize the wizard window to extend the cell width. You can also use the F2 function key to change the values in the field.

- Fusion Applications Custom Variables
  - *Directory on database machine where the FA install dumps are located*: Specify the directory where you have extracted the main data pump export dump files earlier. Note that even if you are running the RCU from a remote machine, the data pump directory must be created on database server only. In this case we extracted them at /app/fusion/provisioning/apps_rcu/dp_dir. Specify the same value here.

  - *Directory for the* APPLCP_FILE_DIR *directory object*: The first directory that we created for the APPLCP_FILE_DIR variable. For example, /app/database/applcp.

  - *Directory for APPLLOG_DIR directory object*: The second directory that we created for the APPLLOG_DIR variable. For example, /app/database/appllog.

  - *Directory for OBIEE backup directory object*: The third directory that we created for the OBIEE backup custom variable. For example, /app/database/obieebkp.

227

- Secure Enterprise Search

  - *Do you have Advanced Compression Option (ACO) License? (Y/N)*: Default value is N (No). You can select the value appropriately. We will not change this at the moment.

  - *Do you have Oracle Partitioning option License? (Y/N)*: Default value is N (No). You can select the appropriate value. We will leave this unchanged at the moment.

- Master and Work Repository

  - *Master repository ID (001)*: The default value is 501. Leave this unchanged.

  - *Supervisor password*: Set up the password for the ODI supervisor here. Make a note of this password since you will need to enter it during Applications Provisioning response file creation.

  - *Confirm supervisor password*: Enter the same password as above.

  - *Work repository type*: Select the work repository type. The available options are (D) Development and (E) Execution. The default value is D and we will keep it the same.

  - *Work Repository ID (001)*: The default value is 501. Leave this unchanged.

  - *Work Repository Name (WORKREP)*: The default value is FUSIONAPPS_WREP. Leave this value unchanged.

  - *Work Repository Password (Default None)*: Enter the same password as the ODI Supervisor here.

  - *Confirm Work Repository Password*: Confirm the same password as above.

- Oracle Transactional BI

  - *Directory on the database server where OTBI import/export files are stored*: We have extracted Business Intelligence Transactional BI export files in the same location as the main export data pump directory. You can specify a different directory as well but we suggest you keep the same data pump directory to avoid any confusion. We will enter /app/fusion/provisioning/apps_rcu/ dp_dir again here.

- Activity Graph and Analytics

  - *Install Analytics with Partitioning (Y/N)*: Default value is N (NO). We will leave this unchanged.

Once all these values are entered and verified, click Next to continue to the Map Tablespaces screen, as shown in Figure 8-28.

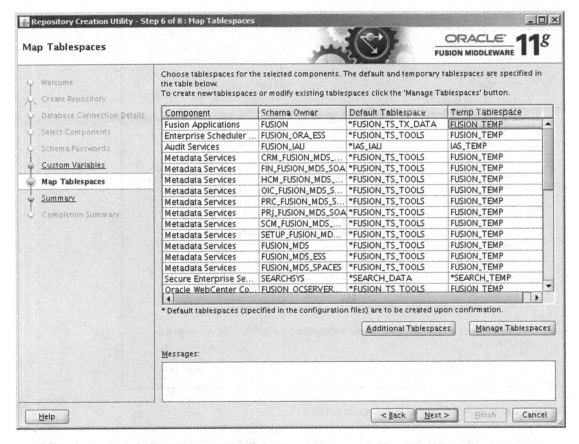

Figure 8-28. Map default and temporary tablespaces for schemas being provisioned

Now you will see the screen for mapping tablespaces for each component schema owner. This screen mainly shows four columns.

- *Component*: This column lists the RCU components selected under the Select Components screen you saw earlier.

- *Schema Owner*: This column lists the default schema owner for the specific component.

- *Default Tablespace*: This column lists the default tablespace for the specific schema's objects. Note that the schema objects could also be stored in different tablespaces as well but the default one is specified here.

- *Temp Tablespace*: This column lists the default temporary tablespace for the given schema.

When you click the default or temporary tablespace name, you will see a list of the values to be selected. You could even select existing tablespaces. Any new tablespaces that are to be created will be prefixed with an asterisk (*) sign.

On the same screen you will see two more buttons—Additional Tablespaces and Manage Tablespaces. When you click Additional Tablespaces button, you will see the pop-up screen shown in Figure 8-29.

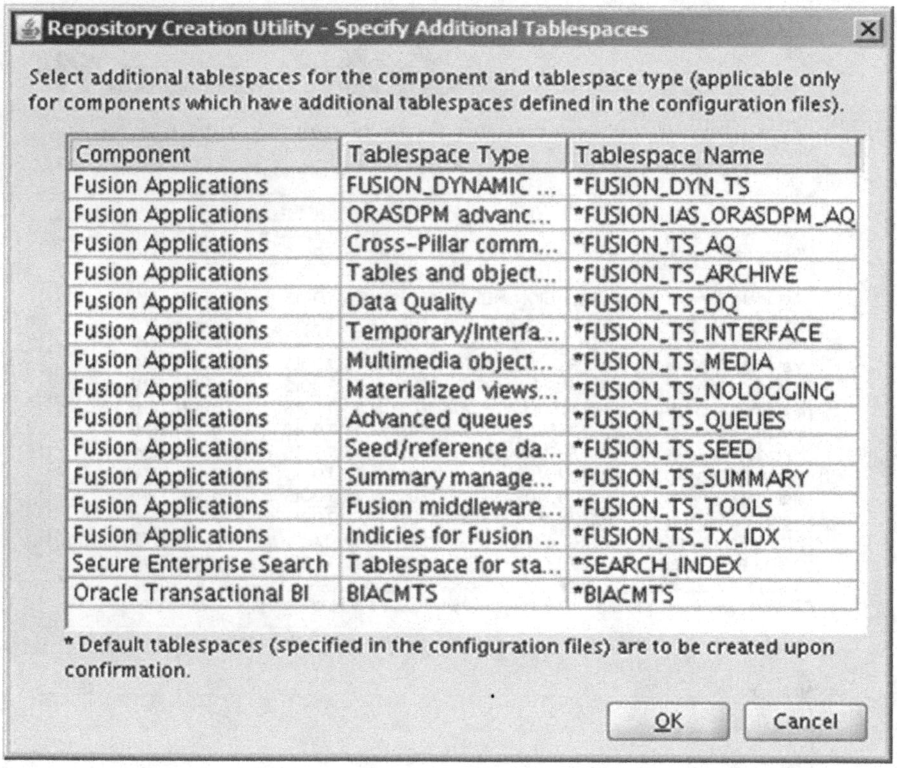

Repository Creation Utility - Specify Additional Tablespaces

Select additional tablespaces for the component and tablespace type (applicable only for components which have additional tablespaces defined in the configuration files).

Component	Tablespace Type	Tablespace Name
Fusion Applications	FUSION_DYNAMIC ...	*FUSION_DYN_TS
Fusion Applications	ORASDPM advanc...	*FUSION_IAS_ORASDPM_AQ
Fusion Applications	Cross-Pillar comm...	*FUSION_TS_AQ
Fusion Applications	Tables and object...	*FUSION_TS_ARCHIVE
Fusion Applications	Data Quality	*FUSION_TS_DQ
Fusion Applications	Temporary/Interfa...	*FUSION_TS_INTERFACE
Fusion Applications	Multimedia object...	*FUSION_TS_MEDIA
Fusion Applications	Materialized views...	*FUSION_TS_NOLOGGING
Fusion Applications	Advanced queues	*FUSION_TS_QUEUES
Fusion Applications	Seed/reference da...	*FUSION_TS_SEED
Fusion Applications	Summary manage...	*FUSION_TS_SUMMARY
Fusion Applications	Fusion middleware...	*FUSION_TS_TOOLS
Fusion Applications	Indicies for Fusion ...	*FUSION_TS_TX_IDX
Secure Enterprise Search	Tablespace for sta...	*SEARCH_INDEX
Oracle Transactional BI	BIACMTS	*BIACMTS

* Default tablespaces (specified in the configuration files) are to be created upon confirmation.

OK   Cancel

Figure 8-29. *Specify Additional Tablespaces screen*

The Specify Additional Tablespaces screen will show the additional tablespaces to be created for the selected components in addition to their existing default tablespaces. These tablespaces are required to store a specific type of additional objects for the selected components. None of these tablespaces exist in a blank Transactional database, hence all these tablespaces will be created in the further screens. In this screen, you can also select from a list of values but it's better to leave these unchanged unless you have a specific reason to change the tablespace.

Table 8-3 shows each of the tablespaces created for Fusion Applications and the contents of the objects created in each. Note that not all of these tablespaces will have objects created during the RCU. We will look at this after the completion of RCU.

Table 8-3. *Summary of Fusion Applications Related Schemas After RCU*

Tablespace Name	Tablespace Contents
FUSION_DYN_TS	FUSION_DYNAMIC tables to store dynamically generated PL/SQL
FUSION_IAS_ORASDPM_AQ	ORASDPM advanced queues JMS data and indices
FUSION_TS_AQ	Cross-pillar communication advanced queues
FUSION_TS_ARCHIVE	Tables and objects that are no longer used by Fusion Applications
FUSION_TS_DQ	Data quality
FUSION_TS_INTERFACE	Temporary/interface data and indices
FUSION_TS_MEDIA	Multimedia objects such as text, video, and graphics
FUSION_TS_NOLOGGING	Materialized views and other temporary/scratch pad objects
FUSION_TS_QUEUES	Advanced queues
FUSION_TS_SEED	Seed/referenced data and indexes
FUSION_TS_SUMMARY	Summary management objects
FUSION_TS_TOOLS	Fusion middleware tables, indices, and data
FUSION_TS_TX_IDX	Indices for Fusion transactional data
SEARCH_INDEX	Tablespaces for statistics tables
BIACMTS	Oracle BI ACM tables
SEARCH_DATA	Secure Enterprise search-related tables
SEARCH_INDEX	Indices for SES related tables
IAS_IAU	Audit services data

Now let's look at the screen that pops up when we click the Manage Tablespaces button. This screen allows you to manage the tablespaces selected in the earlier two screens. We have seen two types of tablespaces—Default and Additional. For default tablespaces, we cannot change any values on the screen including tablespace name, type, block size or storage type, number of datafiles, or the name or size of datafiles, as shown in Figure 8-30.

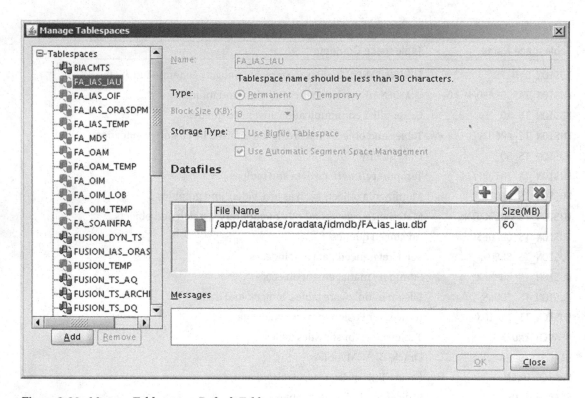

Figure 8-30. Manage Tablespaces: Default Tablespace

When you select an additional tablespace, you will be allowed to change all configuration values of the tablespace, including adding or removing a new tablespace that can be selected for any component. Figure 8-31 shows an example of the Manage Tablespaces screen.

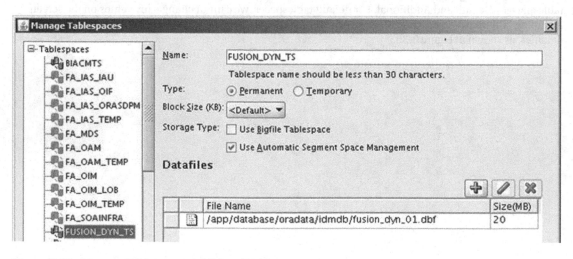

Figure 8-31. Manage Tablespaces: Additional Tablespace

Once you have reviewed the tablespaces and all related screens, click Next to continue creating the tablespaces. Note that the schemas will not be created now since the tablespaces are the prerequisites to create database schemas. The wizard will now prompt you for confirmation in order to create all new tablespaces, as shown in Figure 8-32.

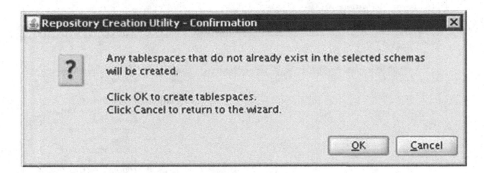

Figure 8-32. *Tablespaces creation confirmation prompt*

This will create the new tablespaces while leaving the existing tablespaces untouched, even if their specification is not as per the default specification required by the RCU. Once you click OK, the tablespace creation will begin as shown in Figure 8-33.

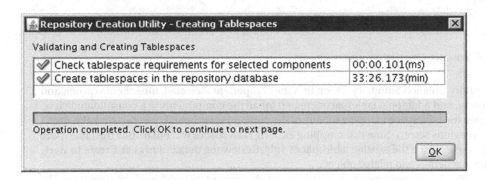

Figure 8-33. *Tablespaces creation progress*

This pop-up screen will show you overall progress of all tablespaces instead of the individual ones. You can connect to the database or OS in different window to monitor the progress of the tablespaces creation if required. Once the tablespaces are created, click OK to proceed with the pre-repository creation summary, as shown in Figure 8-34.

233

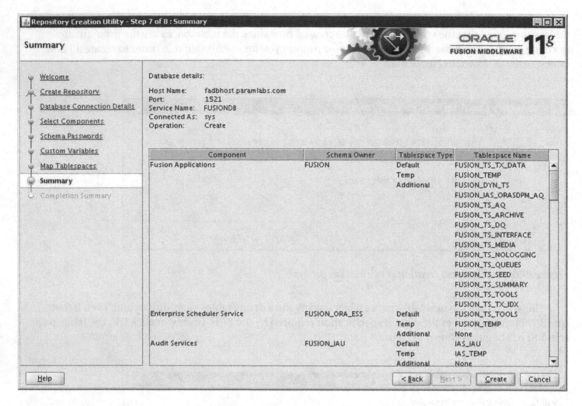

Figure 8-34. *Pre-Repository Creation Summary screen*

The Pre-Repository Creation Summary screen lists the components selected, the schema owner, and the default, temporary, and additional tablespaces created for all the components in a consolidated view. If you want to change the tablespace mapping for any of the component schemas, you can click the Back button to go to the previous screen. Note that mapping existing tablespaces will not invoke the tablespace creation again if you select from the existing tablespaces only. Review the details and click Create to start creating the database schemas and related objects.

Now the RCU will start creating repository schemas and objects and then will load the seed data. The screen will display the progress of each component along with the timing information, as shown in Figure 8-35. This might take long time depending on the machine configuration. Note that this screen will close automatically and move to the next screen once the repository has been created.

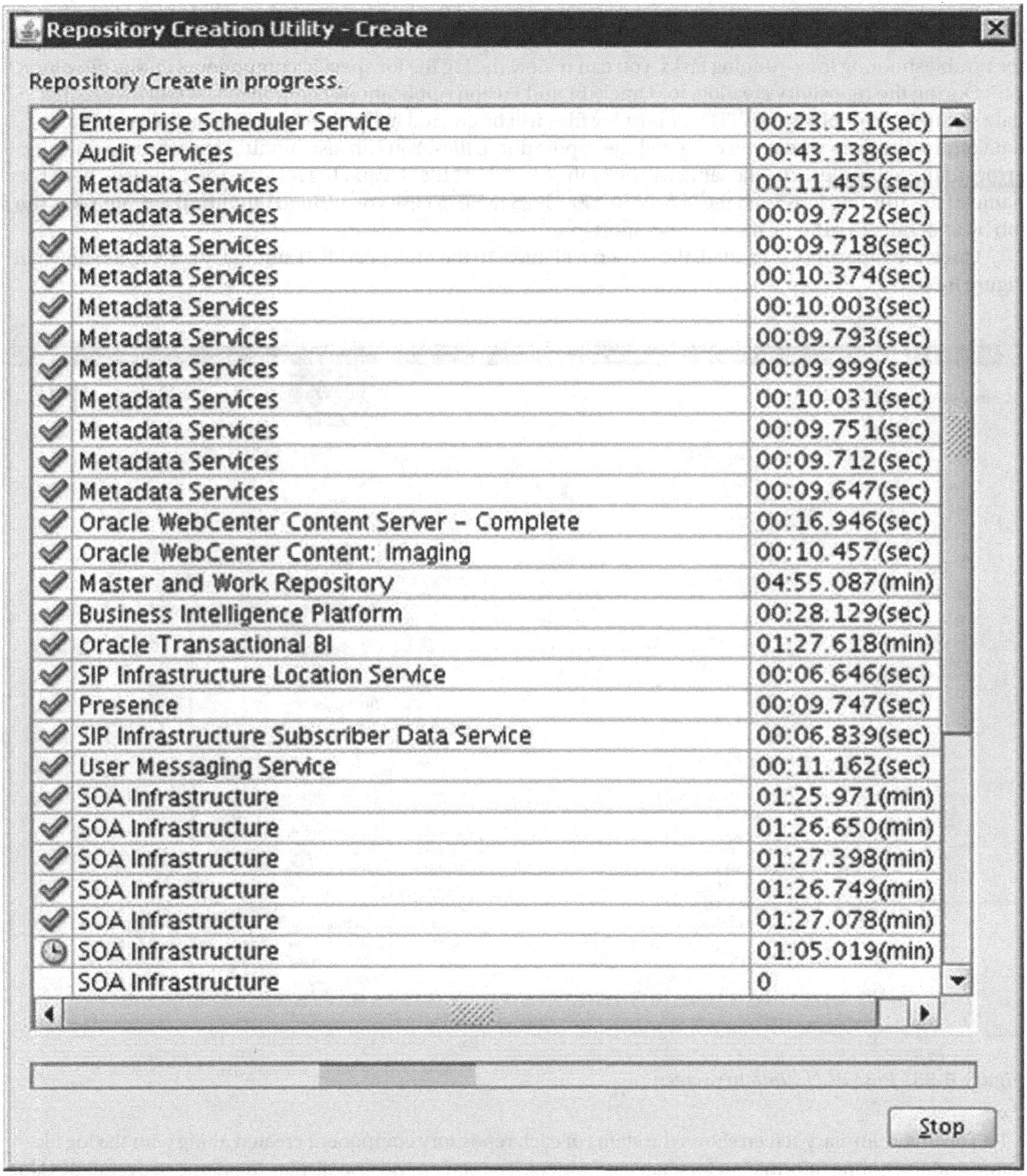

Repository Creation Utility - Create		✕
Repository Create in progress.		
✔ Enterprise Scheduler Service	00:23.151(sec)	▲
✔ Audit Services	00:43.138(sec)	
✔ Metadata Services	00:11.455(sec)	
✔ Metadata Services	00:09.722(sec)	
✔ Metadata Services	00:09.718(sec)	
✔ Metadata Services	00:10.374(sec)	
✔ Metadata Services	00:10.003(sec)	
✔ Metadata Services	00:09.793(sec)	
✔ Metadata Services	00:09.999(sec)	
✔ Metadata Services	00:10.031(sec)	
✔ Metadata Services	00:09.751(sec)	
✔ Metadata Services	00:09.712(sec)	
✔ Metadata Services	00:09.647(sec)	
✔ Oracle WebCenter Content Server - Complete	00:16.946(sec)	
✔ Oracle WebCenter Content: Imaging	00:10.457(sec)	
✔ Master and Work Repository	04:55.087(min)	
✔ Business Intelligence Platform	00:28.129(sec)	
✔ Oracle Transactional BI	01:27.618(min)	
✔ SIP Infrastructure Location Service	00:06.646(sec)	
✔ Presence	00:09.747(sec)	
✔ SIP Infrastructure Subscriber Data Service	00:06.839(sec)	
✔ User Messaging Service	00:11.162(sec)	
✔ SOA Infrastructure	01:25.971(min)	
✔ SOA Infrastructure	01:26.650(min)	
✔ SOA Infrastructure	01:27.398(min)	
✔ SOA Infrastructure	01:26.749(min)	
✔ SOA Infrastructure	01:27.078(min)	
🕐 SOA Infrastructure	01:05.019(min)	
SOA Infrastructure	0	▼

Stop

Figure 8-35. Fusion Applications repository creation progress

You might wonder what exactly happens behind the scenes when the repository is being created. We have two important directories involved at this point. First, the data pump directory where we have extracted the export dump files and second, the directory named <APPS_RCU_HOME>/rcu/integration. This directory contains subdirectories for each of the components being loaded. The subdirectory for each component has a set of XML files along with SQL files that run on the database to create schema objects and load the data. If you remember, we extracted the dump file from this location only.

During repository creation, each of these SQLs runs and the logs are created at <APPS_RCU_HOME>/rcu/log/logdir.<timestamp>. You will see a different log file for each of the components. In case of any errors or for troubleshooting long-running tasks, you can review the log file for specific components in this directory.

During the repository creation, for Oracle BI and Fusion Applications components, it will invoke the data pump import jobs as well. The import log files will be created in the same location as the temporary data pump directory where you extracted the export dump files. You can also monitor the progress and any errors in these log files. The filename will be of the import_<timestamp>.log format. You can also check the name of the running jobs from the DBA_DATAPUMP_JOBS table in case you want to monitor the progress of the job by attaching to running data pump import job.

Once the repository is created, the screen will move to the final post-RCU summary screen, as shown in Figure 8-36.

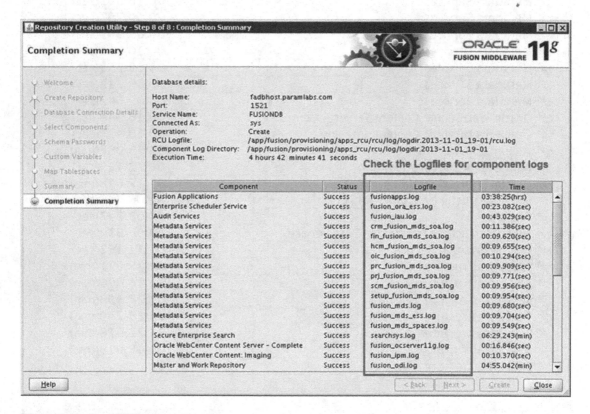

Figure 8-36. *Post-RCU summary screen*

The final summary screen shows the status of each repository component created along with the log file name and the timing information for each component. The screen will also display the name of overall RCU log file and the location of component logs, where you can find the log files mentioned in the grid. It also displays the overall execution time needed to create the repository. The time can vary depending on the configuration of database and host. Review the summary and click Close to finish the Fusion Applications RCU.

Fusion Applications Schemas and Tablespaces

Once the RCU is complete, we can log in to the Fusion Applications database and check the newly created schemas, tablespaces, and so on. Figure 8-37 classifies the tablespaces created by the RCU in two categories. The first group contains the default tablespaces for one or more schemas. The second group of tablespaces contains additional objects from one or more of the schemas. As you can see, some of the tablespaces do not have any objects at the end of the RCU, but once the specific business objects are created in the future, these tablespaces will contain relevant objects.

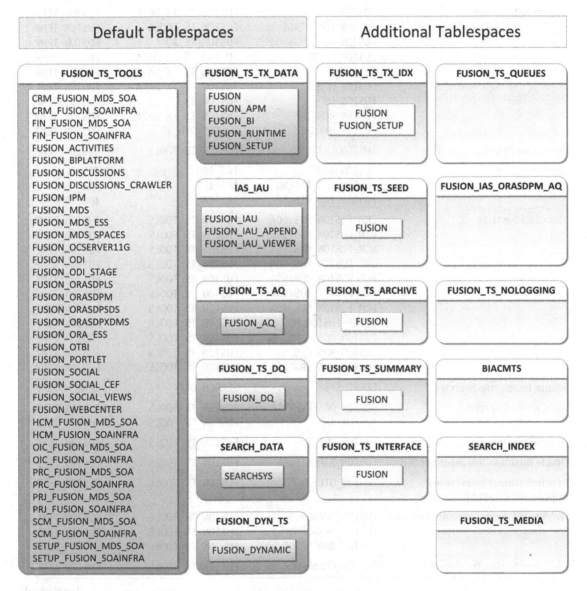

Figure 8-37. Default and additional tablespaces at the schema level

Table 8-4 shows the summary information of all the new schemas and tablespaces created after RCU completion. You should be able to see these schemas in your database in order to validate the RCU. You can use this table as a reference to locate the relevant schemas in the future.

Table 8-4. *Summary of Fusion Applications Related Schemas after RCU*

Component	Schema	Default Tablespace	Temporary Tablespace
Fusion Applications	FUSION	FUSION_TS_TX_DATA	FUSION_TEMP
	FUSION_ODI_STAGE	FUSION_TS_TOOLS	FUSION_TEMP
	FUSION_AQ	FUSION_TS_AQ	FUSION_TEMP
	FUSION_SETUP	FUSION_TS_TX_DATA	FUSION_TEMP
	FUSION_BI	FUSION_TS_TX_DATA	FUSION_TEMP
	FUSION_APM	FUSION_TS_TX_DATA	FUSION_TEMP
	FUSION_DQ	FUSION_TS_DQ	FUSION_TEMP
	FUSION_RUNTIME	FUSION_TS_TX_DATA	FUSION_TEMP
	FUSION_DYNAMIC	FUSION_DYN_TS	FUSION_TEMP
Enterprise Scheduler Service	FUSION_ORA_ESS	FUSION_TS_TOOLS	FUSION_TEMP
Audit Services	FUSION_IAU	IAS_IAU	IAS_TEMP
	FUSION_IAU_APPEND	IAS_IAU	IAS_TEMP
	FUSION_IAU_VIEWER	IAS_IAU	IAS_TEMP
Metadata Services	CRM_FUSION_MDS_SOA	FUSION_TS_TOOLS	FUSION_TEMP
	FIN_FUSION_MDS_SOA	FUSION_TS_TOOLS	FUSION_TEMP
	HCM_FUSION_MDS_SOA	FUSION_TS_TOOLS	FUSION_TEMP
	OIC_FUSION_MDS_SOA	FUSION_TS_TOOLS	FUSION_TEMP
	PRC_FUSION_MDS_SOA	FUSION_TS_TOOLS	FUSION_TEMP
	PRJ_FUSION_MDS_SOA	FUSION_TS_TOOLS	FUSION_TEMP
	SCM_FUSION_MDS_SOA	FUSION_TS_TOOLS	FUSION_TEMP
	SETUP_FUSION_MDS_SOA	FUSION_TS_TOOLS	FUSION_TEMP
	FUSION_MDS	FUSION_TS_TOOLS	FUSION_TEMP
	FUSION_MDS_ESS	FUSION_TS_TOOLS	FUSION_TEMP
	FUSION_MDS_SPACES	FUSION_TS_TOOLS	FUSION_TEMP
Secure Enterprise Search	SEARCHSYS	SEARCH_DATA	SEARCH_TEMP
WebCenter Content	FUSION_OCSERVER11G	FUSION_TS_TOOLS	FUSION_TEMP
	FUSION_IPM	FUSION_TS_TOOLS	FUSION_TEMP
Oracle Data Integrator	FUSION_ODI	FUSION_TS_TOOLS	FUSION_TEMP
Oracle Business Intelligence (BI)	FUSION_BIPLATFORM	FUSION_TS_TOOLS	FUSION_TEMP
Oracle Business Intelligence Applications (OBIA)	FUSION_OTBI	FUSION_TS_TOOLS	FUSION_TEMP
WebLogic Communication Services	FUSION_ORASDPLS	FUSION_TS_TOOLS	FUSION_TEMP
	FUSION_ORASDPXDMS	FUSION_TS_TOOLS	FUSION_TEMP
	FUSION_ORASDPSDS	FUSION_TS_TOOLS	FUSION_TEMP
SOA User Messaging Service	FUSION_ORASDPM	FUSION_TS_TOOLS	FUSION_TEMP

(continued)

Table 8-4. (*continued*)

Component	Schema	Default Tablespace	Temporary Tablespace
SOA Infrastructure	CRM_FUSION_SOAINFRA	FUSION_TS_TOOLS	FUSION_TEMP
	FIN_FUSION_SOAINFRA	FUSION_TS_TOOLS	FUSION_TEMP
	HCM_FUSION_SOAINFRA	FUSION_TS_TOOLS	FUSION_TEMP
	OIC_FUSION_SOAINFRA	FUSION_TS_TOOLS	FUSION_TEMP
	PRC_FUSION_SOAINFRA	FUSION_TS_TOOLS	FUSION_TEMP
	PRJ_FUSION_SOAINFRA	FUSION_TS_TOOLS	FUSION_TEMP
	SCM_FUSION_SOAINFRA	FUSION_TS_TOOLS	FUSION_TEMP
	SETUP_FUSION_SOAINFRA	FUSION_TS_TOOLS	FUSION_TEMP
WebCenter Portal	FUSION_WEBCENTER	FUSION_TS_TOOLS	FUSION_TEMP
	FUSION_PORTLET	FUSION_TS_TOOLS	FUSION_TEMP
	FUSION_ACTIVITIES	FUSION_TS_TOOLS	FUSION_TEMP
	FUSION_DISCUSSIONS	FUSION_TS_TOOLS	FUSION_TEMP
	FUSION_DISCUSSIONS_ CRAWLER	FUSION_TS_TOOLS	FUSION_TEMP
Oracle Social Network	FUSION_SOCIAL	FUSION_TS_TOOLS	FUSION_TEMP
	FUSION_SOCIAL_VIEWS	FUSION_TS_TOOLS	FUSION_TEMP
	FUSION_SOCIAL_CEF	FUSION_TS_TOOLS	FUSION_TEMP

This concludes the Fusion Applications Transaction database creation. We will now proceed to the Fusion Applications Environment provisioning steps in the next chapter.

Summary

This chapter explored the process of creating a Fusion Applications Transaction database. We have seen how to install Fusion Applications provisioning framework on a database node, followed creating a blank starter database. You learned about the steps to create the database manually and what other post-installation steps are required to bring the database to the supported level. In the latter part of this chapter, you learned the steps needed to run the *Repository Creation Utility (RCU)* for the Fusion Applications database.

At the end of the chapter, you saw the tablespace and schema-level view of the Fusion Applications Transaction database after the repository was created. The next two chapters focus on preparing a Fusion Applications environment using the already provisioned Identity Management nodes and Fusion Applications database as the base infrastructure.

CHAPTER 9

■ ■ ■

Preparing for Fusion Applications Provisioning

We are reaching the final and most important phase of the on-premise installation of Oracle Fusion Applications, which is the provisioning of Fusion Applications nodes. We already have an Identity Management environment up and running that provides identity and policy stores for our Fusion Applications environment. Additionally, we have the Fusion Applications database prepared which will now host the Fusion Applications-related transaction data. In this chapter, we will prepare the Fusion Applications host by installing the provisioning framework and creating the provisioning response file. This response file will be later used for provisioning the Fusion Applications environment. Since the provisioning process relies completely on the values entered in the response file, any incorrect values may lead to failure of the installation.

Installing Provisioning Framework

Similar to what we saw with the database nodes, installing the Fusion Applications provisioning framework on all the application nodes of the topology is a prerequisite for the provisioning process. This framework includes the Graphical Provisioning wizard as well as command-line tools that are required to run the provisioning phases on the primary and secondary hosts.

As you know, we have selected two-tier topology with four nodes. So we have single node only for Fusion Applications middle tier and web tier components. Hence, we will install the Fusion Applications provisioning framework only on one node—FAHOST. Note if you have application or web multiple nodes in the selected topology, you must install the provisioning framework on all nodes.

■ **Note**   Since we have already covered installing the provisioning framework on a Fusion Applications database node in a previous chapter, we will not go into the details of the steps here. If you want a refresher, follow the steps and screens in Chapter 8.

As the Fusion Applications provisioning framework installer is available in the Installer Repository under the directory named `faprov`, start the installation of Fusion Applications provisioning framework from `<REPOSITORY_LOCATION>/installers/faprov/Disk1`. For example:

```
[fusion@idmhost ~]$ cd /stage/installers/faprov/Disk1/
[fusion@idmhost Disk1]$ ./runInstaller
...
Specify the JRE/JDK location ( Ex. /home/jre ), <location>/bin/java should exist :/stage/jdk6
```

Since the installation of provisioning framework is identical to what we saw in Chapter 8, you can run through the wizard by following the screens and steps shown in Chapter 8 and finish the installation. Here also we will install the framework at /app/fusion/provisioning.

Fusion Applications Provisioning Framework Directory Structure

We skipped the explanation of the Fusion Applications provisioning framework directory structure in the last chapter since most of its subdirectories are relevant to the applications provisioning but not to the database installation. In this section, we will explore the importance of each subdirectory of the Fusion Applications provisioning framework with respect to the applications provisioning process.

Figure 9-1 shows the major directories of importance under the provisioning framework home that are accessed during the various tasks of the provisioning process.

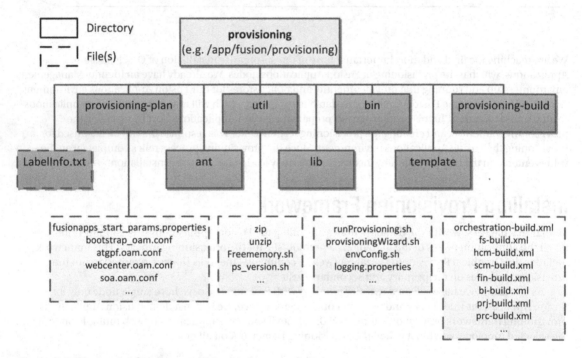

Figure 9-1. *Fusion Applications provisioning framework directory structure*

Let's explore the role of each of these subdirectories of the provisioning framework.

- bin: This is the main directory that you will refer to since it contains all the scripts to run the Provisioning wizard, including provisioningWizard.sh, the command-line tools like runProvisioning.sh, and the environment setup scripts like envConfig.sh and the Windows equivalents in .bat format. The directory also contains various configuration files specific to the execution of these scripts; for example, logging.properties, prov-logging-config.xml, and so on.

- lib: As the name suggests, this directory contains all the required Java class libraries required for the provisioning process in Java Archive (.jar) format. The provisioning scripts transparently set the Java classpath to this directory and its included JAR files.

- ant: The ANT utility provides the seamless orchestration mechanism of the Fusion Applications provisioning process. We learned about the importance of the ANT utility in the provisioning process in Chapter 3. The Provisioning wizard automatically locates the ANT libraries from this location. Only after the ANT home is identified will the installation begin. If this directory is not available, you will see error in identifying the ANT home.

- util: This directory contains OS-specific common utilities like zip, unzip, ps_version.sh, and so on, which are used by the Provisioning wizard at every phase.

- template: This directory is used by the database-creation option of the Provisioning wizard. We have already seen these templates in Chapter 8.

- provisioning-build: This is the most important directory in the Fusion Applications Provisioning process at every stage because it contains all the tasks to be executed for each product in each phase of provisioning. As we saw, the ANT orchestration uses XML files for getting the list of actions, their sequences and error conditions. Each product has a dedicated XML file, for example bi-build.xml, fs-build.xml, soa-build.xml, hcm-build.xml, crm-build.xml, and so on. The complete provisioning process is controlled by orchestration-build.xml. We discuss these files in detail during the provisioning sections.

- provisioning-plan: The name of this directory should not be confused with the internal plan file <ORACLE_BASE>/provisioning/plan/provisioning-plan generated by the wizard after creating the response file. This directory contains some configuration files like fusionapps_start_params.properties, bootstrap_oam.conf, and so on.

- LabelInfo.txt: This is only a text file containing the version details of the provisioning framework. This file is not used by the provisioning process but it helps in identifying any issues specific to the provisioning framework version bundled with the installation media. You may provide the version details from this file to Oracle Support during the troubleshooting process if required.

Install JDK

Since Fusion middleware and applications are based on Java, all installers included in the media require a permanent JDK home to be available on the host machine. Since the JDK version included with the current release of Fusion Applications is JDK 6, we will install there.

The compressed JDK 6 file (jdk6.zip) is included at <REPOSITORY_LOCATION>/installers/jdk. We will unzip it to the provisioning installer root directory /app/fusion, but you can select any location.

```
[fusion@fahost ~]$ cd /app/fusion/
[fusion@fahost fusion]$ unzip /stage/installers/jdk/jdk6.zip
```

This will create a directory named jdk6 at the selected location. In this example, it will be /app/fusion/jdk6. We will specify this directory as the Java home in any further installations on this host. Most of the installers can detect the Java home if it is created in the Oracle Base directory.

Copy Required Libraries to WebGate Installer Directory

If you were installing earlier versions of Fusion Applications, you would have already performed this step during Identity Management provisioning. Since WebGate requires platform-specific GCC and C++ libraries to be available, we used to provide the location of the required libraries as part of manual WebGate installation.

Since for the recent releases of Fusion Applications, the WebGate installation is automated for both Identity Management and Fusion Applications nodes, we need to copy these libraries in the installation repository.

We will need the following libraries in the repository installers webgate directory. Let's first make sure if we have the required libraries. Execute the following commands to confirm the existence of the required libraries. The output of all these should be more than 0.

■ **Note** We will run the required checks for the Linux x86-64 platform. Refer to the platform-specific notes for the required libraries for your selected platform.

```
[fusion@fahost bin]$ strings -a /lib64/libgcc_s.so.1 | grep -v "GCC_3.3.1" | grep -c "GCC_3.3"
2
[fusion@fahost bin]$ strings -a /lib64/libgcc_s.so.1 | grep -c "GCC_3.0"
1
[fusion@fahost bin]$ strings -a /lib64/libgcc_s.so.1 | grep -c "GCC_4.2.0"
1
[fusion@fahost bin]$ strings -a /lib64/libgcc_s.so.1 | grep -v "GCC_3.3.1" | grep -c "GCC_3.3"
1
[fusion@fahost bin]$ file -L /lib64/libgcc_s.so.1 | grep "64-bit" | grep -c "x86-64"
1
[fusion@fahost bin]$ file -L /usr/lib64/libstdc++.so.6 | grep "64-bit" | grep -c "x86-64"
1
```

Let's keep a local copy of the libraries as well (optional). This will prove to be handy if you need to scale the environment up and need to install WebGate manually later. This was mandatory in earlier releases for manual installation of WebGate, but is not required now.

```
[fusion@fahost bin]$ mkdir /app/fusion/oam_lib
[fusion@fahost bin]$ cp -p /lib64/libgcc_s.so.1 /app/fusion/oam_lib/
[fusion@fahost bin]$ cp -p /usr/lib64/libstdc++.so.6 /app/fusion/oam_lib/
[fusion@fahost bin]$ cp -p /usr/lib64/libstdc++.so.5 /app/fusion/oam_lib/
```

We must copy the files in the installation repository webgate directory so that the installer can use these libraries automatically.

```
[fusion@fahost bin]$ cp -pr /app/fusion/oam_lib/* /stage/installers/webgate/
```

Let's make sure that all the required the files have been copied.

```
[fusion@fahost bin]$ ls -ltr /stage/installers/webgate/
-rwxrwxrwx 1 root root 2480 Mar 3 2013 Labels.txt
drwxrwxrwx 1 root root 0 Oct 24 03:01 Disk1
drwxrwxrwx 1 root root 0 Oct 24 03:01 patch
-rwxrwxrwx 1 root root 58400 Oct 27 14:51 libgcc_s.so.1
-rwxrwxrwx 1 root root 825400 Oct 27 14:51 libstdc++.so.5
-rwxrwxrwx 1 root root 976312 Oct 27 14:51 libstdc++.so.6
```

This concludes the prerequisites preparation for creating the provisioning response file.

Creating the Fusion Applications Response File

In earlier versions of Fusion Applications (prior to Fusion Applications 11g, Release 3), the Fusion Applications response file was called the provisioning plan. The term "provisioning plan" is no longer used. Make sure that you are creating the response file from the *primordial host* only since the Provisioning wizard assumes that the node where response file is being generated is the primordial host. Since our selected topology has only a single host for the application tier, we will create the response file from the same host, that is, FAHOST.

The concept of the response file is simple; it gathers all the details of the proposed installation in the form of questionnaire-based wizard and stores your responses in a variable-value based text file. Fusion Applications provisioning allows you to create this file in advance so that the actual installation does not require you to enter those details again. Although you prepare the response file in advance, you can modify most of its parameters later during the response file review process. We will look at this in detail in the appropriate sections.

Although we can provision the Fusion Applications environment using a graphical wizard or via command-line scripts, creation of the provisioning response file must be done using the graphical interface. In order to create a new Fusion Applications response file, we will launch the Provisioning wizard script provisioningWizard.sh from <framework_location>/provisioning/bin. For the Windows platform, the script is called provisioningWizard.bat. <framework_location> is where you have installed the Provisioning framework. In this example, it is /app/fusion/provisioning.

We must set JAVA_HOME before starting the wizard to the location where we have installed JDK in the previous step.

```
[fusion@fahost ~]$ export JAVA_HOME=/app/fusion/jdk6
```

Let's launch the Provisioning wizard now.

```
[fusion@fahost ~]$ cd /app/fusion/provisioning/bin
[fusion@fahost bin]$ ./provisioningWizard.sh &
```

The Provisioning wizard's Welcome screen displays important prerequisites information, as shown in Figure 9-2, in order to make sure that the preceding tasks have completed before initiating this step.

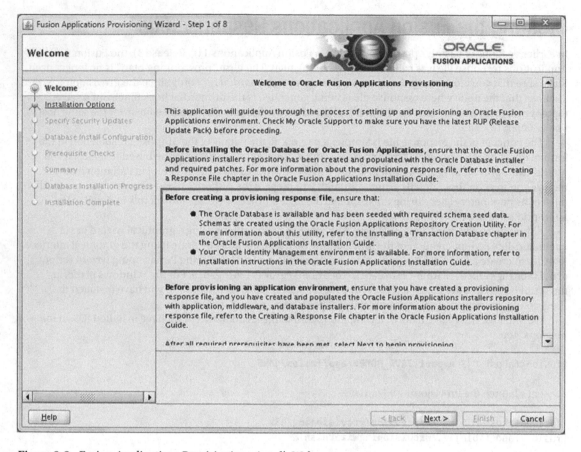

Figure 9-2. *Fusion Applications Provisioning wizard's Welcome screen*

The following prerequisites must be completed before you create a provisioning response file. The wizard will validate the connections to these components during the response-collection process.

- The Fusion Applications provisioning framework must be installed on application nodes. This is an obvious prerequisite since the response file creation option is part of the Provisioning wizard included in the framework.

- Fusion Applications Transaction database must have been installed and the repository creation should have completed. The response file interview process checks for database connectivity and for users validation in order to make sure that the correct details are entered in the response file.

- The Identity Management environment must be created and configured. This includes an Identity Management database as well as Identity and Access Management components. The Response File creation wizard will validate each component port's accessibility and the URLs to make sure that the information stored in the response file is accurate.

Review the information and click Next to proceed to the provisioning option selection, as shown in Figure 9-3.

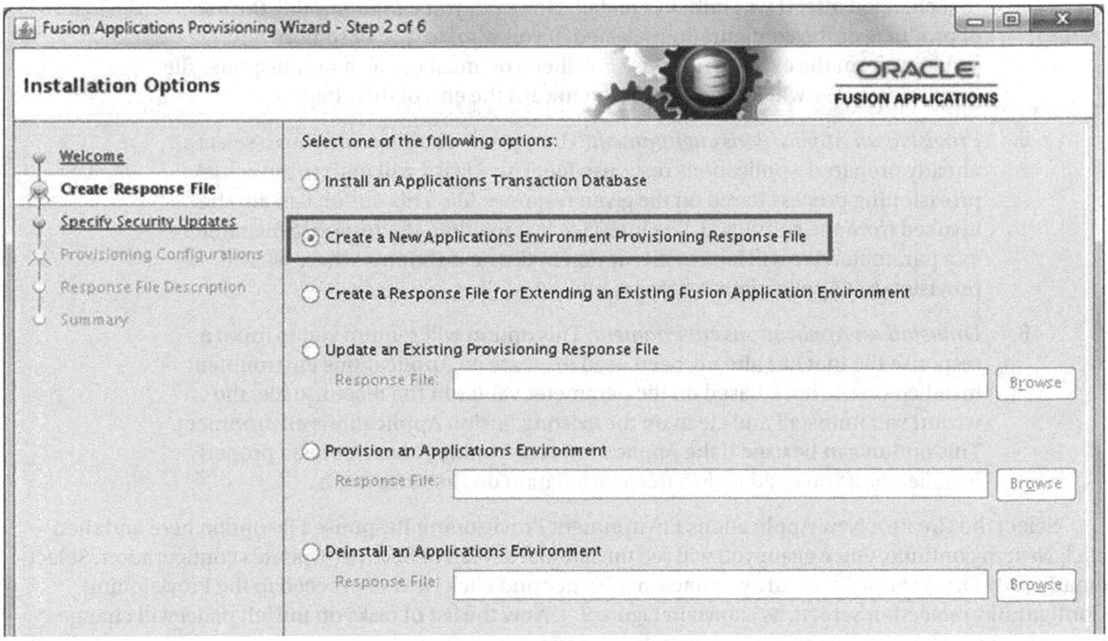

Figure 9-3. *Wizard option selection screen*

This screen allows you to select from following five provisioning options. We saw these options in Chapter 8 but since there we were installing Applications Transaction database, we skipped the discussion of these options. Let's look at the options and the tasks performed by each of them.

1. *Install an Applications Transaction database*: We used this option to create the Fusion Applications Transaction database.

2. *Create a new Applications environment provisioning response file*: We will use this option to create a new Fusion Applications response file from scratch. Once this option is selected, the list of steps on the left panel will be populated accordingly. The first two options do not require any other input since both steps are performed from scratch.

3. *Create a response file for extending an existing Fusion Applications environment (available from Fusion Applications 11.1.9 onward)*: The option to create a response file for extending an existing Fusion Applications environment was not available until 11.1.9, so if you are installing release 11.1.8 or earlier, you may not see this option. This option has to be used only while upgrading Fusion Applications.

4. *Update an existing provisioning response file*: This option requires you to select an existing Applications environment response file that was created earlier. This options allows you to modify any parameter value in the response file that changed after it was initially created. However, you cannot modify the list of products or the configuration selected. If you want to add or remove any products from the existing response file, then you must create a new response file from scratch. We will look at this option toward the end of this chapter.

5. *Provision an Applications environment*: This option also requires you to select an already prepared Applications response file. The wizard will initiate the actual provisioning process based on the given response file. This option can also be invoked from the command-line interface by providing the response filename as a parameter. We will look at this option in the next chapter, where we will provision the Applications environment.

6. *Uninstall an Applications environment*: This option will require you to input a response file that has already been used to create an Applications environment installed on the host. Based on the parameter values in the response file, the wizard will uninstall and clean up the existing Fusion Applications environment. This option can be used if the Applications environment has not been properly installed or if you need to do a fresh installation on the same hosts.

Select the Create a New Applications Environment Provisioning Response File option here and then click Next to continue. Once again you will see the familiar screen of Security Updates configuration. Select email or My Oracle Support security updates preference and click Next to proceed to the Provisioning Configuration selection screen, as shown in Figure 9-4. Now the list of tasks on the left panel will change from six steps to 20 steps specific to creating the response file.

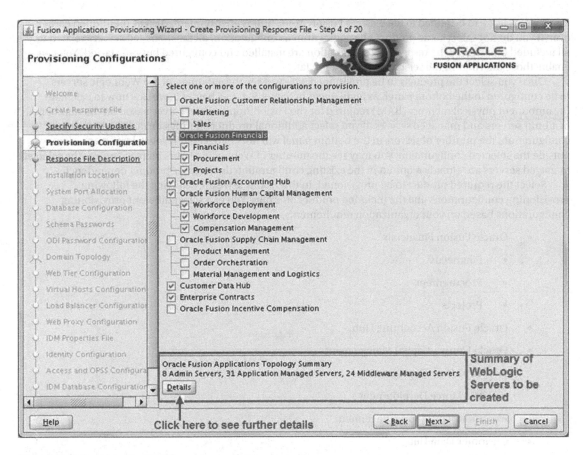

Figure 9-4. Provisioning Configurations selection screen

The next screen is the most important selection screen when creating the response file. This screen allows you to select one or more product configurations. We looked at the relation between Fusion Applications product offerings and configurations in Chapter 2, in the section titled "Deciding the Product Offerings to be Provisioned." Although there are several products available under the Fusion Applications umbrella, we can select from the major groups of product offerings, also called as configurations.

■ **Caution** Note that as of the current Fusion Applications release, you cannot modify the selected list of products and configurations using the Update an Existing Provisioning Response File option. So be careful while selecting the provisioning configurations and freeze the required products list before creating the response file.

It would be crucial to note the important differences between the E-Business Suite installation and Fusion Applications installation. In E-Business Suite, we can select/license a minimal number of products during the installation and then enable more products or components later, based on the business and licensing needs. But in case of Oracle Fusion Applications, as on current architecture, we must decide on the list of products to be provisioned in advance. You cannot add or modify products to/on an existing Fusion Applications environment. However, there is an exception to this restriction if you are upgrading Fusion Applications to a newer release. During upgrade, the wizard allows you to select new products from the newer release to be added to the existing Fusion Applications environment. Also as mentioned earlier, even if you do not select some product offerings within a configuration, all the managed servers related to all included offerings of the respective configuration are installed and configured but not started. You can enable those offerings in the selected configuration later.

Once you select the products to be provisioned, you will see the summary of the WebLogic servers to be configured in the bottom panel, as highlighted in Figure 9-4. In Chapter 2, we saw how to calculate the amount of physical memory (RAM) required for the Fusion Applications server based on the number of admin servers and managed servers. If you select additional product offerings in an already selected configuration, the number of servers in the bottom panel will not change. But if you select any product outside the selected configuration, you may see the number of WebLogic servers increase unless the selected managed servers are already required in the existing configuration due to inter-product dependencies.

Select the required product to be provisioned. In this example we are selecting the following provisioning configurations and the included product offerings. You can select different provisioning configurations based on your organization requirements.

- Oracle Fusion Financials

  - Financials

  - Procurement

  - Projects

- Oracle Fusion Accounting Hub

- Oracle Human Capital Management

  - Workforce Deployment

  - Workforce Development

  - Compensation Management

- Customer Data Hub

- Enterprise Contracts

With this selection you will see the following managed servers in the lower panel.

- Eight admin servers

- Thirty-one application managed servers

- Twenty-four middleware managed servers

Now let's click the Details button to launch the Topology Details pop-up screen, as shown in Figure 9-5. It shows how many managed servers are being configured as part of this offering.

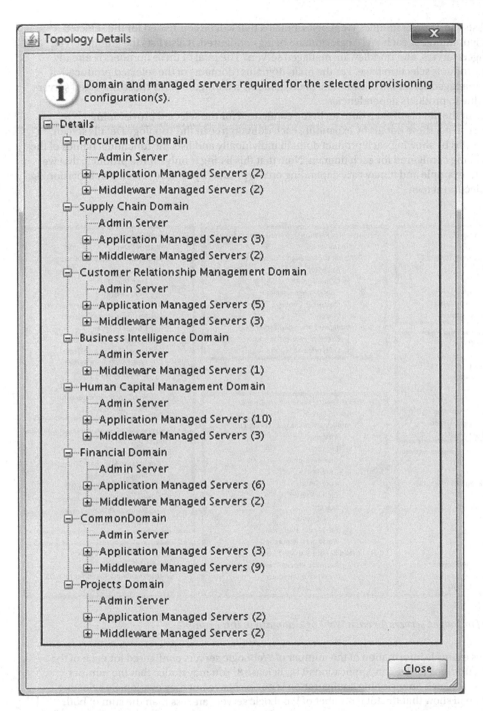

Figure 9-5. Topology details for the selected configuration

This screen lists the product families WebLogic domains that will be configured for the selected provisioning configuration. For each WebLogic domain being configured, it also lists the admin server, application managed servers, and middleware managed servers. The total of these numbers is already mentioned in the products selection page. For the main domains (domains of the selected products), it configures all the managed servers, while for non-main domains it configures only those managed servers that are required due to products dependencies.

Now let's look at the details of each domain being configured for the selected provisioning configuration. You can get these details by expanding each domain tree in the Topology Details screen. Figure 9-6 explains this by showing each product domain individually and lists the functional names of the managed servers being configured for each domain. Note that this listing is only for the products that we have selected in our example and it may vary depending on the products you have selected in Provisioning Configurations selection screen.

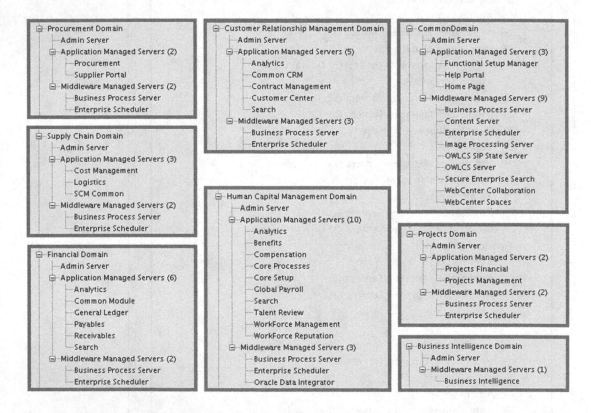

Figure 9-6. *List of managed servers for each WebLogic domain in this example*

Table 9-1 gives example information of the number of WebLogic servers configured for each of the provisioning configurations for Fusion Applications 11g, Release 8. You may notice that the number of WebLogic servers for each provisioning configuration is not exclusive but they overlap. So selecting two configurations will show that the total number of WebLogic servers are less than the sum of both Configurations WebLogic servers. For example, the Fusion HCM configuration requires five admin servers and 34 managed servers, while the Fusion Financials requires eight admin servers and 46 managed servers. But when you select both of them, the total number of WebLogic servers will be much less than the sum of their respective numbers due to the dependencies between Fusion HCM and Fusion Financials product families.

Table 9-1. *WebLogic server counts for each configuration of Fusion Applications 11.1.8*

Provisioning Configuration	Product Offerings	Admin Servers	Application Managed Servers	Middleware Managed Servers
Oracle Fusion Customer Relationship Management	Marketing Sales	6	21	17
Oracle Fusion Financials	Financials Procurement Projects	8	23	23
Oracle Fusion Accounting Hub	Fusion Accounting Hub	5	12	14
Oracle Fusion Human Capital Management	Workforce Deployment Workforce Development Compensation Management	5	19	15
Oracle Fusion Supply Chain Management	Product Management Order Orchestration Material Management and Logistics Supply chain financial orchestration	7	23	18
Customer Data Hub	Customer data hub	5	12	14
Enterprise Contracts	Enterprise contracts	5	14	13
Oracle Fusion Incentive Compensation	Incentive compensation	6	13	15
All configurations selected	All available product offerings	9	41	28

Table 9-1 should help you get a quick estimate of the hardware required in your Fusion Applications implementation projects, especially for those who are installing Fusion applications for proof of concept demo. You will notice that sometimes adding a standalone product offering will not increase any more WebLogic servers in your environment so you may want to include them in your installation.

Now let's look at the details of WebLogic domain dependencies for each provisioning configuration. We will now look at which domains are created for the provisioning configurations. This will help us draw a dependency map between the product families and the dependent WebLogic domains.

Figure 9-7 shows lists the names of the WebLogic domains configured for each provisioning configuration. It reveals an interesting fact here. The following domains are *always* configured regardless of the products selection for provisioning.

- CommonDomain
- BIDomain
- CRMDomain
- FinancialDomain
- HCMDomain

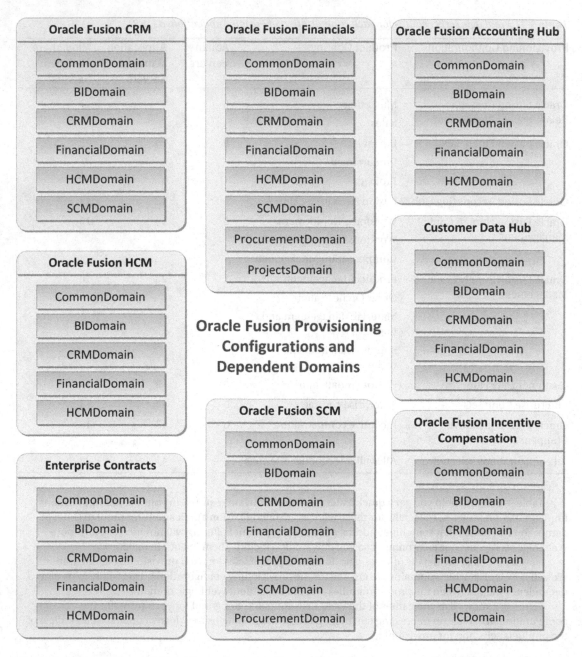

Figure 9-7. Domains provisioned for each provisioning configuration

Similarly, you can see that some domains are configured only when specific provisioning configurations are selected. For example, SCMDomain is created and configured only when you have selected one of the following configurations:

- Oracle Fusion SCM

- Oracle Fusion Financials

- Oracle Fusion CRM

Once you have finalized the provisioning configurations and product offerings, select the appropriate checkboxes in the Configuration Selection screen and click Next to proceed to the Response File Description screen, as shown in Figure 9-8.

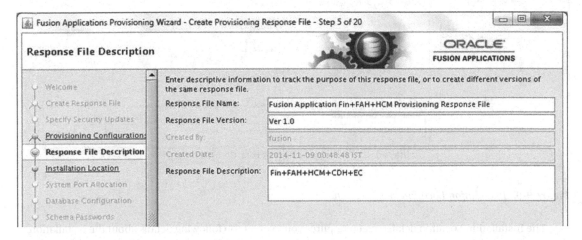

Figure 9-8. *Response File Description screen*

The Response File Description screen requires you to enter the following details to identify the response file in the future. Although the default name, version, and description are already filled in, it is always advisable to modify the values according to your selection so that if you have created multiple provisioning response files, you can simply identify them by reading the name or description in the response file using a text viewer.

It is advisable to provide a version number for the response file manually as it helps if you need to update the file later. Created By and Created Date values are populated automatically with the OS user and system time respectively when the response file creation is started. This value remains the same even if you are updating the existing response file. Review and modify these values and click Next to proceed to the Installation Location screen, as shown in Figure 9-9.

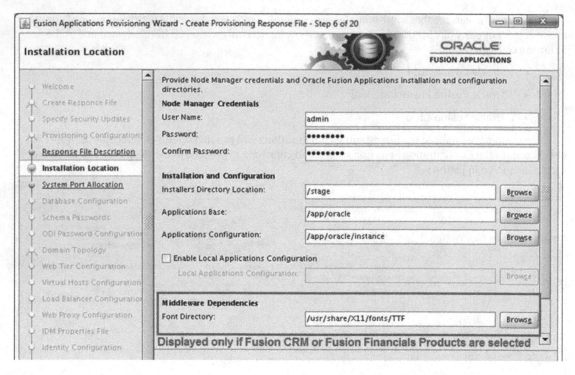

Figure 9-9. Installation Location details screen

The Installation Location details screen requires you to enter the following details about the installation.

Node Manager Credentials

1. *Username and password*: Enter any username and password for the Node Manager Administration role. These values will be used to configure the node manager and secure the WebLogic servers by using encrypted values. These same values will be used in keystore and wallet files.

Installation and Configuration

2. *Installers directory location*: Specify the location of the Fusion Applications Installation Repository where the installation media has been extracted, also referenced as REPOSITORY_LOCATION in earlier examples. In this case, the location is /stage. The wizard will check for a subdirectory named installers in this location. If no such directory is found, the installer will display an error.

3. *Applications base*: Specify a directory for the Applications base, which will act as the top-level directory for all Fusion Applications products. It is mandatory to specify a directory within a mount point instead of the mount point itself. For example, if /app is your mount point, you cannot specify /app. You must create a new directory within the mount point, for example /app/oracle. The installer user must also have permission to create this path in the parent directory. This path is also referred to as APPLICATIONS_BASE.

4. *Applications configuration*: This value will be populated automatically based on the value entered above. If this directory already has files in it, then the installer will throw an error suggesting that the directory be empty. The default value will be `<APPLICATIONS_BASE>/instance`. Leave this value unchanged.

5. *Enable local Applications configuration*: This checkbox is optional. This should be checked only if you want to store the configurations files locally instead of in a shared location.

    Local Applications configuration: This field will be activated only if you have selected this checkbox. You need to specify a local directory on the host for this location. The wizard will copy the configuration files to this location. The directory must exist on a local disk and must be empty.

6. *Middleware dependencies*

    Font Directory: This field will appear only if you have selected Oracle Fusion CRM or Oracle Fusion Financials related products. In all other cases, this field will not be displayed on this screen. Although the value is populated automatically, confirm it by checking the location manually and making sure that the TrueType fonts (TTF) and related files are present.

    - Linux x86-64: `/usr/share/X11/fonts/TTF`

    - Windows: `C:\Windows\Fonts`

    - Solaris/AIX: `/usr/X11R6/lib/X11/fonts/TrueType`

7. *Oracle Business Intelligence repository password*

    RDP password: Enter a complex password to allow access to Oracle Business Intelligence Applications (OBIA) and Oracle Transactional Business Intelligence (OTBI) metadata repositories (RPD). Confirm it next.

Figure 9-10 shows the bottom portion of the screen, which was not visible in Figure 9-9.

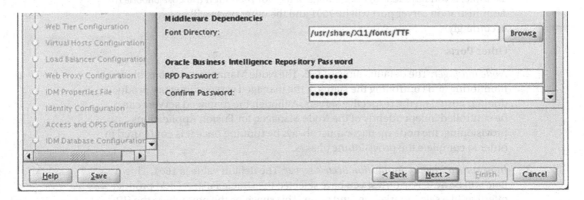

Figure 9-10. *Installation Location details screen (continued)*

Once all these values are entered and manually verified, click Next to proceed to the System Port Allocation screen, as shown in Figure 9-11.

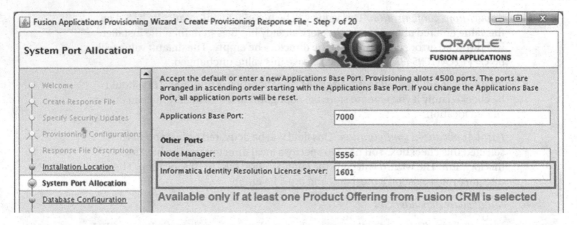

Figure 9-11. *System Port Allocation screen*

The screen requires you to input or verify the following ports. The default values are already populated. So if you do not have anything else running on the selected server or if you do not plan to use non-default ports, you can leave them unchanged. If you are provisioning for production or if your organization has non-default ports policy then you may change the value of the Applications base port.

As the screen suggests, the Fusion Applications provisioning internally allocates 4500 ports, and the ports are arranged in ascending order starting from the Applications base port. If you change the value of Applications base port from 7000 to 7000 + n then all subsequent Applications ports will change to <port number or range> + n as well. This does not apply to the node manager and IIR ports, which you can change independently. The default node manager port is 5556. This can be left unchanged unless you have another service running on the same port since the Node Manager port is not exposed to the users. Here is the list of ports requested on this page.

1. *Applications base port*: The default value is 7000. This is the starting port of the overall range of ports allocated for the Fusion Applications services. For example, if you have left this value to its default of 7000 then the CommonDomain Administration server port will be 7001 and the other ports will be set accordingly.

Other Ports

2. *Node manager*: The default value is 5556. The Node Manager is responsible for monitoring and controlling the status of the managed servers for every product domain hosted on the respective servers. Although the managed servers can be controlled independently of the Node Manager, for Fusion Applications provisioning, the node manager must always be running once it is configured in order to complete the provisioning phases.

3. *Informatica Identity Resolution license server*: The default value is 1601. This field will be available only if you have selected the Oracle Fusion CRM product offerings like sales, marketing, and so on. This specifies the port where the IIR License Server will be running.

Review the ports and click Next to continue to the Database Configuration screen, as shown in Figure 9-12.

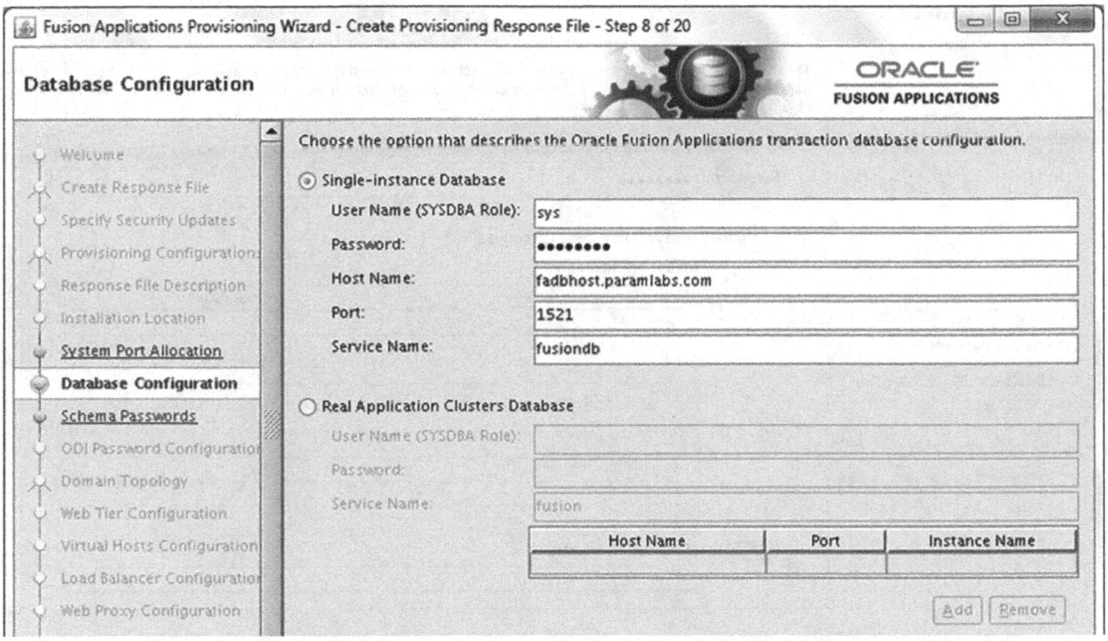

Figure 9-12. *Fusion Applications Transaction Database Configuration screen*

The Database Configuration screen requires you to enter the following connection details of Fusion Applications Transaction Database including the SYSDBA privileged user (preferably SYS) credentials, single node or RAC hostname, service name/SID, and any port details. Once these details are entered, click Next to proceed to the Schema Passwords screen, as shown in Figure 9-13. The wizard will verify the connectivity to the database now and throw a warning if it cannot reach the database with the settings you entered. You can fix the issues and if you are sure that the values are correct but database is not running then you can opt to ignore the warning.

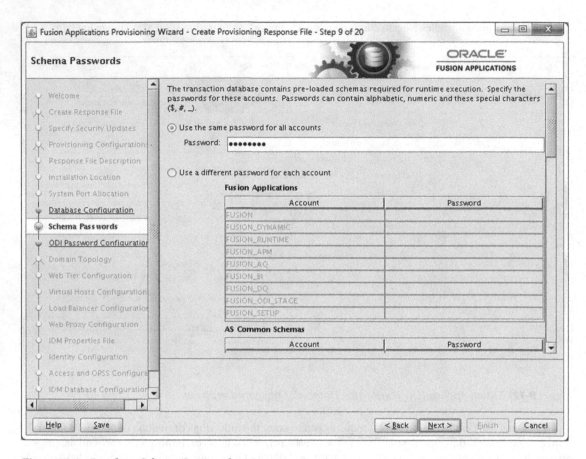

Figure 9-13. *Database Schema Passwords screen*

■ **Tip** If you are unsure of some detail and want to resume the response file creation later, don't cancel the wizard. Instead use the Save button to save the partial response file. This file must be completed before it can be used to provision an Applications environment.

The Database Schema Passwords screen requires you to select from two options. The selection is based on whether you specified the same or a different password for all schemas while running RCU for the Applications transaction database. You can refer to Figure 8-26 in Chapter 8 for more information.

- *Use the same password for all accounts*: This is default option. If you selected the same password during RCU then select this option. You will be required to enter the single password for all schemas. This password must match the RCU password.

- *Use a different password for each account*: If you selected different passwords for each schema while running RCU then you must enter each password individually here. There are two sections under this option. The first is for the Applications schemas and the second section is for middleware-related schemas (AS Common Schemas, SES, WebCenter, SOA, BI, and so on).

The wizard will validate the passwords and show a warning if it cannot validate. You can choose to ignore the warning if the database is not yet running. Click Next to proceed to ODI Password Configuration, as shown in Figure 9-14.

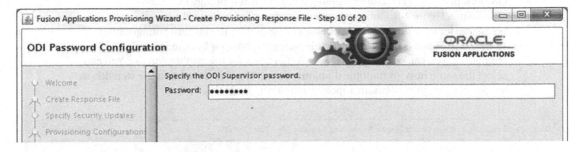

Figure 9-14. *ODI Password Configuration screen*

This screen requires you to enter an ODI supervisor password. Enter the same password that you selected for the supervisor password on the Custom Variables screen of RCU under the Master and Work Repository section. You can refer to Figure 8-27 in Chapter 8 for the Custom Variables screen. The wizard will validate this password as well. Once the password is entered, click Next to Proceed.

On the Topology Selection screen, you are required to select one of the three possible topology options, as shown in Figure 9-15. Of course at this point you already have your topology finalized so you can fill in these details. So far we have not yet started Fusion Applications provisioning, so you can increase the number of application nodes at this point. All you will need to do is to install Fusion Applications provisioning framework on other nodes.

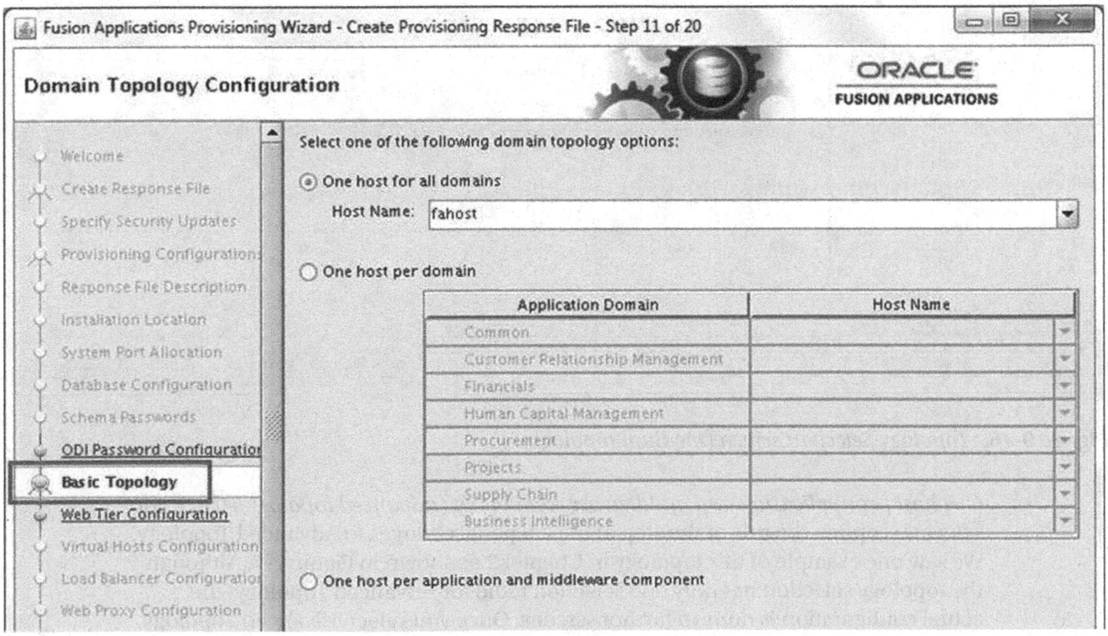

Figure 9-15. *Topology Selection screen (basic topology)*

- *One host for all domains (basic topology)*: This is the default topology and also the selected topology for this example. In this case, all the Product WebLogic domains will be configured on same application host.

- *One host per domain (medium topology)*: We saw this topology in Chapter 2 as shown in Figure 2-8. Once you select this option you will be able to select a hostname for each of the domains being configured for the current configuration, as shown in Figure 9-16. In this example, since you have eight domains being configured, you can select up to eight different hosts for the application tier. You can select the same host for multiple domains as well. You will notice that the step title in left panel changes to Medium Topology when you select this option.

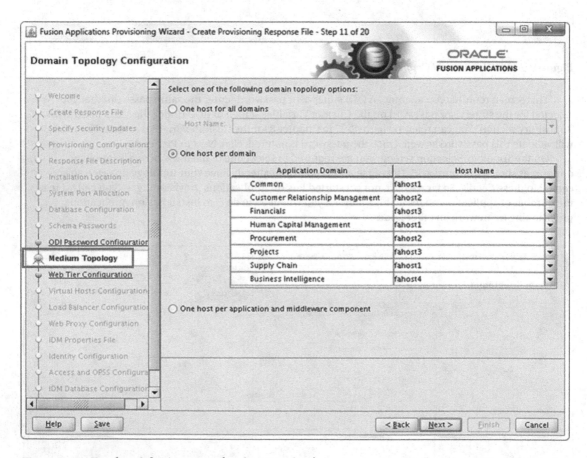

Figure 9-16. Topology Selection screen (medium topology)

- *One host per application and middleware component (advanced topology)*: Once you select this option the title of the step in the left panel changes to Advanced Topology. We saw one example of this topology in Chapter 2 as shown in Figure 2-7. Although the topology selection has only one selection radio for Advanced Topology, the actual configuration is done in further screens. Once you select Advanced Topology and click Next, the number of steps in the left panel increase from 20 to 20 + *n* where *n* is the number of WebLogic domains to be created for the selected configuration, as shown in Figure 9-17.

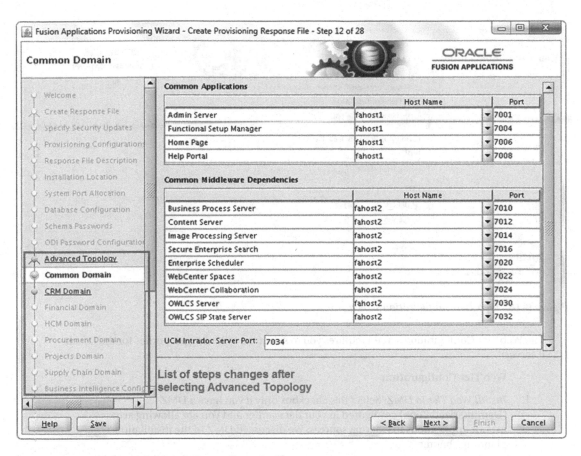

Figure 9-17. Topology selection (advanced topology)

■ **Tip** Note that once you select Advanced Topology and click Next, you cannot change the topology later. The topology selection screen fields will become grayed out.

The Advanced Topology selection brings more screens in the wizard depending on the number of WebLogic domains being created. Figure 9-17 shows the example of CommonDomain where we need to select the host for the admin server and the managed servers. As you can see the list of ports is in ascending order depending on the Application base port selected earlier. Similarly you will see screens for all the product domains.

In this example, we have selected the basic topology with a single host called fahost for all domains, as shown in Figure 9-15. Click Next to continue to the Web Tier Configuration screen, as shown in Figure 9-18.

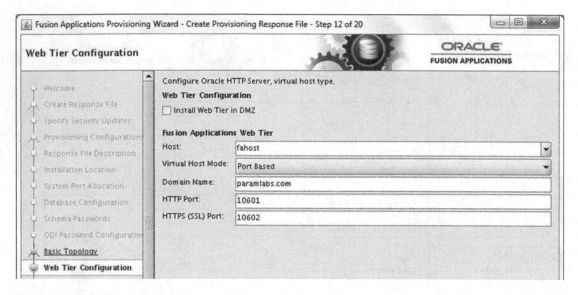

Figure 9-18. *Web Tier Configuration screen*

The Web Tier Configuration screen requires you to select the following properties for the Oracle HTTP server:

Web Tier Configuration

1. *Install Web Tier in DMZ*: Select this checkbox only if you have a DMZ (Demilitarized Zone) configured in your data center and you are allowing access to your applications to external sources. We discussed DMZ in the installation planning chapter.

Fusion Applications Web Tier

2. *Host*: Enter the name of the web tier host in your selected topology. Note that if you have selected DMZ then you must select a different hostname than any of the application tier hosts specified in the previous screens. In this case, we have selected two-tier topology so our web tier is hosted on the same server, called fahost.

3. *Virtual Host Mode*: We have to select from one of these three virtual host mode options.

   • *IP Based*: This is the default option. In this case, the product domain related URLs will be in selected Virtual IP:Port format. We will see this in the next screens.

   • *Name Based*: With this option we can map the product domain related URLs with distinct internal and external virtual names. This is more suitable for a production setup since from the URL we can distinguish the related product functionality.

   • *Port Based*: Use this option when you are not using a virtual hostname and want to distinguish the URLs as dedicated ports for each of the product families. In this case the HTTP server will be set up with aliases where each product-related port will be redirected to related product managed servers. In this example we have selected single host, so we'll use this option.

4. *Domain Name*: Specify the default domain name of your infrastructure. This domain name will receive the Fusion Applications related requests. You will see the same domain name populated automatically in subsequent screens, where any name-based references are used.

5. *HTTP Port*: Depending on the topology selected in the previous screen, the value of default HTTP port will be automatically populated.

6. *HTTPS (SSL) Port*: Depending on the topology selected in previous screen, the value of default HTTPS port will also be automatically populated.

7. *SMTP Server*: SMPT Server related options will be displayed only if you have selected Oracle CRM Configuration as outbound emails are required for email marketing products. Specify the Outgoing Mail Server (SMTP) hostname or IP address. Make sure that the SMTP hostname resolves from DNS or a local hosts file. You also need to specify the outgoing mail server port. The default value for this port is 25.

The next screen will vary depending on the virtual host mode selected in this screen. We will look at the next screen with these virtual host mode selections.

Figure 9-19 shows the Virtual Hosts Configuration screen for port-based virtual host mode. As you can see for each product domain, you can select internal and external ports. For example, the internal URLs related to CommonDomain start with http://fahost.paramlabs.com:10633 and the external URLs will be https://fahost.paramlabs.com:10634. Although you can change the values of these ports, it is advisable to change them through the Applications base port only to avoid any port conflict or overlap. The Virtual Hosts Configuration screen will look as shown in Figure 9-20 if you select name-based virtual host mode for the web tier.

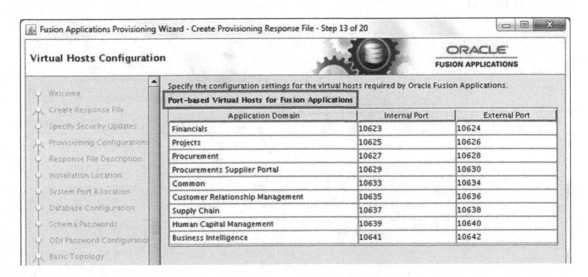

Figure 9-19. *Virtual Hosts Configuration screen (port-based virtual host mode)*

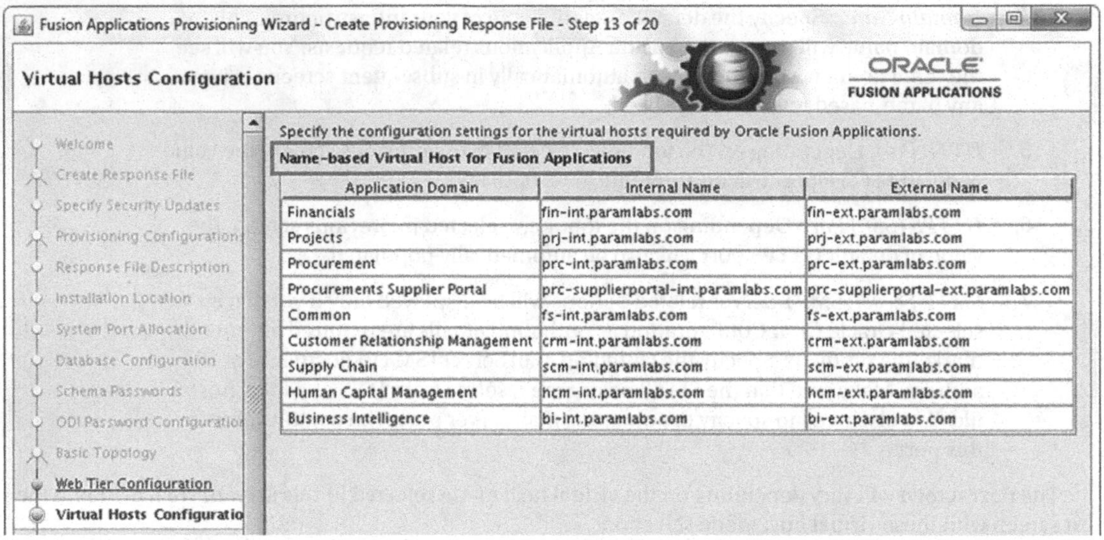

Figure 9-20. *Virtual Hosts Configuration screen (name-based virtual host mode)*

Here you will not specify any ports but virtual hostnames for each product family. You can specify different virtual hostnames for internal and external URLs. The prerequisite for this is to have each of these names registered in your organization DNS server so that the URLs will resolve from servers as well the user's network. Now we will see the same screen with IP-based virtual host mode selected for web tier, as shown in Figure 9-21.

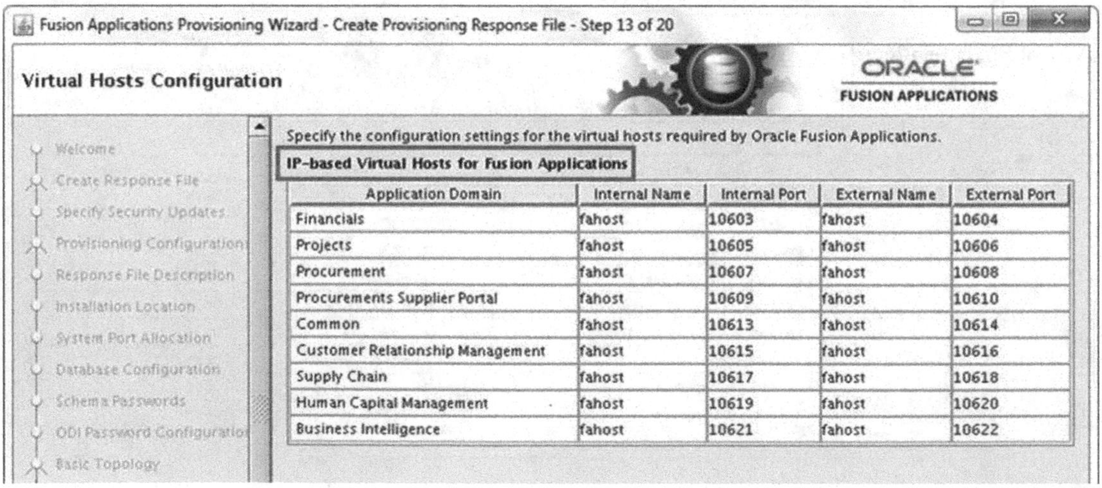

Figure 9-21. *Virtual Hosts Configuration screen (IP based virtual host mode)*

Although the screen initially displays the same hostname as web tier host for all internal and external ports, you can change these internal and external virtual names individually. Here also if you are using a virtual name other than the hostname, you must make sure that these names are registered in the DNS mapped to the server's IP address. You can also specify one virtual name for all internal applications and one virtual name for external URLs. Make sure to document these ports since you may need to configure the network firewall accordingly if you are not planning to use the load balancer in your environment. If you do not change the virtual hostnames for the Application domains, the configuration remains similar to the port-based virtual host mode. However, note that the range of ports is different for IP-based and port-based virtual hosts configuration.

Review and modify the Virtual Hosts Configuration screen and click Next to proceed to the Load Balancer Configuration screen, as shown in Figure 9-22.

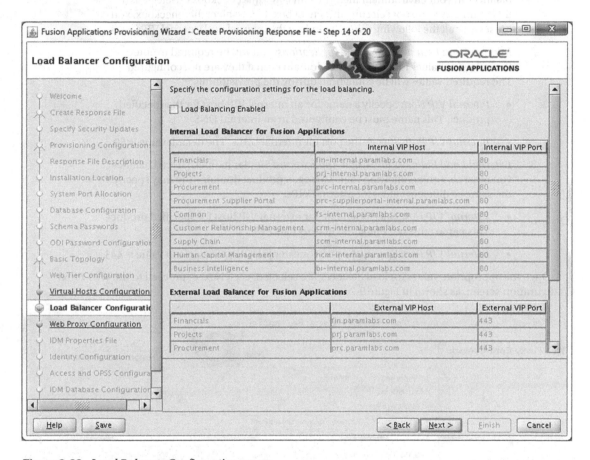

Figure 9-22. Load Balancer Configuration screen

The Load Balancer Configuration screen allows you to select internal and external load balancer virtual hostnames and port details for your Fusion Applications environment.

Although the role of the load balancer is to provide a single point of entry for an environment with multiple hosts for same service, you can also use the load balancer for non-high available environments. Having a load balancer VIP and port simplifies the firewall configuration by reducing the number of ports required to be opened from the user network to Fusion Applications infrastructure. This also allows you to use simple to remember virtual hostnames.

Although you may use common hardware network load balancers in your organization, you may need to allocate different NLB (Network Load Balancer) IP addresses to resolve each internal and external VIP host. The load balancer should be configured to forward the traffic to internal servers on domain-specific ports. You will need to work closely with your network security team in order to configure this seamlessly.

Modern Network Firewalls like F5 BIG-IP and a few other appliances that provide load balancing features for multiple URLs on single source IP as well. These appliances can forward the traffic to servers based on incoming URL requests using preconfigured rules.

The load balancer configurations screen requires the following details to be entered.

1. *Load Balancing Enabled*: All the remaining options on the screen remain grayed out until this checkbox is selected. If you are not planning to use network load balancer in your environment then you can leave this checkbox unselected. In this example we are not selecting this checkbox. If you select this checkbox, you must enter all the following values including the internal and external VIPs.

2. *Internal Load Balancer for Fusion Applications*: You will be required to enter the following values for each product domain even if they are not configured. The required values will be configured during the provisioning.

   • *Internal VIP Host*: Specify a name for an internal VIP host for the specified product. This name must be configured in an internal DNS.

   • *Internal VIP Port*: Specify the port for internal URLs. The default value is 80.

3. *External Load Balancer for Fusion Applications*: Similar to internal load balancer, you must also enter following values for each product domain. You may specify the same or different values for external VIPs.

   • *External VIP Host*: Specify a name for external VIP host for specified product. This name must be configured in external DNS.

   • *External VIP Port*: Specify the port for external URLs. The default value is 443.

Once the appropriate values for load balancer are selected, click Next to proceed to the Web Proxy Configuration screen, as shown in Figure 9-23.

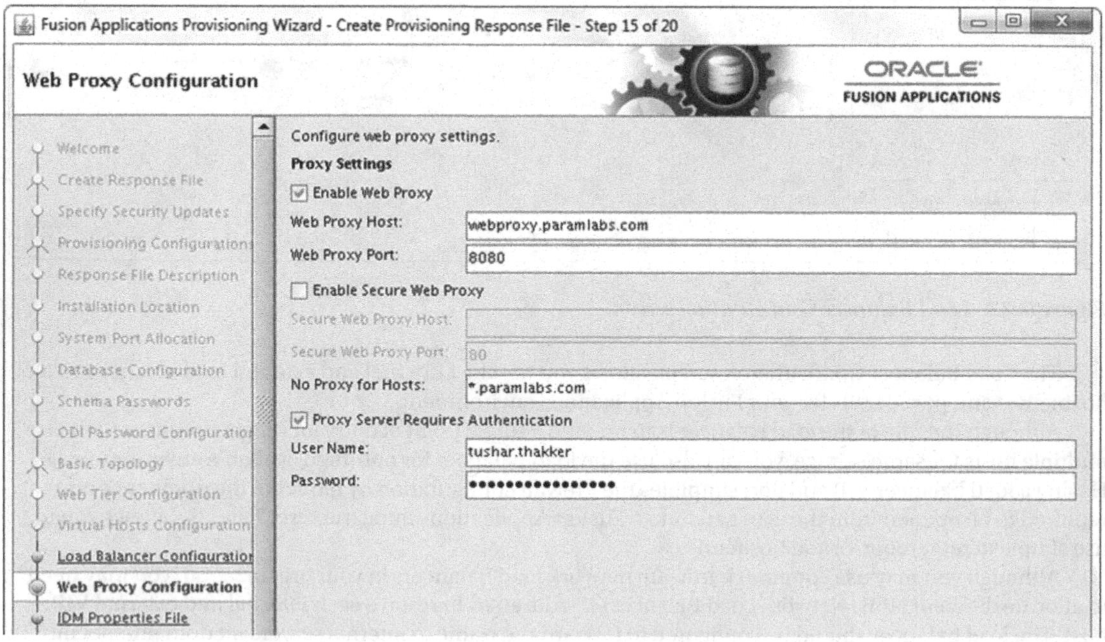

Figure 9-23. *Web Proxy Configuration screen*

The Web Proxy Configuration is an optional selection. This should be enabled only if you have any integration with external applications outside your organization through the Internet. Since servers in data centers generally do not have direct Internet access, you must route the Internet traffic through your corporate web proxy. Figure 9-23 shows an example web proxy configuration for Fusion Applications environment. Let's look at the possible configurations on this screen.

1. *Enable Web Proxy*: If you do not want to enable Internet access from the hosts then you can just leave this checkbox unselected and the rest of the screen will remain grayed out. Once you select this checkbox, the following fields will be enabled.

    a. *Web Proxy Host*: Enter the name of your corporate web proxy server.

    b. *Web Proxy Port*: Enter the port on which the proxy server is configured. You must make sure that the firewall rule for allowing the access to the required proxy server ports from the Fusion Applications nodes is configured and enabled.

2. *Enable Secure Web Proxy*: This checkbox is enabled only if the Web Proxy checkbox is already selected. It is advisable to use Secure Web Proxy to SSL enable the Internet traffic. Once you select the Secure Web Proxy checkbox, the following fields also become active and mandatory.

    a. *Secure Web Proxy Host*: Enter the name of SSL host to provide secure proxy.

    b. *Secure Web Proxy Port*: Enter the configured SSL port for secure proxy.

    c. *No Proxy for Hosts*: This option will allow you to skip web proxy for any hosts included in this list separated by vertical bar (|). By default, all hosts in the same domain are excluded from the proxy.

3. *Proxy Server Requires Authentication*: Most proxy servers require authentication with a domain username and password. If your organization proxy server requires authentication then select this checkbox and provide the following value.

    a. *User Name*: Enter the username of the person allowed to access the proxy server.

    b. *Password*: Enter the password for this username.

Enter the appropriate values and click Next to proceed to another important screen of loading the IDM properties file, as shown in Figure 9-24.

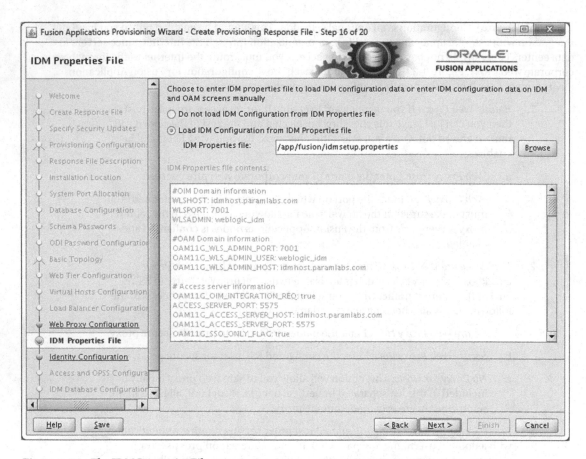

Figure 9-24. *The IDM Properties File screen*

The IDM Properties File screen was introduced in Fusion Applications 11g, Release 5 (11.1.5). Until this release, we were required to enter all parameters related to the Oracle Identity and Access Management manually in the subsequent screens. Due to a large number of parameters required for Identity Management, the process was prone to errors. Oracle had greatly reduced the chances of error in Identity Management related details by introducing the idmsetup.properties file, which contains most of the variables and values required in the subsequent screens.

Now let's refer back to the Identity Management provisioning and you may notice that at the end of Identity Management provisioning the wizard created an IDM properties file named idmsetup.properties under the Identity Management shared configuration directory. The location of the file on Identity Management node is <IDM_CONFIG_DIR>/fa/idmsetup.properties. This file includes all the required details of the Identity Management installation, which can be directly used for populating the required values in the next two screens. If you do not have this file, you can still choose to enter the required values manually in the next screens.

Before we can select the file in the wizard, we must copy the idmsetup.properties file from the IDM node to any desired location on the current node.

```
[fusion@fahost bin]$ cd /app/fusion/
[fusion@fahost fusion]$ scp fusion@idmhost:/app/oracle/config/fa/idmsetup.properties.
```

Now the file should be available at /app/fusion/idmsetup.properties on the primordial host as well. Select Load IDM Configuration from IDM Properties File. You can enter the path manually in the textbox for IDM Properties file or browse for this file as shown in Figure 9-24. If you want to enter the values in subsequent screens, then select the Do Not Load IDM Configuration from IDM Properties File option.

Once you have entered the IDM properties filename, press the Tab key to populate the contents of the idmsetup.properties file in the text area titled IDM Properties File Contents. This textbox is read-only and cannot be modified.

Click Next once the appropriate values are selected. Regardless of whether you have selected the IDM properties file, you will see the warning prompt shown in Figure 9-25 informing you that once you confirm you cannot change the choices in this screen.

Figure 9-25. *Confirmation prompt for loading the IDM properties*

Click Continue to proceed to the Identity Configuration screen, as shown in Figure 9-26.

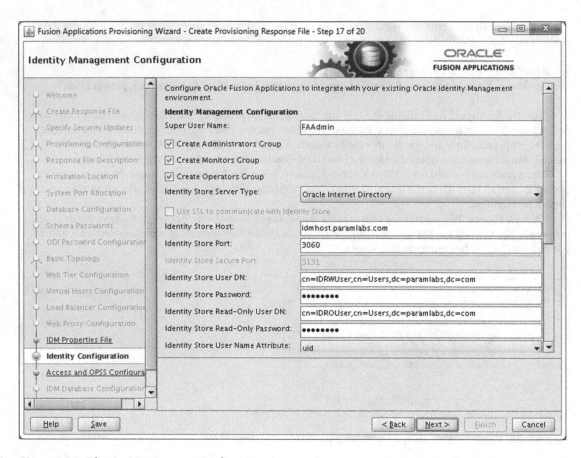

Figure 9-26. *Identity Management Configuration screen*

■ **Tip** Despite entering the values in the screen, as shown in Figure 9-24, sometimes you may see a red error symbol in the left panel against the current step. You may safely ignore it at this point since this is a known issue with this wizard. Due to this warning prompt, it displays an error symbol and does not clear it despite confirming the message box.

If you are creating a provisioning response file for Fusion Applications versions earlier than 11.1.5 or if you have selected *Do Not Load IDM Configuration from IDM Properties File,* then you may need to manually enter all the values in this screen. In all other cases, you will see most of the values already populated in this screen. Let's have a look at the details required to be entered in this screen. Be very careful to verify details in this as well as the next screens since these values determine the integration of Fusion Applications with Identity Management.

Identity Management Configuration

1. *Super User Name*: Specify the name of the Fusion Applications super user who will be created and granted administrator and functional setup privileges. In earlier versions of Fusion Applications, we were required to enter any desired super user name here and the default value was `weblogic_fa`. From recent versions of Fusion Applications the wizard provides the `FAAdmin` as the default name. You can specify any existing user as well, which can be granted these privileges. We will leave this as `FAAdmin`.

2. *Create Administrators Group*: Specify whether you want to create an administrators group in OID. Members of this group have special administrative privileges on all middleware components. If you already created this group in OID then you can deselect this checkbox. Otherwise, it must be selected.

3. *Create Monitors Group*: Specify whether you want to create a monitors group in OID. Members of this group have read-only access to the Oracle WebLogic server console for all domains. If you have already created this group in OID then you can deselect this checkbox. Otherwise, it must be selected.

4. *Create Operators Group*: Specify whether you want to create an operators group in OID. Members of this group can view the WebLogic server configuration except encrypted attributes. These users can also start/stop/resume the WebLogic server but cannot alter any configuration. If you have already created this group in OID then you can deselect this checkbox. Otherwise, this must be selected.

5. *Identity Store Server Type*: OID and OVD both are supported as the identity store server. Select `Oracle Identity Directory` or `Oracle Virtual Directory` here. The default value is already populated if you have selected the `idmsetup.properties` file in an earlier screen.

6. *Use SSL to communicate with the Identity Store*: This field is grayed out since currently it is not supported and is a placeholder for future releases only.

7. *Identity Store Host*: The value is already populated based on your Identity Management configuration file. If you have not specified the Identity Management properties file earlier then enter the identity store hostname here. For example, `idmhost.paramlabs.com`. Leave this value unchanged.

8. *Identity Store Port*: The Identity Store Port value is already populated in this example. The default value is 3060. Leave this unchanged.

9. *Identity Store Secure Port*: Although Identity Store Secure Port value is already selected, it is currently not supported for the Fusion Applications environment. This field remains grayed out.

10. *Identity Store User DN*: The Distinguished Name (DN) of the user with read/write access to the identity store is already selected based on the Identity Management environment properties file. For example, `cn=IDRWUser,cn=Users,dc=paramlabs,dc=com`.

11. *Identity Store Password*: All password fields in this screen are blank since `idmsetup.properties` file is a plain-text file. The passwords are not stored in that for security reasons. Enter the password for the user in this field.

12. *Identity Store Read-Only User DN*: The Distinguished Name (DN) of the user with read-only access to the identity store is already selected based on our Identity Management environment properties file. For example, cn=IDROUser,cn=Users, dc=paramlabs,dc=com.

13. *Identity Store Read-Only Password*: This field is also blank and the password for the user must be entered here. Since we do not have confirm password fields here, be careful to enter the password correctly.

14. *Identity Store User Name Attribute*: The choice of values in this field are uid (user ID) or cn (Common Name). The populated value is uid based on your configuration. Leave this unchanged since it must match your environment.

Figure 9-27 shows the bottom section in continuation of the same screen.

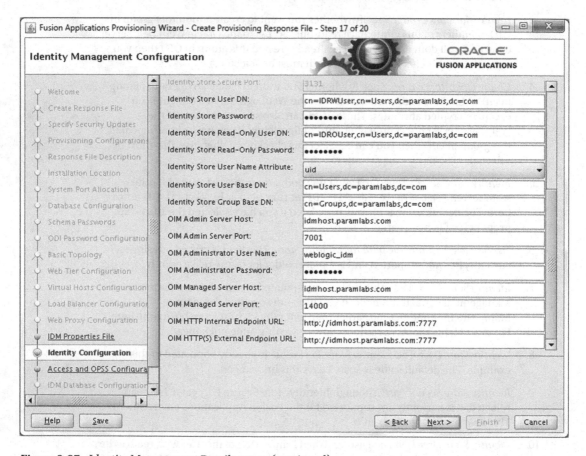

Figure 9-27. *Identity Management Details screen (continued)*

Enter the following values in this section of the Identity Configuration screen.

15. *Identity Store User Base DN*: Mention the Distinguished Name (DN), which will serve as a root node for loading all application users data. Leave it unchanged if the default value is already selected based on our environment. For example, cn=Users,dc=paramlabs,dc=com.

16. *Identity Store Group Base DN*: Mention the Distinguished Name (DN) which will serve as root node for loading all group data. Leave it unchanged if default value is already selected based on our environment. For example, `cn=Groups,dc=para mlabs,dc=com`.

17. *OIM Admin Server Host*: Enter the value of the Identity Management domain administration server host. For example, `idmhost.paramlabs.com`. Leave it unchanged if it's already populated.

18. *OIM Admin Server Port*: Enter the Identity Management Administration Server port value here. The default value 7001 should be filled here if the Identity Management properties file was selected.

19. *OIM Administrator User Name*: Enter the name of the Identity Management WebLogic administrator user here. If you used the Identity Management provisioning framework earlier, the default value of Administration username would be `weblogic_idm` and already populated here. Do not confuse this with the OIM privileged user `xelsysadm` since this field requires the domain administrator username `weblogic_idm` here.

20. *OIM Administrator Password*: As mentioned earlier, all password fields are not filled automatically and no confirm password fields are available. Type the password for the OIM administration user.

21. *OIM Managed Server Host*: Depending on the topology selected, the value of OIM managed server host could be same as OIM admin server host or different. This value is already populated based on your IDM properties file. In our case since we used single host for all Identity Management middleware components, the default value is `idmhost.paramlabs.com`.

22. *OIM Managed Server Port*: The default value for OIM Managed server Port is 14000 if you have used IDM Provisioning Framework for Identity Management installation. Although the OIM related URLs show common HTTP Port but internally it redirects to 14000 port only. So you must enter the port where OIM Server is listening. Leave this unchanged if already populated.

23. *OIM HTTP Internal Endpoint URL*: This URL is used for all communication between Oracle Fusion Applications and the Oracle Identity Manager. This value should be based on internal access point of Identity Management HTTP server. By default this value is in `http://<IMD Web Host>:<web port>` format. The hostname and port values should be either of the web host or the load balancer if you have configured one. For example `http://idmhost.paramlabs.com:7777`

24. *OIM HTTP(S) External Endpoint URL*: Enter the secure URL for Oracle Identity Management HTTP server. This is generally used to access Identity Management from browser or external sources. By default the value should be HTTPS format but if you have not set up the HTTPS endpoint then you can enter HTTP value as well. Note that the communication will remain non-secure. If you have configured an external HTTPS load balancer URL then you must enter it here. In this example, we have not used an external HTTPS URL so we have entered the same as above for demo purposes.

■ **Tip** In general if you have loaded the IDM properties file in the previous step, you need to only select the three checkboxes for creating the administrators, monitors, and operators groups and enter all the required passwords. The rest of the values should be left unchanged in most cases.

Note that the wizard will verify the URLs and port accessibility and if any of these are not reachable then it will display warning message on the screen as well as the bottom panel. You can either choose to fix the errors and if you believe the information entered is correct but the Identity Management environment is not running at the moment then you can skip the warning as well. Note that you must make sure that all Identity Management components as well as Fusion Applications transaction database are running before proceeding to the actual provisioning process.

Once the required values are entered and verified, click Next to proceed to the Oracle Access Manager Configuration, as shown in Figure 9-28.

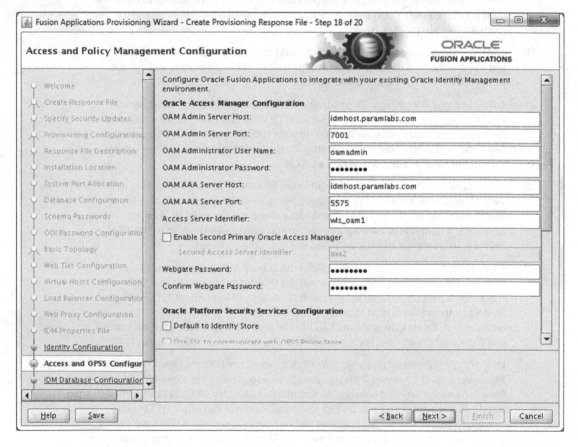

Figure 9-28. *Access Manager and Platform Security Services Configuration*

Similar to the Identity Configuration screen, in Access Manager and OPSS Configuration screen, the values are already populated if you have loaded the IDM properties earlier. If you are creating a provisioning response file for Fusion Applications versions earlier than 11.1.5, you may also need to manually enter all the values in this screen. The following are the list of values to be entered in this screen.

Oracle Access Manager Configuration Parameters

1. *OAM Admin Server Host*: Enter the name of the host where the Administration Server for Oracle Access Manager is configured. Regardless of the topology selected, the admin server host for OIM and OAM will be the same. This value could be either the physical hostname or VIP name. In this case since we have loaded the IDM Properties file, the value is already populated. For example, idmhost.paramlabs.com.

2. *OAM Admin Server Port*: Enter the value of the OAM administration server port. This value will generally be same as the value entered earlier for OIM Admin Server Port. In this example the value has been pre-filled with 7001.

3. *OAM Administrator User Name*: This filed can be confusing since we entered domain administrator username for OIM administrator user while for OAM administrator user we need to enter the name of the user which has been granted OAM Administrator privileges while provisioning Identity Management. If you have used Identity Management provisioning framework then this value defaults to oamadmin. In this case the value has already been populated, so leave it unchanged.

4. *OAM Administrator Password*: Enter the password that you selected for the oamadmin user.

5. *OAM AAA Server Host*: Enter the hostname of the OAM proxy server which is configured with the OAM managed server. This is generally the name of the host where the OAM component has been installed and configured based on the topology selected. Since in this example we have used single host for all Identity Management components, the value remains the same—idmhost.paramlabs.com.

6. *OAM AAA Server Port*: Enter the value of OAM proxy server port used for communication with WebGate. If you have provisioned Identity Management using IDM framework then this value defaults to 5575. Note that this value is not same as the port that OAM Managed Server listens to (14100) so you must leave this value unchanged if it is already populated.

7. *Access Server Identifier*: Enter the name of Oracle Access Server Managed Server which is also called Access Server ID. For Identity Management environment created using Identity Management Provisioning Framework this value defaults to wls_oam1.

8. *Enable Second Primary Oracle Access Manager*: If you have configured second primary instance of OAM then you should select this checkbox. Once this checkbox is selected, the next text field for Second Access Server Identifier becomes active and mandatory.

   - *Second Access Server Identifier*: Enter the second Access Server ID here. Since in our case second Primary OAM Server is not configured, the checkbox is deselected and this field remains grayed out.

9. *WebGate Password*: The WebGate password must be entered since this field is empty by default. Specify a complex password for WebGate resource.

10. *Confirm WebGate Password*: Retype the password.

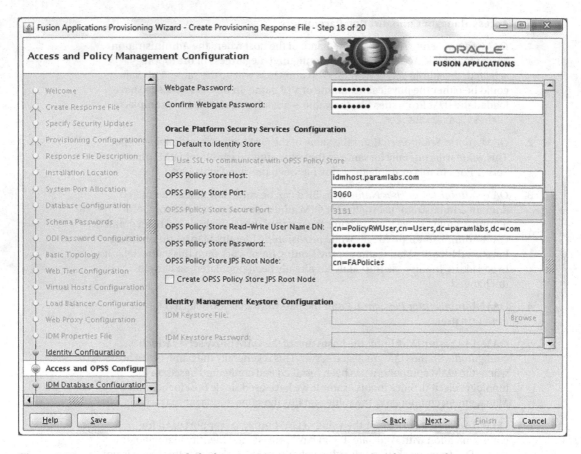

Figure 9-29. *Access manager and platform security services configuration (continued)*

Figure 9-29 shows the bottom section of the same screen.

Enter the following values related to the Oracle Platform Security Services and Identity Management Keystore Configuration sections. If you have loaded the IDM properties file earlier, then in most cases you only need to enter the required passwords without changing other values.

Oracle Platform Security Services Configuration Parameters

11. *Default to identity store*: If you want your policy store to be same as your identity store then you can select this checkbox Note that at the moment the only supported directory for policy store is OID so if you have selected Oracle virtual directory for your identity store earlier then you must not select this checkbox and provide OID details for the policy store. When you select this checkbox, three fields will be automatically populated based on the values selected for identity store, namely OPSS Policy Store Host, OPSS Policy Store Port, and OPSS Policy Store Secure Port (currently disabled). In our case we can select this checkbox but the required values have been populated already based on IDM property file. So we will leave this untouched.

12. *Use SSL to communicate with OPSS Policy Store*: This option is not yet supported in the current release so it remains grayed out. This is a placeholder for future releases.

13. *OPSS Policy Store Host*: If you have selected the previous checkbox or loaded IDM properties file earlier then this and related port values will be filled automatically. If you are having ID Store in OVD and policy store in OID then be sure to enter the appropriate hostname. The value based on the selected topology is the same as the ID store host. For example, `idmhost.paramlabs.com`.

14. *OPSS Policy Store Port*: The default value for this field is 3060, which is same as the ID store port. Or else enter the policy store port or load balancer port value.

15. *OPSS Policy Store Secure Port:* Although this parameter is not yet supported as of the current release, the secure port value is automatically loaded from the IDM properties file.

16. *OPSS Policy Store Read-Write User Name DN*: Even if you have selected the same OID for identity store and policy store, you must enter different value for Oracle Platform Security Services Policy Store. Enter the Distinguished Name (DN) for the user to have read/write access to the OPSS policy store. If you have used IDM provisioning framework then the value defaults to your domain specific value similar to `cn=PolicyRWUSer,dc=paramlabs,dc=com`. Leave this value unchanged.

17. *OPSS Policy Store Password*: Enter the password selected for the OPSS policy store user mentioned above.

18. *OPSS Policy Store JPS root Node*: In older releases JPS root node for Fusion Applications (POLICYSTORE_CONTAINER) was created as `cn=jsproot` while from Fusion Applications 11g, Release 7 onward the value is created as `cn=FAPolicies`. Leave this unchanged if it's already populated based on your IDM properties file.

19. *Create OPSS Policy Store JPS root node*: For some releases the IDM provisioning framework creates the OPSS Policy Store JPS root node. So check if the above already exists in OID then you must deselect this checkbox. Note that depending on the release you are provisioning, this might not already exist. Confirm the existence of JPS root node before selecting or deselecting this checkbox; otherwise, you may receive an error during provisioning suggesting that the JPS root node already exists.

Identity Management Keystore Configuration Parameters

The fields in this section are enabled only if you have enabled SSL for identity store, policy store, or OIM endpoint. In other cases the complete section remains grayed out.

20. *IDM Keystore File*: The location of Java keystore file for IDM, which contains the certificate files for Identity Management components. If you have selected SSL then the value will be automatically filled based on the IDM properties file.

21. *IDM Keystore Password*: You must enter the same password that you have configured for IDM keystore file.

Verify the details on the screen even if they are automatically populated from the properties file, enter the passwords, and click Next to proceed to IDM Database Configuration screen, as shown in Figure 9-30.

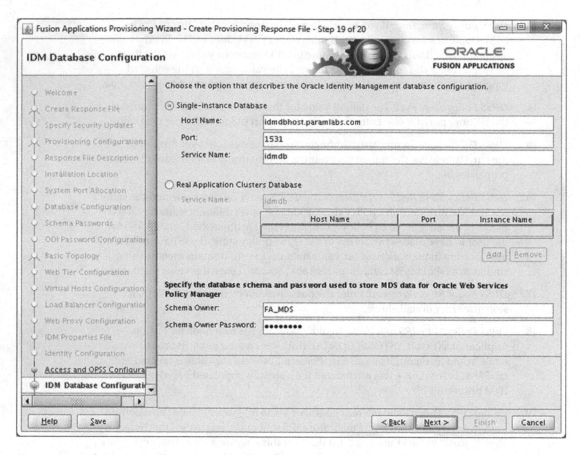

Figure 9-30. Identity Management Database Details screen

In the IDM Database Configuration screen as shown in Figure 9-30, you are required to enter the Identity Management database connection details, including single node or RAC hostname, port, and the service name of the Identity Management database (idmdb in this example).

You also need to specify credentials for MDS data schema in this screen. We had already created MDS data schema for Oracle Web Services Policy Manager during Identity Management RCU. Provide the same details as you provided during RCU in the following fields. Once the database details are entered, click Next to proceed to the Summary screen, as shown in Figure 9-31.

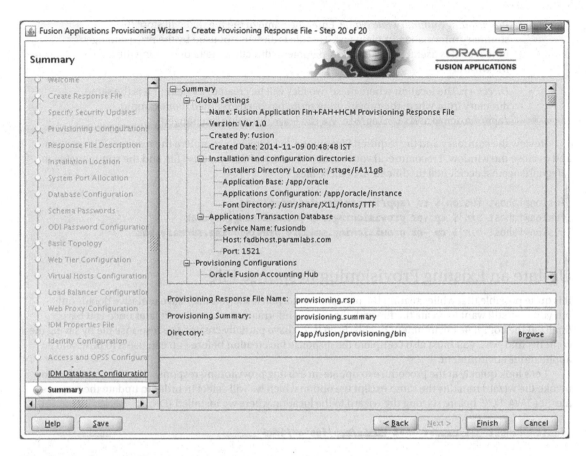

Figure 9-31. *Response file creation summary*

The main summary section shows all the details you entered throughout all screens in plain text format. Although the actual provisioning response file contains a parameter-value format instead of the text, the summary text gives a clear view of the values selected so far.

The summary screen has the following sections. I strongly recommend you go through the summary as you can easily notice any incorrect information in this consolidated view.

- *Summary*: The Fusion Applications Response File creation summary includes a plain text summary of all parameters entered in previous screen. This is a large scrollable read-only text area.

- *Provisioning Response File Name*: Enter the name of the response file to be created. Note that this is the physical filename and should not be confused with the response file name provided in Figure 9-8. The default value is provisioning.rsp. You can change the name of this file if you are creating and storing multiple response files in same location.

- *Provisioning Summary File Name*: Enter the name of the file that will store the summary information in plain text. This file is directly not used by the provisioning process but is useful for reading any parameter directly instead of running through the wizard.

- *Directory*: The location where these two files will be created. By default it is the same directory from where the provisioning script has been executed. For example, /app/fusion/provisioning/bin. We can leave this value unchanged.

Review the summary and the required filenames. Click Finish to complete the response file creation and to close the window. I recommend you to make a backup of the response file and the summary file to safeguard against accidental modification of these files.

```
[fusion@fahost fusion]$ cd /app/fusion/provisioning/bin/
[fusion@fahost bin]$ cp -pr provisioning.rsp provisioning.rsp.bak
[fusion@fahost bin]$ cp -pr provisioning.summary provisioning.summary.bak
```

Update an Existing Provisioning Response File

It is quite possible that while creating the provisioning response file you may have tentative details only but you may still want to create the file with the current information and update it later once you have finalized the complete environment details. Even if you have partially created the response file by saving the contents mid-way, you must also complete the response file creation before you can use it to provision an applications environment.

Let's look quickly at the procedure to update an existing provisioning response file. The command to invoke the wizard remains the same except the option which we will select in order to update the response file. Set JAVA_HOME before starting the wizard to the location where we installed JDK.

```
[fusion@fahost ~]$ export JAVA_HOME=/app/fusion/jdk6
```

Let's launch the Provisioning wizard now from <framework_location/provisioning/bin as follows. After the Welcome screen, the next screen will provide same six provisioning options as shown in Figure 9-32.

```
[fusion@fahost ~]$ cd /app/fusion/provisioning/bin
[fusion@fahost bin]$ ./provisioningWizard.sh &
```

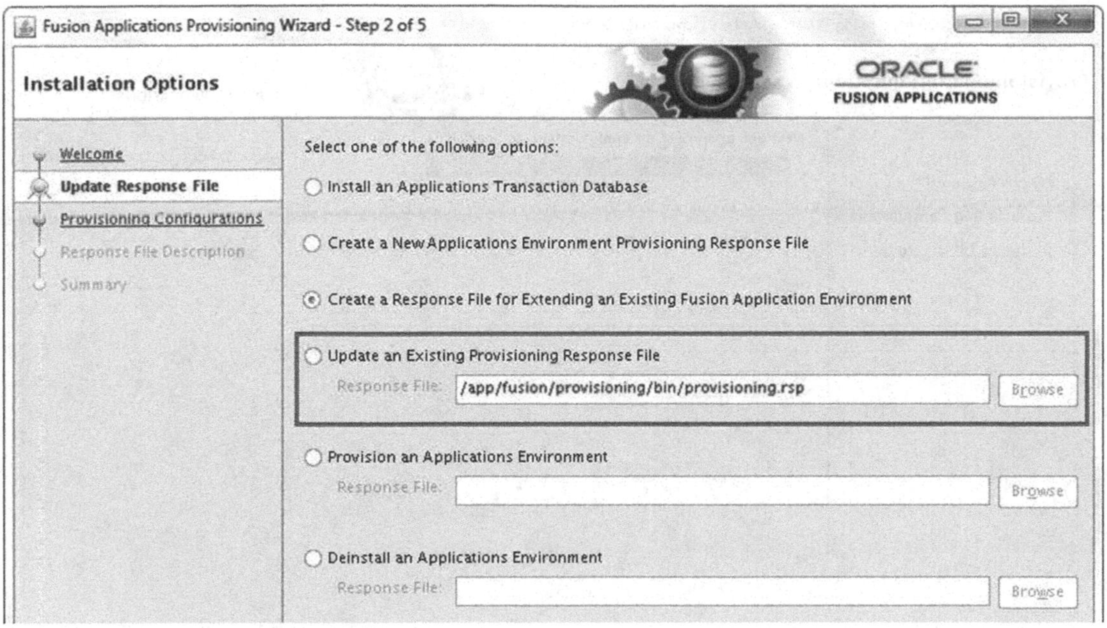

Figure 9-32. Update Response File option in the Provisioning wizard

---

■ **Note** As of the current release it is not possible to add or delete product offerings from the existing response file. You must create a new response file in order to do so.

In this case we will select option 4 (for Fusion Applications release 9 and above) or option 3 (for Fusion Applications release 8 and earlier) which is Update an Existing Provisioning Response File. Additionally, the wizard will require you to enter the full path of the existing response file (complete or partially completed Response File) which you would like to update. You can use the Browse button to locate the file.

Once the response file details are entered, click Next to continue with the wizard. Note that the wizard will be very similar to the wizard for creating a new response file except a few differences which we will see now. It is interesting to see that the Update Response File option does not allow us to modify the product configuration selected for provisioning. Therefore the Provisioning Configuration screen remains grayed out, as shown in Figure 9-33.

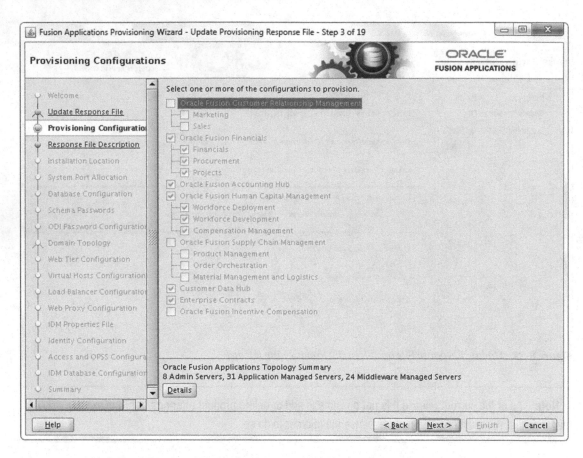

Figure 9-33. *Grayed out Provisioning Configuration window*

In this screen you can only see the list of WebLogic domains and managed servers to be created using the Details option. The reason behind not allowing changes in this screen is that if you change any values in this screen then the further screens which have already been populated with WebLogic domains, topology, and ports details must be modified and they may require a complete rework in terms of responses and may hamper the vary purpose of updating the response file. Review the information on this screen and click Next to proceed to the Response File Description screen, as shown in Figure 9-34.

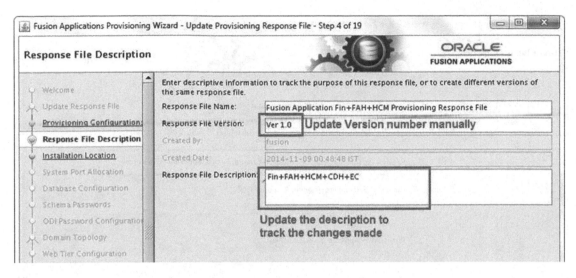

Figure 9-34. Updating Response File Description

The next screen will show the response file description and version as you entered while creating the response file. The Created By and Created Date fields remain the same as the original file and do not get updated even if you update the response file. Make sure to update the response file version number manually for tracking purposes. You may also want to edit the response file description to mention the major changes being done in this response file. Since all the other steps are similar to creating a new response file, we will not discuss them here.

This concludes all the preparation tasks for provisioning a new Fusion Applications environment. Let's quickly look at the additional option provided in Fusion Applications Provisioning wizard in the recent release before completion of this chapter.

Creating a New Response File for Extending an Existing Environment

This option has been introduced from Fusion Applications 11g, Release 9 (11.1.9) onward only and was not available in earlier releases. This option allows you to add new products in your already provisioned existing Fusion Applications environment. These products can either be newly introduced in the new release or existing products from earlier releases which you did not provision earlier and are available as part of new release as well. Since this option is not related to Fusion Applications installation but is only for the upgrade process, I will only give you an introduction to this option here.

Before proceeding with this option you must have an existing Fusion Applications environment running and a complete backup must have been taken. Once you create a new response file for upgrade, you need to provision the new products similar to normal provisioning process. Once the provisioning completes, you must follow the normal upgrade orchestration process.

The step to invoke the wizard is precisely the same since we will run the same Provisioning wizard here as well and select the appropriate option. Launch the Provisioning wizard as we saw earlier.

Select the option called Create a Response File for Extending an Existing Fusion Applications Environment, as shown in Figure 9-35 and then click Next. The subsequent screens will provide you the details of the existing products provisioned in your environment. You'll also see the Configuration selection screen, which will allow you to select additional products that are not already provisioned. The number of WebLogic servers and domains will change accordingly. The subsequent screens will have most fields grayed out except the details for newly configured product domains, ports, and so on. We will skip the discussion of this since it is not related to installation of a new Fusion Applications environment. Once such a response file is created, you can proceed to provisioning the environment followed by the upgrade process.

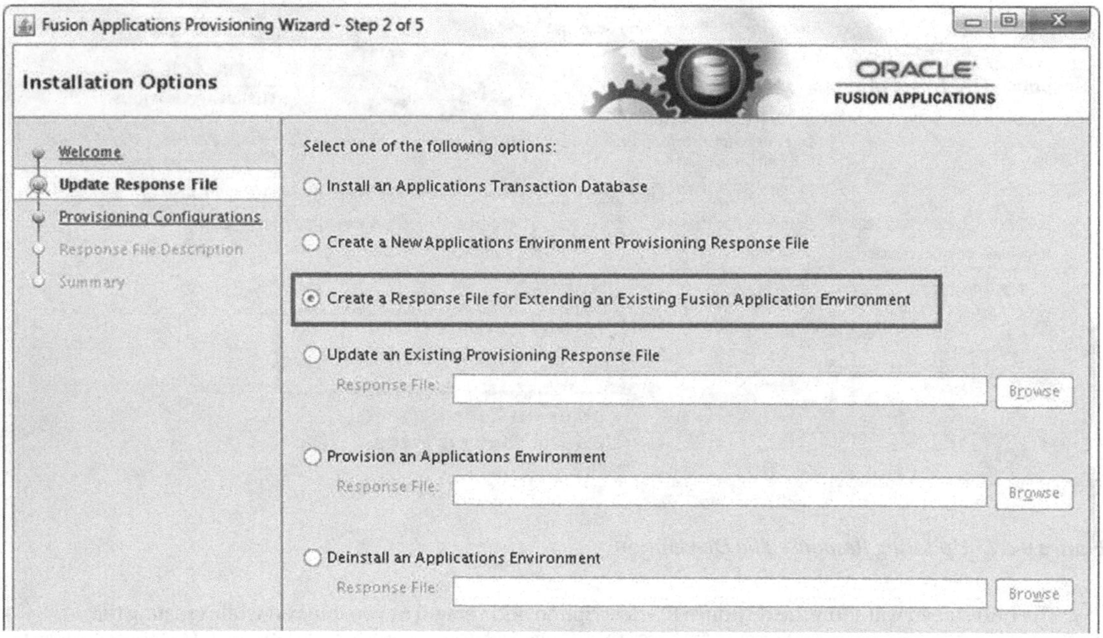

Figure 9-35. *Selecting the option to create a response file for extending existing environment*

Summary

This chapter mainly dealt with preparing for the actual provisioning of Fusion Applications environment. However the response file creation steps should have provided you with a good overview of the components and topology of Fusion Applications environment and explained how they interact with Identity Management components. Creating a correct provisioning response file is of utmost importance in the Fusion Applications provisioning process since the installation of Fusion Applications environment will solely use the response file to perform a seamless installation without prompting for any further details.

In the beginning of this chapter you saw the directory structure of the provisioning framework, which will also help you in the upcoming chapters, since the provisioning process uses the framework extensively for fully automated orchestration of the provisioning phases. You also saw how to update an existing provisioning response file followed by a quick overview of creation of a new response file for extending an existing Fusion Applications environment. Now you will proceed to the final phase of Fusion Applications installation, which is the provisioning of the Fusion Applications nodes.

CHAPTER 10

■ ■ ■

Provisioning Oracle Fusion Applications Environment

Finally we have reached the most important step of the Fusion Applications installation, which is the installation of a Fusion Applications environment using the response file we created in an earlier chapter. From the point of view of the number of steps involved, this process seems fairly straightforward since you only need to initiate the Provisioning wizard in order to perform the provisioning process. However, behind the scenes Fusion Applications provisioning is a complex process with a large number of tasks involving database, middleware, and operating system related activities. If so far your setup is flawless, the provisioning process may be completely transparent and you can simply navigate through the wizard. But in many cases, it requires multiple rounds of troubleshooting at various stages of provisioning, especially if you are installing it for the first time.

As mentioned earlier, patience is a virtue while provisioning a Fusion Applications environment as it is quite a lengthy process and prone to errors due to the high resource consumption and a large number of processes running in parallel. Eight out of 10 people who give up on the on-premise installation of Fusion Applications installation do so at this stage. My aim here is to alter the mindset about on-premise Fusion Applications installation. Let me assure you, if you understand the orchestration mechanism of the provisioning process along with the control files, flags, and log files involved, you can troubleshoot any issues encountered during the provisioning process or at least find a root cause and work with Oracle support to find a way forward.

Current Status of the Provisioning Process

Let's look at what have we completed so far and see where we stand in the overall provisioning process. In other words, let's look at what you should have accomplished by now in order to reach this stage. Refer to Figure 3-5 of Chapter 3, where we discussed the overall process of Fusion Applications provisioning with the help of dependency diagram. Here, you'll look at that same diagram with respect to the current status of provisioning with the list of completed and pending tasks.

Figure 10-1 is the depiction of this earlier diagram with classification of completed and pending tasks. As you can see, all the listed tasks except the last one (Provision Fusion Applications environment) are complete. In other words all the listed tasks except this one must be complete before you can proceed to this task. The diagram may lead you to believe that since we have only one task left out of nearly one and half a dozen of them, the installation is about to finish, but technically this is the start of actual installation. All we did so far was prepare to begin the actual applications installation process. At the same time, this task involves running through the wizard.

© Tushar Thakker 2015

T. Thakker, *Pro Oracle Fusion Applications*, DOI 10.1007/978-1-4842-0983-7_10

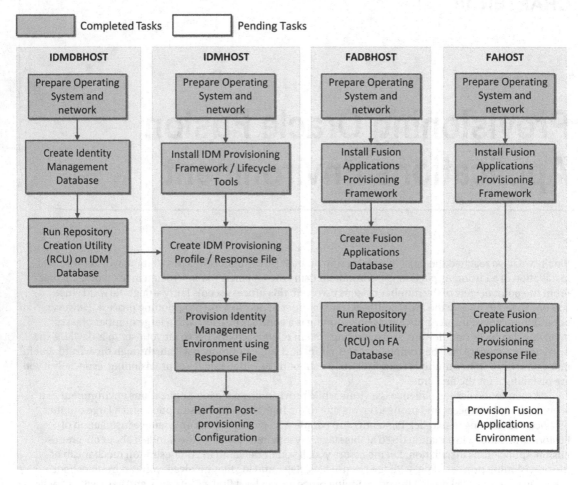

Figure 10-1. *Fusion Applications provisioning prerequisite steps*

You might wonder why you need to wait for all these tasks to completed before you can proceed to the installation in parallel. The answer lies in the dependency diagram. As per Figure 10-1, there are three dependencies or prerequisites for the Provision Fusion Applications Environment task.

- *Identity Management provisioning must be complete*: All the required tasks in Figure 10-1 up to the post-IDM provisioning configuration must be complete. This requires all tasks on IDMDBHOST and IDMHOST to be completed prior to this.

- *Fusion Applications transaction database must be ready*: This also means that the Fusion Applications RCU must have been run on the Applications transaction database. So all steps on FADBHOST must be completed.

- *Fusion Applications Provisioning response file must be created*: In order to create the provisioning response file we must have Fusion Applications provisioning framework installed on FAHOST. So partial activities on FAHOST must also be complete.

Fusion Applications Provisioning Phases

We saw the phases for the Identity Management provisioning process that were introduced in Fusion Applications 11g, Release 7 onward. For Fusion Applications provisioning, we have similar phases right from the initial release. However the tasks performed in each phase are quite different in Fusion Applications provisioning compared to IDM provisioning due to the architectural complexity involved.

The concept of provisioning phases is to perform a similar set of actions for every product domain on every node involved in the provisioning topology, make a backup at the end of the phase, and then move on to the next phase. If there's a failure during any phase, it allows you to fix the underlying cause and then do a proper cleanup of the failed phase, restore from the backup, and restart the phase. All of these actions are seamlessly controlled by the installation orchestration process driven by Apache ANT utility using XML build files. We will look at the build files in a later section.

Let's first look at the phases of Fusion Applications provisioning followed by the flow of provisioning process. Fusion Applications provisioning involves following phases to be run on every application and web tier hosts in selected topology.

■ **Tip** Fusion applications installation phases are actually ANT build targets. The PROVISIONÇING framework calls the ANT utility with the `orchestration.xml` build file by specifying the target to be run. For example, to run the configure phase, the ANT utility is executed with the target name as configured, so the tasks are included in `target name="configure"` from the `orchestration.xml` build file.

---

1. *Preverify*: Prerequisite checks (preverify) phase runs various validation tests to check if the environment meets the installation prerequisites. It checks if installation location is writable, the available physical memory, disk space, swap space, ports availability, JDK version, and kernel parameters, to name a few. It also validates a connection to the FA and IDM databases. It also validates the Identity Management managed servers and URLs reachability. This phase also creates a provisioning plan file from the response file.

2. *Install*: Installation (install) phase installs Fusion Middleware and Fusion Application components in respective home directories. Once installation of each component is done, it applies the tech patches from the patches directories which are bundled with the installation media and extracted to the respective product directory in the installation repository

3. *Preconfigure*: The Preconfigure phase mainly performs the Identity Management related activities including creation of administrator groups, seeding bootstrap of AppID, and so on. We will discuss more about this when we look at the preconfigure phase later in this section. This phase also performs ESS ADF configuration by updating the `connections.xml` file with the Fusion Applications database MDS schema details (`FUSION_MDS_ESS`) so that ADF uses this as the metadata services repository.

4. *Configure*: The Configure phase performs a lot of important activities with respect to Fusion Applications installation. It creates WebLogic domains for all required product families, including CommonDomain and other domains required for the products selected for installation on the selected host. Once the domains are created, it creates WebLogic clusters and managed servers as part of the clusters. It also configures the data sources for each domain and wires the middleware components. It also deploys the application products to the respective managed servers. The Configure phase also registers node managers on servers and enrolls the product domains with the node manager. This phase also creates Oracle HTTP Server Virtual Host configuration files for each domain.

5. *Configure-secondary*: The Configure Secondary phase performs the same configure actions on primary and/or secondary servers if available. The phase runs for each product family, checks whether split domain is enabled for the specific domain and if primary/secondary host is available for the domain, and then performs the configure actions on that domain. Otherwise, it skips the pack/unpack or any other actions. This phase also registers the managed servers with node manager.

6. *Postconfigure*: The Post-Configure (Postconfigure) phase performs tasks that require the components while they are online. It seeds policies and grants and assigns administrator and functional setup privileges to the super user. This phase configures and deploys Oracle SOA composites and performs post-deployment security configurations. For each domain, it sets the value of FusionAppsFrontendHostUrl.

7. *Startup*: The Startup phase essentially brings up all domains administration servers and managed servers including middleware and Application managed servers for the host where the phase is running. Although technically these servers are supposed to be running from the Postconfigure phase, it does a clean restart of all the required servers. The Startup phase also performs GUID reconciliation to make sure the seeded policies and grants are reconciled between the Oracle Fusion data security and policy store.

8. *Validate*: This phase does a variety of checks to validate the installation. These checks include application URLs reachability, validation of data source, and many more.

Now since you know the phases of Fusion Applications provisioning and which tasks run during each phase, let's look at the provisioning process flow. Figure 10-2 shows the flow of Fusion Applications provisioning with respect to the phases involved.

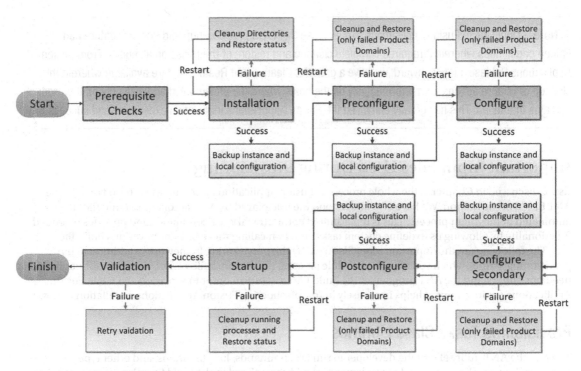

Figure 10-2. *Phases of the Fusion Applications provisioning process*

As you can see, the phases run in sequential manner and a new phase cannot start until the previous phase has completed on each of the hosts involved in the selected topology. After successful completion of each phase, the provisioning framework backs up the instance directory. If the local configuration is enabled then that is also backed up. Since the preverify (prerequisites check), startup, and validation phases do not make any changes to configuration, there is no backup taken during these phases.

■ **Note**   The Provisioning wizard must be started on a primordial host only followed by running the same phase on primary and secondary hosts using the command-line interface.

If any phase encounters an error for any reason, then we must do a cleanup of the existing phase and restore of the previous phase's backup files using the Provisioning wizard or the command-line tools. We will look at this in detail in later sections. Since there are no previous backup available during installation phase, if install phase fails then the cleanup and restore activity will delete the existing directories. It does not need to restore any backup files before restarting the install phase. Similarly for startup phase failure, it may only need to clean up any process that failed to start and restart the phase instead of restoring since there is no configuration change involved in this phase. For Preverify and Validation phase, it only needs to restart the same phase again after fixing the underlying issue without doing any actual cleanup tasks. The cleanup target will run as part of the process but without making any changes.

■ **Note** Until Oracle Fusion Applications 11g, Release 3 (11.1.3), the Cleanup and Restore feature had limited capabilities wherein it required complete cleanup and restore of the phase on all nodes. From Fusion Applications Release 11.1.3 onward, we have a granular Cleanup and Restore feature available wherein the cleanup or restore actions are performed only on the hosts where the phase failed and also only on the product domains that failed. This has greatly enhanced the Fusion Applications installation experience and success rate.

Important Input Files Used During Provisioning

As we discussed in Chapter 3, the whole process of Fusion applications provisioning is based on Apache ANT based orchestration. We have also understood the role played by ANT automation build files in any automated deployment process. This is replacement of traditional make commands and provides extended functionality by allowing us to define custom tasks and then calling these tasks from various build files.

The following are the important input files used by the provisioning framework in addition to the provisioning scripts, which you already saw while creating the response file earlier. Note that although you need not understand the ANT program or the build file structure in order to provision an Oracle Fusion Applications environment, it helps immensely in troubleshooting Fusion Applications installation issues.

Provisioning Tasks Class Libraries

The Apache ANT utility allows the developer to run OS commands, Java programs, and other types of codes, each of which is contained in an element called task defined in the build files. A developer can create custom task definitions using Java classes and bundle the class libraries in .jar (Java Archive) files. Oracle Fusion Applications provisioning related tasks are also bundled in various task definition libraries and available under the <FRAMEWORK_LOCATION>/provisioning/lib path. FRAMEWORK_LOCATION is where we have installed the provisioning framework (/app/fusion). Figure 10-3 lists some of the class libraries in this location that include the actual tasks definitions for the provisioning process. These class libraries contain the tasks which are the actual activity to be performed. These tasks can be directly called from build files, which we will discuss next. The same location also can contain third-party extensions in the form of .jar files, which also can be referenced by ANT build files.

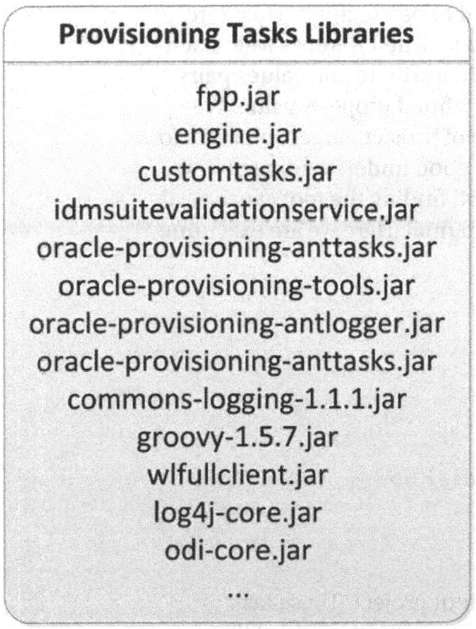

```
Provisioning Tasks Libraries

              fpp.jar
            engine.jar
          customtasks.jar
   idmsuitevalidationservice.jar
   oracle-provisioning-anttasks.jar
    oracle-provisioning-tools.jar
  oracle-provisioning-antlogger.jar
   oracle-provisioning-anttasks.jar
      commons-logging-1.1.1.jar
          groovy-1.5.7.jar
           wlfullclient.jar
           log4j-core.jar
            odi-core.jar

               ...
```

Figure 10-3. Provisioning task definition libraries

Provisioning Build Files

Provisioning build files are located in the `<FRAMEWORK_LOCATION>/provisioning/provisioning-build` directory. These are ANT build automation files or build files written in the XML format. These files contain the logical flow of the provisioning process in the form of various tasks. These tasks can be defined in the build file or can make direct calls to the java program units contained in the custom tasks definition libraries. The following are important elements of an ANT build file.

- *Project*: A logical grouping of related tasks and targets. Each build file will have a distinct project name which will contain a number of targets within it. Project contains a number of targets and only the target which is specified while referencing the build file is executed. Each project has a default target and if no target is specified during the build process, the default target is executed.

- *Targets*: A container of tasks to be performed similar to traditional make utility targets in order to achieve a specific build objective. A target may depend on one or more other targets. So in order to execute one target, the dependency targets are executed from left to right by following any further dependencies. If a dependent target is has already run then it will not run again during this dependency check.

- *Tasks*: The actual code or program unit that is required to be executed. There are many built-in tasks and a developer can write his own task definition as well. Each task can have multiple attributes which are specified in attribute and values pairs. The values could be any string or a reference to a predefined property value. We will look at properties next. Let's take a short example of project, target and tasks to understand how they relate to each other. Note that a good understanding of how ANT works will always help you in troubleshooting and finding the root cause easily. This example is based on Apache ANT open source manual. Here we are executing the built-in ANT tasks javac and mkdir.

```
<project name="AntExample" default="compile">
  <property name="srcdir" location="src"/>
  <property name="destdir" location="dest"/>
  <target name="compile">
    <mkdir dir="${dest}"/>
    <javac srcdir="${srcdir}" destdir="${destdir}"/>
  </target>
</project>
```

- *Taskdefs*: Used to add a new task definition in the current project. These task definitions may include a reference to a Java class that must exist in any of the included .jar files in the ANT library directory (../lib). In Fusion Applications provisioning framework the custom task definitions are created in a build file named common-taskdefs-build.xml. This file is referenced by common-build.xml file and in turn by the provisioning entry point orchestration.xml build file so these tasks remain available to all provisioning targets. For example:

```
<taskdef name="createDomain" \
classname="oracle.apps.fnd.provisioning.ant.
taskdefs.CreateDomainTask" \
classpath="${provisioning.classpath}"/>
```

- *Properties*: The key-value pairs defined either using the <property> task or predefined outside ANT using some input files or one of many possible task. Key acts as a variable which can be used at runtime by ANT by expanding ${key} to a value which is either predefined or generated at runtime. One example of a build file that sets various properties during Fusion Applications Provisioning is common-propertyops-build.xml. For example:

```
<property name="tstamp.format" value="MM/dd/yyyy hh:mm:ss aa z" />
<property name="time.total" value="Total time: " />
```

During provisioning process some properties are also loaded from provisioning plan file. We will look at this in next section. Figure 10-4 shows some of build files contained at <FRAMEWORK_LOCATION>/provisioning/provisioning-build. Although all these files are located in same directory and used in the same fashion as any other build files, we have grouped these files into four categories to help you understand them better.

Provisioning Phases and Orchestration	Fusion Applications Products	Fusion Middleware Products	Common Tasks
orchestration-build.xml listener-build.xml common-install-build.xml common-configure-build.xml common-preconfigure-build.xml common-preverify-build.xml common-restart-build.xml common-validate-build.xml	fs-build.xml crm-build.xml fin-build.xml hcm-build.xml prj-build.xml scm-build.xml prc-build.xml ic-build.xml bi-build.xml crm-sales-build.xml fin-ledger-build.xml hcm-core-build.xml ...	soa-build.xml webcenter-build.xml webgate-build.xml webtier-build.xml odi-build.xml ses-build.xml ...	common-build.xml common-deploy-build.xml common-security-build.xml common-taskdefs-build.xml domain-build.xml common-lifecycle-build.xml common-misc-build.xml common-opatch-build.xml base-product-family-build.xml ...

Figure 10-4. Provisioning build files

- *Provisioning phases and orchestration-related build files*: This category includes the build files containing common actions related to each Provisioning Phase in common-<phase>-build.xml format. This category also includes the main installation build file orchestration-build.xml which is the entry point of any Fusion Applications Provisioning. Any phase will begin with orchestration build which internally calls all other build targets and tasks.

- *Fusion Applications products-related build files*: This category includes all the build files related to a particular product family of Fusion Applications suite. There may be one or more build files for each product family which reference each other from main product build file which is in <product>-build.xml format. We will show an example in coming section for one product family and how the tasks calls are being referenced via multiple build files till the particular task definition.

- *Fusion middleware products-related build files*: Similar to Fusion Applications Products Build Files, there are individual build files for each Fusion Middleware Product in the same directory. The format is again <product>-build.xml for example soa-build.xml, webcenter-build.xml and so on. These build files are referenced every time a middleware component related build action is called in any phase.

- *Common tasks-related build files*: This category includes all the build files which are not related to specific phase or product but contain generic task definitions, targets and properties which are common to most phases and products. In the following build files example we will show you how common tasks are referenced from product or phase related build files.

Provisioning Plan File

This file can be considered as input file as well as output file since it is first created as an output file at the beginning of Preverify stage and then used as input file for all phases. The location of this file is <APPLICATIONS_BASE>/provisioning/plan directory which is also created in the Preverify phase just before creation of provisioning plan file. This file should not be confused with the provisioning response file although many people sometimes use the word provisioning plan interchangeably with the response file. Response file is created from the specific responses you entered during the wizard while provisioning plan file is created internally by the provisioning framework during the Preverify phase after validating the response file and then creating a properties file named provisioning.plan. This file contains values of your provisioning environment specific variables which are used by the provisioning build files in alphabetically sorted order.

■ **Note**   In earlier versions of Oracle Fusion Applications, the provisioning plan was created first and then supplied to the installation orchestration process. In recent releases, the provisioning plan is generated as part of the Preverify phase. The Preverify phase calls the runCLI.sh (or runCLI.bat) script located at <FRAMEWORK_LOCATION>/provisioning/bin by passing the provisioning response file (provisioning.rsp) as input and specifying the provisioning plan file (provisioning.plan) as the output file to be created.

Then following target included in the common-propertyops-build.xml build file loads the properties from provisioning plan during every provisioning phase and the key values are referred by the build files at runtime.

```
<taskdef name="loadplan"
  classname="oracle.apps.fnd.provisioning.ant.taskdefs.LoadPlanTask"
  classpathref="bootstrap.provisioning.classpath"/>
...
<target name="common-load-properties" unless="load.properties.done" \
depends="private-bootstrap-tasks, private-generate-plan-from-response-file">
...
   <loadplan plan="${provisioning.plan}"
      override="${plan.override}"
      invptrloc="${invptr.location}"
      ignoresysprereqs="${preverify.ignore}"/>
...
</target>
```

You will see following entries in each phase log files related to loading of properties from provisioning plan. Once these properties are loaded, the build files can refer the values using ${key} reference which will be expanded at runtime by ANT to a corresponding value.

```
...
[echo] Plan file: /app/oracle/provisioning/plan/provisioning.plan
[loadplan] Loading /app/oracle/provisioning/plan/provisioning.plan
[loadplan] Loaded /app/oracle/provisioning/plan/provisioning.plan
```

The contents of the provisioning.plan file is in <key>=<value> format. Let's look at some examples of these properties set in the provisioning plan file.

Database-Related Property Examples

```
database.fusion.dbhost.host.name=fadbhost.paramlabs.com
database.fusion.dbhost.port=1521
database.fusion.enterprise.servicename=fusiondb
```

IDM Setup-Related Property Examples

```
provisioning.setup.load-idm-properties.load-idm.load.idm.properties=true
provisioning.setup.load-idm-properties.load-idm.validated.and.processed=true
provisioning.setup.load-idm-properties.load-idm.inputfile.location=/app/fusion/idmsetup.
properties
```

Locations-Related Property Examples

```
provisioning.setup.common.core.default.home.top=/app/oracle
provisioning.setup.common.core.phaseguards.dir=/app/oracle/provisioning/phaseguards
provisioning.setup.install-location.locations.default.home.instance=/app/oracle/instance
```

Example of a Provisioning Task Execution Using ANT Build Files

Let's look at an example task execution during the orchestration process shown in Figure 10-5. We have taken an example of createDomain which is used to create a product family domain in the Configure phase before any managed server cluster can be created.

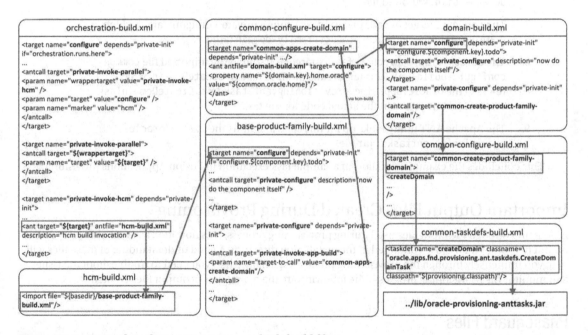

Figure 10-5. Example task execution across multiple build files

As you can see we have taken example of createDomain task. This task is called during the Configure phase for each product family and creates the respective application domain. Here we will look at HCM WebLogic domain creation task. Let's look at the steps involved in this ANT call.

1. The entry point for Fusion Applications provisioning is always the build file named orchestration.xml, as you can see in Figure 10-5. We can see the target named configure in this file. configure target internally calls private-invoke-parallel with value of wrappertarget parameter as private-invoke-hcm and value of target parameter as configure.

2. The private-invoke-parallel in turn runs the target name ${wrapppertarget}, the value of which resolves to private-invoke-hcm.

3. The private-invoke-hcm target then runs another target named {$target}, which resolves to configure. But since the antfile value specified is hcm-build.xml, it looks for this target in this file.

4. hcm-build.xml file imports another build file named base-product-family.xml which contains the target named configure.

5. configure internally calls private-configure target which in turn runs common-apps-create-domain via multiple internal calls not shown here.

6. The target common-apps-create-domain is found in another imported file named common-configure-build.xml. This target runs the configure target within the domain-build.xml build file.

7. The configure target in domain-build.xml runs a private-configure target which in turn runs common-create-product-family-domain target.

8. The common-create-product-family target is found in the imported file common-configure-build.xml. This target runs the Task named createDomain, which refers to the oracle.apps.fnd.provisioning.ant.taskdefs.CreateDomainTask class, which may contain the actual code for the task.

9. The Apache ANT utility looks up for this class and finds the ../lib/oracle-provisioning-anttasks.jar file.

This concludes the example workflow of a sample task execution in Fusion Applications provisioning.

Important Output Files Created During Provisioning

After going through the input files used during provisioning process, let's now look at some of the important output files other than those contained in the installation directory. A good understanding of these files will help you immensely through the provisioning process especially when you need to troubleshoot the issues and monitor the provisioning progress. The following are the main types of output files created.

Phaseguard Files

Phaseguards are created for each host and for every provisioning phase in the <phase>-<hostname>-<status>.grd format. These are blank files acting as flag files for the provisioning framework to detect the current status of the phase. Each phase may have one of the status from STARTED, COMPLETED, ENDED, FAILED, or ABORTSIGNLED.

The directory phaseguards also contains a sub-directory named pf (Product Family) which contains individual status of each product family in every phase. These files are in <phase>-<hostname>-<product family>-<status>.grd format. Product family phaseguards can have STARTED, COMPLETED, or FAILED status. Whenever a phase is restarted after failure, these product family phaseguard files are read and only those which failed earlier are restarted.

■ **Caution**   Since the phaseguard files enable the provisioning framework to monitor and control the provisioning phases to the provisioning framework, these files must not be touched during the provisioning process even though if you are stuck with a particular phase of provisioning since it can lead to incomplete installation or failure in further steps. There is an exception to this which we will see at the end of provisioning process after the Validate phase.

Provisioning Lock Files

Provisioning lock files are also as sensitive as phaseguards and should not be touched manually. Provisioning framework controls the asynchronous flow of certain tasks which should not run at the same time by allowing each product build to obtain a lock in form of these flag files so that other tasks may not run the same tasks at that time and need to wait till the lock is released. There is a specific timeout specified for each of such tasks on how long they need to wait before aborting the task and sending failure signal. Provisioning lock files have extension .lck and are blank files acting as a placeholder or flag file only. Only in case of manual cleanup these files can be deleted if you are fully aware of the root cause or if advised by Oracle Support.

Instance and Local Configuration Backup Files

Upon completion of each provisioning phase related tasks, the provisioning framework creates a backup of the instance directory and local configuration directory (if exists). These files are named instance.tar and placed under respective <APPLICATIONS_BASE>/provisioning/restart/backup_<phase> directory for each completed phase. Depending on the number of phases successfully completed, you will see a number of directories in this location. These backup files are used to do a full or partial restore of instance directory in case of failure during Fusion Applications installation.

Figure 10-6 shows the three types of output files along with their location. Note that this diagram shows the status after a successful completion of provisioning so you do not see any FAILED or ABORTSIGNALED phaseguards. Also although you can see all instance backups for reference only since upon successful completion of next phase the instance backup from previous phase is no longer required and deleted automatically. So you may not see the directories for other earlier phases except the Postconfigure phase under restart directory upon completion of Fusion Applications provisioning.

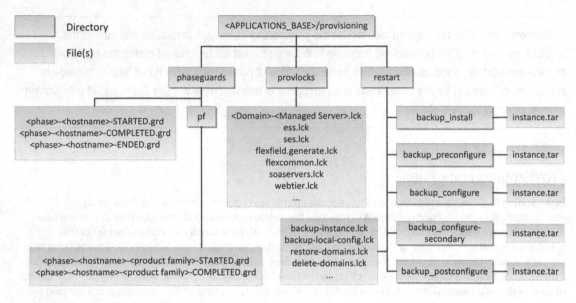

Figure 10-6. *Important files created during provisioning*

Now let's try to relate the Fusion Applications provisioning phases with the output files created during each phase. As you can see the phase proceeds in following stages. Let's see the output files created in each of these stages.

1. *Phase initiation*: Once the phase is initiated, it first creates a phaseguard file named <phase>-<hostname>-STARTED.grd to let other attempts to run the provisioning framework know that the phase has already initiated on this host and not yet completed.

2. *Phase execution*: During the execution of the phase build targets related to each product family (those part of selected configuration) are executed. This begins with first creating a phaseguard file for the respective product family with name as <phase>-<hostname>-<product family>-STARTED.grd. During the execution of the phase several lock files are created to control asynchronous tasks. Once the tasks related to a particular product family completes then a phaseguard file named <phase>-<hostname>-<product family>-COMPLETED.grd is created. The other product families related build targets may still be running at this stage.

3. *Tasks completion*: Once all product families related tasks for the particular phase are complete, the installer creates phase tasks completion phaseguard file named <phase>-<hostname>-COMPLETED.grd and the status column of the phase on the wizard screen shows up as completed with a green tick mark sign. However the Next button to initiate the next phase will not be active yet.

4. *Phase completion*: During the time between tasks completion and phase completion the provisioning framework creates backup of the complete instance directory and local configuration (if available) to the restart directory in the background. It also creates backup lock files to indicate that the backup is going on. Once these tar backups are complete, the framework writes a phaseguard file named <phase>-<hostname>-ENDED.grd. At this stage you will notice that the Next button to proceed to next phase becomes enabled.

Figure 10-7 shows stages of a generic phase as mentioned above in graphical format.

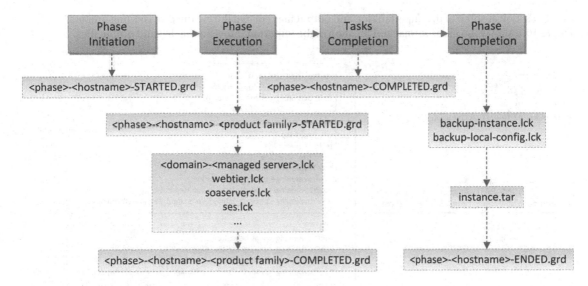

Figure 10-7. Stages of each phase with corresponding files created

Fusion Applications Provisioning Log Files

Provisioning Log files and output files are your most important resources during provisioning process since we will use them heavily to troubleshoot or monitor the provisioning phases. Log files (.log extension) contain details of every task being executed during the provisioning process while the output files (.out extension) contain the standard execution output of each task. The output files are generated for phase only not for each product domain. While log files are crated for each phase as well as every product domain and for some phases there are log files for managed servers as well. Output files generally contain the execution output with timing details while log files contain the verbose messages about the tasks being started, completed or error conditions.

If there are any errors during any of the provisioning phases, you may not find java related exception details in log files so in this case you must refer to the output files since such exception details are found in output files. For individual command-line tasks like cleanup and restore you may see output files containing the console output. In later sections we will see how to clean up the phase and restore to previous state before restarting the same phase again. In this case the provisioning framework creates a directory named <phase>-<timestamp> inside <logfiles location>/archive and moves previous log files related to failed phase. This is done in order to avoid the files from being overwritten and to keep them available for future reference or troubleshooting.

The default logging level in the log files is specified in the configuration file prov-logging-config.xml located at <FRAMEWORK_LOCATION>/provisioning/bin directory, the same directory where from where we run the provisioning wizard scripts. Names of the logger parameters that control the level of logging in the files as well as on the console are runProvisioning-default-main and runProvisioning-console respectively. The default level of these logger is TRACE:1 and NOTIFICATION:1 respectively which are FINE and INFO levels. There are various other levels like TRACE:16 (FINER), TRACE:32 (FINEST) etc. for more detailed log for further debugging purpose. All you need to do is to back up prov-logging-config.xml file and modify the following lines temporarily to change the logging level.

```
<logger name="runProvisioning-default-main" level="TRACE:1">
<logger name="runProvisioning-console" level="NOTIFICATION:1">
```

Let's look at some of the important log and output files created during the provisioning process. Figure 10-8 shows the name format and location of the important provisioning log and output files.

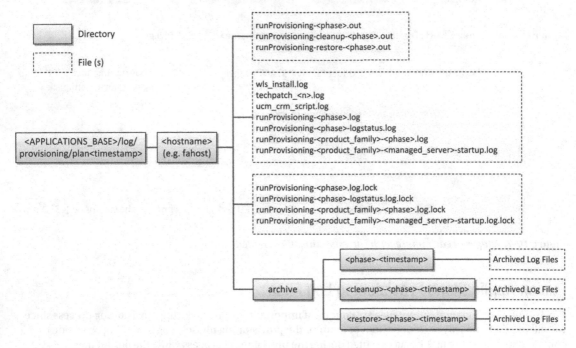

Figure 10-8. *Fusion Applications Provisioning Log files*

As you can see the files are generated at `<APPLICATIONS_BASE>/log/provisioning/plan<timestamp>/<hostname>`, where `hostname` is the host where the current provisioning phase is running and timestamp format is number of milliseconds from `1-Jan-1970 00:00:00` not counting the leap seconds. This value is generated at runtime using `java.lang.System.currentTimeMillis()` method. You can also see the archive folder and corresponding archived log files for each phase.

Provision Fusion Applications Environment

In this crucial section we will look at the step-by-step process to Provision Fusion Applications environment on application and web tier nodes. Once you initiate this process, it may take fairly long time to complete the wizard so be patient as you may need to let some phase run overnight in order to save time. Make full use of the Fusion Applications Provisioning log files and output files as discussed earlier. Make sure to monitor the provisioning process continuously at host level, database level including on Identity Management nodes since there will be a lot of processing on each of the nodes of selected topology during the installation.

■ **Tip** The Fusion Applications provisioning framework invokes the tasks in parallel depending on the number of CPUs installed on the host. If you have fewer CPU cores with more processing power then it is more likely to complete successfully as compared to more cores with less processing power. You can see the number of threads to initiate per CPU core in your provisioning plan file, which was generated automatically.

We have two types of interfaces to run the provisioning process. Let's look at both available options with the associated advantages and restrictions for selecting between these interfaces.

Provisioning Through the Graphical interface

Graphical interface (GUI) wizard is the default installation method used for Single host topology. We need to run the same Provisioning wizard which we used for creating Fusion Applications Transaction database and for creating the provisioning response file. Although we can run the installation using the *command-line interface* as well, installing through the graphical interface allows us to monitor the progress of installation in near real time with status of the phase on each host for each product family. Only for phase running on DMZ host we cannot monitor the progress on the wizard screen since the log status location on DMZ host is not shared with the primordial host. For multi-host topologies we can run the installation using GUI interface on the primordial host while for other hosts we need to run using the command-line interface, as explained in the next section.

In order to install Fusion Applications using a graphical interface we need to run the provisioning wizard using provisioningWizard.sh script (provisioningWizard.bat on the Windows platform) located at <FRAMEWORK_LOCATION>/provisioning/bin directory. The syntax of running the wizard is as follows.

```
./provisioningWizard.sh [-invPtrLoc <inventory pointer file> -ignoreSysPrereqs <true/false>]
```

Note that the arguments ivPtrLoc and ignoreSysPrereqs are optional. Let's look at these arguments.

- invPtrLoc: You may optionally specify the location of Oracle inventory pointer file if it is not at the default /etc/oraInst.loc location. In general you may not need to specify the same for most installations.

- ignoreSysPrereqs: This argument allows you to skip most validation errors in the Preverify phase. For current releases of Fusion Applications installation you may need to specify -ignoreSysPrereqs true since default value is false. If you do not specify this switch then the Next button may not be activated on Prerequisites check screen even if you encountered known errors for the particular release that can be skipped.

Provisioning Through the Command-Line Interface

Installation using the command-line interface (CLI) is optional for a single-host topology and mandatory for multi-host scenarios where you must install using the command-line interface on non-primordial hosts. Even if you run installation using CLI on non-primordial hosts, you can still track the same using GUI wizard screen on the primordial host. Note that until the phase has not completed on all hosts, the Next button will not be activated on the GUI screen to move to next phase.

The command-line interface scripts are located in same location as GUI scripts i.e. <FRAMEWORK_LOCATION>/provisioning/bin. In order to run the installation phase using the command-line interface you need to run the script runProvisioning.sh (runProvisioning.bat for Windows platform) as follows.

```
./runProvisioning.sh -responseFile <Response File path> -target <phase name> \
[-invPtrLoc <Inventory Pointer file> -ignoreSysPrereqs <true/false>]
```

Let's look at these arguments for the command-line interface.

- responseFile: This is mandatory argument for the script. Although we do not need to specify this on GUI since there we manually select the response file, for command-line interface we must specify the response filename with full path as an argument to the script.

■ **Note**   From Oracle Fusion Applications 11g, Release 3 (11.1.3) onward the command-line argument -plan was replaced with -responseFile and the argument provisioning_plan_location was replaced with response_file_location.

- target: This is also mandatory argument for the script. Usually the target name is the name of the provisioning phase except for cleanup and restore where we specify the argument as <cleanup>-<phase> or <restore>-<phase>.

- invPtrLoc: This argument is the same as we discussed in the GUI script and here also it is optional. The default value for Linux is /etc/oraInst.loc, which is true for most installations.

- ignoreSysPrereqs: This argument is also same as we discussed in the GUI script and here also it is optional. Note that if you have specified ignoreSysPrereqs on one host or phase then you must specify the same on other hosts and next phases regardless of whether you had specified this argument in GUI or CLI.

Multi-Host Installation of Fusion Applications

Before you begin the example installation, let's have a quick look at the multi-host scenario. Although we have selected two-tier topology with single-node for Fusion Applications and web tier, let me explain what steps are involved when you have multiple hosts involved in the topology. We will also look at DMZ scenario to get an understanding of additional steps required. Also during our example installation we mention any additional steps in the multi-host topology.

Figure 10-9 shows the list of steps required during the Fusion Applications installation in single host, multi-host, and DMZ scenarios. The diagram legend marks the steps in these three categories so depending on which topology you have selected you need to run the corresponding steps only.

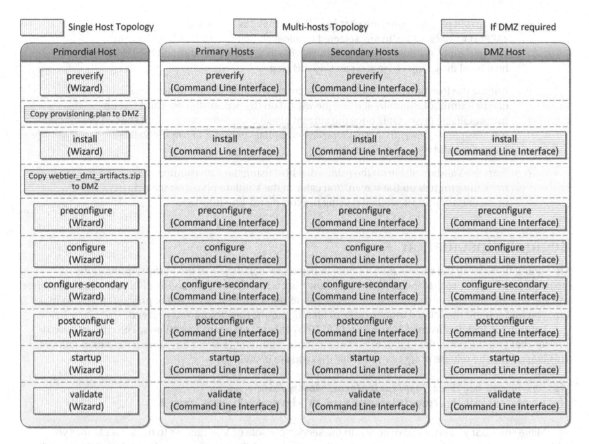

Figure 10-9. List of steps required based on different topologies

For single node scenario you just need to run through the Provisioning wizard and no manual action is required. Let's have a quick summary of the required steps which may help you in the next section of installation.

1. Start the Fusion Applications Provisioning wizard on the primordial host.

2. Once the Preverify phase is kicked off on the primordial host, initiate the Preverify phase on the primary host (if available) and the secondary host (if available) using the command-line interface (CLI) and wait for the phase to complete on all hosts.

3. Since the internal provisioning plan, called provisioning.plan, is generated during the Preverify phase, if you have DMZ set up in selected topology then you must copy the file to DMZ host since DMZ host does not have the shared directory that's available on other hosts. Copy the file provisioning.plan from the <APPLICATIONS_BASE>/provisioning/plan to same local location in the DMZ host. You may skip this step if you do not have a DMZ host.

4. Start the Install phase on the primordial host. Once the progress is visible on the screen, initiate the Install phase on the primary host (if available), the secondary host (if available), and the DMZ host (if available) using the command-line interface (CLI) and wait for the phase to complete on all hosts.

5.   The Install phase creates the `webtier_dmz_artifacts.zip` file at
     `<APPLICATIONS_BASE>` in any selected topology. If you have a DMZ host in your
     selected topology then you must copy this file to the same location on the DMZ
     host local disk. Otherwise you can skip this step.

6.   Initiate the Preconfigure, Configure, Postconfigure, and Startup phases one by
     one in a similar fashion by starting the wizard on the primordial host and CLI on
     the remaining hosts. Only once the current phase completes can you can start
     the next phase. Once all these phases are complete, proceed to run the Validate
     phase for validation of the installation.

7.   Start the Validate phase on the primordial host using the Provisioning wizard and
     track the progress on the screen. You can run the Validate phase on the primary
     or secondary host (if available) using the command-line interface.

Begin the installation

After going through all the theory, now it's time to begin the installation of the Fusion Applications
environment. Make sure that the provisioning framework is installed on the application and web hosts. Once
you start the installation and complete the Install phase, you cannot go back to the previous phase so make
sure you understand the related input or output files for monitoring before you proceed.

Launch the installer from `<FRAMEWORK_LOCATION>/provisioning/bin` as follows. The current release
advises that you start with the `-ignoreSysPrereqs true` argument to avoid any known validation failures.
This is stated in the release notes of the release that you are installing.

```
[fusion@fahost bin]$ cd /app/fusion/provisioning/bin/
[fusion@fahost bin]$ ./provisioningWizard.sh -ignoreSysPrereqs true &
```

Make sure that you either have access to the service console or VNC access to the server before you
initiate the graphical interface. There are several ways to launch GUI screens on a Unix platform so we will
not discuss any specific method here. Once you execute the script, the GUI Provisioning Wizard screen will
pop up. As you can see in Figure 10-10, the Welcome screen displays important prerequisite information
related to each task the wizard can perform.

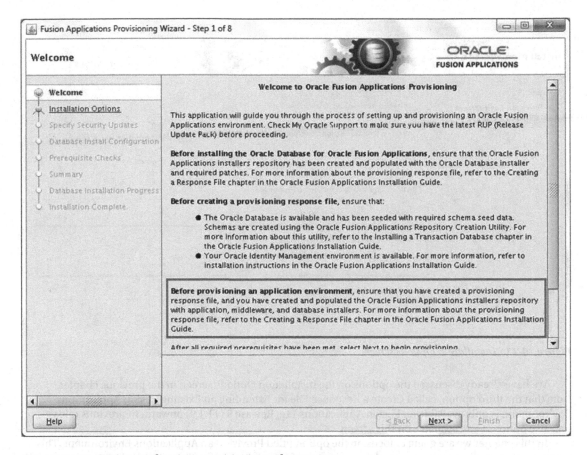

Figure 10-10. *Fusion Applications provisioning welcome screen*

In our case since we are provisioning the Fusion Applications environment, we should read the paragraph on the screen that's highlighted in Figure 10-10 and make sure that all the prerequisites are met. In general, all of the following tasks must be completed before you can initiate Fusion Applications installation.

- The installation media must be extracted to the installation repository location and be available on the shared location that's accessible to all hosts in the selected topology except the DMZ host.

- The Identity Management environment must be provisioned and be running.

- The Fusion Applications transaction database must be created and the Repository Creation Utility must be running on this database.

- You must have already created Fusion Applications provisioning response file since you will need this file in order to initiate the provisioning process.

Once you have made sure that the installation prerequisites are met, click Next to continue to the Installation options screen, as shown in Figure 10-11.

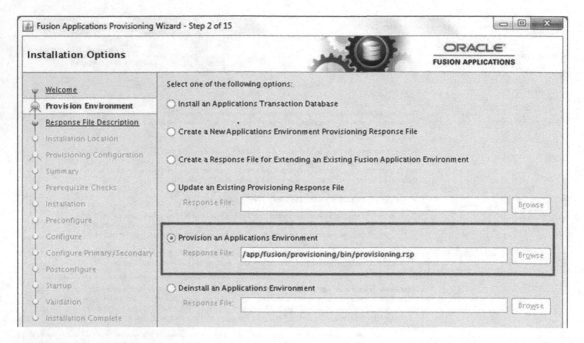

Figure 10-11. *Installation Options screen*

We have already discussed the options on the Installation Options screen in the previous chapter. Note that the third option, called Create a Response File for Extending an Existing Fusion Applications Environment, is only available on Fusion Applications 11g, Release 9 (11.1.9) onward. In previous releases, only five options were available on this screen.

In this chapter we are going to focus on the option titled Provision an Applications Environment. This option requires the name of the provisioning response file as an input in order to proceed. This response file must have been created in advance and must be complete. Incomplete response files (created by using the Save option in middle of Response File Creation wizard) is not supported for Fusion Applications provisioning. Select Provision an Applications Environment and enter the full path of the existing response file in the textbox or use the Browse button to locate the response file.

Once you click Next, the wizard reads the response file and once the response file is validated and loaded, it will initialize the values in other screens. In the next few screens it will allow you to make last-minute modifications or verify the response file (with few exceptions including provisioning configuration selection and so on).

As soon as the response file's values have been loaded, you will see Response File Description screen as shown in Figure 10-12. It allows you to review the response file, version and description and allows you to edit any fields if required. You can see that two fields called Created By and Created Date are grayed out and they show the values as of the creation time of response file and not as of the last update of the response file.

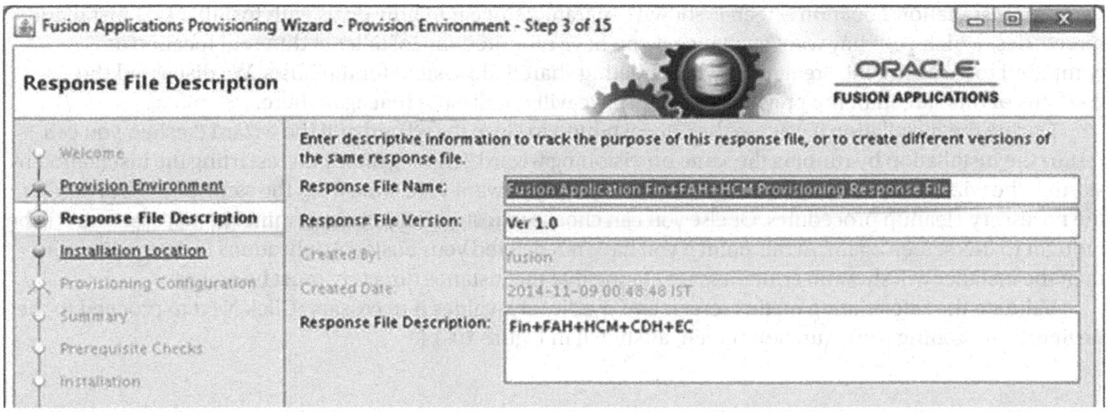

Figure 10-12. Response File Description screen

If you are planning to make any modifications to the response file in the upcoming screens, you can modify the description with changes mentioned for documentation purposes. You can also change the version number to a custom number for the same reasons. Click Next to proceed to installation location screen, as shown in Figure 10-13.

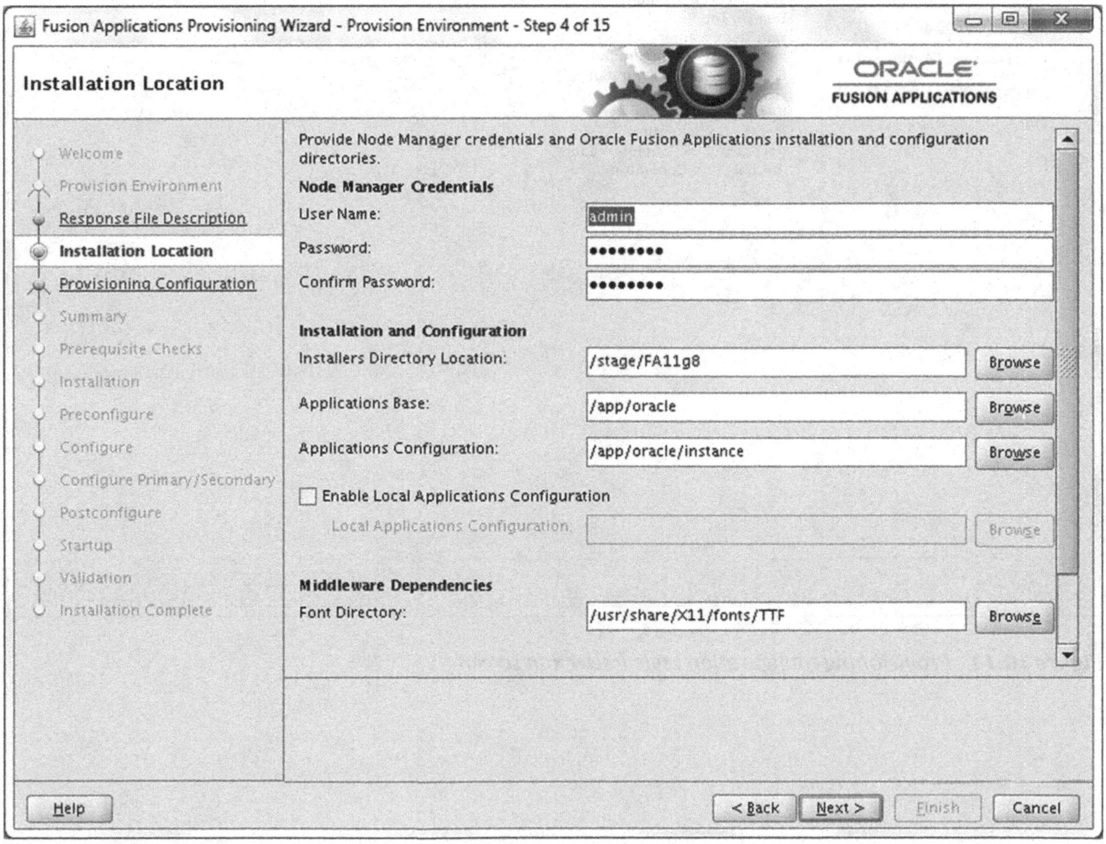

Figure 10-13. Installation Location details screen

The Installation Location screen is shown separately since it mainly deals with installer and installation directories, which you may want to change if you have mounted the installer at different location as compared to response file creation or while creating shared file system for the hosts. We discussed the contents of this screen in the previous chapter so we will not discuss that again here.

During the installation if you use the Cancel button to close the wizard or if the wizard crashes, you can restart the installation by running the same provisioning wizard script again. Upon restarting the installation by starting the wizard again, you may be asked to confirm if you want to resume from the same phase by running the necessary cleanup procedures. Or else you can choose to restart from the beginning. In that case you will be brought to this screen again. At this point if you have not deleted your Fusion Applications instance directory then the installer will show an error message stating that the instance directory must be empty.

Validate the information on this screen and modify any values if necessary. Click Next to proceed to the Review Provisioning Configuration screen, as shown in Figure 10-14.

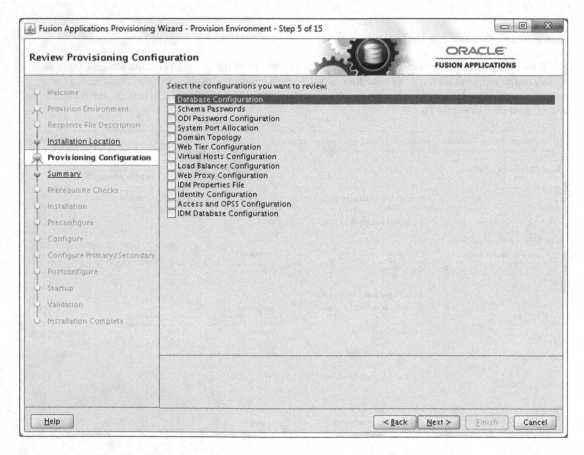

Figure 10-14. Provisioning configuration review selection screen

The Review Provisioning Configuration selection is optional. If you have any doubt about any of the given configuration in the response file or if you want to change any of the previously selected values, select the appropriate configuration which you want to review and/or modify. The options available in this screen are as follows:

- *Database Configuration*: Select this option if you want to make any changes to the Database Configuration parameters selected during response file creation. You can refer to Figure 9-12 from previous chapter to know which screen will be presented again if you select this option.

- *Schema Passwords*: Select this option if you want to change any parameters specified earlier in the Schema Passwords screen, as shown in Figure 9-13 during response file creation.

- *ODI Password Configuration*: Select this option if you want to change any parameters specified in the ODI Password Configuration screen, as shown in Figure 9-14 during response file creation.

- *System Port Allocation*: Select this option if you want to change any parameters specified earlier in the System Port Allocation screen, as shown in Figure 9-11 during response file creation.

- *Domain Topology*: Select this option if you want to change any parameters specified earlier in the Domain Topology and related screens, as shown in Figure 9-15 during response file creation.

- *Web Tier Configuration*: Select this option if you want to change any parameters specified earlier in the Web Tier Configuration screen, as shown in Figure 9-18 during response file creation.

- *Virtual Hosts Configuration*: Select this option if you want to change any parameters specified earlier in the Virtual Hosts Configuration screen, as shown in Figure 9-19 during response file creation.

- *Load Balancer Configuration*: Select this option if you want to change any parameters specified earlier in the Load Balancer Configuration screen, as shown in Figure 9-22 during response file creation.

- *Web Proxy Configuration*: Select this option if you want to change any parameters specified earlier in the Web Proxy Configuration screen, as shown in Figure 9-23 during response file creation.

- *IDM Properties File*: Select this option if you want to change any parameters specified earlier in the IDM Properties File selection screen, as shown in Figure 9-24 during response file creation.

- *Identity Management*: Select this option if you want to change any parameters specified earlier in the Identity Management screen, as shown in Figure 9-26 during response file creation.

- *Access and OPSS Configuration*: Select this option if you want to change any parameters specified earlier in the Access and OPSS Configuration screen, as shown in Figure 9-28 during response file creation.

- *IDM Database Configuration*: Select this option if you want to change any parameters specified earlier in the IDM Database Configuration screen, as shown in Figure 9-30 during response file creation.

If you want to revisit some of these sections of the response file, select the appropriate checkboxes and click Next to continue to the pre-provisioning summary, as shown in Figure 10-15. In this example we will not select any checkboxes for now.

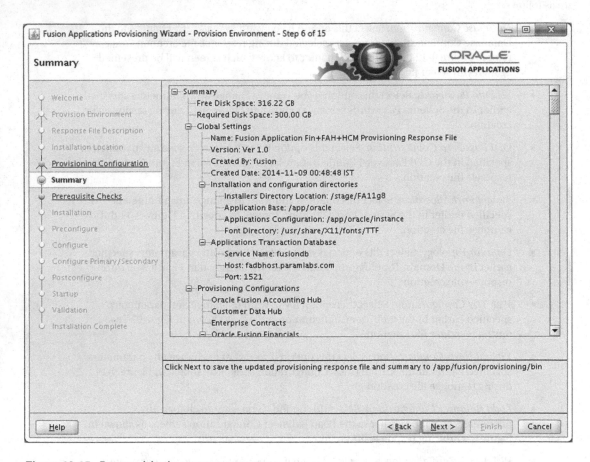

Figure 10-15. *Pre-provisioning summary screen*

The pre-provisioning summary is similar to response file creation summary screen with the only difference being that this screen does not have options to select a response file, a summary filename, or a location to save the files. If you have made any changes to the response file in previous screens, you will see the updated information. Once you review the summary and click Next, the wizard will update the response file and the related summary file.

Note that the further screens do not require any additional inputs from your end except you need to click Next once the phase is complete or Retry if the phase fails.

Preverify Phase

Figure 10-16 shows the Prerequisite Checks screen, which runs the Preverify phase behind the scenes.

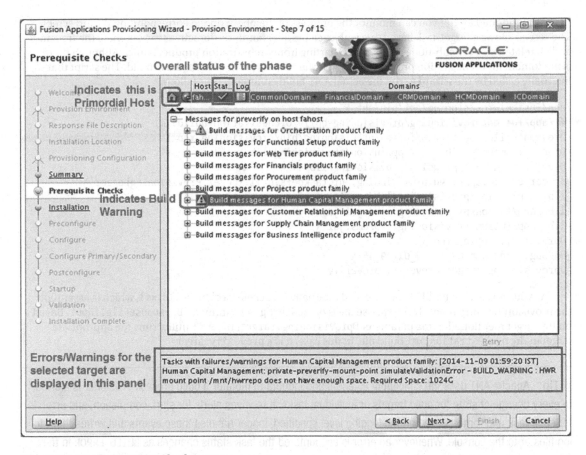

Figure 10-16. *Prerequisite Checks screen*

Once you see the target-tasks tree on the screen, you can initiate the phase from other primary and/or secondary hosts if they are selected in your installation topology. You must initiate the phase on these nodes using the command-line interface only. You can monitor the progress of the phase on each non-DMZ host on this same screen. The following is the script you need to run to initiate the phase on other hosts. Note that you may need to use the -ignoreSysPrereqs true argument on the command line if you have used the same option while invoking the wizard earlier.

```
./runProvisioning.sh -responseFile <Response File path> -target preverify \
[-ignoreSysPrereqs true]
```

For example:

```
[fusion@primaryhost ]$ cd /app/fusion/provisioning/bin
[fusion@primaryhost bin]$ ./runProvisioning.sh -responseFile \
/app/fusion/provisioning/bin/provisioning.rsp -target preverify -ignoreSysPrereqs true
```

Since the selected topology has only one node for the Fusion applications tier, we need not run this command on any host. We will use only the wizard for Fusion Applications installation but we will mention the steps required for multi-host topology as well wherever applicable.

As mentioned earlier you can monitor the progress of the phase on the corresponding Wizard screen. The screen shows a target-task based tree with each product family or domain as the parent of the tree node and all related tasks as sub-nodes of the same starting from orchestration product family. Although there is no domain for orchestration product family, it is the starting point of each phase build. The script that's internally called by the wizard to run the actual ANT build command is as follows.

```
/app/fusion/provisioning/ant/bin/ant \
-f /app/fusion/provisioning/provisioning-build/orchestration-build.xml \
-Dresponsefile.input=/app/fusion/provisioning/bin/provisioning.rsp \
-Dconfigframework.lib.dir=/app/fusion/provisioning/lib \
-Dtools.lib.dir=/app/fusion/provisioning/lib \
-logger oracle.apps.fnd.provisioning.ant.taskdefs.util.logger.ProvisioningLogger \
-lib /app/fusion/provisioning/lib/oracle-provisioning-antlogger.jar \
-lib /app/fusion/provisioning/lib/ojdl.jar \
-lib /app/fusion/provisioning/lib/dms.jar \
-Dpreverify.ignore true \
-Ddebug.timestamp 09_11_14_01_49_46 \
-Dprovisioning.target preverify preverify
```

As you can see, the build file being called internally is orchestration-build.xml, which is essentially the provisioning entry point. The response file is passed using the parameter DresponseFile.input. Based on the target mentioned as the parameter Dprovisioning.target, the ANT utility runs the appropriate target in the orchestration.xml build file. In this case, it is a preverify target.

■ **Tip** Apache ANT uses the concept of listeners and loggers to monitor a build process. A listener is alerted to every change of state for build targets or individual tasks. It receives alerts for start, completion, and error for each task and target. Based on the logging level specified, logger handles these events and writes them to log files or to the console. Whenever an error is encountered the task status changes as BUILD_ERROR in the logstatus file and you may see a message in log file containing listener-log-status-in-error. Do not get confused with this generic error; see the output file for further details about the error.

While the tasks in a target are executing you will see a clock symbol next to the target name. Once all the tasks in any target are complete, you will see a green checkmark next to the target name. Any errors or warnings in the task will be displayed by red x mark or yellow exclamation symbol respectively next to the task as well as the product family tree parent node. The orchestration family node will also reflect the same symbol but if there are errors or warnings then the orchestration node will be marked with error symbol.

You can see the home icon on top of the screen before hosts column, which suggests that the host where the wizard is running is essentially the primordial host. The current provisioning phase is highlighted in the left panel. The bottom messages panel will remain empty until you select any member of the tree. Once you click on any line in the tree, it will show a success, warning, or failure message in the messages tab whenever such message is available.

There are a lot of documented known errors or warnings for this phase depending on the topology. You can refer to the release notes for current release to determine which errors can be skipped. For example, the following was a known error in Fusion Applications 11g, Release 7 and, in some cases, you may see this error even in the latest release. This error can be ignored if you have already validated your Identity Management environment manually.

```
OAM_Validation: Cannot perform OAM Validation as null
```

In such cases if you have not initiated the script with the `ignoreSysPrereqs true` argument then the Next button may not be activated and you may see the Retry button to rerun the phase. If you have used `ignoreSysPrereqs` argument then both the Retry and Next buttons will be activated. Note that this is not applicable for other phases so even if you have used the same argument, you cannot skip the errors in any other phases and any error must be fixed before you can proceed to the next phase. Make sure not to use any workarounds to skip the phase (except validate phase) since it may result in incomplete and erroneous installation of Fusion Applications.

Here are the major activities performed during the Preverify phase.

- Runs various validation tests to check if the environment meets the installation prerequisites.

- It checks if the installation location is writable, checks available physical memory, disk space, swap space, ports availability, JDK version, kernel parameters, and so on.

- Validates connection to FA and IDM databases.

- Validates the Identity Management managed servers and URLs reachability.

- Creates a provisioning plan file from the response file.

- If you did not select the Create Administrators Group checkbox in Identity Management screen of response file creation then it checks whether the Administrator group already exists.

- It also checks whether the super user specified in the same screen already exists in identity store or a new user needs to be created.

In this example the only warning it shows is related to HWR mount point size which is a special file system path where HWR reporting files are stored. The minimum required size is 1024 GB as per documentation. You can ignore the warning about HWR mount point size (1024 GB) if you are not using this functionality.

The following are the important files created during the Preverify phase. If there are any issues with the phase you may need to refer to these files for troubleshooting.

Log files: Created at `<APPLICATIONS_BASE>/logs/provisioning/plan<timestamp>/<hostname>`. For example, `/app/oracle/logs/provisioning/plan1415477981901/fahost`.

```
runProvisioning-preverify.log
runProvisioning-preverify-logstatus.log
runProvisioning-preverify.out
```

Phaseguards: Created at `<APPLICATIONS_BASE>/provisioning/phaseguards`. For example, `/app/oracle/provisioning/phaseguards`.

```
preverify-fahost-STARTED.grd
preverify-fahost-ENDED.grd
preverify-fahost-COMPLETED.grd
pf/preverify-fahost-<phase>-STARTED.grd
pf/preverify-fahost-<phase>-COMPLETED.grd
```

Provisioning Plan: The `provisioning.plan` file is created at `<APPLICATIONS_BASE>/provisioning/plan`. For example, `/app/oracle/provisioning/plan/provisioning.plan`.

As you can see, the Preverify phase creates the internal provisioning plan file
`<APPLICATIONS_BASE>/provisioning/plan/provisioning.plan` from provisioning response file. Since this is a
shared location, this file will be available to primordial, primary, and secondary hosts except a DMZ host since
DMZ uses the local file system. If your architecture involves a DMZ host then you must manually copy this file
to `<APPLICATIONS_BASE>/provisioning/plan` on the DMZ host before you proceed to the Install phase.

Install Phase

Once the Preverify phase is completed successfully, click Next to proceed to the Install phase, as shown in
Figure 10-17.

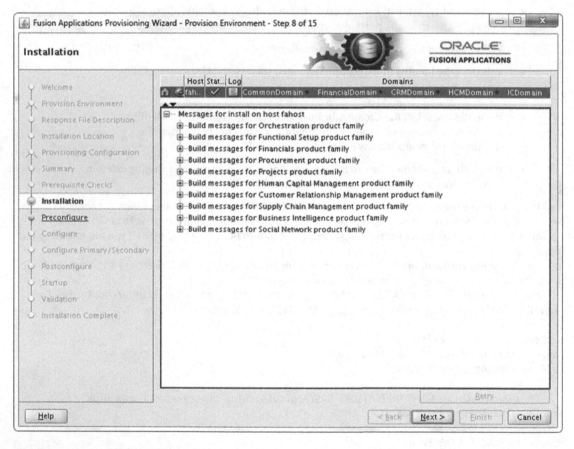

Figure 10-17. *Installation phase status screen*

Now you will see the installation (install) phase progress screen. The interface for all phases looks
exactly the same with same top-level titles in the task tree. Each phase runs on each of the configured
product domains and, depending on the number of physical CPUs on the host, tasks related to multiple
product families may start in parallel.

Once the Install phase has been kicked off on the primordial host, you can initiate the phase on primary
hosts (if present), secondary hosts (if present), and DMZ host (if present) from the command-line interface
as follows.

```
./runProvisioning.sh -responseFile <Response File path> -target install [-ignoreSysPrereqs true]
```

For example:

```
[fusion@primaryhost ]$ cd /app/fusion/provisioning/bin
[fusion@primaryhost bin]$./runProvisioning.sh -responseFile \
/app/fusion/provisioning/bin/provisioning.rsp -target install -ignoreSysPrereqs true
```

■ **Caution** Before starting the Install phase on DMZ host, make sure that you have already copied the provisioning.plan file to the <APPLICATIONS_BASE>/provisioning/plan location.

The following important actions are performed during the Install phase.

- Installs Fusion Middleware and Fusion Application components in respective home directories.

- Once installation of each component is done, it applies the tech patches from the patches directories that are bundled with the installation media and extracted at the respective product directory in the installation repository.

- This phase involves any Identity Management environment-related actions.

The actual ANT command executed behind the scenes is as follows.

```
/app/fusion/provisioning/ant/bin/ant \
-f /app/fusion/provisioning/provisioning-build/orchestration-build.xml \
-Dresponsefile.input=/app/fusion/provisioning/bin/provisioning.rsp \
-Dconfigframework.lib.dir=/app/fusion/provisioning/lib \
-Dtools.lib.dir=/app/fusion/provisioning/lib \
-logger oracle.apps.fnd.provisioning.ant.taskdefs.util.logger.ProvisioningLogger \
-lib /app/fusion/provisioning/lib/oracle-provisioning-antlogger.jar \
-lib /app/fusion/provisioning/lib/ojdl.jar \
-lib /app/fusion/provisioning/lib/dms.jar \
-Dpreverify.ignore true \
-Ddebug.timestamp 09_11_14_02_02_07 \
-Dprovisioning.target install install
```

The following are the important files created during the Install phase. If there are any issues with this phase, you may need to refer to these files for troubleshooting.

Log files: Created at <APPLICATIONS_BASE>/logs/provisioning/plan<timestamp>/<hostname>. For example, /app/oracle/logs/provisioning/plan1415477981901/fahost.

```
runProvisioning-install.log
runProvisioning-install-logstatus.log
runProvisioning-install.out
```

Phaseguards: Created at <APPLICATIONS_BASE>/provisioning/phaseguards. For example, /app/ oracle/provisioning/phaseguards.

```
install-fahost-STARTED.grd
install-fahost-ENDED.grd
install-fahost-COMPLETED.grd
pf/install-fahost-<phase>-STARTED.grd
pf/install-fahost-<phase>-COMPLETED.grd
```

Instance directory Backup: Back up of the instance directory <APPLICATIONS_BASE>/instance is created at <APPLICATIONS_BASE>/provisioning/restart/backup_<phase>. For example, a .tar backup of /app/oracle/ instance directory is created at /app/oracle/provisioning/restart/backup_install/instance.tar.

Installation takes a few hours depending on the type of disk selected and other hardware configuration. Once the Installation phase is complete on all hosts, the Next button will be activated. The Installation phase creates a file named webtier_dmz_artifacts.zip at <APPLICATIONS_BASE>. If you have a DMZ host in your topology, you must copy this file to the same location on the DMZ host before you can proceed.

Preconfigure Phase

Once Install phase has completed successfully, click Next to proceed to the Preconfigure phase, as shown in Figure 10-18.

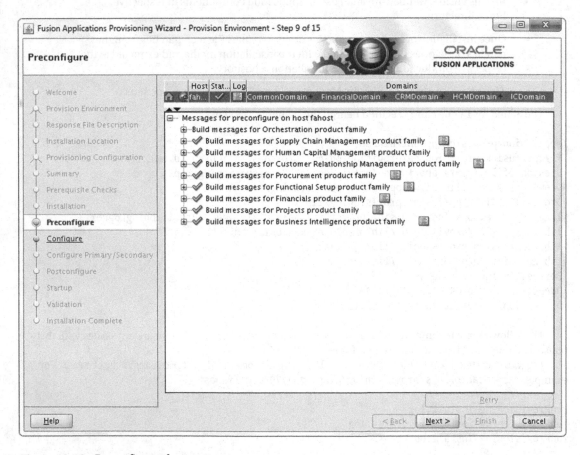

Figure 10-18. *Preconfigure phase status screen*

As you know the phase runs on each of the configured product domains and, depending on the number of physical CPUs on the host, tasks related to multiple product families may start in parallel. But there are some tasks that should not run in parallel. To make sure that these tasks are not run in parallel, the provisioning framework makes use of lock files, which are empty files that act as a flag to indicate that the task is already being executed by another process. So once such a task is initiated, the task creates the appropriate lock file. If any other task wants to run the same action then it will first check if it is possible to acquire a lock on this file and such lock already exists then it will need to wait for the previous task to complete. There is a stipulated time until which the process will wait after which also if it cannot acquire lock then it will fail. These timeout parameters are specified in relevant XML build files and should not be modified as a workaround to get rid of timeout errors unless specified by a provisioning expert or by Oracle Support.

Once the Preconfigure phase has been kicked off on the primordial host, you can initiate the phase on the primary hosts (if present), secondary hosts (if present), and DMZ host (if present) from the command-line interface as follows. In case of single FA host topology, you should skip this step.

```
./runProvisioning.sh -responseFile <Response File path> -target preconfigure \
[-ignoreSysPrereqs true]
```

For example:

```
[fusion@primaryhost ]$ cd /app/fusion/provisioning/bin
[fusion@primaryhost bin]$./runProvisioning.sh -responseFile \
/app/fusion/provisioning/bin/provisioning.rsp -target preconfigure -ignoreSysPrereqs true
```

The following important actions are performed during the Preconfigure phase.

- Performs ESS ADF configuration by updating connections.xml with the Fusion Applications database MDS schema details (FUSION_MDS_ESS) so that ADF uses this as the metadata services repository.

- Uploads the LDIF files containing tasks to create Application administrator groups. These files with the .ldif extension are already copied as part of the Install phase under /app/oracle/fusionapps/applications/com/acr/security/ldif.

- Creates system administrator groups if selected during response file creation and if it does not already exist.

- Seeds AppID users and AppID groups to the identity store using oid_appid_users. ldif and oid_appid_groups.ldif files. Gives the bootstrap AppID membership of the system administrators group.

- Makes the designated super user (FAAdmin in this case) member of the administrator groups and other groups related to the application family.

The actual ANT command executed behind the scenes is as follows.

```
/app/fusion/provisioning/ant/bin/ant \
-f /app/fusion/provisioning/provisioning-build/orchestration-build.xml \
-Dresponsefile.input=/app/fusion/provisioning/bin/provisioning.rsp \
-Dconfigframework.lib.dir=/app/fusion/provisioning/lib \
-Dtools.lib.dir=/app/fusion/provisioning/lib \
-logger oracle.apps.fnd.provisioning.ant.taskdefs.util.logger.ProvisioningLogger \
-lib /app/fusion/provisioning/lib/oracle-provisioning-antlogger.jar \
-lib /app/fusion/provisioning/lib/ojdl.jar \
-lib /app/fusion/provisioning/lib/dms.jar \
-Dpreverify.ignore true \
-Ddebug.timestamp 09_11_14_01_49_46 \
-Dprovisioning.target preverify preverify
```

The following are the important files created during the Preconfigure phase. If you have any issues with the phase you may need to refer to these files for troubleshooting.

Log files: Created at <APPLICATIONS_BASE>/logs/provisioning/plan<timestamp>/<hostname>. For example, /app/oracle/logs/provisioning/plan1415477981901/fahost.

```
runProvisioning-preconfigure.log
runProvisioning-<product_family>-preconfigure.log
runProvisioning-preconfigure-logstatus.log
runProvisioning-preconfigure.out
```

Phaseguards: Created at <APPLICATIONS_BASE>/provisioning/phaseguards. For example, /app/oracle/provisioning/phaseguards.

```
preconfigure-fahost-STARTED.grd
preconfigure-fahost-ENDED.grd
preconfigure-fahost-COMPLETED.grd
pf/preconfigure-fahost-<phase>-STARTED.grd
pf/preconfigure-fahost-<phase>-COMPLETED.grd
```

Instance directory backup: Back up of the instance directory <APPLICATIONS_BASE>/instance is created at <APPLICATIONS_BASE>/provisioning/restart/backup_<phase>. For example, a .tar backup of /app/oracle/instance directory is created at /app/oracle/provisioning/restart/backup_preconfigure/instance.tar.

Configure Phase

Once the Preconfigure phase is complete on all hosts, click Next to proceed to the Configure phase, as shown in Figure 10-19.

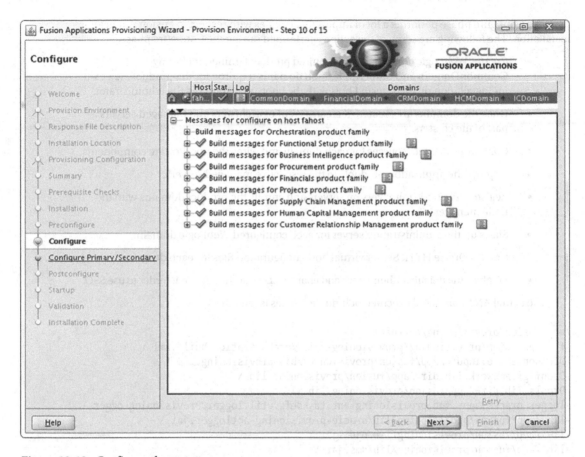

Figure 10-19. *Configure phase status screen*

Configure and Postconfigure are two of the most time-consuming phases after the Install phase. You can monitor this screen to see the progress of the Configure phase for each product family on each host (except DMZ). Once the Configure phase has been kicked off from the primordial host, start it from the primary hosts (if available), secondary hosts (if available), and DMZ host (if available) using the following command-line interface scripts.

```
./runProvisioning.sh -responseFile <Response File path> -target configure \
[-ignoreSysPrereqs true]
```

For example:

```
[fusion@primaryhost ]$ cd /app/fusion/provisioning/bin
[fusion@primaryhost bin]$./runProvisioning.sh -responseFile \
/app/fusion/provisioning/bin/provisioning.rsp -target configure -ignoreSysPrereqs true
```

The Configure phase performs a lot of important activities with respect to Fusion Applications installation. The following are some of the actions performed during the Configure phase.

- Creates WebLogic domains for all required product families, including CommonDomain and other Application domains required for the products selected for installation on the selected host with the bootstrap AppID as the administrator.

- Once the domains are created, it creates WebLogic clusters and managed servers as part of the clusters.

- Configures the data sources for each domain and wires the middleware components.

- Deploys the application products to the respective managed servers.

- Registers the node managers on servers and enrolls the product domains with the node manager.

- Starts up the administration server for each configured WebLogic domain.

- Creates Oracle HTTP Server virtual host configuration files for each domain.

- Disables the default authenticator and enables LDAP authenticator in order to use SSO.

The actual ANT command executed behind the scenes is as follows.

```
/app/fusion/provisioning/ant/bin/ant \
-f /app/fusion/provisioning/provisioning-build/orchestration-build.xml \
-Dresponsefile.input=/app/fusion/provisioning/bin/provisioning.rsp \
-Dconfigframework.lib.dir=/app/fusion/provisioning/lib \
-Dtools.lib.dir=/app/fusion/provisioning/lib \
-logger oracle.apps.fnd.provisioning.ant.taskdefs.util.logger.ProvisioningLogger \
-lib /app/fusion/provisioning/lib/oracle-provisioning-antlogger.jar \
-lib /app/fusion/provisioning/lib/ojdl.jar \
-lib /app/fusion/provisioning/lib/dms.jar \
-Dpreverify.ignore true \
-Ddebug.timestamp 09_11_14_10_46_10 \
-Dprovisioning.target configure configure
```

The following are the important files created during the Configure phase. If there are any issues with the phase you may need to refer to these files for troubleshooting.

Log files: Created at <APPLICATIONS_BASE>/logs/provisioning/plan<timestamp>/<hostname>. For example, /app/oracle/logs/provisioning/plan1415477981901/fahost.

```
runProvisioning-configure.log
runProvisioning-<product_family>-configure.log
runProvisioning-configure-logstatus.log
runProvisioning-configure.out
```

Phaseguards: Created at <APPLICATIONS_BASE>/provisioning/phaseguards. For example, /app/oracle/provisioning/phaseguards.

```
configure-fahost-STARTED.grd
configure-fahost-ENDED.grd
configure-fahost-COMPLETED.grd
pf/configure-fahost-<phase>-STARTED.grd
pf/configure-fahost-<phase>-COMPLETED.grd
```

Instance directory Backup: Back up of the instance directory `<APPLICATIONS_BASE>/instance` is created at `<APPLICATIONS_BASE>/provisioning/restart/backup_<phase>`. For example, a `.tar` backup of `/app/oracle/instance` directory is created at `/app/oracle/provisioning/restart/backup_configure/instance.tar`.

Configure Secondary Phase

The Configure phase takes a few hours to complete. Once the Configure phase is complete on all hosts, click Next to proceed to the Configure-Secondary phase, as shown in Figure 10-20.

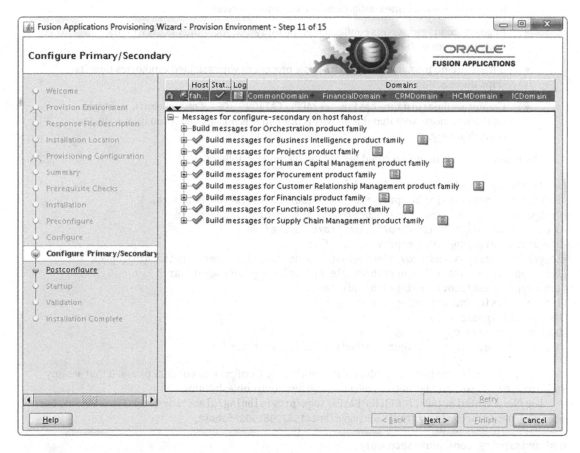

Figure 10-20. *Configure Primary/Secondary phase status screen*

The Configure-Secondary phase is also called Configure Primary/Secondary. It was shown on the screen as Configure Secondary in older releases but the name was changed to Configure Primary/Secondary. Once the Configure-Secondary phase has been kicked off from the primordial host, start it from the primary hosts (if available), secondary hosts (if available), and DMZ host (if available) using the following command-line interface scripts.

```
./runProvisioning.sh -responseFile <Response File path> -target configure-secondary \
[-ignoreSysPrereqs true]
```

For example:

```
[fusion@primaryhost ]$ cd /app/fusion/provisioning/bin
[fusion@primaryhost bin]$./runProvisioning.sh -responseFile \
/app/fusion/provisioning/bin/provisioning.rsp -target configure-secondary \
-ignoreSysPrereqs true
```

The following important actions are performed during the Configure-Secondary phase.

- If there are primary and/or secondary servers in your selected topology then this phase will run the same configure actions on those servers.

- Registers managed servers configured on primary and secondary hosts with the node manager of the respective host.

- If there are no primary or secondary hosts present in your selected topologies then it skips these actions.

- Creates web tier instance ohs1 under <APPLICATIONS_TOP>/CommonDomain_webtier on the web host. Note that this activity is done in this phase even if you have a single-node topology.

The actual ANT command executed behind the scenes is as follows.

```
/app/fusion/provisioning/ant/bin/ant \
-f /app/fusion/provisioning/provisioning-build/orchestration-build.xml \
-Dresponsefile.input=/app/fusion/provisioning/bin/provisioning.rsp \
-Dconfigframework.lib.dir=/app/fusion/provisioning/lib \
-Dtools.lib.dir=/app/fusion/provisioning/lib \
-logger oracle.apps.fnd.provisioning.ant.taskdefs.util.logger.ProvisioningLogger \
-lib /app/fusion/provisioning/lib/oracle-provisioning-antlogger.jar \
-lib /app/fusion/provisioning/lib/ojdl.jar \
-lib /app/fusion/provisioning/lib/dms.jar \
-Dpreverify.ignore true \
-Ddebug.timestamp 09_11_14_15_56_16 \
-Dprovisioning.target configure-secondary configure-secondary
```

The following are the important files created during the Configure-Secondary phase. If that are any issues with the phase you may need to refer to these files for troubleshooting.

Log files: Created at <APPLICATIONS_BASE>/logs/provisioning/plan<timestamp>/<hostname>. For example, /app/oracle/logs/provisioning/plan1415477981901/fahost.

```
runProvisioning-configure-secondary.log
runProvisioning-<product_family>-configure-secondary.log
runProvisioning-configure-logstatus-secondary.log
runProvisioning-configure-secondary.out
```

Phaseguards: Created at <APPLICATIONS_BASE>/provisioning/phaseguards. For example, /app/oracle/provisioning/phaseguards.

```
configure-secondary -fahost-STARTED.grd
configure-secondary -fahost-ENDED.grd
configure-secondary -fahost-COMPLETED.grd
pf/configure-secondary -fahost-<phase>-STARTED.grd
pf/configure-secondary -fahost-<phase>-COMPLETED.grd
```

Instance directory Backup: Back up of the instance directory `<APPLICATIONS_BASE>/instance` is created at `<APPLICATIONS_BASE>/provisioning/restart/backup_<phase>`. For example, a `.tar` backup of `/app/oracle/instance` directory is created as follows: `/app/oracle/provisioning/restart/backup_configure-secondary/instance.tar`.

Postconfigure Phase

The Configure Primary/Secondary phase may take a few minutes. Click Next to proceed to the Postconfigure phase, as shown in Figure 10-21.

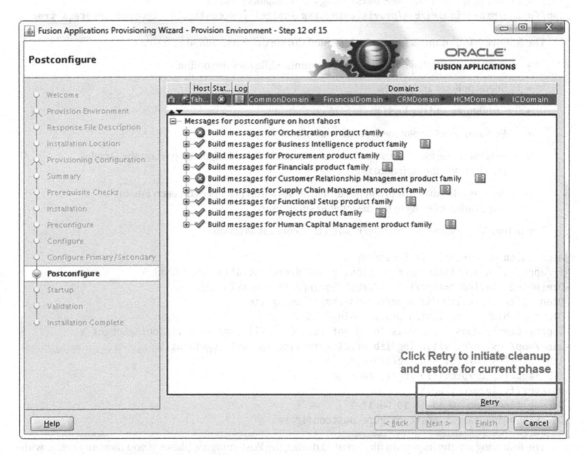

Figure 10-21. *Postconfigure phase status screen*

The Postconfigure phase is the most error-prone phase if you do not have the right hardware or if the process parallelism does not initiate correctly. In such cases it may cause timeout errors. We will discuss that soon. The Postconfigure phase takes a very long time. Do not panic if you see errors during this phase since most of the errors are transient and can be fixed upon rerunning based on the error. In the previous example you saw that the CRM postconfigure failed and the error was related to a timeout during high CPU activity.

Once the Postconfigure phase has been kicked off from the primordial host, start it from the primary hosts (if available), secondary hosts (if available), and DMZ host (if available) using the following command-line interface scripts.

```
./runProvisioning.sh -responseFile <Response File path> -target postconfigure \
[-ignoreSysPrereqs true]
```

For example:

```
[fusion@primaryhost ]$ cd /app/fusion/provisioning/bin
[fusion@primaryhost bin]$./runProvisioning.sh -responseFile \
/app/fusion/provisioning/bin/provisioning.rsp -target postconfigure -ignoreSysPrereqs true
```

The following important actions are performed during the Postconfigure phase.

- Performs tasks that require the components while they are online.

- Seeds policies and grants.

- Configures and deploys Oracle SOA composites.

- Performs post-deployment security configurations.

- Sets the value for FusionAppsFrontendHostUrl to the designated port on the Oracle HTTP Server for each domain.

- Assigns administrator privileges and function setup privileges on each Fusion Application offering to the designated super user.

The actual ANT command executed behind the scenes is as follows.

```
/app/fusion/provisioning/ant/bin/ant \
-f /app/fusion/provisioning/provisioning-build/orchestration-build.xml \
-Dresponsefile.input=/app/fusion/provisioning/bin/provisioning.rsp \
-Dconfigframework.lib.dir=/app/fusion/provisioning/lib \
-Dtools.lib.dir=/app/fusion/provisioning/lib \
-logger oracle.apps.fnd.provisioning.ant.taskdefs.util.logger.ProvisioningLogger \
-lib /app/fusion/provisioning/lib/oracle-provisioning-antlogger.jar \
-lib /app/fusion/provisioning/lib/ojdl.jar \
-lib /app/fusion/provisioning/lib/dms.jar \
-Dpreverify.ignore true \
-Ddebug.timestamp 10_11_14_10_06_17 \
-Dprovisioning.target postconfigure postconfigure
```

The following are the important files created during the Postconfigure phase. If you have any issues with the phase you may need to refer to these files for troubleshooting.

Log files: Created at <APPLICATIONS_BASE>/logs/provisioning/plan<timestamp>/<hostname>. For example, /app/oracle/logs/provisioning/plan1415477981901/fahost. You may notice that some startup log files are also created during this phase. This is because the Postconfigure phase brings up these managed servers for processing.

```
runProvisioning-postconfigure.log
runProvisioning-<product_family>-postconfigure.log
runProvisioning-postconfigure-logstatus.log
runProvisioning-postconfigure.out
runProvisioning-<product_family>-<managed_server>-startup.log
```

Phaseguards: Created at <APPLICATIONS_BASE>/provisioning/phaseguards. For example, /app/oracle/provisioning/phaseguards.

```
postconfigure-fahost-STARTED.grd
postconfigure-fahost-ENDED.grd
postconf/igure-fahost-COMPLETED.grd
pf/postconfigure-fahost-<phase>-STARTED.grd
pf/postconfigure-fahost-<phase>-COMPLETED.grd
```

Instance directory Backup: Back up of the instance directory <APPLICATIONS_BASE>/instance is created at <APPLICATIONS_BASE>/provisioning/restart/backup_<phase>. For example, a tar backup of /app/oracle/instance directory is created at /app/oracle/provisioning/restart/backup_postconfigure/instance.tar.

We can rerun the phase by clicking on Retry and it will do cleanup/restore to the previous step (only for the failed product domains).

Restarting the Installation After a Failure in a Phase

Fusion Applications provisioning allows granular restart functionality for each phase. If a phase fails due to errors in executing some tasks or a task timed out waiting for locks, you will see the product domain status for that phase marked as FAILED and it will stop any further processing of that particular product domain. However it will continue to process the remaining product domains until their completion. At the end of the processing, the installer will display successful and failed targets (product domains) with the relevant symbol with overall phase status also as FAILED. You will see appropriate phaseguard files being generated in <APPLICATIONS_BASE>/provisioning/phaseguards. At this stage, the wizard will activate the Retry button. Once you click on the Retry button, the wizard will initiate the cleanup and restore operations on the failed host, as shown in Figure 10-22.

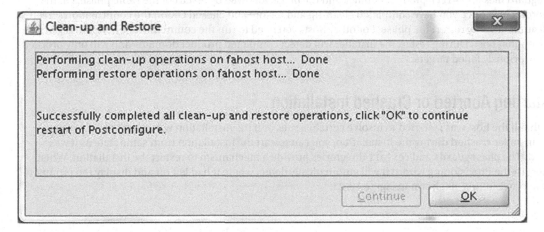

Figure 10-22. *Cleanup and Restore status screen*

Sometimes, the cleanup or restore or both may fail to complete. In that case you may need to run the cleanup and restore from command-line tools even on the primordial host. Also for the other hosts, you will need to run cleanup and restore using the same command-line options. The syntax of running this using CLI is as follows. Note that once the cleanup operation completes on all hosts you can only initiate the Restore operation.

```
cd <FRAMEWORK_LOCATION>/provisioning/bin
./runProvisioning.sh -responseFile <Response File path> -target cleanup-<phase>
./runProvisioning.sh -responseFile <Response File path> -target restore-<phase>
```

For example:

```
[fusion@fahost ]$ cd /app/fusion/provisioning/bin
[fusion@fahost bin]$./runProvisioning.sh -responseFile \
/app/fusion/provisioning/bin/provisioning.rsp -target cleanup-postconfigure
[fusion@fahost bin]$./runProvisioning.sh -responseFile \
/app/fusion/provisioning/bin/provisioning.rsp -target restore-postconfigure
```

You can see the following cleanup and restore log files generated at <APPLICATIONS_BASE>/logs/provisioning/plan<timestamp>/<hostname>. The log files are moved to the archive directory upon restart.

```
runProvisioning-cleanup-<phase>.out
runProvisioning-cleanup-<phase>.log
runProvisioning-restore-<phase>.out
runProvisioning-restore-<phase>.log
```

During restore, the installer will restore the failed domains' subdirectories from backup_<previous_phase>/instance.tar located at <APPLICATIONS_BASE>/provisioning/restart. It will also remove the phaseguard files for FAILED product families and the phase followed by restart of the same phase. On the primordial host once you have completed clean-up and restore and clicked OK on the confirmation screen, it will automatically restart the phase. For other hosts you need to run the command-line script to restart the phase on that host. During restart the installer will detect completed product domains and will only proceed to the previously failed targets.

Restarting Aborted or Crashed Installation

Note that if the host was restarted to resolve certain issues or if the installation was canceled in between or the installer crashed during the installation, you can restart the installation from same state as it was aborted. The phaseguards and restart directories provide a mechanism to restart the installation. When you restart the Provisioning wizard it will automatically detect where it had left off and display the prompt to resume provisioning, as shown in Figure 10-23.

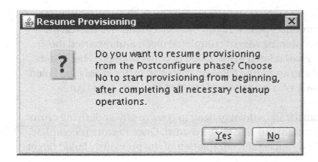

Figure 10-23. *Resume Provisioning prompt*

As you can see in Figure 10-23, you have two options to select from by clicking Yes or No. Be very careful before choosing.

- *Start provisioning from beginning*

    If you select No the installer will reset all the status information and take you back to the first screen of installation location details. You must kill all running processes related to the Fusion Applications environment, clean up the `<APPLICATIONS_BASE>` directory, and restore the Fusion Applications transaction database to its post-RCU stage. If you do not have any backup of the database then you must create a fresh database and run RCU on that.

- *Resume provisioning from previously running or failed phase*

    If you select Yes then the installation will resume from where it left off. It could be an already running, failed, or successful phase. If the last phase was successful and the installation was aborted before proceeding to the next phase, you will see the success screen again and you will be able to click Next to proceed to the next phase. If the phase was failed or running while installation was aborted, it will show the failed phase screen and allow you to initiate cleanup and restore by clicking on the Retry button.

Before running the cleanup target, make sure that Identity Management environment is running and the Fusion Applications Transaction database is up. For the Configure phase onward, you must also ensure that the node manager has been started on the host. This also applies to the scenario when a phase had completed successfully and before starting the next phase you had restarted the host. Before any new provisioning target including cleanup or restore can start, the installer will need to connect to the node manager to check the status of the WebLogic servers status on that node. It will start them if required. You can start the node manager by running the following script. For all startup steps, including Identity Management and Fusion Applications components, refer to the components startup section in Chapter 12.

```
[fusion@fahost ~]$ cd /app/oracle/instance/nodemanager/fahost/
[fusion@fahost fahost]$ nohup ./startNodeManagerWrapper.sh &
```

You can monitor the progress in the nohup.out file until you see the following message:

```
INFO: Secure socket listener started on port 5556
```

Let's move the focus back to the Postconfigure phase error. As you saw in Figure 10-21, the CRM postconfigure encountered error while rest of the products postconfigure was successful. We clicked the Retry button and, as shown in Figure 10-22, the Provisioning wizard completed clean and restarted the operation. The Cleanup phase shut down any processes related to the failed product domain. The Restore phase deletes any identity and policy store-related entries for the CRM product and restores only the failed CRM domain directory from the <APPLICATIONS_BASE>/provisioning/restart/backup_configure-secondary/instace.tar backup file.

If the cleanup or restart fails to complete automatically, you may need to resolve any underlying errors followed by running cleanup and restore using the command-line or the wizard. Once Restore is complete, click OK to restart the failed phase. Figure 10-24 shows successful completion of the previously failed target (CRM product domain).

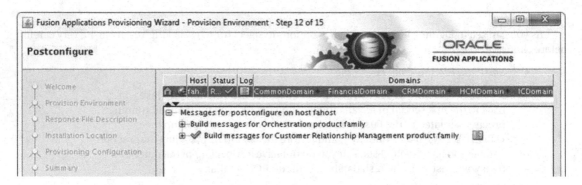

Figure 10-24. *Postconfigure phase post-restart screen*

Before activating the Next button, the wizard will take a full backup of instance directory and place the instance.tar backup file in the <APPLICATIONS_BASE>/provisioning/restart/backup-postconfigure directory. This will create the following phaseguard files to record the phase status as completed:

```
postconfigure-<hostname>-COMPLETED.grd
postconfigure-<hostname>-ENDED.grd
```

Before you proceed to the next phase, take a look at an an example of false errors during the provisioning phase. Figure 10-25 shows an example. This might not occur during your installation.

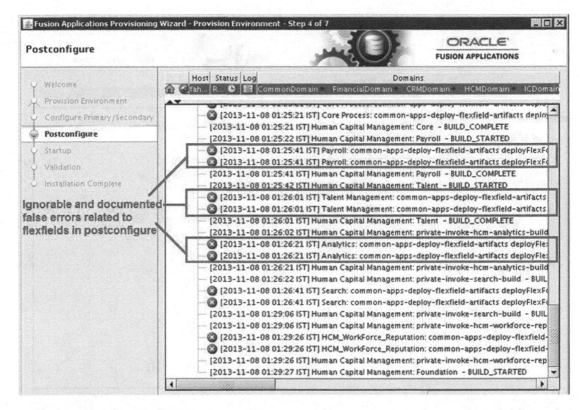

Figure 10-25. *Ignorable errors example*

Here you can see that, despite the red mark against various tasks in HCM postconfigure, the phase has not failed and it continues processing. This is due to known flexfield related errors that are not actually "errors" but the Provisioning wizard incorrectly shows them as so. This does not affect the phase at all and installation continues. For example, the demo installation did not face this error. These errors can be ignored and no action is necessary. Although the product family tree node will show the error symbol, the overall postconfigure phase will show a completed status.

Startup Phase

Once the Postconfigure phase is complete on all nodes, click Next in the wizard to proceed to the Startup phase shown in Figure 10-26.

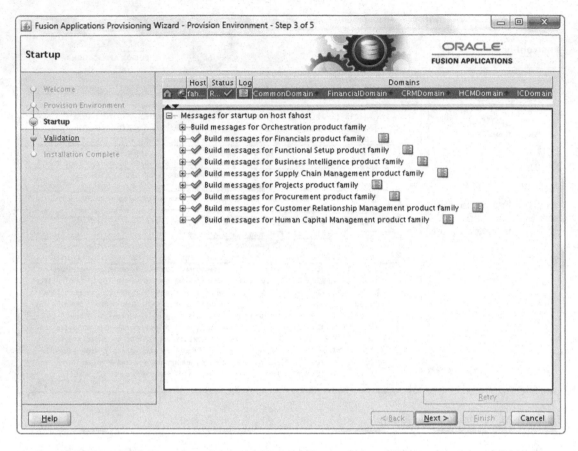

Figure 10-26. *Startup phase status screen*

After completion of the Postconfigure phase your installation is near complete and there is no further backup taken from here onward. Once the Startup phase has been kicked off from the primordial host, start the same from primary hosts (if available), secondary hosts (if available), and DMZ host (if available) using following command-line interface scripts.

```
./runProvisioning.sh -responseFile <Response File path> -target startup \
[-ignoreSysPrereqs true]
```

For example:

```
[fusion@primaryhost ]$ cd /app/fusion/provisioning/bin
[fusion@primaryhost bin]$./runProvisioning.sh -responseFile \
/app/fusion/provisioning/bin/provisioning.rsp -target startup -ignoreSysPrereqs true
```

The following important actions are performed during the Startup phase.

- Startup phase essentially brings up all domains administration servers and managed servers including middleware and Application managed servers for the host where the phase is running. Although these servers are supposed to be running from the Postconfigure phase, it does a clean restart of all required servers just in case the host was restarted after successful completion of postconfigure.

- Performs GUID reconciliation to make sure the seeded policies and grants are reconciled between the Oracle Fusion Data Security and policy store.

The actual ANT command executed behind the scenes is as follows.

```
/app/fusion/provisioning/ant/bin/ant \
-f /app/fusion/provisioning/provisioning-build/orchestration-build.xml \
-Dresponsefile.input=/app/fusion/provisioning/bin/provisioning.rsp \
-Dconfigframework.lib.dir=/app/fusion/provisioning/lib \
-Dtools.lib.dir=/app/fusion/provisioning/lib \
-logger oracle.apps.fnd.provisioning.ant.taskdefs.util.logger.ProvisioningLogger \
-lib /app/fusion/provisioning/lib/oracle-provisioning-antlogger.jar \
-lib /app/fusion/provisioning/lib/ojdl.jar \
-lib /app/fusion/provisioning/lib/dms.jar \
-Dpreverify.ignore true \
-Ddebug.timestamp 11_11_14_10_07_32 \
-Dprovisioning.target startup startup
```

The following are the important files created during the Startup phase. If you have any issues with the phase you may need to refer to these files for troubleshooting.

Log files: Created at <APPLICATIONS_BASE>/logs/provisioning/plan<timestamp>/<hostname>. For example, /app/oracle/logs/provisioning/plan1415477981901/fahost.

```
runProvisioning-startup.log
runProvisioning-<product_family>-startup.log
runProvisioning-<product_family>-<managed_server>-startup.log
runProvisioning-startup-logstatus.log
runProvisioning-startup.out
```

Phaseguards: Created at <APPLICATIONS_BASE>/provisioning/phaseguards. For example, /app/oracle/provisioning/phaseguards. You may notice that there are no product domains related phaseguard files created in this phase. Hence the cleanup and restore are done for complete phase instead of failed product domains.

```
startup-fahost-STARTED.grd
startup-fahost-ENDED.grd
startup-fahost-COMPLETED.grd
```

Validate Phase

Once the Startup phase is complete on all hosts, click Next in the wizard to proceed to the Validate phase, as shown in Figure 10-27.

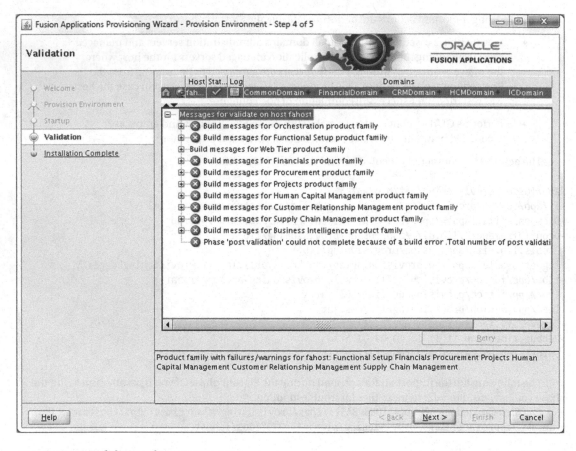

Figure 10-27. *Validation phase status screen*

Once all the services are started, the installer will proceed to the final phase of provisioning—the Validate phase. You may see the errors shown in Figure 10-27 but be patient since these errors are expected on current release. We will discuss this in a little while. Once the Validate phase has been kicked off from the primordial host, start it from the primary hosts (if available), the secondary hosts (if available), and the DMZ host (if available) using the following command-line interface scripts.

```
./runProvisioning.sh -responseFile <Response File path> -target validate \
[-ignoreSysPrereqs true]
```

For example,

```
[fusion@primaryhost ]$ cd /app/fusion/provisioning/bin
[fusion@primaryhost bin]$./runProvisioning.sh -responseFile \
/app/fusion/provisioning/bin/provisioning.rsp -target validate -ignoreSysPrereqs true
```

The Validate phase does a variety of checks to validate the installation. These checks include application URLs reachability, validation of data sources, and more. Similar to the Preverify phase, the Validate phase also does not stop processing if a particular build target or product domain validation if any errors or warnings are encountered. Instead it keeps track of the errors and displays a consolidated list of errors at the end. Also similar to the Startup phase, this phase needs to be restarted as a whole even when only specific product domains encountered errors.

The actual ANT command executed behind the scenes is as follows.

```
/app/fusion/provisioning/ant/bin/ant \
-f /app/fusion/provisioning/provisioning-build/orchestration-build.xml \
-Dresponsefile.input=/app/fusion/provisioning/bin/provisioning.rsp \
-Dconfigframework.lib.dir=/app/fusion/provisioning/lib \
-Dtools.lib.dir=/app/fusion/provisioning/lib \
-logger oracle.apps.fnd.provisioning.ant.taskdefs.util.logger.ProvisioningLogger \
-lib /app/fusion/provisioning/lib/oracle-provisioning-antlogger.jar \
-lib /app/fusion/provisioning/lib/ojdl.jar \
-lib /app/fusion/provisioning/lib/dms.jar \
-Dpreverify.ignore false \
-Ddebug.timestamp 11_11_14_17_11_07 \
-Dprovisioning.target validate validate
```

The following are the important files created during the Configure phase. If you have any issues with the phase, you may need to refer to these files for troubleshooting.

Log files: Created at <APPLICATIONS_BASE>/logs/provisioning/plan<timestamp>/<hostname>. For example, /app/oracle/logs/provisioning/plan1415477981901/fahost:

```
runProvisioning-validate.log
runProvisioning-validate-logstatus.log
runProvisioning-validate.out
```

Phaseguards: Created at <APPLICATIONS_BASE>/provisioning/phaseguards. For example, /app/oracle/provisioning/phaseguards. You may notice that there are no product domains related phaseguard files created in this phase. Hence the cleanup and restore are done for the complete phase instead of failed product domains.

```
validate-fahost-STARTED.grd
validate-fahost-FAILED.grd (if validate phase has failed)
validate-fahost-ENDED.grd (if validate phase is successful)
validate-fahost-COMPLETED.grd (if validate phase is successful)
```

As of the current release, the Validate phase may encounter some of the known errors as mentioned next. These and a few more expected error messages are documented in the Oracle Support Document ID 1487115.1 and 1404577.1. If there are any other validation errors you must resolve them before proceeding to the Summary phase.

```
MESSAGE=Failed connecting to http://fahost:7010/integration/worklistapp/faces/login.jspx,
Server redirected too many times (20)!DETAIL=Failed connecting to http://fahost:7010/
integration/worklistapp/faces/login.jspx, Server redirected too many times (20)
```

The following error is also ignorable.

```
The web page http://fahost:7001/em/faces/fa-faLogin;jsessionid=UUk-
ZidyFeG2FHkJupePpadc6Jwez7Iy9yk5uqIxxteJK7VQDv_d!-
1008637013?target=Farm_CommonDomain&type=oracle_ias_farm&FromContextInitFilter=true does
not contain the text, html
```

After resolving all the validation errors, the Next button on the Provisioning wizard will still not be enabled as the status of the phase is still FAILED. Perform these steps from the command-line to enable the Next button and manually change the phase status to completed successfully.

■ **Caution**   Deleting and creating files in the phaseguard directory should be used as a workaround to resolve validation phase issues *only* if none of the other options works. In any other case, you should never modify or make changes to the phaseguard files.

```
cd <APPLICATIONS_CONFIG>/phaseguards
rm validate-<host>-FAILED.grd
touch validate-<host>-COMPLETED.grd
```

The previous command will change the phase status as completed successfully and disable the Retry button. The Next button will still be disabled.

```
touch validate-<host>-ENDED.grd
```

The previous command will change the phase status as ended and enable the Next button. For example,

```
[fusion@fahost ~]$ cd /app/oracle/provisioning/phaseguards/
[fusion@fahost phaseguards]$ ls -ltr validate-fahost-*
-rwx— 1 fusion dba 0 Nov 10 13:02 validate-fahost-STARTED.grd
-rwx— 1 fusion dba 0 Nov 10 14:23 validate-fahost-FAILED.grd
[fusion@fahost phaseguards]$ rm validate-fahost-FAILED.grd
[fusion@fahost phaseguards]$ touch validate-fahost-COMPLETED.grd
[fusion@fahost phaseguards]$ touch validate-fahost-ENDED.grd
```

Now you can see that the Next button is enabled. Click Next to proceed to the final screen of post-installation summary, as shown in Figure 10-28.

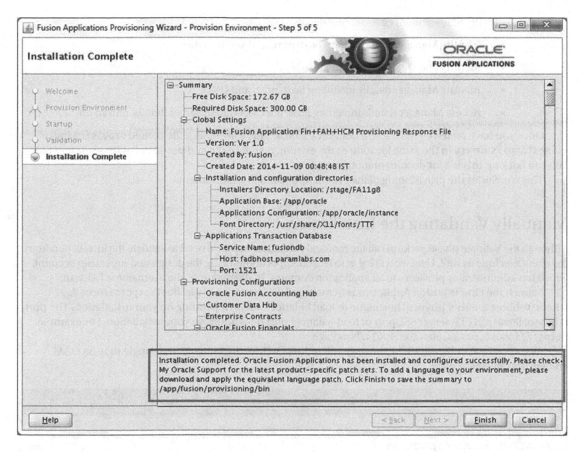

Figure 10-28. Post-installation summary screen

The post-installation summary screen provides vital information about your Fusion Applications environment. The following are the few important details that the screen displays. You need not copy the content manually since once you click Finish, it will create a provisioning summary file that contains this information.

- Disk space information

- Response file details

- Applications transaction database host, port, and service name

- List of products and configurations provisioned

- Details of each domain, respective admin server, each managed server and related ports, URLs, and home directories

- Web tier host detail

- Identity Management environment details

    - Identity Management database host, port, and service name

    - Identity and OPSS policy store details

    - Identity Manager details including host, port, and URLs

    - Access Manager details including host, port, OAM AAA server details, and so on

Once you have reviewed the information, click Finish. This will create a file named `provisioning-<timestamp>.summary` in the same location as the existing response file and pre-installation summary file. You can back up this file for documentation purposes.

This concludes the provisioning of the Fusion Applications environment.

Manually Validating the Installation

Although the Validate phase performs all the required validation steps, we need to validate the installation from the client machine as well. Here we will log in to Fusion Applications using the designated super user account, which has administrator privileges to all application domains. In this example, the username is `FAAdmin`.

Launch the Oracle Fusion Applications homepage URL at `https://<webhost>:<port>/homePage` where webhost is either physical hostname or load balancer name depending on your installation. The port is `CommonDomain` HTTP server SSL port or load balancer port depending on your installation. For example, `https://fahost.paramlabs.com:10634/homePage`.

As you can see in Figure 10-29, the page will redirect to Identity Management single sign-on OAM credentials collection page.

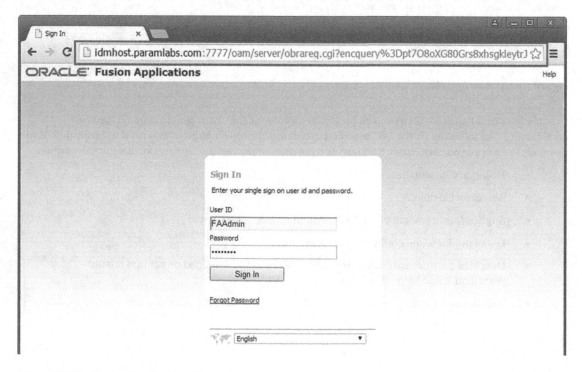

Figure 10-29. *Fusion Applications Login screen*

Log in as the FAADMIN user here. Once the login is successful you will be redirected to the Fusion Applications homepage, as shown in Figure 10-30.

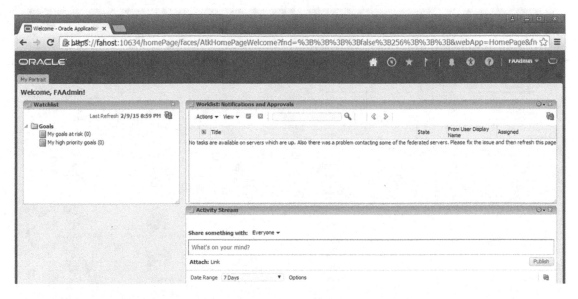

Figure 10-30. *Oracle Fusion Applications homepage*

We will discuss about the Fusion Applications interface in coming chapters. For now our focus is only to validate the installation. Click on Navigator to see list of functions available for the user. Once you have clicked on the Navigator icon you will see a menu that contains specific functions for the user (in this case FAAdmin), as shown in Figure 10-31.

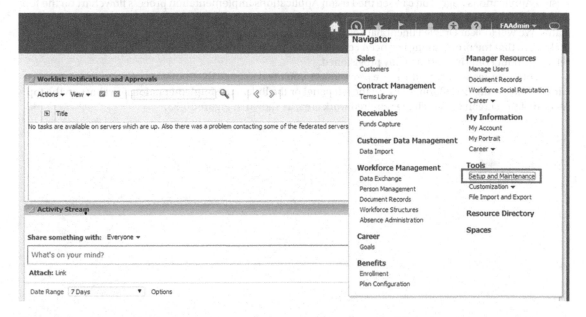

Figure 10-31. *Fusion Applications Navigator menu*

Click on the Setup and Maintenance link to go to the Oracle Fusion Functional Setup Manager screen, as shown in Figure 10-32.

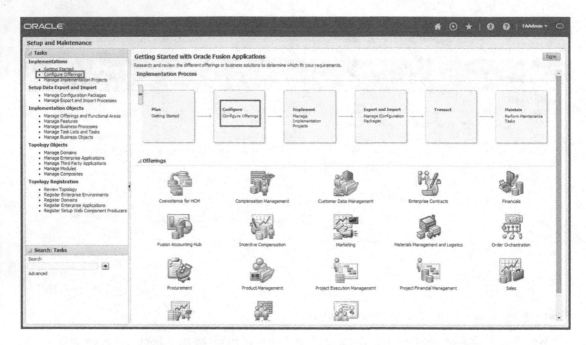

Figure 10-32. *Fusion Applications Setup and Maintenance screen*

Figure 10-32 shows the homepage for setup and maintenance, which is the Getting Started with Oracle Fusion Applications page. You can see the Fusion Applications implementation process flowchart on the top along with the list of all Fusion Applications product offerings at the bottom regardless of their provisioning status. We will look at Oracle Functional Setup Manager in detail in later chapters but here our aim is to make sure that the provisioning has been completed normally and that all the selected product families and related product offerings are actually provisioned.

In order to see which products are provisioned, you need to go to the Configure Offerings page. You can click on the Configure Offerings link on the left panel or the link in the implementation flowchart on the top section of the screen to launch the required work area, as shown in Figure 10-33.

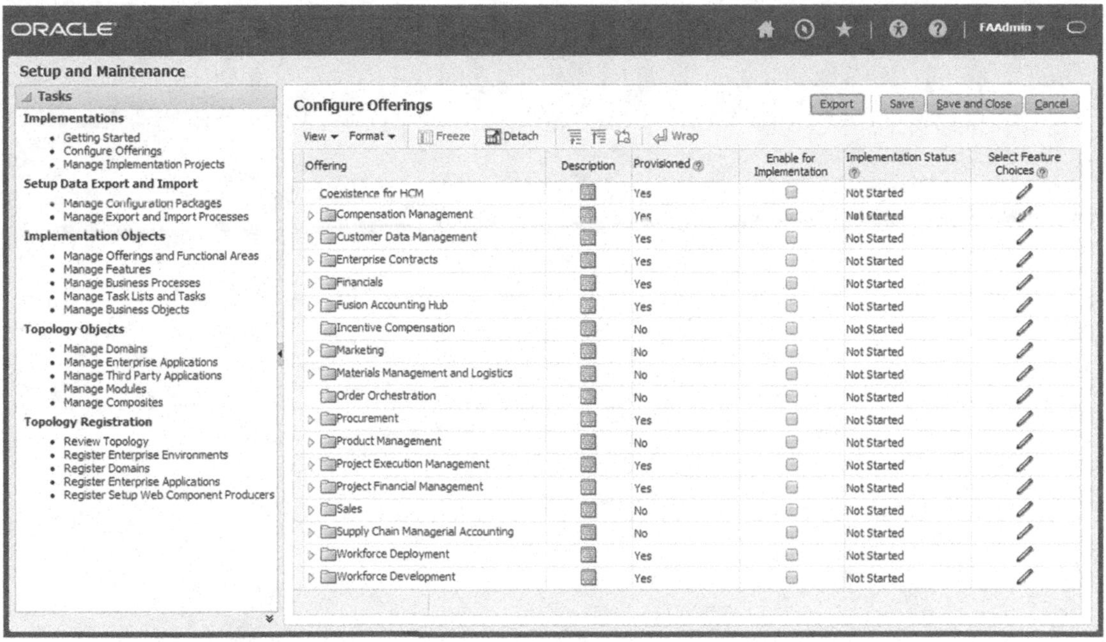

Figure 10-33. Configure Offerings page

The Configure Offerings page shows you list of all Fusion Applications products available for the release along with the Provisioned column which suggests whether the product offering has been provisioned or not. There are other columns like Enable for Implementation and Implementation Status, Select Feature Choices, and so on, which are required in order to do the functional implementation of the Fusion Applications product. We will look at this in later chapters. You can see that the selected products are Provisioned but the implementation status is Not Started. This is the expected status. You can refer to individual product implementation guide to further implement the products.

This concludes the Fusion Applications installation. The following chapters look at the Fusion Applications administration activities.

Summary

In this final chapter of installation you saw the main installation actions for provisioning an Oracle Fusion Applications environment. You saw both the command-line as well as graphical interface options for provisioning on single-node and multi-node topologies. You also explored the basics of Apache ANT and learned how the build process works. You explored the concept of ANT projects, targets, tasks, properties, and so on, and the vital role they play in the Fusion Applications provisioning process.

We saw the important input files used by the provisioning framework, including XML build files, tasks, and libraries, and learned about their location in the provisioning framework home. You also explored the important output files generated during provisioning and how they help you troubleshoot any issues encountered during provisioning. You also saw how to restart a failed or aborted installation using automated and manual cleanup/restore. At the end of the chapter, you saw how to manually make sure that the provisioning was complete and consistent with the product configurations you selected earlier.

PART IV

Administration

CHAPTER 11

■ ■ ■

Understanding Oracle Fusion Applications Interface

At this stage we have our Oracle Fusion Applications Environment ready and running. Before we begin with Fusion Applications administration, you must understand the Fusion Applications interface if you are not already aware of it. If you are aware of Fusion Applications interface, this chapter will provide a quick reference for you to various sections of the screens and will explore the common functionality provided with every Fusion Applications product. Since this is an intermediate chapter between Fusion Applications installation and administration, we will only have a quick look at the various features.

Getting Started with Fusion Applications Interface

As we saw earlier, Oracle Fusion Applications was built by incorporating the best practices and processes of various existing ERPs from Oracle. Fusion Applications interface also incorporates the best of the possible features from these application suites, including Oracle E-Business Suite, PeopleSoft, Siebel, JD Edwards, and so on. If you have been working on any of the ERPs from Oracle, then you are familiar with specific interface of the ERP you have used. These interfaces differ a lot and are based on different technologies, including Oracle Forms, OA Framework, Java, and many other web based technologies. If your organization is using multiple ERP suites for different products then the user must learn all these interfaces. Fusion Applications provides the best features of these ERPs in a unified interface, which eliminates the need for using different tools for business transactions, reporting, analytics, and so on. We will look at these features of Fusion Applications interface in the next section.

Figure 11-1 provides a glimpse at the various Oracle interfaces, including PeopleSoft, Siebel, E-Business Suite, JD Edwards, and so on, and still does not include all the interface types for these application suites. As mentioned earlier, all these application suites were built on numerous development technologies, so they vary from each other drastically. That is, until Oracle acquired these companies over a period of time. Oracle has constantly tried to bring synergy to these interfaces by evolving the look and feel of these products to at least a similar theme. The latest releases of all these ERPs have a similar layout, including similar UI areas and color combinations. However, the functionalities and processes still carry the legacy of the original products. Fusion Applications aims at providing a consolidated view of these different processes in unified application dashboards. Since the Fusion Applications interface was built from ground up, Oracle has been able to invest ample time in building the Fusion Applications user interface (UI) around the new user experience (UX) strategy. We will look at these concepts in the upcoming section.

© Tushar Thakker 2015
T. Thakker, *Pro Oracle Fusion Applications*, DOI 10.1007/978-1-4842-0983-7_11

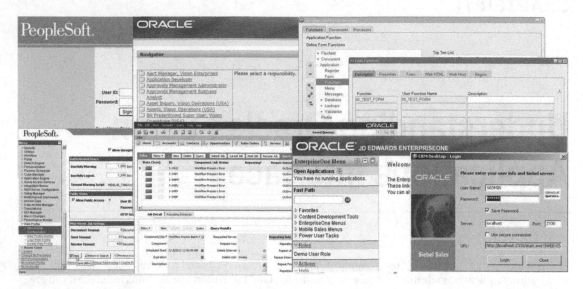

Figure 11-1. *Interfaces of various ERPs from Oracle*

We can see in Figure 11-1 that the enterprises use different interfaces for selected modules from various ERPs. For example, if your organization is using PeopleSoft for HRMS, Oracle EBS for financials, and so on, you may have been using different interfaces that are built on different frameworks. Each of these products also provides multiple interfaces including web, desktop client, forms-based interfaces, and so on. Oracle Fusion Applications is developed on a flexible UI shell based on ADF and WebCenter, which encompasses the best of the products and interface features of these products.

Now let's look at Figure 11-2, which shows the major differences between a traditional applications suite product and the Oracle Fusion Applications interface.

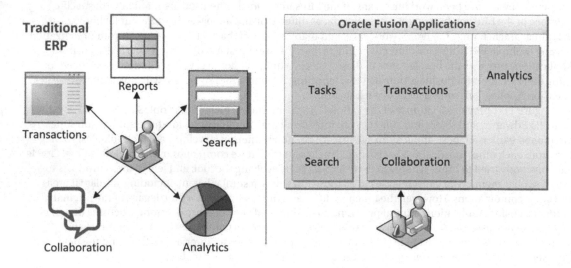

Figure 11-2. *Other ERPs versus the Oracle Fusion Applications interface*

Even if we look at a single ERP product like E-Business Suite, Siebel, PeopleSoft, and so on, we have to go through different screens for common functionalities like search, reports/analytics, collaboration, and the main work area/transaction related pages. So we must navigate from one page to another in order to have a holistic view of the business area. But Oracle has made an impressive user interface keeping the user experience in mind, which allows you to have a consolidated view of business area in single screen. That single screen is divided into multiple sections covering transactions, reports/analytics, and collaboration within the organization and Enterprise search features. This eliminates the need to navigate through a number of screens to complete a particular business task.

Fusion Applications User Interface Layout

Before going through the common functionalities available in the Fusion Applications interface, let's first look at the Fusion Applications UI shell areas. These are the logical sections of the screen where a developer may place different functional blocks like Tasks, Search, Cart, Business Intelligence reports, and so on. Not all of these areas are mandatory in all the screens of Fusion Applications, but all the objects on the Applications screen will fall into one of these categories.

The following are the important goals of these UI areas.

- Provide *consistency* across the entire application suite by placing the functional blocks in the same logical place across various screens to improve familiarity and simplicity of the interface.

- Minimize the need to go through multiple pages to complete single tasks or business functions. Ideally the users can initiate any task in Fusion Applications using a maximum of 2-3 clicks and complete the tasks in same screen with different regions and panes.

- Provide role-based interface by dynamically populating relevant application dashboards, reports, and collaboration tools depending on the applications and management role of the user.

- Provide an exception-based interface, which will alert the user about the pending tasks instead of the user having to go through tedious methods of locating the tasks of importance. This applies for reporting where exception-based reports and analysis provide a quick overview of the business goals and related actions to be taken. Management by exception drastically improves the productivity of the users or specialists by focusing only on what needs to be done instead of monitoring a large number of business objects and transactions.

Figure 11-3 shows an example page of Fusion Applications along with the classification of various user interface areas.

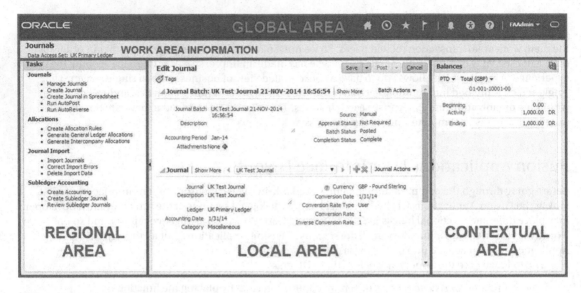

Figure 11-3. *Oracle Fusion Applications user interface layout*

Let's look at the Fusion Applications UI shell areas, as shown in Figure 11-3.

- *Global area*: This area covers the top of the screen across its full width. It generally remains static across all screens for the user or for the particular product-related pages. It contains global functional controls and menus that drive the contents of remaining areas of the screen. The major UI elements in the Global area are application branding (the default is Oracle Fusion Applications but we can customize the logo and color scheme based on organization's branding patterns), navigator, application home, favorites/recent items, notifications, logged on username (with Global area context menu for personalization, help and sign out), global search (optional), Watchlist, accessibility, and so on. We will discuss these elements in the coming sections.

- *Work Area Information area*: This area occupies a narrow panel with a full-screen width below the Global area. It contains text labels, including the current page's work area title as well as any relevant information about the work area.

- *Regional area*: This area is the collapsible left panel of the screen under Work Area Information panel. Most of the screens will have a Regional area, except the some dashboard screens. This area contains tasks related to the application role. These tasks define and control the content being populated on the Local area. Certain tasks may be in navigation tree format if there are any sub-tasks available in the main category. It may also contain a Regional Search pane as well as collaboration tools. The Regional Search may have additional tabs in the Local area. Certain screens for the application administrator or manager roles may have high-level analytics panes as well in this area.

- *Local area*: This area is the default and most important area of any Fusion Applications screen. This is where the users will perform most of their activities, analysis, and transactions. The Local area contains all related control buttons and links to complete the entire task without referring back to Regional area most of the time since the user can collapse the Regional area during the routine operation. The Local area may have static tabs and dynamic tabs. The dynamic tabs could be generated based on the flow from the Local area or based on a search from the Regional area. The Local area may have multiple regions for various activities, including local search (with search by example option), analytics related to particular task, collaboration panels, and so on. Sections of the Local area may be derived from saved searches as well. We will look at these functions in the coming sections.

- *Contextual area*: This area occupies the right panel of the Fusion Applications screen. This is an optional area and available in specific screens only. The contents of this area are dependent on the selected context in the Local area. For example, it may contain an analytics or Business Intelligence pane that may be populated based on the data in local area. In Fusion UI context, it may contain consolidated data or container like a shopping cart for external facing websites, and so on. The content of this area is driven by the Local area and it might not be part of the overall workflow of a task but may be used as a reference. This panel can be collapsed if it's not required during the regular functional tasks.

Logging into Oracle Fusion Applications

Before we start looking at the Oracle Fusion Applications interface, let's first see how to log in to the Fusion Applications and launch the homepage. If you are the administrator and are trying to access the applications just after the provisioning is complete, use the FAAdmin or whichever super user you had selected during provisioning process. If the administrator gave you a login account, then use it to log on to the applications interface. The login URL for launching the Fusion Applications homepage is similar to the following.

```
https://<hostname or load-balancer name>:<port>/homePage
```

Note that the homepage login URL depends on your selection of load balancer, internal/external URLs, and so on, and it was displayed in the post-provisioning summary screen. If you have not captured the URL then you can get the details from the saved summary file provisioning-<timestamp>.summary file located at <FRAMEWORK_LOCATION>/provisioning/bin. If you selected the different summary filename and location, check the respective file and locate the link.

```
Home Page
   Host: fahost.paramlabs.com
   Managed Server Port: 7006
   Application URLs
      https://fahost.paramlabs.com:10634/homePage
      https://fahost.paramlabs.com:10634/homePageApi
```

As you can see, the URL for the Fusion Applications homepage in this example is https://fahost.paramlabs.com:10634/homePage. Locate the URL corresponding to your setup and launch it. We have already seen the Fusion Applications Login screen and homepage screen example in the previous chapter.

Common Features Across Fusion Applications

In this section we look at the common features and functionalities available throughout the Fusion Applications interface regardless of the product family. Most of these features are available to all users so we will discuss these common features here. This will help you understand and navigate through the applications interface for effective administration.

Oracle Fusion Applications interface is built using Oracle WebCenter technology, which provides a powerful and highly customizable user interface using WebCenter UI shell components. It also provides a desktop integration for power Excel users and seamless integration to and from Excel worksheets. Figure 11-4 provides a summary of the common features of the Fusion Applications interface.

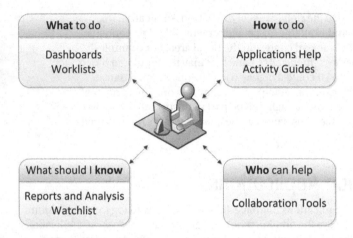

Figure 11-4. *Example of Fusion Applications common features*

■ **Note** The Fusion Applications interface got a major facelift from Oracle Fusion Applications 11g, Release 8 (11.1.8) onward. The common functionalities were available as a menubar in Global area until release 7, but from release 8 onward, these are available as a set of icons on top-right portion of the Global area.

These common features allow you to answer the most important questions related to the user interface, such as what the user's role is related to the business based on the applications dashboards and worklist notifications, how the task needs to be done (using Fusion Applications embedded help and activity guides), what the user should know (exceptions on based reports and watchlist), and who can help from within the organization or team to resolve issues (using collaboration tools like discussion forums, activity streams, and so on).

Settings and Actions Menu

You can use the Settings and Actions menu to access many of the features discussed here. This menu is always available in the Global area of any screen. You can access this menu by clicking on the currently logged on user name on right corner of Global area. This menu contains links to user specific Settings and Actions for Personalization, Administration, and Troubleshooting. We will discuss the individual contents of this menu in the next section. This menu also contains the Log Out link, so you may need to access this menu and then click on Sign Out on top-right corner in order to log out of the applications.

Figure 11-5 shows an example of Settings and Actions menu in the Global area.

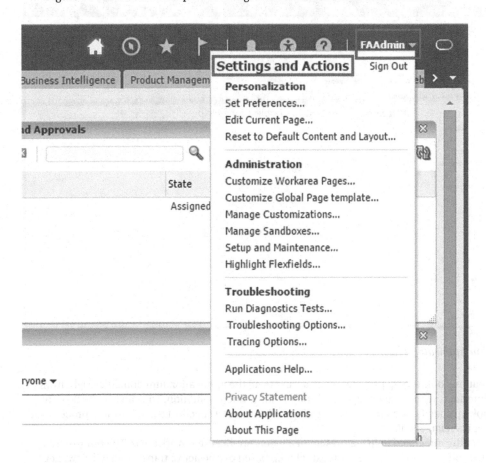

Figure 11-5. *Fusion Applications Settings and Actions menu*

Help

The Fusion Applications Help Feature has been integrated throughout the applications interface. This eliminates the need for the user to go through user documentation while using the applications functionalities.

■ **Tip** Help-related pages are served by a dedicated WebLogic cluster in the common domain named `HelpPortalServerCluster`. If this service is down then some help-related features may not work.

You can access Fusion Applications Help either manually using Global Area ➤ Settings Menu ➤ Applications Help or directly using integrated help features in the transaction window. Let's first look at the Fusion Applications Help home screen, which is displayed when you use the Applications Help link in the Global Area menu. Figure 11-6 provides a glimpse of the Fusion Applications Help home screen when launched from the Global Area menu.

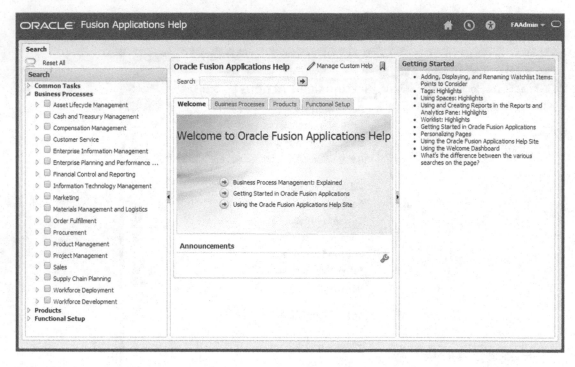

Figure 11-6. *Fusion Applications help*

Fusion Applications online help provides quick access to all the application functionalities right from the Applications interface, without needing to go through offline documentation. You can use the Search functionality to look up specific subjects or use the left panel to select a specific task or business process and look up the help topics related to it.

Now let's look at the integrated help features in the Fusion Applications Work areas. The built-in help integration provides you a means to look up contextual help based on the active transaction window. Let's understand these integrated help options using an example screen of a journals-related work area and the types of help features available in the example screen, as shown in Figure 11-7.

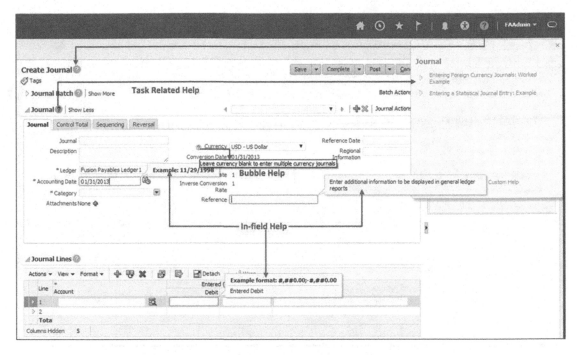

Figure 11-7. *Fusion Applications user help features*

As you can see in Figure 11-7, the transaction screen has multiple options to look up help related to the tasks, fields, and types of values to be entered.

- *Task-related help*: When you click the Help icon in the Global area on any page, you will see a yellow Help icon in front of every section of the screen. Clicking on this icon will bring up the Fusion Applications help frame with a list of related tasks.

- *Bubble help*: Some fields have dedicated help icons to provide additional information or notes about the field. Bubble help pops up when you mouse over the built-in Help icon next to the field.

- *In-field help*: Clicking in the blank area of the field pops up an in-field help, which provides example of valid values for the specific field along with the format of the value to be entered.

Dashboards

Fusion Applications dashboards provide you with a one-stop overview of all that you need to know for the relevant business role for example manager, administrator, specialist, analyst, and so on. Once you log in to Fusion Applications you will notice a tabbed interface where each tab links to the dashboard for the particular product and application role.

The default dashboard is the Welcome Dashboard and it's available with every Fusion Applications user regardless of the application roles. This dashboard provides you with important notifications through the watchlist and quick access to tasks that you may need to complete or reports of importance using the worklist. It also provides quick access to collaboration events within the organization using activity streams. We will look at all these elements next. Now let's look at the application-specific dashboard example, as shown in Figure 11-8.

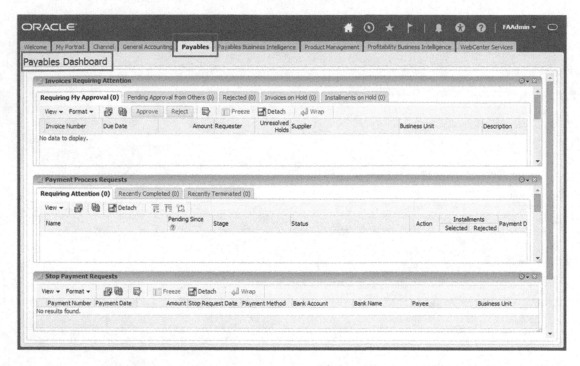

Figure 11-8. *Dashboard without Regional area*

A dashboard might not have Regional area since the purpose of dashboard is to give you an overview of all critical activities that fall under your responsibility. Figure 11-8 shows an example of a product-specific dashboard without a Regional area. You can see multiple collapsible blocks here to give a quick access to the areas of interest depending on the application role assigned to the user.

Now let's look at an example dashboard with a Regional area as well. Figure 11-9 shows an example dashboard with a Regional area. As you can see the specific application role requires the user to perform certain tasks related to general accounting often, so the dashboard provides quick links to those tasks for the users in order to reduce the number of pages they have to navigate to perform day-to-day functional tasks.

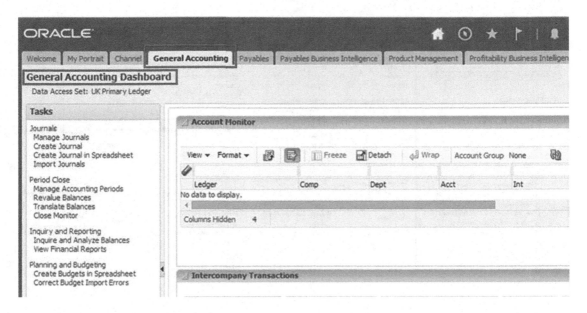

Figure 11-9. *Dashboard with Regional area*

Navigator

The Navigator is available throughout the Fusion Applications interface. The Navigator provides quick links to application-specific work areas depending on your assigned roles and responsibilities. Since a user may have multiple application roles, you may see various application-related links grouped under corresponding product names. Let's look at how to access the Navigator and see how it works.

Figure 11-10 shows how to access the Navigator menu in any screen by clicking on the Navigator icon in the Global area. This will bring up a menu with various task-related links specific to the roles assigned to the user. The navigator has a few common tasks that are always available to each user created in Fusion Applications and the remaining tasks are specific to the application roles. For example, scheduled processes or reports are available to all users having an employee role assigned to them. We can also customize the Navigator menu by using Manage Customization task. The Manage Customization task allows you to add, remove, hide, or display certain menu items. We will look at how to locate and execute such administrative tasks in the administration-related chapters.

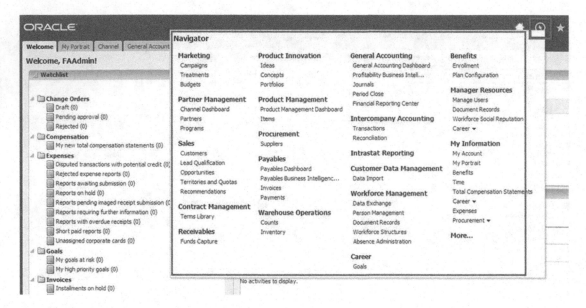

Figure 11-10. *Fusion Applications Navigator menu*

Watchlist

The Watchlist is an additional navigation feature available in the Oracle Fusion Applications user interface. The Watchlist region is available on the Fusion Applications welcome dashboard for all users. It allows you to have a quick look at the important counts related to your business role based on predefined criteria. Practically speaking, Watchlist links are predefined count-based searches that provide a shortcut to relevant work areas, allowing you to monitor your areas of interest. For example, a manager needs to see the expense reports submitted by the team for approval so instead of going to the expenses screen every time, he would prefer to see the number of pending expense reports in the Watchlist and, if the count of pending requests is more than zero, then only go to the relevant screen by clicking on the link. Depending on the application roles assigned to the user there will be set of predefined Watchlist items already populated for the user. But the user can always create custom saved searches in the application and add the saved search as a Watchlist item using the Set Watchlist Options administrative task. Figure 11-11 shows an example of a Watchlist on the welcome screen.

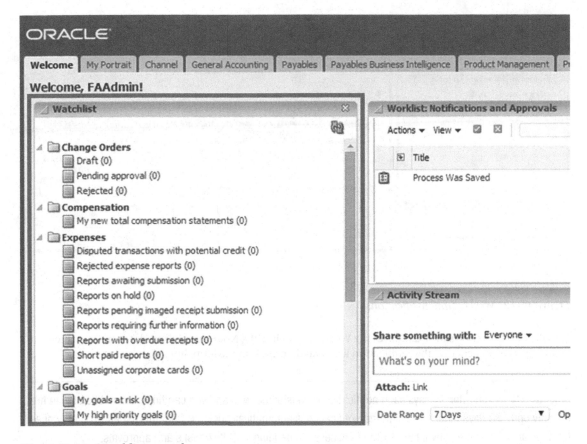

Figure 11-11. Watchlist example

You can use the Preferences ➤ Watchlist personalization option to select or deselect the items you want to display in the Watchlist.

Worklist and Notifications

The Worklist region is available on the welcome page and it displays new notifications and approvals specific to the currently logged on user ordered by the notification creation date. While the Watchlist presents the counts of important tasks or alerts, the Worklist provides individual workflow alerts and notifications as and when they are available. When you click on an individual worklist item, it will take you to the related work area for viewing the details or taking an action on the workflow. You may find a lot of similarities between the Worklist and Watchlist with the difference being that the Worklist has dynamic content based on the availability of new notifications while the Watchlist will always have the saved searches displayed regardless of the result count (unless you have selected the option to hide non-zero results in the Watchlist personalization preferences).

While the Worklist is available on the home dashboard for the user, for all other screens Fusion Applications provides a Notification icon in the Global area. Clicking on the Notification icon in any screen will bring up a drop-down menu with list of recent *unread* notifications. When you click on the More link, it shows a list of all available notifications, as shown in Figure 11-12. With the default settings, any new notifications will automatically appear in the Global area.

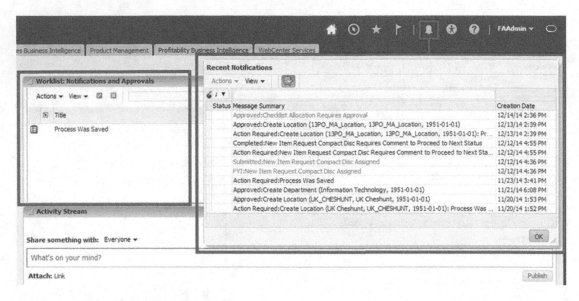

Figure 11-12. *Worklist and notifications*

Figure 11-12 shows the example of the Worklist as well as the Notification drop-down menu, which shows up after you click on the Notification icon and then click on the More link.

■ **Note** Note that after 14 days each notification is considered read and you can find each notification in this list only up to 30 days. After that point, the notification is automatically deleted from this list and you may need to manually access the relevant work area to access the pending workflow tasks and approvals.

Personalization

As the name suggests, the Personalization area allows you to customize the layout display by adding, removing, or modifying panels or regions, setting language preferences and accessibility preferences, or changing the way the tables show up on specific pages, including the default search criteria. All these changes affect only the user performing the personalization and not the application in general. Certain personalization tasks are effective at the global level for the user so they will be applicable throughout every screens of the application, whereas other personalization options are specific to the pages that you personalize. We will look at each of the personalization option available in Fusion Applications. Before that let's look at how to access the personalization options in the Fusion Applications common interface.

Figure 11-13 provides a glimpse at the Personalization section of the Settings and Actions menu in the Global area.

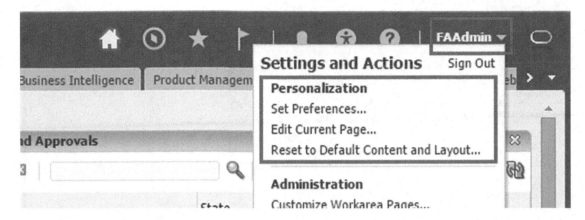

Figure 11-13. *Personalization options in the Global area*

When you click on the username in the Global area, you can see the following main commands related to personalization.

- Set Preferences

- Edit Current Page

- Reset to Default Content and Layout

Let's understand each of these commands one-by-one since as an Applications user or even an administrator you will be required to use these options often. Note that other than the Global menu, there is an additional icon next to notification for bringing up the Accessibility screen, which is also related to personalization. We will discuss that when we talk about the Accessibility feature.

Preferences

The Oracle Fusion Applications Preferences page allows you to set user preferences for a number of categories, including choice of default language, regional formats, as well as many function-specific preferences. The left pane of the Preferences page has two sections. The first section contains common preferences categories including regional, language, accessibility, password, and so on. The second section contains application-specific preferences, for example, expense preferences, sales preferences, calendar and appointments preferences, and so on.

Figure 11-14 shows an example of the landing page when you choose Set Preferences in the Global area Settings menu. This takes you to the General Preferences screen.

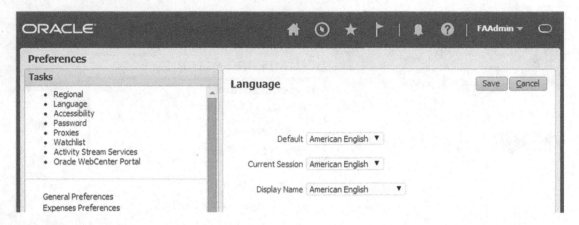

Figure 11-14. *Language Preferences screen*

By default, the General Preferences page contains language-specific preferences, and this is essentially the same screen as when you click the Language link in the Tasks region on the left. This allows you to choose a display language for the current session or set the default language option for the currently logged on user.

The other preferences you can set are as follows:

- *Regional*: Allows you to personalize regional settings like date format, currency, and so on.

- *Password*: Allows you to change your Fusion Applications password. Clicking on this link will take you to the Oracle Identity Management Password screen.

- *Proxies*: The Proxies Personalization option allows you to add a list of people who can act as your proxy in your absence. These people will have access to your roles and can perform certain activities on your behalf.

- *Activity Stream Services*: Allows you to select and follow any of the activities that are visible to you and you may want to see those activities on your homepage under the Activity Streams region.

- *Watchlist*: The Watchlist preferences allow you to select the list of important count-related queries in your user specific Watchlist in the welcome dashboard. For all the enabled Watchlist items, the result will be displayed even if the count is 0. If you want to monitor only those items or saved searches for which there are non-zero results, you can select the Hide Items With no Results Found checkbox at the bottom of the Watchlist preferences screen. Figure 11-15 shows the Watchlist Preferences screen.

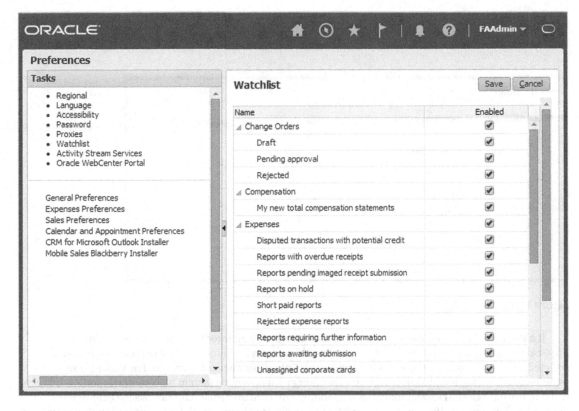

Figure 11-15. *Watchlist Preferences screen*

- *Accessibility*: The Fusion Applications interface provides Accessibility preferences via a dedicated Accessibility icon in the Global area as well as through the Global Settings menu. It allows you to optimize the screen-viewing experience for people with disabilities or visual difficulties. Figure 11-16 shows the Accessibility screen, which can be invoked using either of these links.

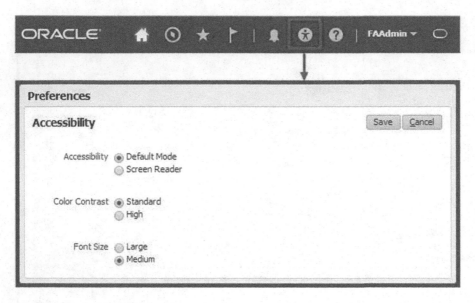

Figure 11-16. *Accessibility preferences*

It allows you to select if the user is using assistive Screen Reader technology while using Fusion Applications interface. It may also provide additional shortcuts for Screen Reader users if this option is selected. The other available accessibility options are Color Contrast and Font Size. The Color Contrast preference allows the user to select high contrast along with operating system high contrast mode, which will dim the background images for easier readability. The Font Size preference allows the user to let Fusion Applications interface display the content according to the browser's large font setting since this setting scales up the complete layout. This preference will allow Fusion Applications interface to render in accordance with the browser's large font settings. If you are not using large font settings in your browser, leave this preference at medium.

Edit Current Page

The Personalization settings that we have discussed so far are applicable at the global level for the given user, regardless of the screen the user is accessing. But at times the user needs to customize certain screens or dashboards according to user's personalization requirements. Although Fusion Applications interface supports ad hoc changes in table width, layout, and so on, any such changes applied without using personalization options might not persist when the user logs off, depending on what was modified. The Edit Current page link in the Global area settings brings up the customization screen for the current page.

This personalization option allows you to design a custom layout of your page, as shown in Figure 11-17. It displays the title of the page being edited along with the user's details for which the page layout is being personalized. You can choose the regions to be displayed or hidden, add new regions, or modify the placement of the panels. Once you have made the required changes, you can save the preferences for the particular page and these changes will persist even after logoff.

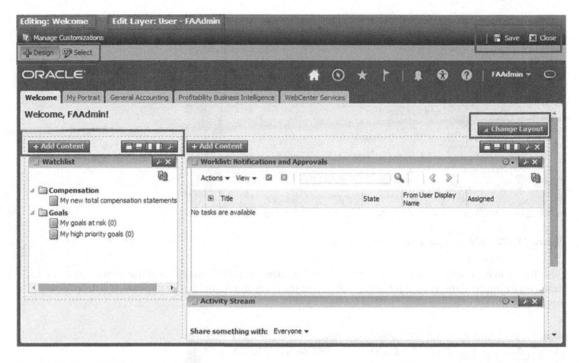

Figure 11-17. *Edit Current Page screen*

In addition to the Edit Current Page option, you can also customize the default search queries to be run when the specific page loads. For this, you can create a Saved Search and then set the search criteria as the default for the page. We will cover Saved Search when we look at the Search feature next.

The last option in the Personalization section of the Global Settings menu is Reset to Default Content and Layout. You can use this option to reset all customizations done by the user for every customized page. However, this does not affect the Saved Searches or if any page has any Saved Search set as the default or set to run automatically on page load.

Favorites and Recent Items

The Favorites and Recent Items menu is another Fusion Applications navigation-related feature. These features allow you to refer to your most visited links quickly as compared to navigating to them manually or through the Navigator menu. The Favorites feature is particularly more useful for the important daily tasks that are not part of the Navigator menu. Adding those tasks to the Favorites menu helps you gain quick access to the specific task screen without accessing the application dashboard and then subsequent task links.

By default, the Favorites menu has no predefined items. To add any page to the Favorites menu, first open the page that needs to be added and then click on the Favorites icon in the Global area. Once it brings up the Favorites menu, click on Add to Favorites to add the current page in the list. Similar to a browser favorites menu, in Fusion Applications you can add a page directly under the Favorites menu or add it under an existing folder. You can also create a new folder if you want to group the favorites by product families, roles, or any other classification. In the example shown in Figure 11-18, we created a demo folder and added the Manage Implementation Projects page to it.

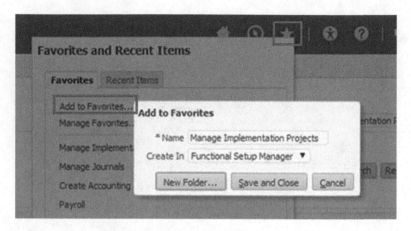

Figure 11-18. *Adding a page to the Favorites list*

Once you have added the required pages to the Favorites menu, let's now look at the menu. Figure 11-19 shows an example of the Favorites menu. Notice that the recently created folder appears as a drop-down menu with the list of pages added to that folder.

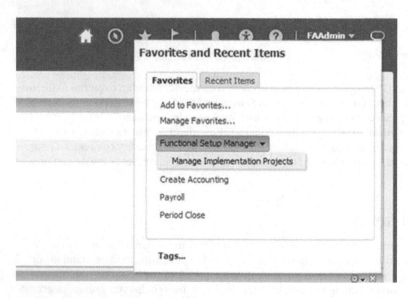

Figure 11-19. *Favorites menu example*

Favorites can be modified at any time during the regular use of the application and the changes come into effect immediately. Also the scope of this menu is limited to the user and it does not affect the other application users.

■ **Note**   For Fusion Applications release 7 and earlier, Favorites, Recent Items, and Tags were separate menus, while from release 8 onward, Favorites and Recent Items are part of single menu with two separate tabs. Tags is at the bottom of the same menu.

Now let's look at the second tab of the same menu, which is Recent Items. This list is also specific to the user only and does not affect the other application users. Unlike Favorites, this list cannot be modified manually but is populated every time you visit an application page by putting the recently visited page on the top. This helps you quickly refer to the most used pages even if they are not in your Favorites list. Figure 11-20 shows an example of Recent Items list. If you want to go back to one of the previously visited page, you may be want to use browser's Back button, but I strongly recommend you to use this feature since, this way, the application remains aware that you are navigating away from the current transaction and will display appropriate messages if any action needs to be taken on the current page before navigating to a different page.

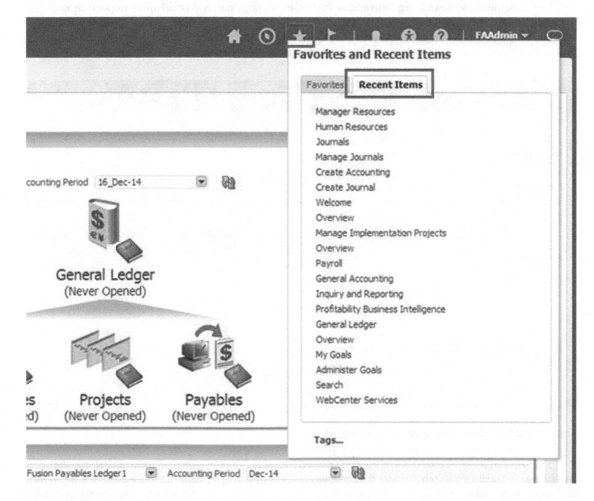

Figure 11-20. *Recent Items menu example*

Search

The Oracle Fusion Applications Search is based on the Oracle Secure Enterprise Search (SES) product. Oracle SES provides sub-second query performance for enterprise-wide content search. The Internet-like features of the Oracle Fusion Applications search also provide quick suggestions based on the partially entered query terms. The Search feature allows you to use various options including, wildcard, begins with, contains, and so on, to retrieve specific results.

■ **Note**   Since Oracle has a strategy to use Secure Enterprise Search as the indexing technology for its applications suite products only, as of early 2014 Oracle is no longer selling Oracle Secure Enterprise Search as a standalone product (with some exceptions). Oracle Fusion Applications licensing includes a restricted uses license for SES.

Fusion Application Search can be available in the Global, Regional, and Local areas, depending on the page content and context. For example, Figure 11-21 shows an example of items related the Work area, which has a Regional as well as a Local area. In this example, it allows you to directly search for the items from the regional area, which will take you directly to an item-specific page in the Local area.

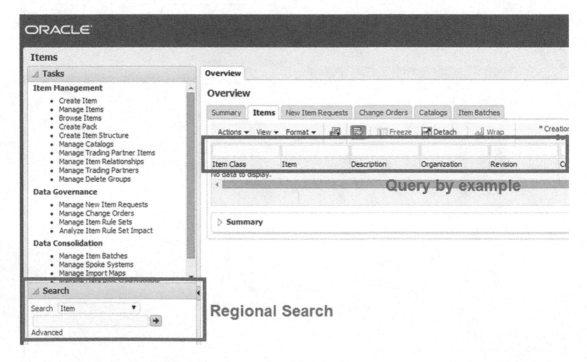

Figure 11-21. *Fusion Applications Search example*

The Local area search provides a more specific search based on more criteria than those available in the Global area. A Local area search provides the capability to query by example. Siebel interface users may be aware of a similar functionality. In this case you can enter one or more values or part of a value for multiple columns and it will immediately update the table beneath the search box with the rows matching those values or patterns.

Generally the search in the Regional area overwrites or refreshes the current search conditions in the Local area, including the query by example values. This is because most search results update the existing screen content of the Local area. However, certain Regional area search results may appear in an additional tab instead of overwriting the Local area content.

■ **Note** Note that Fusion Applications search results are not realtime since the search-related indexes are updated at certain intervals. As an administrator, you can set the indexing frequency and make sure it does not affect the application's performance.

The Oracle Fusion Applications interface also allows you to save a search query that you are using often as part of your job. These types of queries are called Saved Searches. The Saved Search feature does not contain any actual data but only the search criteria so every time it is run the results may not be the same. You can also personalize Saved Searches by adding them to the Watchlist. You can select any Saved Search as the default for the page as well, so whenever the default search runs manually you may see the results retried by the saved search query. Fusion Applications also allows you to run the Saved Search automatically, provided it is set to default. In this case as soon as you launch the page containing this Saved Search, it will automatically run the Saved Search and retrieve the query results. Figure 11-22 shows an example of creating a Saved Search.

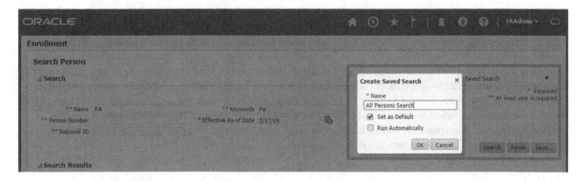

Figure 11-22. *Creating a Saved Search*

Analytics/Reports

Oracle Business Intelligence Reports and Analytics are embedded in various work areas of Oracle Fusion Applications interface. Since the reporting and analysis functionality is based on the Oracle Business Intelligence Enterprise Edition (OBIEE) and the Oracle BI Applications (OBIA), it allows users to access relevant analytical information in graphical format on the application dashboards as well as transaction pages wherever applicable. This allows the data to be presented in a meaningful format for end users. The same reports are also available from Oracle Business Intelligence Analytics homepage as well. This can be accessed from the Global area using Navigator ➤ Tools ➤ Reports and Analytics.

If the report is available in a dashboard, then you will be allowed to open it in the same work area or use More link to open it to the Oracle Business Intelligence screen, where the user will be allowed more actions including editing and copying the report. If the report is accessed from the Reports and Analytics screen then you may also see an option to edit the report using OBIEE or edit the analysis using BI Composer. Figure 11-23 shows the Create Analysis screen.

Figure 11-23. Fusion Applications Create Analysis example

ADF Desktop Integration

ADF Desktop Integration is one of the optional but salient features of Oracle Fusion Applications user interface. This allows users to have a desktop-like interface for using spreadsheets and such for uploading or editing the data in the Fusion Applications Transactional screens. There are many users who feel more comfortable using desktop spreadsheet software like Microsoft Excel to enter or edit transaction data. ADF Desktop Integration comes in the form of a Microsoft Excel plugin. In order to use this feature you must run the ADF Desktop Integration installer. This installer can either be downloaded from the Navigator menu ➤ Tools ➤ Download Desktop Integration Installer or as an administrator you can share the installer on a network drive from where the users can run the installer.

Collaboration

Fusion Applications provides a lot of collaboration tools that allow users to interact with other users in the organization, including share information, participate in discussions and receive updates, and so on. It is important to note that these collaboration-related objects might not be associated with Fusion Applications business objects. This allows the enterprise users to use Fusion Applications as single platform for business transactions as well as social interaction with other users based on projects or special interest groups.

Let's look at some of the collaboration options available in Fusion Applications.

Spaces

The Fusion Applications Spaces feature is provided through the integrated WebCenter Spaces service. It allows the users to create their own collaborative pages by using various WebCenter Portal Services based on many available page templates. Although it is not the only collaboration method available, the Spaces feature is the preferred method of collaborating in Fusion Applications. Although Spaces can be used as independent pages, a developer can also integrate Spaces content in the work area. Figure 11-24 shows an example of the Spaces screen, which can be accessed through the WebCenter Services tab, the Global Settings menu, dashboards, or even from transactional screens.

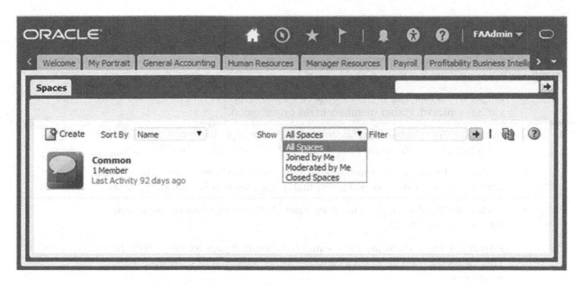

Figure 11-24. *Fusion Applications Spaces screen*

The following are some of the collaboration components that can be used in WebCenter Spaces. Each of these components is part of Oracle WebCenter Portal Services:

- *Announcements*: Provides a mechanism to communicate with a group of people about important events and activities. Announcements can be sent immediately or scheduled for a specific time.

- *Discussions*: Facilitates discussion-based communication with the users within the application or those subscribed to the specific space. It allows quick resolution of issues by forum-like community discussions as well as a searchable knowledge base.

- *Documents*: Enables storing, sharing, and attaching documents in a content repository. Documents are only available within the spaces.

- *Events*: Provides group calendar services to enable sharing of appointments, meetings, and important activities within the team.

- *Lists*: Provides a generic mechanism to create a list of items, ideas, to-do tasks, meeting activities, and a number of other possible actions. Lists are also only available within spaces.

- *Links*: Enables sharing any other related or unrelated WebCenter components mentioned in this list on a page in the form of related links. For example, you can link to knowledge base lists, wikis, discussions, documents, and so on, in your page, blog, or portal.

- *Wiki*: Allows users collaborative publishing and editing of knowledge base documents specific to the application or product using a WYSIWYG editor.

- *Tags*: Allows users to mark/tag related contents with custom labels. This allows them to quickly locate the relevant information.

Space Templates

Fusion Applications users can use any of these collaboration components to build a social Space page. These pages can be public or set up by invitation basis only (visible or hidden from search). The following are the default available templates for creating a new space.

- *Blog*: Use this template to publish and share knowledge, events, and opinions on various topics with other members in the organization.

- *Discussion Site*: Use this template to create a forum-type discussion board to allow users to exchange ideas and discuss various topics in a thread-based model.

- *Document Exchange*: Use this template to publish and share project-related or other documents within the group of individuals using attachments and sharable links.

- *Portal Site*: Use this template to create a portal-like interface for the page with a number of subsections.

- *Project Site*: Use this template to create a collaboration page for the specific project. This allows the team to access a common project calendar to share events and schedules.

- *Team Site*: Use this template to create a collaboration page for a group of people working in a team by allowing document sharing, wiki pages, announcements, and discussion forums.

Activity Stream

Activity Stream provides a social networking collaboration feature for Fusion Applications users. Activity Stream is by default available on the Welcome dashboard for all Fusion Applications users. Similar to Internet-based social networks, Activity Stream allows users to connect to other people within or outside the application group, share information with all or selected people, view the updates, like or share other's updates from other users, and so on, from Fusion Applications interface. It also allows users to attach media via links while sharing updates with others. Figure 11-25 shows an example of the Activity Stream region on the Fusion Applications welcome dashboard.

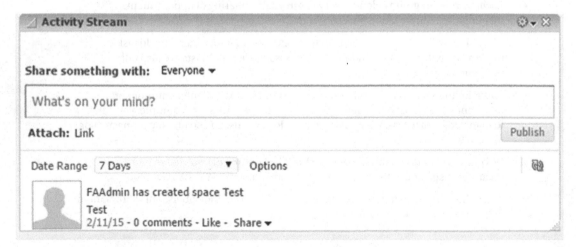

Figure 11-25. Activity Stream region

Scheduled Processes

Scheduled Processes are similar to concurrent requests in the Oracle E-Business Suite. In the E-Business Suite, the concurrent requests and processes are managed by the Concurrent Manager, while in Oracle Fusion Applications, this task is completed by the Oracle Enterprise Scheduler. Oracle Enterprise Schedule provides a robust mechanism to execute, control, monitor, and schedule the user's jobs. Each product domain has a dedicated Enterprise Scheduler WebLogic cluster that handles the relevant jobs. We will look at Enterprise Scheduler in more detail in the administration chapters. Let's explore the Scheduled Processes from a user's point of view first.

During implementation and the day-to-day operations with Fusion Applications, every user or administrator needs to run various scheduled jobs or batches of jobs. For example, as an administrator you might need to retrieve the latest LDAP changes from OIM after a user is assigned roles using Oracle Identity Manager that are either delayed or failed due to any reason. Although all users created in Fusion HCM are always being created in Oracle Identity Management, there will be many cases when you need to manually send any pending LDAP requests to Identity Management and eventually to the identity store. For example, if you select a future date for de-provisioning for a user in HCM, it needs to be reflected in OIM. Figure 11-26 shows an example of two LDAP-related Scheduled Processes—Send Pending LDAP Requests and Retrieve Latest LDAP Changes—which may help you in completing these tasks.

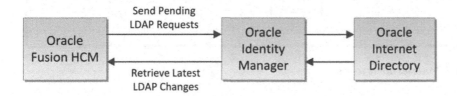

Figure 11-26. LDAP-related Scheduled Process example

Let's look at how to view, monitor, or run a Scheduled Process using the Fusion Applications interface. All the users with the Employee role will have a link titled Scheduled Processes in the Navigator menu under the Tools category. Clicking on this link will launch the Scheduled Processes home screen, as shown in Figure 11-27.

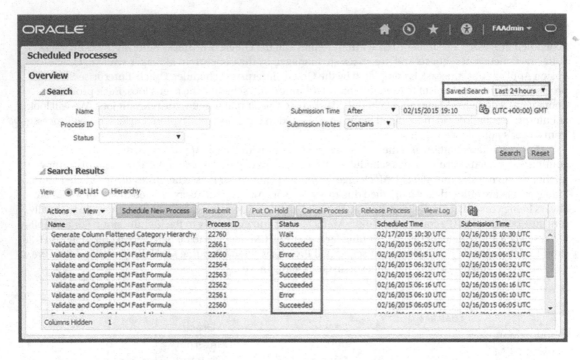

Figure 11-27. *Scheduled Processes home screen*

The Scheduled Processes screen allows you to monitor previously executed or scheduled processes as well as schedule a new process. The default search covers the last 24 hours, so the search will display the list of processes executed in the last 24 hours along with the current status. The status could be Wait, Ready, Running, Succeeded, Error, and so on. Clicking on the status value will display more information about that specific process. You can alternatively specify other search filters like name or processes with Wait or Error status to monitor the scheduled jobs.

To run or schedule a new process, click the Schedule a New Process button. This will bring up a pop-up window, as shown in Figure 11-28. First you must first select whether you want to run a scheduled job or job set and use the Search box to type the name of the job/job set or use the automatic search suggestion based on a partial query. If you do not find the job listed here, it will invoke the search interface where you can provide filters to locate the job or job set.

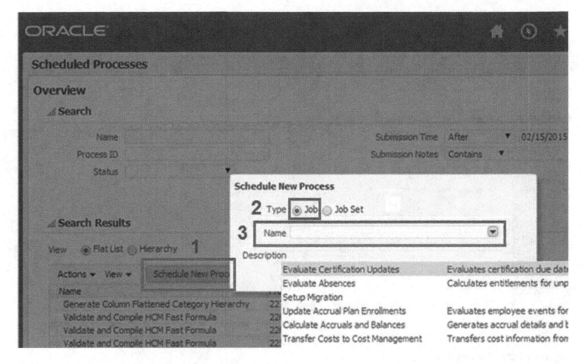

Figure 11-28. *Schedule a new process*

The Fusion Applications Scheduled Process (based on a job) and Process Set (based on a job set) commands are comparable to the Oracle E-Business Suite's Concurrent Request (based on a concurrent program) and Request Set (based on a set of concurrent programs). A job contains a single task that will run independently of other jobs. A job set is a group of multiple other jobs that need to be run in a specific order to achieve a specific result. A job set can contain other nested job sets as well. A job set is considered the parent process for the included jobs or job sets so when you switch the Scheduled Processes Search result view to Hierarchy view, you will see the job set ID as the parent ID while the included jobs will display in the same hierarchy.

Once you have selected a job or job set to be run or scheduled, you will see Process Details screen, as shown in Figure 11-29, in order to provide the runtime parameters for the job being submitted.

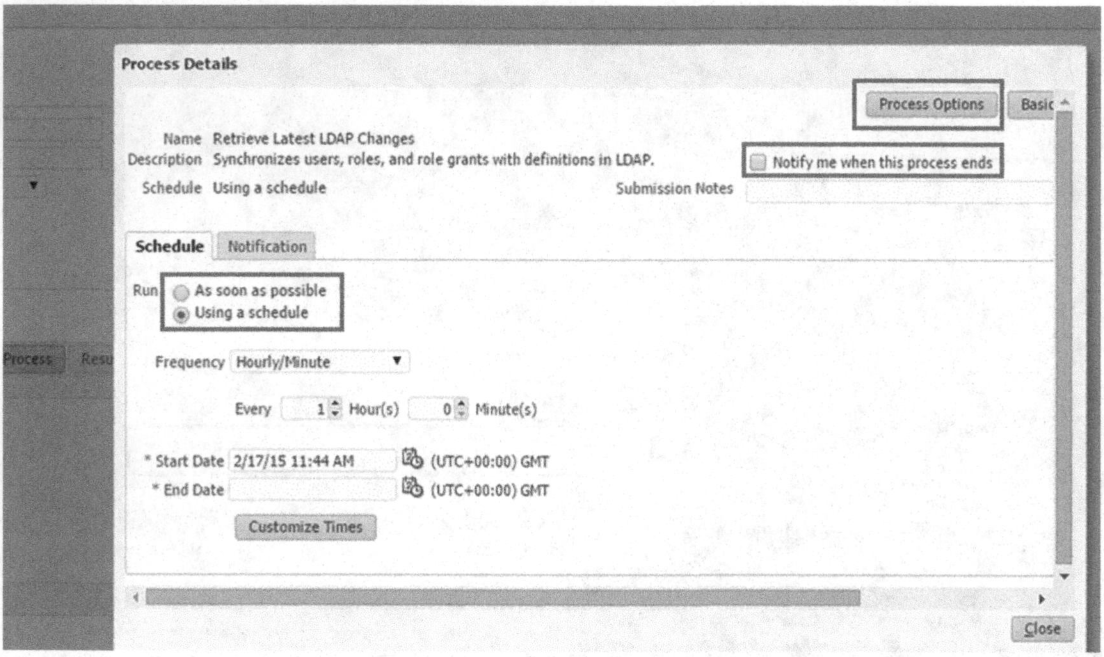

Figure 11-29. *Process details*

You can either schedule the process to run as soon as possible, schedule it at a later date/time, or define a regular interval schedule for the job. This screen provides various options to receive notification, output formats, and so on. Once you submit the process it goes to Wait status if it is scheduled for a later time. Once the process is ready to run, it goes to Ready status, followed by Running and eventually Successful or Error status. We will look at these statuses in more detail during the Fusion Applications Administration chapters.

Summary

This chapter provided a bird's eye view of Fusion Applications interface. Understanding the common interface features enables you to use the Fusion Applications interface efficiently for business-related tasks as well as administrative tasks. You saw how Fusion Applications differs from other traditional application suites and how it helps you increase your productivity by bundling various reporting/analytical, social, and business objects together in a single interface.

At this point you should be able to identify and use the navigation icons and menus in the Fusion Applications Global area. Although you have not yet seen how to assign the application roles to the users (which you will explore in upcoming chapters), you should be able to use the application dashboards once you have been assigned the appropriate application roles and dashboards are populated on the screen. You have also seen the importance of Scheduled Processes and how they map to Oracle E-Business Suite equivalent concurrent requests. You should now be able to schedule a new request as well as monitor it. We will look at Enterprise Scheduled in detail in upcoming chapters.

With Fusion Applications installed in earlier chapters and having seen the Fusion Applications interface in this chapter, at this stage you should be ready to move to Fusion Applications administration. The next chapters discuss monitoring, troubleshooting, diagnosing, and patching Fusion applications.

■ ■ ■

## CHAPTER 12

Getting Started with Fusion Applications Administration

The earlier chapters of this book provided an overview of the end-to-end provisioning of an Oracle Fusion Applications instance in your environment, whether on-premise or via a private cloud. The last chapter brought a logical switch to the contents of this book from installation to management of the installed applications where you got an idea of the basic interface of Fusion Applications and how the screen elements and UI components are placed in the common interface and their importance in the overall application suite. If you have followed the chapters sequentially, you should have your own Fusion Applications instance running on your servers depending on the topology you selected. You are also aware of how to navigate through various logical sections of the applications interface and know how to locate the important functionalities.

This and the next few chapters will focus on the day-to-day administration of Fusion Applications. This chapter includes only a part of the overall Administration tasks and the further chapters will continue to complement the discussion related to the day-to-day administration of Fusion Applications. In this chapter, we will focus on the most obvious and common administration tasks, for example starting and stopping the complete Fusion Applications and Identity Management environment, understanding the implementation process, creating new users and assigning required roles, managing important components of Fusion Applications, and so on. The next chapters will focus on other important administration tasks like monitoring, diagnosing, and troubleshooting, patching fusion applications components, and so on. Because of the complexity of the Fusion Applications environment due to the number of components involved, despite covering these mentioned topics, there will be many administration tasks that may remain left out from our discussion so we will not define the boundaries of Fusion Applications Administration only by the topics discussed in this and the next few chapters.

Starting Fusion Applications Environment

Once the Fusion Applications installation is complete, by default all the application and middleware components would be running and you can browse through the applications interface. However you need to create and document a procedure for shutting down and starting up the complete Fusion Applications environment including Identity Management and corresponding databases. We will discuss many of the recommended options of starting up and shutting down the components; however, there are many additional component specific ways to start/stop the components. At the logical end of each tier discussion, I will also provide consolidated scripts to automate the startup or shutdown procedure. You may want to integrate the startup and shutdown procedures with your existing operations downtime scripts, integrate them with a backup infrastructure, or any other documented bounce procedures specific to your enterprise.

© Tushar Thakker 2015
T. Thakker, *Pro Oracle Fusion Applications*, DOI 10.1007/978-1-4842-0983-7_12

Before proceeding to the actual management of Fusion Applications services, let's first understand how the dependencies between the components affect the startup sequence. Note that the shutdown sequence is exactly opposite of this; however, the methods used can vary since Fusion Applications components shutdown is relatively quicker than startup, which usually takes a reasonable amount of time. Figure 12-1 illustrates a high-level understanding of Fusion Applications components startup sequence.

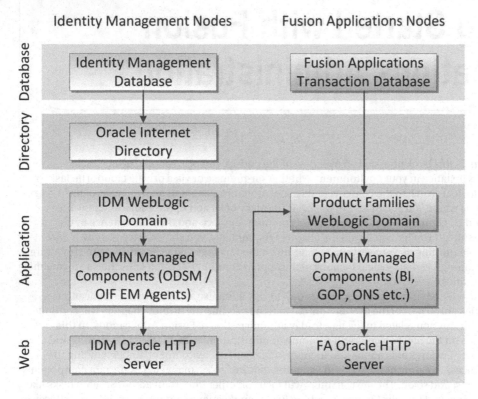

Figure 12-1. *Fusion Applications Environment startup sequence*

Figure 12-1 shows the components located at each logical tier of your environment. As you can see, the database tier including both IDM and FA databases can be started first since they don't have any dependencies. There are a few components like Oracle HTTP Server that can be started out of sequence also but then you may see false alerts on console and browser until all the other components have started successfully. Be patient during Fusion Applications startup since, unlike Oracle E-Business suite and other applications suites, it takes much longer time to start up due to large number of WebLogic Managed Servers. If some component's startup times out through seeded scripts, it may still be starting up in the background so make sure to clean up existing processes before attempting another startup.

At the same time, keep monitoring the server resources including CPU, memory, and so on, since you may see a temporary spike in CPU usage during components startup. Depending on the speed of IO devices, you may see some wait events as well. It may take some time to get used the startup procedure along with estimated time it may take for your environment.

■ **Note**   From Fusion Applications 11g, release 9 onward Oracle recommends you use Enterprise Manager Cloud Control as the administrative interface for managing Fusion Applications. Although in this chapter you may see references to Enterprise Manager Cloud Control, its installation and configuration is explained in Chapter 14 due to relevance with the content. Any references to EM in this chapter assume that it has already been configured in your environment.

We will look at the Fusion Applications environment startup in following steps.

- Starting Identity Management Database
- Starting Identity Management Middle Tier Components
- Starting Fusion Applications Transaction Database
- Starting Fusion Applications Middle Tier Components

Starting Identity Management Database

Oracle Database is the first component to be started for Identity Management or Fusion Applications Nodes startup. Although starting the database through the command line is the generally preferred option for most database administrators, we will see the command line and the EM Cloud Control here since EM Cloud Control can start the entire technology stack involved in Fusion Applications environment and at times it may be handy to start up everything from a single interface.

At some point during the following discussion you may feel that the explanation is more detailed for the startup methods which are common between Identity Management and Fusion Applications components. So we will discuss them in detail during Identity Management startup but skip the detailed explanation when a similar startup method is explained later for Fusion Applications components.

Using the Command-Line Interface

Let's start the Identity Management database using the command-line interface (which most database administrators prefer). The advantage of the command-line interface methods is that they can be automated using consolidated scripts. If you are using GUI interface like Enterprise Manager, the procedure remains largely manual.

Setting Up Environment Variables

In order to start Oracle Database or a listener service, we must set the mandatory environment variables like ORACLE_HOME, PATH, ORACLE_SID, and so on, in order to identify the database name and location of the binaries. We can set the environment variables using any of the following methods.

1. Setting the environment variables in the current session.

You can set the temporary environment variable in the current startup session as follows.

    a. Set the ORACLE_HOME variable to the full path of the Oracle Database home directory. Use the set command for the Windows host and the export command for Linux/Unix host. For example:

```
[fusion@idmhost ~]$ export ORACLE_HOME=/app/database/product/11.2.0/dbhome_1
```

    b. Append the <ORACLE_HOME>/bin directory to the existing PATH environment variable. Note that you must append this path in the beginning instead of the end since the PATH variable is searched by the operating system in sequential order. For example:

```
[fusion@idmhost ~]$ export PATH=$ORACLE_HOME/bin:$PATH
```

    c. Set the ORACLE_SID and ORACLE_UNQNAME variables pointing to the Local Oracle System Identifier (SID) of the database (local instance name in case of RAC) and unique name of the database, respectively. ORACLE_SID is used by the commands like sqlplus to identify the local instance for administering the database without using the net service name, while ORACLE_UNQNAME is used by Enterprise Manager commands like emctl to identify the unique database identifier. For example:

```
[fusion@idmhost ~]$ export ORACLE_SID=idmdb
[fusion@idmhost ~]$ export ORACLE_UNQNAME=idmdb
```

    d. Set JAVA_HOME to point to the Java home directory that we created earlier. This may not be required for database startup/shutdown, but it is always good practice to set the JAVA_HOME environment variable. For example:

```
[fusion@idmhost ~]$ export JAVA_HOME=/app/oracle/jdk6
```

2. Using a custom profile setup script.

You can also put these environment variables in a single environment setup script that can be sourced within a session or from another script. For example, we have created a script named dbprofile.sh that sets these variables.

```
#!/bin/bash
# Script name: dbprofile.sh v1.0_TT
# Change the following path to the actual path in your environment
ORACLE_HOME=/app/database/product/11.2.0/dbhome_1
export ORACLE_HOME

PATH=$PATH:$ORACLE_HOME/bin
export PATH

ORACLE_SID=idmdb
export ORACLE_SID

# Change the following path to the actual path in your environment
JAVA_HOME=/app/oracle/jdk6
export JAVA_HOME
```

Let's assign execute permission for this script so that this file can be sourced from any other script.

```
[fusion@idmhost ~]$ chmod +x dbprofile.sh
```

We can source this profile using the following command whenever required considering the profile was created in the home directory of the user.

```
[fusion@idmhost ~]$ . $HOME/dbprofile.sh
```

or

```
[fusion@idmhost ~]$ . ~/dbprofile.sh
```

3. Appending the variables assignment in the user's default login profile Alternatively we can add the same environment variables in the user's default login profile, for example .bash_profile (for users with bash as the default login shell).

Starting Up Oracle Database and Listener

Assuming that the database is created using the Provisioning wizard, it will be single-node database initially. Hence, the following procedure applies to a single-node database. For RAC databases, use srvctl commands to start the database and the listener.

1. Start the IDM database listener service.

First let's set the environment variables related to the IDM database as discussed in an earlier section.

```
[fusion@idmhost ~]$. $HOME/dbprofile.sh
```

Start the listener now. Make sure to pass the correct listener name. If you are not sure about the listener name, refer to <ORACLE_HOME>/network/admin/listener.ora for the correct name.

```
[fusion@idmhost ~]$ lsnrctl start listener_idmdb
```

2. Start the IDM database.

Considering that the database is a single-node DB, environment variables are already set in the current session and the OS user is the database owner. Start the database now.

```
[fusion@idmhost ~]$ sqlplus / as sysdba
SQL> statup
```

Consolidated Startup Script for IDM Listener and Database

To keep it simple, let's create a single startup script for both the database and listener in order to start them using a single command. The following is an example of such script. Save it as startDB.sh.

```
#/bin/bash
# Script Name: startDB.sh v1.0_TT
# Source the db environment file created in previous step
. /home/fusion/dbprofile.sh
echo "Starting database listener"
lsnrctl start listener_idmdb
```

```
echo "Starting Database"
sqlplus / as sysdba << EOF
startup
exit;
EOF
```

Remember to add execute permission for the user to this script. After that you can run this script from a shell prompt or within another script as follows.

[fusion@idmhost ~]$ **./startDB.sh**

Using Oracle Enterprise Manager Cloud Control

As mentioned in an earlier section, Oracle recommends you use the Enterprise Manager Cloud Control to manage and administer the Fusion Applications environment since it provides a single interface to manage, monitor, and troubleshoot your complete Oracle infrastructure. Assuming that you already have EM installed and configured to manage the Identity Management and Fusion Applications nodes, let's explore how you can use it to start the database tier components. Refer to Chapter 14 for how to install and configure EM Cloud Control.

In order to start the listener service, log in to Oracle Enterprise Manager Cloud Control using the SYSMAN user, click on the Targets menu, and select the Listener target type in the left panel. The screen will now look as shown in Figure 12-2.

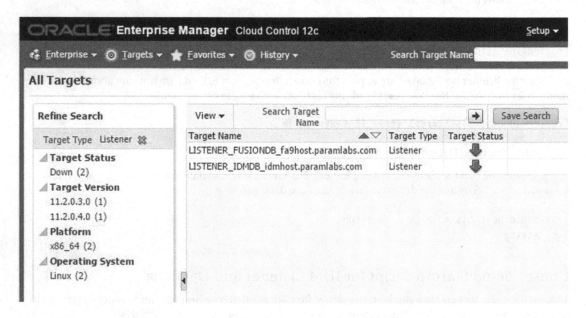

Figure 12-2. *List of configured listeners*

In this screen you will see the list of configured listeners, which are IDM and FA listeners in our case. Click on the IDM listener to open the IDM listener home screen, as shown in Figure 12-3.

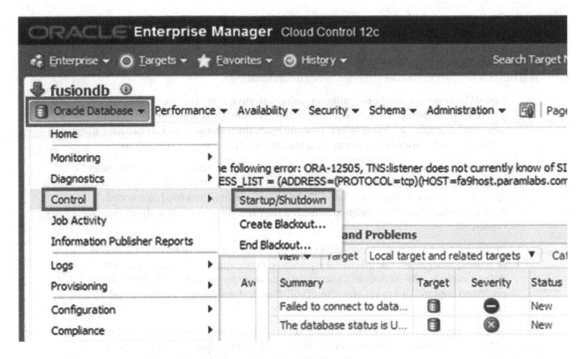

Figure 12-3. *Starting up the listener using EM Cloud Control*

Click on the Oracle Listener menu followed by Control Submenu. You can see Startup/Shutdown options here. You need to select this option even if you want to start up or shut down the service. This will lead to the Host Login details screen, as shown in Figure 12-4.

Figure 12-4. *Host credential screen for listener startup/shutdown*

In the Host Credential screen, you will be prompted to enter the login details of the database owner user on database host. This is mandatory in order to allow the enterprise manager agent to start the database listener service on the local host. Such credentials are not only asked for listener startup/shutdown but for all the Oracle components that we will see in the coming sections. Let me explain each of these options for providing host credentials in reverse order for better understanding.

- *New*: Whenever you are performing any administrative action on a component, you must provide the host login details for the first time since there are no default stored credentials. Once you select New and enter the login details, you can save the credential with a user-defined name and set as preferred credential if required.

- *Named*: After you save the host credential in a user defined name, you need not enter it again but you can select the Named option and then select the credential from the drop-down menu, as shown in Figure 12-4. Use this option when you have stored the login details in the user defined name but have not yet selected it as the preferred credential.

- *Preferred*: After a named credential is set as preferred one, you need not select new or named credentials, but just use the preferred credentials screen to go with the default value for the component and move to next screen immediately. Until the preferred credentials are set, the screen will display the message "Default preferred credentials are not set."

Once you select appropriate credential in this screen, click Login. Confirm the action on the next screen in order to let the EM perform the required action (start the listener in this case) on the host.

Now let's look at how to start up the IDM database using the EM Cloud Control interface. On any screen of EM, click on Targets menu followed by the Databases menu option. This will launch the Databases dashboard, as shown in Figure 12-5.

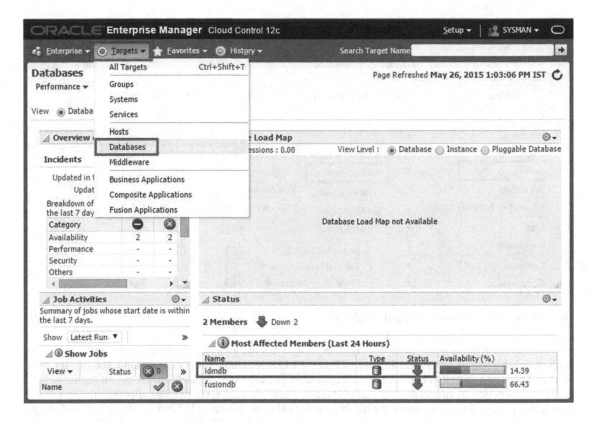

Figure 12-5. *Databases common dashboard*

This screen shows a consolidated summary of all the Oracle Databases configured with Enterprise Manager along with the status, availability in the last 24 hours, any critical incidents noticed in the last seven days, and so on. You may notice the list of databases configured with EM in the database status region of the screen. As you can see, the current status of the database is Down. Click on the database name idmdb to launch the home screen of the idmdb database, as shown in Figure 12-6.

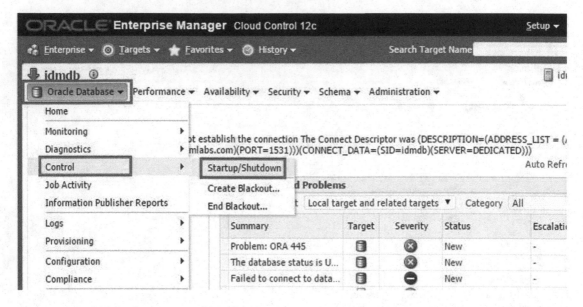

Figure 12-6. *IDM database startup through EM*

The database home screen may display an expected error at the top, suggesting that the agent can't establish a connection to the database. Choose the Oracle Database ➤ Control menu. You can see Startup/Shutdown as well as blackout-related options in this submenu. A blackout is required during any maintenance period to inform the Enterprise Manager Cloud Control agent to stop collecting statistics during this period. If you shut down the database using EM earlier, then a blackout would have already been there which will be removed upon startup. We will look at blackouts in detail in the next chapter where we will discuss Fusion Applications monitoring. Click on the Startup/Shutdown from the submenu to launch the Host and Database Credential screen, as shown in Figure 12-7.

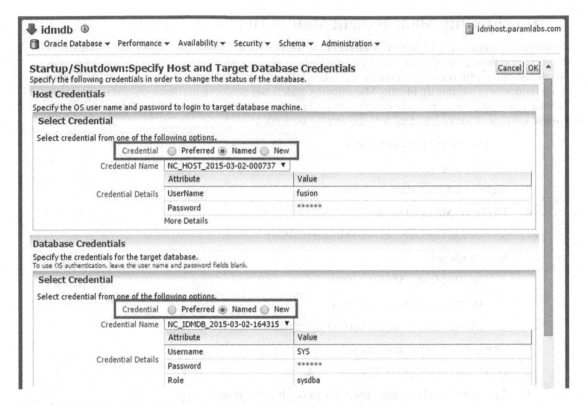

Figure 12-7. Host and database credential screen for database startup/shutdown

We have seen the Host Credential screen earlier during the Listener startup where it prompted for only host OS user login details since listener startup commands are executed directly in the host shell. However in order to start the database you will need database credentials in addition to the host credential. The host credential is used to execute the commands like sqlplus in the host default shell. Database credentials are required to connect to the database instance or to bring up the database prompt in order to execute startup/shutdown commands.

You are also prompted for preferred, named, or new credentials. Regardless of whether it is host, database, or WebLogic credential, the types of credentials remain the same, as explained earlier. Create the new or use existing credential for the host and database. Make sure you select a database user with sysdba privilege for the startup/shutdown tasks.

The next screen will show the SQL being executed in the background (which is essentially STARTUP only) followed by the screen that allows you to select specific startup options like Restricted mode or STARTUP FORCE, which can abort the running instance that's hung and start it up. (Use this with caution and only when there is no other option available.) You can also specify a custom parameter file if you want to troubleshoot some issue.

This concludes the database startup on the IDM database tier. Now let's move on to Identity Management components startup.

Starting Identity Management Middle Tier Components

Before you proceed to the Identity Management Middle Tier components, the Identity Management database and listener must be started. Since the Fusion Applications Transaction database does not have any dependency with other components, it can be started along with Identity Management. The following is the sequence of starting up Identity Management middle tier components manually. Even if you are using automation script, this is the same order in which the script will start components on the respective server. We will see how to start each of these in the coming sections.

1. Oracle Internet Directory (OID)

2. Node Manager

3. WebLogic Administration Server

4. WebLogic Managed Servers

    a. Oracle Directory Service Manager (ODSM)

    b. Oracle SOA

    c. Oracle Identity Manager (OIM)

    d. Oracle Access Manager (OAM)

    e. Oracle Identity Federation (OIF) (if configured)

5. Oracle HTTP Server instance (OHS)

6. Oracle Directory Service Manager EM Agent

7. Oracle Identity Federation EM Agent (if OIF is configured)

Manual Startup

Although Oracle suggests you use `startall.sh` and `stopall.sh` scripts (generated during the provisioning process) in order to start or stop the Identity Management environment, we must also see how to start the components manually. We will explain the pros and cons of each methods at the end of the startup section. You may also prefer to use the script we provided in this section or create your own to start the environment.

Oracle Internet Directory

Since Oracle Internet Directory is the default identity store, it must be started up first in order to authenticate the bootstrap users before starting the WebLogic domain. The provisioning process installs the OID in IDM_BASE/products/dir/oid directory and creates a local instance of it named oid1 in the IDM_CONFIG directory. We need to start up OID from the instance directory. The syntax to start up OID using the command line is as follows. Execute this command on the host where Directory Services are installed. Since we have installed Identity Management components on the same node, we will run it on the IDM host. Depending on the number of hosts used in your environment, you need to run these commands on the appropriate hosts.

```
<IDM_CONFIG>/instances/<OID_Instance>/bin/opmnctl startall
```

For example:

```
[fusion@idmhost ~]$ /app/oracle/config/instances/oid1/bin/opmnctl startall
opmnctl startall: starting opmn and all managed processes...
```

Once the command completes successfully without error, proceed to the next startup task.

Node Manager

Although in theory Node Manager is an optional component, it is mandatory if you want to start WebLogic Managed Servers using Administration Console or using EM Cloud Control. However, if you are starting the instance using default WebLogic scripts, then Node Manager may not be required. In that case you will lose the monitoring and automatic restart functionality. You can start the Node Manager from the Node Manager home directory or from the local configuration directory. The syntax to start up Node Manager is as follows. Node Manager must be started on each host where WebLogic managed servers are configured.

■ **Note**   You must use the nohup command on the Linux/Unix platform to start the components or else, once you close the current session, the process may terminate depending on the operating system. This will create a file named nohup.out, which captures the output from this command.

```
cd <IDM_CONFIG>/nodemanager/<hostname>
nohup ./startNodeManagerWrapper.sh &
```

For example:

```
[fusion@idmhost ~]$ cd /app/oracle/config/nodemanager/idmhost.paramlabs.com/
[fusion@idmhost idmhost.paramlabs.com]$ nohup ./startNodeManagerWrapper.sh &
```

If you want to start from the WebLogic home then you can use following syntax.

```
cd <IDM_BASE>/products/app/wlserver_10.3/server/bin
nohup ./startNodeManager.sh &
```

For example:

```
[fusion@idmhost ~]$ cd /app/oracle/products/app/wlserver_10.3/server/bin
[fusion@idmhost bin]$ nohup ./startNodeManager.sh &
```

■ **Caution**   If the WebLogic servers were not shut down gracefully earlier, the Node Manager will automatically start all those servers up. So monitor the Node Manager output file to show a line similar to "Plain socket listener started on port 5556" before proceeding to manual startup of WebLogic servers to avoid duplicate startup commands.

Oracle WebLogic Server Domain for Identity Management

In an environment where Oracle Enterprise Manager Cloud Control is not installed, WebLogic Administrator Server must be started using the command line. However, the managed servers can be started using the Administrator console as well.

WebLogic Administration Server

We must start the IDM Domain Administration Server first on the node where Admin Server has been configured. Since in this case we have all IDM domain components configured on the same node we will start the same on IDM host but you may need to make sure in your environment which host is configured to run the admin server.

To start admin server, run the startWebLogic.sh script from <IDM_CONFIG>/domains/IDMDomain/. As mentioned earlier, we need to use the nohup command to let it run after leaving the session as well. You can monitor the nohup.out log file for the progress of the startup command.

```
[fusion@idmhost ~]$ cd /app/oracle/config/domains/IDMDomain/bin
[fusion@idmhost ~]$ nohup ./startWebLogic.sh &
```

Note that we can start up the WebLogic domain including the administration and managed servers using Enterprise Manager as well. We will see the same in the next section of starting up the WebLogic Managed Servers.

WebLogic Managed Servers

By default the following four managed servers are configured for the Identity Management domain. If you have created a high available setup then you may have more than one managed server for each WebLogic cluster. By default, the Oracle Identity Federation (wls_oif1) managed server remains down unless you have enabled and configured it.

1. Oracle Directory Service Manager (wls_ods1)

2. Oracle SOA (wls_soa1)

3. Oracle Identity Manager (wls_oim1)

4. Oracle Access Manager (wls_oam1)

We have three options to start these managed servers up manually. Of course if you use automatic startup script (startall.sh) explained later in this section, you need not use any of these manual methods

1. Using the command-line interface.

We can use the default WebLogic scripts to start up the managed servers. The prerequisite for using this method is to have the boot identity file called boot.properties present in the IDMDomain/server/<ManagedServer>/security directory to allow the script to run in the background without prompting for WebLogic server username and password. Since this file contains encrypted credentials, it is safe to keep the credentials stored in this file. If the boot identity file does not exist for any managed server then you can choose any of the following methods to create one.

a. Copy the existing boot.properties from a different directory.

You can copy the existing boot.properties file from the <ManagedServer>/data/nodemanager directory or from the AdminServer/security directory to the <ManagedServer>/security directory. This file already has encrypted credentials to start up the managed server and the same file can be copied safely.

b.   Create a new boot.properties file.

If there is no existing boot.properties file, then you can simply create a new file with the following content.

```
username=weblogic_idm
password=<password  of the weblogic_idm user>
```

Save this content as the boot.properties file. After you start the managed server the first time, it will automatically encrypt the values in the file. Now let's start each managed server one by one. The advantage of using this method is that you need not wait for one managed server to start up completely before proceeding to the next one. Make sure to use nohup and & in order to let it run in background after you leave the session. Use the startManagedWebLogic.sh script in the <IDM_CONFIG>/domains/IDMDomain/bin directory to start the managed servers. Although Oracle's automated startup script uses the following order to start the managed servers, you can start in any order.

```
[fusion@idmhost ~]$ cd /app/oracle/config/domains/IDMDomain/bin
```

Let's first start Oracle Directory service manager.

```
[fusion@idmhost ~]$ nohup ./startManagedWebLogic.sh wls_ods1 &
```

Now start Oracle SOA.

```
[fusion@idmhost ~]$ nohup ./startManagedWebLogic.sh wls_soa1 &
```

Now let's start Oracle Identity Manager.

```
[fusion@idmhost ~]$ nohup ./startManagedWebLogic.sh wls_oim1 &
```

Finally, start the Oracle Access Manager.

```
[fusion@idmhost ~]$ nohup ./startManagedWebLogic.sh wls_oam1 &
```

You must allow some time for the managed servers to start up. You can refer to the log file nohup.out as well as the individual managed server log file at the IDMDomain/servers/<ManagedServer>/log directory to check the status until it shows the message, "Server started in RUNNING mode."

2.   Using the Oracle WebLogic administration console.

You can use Oracle WebLogic administration console to start or restart an individual managed server. But when you need to start all the managed servers then this is not the recommended method since it requires Admin Server and OAM Managed Server to be running due to the admin console's integration with Access Manager. Additionally it requires Oracle HTTP server to be running since Oracle Access Manager SSO Login page uses HTTP server as front end. At the same time you also need to make sure that the Node Manager has been started on the hosts. However using the WebLogic admin console is very handy while manually stopping or starting individual managed servers and most administrators find this interface a simple and quick way to manage WebLogic managed servers.

Log in to the administration console at `http://<AdminHost>:<AdminPort>/console` as the administration user. For example, log in to `http://idmhost.paramlabs.com:7777/console` using the `weblogic_idm` user. Once you're logged in, you will see the WebLogic Administration console homepage. Click on the Servers link in the main area or in the left panel under Domain Structure region using IDMDomain ➤ Environment ➤ Servers. You will see the summary of all WebLogic servers in the IDMDomain, as shown in Figure 12-8.

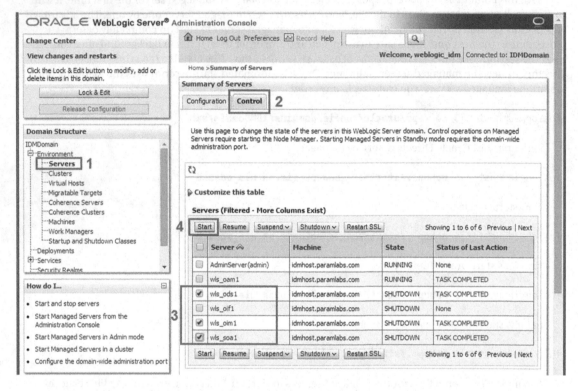

Figure 12-8. *Starting up the managed servers using the administration console*

As you can see, `AdminServer` and `wls_oam1` are already started. You can start other managed servers from here by selecting them and clicking on the Start button. The next screen will prompt for confirmation to start the selected managed servers.

3. Using Oracle Enterprise Manager Cloud Control.

Once you have configured Oracle Identity Management environment with Enterprise Manager Cloud Control, you can manage each of its components using EM. Note that this includes all middleware components including HTTP Server, OID, OVD and so on, as well and not just WebLogic servers. In this example, let's see how to start up IDM WebLogic domain using EM Cloud Control. The advantage of this method is that we need not start the administration server in advance since starting through EM provides us an option to start the complete WebLogic domain including the admin server at the same time.

Log in to Enterprise Manager Cloud Control URL at `http://<em_host>:<em_port>/em` using EM Administration user SYSMAN. Once you have logged on to EM, click on the Middleware link from the Targets menu. You will see Middleware summary screen, as shown in Figure 12-9.

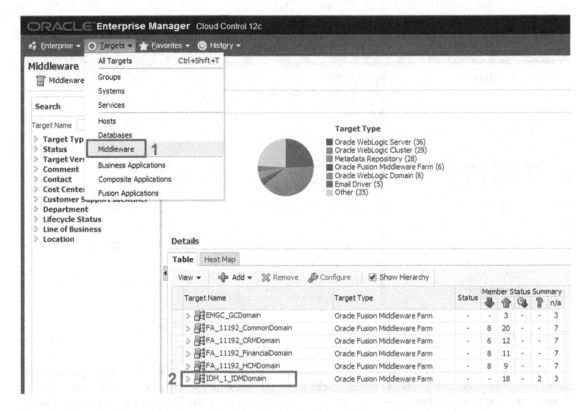

Figure 12-9. *Selecting a IDM domain target in Enterprise Manager*

You will see all the configured and monitored WebLogic domains in the Details table. Click on the IDMDomain target in this list to bring up the Identity Management homepage.

The Identity Management homepage allows you start up, shut down, and manage the complete WebLogic domain, individual WebLogic managed servers, application deployments, directory services, and even web tiers. You will use this screen very often during monitoring, troubleshooting, and day to day administration of Identity Management components. This example shows you how to start the complete WebLogic domain called IDMDomain, including the administration server as well as managed servers that are enabled for startup.

In the Target Navigation region, click on the WebLogic domain followed by the IDMDomain node of the navigation tree. You can see individual managed servers under IDMDomain but we will select IDMDomain only at this moment. It will bring up the home screen for IDM WebLogic domain, as shown in Figure 12-10.

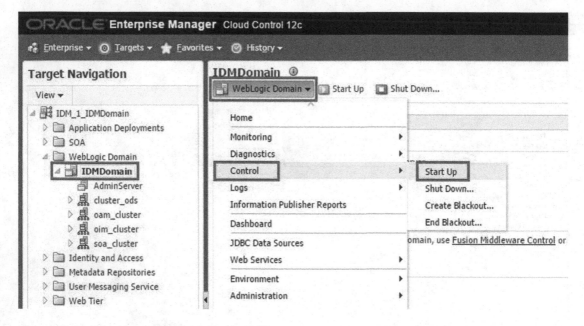

Figure 12-10. *Starting up IDM domain using EM*

From the IDM domain homepage, choose WebLogic Domain ➤ Control. This will bring up the Startup/ Shutdown and Create/End Blackout options. Click on Startup to initiate the startup of the WebLogic domain. Alternatively you can also click the Startup button located at top of the page. This will lead to Startup options and Credentials screen, as shown in Figure 12-11.

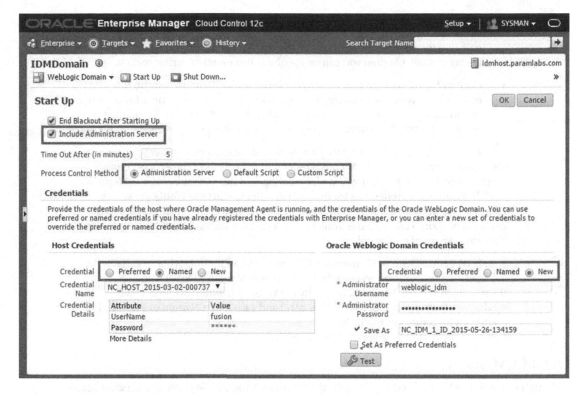

Figure 12-11. *IDM domain startup options and credentials screen*

Let's look at the important startup options required in the domain startup screen.

- *End Blackout After Starting Up*: By default it is checked. If you are planning to perform further maintenance even after starting up then you can uncheck this. Remember to manually end the blackout using the Control Submenu ➤ End Blackout option.

- *Include Administration Server*: This is very useful option since unlike the WebLogic administration console, EM allows you to start up the domain including admin server. This is also mandatory option while selecting Administration Server Process Control Method discussed next. The same option is available while shutting down as well so you can choose whether to keep admin server running after shutting down the managed servers or not.

- *Process Control Method*: Since Enterprise Manager effectively runs the commands at the host using EM agent, the process control method defines the set of commands to be executed in order to start the domain up. It provides the following three process control methods to choose from.

    - *Administration Server*: This is the default method that uses the currently running administration server to manage startup of the managed servers. You need to make sure that admin server is already running or the checkbox Include Administration Server is selected.

- - *Default Script*: If you want to use the default WebLogic scripts like startWeblogic.sh and startManagedWebLogic.sh to start up the domain. Make sure that the boot.properties file is available for each managed server and if the file is not available then you can create one as discussed in earlier section.

    - *Custom Script*: You can also create your own custom script to start up the managed servers. For example, if you want to add custom logging information or you have some pre- and post-scripts to be executed along with managed servers, you can do so here.

  - *Host Credentials*: Similar to what we have seen in database and listener startup, here also you need to specify the IDM host credentials regardless of the process control method selected. In this example we have configured the idmhost as the IDMDomain host. It requires the credentials for this host in order to start the WebLogic server. Here also we need to select from the Preferred or Named credentials as discussed earlier. If no stored credential is available (for first time startup) then you can create a New stored named credential.

  - *Oracle WebLogic Domain Credentials*: This frame shows up only when you have selected Administration Server as the Process Control method for starting up the managed servers. You need to specify the WebLogic administration server credentials (weblogic_idm user in this case) and save it as a Named or Preferred credential for future startup tasks.

ODSM EM Agent

Although starting ODSM managed servers will allow you to use the Oracle Directory Services Manager URL to manage OID or OVD instances, you also need to start ODSM agent process in order to manage the ODSM instance through Fusion Middleware control. The command to start ODSM process manager instance is as follows.

```
<IDM_CONFIG>/odsm/bin/opmnctl startall
```

For example:

```
[fusion@idmhost ~]$ /app/oracle/config/instances/odsm/bin/opmnctl startall
opmnctl startall: starting opmn and all managed processes...
```

OIF EM Agent

If you have configured and enabled Oracle Identity Federation (OIF) then you need to start the OIF EM agent service in order to manage the OIF instance through middleware control. This is an optional service. The command to start the OIF instance through process manager is as follows.

```
<IDM_CONFIG>/oif_inst/bin/opmnctl startall
```

For example:

```
[fusion@idmhost ~]$ /app/oracle/config/instances/oif_inst/bin/opmnctl startall
opmnctl startall: starting opmn and all managed processes...
```

Oracle HTTP Server

Although Oracle HTTP Server can be started any time and out of sequence as well, it is recommended to start it last to allow Oracle Access Manager to start up completely due to Oracle HTTP Server integration with Access Manager through WebGate. If you start it before Access Manager (wls_oam1 managed server) has completed startup, you may see false errors on the Unix console similar to the following. Although these messages can be annoying while working on the Unix shell, you can ignore them until OAM is completely started and the status changes to RUNNING. If these message continue to appear even after OAM is started then it may need further troubleshooting.

```
"Exception thrown during WebGate initialization"
"The AccessGate is unable to contact any Access Servers."
```

The syntax of starting the Oracle HTTP Server (OHS) instance is as follows.

```
<IDM_CONFIG>/<OHS_INSTANCE>/bin/opmnctl startall
```

For example:

```
[fusion@idmhost ~]$ /app/oracle/config/instances/ohs1/bin/opmnctl startall
opmnctl startall: starting opmn and all managed processes...
```

Automated Startup

Having seen the manual methods of starting Identity Management components, let's now look at the automated and simpler methods of starting the components. Why did we look at the manual methods first? The answer is that because in automated startup we are simply going to put the manual methods in automation scripts so it is important to understand the manual startup first followed by understanding the automated startup.

We have two options to start up the Identity Management environment automatically or by calling a single script. The first option is provided by Oracle itself while the second option is to create your own automated startup script. Why do we need to create automated startup script? Well, you will see the advantage of one method over the other soon.

Using the Startup Script Generated During Provisioning

From Oracle Fusion Applications Release 7 onward, the Identity Management environment installation is done by the IDM provisioning process, which generates the automated startup and shutdown scripts at the end of the provisioning process. We can use the same script to cleanly start up or shut down the Identity Management environment. The advantage of this method is that the script already includes all the enabled managed servers and instance details in your environment and it is aware of the dependencies between components. At the same time the drawback is that this script runs in serial mode by completing each task before moving forward with the next one. If one startup task has failed, it will not proceed to the next task by default.

The syntax of the startall.sh script is as follows.

```
<IDM_CONFIG>/scripts/startall.sh [<Node Manager Password> <WebLogic Admin Password>]
```

Note that the passwords can either be specified on the command-line or can be entering manually when the script prompts for them. For automated startup you need to specify the passwords in the command line. The following is the example startup log for the startall.sh script. You can see in which order the script starts the IDM components. The log files for the startup/shutdown operations are available from the <IDM_CONFIG>/scripts/logs directory.

```
[fusion@idmhost ~]$ cd /app/oracle/config/scripts/
[fusion@idmhost scripts]$ ./startall.sh
Enter NodeManager Password:
Enter Weblogic Admin Password:
Executing on host :idmhost.paramlabs.com
Starting Instance : /app/oracle/config/instances/oid1 of Instance Type :OID on machine
: idmhost.paramlabs.com
Starting Instance : /app/oracle/config/nodemanager/idmhost.paramlabs.com of Instance Type
:NM on machine : idmhost.paramlabs.com
Starting Instance : AdminServer of Instance Type :AS on machine : idmhost.paramlabs.com
Starting Instance : /app/oracle/config/instances/odsm of Instance Type :ODSM_OPMN on machine
: idmhost.paramlabs.com
Starting Instance : wls_ods1 of Instance Type :ODSM on machine : idmhost.paramlabs.com
Starting Instance : wls_soa1 of Instance Type :SOA on machine : idmhost.paramlabs.com
Starting Instance : wls_oim1 of Instance Type :OIM on machine : idmhost.paramlabs.com
Starting Instance : wls_oam1 of Instance Type :OAM on machine : idmhost.paramlabs.com
Starting Instance : /app/oracle/config/instances/ohs1 of Instance Type :OHS on machine
: idmhost.paramlabs.com
```

Using Custom Scripts with Consolidated Manual Startup

As you saw, the automated script takes longer to start up the all components since it waits for the current component startup to finish before proceeding with the next component even if the server resources are idle. At the same time if one component startup fails, it will stop processing further even if the error is ignorable due to a false alert. In such cases you may want to create a custom startup script to start the components in the same order and at the same time by allowing multiple managed servers to start in parallel. The following is an example of a custom script we have created. Save this script as startIDM.sh and then provide execute permission to this script using the chmod +x startIDM.sh command.

```
#!/bin/bash
# Script Name: startIDM.sh v1.0_TT
# Start OID
echo "Starting Oracle Internet Directory (OID)"
/app/oracle/config/instances/oid1/bin/opmnctl startall
# Start Node Manager
echo "Starting Node Manager"
# Change this path as per your environment
cd /app/oracle/config/nodemanager/idmhost.paramlabs.com
nohup ./startNodeManagerWrapper.sh &
# Start WebLogic Domain Services
cd /app/oracle/config/domains/IDMDomain/bin
echo "Starting Weblogic Admin Server"
nohup ./startWebLogic.sh &
echo "Starting ODSM Agent service"
app/oracle/config/instances/odsm/bin/opmnctl startall
```

```
echo "Starting Managed Servers"
nohup ./startManagedWebLogic.sh wls_ods1 &
nohup ./startManagedWebLogic.sh wls_soa1 &
nohup ./startManagedWebLogic.sh wls_oim1 &
nohup ./startManagedWebLogic.sh wls_oam1 &
cd /app/oracle/products/app/wlserver_10.3/server/bin
echo "Waiting for 180 seconds to start Web server to avoid getting false WebGate alerts on
console"
sleep 180
# Start Web Server
echo "Starting Oracle HTTP Server (web)"
/app/oracle/config/instances/ohs1/bin/opmnctl startall
# Display informative messages
echo "Now you can monitor the status of Weblogic services startup by executing following
command"
echo "tail -f /app/oracle/config/domains/IDMDomain/bin/nohup.out"
echo "Once you see RUNING in following 2 log files, you can check the status at
http://`hostname`:7777/console or  http://`hostname`:7777/em"
echo "/app/oracle/config/domains/IDMDomain/servers/AdminServer/logs/AdminServer.log"
echo "/app/oracle/config/domains/IDMDomain/servers/wls_oam1/logs/wls_oam1.log"
```

■ **Tip**   Note that the database must be started before running this script. You may want to create another consolidated script that calls the database startup script startDB.sh (created earlier) and IDM startup script startIDM.sh sequentially.

Validating the Identity Management Nodes OS Processes

Once you have issued startup commands for the Identity Management components, you must make sure that the components have indeed started up. If you are starting the components manually, you could validate each component immediately after staring up but if you are starting up using single consolidated script then you can validate the OS processes one by one, as follows.

Validating OID

Run the following command to make sure that the OID has been started successfully. Depending on the number of server processes configured, you may see multiple processes of oid1 component, an OVD process and EM Agent process for OID. If any of these components status is not Alive, then you need to troubleshoot the cause.

```
<IDM_CONFIG>/instances/<OID_INSTANCE>/bin/opmnctl status
```

For example:

```
[fusion@idmhost scripts]$ /app/oracle/config/instances/oid1/bin/opmnctl status
Processes in Instance: oid1
--------------------------------+--------------------+---------+---------
ias-component                   | process-type       |    pid  | status
--------------------------------+--------------------+---------+---------
ovd1                            | OVD                |  20959  | Alive
oid1                            | oidldapd           |  21222  | Alive
oid1                            | oidldapd           |  21116  | Alive
oid1                            | oidldapd           |  21050  | Alive
oid1                            | oidmon             |  20958  | Alive
EMAGENT                         | EMAGENT            |  20957  | Alive
```

You can also telnet to the OID host with port 3060 (or the OID port in your environment) to make sure the process is already listening to requests on the specified port.

Validating ODSM EM Agent

Run the following command to make sure that the ODSM EM agent has started successfully. This is not a mandatory process for the Identity Management to work properly but if this is not started, the Middleware Control may not get updated status information about the Oracle Directory Service Manager.

```
<IDM_CONFIG>/instances/<ODSM_INSTANCE>/bin/opmnctl status
```

For example:

```
[fusion@idmhost scripts]$ /app/oracle/config/instances/odsm/bin/opmnctl status
Processes in Instance: wls_ods1
--------------------------------+--------------------+---------+---------
ias-component                   | process-type       |    pid  | status
--------------------------------+--------------------+---------+---------
EMAGENT                         | EMAGENT            |  22297  | Alive
```

Validating Oracle HTTP Server

Since we are only validating the OS processes here, run the following command to make sure that Oracle HTTP Server component has started successfully. However, in realtime you may be able to validate it by launching OHS static homepage as well. Run this command on the node where the Oracle HTTP server is configured to run.

```
<IDM_CONFIG>/instances/<OHS_INSTANCE>/bin/opmnctl status
```

For example:

```
[fusion@idmhost scripts]$ /app/oracle/config/instances/ohs1/bin/opmnctl status
Processes in Instance: ohs1
------------------------------+--------------------+---------+---------
ias-component                 | process-type       |   pid   | status
------------------------------+--------------------+---------+---------
ohs1                          | OHS                |  28854  | Alive
```

You can also telnet the web host to port 7777 (or the OHS port in your environment) to make sure the HTTP server is accepting requests.

Validating Node Manager

In order to validate Node Manager, you can simply run a grep command on the running processes to make sure that Node Manager is running.

```
[fusion@idmhost scripts]$ ps -ef | grep NodeManager
fusion    20652 20620 31 01:01 pts/3    00:00:03 /app/oracle/products/app/jdk6/bin/java
-jrockit -Xms128m -Xmx256m -Dcoherence.home=/app/oracle/products/app/coherence_3.7 -Dbea.
home=/app/oracle/products/app -DNodeManagerHome=/app/oracle/config/nodemanager/idmhost.
paramlabs.com -Xverify:none -Djava.security.policy=/app/oracle/products/app/wlserver_10.3/
server/lib/weblogic.policy -Dweblogic.nodemanager.javaHome=/app/oracle/products/app/jdk6
weblogic.NodeManager -v
```

You can telnet to each host with WebLogic servers configured with port 5556 to make sure that the node manager is reachable.

Validating WebLogic Server Processes

While we can simply log in to the WebLogic administration console to see the current status of all processes, you may want to validate the OS process in order to validate the correctness of the status derived from Node Manager state information or to troubleshoot issues with the WebLogic server. The OS processes for the WebLogic servers are individual JVM processes with the name of Managed Server as the value for the argument -Dweblogic.Name.

For example, to find the OS process for Admin Server, we can simply run grep for all running processes with the AdminServer value as follows. The full ps command output is long, so here is a truncated example.

```
[fusion@idmhost scripts]$ ps -ef | grep AdminServer
fusion    10652 10310  9 Mar06 ?        02:27:56 /app/oracle/products/app/jdk6/bin/java
-jrockit -Xms768m -Xmx1536m -Dweblogic.Name=AdminServer
```

Similarly you can run look for other managed server processes as well. For example for OAM Managed Server we can look for process with wls_oam1 argument. The same way you can search for wls_ods1, wls_oim1, and wls_soa1.

```
[fusion@idmhost scripts]$ ps -ef | grep wls_oam1
fusion    10650 10326  5 Mar06 ?        01:35:47 /app/oracle/products/app/jdk6/bin/java
-jrockit -Xms768m -Xmx1536m -Dweblogic.Name=wls_oam1
```

Comparison of Different Startup Options for Identity Management

At this stage you have learned about the various methods of starting up an Identity Management environment. While all of these methods are valid and applicable for starting up the components, you may want to choose one option for your routine operations. Table 12-1 shows a quick comparison of the methods with the pros and cons of each. You may want to choose one of the methods based on your priorities and organizational practice.

Table 12-1. *Comparison of Different Startup Options for Identity Management*

Startup Option	Advantages	Disadvantages
Command Line	1) Runs the startup tasks in background in parallel. 2) Commands can be placed in a consolidated automation script.	Post-execution status of components must be checked through the graphical interface or through lengthy log files.
WebLogic Administration Console	Simple interface with automatic refresh of current status.	1) Needs Admin Server and OAM to be started beforehand. 2) Cannot start HTTP Server and OID (since both are prerequisites to start the console).
EM Cloud Control	Single interface to start all IDM and FA components.	Manual task. Needs to navigate to relevant components pages.
Common Startup Script (`startall.sh`)	Completely automated startup of all IDM middle tier and web tier components.	Runs the startup tasks sequentially. Takes longer since it waits until the previous action completes.

Starting Fusion Applications Transaction Database

You must start the Fusion Applications transaction database before proceeding with the Fusion Applications components startup. Since we have already discussed database and listener startup options while looking at the IDM database, we will quickly go through the Fusion Applications database startup options without going into much details.

Using the Command-Line Interface

Once again, similar to the Identity Management database, we can comfortably start the Fusion Applications Transaction database using the command-line interface. This is the method that most database administrators prefer depending on whether the database is single node or RAC. Let's quickly go through the steps followed by the consolidated startup scripts.

Setting Up the Environment Variables

In order to start Oracle Database or the Listener service, we must set the mandatory environment variables like ORACLE_HOME, PATH, ORACLE_SID, and so on, in order to identify the database name and the location of the binaries. We can set the environment variables using any of the following methods.

Let's create a script to set minimum required environment variables on the database tier before starting the database and listener manually. Save it as dbprofile.sh on the FA database node.

```
#!/bin/bash
# Script name: dbprofile.sh v1.0_TT
# Change the following path to the actual path in your environment
ORACLE_HOME=/app/database/product/11.2.0/dbhome_1
export ORACLE_HOME

PATH=$PATH:$ORACLE_HOME/bin
export PATH

ORACLE_SID=fusiondb
export ORACLE_SID

# Change the following path to the actual path in your environment
JAVA_HOME=/app/oracle/jdk6
export JAVA_HOME
```

Let's assign execute permission to this script so that this file can be sourced from any other script.

```
[fusion@idmhost ~]$ chmod +x dbprofile.sh
```

Starting Up Oracle Database and Listener

Assuming that the database is created using the Provisioning wizard, it will be a single node database initially. Hence, the following procedure applies to single node database. For RAC databases use srvctl commands to start database and listener. You already know how to start up database and listener services. So we will directly go ahead with creating the consolidated startup script for Fusion Applications Transactional DB.

Startup Script for Fusion Applications Database and Listener

Let's create a script to start the Fusion Applications Transaction database and listener together. Save this as startDB.sh on the Fusion Applications Database server.

```
#!/bin/bash
# Script Name: startDB.sh v1.0_TT
. /home/fusion/dbprofile.sh
echo "Starting database listener"
lsnrctl start listener
echo "Starting Database"
sqlplus / as sysdba << EOF
startup
exit;
EOF
```

Remember to add execute permission for the user to this script. After that you can run this script from a shell prompt or within another script as follows.

```
[fusion@idmhost ~]$ ./startDB.sh
```

401

Using the Oracle Enterprise Manager Cloud Control

Assuming that you have already configured Fusion Applications database and other components with Enterprise Manager Cloud Control 12c and you have already gone through the database and middleware startup using EM in previous section, we will keep the sections related to EM-based startup compact to avoid any repetition.

In order to start the Fusion Applications database listener service, log in to Oracle Enterprise Manager Cloud Control using SYSMAN, click on the Targets menu and select Listener target type in the left panel. Select LISTENER_FUSIONDB_<DBHOST> from the list of targets. It will take you to the FUSIONDB listener home screen, as shown in Figure 12-12.

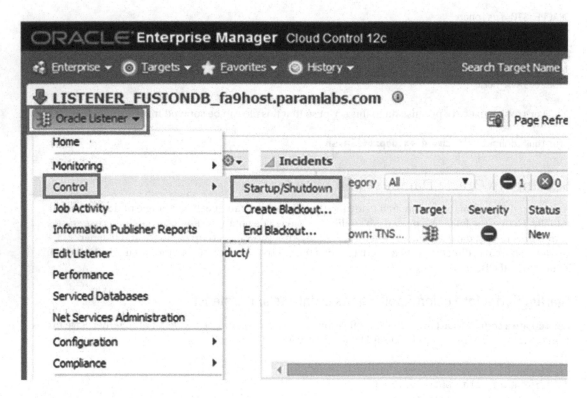

Figure 12-12. *Fusion Applications Database Listener startup screen*

Click on the Oracle Listener menu followed by the Control submenu. You can see the Startup/ Shutdown options here. You need to select this option even if you want to start up or shut down the service. This will lead to the Host Login details screen, as we saw earlier during the IDM Database startup. The Host Credential screen prompts for the database owner and again we have option to select from Preferred, Named, or New credential. You can refer to the IDM Database startup section if you want to review the details of the types of credentials prompted in this screen.

Let's now move on to Fusion Applications Transaction Database startup using the Enterprise Manager Cloud Control interface. Click on the Targets menu in the Global area of EM screen and then click on the Databases menu option. This will lead to the Database summary screen, which will display all configured databases in your environment. You will see that IDM database is already running and the fusiondb database is currently down. Click on fusiondb to launch Fusion Applications Database Home screen, as shown in Figure 12-13.

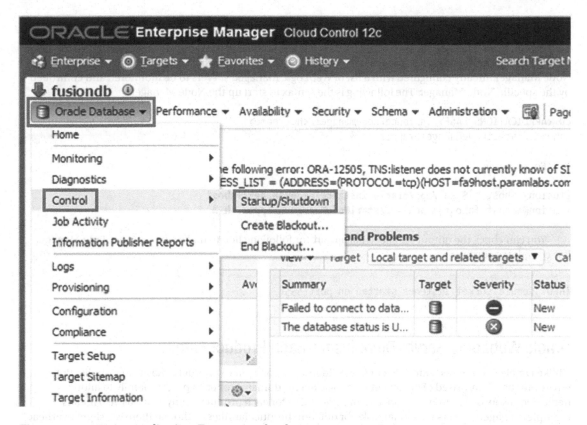

Figure 12-13. Fusion Applications Transaction database startup using EM

You may see an expected error on top suggesting the agent is unable to establish a connection to the database, which is expected since the database is down. Click on the Oracle Database menu, followed by the Control submenu, as shown in Figure 12-13. Click on Startup/Shutdown from the submenu to launch the Host and Database Credential screen. The Host/Database credentials screen is identical to what we have seen in IDM Database startup. Specify the database owner credentials as well as database user credentials with SYSDBA privilege.

In the next screen, you may see advanced startup options for the database, including specifying a custom parameters file, specifying different startup options for maintenance or force startup, and so on. Refer to the IDM Database startup section if you need more information about these screens. This concludes the startup of Fusion Applications transaction database and listener. Let's move on to understanding the Fusion Applications Components startup.

Starting Fusion Applications Middle Tier Components

We mentioned earlier that the startup of complete Fusion Applications environment takes quite a long time compared to traditional ERPs you have used, but you may have noticed that so far all the components started came up very quickly and we are already at the last phase of startup. Note that most of the time taken for the Fusion Applications environment is spent during Fusion Applications middle tier components. You should try to parallelize the startup tasks as much as possible and make maximum use of server resources for startup but at the same time you must monitor the server resources usage during startup and take necessary action if the CPU remains unavailable for startup processes. Let's look at each component's startup one by one along with the recommended as well as alternate methods.

Node Manager

Starting the Node Manager on each configured host is a prerequisite to WebLogic domains startup for all Fusion Applications startup methods that we are going to discuss. Each host has an instance directory for Node Manager already configured with a list of WebLogic managed servers to be monitored and controlled by the specific Node Manager. The following is the syntax to start up the Node Manager:

```
cd <APPLICATIONS_BASE>/instance/nodemanager/<hostname>
nohup ./ startNodeManagerWrapper.sh &
```

For example:

```
[fusion@fahost ~]$ cd /app/oracle/instance/nodemanager/fahost
[fusion@fahost fahost]$ nohup ./startNodeManagerWrapper.sh &
```

You can check the output file called nohup.out for following line to make sure that the Node Manager has completed startup.

```
INFO: Secure socket listener started on port 5556
```

Oracle WebLogic Server Domains for Each Product Family

Unlike Oracle E-Business Suite R12.2 or Oracle Identity Management products, the Fusion Applications environment is comprised of dedicated WebLogic Server domains for each product family to allow dedicated resources, administration, and manageability for each product family. But this also means multiple managed servers for similar tasks for different product families. Although there is a slight overhead in starting up all these number of WebLogic domains and managed servers, eventually it helps a lot in the day-to-day operations. Depending on the number of products provisioned, your environment may have 25 to 65 managed servers. Since it may take quite some time to start them all up, using the default WebLogic scripts is not recommended since invoking startup script for all of them at same time can put a lot of load on the server CPUs. We will rely on Oracle's specialized scripts or Enterprise Manager. Let's look at the recommended methods of starting up the Fusion Applications WebLogic domains.

Using the fastartstop Utility

The fastartup utility provided by Oracle can start or stop most of the components of Fusion Applications environment even if they are configured on more than one server. We can either use the same utility to manage all services or use fastartstop to manage WebLogic servers while other methods for remaining components. In fact we have multiple options of starting WebLogic managed servers as well, the fastartstop utility is most versatile and recommended method of all. The most obvious reason is that the fastartstop utility provided by Oracle is aware of internal dependencies of domains so it can start the managed servers in appropriate order. It also controls the load on CPU by staring the services in batches instead of starting all of them together.

Although `fastartstop` has many optional switches, the following is the compact and simplified syntax of the utility that administrators use most of the time. The script is located at `<AD_TOP>/bin`. Note that with the Windows platform the utility name is `fastartstop.cmd`.

```
<AD_TOP>/bin/fastartstop.sh \
-Start | -Stop | -Bounce \
-all \
| -domains <comma separated domain names> \
| -domains "<domain_name>(server:all | <managed_server> | AdminServer)" \
| -componentType <OHS | BI | GOP | OSN> \
[-username <FA Admin User name>] \
-fa_oracle_home <FA Oracle Home location> \
[-adminServersOnly | -startAdminServer <true | false>]
```

The following sections will help you understand the `fastartstop` utility, including its available switches, and when to use which options or parameters.

Starting All WebLogic Domains

Since Oracle Fusion Applications involves multiple Oracle WebLogic domains for more than one product family, using default scripts to start up the domains would be a tedious and time-consuming job. Hence Oracle has provided a special startup utilities that can start all the domains configured on multiple physical servers instead of logging on to each server manually. This also eliminates the need to configure individual `boot.properties` file manually in the `secure` directory of each managed server.

■ **Note**   Some documents suggest that using the -`all` switch with the `fastartstop.sh` script starts all the components including the WebLogic domains as well as OPMN-based components, but as of the current release, this does not start the OPMN-based components like OHS, BI, and so on. You need to specify the -`componentType` switch manually in order to start these components.

Use the following command in order to start the WebLogic domains for all the configured product families. Remember to use only -`all` and not -`domains` in the script.

```
<AD_TOP>/bin/fastartstop.sh -Start -all -username <FA Administration user> \
 -fa_oracle_home <FA Oracle Home path> [-adminServersOnly | -startAdminServer <true |
false>]
```

For example:

```
[fusion@fahost ~]$ cd /app/oracle/fusionapps/applications/lcm/ad/bin
[fusion@fahost bin]$ ./fastartstop.sh -Start -all -username FAADMIN -fa_oracle_home \
/app/oracle/fusionapps/applications -startAdminServer true
```

Now let's look at the two optional arguments in the command.

- -adminServersOnly: This option only starts up the administration servers for all WebLogic domains. This allows you to log in to the Administration console of each WebLogic domain manually to perform any required maintenance. The default value is false, which means it will start all managed servers as well in addition to administration servers.

- -startAdminServer: By default the value of this option is false, which means the administration servers for each domain are only used to bring the managed servers up. Upon completion of the Start/Stop command, the administration servers are stopped. If you set this parameter to true, the administration servers will remain up after completion of the fastartstop.sh script execution.

Starting Specific Domains

In many cases you may want to only start or bounce specific WebLogic domains. In this case, instead of using the -all option, you need to use the -domain option with a comma-separated list of domain names that you want to start. Use the following syntax to start specific domains using the command line:

```
<AD_TOP>/bin/fastartstop.sh -Start -domains <Comma Separated list of Domains> \
-username <FA Administration user> -fa_oracle_home <FA Oracle Home path> \
[-adminServersOnly | -startAdminServer <true | false>]
```

For example:

```
[fusion@fahost bin]$ ./fastartstop.sh -Start -domains CommonDomain,HCMDomain \
-username FAADMIN -fa_oracle_home /app/oracle/fusionapps/applications -startAdminServer true
```

Starting Specific Managed Servers

If you want to start, stop, or bounce one or more specific managed servers of one or more product family domains, then the fastartstop utility is flexible enough to allow you to do this. All you need to do is to specify the -domains switch with a comma-separated list of domains to be started with comma-separated names of managed servers for each domain. Use the following syntax to start the specific managed servers using the command line.

```
<AD_TOP>/bin/fastartstop.sh -Start \
-domains "<domain_name>(server:all | <managed_server> | AdminServer)" \
-username <FA Administration user> -fa_oracle_home <FA Oracle Home path> \
[-adminServersOnly | -startAdminServer <true | false>]
```

For example:

```
[fusion@fahost bin]$ ./fastartstop.sh -Start -domains \
"CommonDomain(server:HomePageServer_1)" -username FAADMIN -fa_oracle_home \
/app/oracle/fusionapps/applications -startAdminServer true
```

Note that you can use the all option for some domains for which you want to start all managed servers, while for other domains you can specify the specific list of managed servers to be started.

Using Enterprise Manager Cloud Control

As you now know, Enterprise Manager Cloud Control can start all the configured components in your environment including database, middleware, OPMN managed components and so on. However starting components through EM may be time consuming due to the number of screens to navigate through for multiple WebLogic domains and large number of managed servers. It is generally recommended to limit the use of EM Cloud Control based startup for specific domains or managed servers only but technically you can start up each domains manually using EM interface.

We have already seen Identity Management domain startup using EM Cloud Control interface and the Fusion Applications Domains startup is no different. We will quickly go through how to navigate to specific WebLogic domains and start up complete domain or specific WebLogic cluster manually using EM interface.

Log in to EM Cloud Control using the SYSMAN account and navigate to the Targets ➤ *Fusion Applications* Global menu item. You will see the Fusion Applications Summary screen, as shown in Figure 12-14.

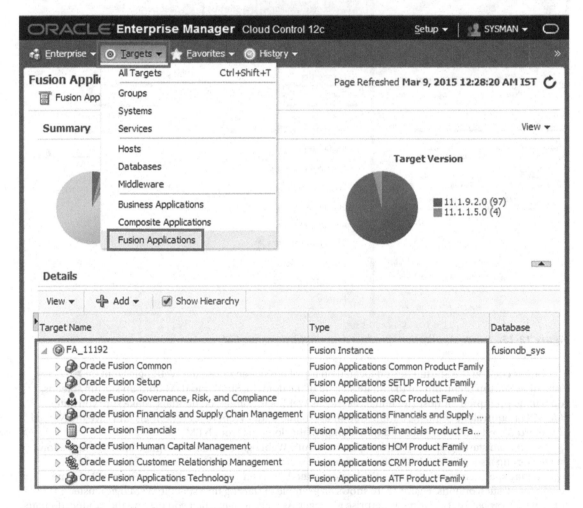

Figure 12-14. Fusion Applications EM Summary screen

You can see the name of the Fusion Applications Instance Target in the Details region of the screen. In this example we have configured the same with FA_11192, as shown in Figure 12-14. You can expand the tree to see the list of product families domains installed in your environment. Click on the product domain which you want to manage and it will navigate to the Product Family home screen. Now you can click on the Target Domain name on the left panel (FA_11192_FinancialDomain in this example) followed by the WebLogic Domain ➤ <ProductDomain> sub-tree entry (FinancialDomain in this example) to bring up the specific domain's home screen, as shown in Figure 12-15.

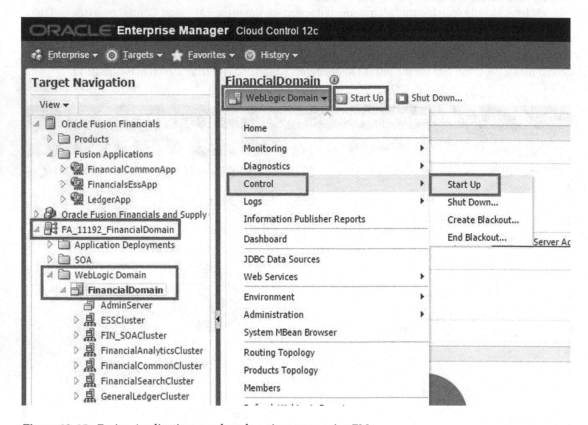

Figure 12-15. *Fusion Applications product domain startup using EM*

Either click on the Startup button located on top of the screen or use the WebLogic Domain ➤ Control ➤ Startup menu option to initiate startup of the domain. Similar to IDM domain startup screens, you will be prompted for host credentials as well as WebLogic domain credentials. Make sure you enter FAADMIN or equivalent Domain Administration username under WebLogic credentials and save the Named or Preferred credentials for future administration of the domain through EM.

Apart from starting up the complete product family WebLogic domain, Enterprise Manager also allows you to start up a specific WebLogic cluster, managed server, or even deployed Fusion cluster application (which may span across one or more WebLogic clusters). You can explore the Product Family EM Home screen for all such options. Figure 12-16 shows an example of starting up a specific WebLogic cluster (FinancialCommonCluster) using Enterprise Manager. As you can see, when you expand the product domain sub-tree, you will see the list of WebLogic clusters under that domain. Click on the cluster that you want to start up, which will bring up the home screen for that cluster. Click Startup or choose the WebLogic Cluster ➤ Control ➤ Startup menu option in order to start the cluster on all the nodes where it is configured to run.

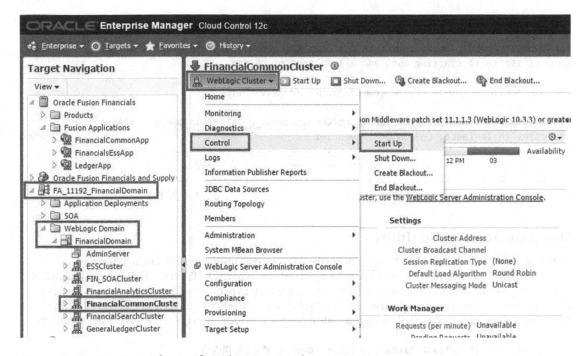

Figure 12-16. *Starting up the specific WebLogic server cluster using EM*

Oracle HTTP Server

Fusion Applications web tier can be started at any point after the Identity Management environment has been started. However it is recommended to startup web tier (Oracle HTTP Server) after all the product domains have been started to restrict users from trying to access the application when it is not yet completely started. The HTTP server in Fusion Applications web tier is also integrated with Oracle access manager through WebGate plugin and all the applications related URLs are protected by the access manager. You can refer to the Oracle HTTP Server Virtual Host configuration files for each product family with the name **FusionVirtualHost_<product_family>.conf** at the following location. These files will include the Oracle HTTP Server aliases and WebLogic redirection rules. You can refer to these files for troubleshooting redirection related issues.

```
<APPLICATIONS_BASE>/instance/CommonDomain_webtier/config/OHS/ohs1/moduleconf/
```

Now let's see how to start up the Oracle HTTP Server on the Fusion Applications web host. We have the following two options for OHS startup.

Using Oracle Process Manager

Starting Oracle HTTP Server using OMPN (Oracle Process Manager and Notification Server) is the simplest and recommended method of starting it up. Run the following command on the web tier to start OHS up.

```
<APPLICATIONS_BASE>/instance/CommonDomain_webtier/bin/opmnctl startall
```

For example:

```
[fusion@fahost ~]$ /app/oracle/instance/CommonDomain_webtier/bin/opmnctl startall
opmnctl startall: starting opmn and all managed processes...
```

Now let's make sure that the process has started up successfully.

```
[fusion@fahost ~]$ /app/oracle/instance/CommonDomain_webtier/bin/opmnctl status
Processes in Instance: CommonDomain_webtier
---------------------------------+--------------------+---------+---------
ias-component                    | process-type       |    pid | status
---------------------------------+--------------------+---------+---------
ohs1                             | OHS                |   6474 | Alive
```

Using the fastartstop Utility

Although we can start Oracle HTTP Server using the fastartstop utility, it is not a straightforward procedure since it needs the OPMN server to be up in order to start the OHS server. So it is more practical to start OPMN as well as OHS together instead of starting them up in two steps. However, if you want to keep the components startup uniform by using the fastartstop utility, you can use this startup method. The following is the syntax to start OHS using this utility. Note that it does not require the -username argument.

```
[fusion@fahost ]$ ./fastartstop.sh -Start -componentType OHS \
-appbase /app/oracle/fusionapps/applications
```

In case of the OPMN server is not already started then you may see following error.

```
Failed to create secure socket for OPMN at fahost.paramlabs.com:7043; OPMN server might be
down on fahost, please start OPMN server
```

In that case you may need to first execute the following command before running the fastartstop utility.

```
[fusion@fahost bin]$ /app/oracle/instance/CommonDomain_webtier/bin/opmnctl start
```

This will only start the OPMN server not the OHS process, as you can see here.

```
[fusion@fahost bin]$ /app/oracle/instance/CommonDomain_webtier/bin/opmnctl status
Processes in Instance: CommonDomain_webtier
---------------------------------+--------------------+---------+---------
ias-component                    | process-type       |    pid | status
---------------------------------+--------------------+---------+---------
ohs1                             | OHS                |    N/A | Down
```

Now you can start the HTTP server process using the fastartstop utility, as you saw.

Oracle Business Intelligence Components

Oracle BI Instance can be started in a similar manner as we started OHS in the previous section. Here also we have two options to start up the Oracle BI processes with OPMN being the recommended option.

Using Oracle Process Manager

Run the following command on the web tier to start up the Oracle BI instance using the OPMN server.

```
<APPLICATIONS_BASE>/instance/ BIInstance/bin/opmnctl startall
```

For example:

```
[fusion@fahost bin]$ /app/oracle/instance/BIInstance/bin/opmnctl startall
opmnctl startall: starting opmn and all managed processes...
```

Let's check the status of the processes after startup.

```
[fusion@fahost bin]$ /app/oracle/instance/BIInstance/bin/opmnctl status
Processes in Instance: BIInstance
---------------------------------+--------------------+---------+---------
ias-component                    | process-type       |   pid | status
---------------------------------+--------------------+---------+---------
coreapplication_obips1           | OracleBIPresentat~ |  17656 | Alive
essbaseserver1                   | Essbase            |  17659 | Alive
coreapplication_obiccs1          | OracleBIClusterCo~ |  17661 | Alive
coreapplication_obisch1          | OracleBIScheduler~ |  17658 | Alive
coreapplication_obijh1           | OracleBIJavaHostC~ |  17657 | Alive
coreapplication_obis1            | OracleBIServerCom~ |  17662 | Alive
```

Using fastartstop Utility

If you want to use single utility for all components startup, use the fastartstop.sh script to start the BI instance up as follows.

```
[fusion@fahost bin]$ ./fastartstop.sh -Start -componentType BI \
-appbase /app/oracle/fusionapps/applications
```

This command may fail if the corresponding OPMN server is down so run the following command in that case.

```
[fusion@fahost bin]$ /app/oracle/instance/BIInstance/bin/opmnctl start
```

Global Order Promising (GOP): Only if Using Supply Chain Management (SCM)

If you have provisioned Oracle Fusion Supply Chain Management (SCM) products, then you may need to start the Global Order Promising (GOP) component. Note that although the fastartstop utility supports stopping the GOP component, it does not support startup of GOP as of the current release (Release 9). If you try to start up GOP using fastartstop.sh, you may see following error.

```
[Warning:1] [oracle.apps.startstop.cli.CLIParser: validateCommandLineArguments.793]
[tid:10] Option Start not supported for GOP
```

The only supported method to start the GOP service is using OPMN-based startup as follows.

```
<APPLICATIONS_BASE>/instance/<gop_instance>/bin/opmnctl startall
```

For example:

```
[fusion@fahost bin]$ /app/oracle/instance/gop_1/bin/opmnctl startall
```

Oracle Social Network (OSN): Only If Configured

If you have configured the Oracle Social Network (OSN) then you can start it up as well using the fastartstop utility. Use the following command to start up OSN.

```
[fusion@fahost bin]$ ./fastartstop.sh -Start -componentType OSN \
-appbase /app/oracle/fusionapps/applications
```

Informatica Identity Resolution (IIR): Only If Using CRM

If you have provisioned Oracle Fusion CRM modules, then you need to start up the Informatica Identity Resolution (IIR) component manually. Use the following commands to start up IIR on the CRM node. Note that IIR needs the DISPLAY variable to be set and the VNC server to be running on the selected port.

```
[fusion@fahost ~]$ export DISPLAY=fahost:0
[fusion@fahost ~]$ cd /app/oracle/InformaticaIR/bin/
[fusion@fahost bin]$ . ./setfusionEnv.sh
[fusion@fahost bin]$ ./liup
[fusion@fahost bin]$ ./idsup
[fusion@fahost bin]$ ./idsconc -a
```

Validating the Fusion Applications Nodes OS Processes

Of course you would have been making sure that each component has started up completely after startup. If you want to troubleshoot any false "component down alerts" and make sure that the OS process is indeed running, you can locate each process as follows.

Oracle WebLogic Server Processes

You can simply run the process status command and look for the specific administration server or WebLogic managed server processes as follows. You should see a Java process with the -Dweblogic.Name parameter pointing to the managed server name.

```
ps -ef | grep <DomainName> | grep <ManagedServer_Name>
```

For example:

```
[fusion@fahost ~]$ ps -ef | grep CommonDomain | grep FunctionalSetupServer_1
```

This should show an output as follows (truncated for better readability):

```
fusion   24848 21540  7 Mar08 ?        02:15:22 /app/oracle/fusionapps/jdk6/bin/java
-jrockit -Xms512m -Xmx2048m -Xgc:genpar -XX:+HeapDumpOnOutOfMemoryError -XX:HeapDumpPath=
/app/oracle/instance/debug -XX:+ExitOnOutOfMemoryError -Xverbosedecorations=level,module,time
stamp,millis,pid -Xverbose:gc -Dweblogic.Name=FunctionalSetupServer_1
...
```

OPMN-Based Components Processes

As seen earlier, after starting up the OPMN-based components we can check the status using the opmnctl status command but at times due to some issues it may continue to show process status even if the process has ended or become defunct in background. In this case first run the status command, then pick up the OS process ID (pid) from the output and then manually check for the PID using the Process Status command.

For example:

```
[fusion@fahost ~]$ /app/oracle/instance/CommonDomain_webtier/bin/opmnctl status

Processes in Instance: CommonDomain_webtier
--------------------------------+--------------------+---------+---------
ias-component                   | process-type       |     pid | status
--------------------------------+--------------------+---------+---------
ohs1                            | OHS                |   27999 | Alive
```

Now let's look up for the process ID mentioned under the pid column using the process status (ps) command. You will notice the process as well as all the child processes spawned by the main component process. The following is the truncated output of the same with a few HTTP processes only.

```
[fusion@fahost ~]$ ps -ef | grep 27999
fusion   27999 27955  4 23:12 ?        00:00:01 /app/oracle/webtier_mwhome/webtier/ohs/bin/
httpd.worker -DSSL
fusion   28008 27999  0 23:12 ?        00:00:00 /app/oracle/webtier_mwhome/webtier/ohs/bin/
odl_rotatelogs -l /app/oracle/instance/CommonDomain_webtier/diagnostics/logs/OHS/ohs1/ohs1-
%Y%m%d%H%M%S.log 10M 70M
fusion   28009 27999  0 23:12 ?        00:00:00 /app/oracle/webtier_mwhome/webtier/ohs/bin/
odl_rotatelogs /app/oracle/instance/CommonDomain_webtier/diagnostics/logs/OHS/ohs1/access_
log 43200
fusion   28010 27999  0 23:12 ?        00:00:00 /app/oracle/webtier_mwhome/webtier/ohs/
bin/odl_rotatelogs -l /app/oracle/instance/CommonDomain_webtier/diagnostics/logs/OHS/ohs1/
deflate_log-%Y%m%d 86400
```

```
fusion    28018 27999  0 23:12 ?         00:00:00 /app/oracle/webtier_mwhome/webtier/ohs/bin/
odl_rotatelogs /app/oracle/instance/CommonDomain_webtier/diagnostics/logs/OHS/ohs1/weblogic.
log 43200
...
fusion    28020 27999  0 23:12 ?         00:00:00 /app/oracle/webtier_mwhome/webtier/ohs/bin/
httpd.worker -DSSL
fusion    28023 27999  0 23:12 ?         00:00:00 /app/oracle/webtier_mwhome/webtier/ohs/bin/
httpd.worker -DSSL
...
```

Consolidated Startup/Shutdown Script Example

Having looked at all the methods of staring up the Fusion Applications environment, it is clear that starting the environment using the command-line interface is the best option since the fastartstop utility takes care of all the required dependencies within the products' WebLogic domains. So let's create a consolidated startup script to start all these components using a single script for quick and comfortable Fusion Applications environment startup. Feel free to customize this script if your OPMN components are hosted on different hosts. Also change the paths and passwords in the script as per your environment.

```
#!/bin/bash
# Script name: startFA.sh v1.0_TT
echo "Starting Node Manager Process"
cd /app/oracle/instance/nodemanager/fahost
nohup ./startNodeManagerWrapper.sh &
# Wait for Node Manager to complete the startup
sleep 30
# Start Product Domains
cd /app/oracle/fusionapps/applications/lcm/ad/bin/
echo "Starting all Fusion Applications Domains"
./fastartstop.sh -Start -all -username FAADMIN -appbase \
/app/oracle/fusionapps/applications -startAdminServer true <<EOF_PASS
MyPassword
EOF_PASS
# Start OPMN based components
echo "Starting Web server"
/app/oracle/instance/CommonDomain_webtier/bin/opmnctl startall
echo "Starting BI services"
/app/oracle/instance/BIInstance/bin/opmnctl startall
echo "Starting informatica IR services"
#If idsconc exists with X display error then run vncserver :0 and xhost + as root and then
rerun the command
export DISPLAY=fahost:0
# Start IIR only if CRM is provisioned or else comment these lins
cd /app/oracle/InformaticaIR/bin/
. ./setfusionEnv.sh
./liup
./idsup
./idsconc -a
echo "All components started"
```

Save this script as `startFA.sh` and add `execute` permission to the script so that you can run it from other wrapper scripts as well.

```
[fusion@fahost scripts]$ chmod +x startFA.sh
```

Comparison of Different Startup Options for Fusion Applications

While you may find one startup/shutdown method more suitable than other, all methods have certain advantages and disadvantages. Table 12-2 lists the major differences between these methods. You may decide on one method and implement it in your organization best practices accordingly since it is always recommended that everyone in the organization follow the same process to manage the applications services. Running multiple commands at same time in such a complex environment may cause unexpected issues.

Table 12-2. *Comparison of Different Startup Options for Fusion Applications*

Startup Option	Advantages	Disadvantages
Command line using `fastartstop` script	1) Can start all domains using a single command. 2) Multiple startup commands can be placed in consolidated automation script.	Must wait for the current `fastartstop` script execution to complete before further commands can be executed.
Command line using default WebLogic scripts	Multiple WebLogic servers can be started in parallel without waiting for the previous one to complete.	1) The `boot.properties` file must be created for all managed severs. 2) Can only start on WebLogic servers.
WebLogic Administration Console	Simple interface. Multiple domains can be started without waiting for other domains to start up.	1) Administration server must be started beforehand. 2) Cannot start the HTTP server and BI instance.
Oracle Enterprise Manager Cloud Control	Single interface to start all IDM and FA components.	Manual task. Need to navigate to relevant domains and components.

Stopping Fusion Applications Environment

You should stop the Fusion Applications environment in reverse order of the startup sequence. The following is the shutdown sequence we will follow in order to stop all the components in Fusion Applications environment. Of course, Oracle Enterprise Manager Cloud Control provides a simple interface to stop all products using a single interface but it should be noted that stopping the Fusion middleware components takes a fraction of the time as compared to startup so you may choose to go with seeded shutdown scripts instead of going with manual shutdown procedure. The following is the generic sequence for shutting down all components involved in a Fusion Applications environment. Depending on your custom integrations and dependencies you may want to add or modify these steps.

1. Stop Fusion Applications tier components.

    a. Oracle HTTP Server

    b. BI, GOP, ONS, IIR components

    c. WebLogic Server domains for each product family

    d. Node Manager

415

2. Stop Fusion Applications transaction database and listener.

3. Stop Identity Management tier components.

    a. Oracle HTTP Server

    b. OIF, ODSM EM Agents

    c. IDM WebLogic Domain

    d. Oracle Internet Directory

    e. Node Manager

4. Stop Identity Management database and listener.

Stopping Fusion Applications Middle Tier Components

Let's take a quick look at the steps to stop the Fusion Applications Tier components. The steps for shutting down are very similar to start up, so we will not go into details of each method again but simply run through the commands. Replace /app/oracle with the actual value of APPLICATIONS_BASE in your environment. We will first start with OPMN-based components followed by WebLogic domains. Note that all these components can be stopped using Enterprise Manager Cloud Control in a similar manner as we have seen their startup using EM.

Informatica Identity Resolution (IIR): Only if Using CRM

If you have provisioned CRM modules then you need to shut down the Informatica Identity Resolution component. Use the following commands to stop IIR;

```
[fusion@fahost ~]$ cd /app/oracle/InformaticaIR/bin/
[fusion@fahost bin]$ . ./setfusionEnv.sh
[fusion@fahost bin]$ ./idsdown
[fusion@fahost bin]$ ./lidown
```

Oracle Social Network (OSN): Only if Configured

If you have configured Oracle Social Network (OSN), then you can stop it using the fastartstop utility as follows.

```
[fusion@fahost bin]$ ./fastartstop.sh -Stop -componentType OSN \
-appbase /app/oracle/fusionapps/applications
```

Global Order Promising (GOP): Only if Using Supply Chain Management (SCM)

If you have provisioned the Oracle Fusion SCM modules, then you must stop the Global Order Promising (GOP) component. The recommended way to stop the GOP component is to use the Oracle Process Manager (OPMN) as follows.

```
[fusion@fahost bin]$ /app/oracle/instance/gop_1/bin/opmnctl stopall
opmnctl stopall: stopping opmn and all managed processes...
```

Unlike the startup of GOP, shutdown is already supported by the fastartstop utility. We can simply provide componentType as GOP as an argument to stop the component.

```
[fusion@fahost bin]$ ./fastartstop.sh -Stop -componentType GOP -username FAADMIN -appbase
/app/oracle/fusionapps/applications
```

Oracle Business Intelligence Components

Unlike starting up an Oracle BI instance, the shutdown is relatively quick. The BI components can be stopped using either OPMN or the fastartstop utility but OPMN is the recommended option to shut down the Oracle BI components. Use the following command to stop it using OPMN.

```
[fusion@fahost bin]$ /app/oracle/instance/BIInstance/bin/opmnctl stopall
opmnctl stopall: stopping opmn and all managed processes...
```

If you want to use the fastartstop.sh script then you can specify BI as the -componentType argument, as shown in the following example.

```
[fusion@fahost bin]$ ./fastartstop.sh -Stop -componentType BI \
-appbase /app/oracle/fusionapps/applications
```

Oracle HTTP Server

Ideally, Oracle HTTP Server should be stopped as soon as you plan to bring the complete Fusion Applications Environment down in order to prevent users from logging into the application. OPMN is the recommended method to stop the Oracle HTTP Server quickly. The following is the command to stop OHS using OPMN. However if you are planning to start it later using the fastartstop script then you can only stop OHS component and leave OPMN running.

```
[fusion@fahost ~]$ /app/oracle/instance/CommonDomain_webtier/bin/opmnctl stopall
opmnctl stopall: stopping opmn and all managed processes...
```

Use the following command in order to stop OHS using the fastartstop utility instead.

```
[fusion@fahost ]$ ./fastartstop.sh -Stop -componentType OHS \
-appbase /app/oracle/fusionapps/applications
```

Oracle WebLogic Server Domains for Each Product Family

We have already seen how to start WebLogic domains for all product families, selected product families as well as only a selected managed servers of specific WebLogic domains. The shutdown of WebLogic server domains can also be done in exactly same way by simply replacing -Start with the -Stop argument while running the fastartstop.sh script. Since we have already discussed multiple uses of the fastartstop utility to manage WebLogic Server domains, we will only look at how to stop all product domains. You can always manage selected servers by providing -domains argument as we have seen during startup. Note that this utility can stop the WebLogic domains on each Fusion Applications host where a product domain or WebLogic cluster is configured to run. Make sure that the Node Manager on each node is running before running this command.

```
[fusion@fahost bin]$ ./fastartstop.sh -Stop -all -username FAADMIN -fa_oracle_home \
/app/oracle/fusionapps/applications
```

This will prompt for the WebLogic Servers Administration user specified above. If you want to leave the Administration Servers running then you can specify the **-startAdminServer true** argument at the end of the command. If you are going to restart the physical servers then you should not specify this argument.

Node Manager

Once all the WebLogic Server domains have been stopped, if you are planning to restart the servers then you can stop the Node Manager processes on each Fusion Applications host. If you are only going to bring up the components up after maintenance without restarting the physical servers then you can leave this running since you will need the Node Manager to be up in next startup cycle. At this moment there is no command to shut down Node Manager so we need to locate the background process for Node Manager and kill the process using the kill command. Following is the single-line command to do both these tasks.

```
[fusion@fahost ]$ ps -ef | grep NodeManager | awk '{print $2}' | xargs kill -9
```

Consolidated Script for Stopping the Fusion Applications Tier

For your convenience, we have created following consolidated script for stopping all the Fusion Applications components. Make sure you change the paths and password to actual ones, as per your environment. Feel free to modify the script to your requirements.

```
#!/bin/bash
# Script Name: StopFA.sh v1.0_TT
# Stop  OPMN Based Components
echo "Stopping informatica IR services"
cd /app/oracle/InformaticaIR/bin/
. ./setfusionEnv.sh
./idsdown
./lidown

echo "Stopping BI services"
/app/oracle/instance/BIInstance/bin/opmnctl stopall

echo "Stopping Web Server"
/app/oracle/instance/CommonDomain_webtier/bin/opmnctl stopall

# Stop WebLogic Server Domains
cd /app/oracle/fusionapps/applications/lcm/ad/bin/
echo "Stopping all Fusion Applications Domains"
./fastartstop.sh -Stop -all -username FAADMIN -appbase /app/oracle/fusionapps/applications
<<EOF_PASS

MyPassword
EOF_PASS
# Stop Node Manager
echo "Killing Node Manager process"
ps -ef | grep NodeManager | awk '{print $2}' | xargs kill -9
echo "All components stopped"
```

Save this script as stopFA.sh and provide execute permission for this file as follows so that this file can be run from other wrapper scripts as well.

```
[fusion@fahost scripts]$ chmod +x stopFA.sh
```

Manual Shutdown Using Enterprise Manager Cloud Control

We have already seen how to start up Identity Management components using Enterprise Manager so we will skip a detailed discussion of the EM interface here. In order to shut down IDM components, follow these steps:

1. Log in to EM Cloud Control 12c with SYSMAN user.

2. On the home screen, click Targets menu ➤ Fusion Applications. This will open the Fusion Applications summary screen.

3. Expand the configured Fusion Applications instance in the targets details region. This will show the list of Fusion Applications Product Families configured with Enterprise Manager under the given Fusion instance. Click on any product family that you want to shutdown or manage. This will launch the Product Family Home screen.

4. In the Product Family Home screen, you can stop the entire WebLogic domain, specific WebLogic clusters, or even specific application deployments by selecting from the Regional area menu.

Stopping the Fusion Applications Transaction Database

Once the Fusion Applications Application and Web Tier components have been stopped, you can shut down the FUSIONDB database and listener. You can use Enterprise Manager to stop the database in a similar way as we have seen the database and listener startup. Since the screen is exactly the same we will not repeat the walkthrough here.

Shut down the database using the shutdown immediate command or if you are using RAC database then use srvctl stop database -d fusiondb to stop the database. Similarly stop listener using the lsnrctl stop command or for RAC use the srvctl stop listener -l <listener_name> command to stop the listener. Alternatively, you can use following script to stop the database and listener in one go. Make sure to change the listener name as per your environment.

```
#!/bin/bash
# Script Name: stopDB.sh v1.0_TT
# Source the database environment file
. /home/fusion/dbprofile.sh

echo "Stopping Database"
sqlplus / as sysdba << EOF
shutdown immediate;
exit;
EOF

echo "Stopping database listener"
lsnrctl stop listener
```

Save this script as stopDB.sh and provide execute permission to the script in order to use it in consolidated shutdown scripts in your organization.

Stopping Identity Management Middle Tier Components

Unlike the startall.sh script, which takes a long time to complete due to serial execution of startup tasks, the stopall.sh script completes quite quickly since the shutdown tasks do not take a long time. Hence the recommended method to stop all Identity Management components is to use the stopall.sh script created during the provisioning process. However during day-to-day administration of the environment you may need to stop certain components only. In that case, the stopall.sh script does not help so we will have a look at how to manually shut down the individual Identity Management components.

Automatic Shutdown Using the stopall.sh Script

The seeded shutdown script is already created by the Provisioning wizard at <IDM_CONFIG>/scripts. You can run the script as follows in order to shut down the Identity Management application and web tier components sequentially. Note that the password arguments are optional so if you do not specify them on the command line then the script will prompt you for them. If you are planning to run the script inside the consolidated shutdown script, you need to provide the passwords as an argument but you must check your IT security policy before specifying passwords in the plaintext script file.

<IDM_CONFIG>/scripts/stopall.sh <Node Manager Password> <WebLogic Administrator Password>

In following example, we are not specifying the passwords on the command line.

```
[fusion@idmhost ~]$ cd /app/oracle/config/scripts/
[fusion@idmhost scripts]$ ./stopall.sh

Enter NodeManager Password:
Enter Weblogic Admin Password:
```

Manual Shutdown Using Command Line

If you want to stop all the Identity Management components manually or if you want to stop only a few selected components, then use the following manual shutdown methods.

Oracle HTTP Server

You must stop Oracle HTTP Server first if you are planning to shut down the complete Identity Management environment manually in order to reject any requests to the Identity Management components while they are still shutting down. The syntax for stopping Oracle HTTP Server (OHS) instance is as follows.

<IDM_CONFIG>/<OHS_INSTANCE>/bin/opmnctl stopall

For example:

```
[fusion@idmhost ~]$ /app/oracle/config/instances/ohs1/bin/opmnctl stopall
opmnctl stopall: stopping opmn and all managed processes...
```

OIF EM Agent

If you have configured the component Oracle Identity Federation (OIF), you need to shut down the OIF EM agent as follows.

```
<IDM_CONFIG>/<OIF_INSTANCE>/bin/opmnctl stopall
```

For example:

```
[fusion@idmhost ~]$ /app/oracle/config/instances/oif_inst/bin/opmnctl stopall
opmnctl stopall: stopping opmn and all managed processes...
```

ODSM EM Agent

Stop Oracle Directory Service Manager EM agent using the following command. Note that this command does not stop the ODSM service but only the EM agent.

```
<IDM_CONFIG>/<ODSM_INSTANCE>/bin/opmnctl stopall
```

For example:

```
[fusion@idmhost ~]$ /app/oracle/config/instances/odsm/bin/opmnctl stopall
opmnctl stopall: stopping opmn and all managed processes...
```

IDM WebLogic Server Domain

Now let's go ahead and stop the IDM WebLogic Server domain (IDMDomain), including all managed servers as well as the administration server. We will use the default WebLogic scripts in order to shut down these servers. Make sure not to run these commands in the background and also stop the administration server at the end. This allows the managed servers to shut down sequentially and lets them communicate with the admin server while they are going down.

```
stopManagedWebLogic.sh <ManagedServer_Name>
```

Stop the managed servers (ODSM, OIM, SOA, and OAM sequentially as follows). For example:

```
[fusion@idmhost ~]$ cd /app/oracle/config/domains/IDMDomain/bin/
[fusion@idmhost bin]$ ./stopManagedWebLogic.sh wls_ods1
[fusion@idmhost bin]$ ./stopManagedWebLogic.sh wls_oim1
[fusion@idmhost bin]$ ./stopManagedWebLogic.sh wls_soa1
[fusion@idmhost bin]$ ./stopManagedWebLogic.sh wls_oam1
```

If you have configured Oracle Identity Federation then you need to stop the OIF managed server as follows.

```
[fusion@idmhost bin]$ ./stopManagedWebLogic.sh wls_oif1
```

If you have not configured the encrypted boot identity file boot.properties for any managed server then it may prompt for WebLogic Server credentials. Once all the managed servers have shut down successfully, you can shut down the Administration Server as follows.

```
[fusion@idmhost bin]$ ./stopWebLogic.sh
```

421

Node Manager

Similar to Fusion Applications hosts Node Manager, we should manually kill the Node Manager process in the IDM hosts since there is no script to shut down the Node Manager at the moment. If you are not going to restart the physical server during the maintenance then you can leave the process running. The following is an example of identifying and ending the running node manager process using the Unix command kill -9.

```
[fusion@idmhost ~]$ ps -ef | grep NodeManager | awk '{print $2}' | xargs kill -9
```

Oracle Internet Directory (OID)

Oracle Internet Directory is the last application tier component that should be stopped since all the components communicate with OID directly or indirectly. Once you have stopped all other components, you can go ahead and stop OID using the following OPMN command.

```
<IDM_CONFIG>/instance/<OID_instance>/bin/opmnctl stopall
```

For example:

```
[fusion@idmhost ~]$ /app/oracle/config/instances/oid1/bin/opmnctl stopall
opmnctl stopall: stopping opmn and all managed processes...
```

Consolidated Script for Stopping Identity Management Components

Once again, here is the consolidated script to stop all the Identity Management components using the manual method. If you have configured Oracle Identity Federation then you can uncomment the OIF shutdown line from the script. Make sure to modify the paths as per your environment.

```
#!/bin/bash
# Script Name: stopIDM.sh v1.0_TT
. /home/fusion/.bash_profile
# Stop OPMN Based components
echo "Stopping Oracle HTTP Server (web)"
/app/oracle/config/instances/ohs1/bin/opmnctl stopall

echo "Starting ODSM Agent service"
app/oracle/config/instances/odsm/bin/opmnctl stopall

# Stop IDM WebLogic Server Domain
echo "Stopping Managed Servers"
cd /app/oracle/config/domains/IDMDomain/bin/
./stopManagedWebLogic.sh wls_ods1
./stopManagedWebLogic.sh wls_oim1
./stopManagedWebLogic.sh wls_soa1
./stopManagedWebLogic.sh wls_oam1
#./stopManagedWebLogic.sh wls_oif1

echo "Stopping Weblogic Admin Server"
./stopWebLogic.sh

# Stop OID
echo "Stopping Oracle Internet Directory (OID)"
```

```
/app/oracle/config/instances/oid1/bin/opmnctl stopall

# Stop Node Manager
echo "Manually killing Node Manager process"
ps -ef | grep NodeManager | awk '{print $2}' | xargs kill -9
```

Save the script as stopIDM.sh and provide execute permission to the script for the reason explained earlier.

Manual Shutdown Using Enterprise Manager Cloud Control

We have already seen how to start up Identity Management Components using Enterprise Manager so we will skip a detailed discussion of EM interface here. In order to shut down IDM components, follow these steps:

1. Log in to EM Cloud Control 12c with the SYSMAN user.

2. On the home screen, choose Targets menu ➤ Middleware. This will open the Fusion Applications Middleware targets summary screen.

3. From the Oracle Fusion Middleware Farm targets listed in the main screen, click on the IDM Middleware farm. This will open IDM Middleware targets home screen.

4. In the IDM Middleware targets screen you can stop the WebLogic domain, directory server, Oracle HTTP server and so on.

Stopping Identity Management Database

Once all the IDM and FA nodes components have been stopped, you can shut down the IDMDB database and listener. You can use the Enterprise Manager to stop the database in a similar way as we have seen the database and listener startup.

Shut down the database using the shutdown immediate command or if you are using RAC database then use srvctl stop database -d idmdb to stop the database. Similarly, stop listener using the lsnrctl stop command or for RAC use srvctl stop listener -l <listener_name> to stop the listener. Alternatively you can use following script to stop the database and listener in one go. Make sure to change the listener name as per your environment.

```
#!/bin/bash
# Script Name: stopDB.sh v1.0_TT
# Source the database environment file
. /home/fusion/dbprofile.sh
echo "Stopping Database"
sqlplus / as sysdba << EOF
shutdown immediate;
exit;
EOF
echo "Stopping database listener"
lsnrctl stop listener_idmdb
```

Save the file as stopDB.sh and assign execute permission to this script using the chmod +x stopDB.sh command.

Overview of the Fusion Functional Setup Manager

The first functionality that you may access after provisioning an Oracle Fusion Applications environment is the Oracle Functional Setup Manager. The name Functional Setup Manager doesn't do justice to the incredible functionalities and importance of this manager in the functional implementation and ongoing maintenance of the Fusion Applications environment. It is probably the most important feature introduced in Fusion Applications as compared to traditional ERP systems, especially for those who have already worked on E-Business Suite applications.

■ **Note**   Since the Oracle Fusion Functional Setup Manager is one of the key applications that's used not only by administrators but also by functional implementers, application specialists, users, and application developers, this section is important for all the audiences of this book. For most of the users this is the starting point of their interaction with Oracle Fusion Applications interface.

Let's first understand what the Fusion Functional Setup Manager is all about. By definition, the Functional Setup Manger is a single interface that allows multiple lines of business to setup and implement the required product offering in the most agile, efficient, and transparent way. However, apart from the setup-related tasks, the Functional Setup Manager also provides an interface to perform day-to-day administrative maintenance tasks as well, hence the work area is not just Setup but Setup and Maintenance. The Functional Setup Manager allows you to manage the end-to-end lifecycle of the Fusion Applications implementation right from planning, configuring the products to be implemented, creating an implementation plan, running implementation tasks, deploying the setup artifacts from one system to another, and thus managing the application implementation like a full-fledged project.

Navigating Through the Functional Setup Manager

Figure 12-17 shows how to navigate to the Fusion Functional Setup Manager work area. Log in to the Fusion Applications homepage using the super user FAAdmin (the one selected during the provisioning process). Choose Navigator Menu ➤ Tools Category ➤ Setup and Maintenance or click on the Username in Global area followed by choosing Settings and Actions menu ➤ Administration category ➤ Setup and Maintenance to launch the Fusion Functional Setup Manager home screen.

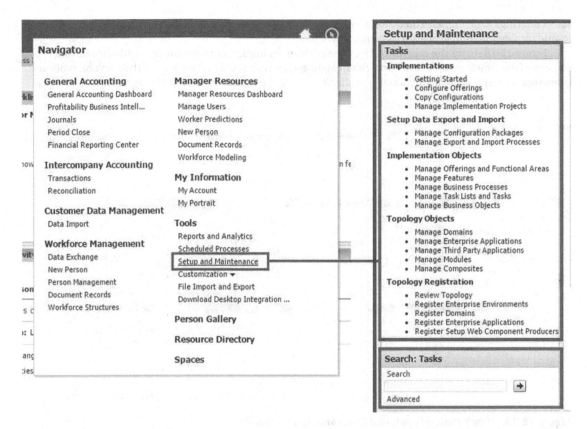

Figure 12-17. *Navigating through the Oracle Fusion Functional Setup Manager*

■ **Note** Fusion Functional Setup Manager is deployed on the `FunctionalSetupServer_1` WebLogic managed server of `CommonDomain`. If this managed server is not running or having issues, then you may not be able to access any of the pages related to the Functional Setup Manager.

Once you launch the Functional Setup Manager work area, you will see a fixed Regional area along with a variable Local area screen based on which functionality of Setup and Maintenance you are working on. Use the Tasks list in the Regional area to navigate to various functionalities during Fusion Applications Implementation. The Tasks search box at the bottom provides access to a number of maintenance tasks after the implementation is complete. We will look at each of these functionalities in the upcoming sections of this chapter.

Fusion Applications Implementation Overview

Functional Setup Manager is the primary interface that you will require in order to plan, configure, implement, deploy, and maintain the Fusion Applications Setup. Functional Setup Manager is independent of any product family and is usable out of the box. Hence, it can manage any product implementation as a management and control point. In this section, we will see how we can use Functional Setup Manger to understand the Fusion Applications product offerings, review the list of implementation tasks involved, select offerings to be implemented along with optional features, run functional setup tasks, and oversee end-to-end implementation processes as projects.

Figure 12-18 shows the mapping of Fusion Applications implementation process with the relevant screens of the Oracle Fusion Functional Setup Manager. You can see that each step of the implementation processes corresponds to a functionality available through the Functional Setup Manager.

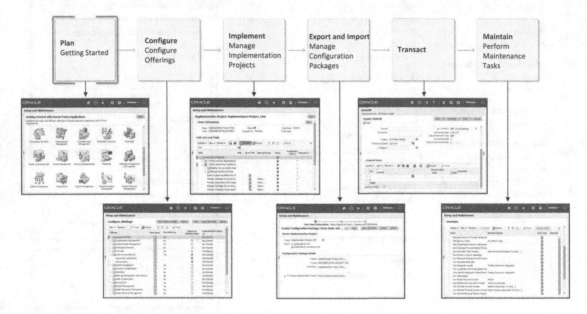

Figure 12-18. *Oracle Fusion Functional Setup Manager overview*

Planning for an Implementation

If you are navigating to Fusion Functional Setup work area for the first time or if you have not created an implementation project, then you will be presented with the default Getting Started with Oracle Fusion Applications screen. Once you have initiated or completed an applications implementation project, the default screen will change to the All Tasks screen. We will look at that later. For now, let's see what the Getting Started screen has to offer.

Figure 12-19 shows an example of the Getting Started screen in Oracle Fusion Applications 11g, Release 9. Except for a small difference, in general all the regional area tasks list between 11.1.9 and earlier releases are the same. This introductory screen provides a quick overview of the implementation process flow at the top of the page. Clicking on each step of the flow leads to the appropriate work areas for those tasks.

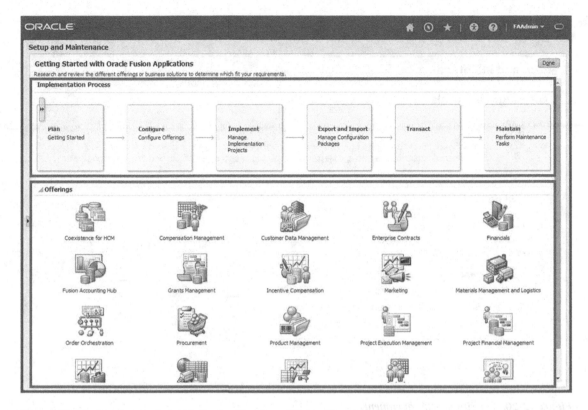

Figure 12-19. *Getting started with Fusion Functional Setup Manager*

This screen also allows you to learn about the Fusion Applications' product offerings regardless of whether they are selected for provisioning or not. As we know already, offerings are the highest level of grouping of application functionalities that can be selected for provisioning. So offerings are the initial decision point for Fusion Applications installation and implementation. Offerings include multiple business processes, which are represented as a one or more functionalities of the particular offering.

You can navigate to any of the offerings displayed in the lower panel to access documents specific to that offering. As you can see in Figure 12-20, the Documents page provides a number of documents for each of the product offering displayed. You can download the documents in PDF, HTML, or Excel formats. These documents immensely help an implementer understand the product features, dependencies, and the complete list of tasks involved in implementation process. By reviewing these documents, you can collect business requirements for the upcoming implementation project.

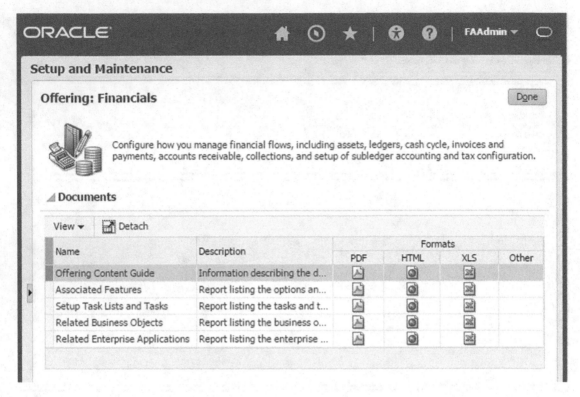

Figure 12-20. *Offering specific documents*

Table 12-3 displays the list of documents available in this screen along with their importance.

Table 12-3. *List of Documents Available in Offering Specific Pages*

Document Title	Description
Offering Content Guide	Provides detailed contents of the offering based on the current version of the application.
Associated Features	This report helps make decisions about options and features for the selected offering.
Setup Task Lists and Tasks	Lists all the implementation Tasks and Task Lists that will be generated if this offering is selected for implementation.
Related Business Objects	Lists all the business objects that this offering uses for functional setup and transactions.
Related Enterprise Applications	This report provides list of Enterprise Applications this offering requires for setup and transactional tasks.

Configuring Products for Implementation

Once you have provisioned a number of product offerings and gone through the implementation steps and other documents in Offerings Documentation page, you can go ahead and select the provisioned offerings or selected functional areas of an offering for implementation. You can launch the Configure Offerings section of the Functional Setup Manager by using the link in the process flow diagram shown on the Getting Started page or from the list of tasks in the Regional area of Setup and Maintenance application.

Figure 12-21 shows an example of Configure Offerings screen with financials, Fusion accounting hub, and HCM products provisioned. This screen displays the following information for each of these offerings for the current version of Fusion Applications.

- *Offering*: Name of Fusion Applications product offering with optional functional areas.

- *Description*: Clicking on this icon will launch a small pop-up with more details of the offering.

- *Provisioned*: By default the field remains blank. If the product offering has been provisioned as part of the Fusion Applications provisioning process, then it will show the value as Yes.

- *Enable for Implementation*: By default, all checkboxes are unchecked including those offerings that are already provisioned. Select this option if you are planning to include this product offering in your upcoming implementation plan. This will enable this product specific implementation tasks to be generated.

- *Implementation Status*: This field tracks the status and progress of the specific offering's implementation. Initially all values are set to Not Started. Once the implementation is complete, it will change to Implemented.

- *Select Feature Choices*: This option allows you to select from a list of optional feature choices available for that specific offering. Note that the feature choices may be different for individual offerings.

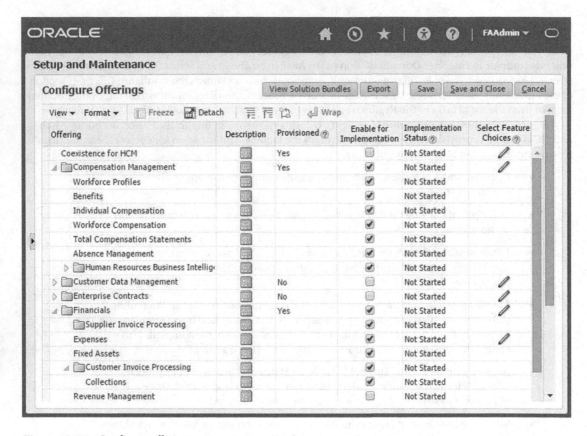

Figure 12-21. *Configure offerings screen*

Select the checkmark against each offering and functional area that you want to implement, select, or modify the optional feature choices (explained in next section) and click the Save button to freeze the selection. Figure 12-22 shows an example of Feature Choices selection for one example offering Compensation Management.

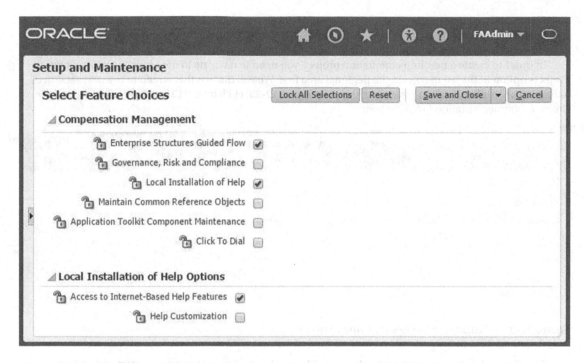

Figure 12-22. *Select Feature Choices screen*

The offering includes a set of business processes that need to be implemented, whereas features are optional or alternative business rules for the selected offering. There are two types of features.

- *Single feature option selection*: When you must select only one feature out of a list of options, then the list is provided as a set of radio buttons to restrict the selection to one only.

- *Multiple features option selection*: When you are allowed to select more than one options for one feature then the list is provided as a set of checkboxes that allow multiple selections.

As you can see in Figure 12-22, in the Select Feature Choices screen you may notice a button titled Lock All Selections. Once you have selected the features, you can click this button which replaces checkboxes with text or tick marks suggesting whether the feature has been selected. Once the Feature Choices are selected, you will return to the previous screen or offering selection. Click Save once you're finished selecting offerings and feature choices for each of the offerings.

Creating an Implementation Project

Although creating and managing an implementation project is role of Application Implementation Manager, at times it is a collaborative activity between Fusion Applications Administrators and Application Implementation Managers when it comes to creating an implementation project or necessary initial setup.

Creating and managing implementation project features are one of the biggest improvements in Fusion Applications as compared to traditional ERPs, including Oracle E-Business Suite. Fusion Applications provides a completely automated and still customizable process of creating an implementation plan for your organization's functional setup of product offerings. Based on the offerings we have selected for implementation in earlier sections, you can automatically generate a completely transparent end-to-end implementation project that can be later driven by the implementation manager and assigned to a project team based on specific tasks and individual skillsets.

In order to create a new implementation project, you need to navigate to the Manage Implementation Projects option in the list of tasks in the Regional area first. We will discuss this screen in the next section of managing an implementation project. As shown in Figure 12-23, click on the Create icon to proceed to the Create an Implementation Project screen.

Figure 12-23. *Creating a new implementation project*

Creating an implementation project begins with specifying a name, description, start and end dates, and so on, for the project, as shown in Figure 12-24. The code or internal name of the project will be generated automatically based on the name provided. As you will see in next section, implementation project is managed in a typical project management methodology and you may assign the project to a specific Implementation manager and assign project deadlines here. However, the deadline can be assigned or changed later as well. Click Next once you have entered this information to proceed with selecting offerings for this implementation project. Figure 12-25 shows an example of the Offerings selection page for a new implementation project.

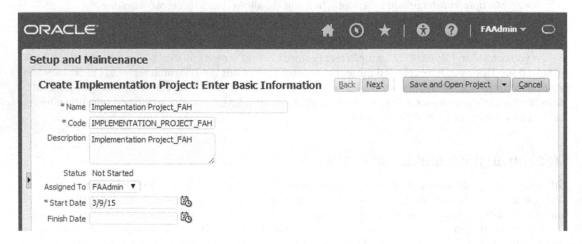

Figure 12-24. *New Implementation Project details screen*

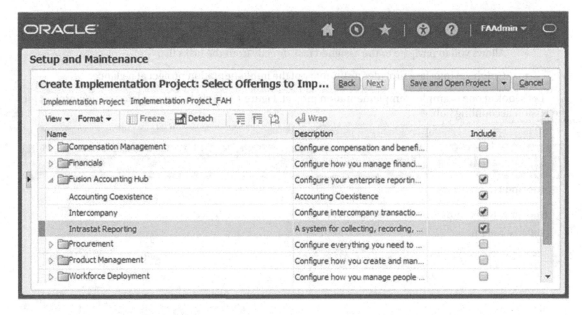

Figure 12-25. *Select offerings to implement*

Based on the offerings that you have selected for implementation in an earlier screen, you may include all or some of those offerings for this implementation project. You may select all or selected functional areas of an offering as well if you do not need to use some business processes in your organization.

Once you select the offerings and click Save and Open Project, it will automatically generate a list of all end-to-end functional and technical tasks for implementing the selected offerings. If there are any tasks required to be performed on other offerings that are not selected here but the current offerings have dependency on them, then those related tasks are also added in the implementation plan.

Managing an Implementation Project

Once an implementation project has been created, you can search for it from Manage Implementation Project work area. This functionality of Functional Setup Manager immensely helps functional implementers as well as system administrators manage the implementation as a full-fledged project with assigned resources, timeframe, dependency rules, task status, management, and reporting of the complete application implementation cycle. The following are a few of the salient features of implementation project management using the Fusion functional setup manager.

- A complete project management suite to create, assign, track, share and manage the end-to-end implementation project.

- Completely automated and transparent generation of all required setup tasks.

- Single and guided tasks lists for multiple offerings.

- All prerequisites and dependencies automatically are taken in account during the tasks list generation.

- Customizable tasks list to suite organization requirements to add or remove specific task to take care of exception cases.

- Eliminates the need of looking up user guides and documentation to understand the tasks involved in an implementation.

- Allows you to navigate to the assigned task directly from the tasks list.

- Graphical interface provides a summary of the implementation project at a glance.

Let's look at one example of implementation project. Figure 12-26 shows an implementation project for the Fusion accounting hub.

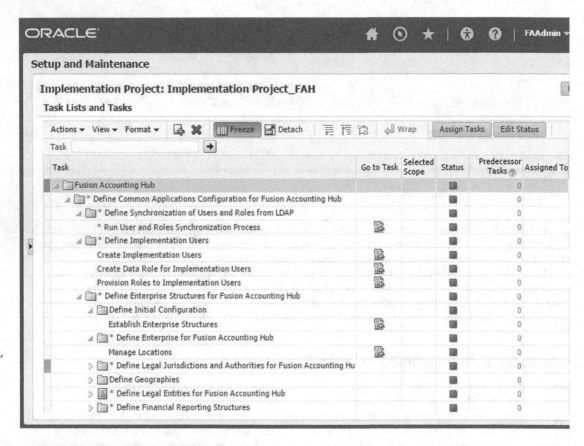

Figure 12-26. *Manage implementation project*

As you can see, the list of implementation tasks has been generated along with individual tasks as well as the grouping of task (also called a *task list*) along with current status of the task and other information like number of predecessors and name of one or resources assigned the task. Note that the automatically generated tasks list is based on the offerings that you have selected for this specific project only and not all the enabled offerings.

As mentioned earlier, the generated tasks list is aware of inter-product dependencies as well as prerequisites, so it follows a specific pattern for generating the tasks list. Figure 12-27 explains how the tasks list is generated based on multiple offerings selected from more than one product families.

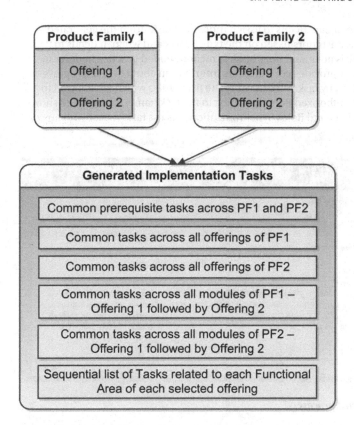

Figure 12-27. *Generic sequence of implementation tasks*

As you can see in Figure 12-27, all the common setup tasks are listed in the beginning and gradually remaining dependent tasks are listed in order. Once the common tasks for an offering, product family, or complete selection are listed, the individual offerings related tasks are generated in sequential order. Any dependency information is also updated in the implementation plan so that the implementation manager can monitor the progress of dependency tasks accordingly.

Now the Application Implementation manager needs to assign individual tasks from the generated list to functional specialists or technical administrators based on the type of task and where it needs to be performed. However, assigning each task is not mandatory but it is recommended practice in order to make sure the project management summary provides correct status information about overall progress of the implementation project. Before assigning any task you can verify the list of roles which are allowed to perform the specific task by clicking on the Authorized Roles icon next to the task name. Figure 12-28 shows an example of authorized roles for the Run User and Roles Synchronization Process task. A user with any of the listed roles can be assigned this task.

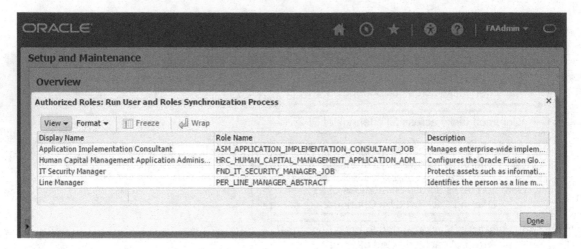

Figure 12-28. Authorized roles for the selected process

Once you have identified the roles required for the functional users, the Fusion Applications Security Administrator can create users with such privileges and then you can assign tasks to the newly created users. While assigning tasks we can also add notes to share important project information with other resources who are part of the same implementation project. We will look at user creation and role assignment in the next chapter.

Migrate and Deploy Configuration on Other Instances

While many administrators and implementers may find the automatic implementation tasks list generation as the most useful feature of the Fusion Functional Setup Manager, especially those moving from other ERPs to Fusion, a large number of implementers may find the Migration and Deployment features of Functional Setup Manager the most useful. The prime reason is the simplicity of migrating the functional setup from one environment to another. This results in a great deal of cost savings mainly due to the amount of time saved in production deployment.

Unlike traditional ERPs, Fusion Applications allows you to export complete setup data from the development or staging instance to production for initial implementation of Fusion Applications. This process is highly customizable and we can exclude or include selected setup data during the migration. This also eliminates the need of cloning complete environments when we only need to deploy setup and configuration-related data.

Once you have completed the basic implementation on a non-production environment and you want to deploy the same setup on production, you can create a new configuration package in order to export the setup data to a downloadable file. You can begin by clicking on the Manage Configuration Packages task from the regional area of Functional Setup Manager followed by clicking the Create New Configuration package icon. This will launch the basic information screen for the New Configuration package, as shown in Figure 12-29.

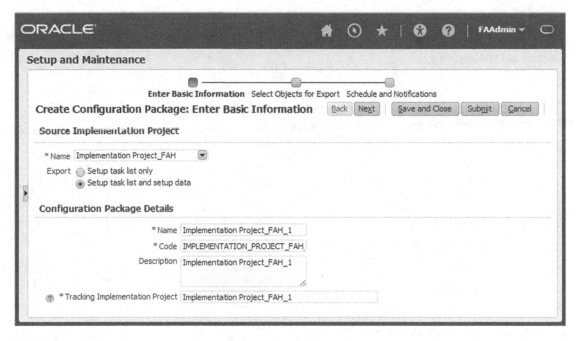

Figure 12-29. *Create Configuration Package: Basic Information screen*

From the list of existing implementation packages, select the project you want to export to the new environment. You can select only the Setup Tasks List or include Setup Data in this package depending on your requirement. The remaining details are populated automatically but you can change them if required. Click Next to proceed to the next screen where we can select objects for inclusion in the configuration package.

Figure 12-30 shows an example of the selection section for exporting setup objects. You should leave the export sequence as is unless you have a strong reason to change it. The checkbox next to each object can be selected or deselected for inclusion or exclusion from the configuration export.

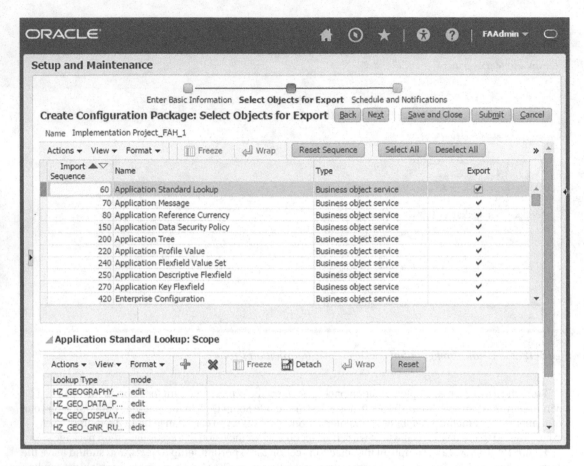

Figure 12-30. *Select objects to be exported in the configuration package*

Once you have created the configuration package, it is ready to be exported and you can look it up under the Manage Configuration Packages work area. In order to export the Configuration package, search for the existing packages, select the one you want to export, and click the Export Setup Data button to initiate the package export.

Note that you can export the same setup information with updated data as many times as you want. Every time you run the export process, a new version of the export file is generated. You can download the latest export file in a zipped format which contains a series of XML files. This file eventually needs to be moved to a target system where it will be imported. Once the downloaded file has been copied to the target system, it will show up in the search results on the same page in the target system. You can click on Import Setup Data to initiate the setup tasks as well as the data (if exported) import. Import will insert the new data from the export file to the target. If any setup data exists in the target, it updates the existing data while leaving the data on target unchanged.

While export or import is running, you can monitor the progress using manage export and import processes task from regional area of Functional Setup Manager. Figure 12-31 shows an example of the Manage Configuration Packages screen, which shows an exported configuration file. As you can see, once the file has been exported successfully, the status changes to Locked.

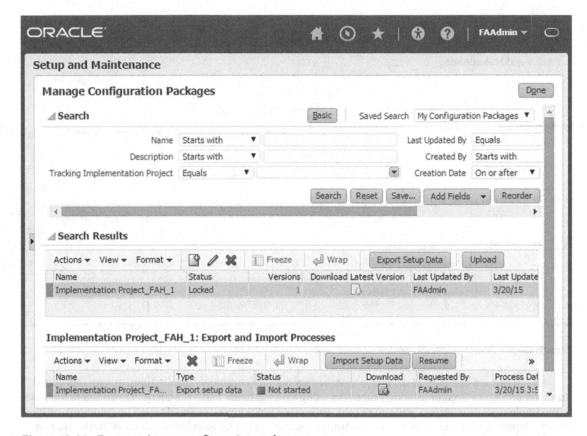

Figure 12-31. *Export or import configuration packages*

Introduction to Maintenance Tasks

As mentioned earlier, Functional Setup Manager has two major functionalities—functional setup of and ongoing maintenance of the applications. The maintenance tasks can be accessed from the Tasks Search panel in the Regional area or from the All Tasks tab under the Maintain Implementation Projects work area. Once you have created an implementation project, the default landing page for the Functional Setup Manager changes from Getting Started page to the All Tasks page. So whenever you access the Setup and Maintenance work area from Navigator it will launch the All Tasks page first. This is appropriate since once functional setup is completed, you need to have maintenance tasks as your default screen.

Figure 12-32 shows the default tab for Maintenance Tasks, which allows you to search and execute various administrative, functional, and developer related tasks from a single interface. You will notice that these tasks are not new for you since we have already seen setup related tasks that were automatically generated as part of implementation project, while in this case you will manually search and execute the relevant maintenance task.

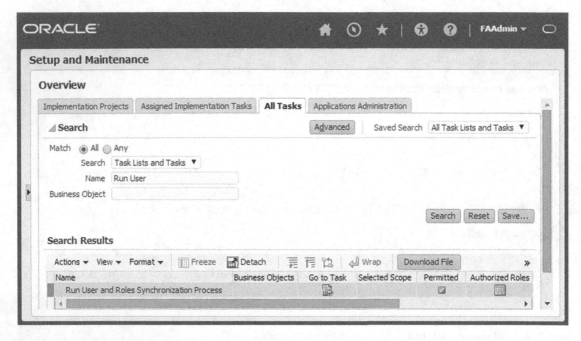

Figure 12-32. Search a specific administrative task

As you can see in Figure 12-32, I have searched for the very commonly used Administrative task called Run User and Roles Synchronization Process by using a partial name in the search query. Similar to the tasks in the implementation project, you can see the Authorized Roles for the selected task. The column Permitted shows whether you already have one of the Authorized roles or not by showing tick or cross mark. You may click on Go to Task in order to navigate to the task-specific page.

Summary

This introductory chapter to Fusion Applications administration gave you a glimpse of what is the immediate next step after the installation is complete. This includes how to start and stop Fusion Applications Services and how to use Oracle Fusion Functional Setup Manager. You saw the various ways of managing Identity Management as well as Fusion Applications environment services, including command-line tools, Oracle Enterprise Manager Cloud Control, and the local management tools. You should now also know how to collaborate with other functional implementation teams and which ones are the common areas of interest in Functional Setup Manager for the administration and application implementation teams.

In the next chapter, you will see how to prepare initial security setup, including provisioning of necessary users and roles for administration, implementation, and regular operations. The remaining chapters will talk more about Fusion Applications administration including monitoring, troubleshooting, diagnosing, patching, and so on.

CHAPTER 13

■ ■ ■

Managing Fusion Applications Security

Fusion Applications Security is a vast subject and this chapter introduces some of the mandatory Security setup tasks in the initial implementation of Fusion Applications. As you learned earlier, Fusion Applications is based on Role Based Access Control (RBAC) and Segregation of Duties (SOD). This chapter helps you understand how Oracle achieves role-based access control at the same time applying segregation of duties policies in order to avoid unauthorized access to Fusion Applications transaction data or functional screens.

Components Involved in Common Security Setup

During the following discussions we will see a lot of different interfaces for specific activities. So let's first understand the components involved in setting up and managing Fusion Applications Security. We have already seen these components earlier so we will only look at what role they play in the Users or Roles provisioning and management processes and how they relate to Fusion Applications Security.

Oracle Internet Directory

Oracle Internet Directory provides the LDAP identity store for Oracle Fusion Applications. Although Oracle Identity Management supports other LDAP directories as well, we discuss it here with reference to OID. Oracle currently supports only OID as a policy store so in this case both the identity and policy stores are hosted in OID. Regardless of the interface from where user or roles are being created, OID stores all these values in the identity and policy stores.

Oracle Directory Service Manager

Oracle Directory Service Manager (ODSM) provides a graphical interface to access Oracle Internet Directory (OID) or Oracle Virtual Directory (OVD). We have already discussed ODSM during the IDM provisioning process. All references and screens in the following sections of this chapter related to OID identity and policy store browsing use ODSM as the interface.

© Tushar Thakker 2015
T. Thakker, *Pro Oracle Fusion Applications*, DOI 10.1007/978-1-4842-0983-7_13

Oracle Identity Manager

Oracle Identity Manager (OIM) manages the identity information and allows us to provision Users and Roles using a simple graphical interface. OIM maintains its own database for storing the identity information and it should be synchronized with LDAP for updated information of newly provisioned or deprovisioned Users or Roles.

Fusion Functional Setup Manager

As you saw earlier, the Fusion Functional Setup Manager provides a host of functionalities for implementation and administration purposes. We will be using the Manage Implementation Projects work area as well as running tasks manually using Fusion Functional setup manager. In order to access the work areas related to Functional setup manager, users must have the Functional Setups user role assigned either directly or indirectly via another role.

Authorization Policy Manager

While Oracle Identity Manager allows you to manage identity stores, Authorization Policy Manager (APM) allows you to manage policy store information. It allows you to create, configure, and manage application policies using a simple-to-use graphical interface. Once we look at the types of roles, you will understand that we can manage duty roles through APM while other Enterprise roles using OIM.

Table 13-1 shows summary of these components and the example URL to launch individual components along with the default login username. You will need to use these interfaces often in the following sections so you should keep these URLs handy.

Table 13-1. *Important URLs for Fusion Applications Security Setup*

Component	Example URL	Username
Oracle Directory Service Manager (For Managing OID)	`http://idmhost:7777/odsm`	`cn=orcladmin`
Oracle Identity Manager	`http://idmhost:7777/oim`	`xelsysadm`
Fusion Functional Setup Manager	`https://fahost:10634/homePage`	FAADMIN (or equivalent)
Authorization Policy Manager	`https://fahost:7777/apm`	FAADMIN (or equivalent)

Fusion Applications Roles

By default, Oracle Fusion Applications users do not have access to any data or functionalities. Roles provide a mechanism to allow selective access to data and required applications functions. Unlike traditional applications suites, Fusion Applications provides granular control over resources based on functional and data security roles. This section looks at the types of roles available in Fusion Applications, including specific types of access control provided by each of these roles and how they relate to traditional applications suites including Oracle E-Business Suite.

Types of Fusion Applications Roles

Before we proceed with the Fusion Applications security setup, it is essential to understand how functional and data security on Fusion Applications Resources is provided using different types of roles. The following are main categories of roles we will discuss here. Duty Role, Job Role, and Abstract Roles provide basic functional security while Data Roles provide data security in addition to function security. Note that certain administrative job or abstract roles may allow restricted or unrestricted access to data as well. Let's look at each of these roles and see how they are stored or accessed by various components of Fusion Applications.

Duty Role

Fusion Applications security provides the individual function or task level access control through Duty Roles. The lowest level function is called the Duty. We can compare Fusion Applications Duties with the Functions feature of Oracle E-Business Suite applications. An employee may have multiple duties as part of his/her job. Each of these duties are controlled as part of individual Duty roles. Duty roles are generally not assigned directly to users but instead are provided as part of other roles that we will discuss next. Duty roles are managed by the Authorization Policy Manager (APM), where you can see the mapping of other external roles with individual Duty roles.

Data roles are stored in the Oracle Internet Directory (OID) as follows. The given naming convention is not mandatory.

```
cn=<Name>_DUTY_<Application>,cn=Roles,cn=crm,cn=FusionDomain,cn=JPSContext,cn=FAPolicies
```

For example:

```
cn=AR_BILL_CREATION_DUTY_CRM,cn=Roles,cn=crm,cn=FusionDomain,cn=JPSContext,cn=FAPolicies
```

Job Role

We know that the definition of job in the real world is to perform a set of duties in an organization. Similarly Fusion Applications has predefined *Job roles* which inherit a set of Duty roles to combine the set of related duties to be performed as part of one's job. We can compare this with the *Responsibility* feature of Oracle E-Business Suite Applications. For example, there is the Application Developer Job Role and General Accounting Manager Job Role. Job roles are also called Enterprise roles but in Authorization Policy Manager (APM) they are considered External roles. Job roles are managed and assigned through the Oracle Identity Manager (OIM). In OIM you can view the details of Job roles and other roles that they inherit or the other roles that inherit these roles. While in APM you can review the Job roles along with the set of duties allowed through the particular Job role.

Job roles are stored in Oracle Internet Directory (OID) as follows. The given naming convention is not mandatory.

```
cn=<NAME>_job,cn=fusiongroups,cn=groups,dc=<domain>,dc=<com>
```

For example:

```
cn=asm_application_implementation_manager_job,cn=fusiongroups,cn=groups,dc=paramlabs,dc=com
```

Abstract Role

We have seen that Job roles are created to combine a set of functional duties in an organization. Abstract roles are independent of specific functional duties but are generic roles that allow a user access to multiple functions which might not be related. For example, Employee role or Line Manager role. These roles are not tied to specific applications but they can perform a set of duties across multiple applications. Abstract roles are also managed through the Oracle Identity Manager in a similar way as Job roles. Abstract roles are also called Enterprise roles and, similar to Job roles, they are also referred to as External roles in Authorization Policy Manager in order to map them with specific duties across multiple applications.

Abstract roles are stored in Oracle Internet Directory (OID) as follows. The given naming convention is not mandatory.

```
cn=<NAME>_abstract,cn=fusiongroups,cn=groups,dc=<domain>,dc=<com>
```

For example:

```
cn=asm_application_implementation_admin_abstract,cn=fusiongroups,cn=groups,dc=paramlabs,
dc=com
```

Data Roles

While Job and Abstract roles can be assigned to a user to provide functional access to the Fusion Applications interface, Data roles are required to provide access to the transaction data for the relevant application. By default, the access to all data is restricted unless explicitly provided through a specific Job role. We can consider a Data role as a set of SQL commands on top of a Job role to restrict data access to a specific set of transactions based on various dimensions. For example, you may want to restrict access to the General Ledger based on specific business units. So you may generate a set of Data roles on top of the existing General Accounting Manager Job roles which will be specific to each business unit and grant only specific Data roles to a user. Such Data roles can be generated from Data Role templates from Authorization Policy Manager. Additionally, custom Data roles can be generated as part of Setup tasks using HCM security profiles and stored in the OID identity store.

Data roles are stored in Oracle Internet Directory (OID) in one of the following namespaces and formats. The given naming convention is not mandatory.

```
cn=<Name>_DATA,cn=Groups,dc=paramlabs,dc=com
```
(If created using HCM Security Profiles)

```
cn=<Name>_DATA, cn=FusionGroups, cn=Groups,dc=paramlabs,dc=com
```
(If created using Generate Data Roles in APM)

For example:

```
cn=VIEW_ALL_FINANCIAL_APPLICATION_ADMINISTRATOR_DATA,cn=Groups,dc=paramlabs,dc=com
```

Figure 13-1 shows a graphical representation of how the roles are inherited from each other and provides a few examples of role assignment. However, these are only a few possible assignments and are only for understanding purposes.

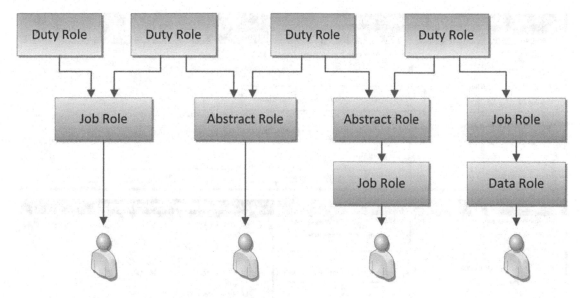

Figure 13-1. *Examples of role assignment options*

Accessing the Roles from Multiple Interfaces

To better understand the concept of Duty roles (Application roles) and Job roles or Abstract roles (Enterprise or external roles), let's see how we can access and relate them to various interfaces. As you know, all the roles are stored in the Oracle Internet Directory under either identity store or policy store. While the Enterprise roles can be accessed and assigned from the Oracle Identity Manager, Duty roles may be managed from the Authorization Policy Manager.

Let's take an example of a Job role—Application Implementation Consultant. This is the role that we will assign to the functional implementation user in the latter part of the chapter. Figure 13-2 provides an example walkthrough of how we can access the role in OIM, APM, and OID. In order to access the role in OIM, we can search for the role on the OIM Administration homepage. In the Details pane for this role, you can see the distinguished name for this role in LDAP. Using this DN, we can locate the same role in OID.

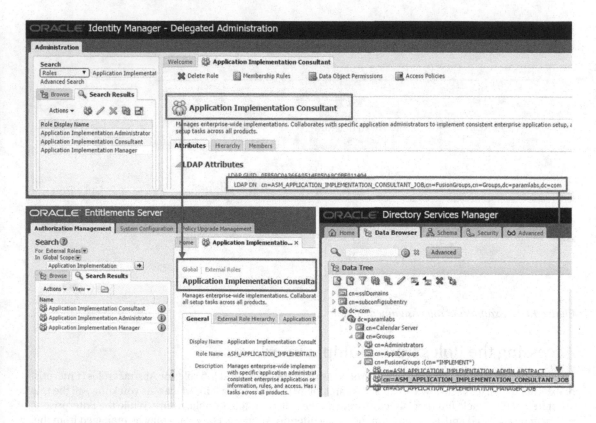

Figure 13-2. *Example of a role in OIM, OID, and APM*

In order to look up the same role in Authorization Policy Manager (APM), you can search the same role using the External Roles Search function since Job and Abstract roles are treated as external roles in APM. Figure 13-2 shows how we can access them in APM and validate the role, which may match a role in OID as well under the **cn=FusionGroups, cn=Groups, dc=paramlabs, dc=com** namespaces.

After having seen these Job roles in OID, OIM and APM, let's move on to Duty roles. As mentioned earlier, Duty roles are managed by the APM only so they are not available through the OIM interface. Duty roles are referred to as Application roles, so we can search for specific Duty roles using the Application Roles Search functionality. If you are not sure which Duty roles are part of a particular Job/External role then you can use the same External Role details screen and click on the Application Role Mapping tab, as shown in Figure 13-3.

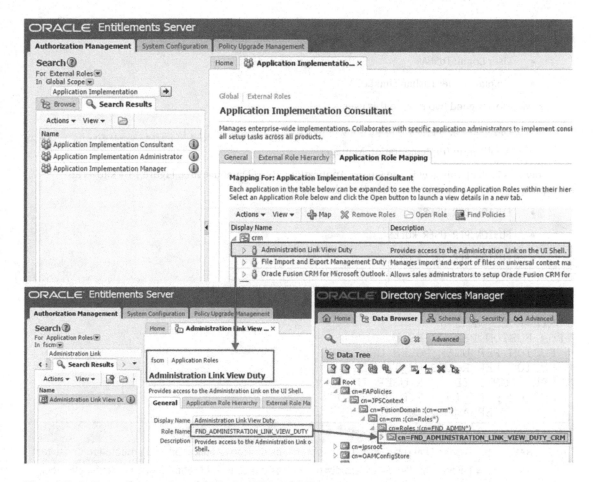

Figure 13-3. *Example mapping of duties in APM and OID*

Let's take the same example role and look up the related Duty roles in APM as well as OID. Click on the Application Role Mapping tab as mentioned and you can go through the list of Duty/Application roles assigned to it. Let's take example of a Duty role from the list, say Administration Link View Duty under the CRM application. We can look up the same Duty using the Application role search as shown in Figure 13-3 and locate the Duty role name in OID. Now we can navigate to the same Duty role in OID under the **cn=FAPolicies, cn=JPSContext, cn=FusionDomain, cn=crm, and cn=Roles** namespaces.

Looking Up Users and Roles in Database Tables

Although this is not required during most of the administration activities, at times you may want to troubleshoot the users/roles creation and assignment. If you want to generate user security reports from the database, knowing the relevant database tables for each components may become handy for Fusion Applications security administrators. Oracle does not recommend making any changes to any of these tables so you can use these or similar queries for reporting or understanding purposes only.

Let's look at each of the components one by one and look up their users and assigned roles. In order to keep the output limited, I have created a user with the following details.

- User Login: TUSHAR

- Display name: Tushar Thakker

I have also assigned two roles to this user.

- Application Implementation Consultant

- Application Implementation Manager

Now let's look up this user in the Fusion Applications HCM Database first. Figure 13-4 shows an example query to look up this user using the following tables.

- FUSION.PER_USERS

- FUSION.PER_USER_ROLES

- FUSION.PER_ROLES_DN_TL

```
SELECT U.USERNAME,
  U.USER_DISTINGUISHED_NAME,
  RTL.ROLE_NAME
FROM FUSION.PER_USERS U,
  FUSION.PER_USER_ROLES UR,
  FUSION.PER_ROLES_DN_TL RTL
WHERE U.USER_ID = UR.USER_ID
  AND UR.ROLE_ID = RTL.ROLE_ID
  AND U.USERNAME LIKE '%TUSHAR%';
```

USERNAME	USER_DISTINGUISHED_NAME	ROLE_NAME
TUSHAR	cn=Tushar Thakker,cn=Users,dc=paramlabs,dc=com	Application Implementation Consultant
TUSHAR	cn=Tushar Thakker,cn=Users,dc=paramlabs,dc=com	Application Implementation Manager

Figure 13-4. *Looking up users and corresponding roles in the Fusion HCM tables*

Now let's look up the same user and assigned roles in the OIM database. You may notice that the OIM query shows the default role of ALL_USERS as well, which is assigned to all users created in the OIM.

Figure 13-5 shows an example query to retrieve the User and Assigned role details from the following OIM schema (FA_OIM) tables:

- FA_OIM.USR

- FA_OIM.UGP

- FA_OIM.USG

```
select USR·USR_LOGIN "User Login",
  USR·USR_EMAIL "Email",
  USR·USR_LDAP_DN "User DN",
  UGP·UGP_DISPLAY_NAME "Role"
FROM FA_OIM·USR,
  FA_OIM·UGP,
  FA_OIM·USG
WHERE USR·USR_KEY = USG·USR_KEY
  AND USG·UGP_KEY = UGP·UGP_KEY
  AND USR·USR_LOGIN='TUSHAR';
```

User Login	Email	User DN	Role
▶ TUSHAR	tushar@paramlabs.com	cn=Tushar Thakker,cn=Users,dc=paramlabs,dc=com	ALL USERS
TUSHAR	tushar@paramlabs.com	cn=Tushar Thakker,cn=Users,dc=paramlabs,dc=com	Application Implementation Manager
TUSHAR	tushar@paramlabs.com	cn=Tushar Thakker,cn=Users,dc=paramlabs,dc=com	Application Implementation Consultant

Figure 13-5. *Looking up users and corresponding roles in the OIM database tables*

Finally, let's see how to access User, Role, and Role Membership details in OID. The first two queries in Figure 13-6 can be used to look up User and Roles details individually from OID, while the last query shows how to look up the assigned roles and the namespaces in which the roles are located. These queries retrieve data from the following OID tables. There are many other tables also involved in each of these components.

- ODS.CT_DN

- ODS.CT_HRCH_QUERY

```
SELECT RDN,
   PARENTDN
FROM ODS.CT_DN
WHERE UPPER(RDN) LIKE '%TUSHAR%';
```

RDN	PARENTDN
► cn=tushar thakker	dc=com,dc=paramlabs,cn=users,

```
SELECT RDN,
   PARENTDN
FROM ODS.CT_DN
WHERE UPPER(RDN) LIKE '%APPLICATION%IMPLEMENTATION%';
```

RDN	PARENTDN
► cn=asm_application_implementation_consultant_job	dc=com,dc=paramlabs,cn=groups,cn=fusiongroups,
cn=asm_application_implementation_admin_abstract	dc=com,dc=paramlabs,cn=groups,cn=fusiongroups,
cn=asm_application_implementation_manager_job	dc=com,dc=paramlabs,cn=groups,cn=fusiongroups,
cn=asm_application_implementation_consultant_duty	cn=fapolicies,cn=jpscontext,cn=fusiondomain,cn=fscm,cn=roles,

```
SELECT ENTRYDN "Role",
   ATTRVALUE "Member"
FROM ODS.CT_HRCH_QUERY
WHERE ATTRVALUE LIKE '%tushar%'
   AND RELATION=1;
```

RDN	PARENTDN
► cn=asm_application_implementation_consultant_job	dc=com,dc=paramlabs,cn=groups,cn=fusiongroups,
cn=asm_application_implementation_admin_abstract	dc=com,dc=paramlabs,cn=groups,cn=fusiongroups,
cn=asm_application_implementation_manager_job	dc=com,dc=paramlabs,cn=groups,cn=fusiongroups,
cn=asm_application_implementation_consultant_duty	cn=fapolicies,cn=jpscontext,cn=fusiondomain,cn=fscm,cn=roles,

Figure 13-6. Looking up users, roles, and hierarchies in the OID database tables

Setting Up Users and Roles Synchronization

Ideally all the previously discussed identity information, including the internal tables, should be in sync at any point in time, but whenever any provisioning activity is performed using external applications, HCM new hire process, or OID bulk load the identity information may remain out of sync for a brief period. In order to keep all these components in sync, Oracle has provided some built-in jobs that analyze OID/OIM/ Fusion tables for any changes and apply those changes to the other components. Although most of these processes are scheduled automatically, you may need to run them on demand to synchronize the identity (between OID/Fusion HCM to OIM) and policy information (between Fusion HCM to OID).

Figure 13-7 provides a quick overview of which components are involved in each of these synchronization jobs and in which direction the synchronization is done between the components involved. We will explore these processes here and discuss how you can schedule or use them on demand.

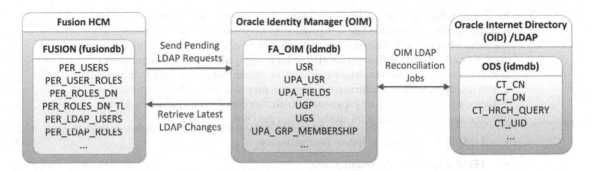

Figure 13-7. Identity synchronization process and relevant database tables

Oracle Identity Manager LDAP Reconciliation Jobs

Oracle Identity Manager includes predefined scheduled jobs for reconciliation of identity data between OIM and OID. You may need a user with either the SYSTEM ADMINISTRATORS or SCHEDULER ADMINISTRATOR role in order to access and run these reconciliation Jobs. Otherwise, we can log in with OIM Administrator user xelsysadm to perform these activities.

We can classify these LDAP reconciliation jobs into two major categories based on the way they synchronize the identity information between OIM and LDAP.

- *Full Reconciliation Jobs*: The LDAP full reconciliation jobs perform a full synchronization of identity store entries between OIM and LDAP. These jobs should never be scheduled to run automatically but should be run on demand if the incremental reconciliation jobs are failing due to some missing entries or in the event that a bulk load has changed a large percentage of identity information. In such cases, full reconciliation jobs ensure that OIM and OID are in sync so that the future incremental jobs will run successfully. You should only run them when there is an absolute necessity or incremental jobs are failing. Full reconciliation jobs do not use the LDAP changelog entries so any errors related to unavailable changelogs will be fixed after these jobs are run. The following is the list of full reconciliation jobs available from the OIM scheduler.

  - LDAP Role Create and Update Full Reconciliation

  - LDAP Role Delete Full Reconciliation

  - LDAP Role Hierarchy Full Reconciliation

  - LDAP Role Membership Full Reconciliation

  - LDAP User Create and Update Full Reconciliation

  - LDAP User Delete Full Reconciliation

- *Incremental Reconciliation Jobs*: As the name suggests, incremental reconciliation jobs apply changes from the last successful sync between OIM and OID related to the entries being synchronized. These jobs should be enabled and scheduled to run automatically (default is five minutes) in order to apply all changes transparently within the maximum five-minute window. If the incremental reconciliation jobs fail due to missing changelog information then you may run related full reconciliation job once and the incremental jobs would finish successfully. The following are the incremental reconciliation jobs available from the OIM scheduler.

  - LDAP Role Create and Update Reconciliation

  - LDAP Role Delete Reconciliation

  - LDAP Role Hierarchy Reconciliation

  - LDAP Role Membership Reconciliation

  - LDAP User Create and Update Reconciliation

  - LDAP User Delete Reconciliation

Let's look at how to view all the LDAP-related OIM scheduled jobs and make sure that they have been set up with recommended settings. Log in to Oracle Identity Manager Service homepage using the OIM Administration user (xelsysadm). In the Self-Service homepage, click on the Advanced link in the top-right area, as shown in Figure 13-8, to launch the Identity Manager Advanced Administration console.

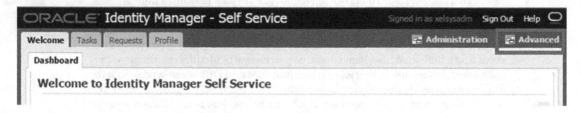

Figure 13-8. *Navigating to the OIM Advanced Administration*

On the Advanced Administration page, you will see a list of dashboards. Click on the System Management tab and you will see a list of sub-tabs. Click on the Scheduler link to launch the Scheduled Jobs regional area, as shown in Figure 13-9.

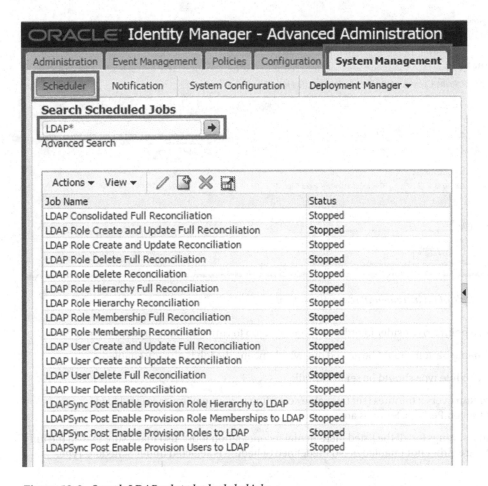

Figure 13-9. *Search LDAP related scheduled jobs*

In the Scheduled Jobs search box, type LDAP and run the search. You can also run an empty search to fetch all the scheduled jobs. Here we are going to focus specifically on job names starting with LDAP since those jobs are related to user and role synchronization with LDAP.

■ **Caution** The name "scheduled jobs" may be misleading here since not all of these jobs are scheduled to run automatically or even enabled. Some of these jobs are scheduled by default while the remaining run on demand.

As I mentioned earlier, it is good practice to keep incremental LDAP reconciliation jobs scheduled to run at regular intervals to synchronize the data transparently without any manual intervention. Let's see how to enable these jobs and select an automatic sync schedule. Click on any incremental job from the list, as seen in Figure 13-9. It will open the job details page as an additional tab in the main local region, as shown in Figure 13-10.

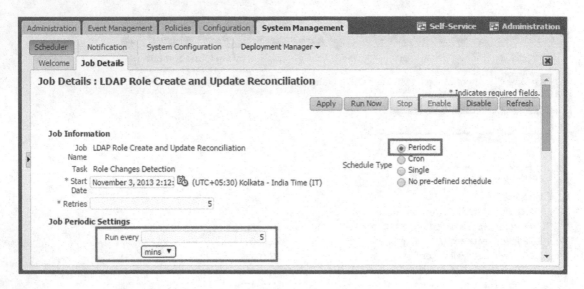

Figure 13-10. *Example of an incremental reconciliation job*

There are three points to consider in order to enable this job to run automatically at regular intervals.

- The Enable button should be grayed out, which means the job is already enabled.

- The Schedule type should be set to Periodic.

- Select Run every x minutes (set this value according to your environment and load) from the Job Periodic Settings area.

Apply the same settings for all the listed incremental reconciliation jobs. Also make sure that all the full reconciliation jobs are either not Enabled or No Predefined Schedule is selected under Schedule Type.

Manually Running OIM Reconcile Jobs

After the Fusion Applications installation is complete, it is a good practice to run the following full reconciliation jobs one time before you provision any additional users or roles for Fusion Applications. This is because sometimes the default seeded roles are not visible in OIM after the provisioning process.

- LDAP Role Create and Update Full Reconciliation

- LDAP Role Hierarchy Full Reconciliation

- LDAP Role Membership Full Reconciliation

- LDAP User Create and Update Full Reconciliation

Open these jobs one by one and click Run Now at the top to run them manually. The status of the job will change to Running for a brief period. Click the Refresh button to check the job status until the status changes to Stopped.

Fusion Applications LDAP Synchronization Tasks

Similar to OIM and LDAP synchronization, we may also need to periodically synchronize Identity information from Fusion HCM Users and Roles tables to LDAP via OIM. Once new users are provisioned through Fusion HCM, the user information is stored in PER_LDAP_USERS, PER_LDAP_ROLES, and a couple of other tables to enable pushing this data to the identity store. Oracle has provided two Scheduled Processes in order to synchronize between Fusion HCM and OID/OIM.

- *Send Pending LDAP Requests*: This scheduled job pushes the incremental data from the Fusion HCM tables (including those with the prefix PER_LDAP_, which already contain the differential data) to the Oracle Identity Manager, which is in turn saved into the OID identity store. In most cases the data gets pushed to OIM transparently but we should make sure that this job runs frequently to make sure there is no pending update from Fusion Applications to Identity Management.

- *Retrieve Latest LDAP Changes*: When a user or role is created outside Fusion HCM directly using OIM interface, we may need to bring those new identity data to Fusion HCM. This scheduled process may be run at least once daily in order to make sure that the identity information is in sync. During initial security setup of Fusion Applications, we may need to run this job after creation of implementation users using Oracle Identity Manager. We will look at that in upcoming sections. As you saw in Figure 13-7, this job pushes the data to the default identity tables in Fusion HCM— for example, PER_USERS, PER_USER_ROLES, PER_ROLES_DN, and so on.

Manually Running Fusion Applications LDAP Synchronization Tasks

You may schedule these Fusion Applications LDAP synchronization tasks to run at least once a day or more frequently. But at times you may need to run these tasks manually especially during the implementation phase when you create multiple users and roles directly in Identity Management. When you are running these jobs as part of the assigned implementation tasks, you get a link that points directly to the synchronization task execution page. You can also invoke these jobs in one of the following two ways.

- Running the scheduled jobs directly using the Scheduled Processes work area

- Invoking Users and Roles synchronization from the Tasks work area

Both of these yield the same result since the task also in turn redirects to the Scheduled Process. Let's take a quick look at how to run these jobs and validate that they have completed successfully. First we will start with manual execution of the LDAP Scheduled Process. You can open the Scheduled Processes work area using Navigator ➤ Scheduled Processes. In the Overview screen, click on the Schedule new Process button, which launches the Search and Select pop-up window, as you can see in Figure 13-11.

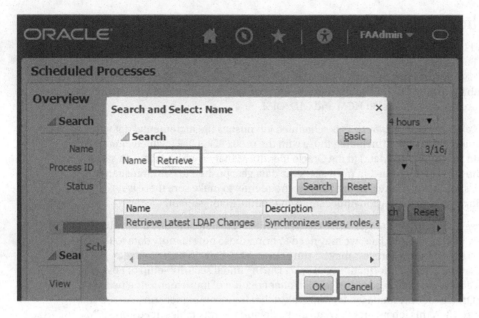

Figure 13-11. Search and run an LDAP sync scheduled process

In the pop-up screen, enter full or partial name of the Scheduled Process—for example Retrieve Latest LDAP Changes—and click Search. Select the appropriate job from search results and click OK to schedule the same. Alternatively you can invoke the same screen using the assigned implementation task or by searching for the task manually in the All Tasks work area, as shown in Figure 13-12.

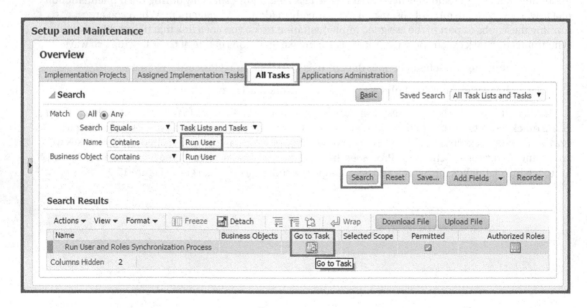

Figure 13-12. Search and run users and roles synchronization process task

Click on the Go to Task icon to launch the Scheduled Process specific screen, as shown in Figure 13-13. In fact, clicking on the OK button in the Search and Select screen will launch the same screen. Follow the same steps to schedule a new process as you learned in Chapter 11.

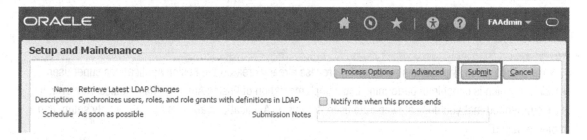

Figure 13-13. Retrieving the latest LDAP changes

In this case, we are going to run the job immediately so you can just click the Submit button to run the job with the default parameters. However, as discussed in Chapter 11, you can select Advanced Options to select job output, notifications, and scheduling parameters. Make sure to run both Scheduled Processes discussed in order to synchronize in both directions. Once you are back to the main work area, search for both scheduled tasks and wait for the job to complete execution, as shown in Figure 13-14.

Scheduled Processes

Overview

⊿ Search

Saved Search Last 24 hours ▼

Name			Submission Time	After	▼	3/13/15 6:09 PM
Process ID			Submission Notes	Contains	▼	
Status		▼				

Search   Reset

⊿ Search Results

View   ● Flat List ○ Hierarchy

Actions ▼ View ▼   Schedule New Process   Resubmit   Put On Hold   Cancel Process   »

Name	Process ID	Status	Scheduled Time	Submission Time
Retrieve Latest LDAP Changes	601	Succeeded	3/14/15 6:08 PM UTC	3/14/15 6:08 PM UTC
ⓘ	501	Wait	3/20/15 7:30 PM UTC	3/13/15 7:32 PM UTC

Figure 13-14. Validate successful completion of the scheduled process

Make sure that the job completes with the status Succeeded to make sure that all pending LDAP changes are applied in both directions.

Fusion Applications Initial Security Setup

After going through the Fusion Applications Users and Roles Security concepts, it's now time to set up the initial users and roles for the pilot implementation of the Fusion Applications modules. Regardless of which offerings are selected for the implementation project, the following User Administration tasks are mandatory and you may not need to do all these tasks in all future implementations.

■ **Note** The Fusion Applications provisioning process already created the Fusion Applications super user (FAAdmin), which is capable of performing initial implementation of Fusion Applications modules. However, it is recommended that you dedicate separate users for Fusion Applications administration, security setup, and implementation.

Before we go ahead with the Security Setup tasks, let me give a quick overview of all the tasks that we are going to look at in this section. Figure 13-15 shows the step-by-step flow of Fusion Applications Security Setup tasks.

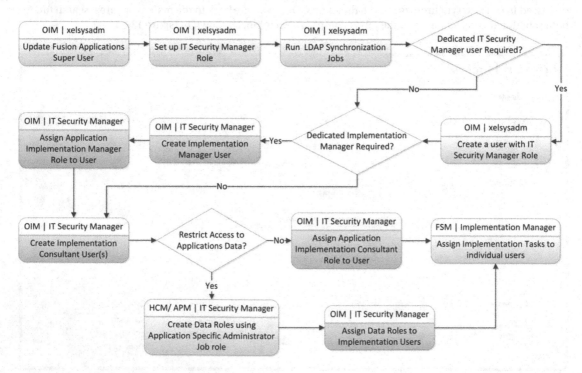

Figure 13-15. *Fusion Applications initial security setup tasks*

You may notice a header block in each of the steps shown in Figure 13-15. I have mentioned the name of the component where the task needs to be performed along with the user who needs to be logged on to perform the selected task. All these mentioned tasks are related to the initial Security Setup of Fusion Applications and there will be additional advanced security-related tasks involved during and after the Applications implementation.

Update Fusion Applications Administration Super User

By default there is no valid e-mail ID assigned to the Fusion Applications super user FAAdmin created during the provisioning process. It is mandatory to have a valid e-mail ID assigned to the super user. Look up for the FAAdmin super user in Oracle Identity Manager and add a valid e-mail to the Email ID Identity Attribute. Figure 13-16 shows an example value for the FAAdmin e-mail address, which was changed from the default value of FAAdmin@company.com.

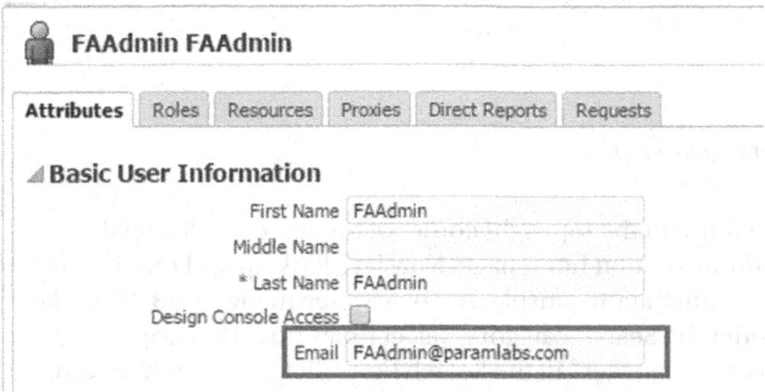

Figure 13-16. *Modify the e-mail attribute for the Fusion Applications super user*

Setting Up the IT Security Administrator Role

The main role of IT Security Administrator user is to provision Fusion Applications Users and Roles using the Oracle Identity Manager (OIM) interface. Although in general the users will be created using the HCM interface, during the Implementation phase we need a dedicated user to provision users and roles outside the Fusion Applications interface.

Before we can create an IT Security Administrator user, we must prepare the IT Security Administrator role. By default the provisioning process creates this role with basic privileges to access the functional setup work area but not with identity Management-related privileges. Hence we must manually add Identity Management-related privileges to this user. Note that if there are any existing roles that already have required privileges then we should always assign that role as a parent role to other roles that require the same privileges. In this case we are going to add existing User Administrator and Role Administrator roles as parent roles to the IT Security Manager.

In order to achieve this, first we need to log in to the OIM homepage using the OIM Administrator user (the default value is xelsysadm). The URL for OIM is http(s)://<IDM Web Host or LB>:<Web Port>/oim.

For example:

http://idmhost.paramlabs.com:7777/oim

Once you log in to OIM using the xelsysadm user, you will see the Oracle Identity Manager Self-Service homepage, as shown in Figure 13-17.

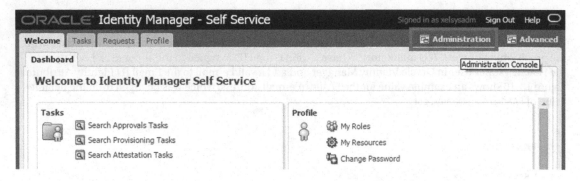

Figure 13-17. Oracle Identity Manager Self-Service homepage

You can see Advanced and Administration links on the top-right corner of the screen. Click on the Administration link to launch the Delegated Administration homepage. Now let's look up and modify the existing IT Security Manager role in the OIM Administration console. As you can see in Figure 13-18, make sure that the Administration tab is selected. Under the Search category, select Roles from the drop-down menu and type the full or partial text of "IT Security Manager" in the Search box. Click the Search button. This will populate the list of users containing the search term. Since in this case we have entered full role name, we see only that specific role as the search result.

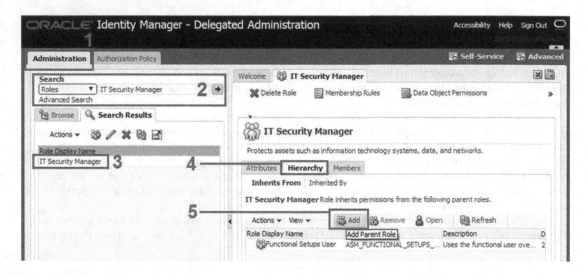

Figure 13-18. Edit the IT Security Manager role

Click on the IT Security Manager role name from the search results. This will bring up details of the role in the main window as an additional tab. Click on the Hierarchy tab. You will see the existing parent roles assigned to this role. As you can see, by default this role has only one parent role, which is Functional Setup User. We need to add roles that are specifically required to manage users and roles in the Oracle Identity Manager. Click on the Add button to launch the Parent Roles selection pop-up frame, as shown in Figure 13-19.

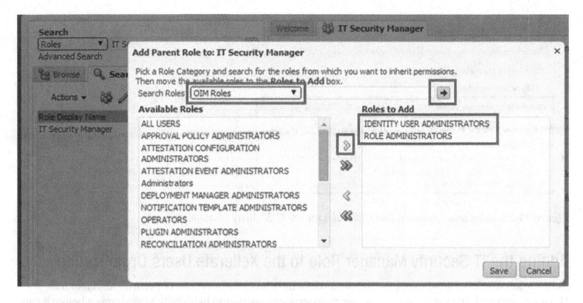

Figure 13-19. *Add parent roles to the IT Security Manager role*

As you can see in Figure 13-19, the roles are grouped by role categories (stored in the ROLE_CATEGORY database table in OIM schema). Since we are only interested in OIM-related roles at the moment, select OIM Roles from the drop-down menu. Select the following two roles from the left pane and move them to right using the arrow buttons.

- IDENTITY USER ADMINISTRATORS

- ROLE ADMINISTRATORS

The first role allows the user to create or modify users in Identity Manager while the later allows you to manage new or existing roles in Identity Manager. Note that these are bare minimum roles required for the IT Security Manager role during the Fusion Applications implementation and you may want to add more OIM related roles to this user, for example SCHEDULER ADMINISTRATORS, REQUEST ADMINISTRATOR, and so on.

■ **Caution**   Some external documents or blogs may suggest that you add the SYSTEM ADMINISTRATORS role to the IT Security Manager role. Note that although this role is a superset of IDENTITY USER ADMINISTRATORS and ROLE ADMINISTRATORS, it contains more privileges on Identity Management than required for the Fusion Applications implementation. Do not assign this role to the IT Security Manager unless you have a specific reason for doing so.

Figure 13-20 shows the post role-addition view of the IT Security Manager role. The first role, called *Functional Setup Manager,* is related to Fusion Applications. It allows the user to log in to Fusion Applications and access the Functional Setup Manager work area and access the tasks that are assigned to the user.

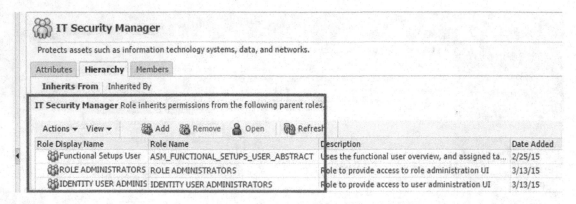

Figure 13-20. Minimum required inherited roles for the IT Security Manager

Adding the IT Security Manager Role to the Xellerate Users Organization

At this point we have already assigned user and role administrator roles to the IT Security Manager role. However, we must first assign this user to the appropriate organization in Identity Management before it can manage the users in that organization. By default all users created for Fusion Applications should be created in the already existing Xellerate Users organization only. So we will add the IT Security Manager role as an administration role to this organization.

■ **Note**   The name *Xellerate* was inherited from Oracle's acquisition of Thor Technologies in 2005. Thor's *Xellerate Identity Provisioning* or *Xellerate Identity Manager* product is now transformed to today's Oracle Identity Manager (OIM).

Let's look at how to add this role as an administrative role to the Xellerate Users organization. In the OIM Delegated Administration console (which should be already open from the previous step), under the Administration tab in the regional area, select the search type as Organizations and perform an empty search. This will show you the list of existing organizations in your Identity Management environment, as shown in Figure 13-21.

Figure 13-21. *Accessing Xellerate Users Organization details*

Click on the name Xellerate Users from the search results. This will launch the Xellerate Users details page as an additional tab in the main area of page. Click on Administrative Roles to launch the list of existing administrative roles, as shown in Figure 13-22.

Organization Detail >> Administrative Roles

The following is a list of the roles (and associated permissions) that can administer this organization:

Organization Name: Xellerate Users

Filter By Role Name [   ]   [Search]

Results 1-2 of 2   First | Previous | Next | Last

Role Name	Read	Write	Delete	Unassign ☐
SYSTEM ADMINISTRATORS	✓	✓	✓	☐
SELF OPERATORS	✓	✓	✗	☐
				[Unassign]

First | Previous | Next | Last

[Assign] [Update Permissions]

Figure 13-22. *Default administrative roles for the Xellerate users organization*

As you can see in Figure 13-22, by default only SYSTEM ADMINISTRATORS are allowed full administration access on this organization. ROLE OPERATORS have limited administration access on the same. We will add the IT Security Manager role with full administration rights in addition to these roles. Click on the Assign button at the bottom of screen to proceed. In the Search and Assign role screen shown in Figure 13-23, you can perform an empty search or filter with name of the role to be added.

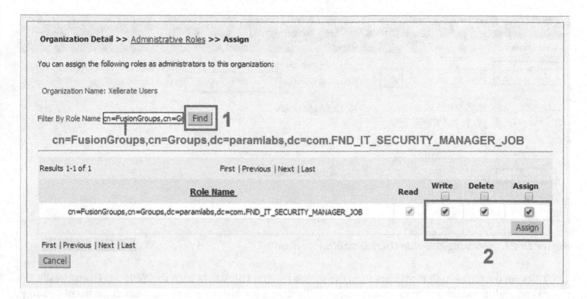

Figure 13-23. *Search and add the new administrator role to the organization*

Note that the role names being displayed in this screen are displayed in <parent_DN>.<ROLE_NAME> format. We performed the search with the same format to filter only the IT_SECURITY_MANAGER role.

For example, the full DN for the IT Security Manager is cn=FND_IT_SECURITY_MANAGER_JOB, cn=FusionGroups,cn=Groups,dc=paramlabs,dc=com and it is displayed as cn=FusionGroups,cn=Groups, dc=paramlabs,dc=com.FND_IT_SECURITY_MANAGER_JOB.

Once you have located the role to be added, select all three checkboxes for Write, Delete, and Assign permissions on this organization (Read is already checked and grayed out) and click the Assign button.

As you can see in Figure 13-24, it will prompt you with the list of roles selected for assignment. If you have performed an empty search and selected multiple roles across different pages then this screen becomes handy to get a summary of all roles to be added before the actual assignment. In this case, we are adding only one role so verify the name and click Confirm to assign the Administrative role.

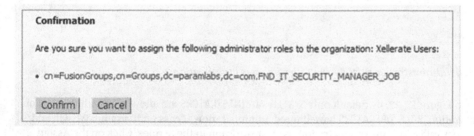

Figure 13-24. *Administrative role assignment confirmation*

Creating the IT Security Administrator User

Once you have set up the IT Security Manager role, you should create a new dedicated IT security manager/administrator user and assign this role to them. As mentioned earlier, the already provisioned super user FAAdmin has all the require permissions administer users/roles (via pre-assigned IT Security Manager role) and can manage the implementation project. But in order to segregate the duties and audit effectively, we must create a dedicated IT security manager user. It is also a good practice to create a new user for Fusion Applications Administration instead of using the FA super user (FAAdmin), since it has much more access privileges than day-to-day administration may require. You may also create a single user with administration as well as IT security role. This example shows you how to create the IT security manager/administrator user and assign required roles to them.

Open the OIM Administration homepage and click on Create User in the page main area or click on Create User in the search region. This will launch new user creation screen, as shown in Figure 13-25.

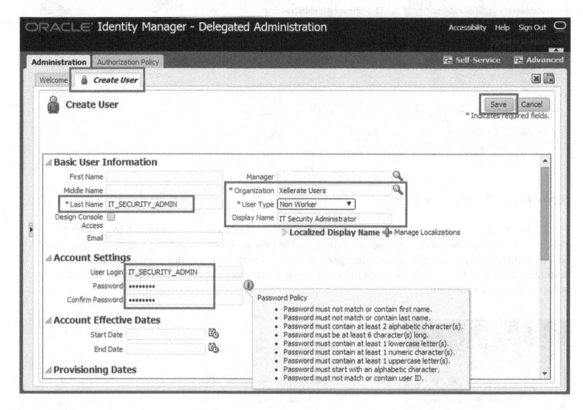

Figure 13-25. *Create new user screen*

Table 13-2 describes the mandatory fields in this screen. Enter the values as shown in the Example column of this table and click the Save button to create the IT Security Administrator user.

Table 13-2. *The Create New User Screen Parameters*

Attribute	Input Type	Example
Last Name	`<Valid String>`	`IT_Security_Admin`
Organization	`Xellerate Users (mandatory)`	`Xellerate Users`
User Type	`Non Worker (mandatory)`	`Non Worker`
User Login	`<Alphanumeric String>`	`IT_SECURITY_ADMIN`
Login Password	`<Valid String>`	`Str0ngP#$$w0rd`
Display Name	`<Valid String>`	`IT Security Administrator`

Once the user is created you will be directed to the user details screen, as shown in Figure 13-26. Click on the Roles tab to access the list of currently assigned roles. By default, the newly created users have the ALL_USERS role only, so you must assign additional roles to this user in order to provide the required privileges.

Figure 13-26. *Post user creation screen*

Click on the Assign button in the Roles tab to launch the Add Role screen, as shown in Figure 13-27. This screen requires you to enter the search criteria to filter the roles with matching names. You can search based on display name, role name, or namespace (parent DN of the role), either beginning with or exactly matching the value. However if you want to use the Containing search option, you can use wildcard "*" before and/or after the value.

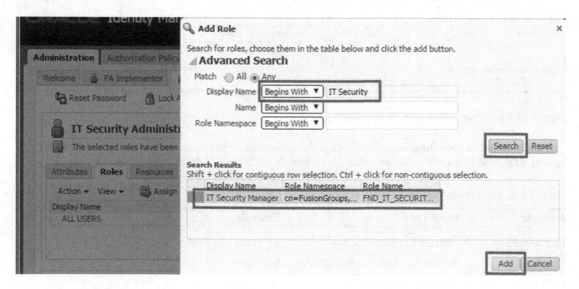

Figure 13-27. *Search and add new role to an existing user*

As shown in Figure 13-27, search for IT Security Manager role by entering and select the required row from the search results. Click Add to add the selected role to the user. The pop-up screen will close automatically. Figure 13-28 shows the list of direct and inherited roles now assigned to the IT Security Administrator user. Wait for a while to make sure that the LDAP incremental synchronization jobs have completed. You could use this user now to provision new Users and Roles in Fusion Applications. If you want a single user for administering the Fusion Applications environment as well as for provisioning users, then you can selectively add administrative roles that are already assigned to the FAAdmin super user to this user as well.

Figure 13-28. *Assigned roles for IT Security Administrator user*

Assigning Users/Roles Provisioning Tasks to Security Administrator

Although this user can manually run users or roles provisioning related tasks, we must assign the related tasks from ongoing implementation projects to this user so that those tasks show up in the Assigned Implementation Tasks tab for this user. Let's assign some tasks from an already created implementation project to the IT Security Administration assuming that this user is dedicated to security administration only.

Log in to Fusion Applications using the FAAdmin super user or the custom administration user (if one is created) and open the current implementation project. From the list of tasks, select the task or task list to be assigned and click on the Actions menu for the list of available actions for the task or list selected, as shown in Figure 13-29.

Task Lists and Tasks

Actions ▾	View ▾	Format ▾	⬚ ✖	⧉ Freeze	⧉ Detach	⯐
Select and Add		➜				
Remove			He	Go to Task	Selected Scope	
Assign Tasks	b					
Edit Status	Applications Config					
Reorder	ronization of Users					
Download File	l Roles Synchronizal	🖹				
Upload File	mentation Users					

Figure 13-29. *Implementation Project Tasks actions menu*

Click Assign Tasks to launch the assignment screen. By default, no user is assigned to a task until the task execution has been started. Click on the Add icon as shown in Figure 13-30 to search and add users to the task.

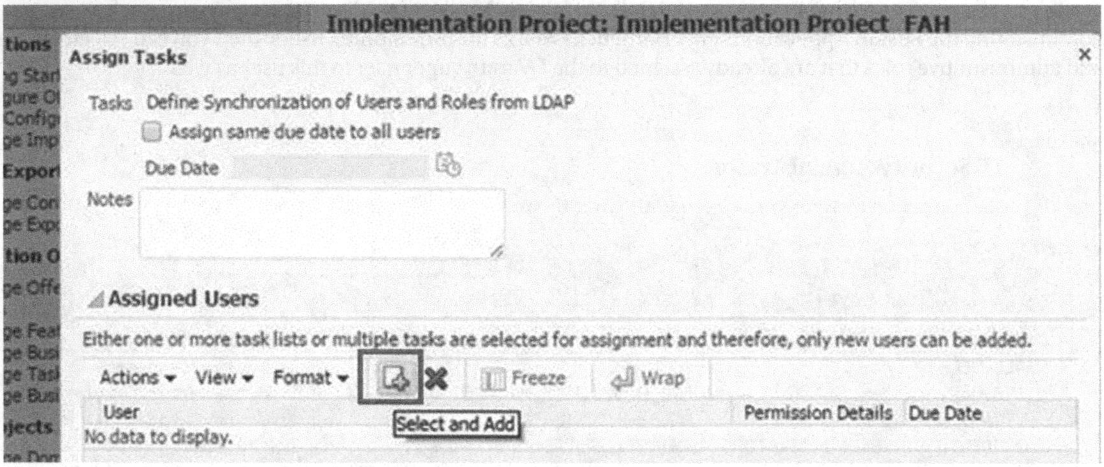

Figure 13-30. *Tasks assignment screen*

The Search and Add users screen allows you to search an existing user using user ID, first or last name, or e-mail. Enter one of the criteria to look up the IT Security Administrator user, as shown in Figure 13-31, and click Search.

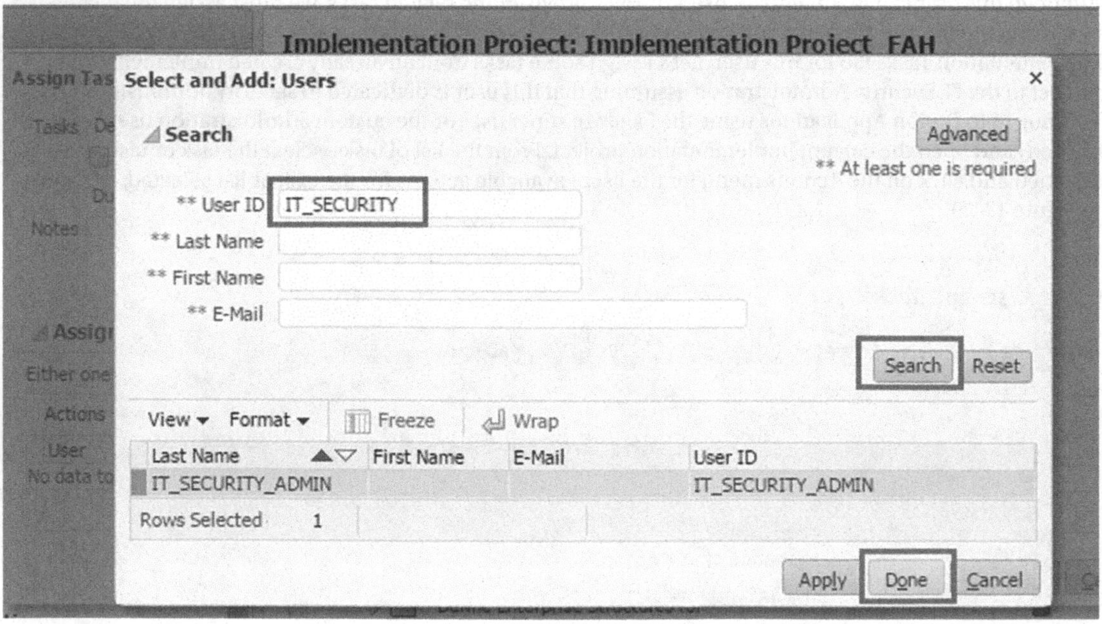

Figure 13-31. *Search and assign users to a task*

Select the IT_SECURITY_ADMIN user from the search results and click Done. If you want to add more than one user using multiple search criteria then click Apply to let the screen remain open for another user assignment. Once the user has been assigned to the task, you can optionally add notes to the task, as shown in Figure 13-32, which can be viewed by the members of the implementation project team and can be used for documentation purposes.

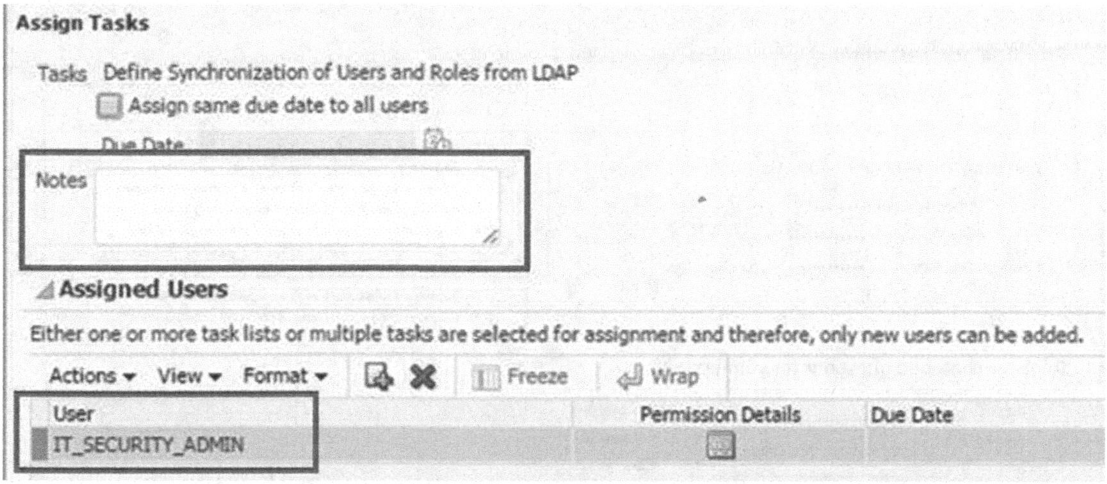

Assign Tasks

Tasks   Define Synchronization of Users and Roles from LDAP
☐ Assign same due date to all users

Due Date

Notes

▲ **Assigned Users**

Either one or more task lists or multiple tasks are selected for assignment and therefore, only new users can be added.

Actions ▾   View ▾   Format ▾   [icons]   Freeze   Wrap

User	Permission Details	Due Date
IT_SECURITY_ADMIN	[icon]	

Figure 13-32. Adding notes to the task

Once the tasks have been assigned to the IT Security Administrator, this user can log in to the Fusion Applications homepage URL (for example, https://fahost:10634/homePage) and view the assigned tasks. Note that for every new user created in Identity Management, upon the first successful log in to Fusion Applications, the Identity Manager will request that the user to provide a new password and register security questions for future account recovery, as shown in Figure 13-33. It also shows the default password policy for selecting new passwords. Note that the default policy does not prevent the user from selecting the same password again. However, you can change the password policy as per your organization security requirements.

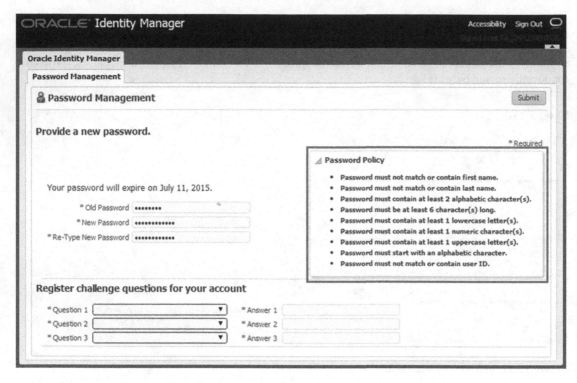

Figure 13-33. *Password Management screen upon first login*

Once the you have logged in to Fusion Applications as the IT security administrator user, launch the Functional Setup manager page using Navigator ➤ Setup and Maintenance. The landing page will display the list of assigned implementation tasks for this user regardless of which implementation project they are assigned. The main implementation tasks for IT security manager/administrator are as follows.

- Run User and Roles Synchronization Process
- Create Implementation Users
- Create Data Role for Implementation Users (optional)
- Provision Roles to Implementation Users

Figure 13-34 shows the Assigned Implementation Tasks screen for the IT Security Administrator user. You can click on Go Task one by one to complete these implementation tasks. Make sure to update the status of the task after it is completed successfully.

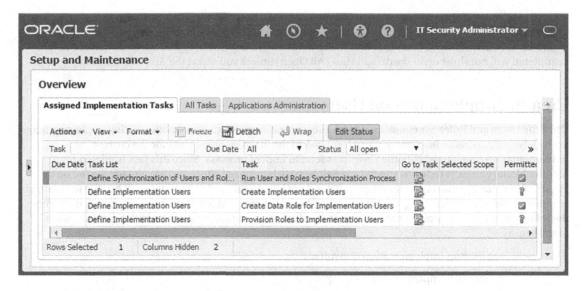

Figure 13-34. Assigned Implementation Tasks screen

Run User and Roles Synchronization Process

The first step in an implementation project before creating any implementation users or assigning new roles is to synchronize Users and Roles information between the identity store and the Fusion Applications. The User and Roles Synchronization Process task is configured to run the LDAP synchronization Scheduled Process called Retrieve Latest LDAP Changes, which you saw earlier. Refer to the earlier section in this chapter for more details on this task.

Click on Go to Task for the Run User and Roles Synchronization Process task to launch the LDAP scheduled process screen and submit the request. Refresh the process status screen until the request status is Succeeded. Make a note of the request ID for documentation purposes. Since this task is now complete, click the Actions menu and select Edit Status to update the status of the task with optional notes, as shown in Figure 13-35.

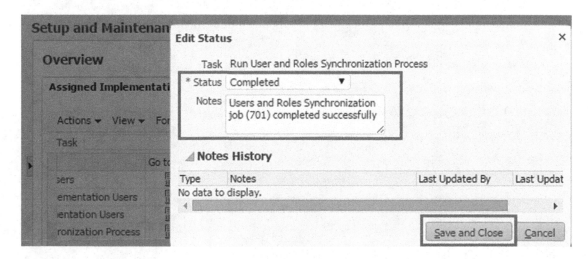

Figure 13-35. Updating the task status

Change the status from Not Started to Complete to make sure that the Implementation project is updated with the completed security tasks. You can add notes for documentation purposes, as shown in Figure 13-35. Click Save and Close to return to the list of assigned tasks. Note that the tasks that are set as Completed will not show up in the default view (All Open) unless you select the All Tasks option.

Creating Implementation Users

Once the Users and Roles Synchronization task is complete, you can go ahead with creating implementation user(s). Select the Create Implementation Users task in the list of assigned tasks for the current implementation project and click the Go to Task icon in front of this task. Since this task is related to Identity Management, it redirects you to OIM Self-Service homepage. Since you are already logged on as IT_SECURITY_ADMIN or an equivalent user, you need not log in again to OIM and you will be able to create or administer users and roles using Identity Manager. You must create at least one implementation user with the following roles if you want to provide unrestricted access to implementation users for the duration of initial setup.

- Application Implementation Consultant

- Application Implementation Manager

Since these roles have a wide range of functional and data security access on Fusion Applications Resources, you may want to restrict the access for the implementation users. In that case, we will not assign these roles but will create Data roles based on specific Applications administrator roles and assign them to the user. We will look at this in the next section.

Once you are redirected to OIM Self-Service homepage, click on the Administration link on top-right side and then click Create User in the main area to launch a new user creation screen, as shown in Figure 13-36. We have already seen this screen earlier when creating the IT Security Administration user so we need not explain the parameters again. You can refer to Table 13-2 for the list of mandatory parameters and acceptable values. In this case, we will name the user FA_IMPLEMENTOR with the display name of FA Implementor (different countries use the term *implementor* and *implementer* interchangeably), as shown in Figure 13-36. You may also set other optional parameters including Begin Date, End Date, and so on, for the user in order to disable such access after implementation is complete.

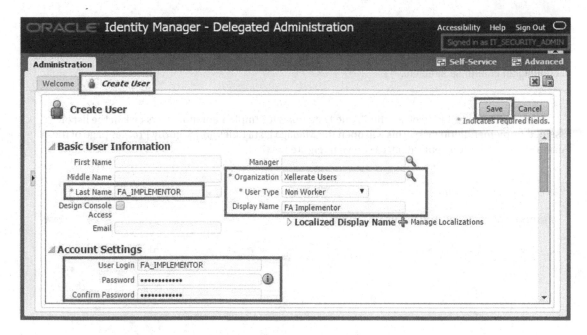

Figure 13-36. *Creating a new application implementation user*

Create Data Roles for Implementation Users

The Application Implementation Consultant role has a wide range of access to Fusion Applications, including necessary access to all secure objects or resources. You may optionally want to restrict this access by creating Data roles that allow access only to a set of data based on the implementation requirement. As per the implementation requirement, we need to create View All and Set ID Data roles based on specific Applications Job roles. We can create Data roles using the following two methods.

- Create a Data role using HCM security profiles in order to restrict or allow data access based on HCM conditions including Legislative Data Group, Persons, and Payrolls. This is the recommended method for creating a Data role for initial implementation users since they require View All permissions to set up the applications.

- Generate Data roles using Data Role templates available in Authorization Policy Manager (APM), which secure data access based on multiple data dimensions and provide further granular control. This method is more suitable for granting access to regular Fusion Applications users instead of the initial implementation users.

The Generate Data Roles task is required to be performed at a later stage of the implementation project. For the initial application setup, the task by default leads to option 1 only. So let's have a quick look at how to create a Data role for a specific application administrator Job role. Note that depending on the implementation tasks you may need to create one or more data roles that need to assigned to the implementation users in the next step.

■ **Note** HCM domain WebLogic managed server `hcmCoreSetupServer_1` is required to be available in order to generate data roles using HCM security profiles as well as to access the next functional implementation task of creating an enterprise structure.

Click on the Go to Task icon for the Create Data Roles for Implementation users task in the list of assigned implementation tasks. This will open the Manage Data Roles and Security Profiles page of the Fusion HCM core setup application, as shown in Figure 13-37.

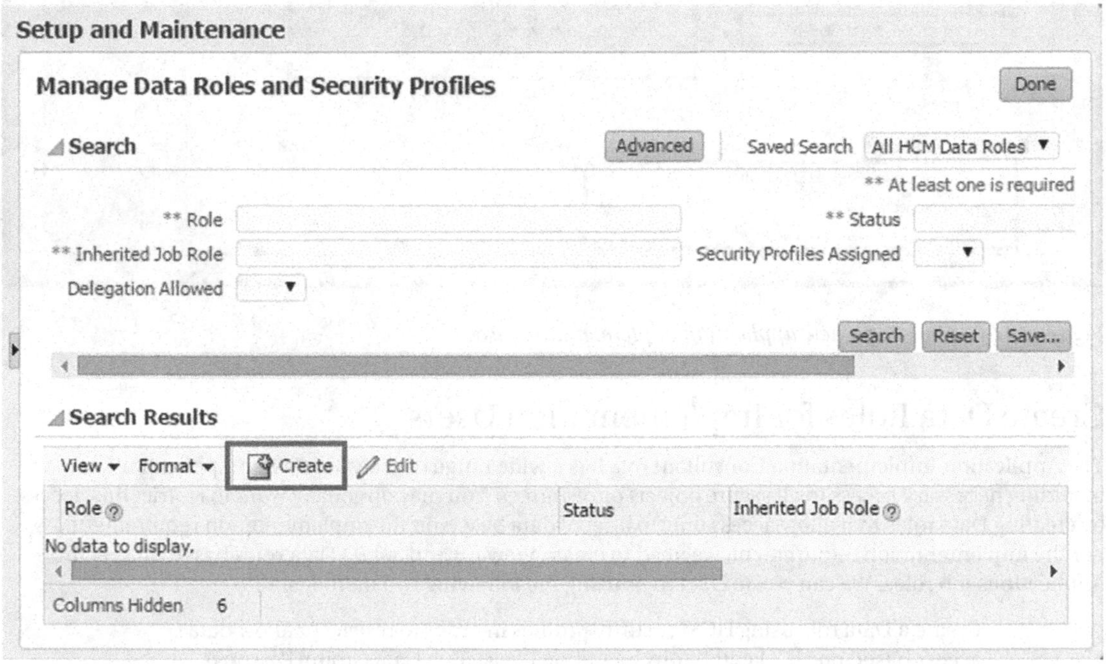

Setup and Maintenance

Manage Data Roles and Security Profiles   Done

⊿ **Search**   Advanced | Saved Search All HCM Data Roles ▼

                                                              ** At least one is required

              ** Role [   ]   ** Status [   ]

** Inherited Job Role [   ]   Security Profiles Assigned [▼]

  Delegation Allowed [▼]

                                                       Search   Reset   Save...

  ◄ ▬▬▬▬▬▬▬▬▬▬▬▬▬▬▬▬▬▬▬▬▬▬▬   ►

⊿ **Search Results**

  View ▼   Format ▼   [Create]   ✎ Edit

  Role ⑦   Status   Inherited Job Role ⑦

  No data to display.

  ◄ ▬▬▬▬▬▬▬▬▬▬▬▬▬▬▬▬▬▬▬▬▬   ►

  Columns Hidden   6

Figure 13-37. Manage Data Roles and Security Profiles page

In the Search Results section, click on the Create button to create a new Data role based on an existing Job role. This will lead to the Create Data Role page, as shown in Figure 13-38. This screen requires an existing Job role be selected. We created the View All Financial Application Administrator Data role based on the Financial Application Administrator Job role in this example.

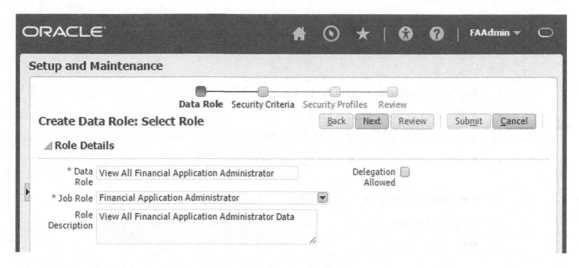

Figure 13-38. *Create View All Data Role for financials application*

The next screens allow you to select HCM security profiles based on the Persons, Payrolls, and Legislative Data groups. This role will be saved in the OID as follows.

```
cn=VIEW_ALL_FINANCIAL_APPLICATION_ADMINISTRATOR_DATA,cn=Groups,dc=paramlabs,dc=com
```

Assign Roles to Implementation Users

Once the user is created, it will now show the User details screen as shown in Figure 13-39. You can see that by default the user does not have any additional roles except ALL_USERS. Click on the Roles tab followed by the Assign button to add more roles to the FA administrator user.

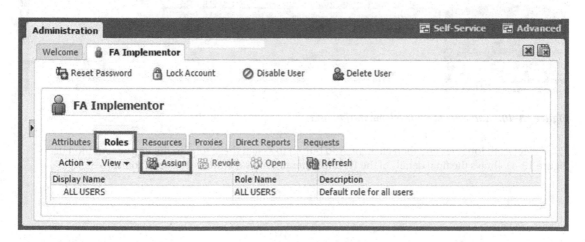

Figure 13-39. *Implementation user details screen*

We have seen the Add Role screen before. As shown in Figure 13-40, enter Application Implementation in the search box to display all roses that begin with this title. The following two Job roles should be displayed in the search results in addition to the Applications Implementation Administrator Abstract role.

- Job roles

  - Application Implementation Consultant

  - Application Implementation Manager

- Abstract role (optional)

  - Application Implementation Administrator

Or

- Previously generated Data roles

  - View All Data roles

  - Set ID Data roles

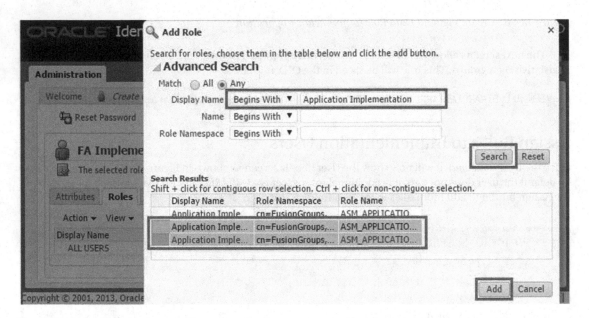

Figure 13-40. *Add roles to the implementation user*

Select both Job roles and then click the Add button to assign these roles to the implementation user. Figure 13-41 shows the final details of the FA implementation user with the required roles.

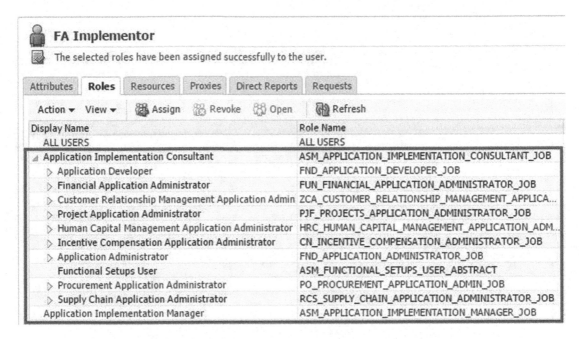

Figure 13-41. *List of assigned roles for the Fusion Applications implementation user*

Rerun the LDAP Synchronization Scheduled Process

It is good practice to run the LDAP synchronization scheduled process after the required users and roles are provisioned. The synchronization may happen automatically but you can speed up the sync by manually running the scheduled process.

Summary

This chapter explored the initial security setup for Fusion Applications implementation. However this does not completely cover the Oracle Fusion Applications security tasks since many of them are beyond scope of this book. At this point you should understand the Role Based Access Control of Fusion Applications and how each component is involved in the Fusion Applications security architecture stores, and how it manages and synchronizes Users and Roles. You saw the various LDAP synchronization jobs between OIM and OID as well as between Fusion HCM and OIM.

Next you saw the mandatory security setup-related steps involved in Fusion Applications implementation project. At this point, your environment should have a security administrator user, an application implementation consultant user, and optionally a Fusion Applications administration user in addition to the initial FAAdmin super user. You got a bird's eye view of how Data roles are created and assigned to existing users. The next tasks in the implementation project are performed by application implementation consultant and once the Fusion Applications environment is in operation, you or the Fusion Applications Administrator needs to monitor and maintain the environment. In next few chapters, you will learn about these important administrative tasks.

■ ■ ■

## CHAPTER 14

Monitoring Fusion Applications Environment

This chapter covers the next important administrative task—Monitoring. In this chapter, we will look at monitoring the complete technology stack of the Fusion Applications infrastructure and application components, including manual as well as automatic monitoring. You must first understand the relationship between the Fusion Applications monitoring and troubleshooting activities. It is important to note that Fusion Applications monitoring and troubleshooting activities are tightly coupled and you mainly need to use similar interfaces to perform both activities and most often troubleshooting is preceded and invoked by monitoring activities.

Although it is difficult to draw a clear line between monitoring and troubleshooting activities, we will see monitoring activities in this chapter followed by diagnosing and troubleshooting in the next chapter to explain each of them as an exclusive administrative task. The reason to explain them separately is that in large organizations there will be different teams dedicated to Enterprise monitoring. In general, monitoring is a proactive administrative task whereas diagnosing and troubleshooting are reactive.

Understanding the Role of Cloud Control

Enterprise Manager Cloud Control is not a new tool for Fusion Applications management but in earlier versions of Fusion Applications it was an optional tool. From the recent versions of Fusion Applications (11g, Release 9 onward) Oracle recommends you use Cloud Control as the primary management tool for complete Oracle Fusion Applications infrastructure. The other tools that come by default with Fusion Applications installation can still perform the same tasks similar to previous releases but you should focus more on using Cloud Control for the obvious benefits achieved through it. Most importantly, Cloud Control allows you to see more historical graphs as compared to the default Enterprise Manager tools like Fusion Application Control. For example, in Fusion Applications Control you can see the last 15 minutes of a job run in Enterprise scheduler service, but from Cloud Control you can see daily, weekly, monthly, or all the requests for which the monitoring information has not yet been purged from repository.

Before we discuss more about cloud control benefits or compare them with pre-installed tools like Fusion Applications Control, let's look at the image shown in Figure 14-1.

© Tushar Thakker 2015

T. Thakker, *Pro Oracle Fusion Applications*, DOI 10.1007/978-1-4842-0983-7_14

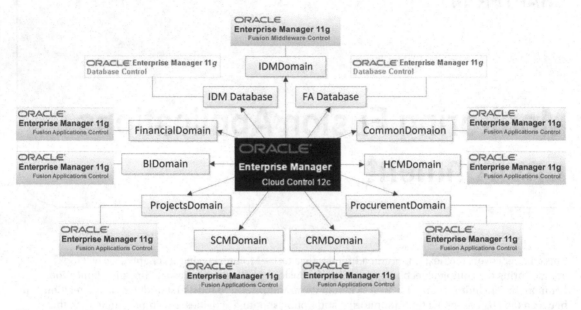

Figure 14-1. *Enterprise Manager Cloud Control versus default management tools*

As you can see, the following three components are pre-installed and available by default in the Fusion Applications environment.

- *Enterprise Manager Database Control*: This is the default Enterprise Manager that's configured with Oracle database (unless explicitly unchecked during installation) and most DBAs have been using it quite extensively.

- *Enterprise Manager Fusion Middleware Control*: This component is configured automatically with Identity Management and is accessible through the WebLogic domain administration server port. It is the default tool used by middleware administrators for Fusion middleware administration in Identity Management or any Fusion middleware environments.

- *Enterprise Manager Fusion Applications Control*: The Fusion Applications Control is configured in the same way as the middleware control on the WebLogic domain of each product family and accessible through the administration port for the specific domain. It provides more capabilities as compared to the middleware control and we can monitor application deployments as well as WebLogic infrastructure components using the same interface. It includes individual homepages for the WebLogic domain, each WebLogic cluster, managed server, and the application deployments as well as the complete farm.

So if you look at Figure 14-1, before configuring EM Cloud Control, you need to use the EM Database control to manage the Identity Management and Fusion Applications transaction databases and the EM Fusion middleware control to monitor Identity Management Middleware components. At the same time for managing Fusion Applications Middleware and Application components, we have the EM Fusion Applications control as the default available tool. For each product family, a dedicated instance of Fusion Applications control is configured. As you can see, we need too many tools to manage this complex environment and we need to keep switching between tools in order to monitor or troubleshoot the issues.

This complexity can greatly be reduced by using Enterprise Manager Cloud Control to configure all of the components. This will allow you to monitor, manage, and troubleshoot each component involved in the Fusion Applications architecture from a single interface in a consolidated or component level drilled down view.

Installing and Configuring Cloud Control

Enterprise Manager Cloud Control is not installed or configured during Fusion Applications provisioning. In order to use it to manage the complete Fusion Applications environment, you need to install and configure EM Cloud Control separately on a different.

■ **Note** You must license the Fusion Applications plugin separately since you need to configure this plugin in Cloud Control order to achieve Fusion Applications monitoring and management capabilities.

Figure 14-2 shows an overview of the steps required to install and configure Enterprise Manager Cloud Control with the Fusion Applications environment.

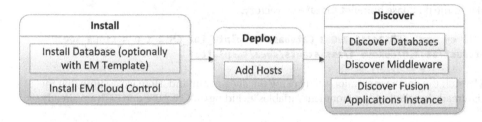

Figure 14-2. Deployment methodology for Cloud Control

This diagram assumes that you do not have EM Cloud Control already installed in your infrastructure. If you already have Cloud Control in your environment, then you can skip the Install step and its related tasks and proceed with the Deploy and Discover steps.

Installing Oracle Database for Cloud Control

In order to host an Enterprise Manager repository, we must install a blank database for EM. We are not going to discuss the database software installation steps here but we will see how we can efficiently create the database for using with Cloud Control. Oracle provides database templates for the latest version of Enterprise Manager Cloud Control so we can download them before creating the database and later use these templates to create the EM database with the repository related schemas preloaded. However, this is optional and you may want to create a regular database as well. In that case, the EM Cloud Control installer will create an EM repository on the blank database. In this example we will use the readily available EM database templates. You can download them from Oracle's software delivery cloud from the same location where you download the Cloud Control installer.

Install the Oracle database software on the server first and make sure that the Create Database option is not selected since we will manually create the database next. Next, download the database template for the matching version of EM to be installed. Once the template ZIP file has been downloaded and extracted, the directory will look as follows.

```
[fusion@emhost ~]$ ls -ltr ./EM12c/11.2.0.3_Database_Template_for_EM12_1_0_4_Linux_x64/
total 241053
-rwxrwxrwx 2 root root 237051904 May 24  2014 11.2.0.3_Database_Template_for_EM12_1_0_4.dfb
-rwxrwxrwx 2 root root   9748480 May 24  2014 11.2.0.3_Database_Template_for_EM12_1_0_4.ctl
-rwxrwxrwx 2 root root        46 May 24  2014 shpool_11.2.0.3_Database_SQL_for_EM12_1_0_4.sql
-rwxrwxrwx 2 root root      1878 May 24  2014 set_repo_param_11.2.0.3_Database_SQL_for_
EM12_1_0_4_Small_deployment.sql
-rwxrwxrwx 2 root root      1989 May 24  2014 set_repo_param_11.2.0.3_Database_SQL_for_
EM12_1_0_4_Medium_deployment.sql
-rwxrwxrwx 2 root root      1990 May 24  2014 set_repo_param_11.2.0.3_Database_SQL_for_
EM12_1_0_4_Large_deployment.sql
-rwxrwxrwx 2 root root      5547 May 24  2014 11.2.0.3_Database_Template_for_EM12_1_0_4_
Small_deployment.dbc
-rwxrwxrwx 2 root root      5548 May 24  2014 11.2.0.3_Database_Template_for_EM12_1_0_4_
Medium_deployment.dbc
-rwxrwxrwx 2 root root      5551 May 24  2014 11.2.0.3_Database_Template_for_EM12_1_0_4_
Large_deployment.dbc
```

Copy these files to the database home's templates directory.

```
[fusion@emhost ~]$ cp -pr ./EM12c/11.2.0.3_Database_Template_for_EM12_1_0_4_Linux_x64/*
/app/database/product/11.2.0/dbhome_1/assistants/dbca/templates/
```

Now you can launch the database creation utility using the dbca command. Here we assume that the database software is already installed and environment variables including ORACLE_HOME and PATH are already set.

```
[fusion@emhost bin]$ dbca &
```

We will look at only the screens that are related to the database templates. As you can see in Figure 14-3, in the Database Templates selection screen, we will now see three additional options—Small, Medium, and Large for Enterprise Manager (12c, Release 4 in this case).

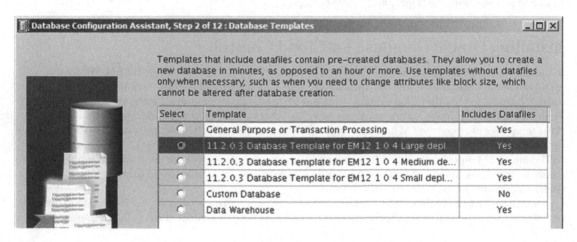

Figure 14-3. *Selecting a database template with pre-configured EM respisotry*

Small, Medium, and Large should be selected based on the size of the infrastructure to be monitored in your organization. Since EM Cloud Control can monitor non-Fusion or even non-Oracle systems as well, you may select from Small, Medium, or Large deployments that support up to 100, up to 1,000, or more than 1,000 agents, respectively.

■ **Note**   Be careful while selecting the deployment size here since during the Cloud Control installation you must specify the same deployment size.

The next important screen is the Enterprise Manager configuration shown in Figure 14-4. Since you are creating the database for Cloud Control, the native Enterprise Manager database control must be deselected.

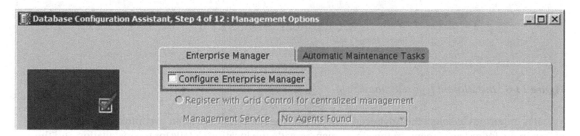

Figure 14-4. *Deselect the Configure Enterprise Manager option*

The next and last important screen to notice is the custom scripts screen shown in Figure 14-5. The installer will automatically populate the post-database creation script details. It is crucial to leave this untouched since these scripts tune the database as per the required deployment size.

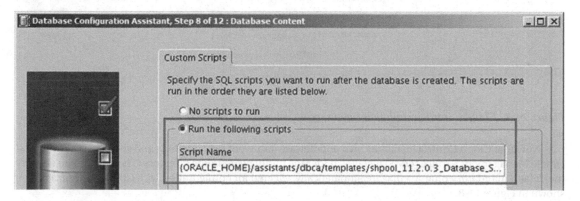

Figure 14-5. *Run mandatory scripts*

Installing Enterprise Manager Cloud Control

The next step is to install the Cloud Control 12c. Note that you can install the current latest release of EM Cloud Control. In this example, we will look at 12c, Release 4. We will look at only the important screens of the installation here.

Launch the installer by executing the runInstaller script. Proceed with the initial screens followed by the environment prerequisites checks. Once the prerequisites checks are successful, you will need to select the installation type, as shown in Figure 14-6.

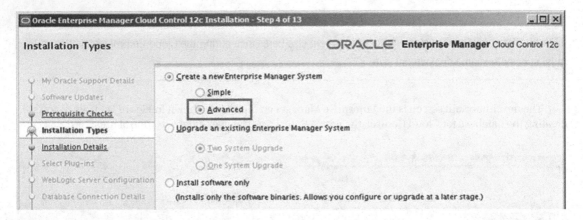

Figure 14-6. Installation type selection screen

It is important to select the Advanced installation type here since we need to configure an additional plugin in the following screens. In the next screen, provide the location details for the installation and the hostname that will run the Cloud Control management services, as shown in Figure 14-7.

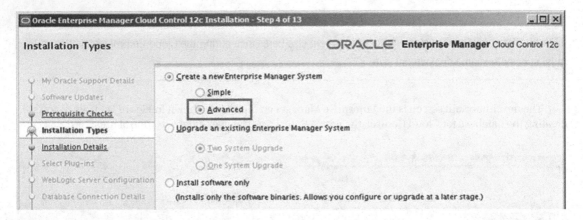

Figure 14-7. Cloud Control Installation Details screen

Note that Cloud Control installs its own middleware and WebLogic domains and you may see the Oracle Management Service (OMS) installed under the middleware home directory. The next screen shows the default mandatory plug-ins that are automatically selected for configuration with Cloud Control, as shown in Figure 14-8.

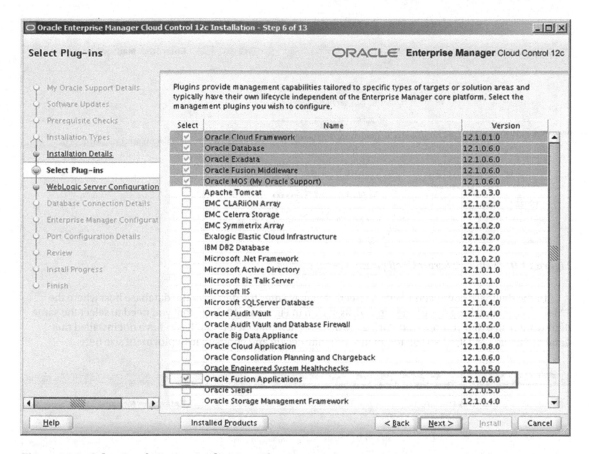

Figure 14-8. *Select Oracle Fusion Applications Plug-Ins*

We must select Oracle Fusion Applications in addition to the default selected ones shown in Figure 14-8. This is the reason we selected the Advanced installation in the beginning, since the Simple installation does not bring up this screen and goes with default plug-ins only. You need to make sure that you have appropriate licenses for Applications Management pack for Fusion Applications and the number of licenses must match the WebLogic Server domains in all Fusion Applications hosts being monitored.

Next you need to select the credentials for the WebLogic domain and Node Manager to be configured on EM host, as shown in Figure 14-9. You cannot change the default domain name (GCDomain) and the instance directory will be automatically populated in the same screen. Make a note of it for future administration purposes. In this example, it is /app/oracle/em/gc_inst based on earlier entered middleware and agent directory information. You will see that the paths still carry the old grid control (gc) prefix in the domain name and path values.

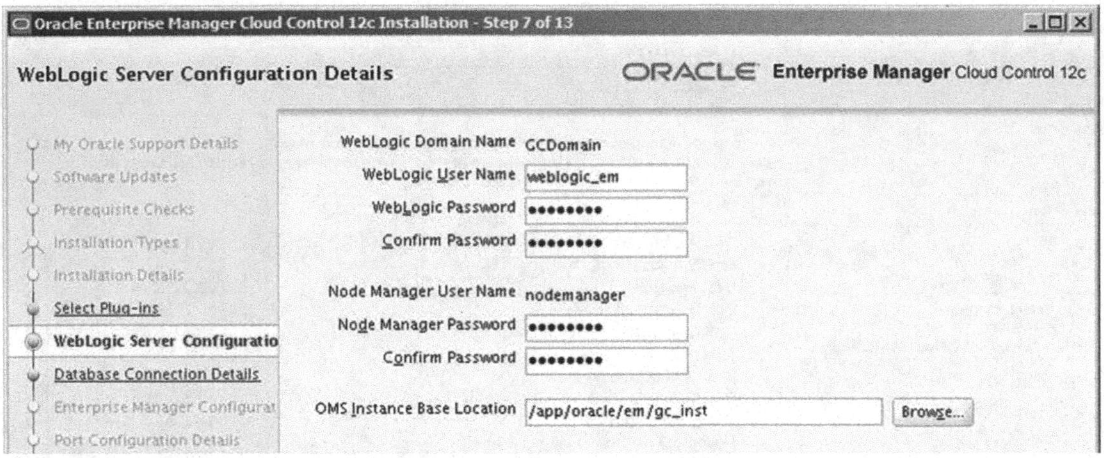

Figure 14-9. WebLogic Server Configuration Details screen

In the database connection details screen, you may enter the details of the database host where the EM repository database has been installed, as shown in Figure 14-10. Note that you need to select the same deployment size that you selected during the database template selection. If you have not installed the database using EM DÇATABASE templates, you may decide and choose the deployment size here.

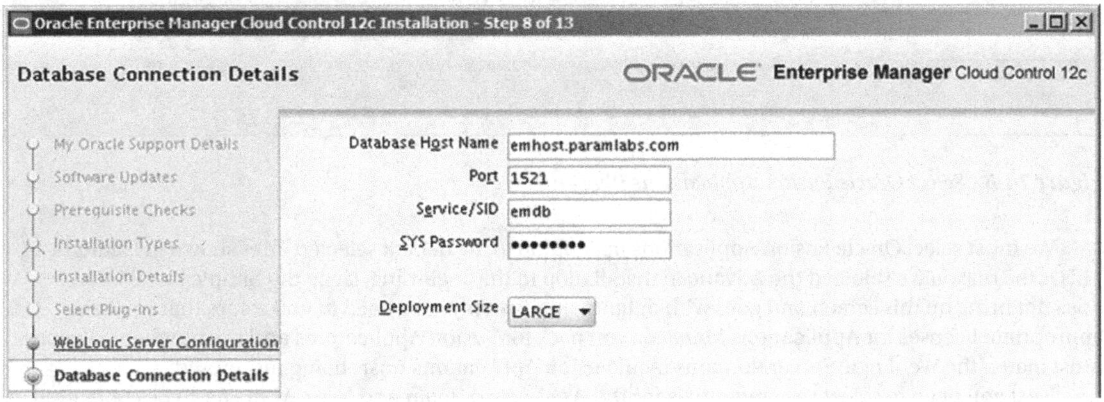

Figure 14-10. Database Connection Details screen

We will now skip to the next important screen, which is the installation progress details screen, as shown in Figure 14-11. Although you need not make any changes in this screen, you may notice different steps and messages on this screen depending on whether you have installed a blank database or used the database templates with the EM repository included.

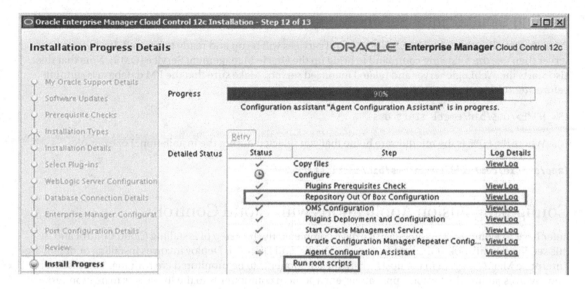

Figure 14-11. *Installation Progress Details screen*

If you look at the installation progress screen shown in Figure 14-11, you will notice that it is not creating the repository again since it has already detected that the database was created using the EM repository template. If you used a general-purpose database template then you may see a Repository Configuration message while in this case the task name changes to Repository Out of Box Configuration. You may also see a task called MDS Schema Configuration in the case of a blank database. Pre-configured databases skip this step. Once the installation is complete, proceed to the Installation Summary screen, as shown in Figure 14-12.

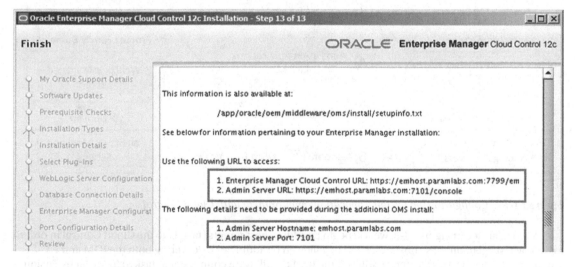

Figure 14-12. *EM Cloud Control installation Summary*

The post-installation summary screen shows the important URLs for accessing Cloud Control interface as well as the local WebLogic administration server URL for managing the services.

Starting Cloud Control Services

Once the installation is complete, Cloud Control services will be up and ready to be used. If you restart the server then use the following command to bring up the Oracle Management Service (OMS). Note that this also starts the WebLogic server and related managed servers. Make sure that the EM database is running before attempting to start OMS.

`<MW_HOME>/oms/bin/emctl start oms`

Where `MW_HOME` is the middleware home that you selected during the installation. For example:

/app/oracle/oem/middleware/oms/bin/emctl start oms

Configuring Fusion Applications with Cloud Control

Refer back to Figure 14-2. At this stage we have completed the first step of installing Cloud Control and in this section we will look at the next two steps—Deploy and Discover. Deploy involves installing or deploying Enterprise Manager agent in the hosts where the components to be monitored are running. The Discover step involves adding the Fusion Applications environment components to the list targets to be monitored.

Figure 14-13 shows a summary of tasks involved in the Deploy and Discover stages.

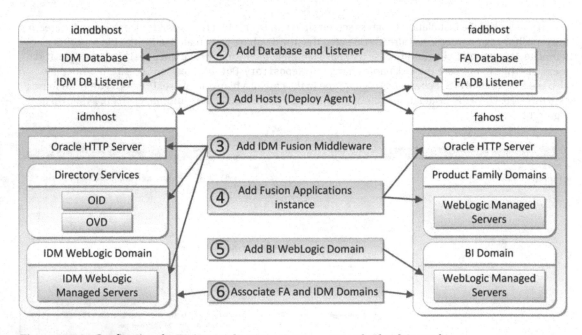

Figure 14-13. *Configuring the Fusion Applications environment with Cloud Control*

As you can see in Figure 14-3, we will begin by adding host targets (task 1) to the Cloud Control in order to deploy EM agent on these hosts. This will be followed by adding or discovering both the IDM and FA database instances (task 2). Later we will add the IDM middleware components (task 3) followed by Fusion Applications instance (task 4). Since BI-related components are not automatically detected as part of the Fusion Applications instance discovery, we will add those later (task 5). At the end, we will associate all these components with Fusion Applications instance in order to manage them as single group (task 6). Let's look at these tasks in the mentioned order, starting with the agent deployment.

Deploying Agent on Hosts

Since this chapter is dedicated to Fusion Applications monitoring, we will only look at those functionalities of Cloud Control that are required to set up the monitoring consoles. In order to deploy the agents on the hosts to be monitored, we will add all the hosts in our Fusion Applications environment in Cloud Control.

Click on the Setup menu in the Global area and then choose the Add Target ➤ Add Targets Manually menu item. This will open the Add Host Targets screen, as shown in Figure 14-14.

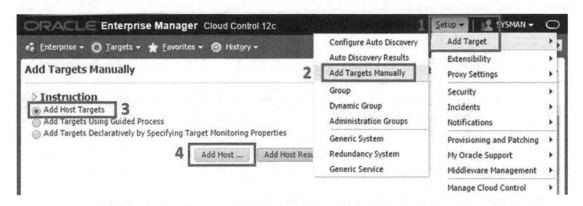

Figure 14-14. *Add Host Targets*

Here we have three options to choose from. For adding the host we will select the first option called Add Host Targets. Once you click the Add Host button, it will launch the Host Details screen, as shown in Figure 14-15.

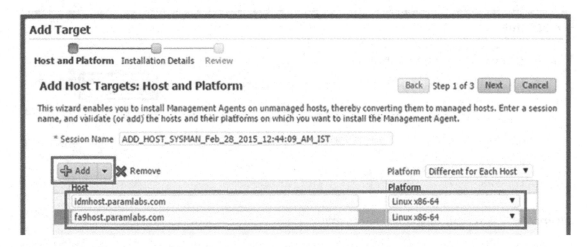

Figure 14-15. *Adding host details*

Add all the hosts to your selected topologies where Identity Management or Fusion Applications components are configured to run. Also specify the operating system for each host. We added two hosts in this example with the Linux x86-64 platform. You can choose Same for All Hosts from the combo box above this table in order to avoid specifying the same platform again for each host. Next it displays the agent installation details screen, as shown in Figure 14-16.

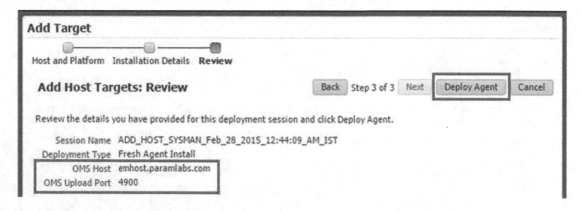

Add Target

Host and Platform   **Installation Details**   Review

Add Host Targets: Installation Details   [Back] Step 2 of 3 [Next] [Cancel]

On this screen, select each row from the following table and provide the installation details in the Installation Details section.

▷ **Deployment Type: Fresh Agent Install**

Platform	Agent Software Version	Hosts	Mandatory Inputs
Linux x86-64	12.1.0.4.0	idmhost.paramlabs.com, fa9host.paramlabs.com	

Linux x86-64: Agent Installation Details

* Installation Base Directory	/app/oracle/emagentHome
* Instance Directory	/app/oracle/emagentHome/agent_inst
* Named Credential	NC_HOST_2015-02-28-004952(SYSMAN) ▼ ⊕ ◄——— **Click here to add host credentials**
Privileged Delegation Setting	/usr/bin/sudo -u %RUNAS% %COMMAND%
Port	3872

Figure 14-16. *Agent installation details*

It is recommended to keep local file system path for agent installation and instance directories. Enter the credentials to log in to the host in order to install the agent. Although it requires you to enter any user with root or sudo privileges, you may specify a regular user as well. in the next screens, we will see the impact of the same and a workaround as well. The default port for agent is 3872 and you can change this if required. Make sure that network firewall rule to allow this port from OMS server to this host is created. Once you click Next, the next screen will display the summary, as shown in Figure 14-17.

Add Target

Host and Platform   Installation Details   **Review**

Add Host Targets: Review   [Back] Step 3 of 3 [Next] [Deploy Agent] [Cancel]

Review the details you have provided for this deployment session and click Deploy Agent.

Session Name   ADD_HOST_SYSMAN_Feb_28_2015_12:44:09_AM_IST
Deployment Type   Fresh Agent Install
OMS Host   emhost.paramlabs.com
OMS Upload Port   4900

Figure 14-17. *Add Hosts Targets Summary screen*

Make sure that the OMS upload port (default value 4900) from the host where the agent is being installed to the OMS server is also allowed in the network firewall. Review the host details and click Deploy Agent to proceed.

The agent installation is completed in three steps for each host, namely initialization, remote prerequisite check, and agent deployment, as shown in Figure 14-18. Each phase must complete on each host before the next phase starts.

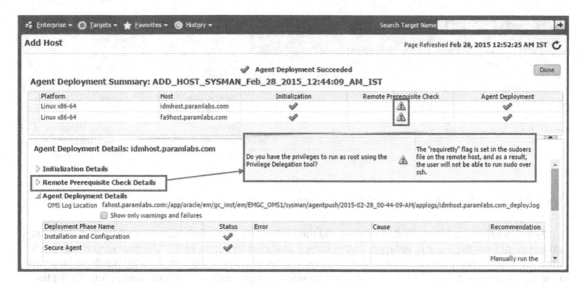

Figure 14-18. *Post-deployment summary*

If you have chosen to use a non-root privilege user for installation then you may see warning messages in between related to the user privileges. You may ignore them. But once the agent deployment is complete, it may prompt you to run the root.sh script from the following location.

```
<EMAgent_Home>/core/12.1.0.4.0/root.sh
```

This concludes the Deploy phase from the list of phases that we have seen in Figure 14-2. We will now move on to the Discover phase. Note that we can use Auto Discovery option to discover all the configured services on each host automatically but since Fusion Applications is a complex environment and quite less prone to frequent infrastructure changes, it is strongly recommended by Oracle that you use manual discovery for Fusion Applications components.

Adding Databases and Listeners

We must add Identity Management as well as the Fusion Applications transaction database in Cloud Control in order to monitor both using a single interface. Let's add the Identity Management database and listener first. Navigate to Setup ➤ Add Target ➤ Add Targets Manually to launch the same screen that we used for adding hosts, as shown in Figure 14-19.

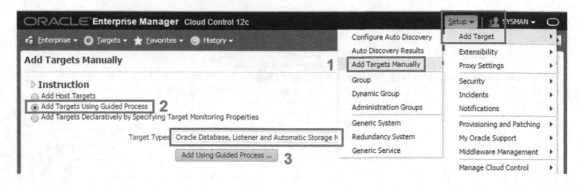

Figure 14-19. Adding the database and listener manaully

Select Add Targets Using Guided Process and then select Oracle database, listener, and automatic storage management from the list of target types in this screen, as shown in Figure 14-19. The next screen will require only a hostname, where the database and listener need to be discovered. Specify the IDM database hostname in the next screen and click Next. The wizard will initiate the target discovery process and eventually list the detected database (idmdb) and listener on the specified host, as shown in Figure 14-20.

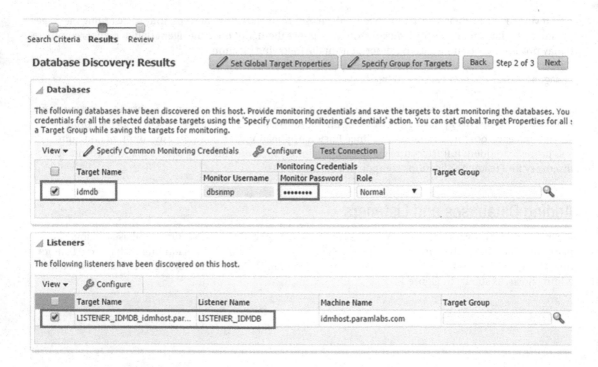

Figure 14-20. IDM database discovery

Select listener as well as database in this screen, enter the password for the dbsnmp user, and then click Next. The last screen will display the summary of targets being added. Review the summary and click Save to add the IDM database and listener.

Perform the same steps for the Fusion Applications transaction database (fusiondb) as well. Figure 14-21 shows the similar screen for the Fusion Applications database. The steps remain the same.

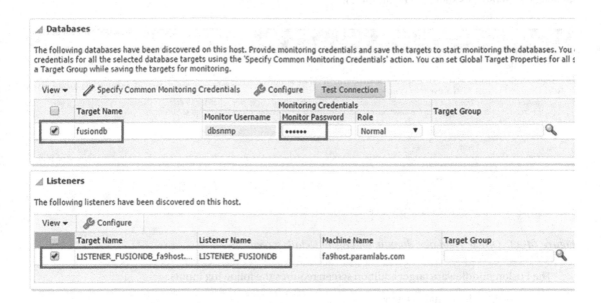

Figure 14-21. *Fusion Applications transaction database discovery*

Adding Identity Management Fusion Middleware Components

The next discovery phase task is to add a complete IDM middleware stack. Note that Fusion Middleware/ WebLogic domain and Fusion Applications instances are specialized components that can be discovered using dedicated discovery methods instead of going through the method that you followed for hosts or databases. However, both of these methods work just fine.

From any page of Cloud Control, choose Targets ➤ Middleware in the Global area menu. This will open the Fusion Middleware Summary page shown in Figure 14-22. We will look at this screen in detail once we have discovered all the required components.

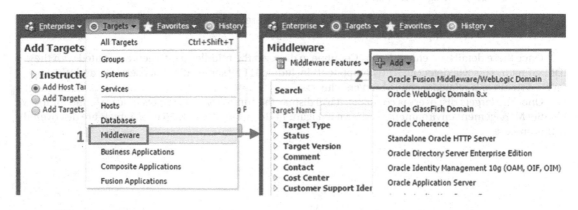

Figure 14-22. *Add an Oracle Fusion middleware target*

Choose Add ➤ Oracle Fusion Middleware/WebLogic domain menu item from the top of the page to add a new middleware target using dedicated discovery process. This will bring up the Fusion middleware details input screen, as shown in Figure 14-23.

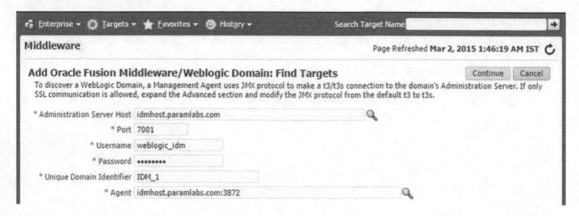

Figure 14-23. Oracle WebLogic domain and Agent Details screen

The Fusion middleware target addition screen requires the following inputs:

- WebLogic Domain Details

    - *Administration Server Host*: Enter the hostname of the server that contains the IDM domain administration server.

    - *Administration Server Port*: Enter the Administration Server port. The default value is 7001.

    - *WebLogic Administration Username and Password*: Enter the credentials for the IDM domain administration user. The IDM provisioning process has a default username as `weblogic_idm`.

    - *Unique Domain Identifier*: Enter any unique name to identify this target in the list of middleware targets in the future. IDM_1 is an appropriate identifier.

- Existing EM Agent Details

    - *Agent*: Enter the agent details in the `<hostname>:<agent port>` format. For example, `idmhost.paramlabs.com:3872`.

Once these details are entered, click Continue to discover the middleware targets associated with the IDM domain. This will detect all IDM components including HTTP server, directory services, and WebLogic server domain and related managed servers/clusters.

Once the targets discovery is complete, it will display the summary of all targets that are found for the Identity Management environment, as shown in Figure 14-24. Approximately 55 to 65 targets are discovered in this process.

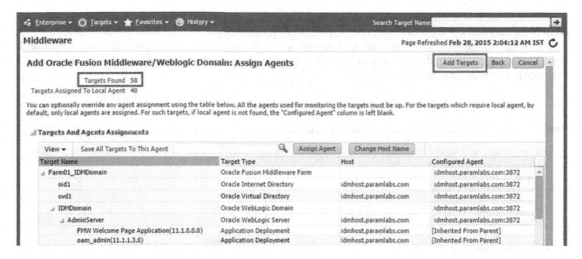

Figure 14-24. Middleware targets discovery summary

Review the summary, modify the agent or host details if required, and click Add Targets to save these targets in Cloud Control. This concludes the Identity Management middleware discovery step.

Run Diagnostic Pre-Checks for Fusion Applications

The last step in the discovery process is adding a Fusion Applications Instance. This includes all Fusion Applications product families, the corresponding WebLogic domains, and HTTP Server. Before we proceed with the Fusion Applications instance discovery, we must run diagnostic pre-checks to make sure that the targets discovery and addition will be smooth later. This is optional but highly recommended in order to prevent partial completion of the Fusion Applications instance discovery.

Launch the Fusion Applications Target Management Best Practices page by navigating to the Targets ➤ Fusion Applications ➤ Fusion Applications Features ➤ Target Management Best Practices menu link, as shown in Figure 14-25.

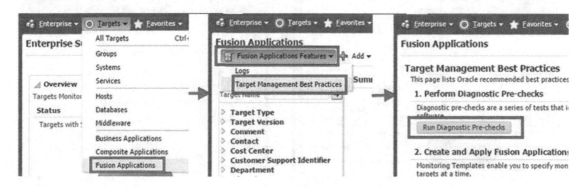

Figure 14-25. Invoking the Fusion Applications diagnostic pre-chceks

On the Target Management Best Practices page, click on the Run Diagnostic Pre-Checks button to launch the diagnostic tests. In the next screen, you will be prompted to enter the administration server details. Make sure to enter the Fusion setup WebLogic server domain CommonDomain details in the screen and it will automatically populate the complete infrastructure details through the same. Figure 14-26 shows an example result of the diagnostic pre-checks.

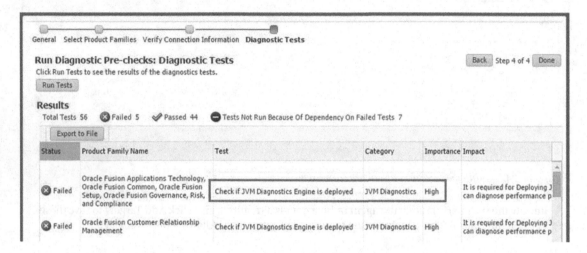

Figure 14-26. *Running diagnostics pre-checks*

As you can see, it suggests that you check if JVM diagnostics engine is deployed. Since the importance level for this test is high, we must fix this before proceeding with the Fusion Applications instance discovery. Since the JVM diagnostics engine is required to diagnose JVM related performance issues and as an Administrator you may use this functionality often, we will deploy it on the OMS server. As shown in Figure 14-27, navigate to Setup ➤ Middleware Management ➤ Application Performance Management first.

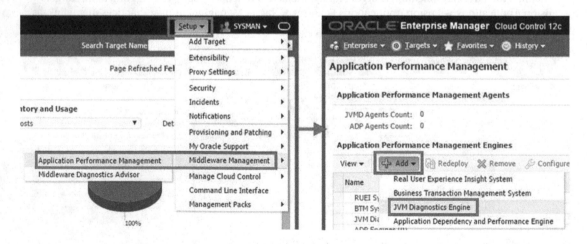

Figure 14-27. *Launching JVM diagnostics engine deployment page*

On the Application Performance Management page, choose the Add ➤ JVM Diagnostics Engine menu item to initiate the deployment process. As you can see in Figure 14-28, in the next screen you need to enter the host credential for the OMS Server as well as the WebLogic administration user credentials for the Cloud Control domain that you selected during installation in Figure 14-9.

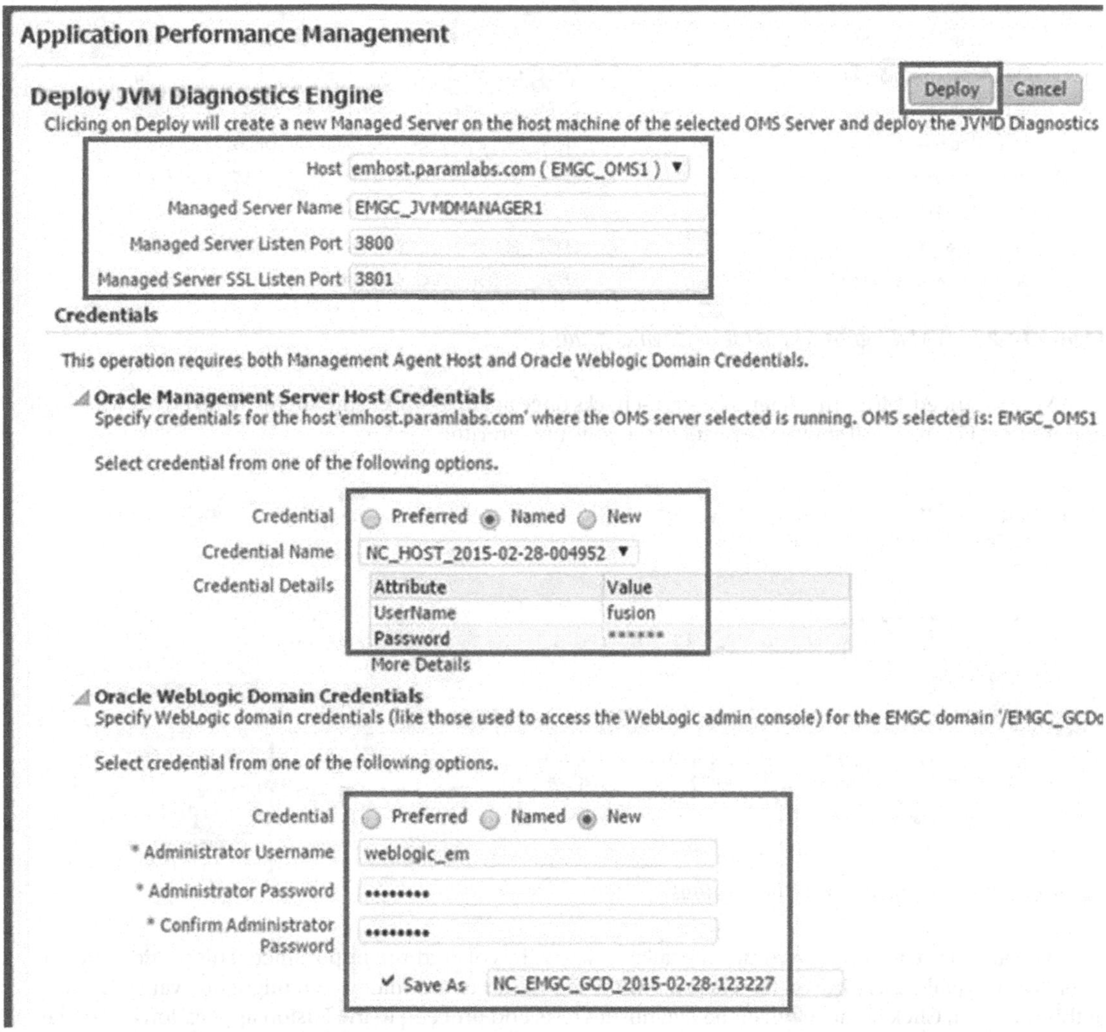

Figure 14-28. *Deploying the JVM diagnostics engine*

The screen displays the managed server name that will be created (the default name is EMGC_JVMDMANAGER1) as well as the listen ports that will be configured for this managed server. Click the Deploy button to create the new managed server and start the deployment of the JVM diagnostics engine. Now the screen will now display a link pointing to the deployment job in Cloud Control and you can monitor the status of the deployment job until it completes successfully. Figure 14-29 shows the successful deployment of the JVM diagnostics engine on the OMS server.

Name	Targets	Status
▽ Execution: /EMGC_GCDomain/GCDomain/EMGC_OMS1	/EMGC_GCDomain/GCDomain/EMGC_OMS1	Succeeded
Previous		
Step: Create Stage Directory	/EMGC_GCDomain/GCDomain/EMGC_OMS1	Succeeded
Step: Copy JVMD Engine Zip file	/EMGC_GCDomain/GCDomain/EMGC_OMS1	Succeeded
Step: Copy Deployment Scripts zip	/EMGC_GCDomain/GCDomain/EMGC_OMS1	Succeeded
Step: Unzipping diagnostic zip file	/EMGC_GCDomain/GCDomain/EMGC_OMS1	Succeeded
Step: Run Prerequisite Checks	/EMGC_GCDomain/GCDomain/EMGC_OMS1	Succeeded
Step: Repackage policy	/EMGC_GCDomain/GCDomain/EMGC_OMS1	Succeeded
Step: Deploy JVMD Engine	/EMGC_GCDomain/GCDomain/EMGC_OMS1	Succeeded
Step: Checking Status		Succeeded
Step: Cleanup	/EMGC_GCDomain/GCDomain/EMGC_OMS1	Succeeded
Step: Refresh targeted WebLogic domain	/EMGC_GCDomain/GCDomain	Succeeded

Figure 14-29. *JVM diagnostics engine deployment status*

Now you need to run the diagnostics pre-checks once again to make sure there are no errors with high importance. Figure 14-30 shows the result of the tests upon rerun.

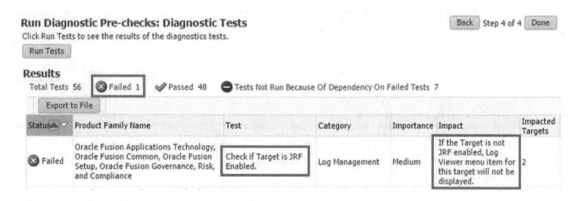

Figure 14-30. *Diagnostics pre-check results*

As you can see now we have only one failed test which is of medium importance. This particular error is related to enabling the JRF on targets to allow the log viewer functionality. You might not want to fix it at this moment. Click Done to finish the diagnostics tests and proceed to the Fusion applications instance discovery using Cloud Control.

Adding Fusion Applications Instance

You should now be able to add the Fusion Applications instance and all related components in Enterprise Manager Cloud Control. As mentioned earlier, you must have the Fusion Applications Application management pack (plugin) installed in order to manage Fusion Applications components using Cloud Control. If you have Fusion Applications plugin deployed in Cloud Control then you will see additional link called Fusion Applications under the Targets menu in the Global area, as shown in Figure 14-31.

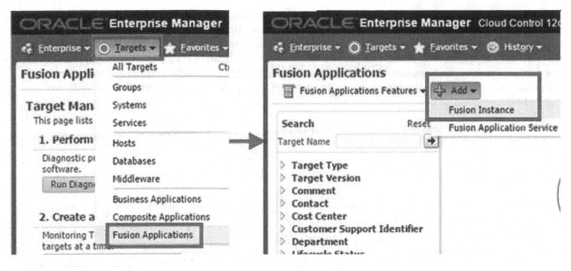

Figure 14-31. Navigating to the Add Fusion Applications instance screen

---

■ **Tip** If you missed adding this plug-in earlier, you can install it using the *Setup* ➤ *Extensibility* ➤ *Plugins* page. Choose *Deploy On* ➤ *Management Servers* and then select *Add* ➤ *Fusion Applications* on the next page to deploy the applications management pack for Fusion Applications.

Choose Targets ➤ Fusion Applications to navigate to the Fusion Applications instance summary screen. Now choose Add ➤ Fusion instance, as shown in Figure 14-31, to start the instance discovery process. The first screen for adding a Fusion Applications instance requires you to enter the details of Administration Server of CommonDomain, as shown in Figure 14-32. This is because it can detect the complete topology of your Fusion Applications instance by connecting to the CommonDomain and then discover each product family and its corresponding WebLogic domains.

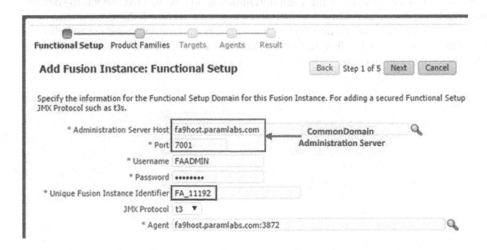

Figure 14-32. Specify Common Domain Admin Server details

Assign a unique identifier for the Fusion Applications instance to be added. If you are planning to monitor multiple Fusion Applications instances later, make sure to use an appropriate naming convention. Once you click Next it will discover all the product families in your Fusion Applications environment and show the list for your review. At the same time it also detects the already configured Fusion Applications transaction database and associates it with the instance being added. Click Next again to confirm or modify the details of each product domain as well as the assigned EM agents on the respective hosts, as shown in Figure 14-33.

Add Fusion Instance: Targets

Back Step 3 of 5 Next Cancel

To find the targets for the product families you selected, enter the information for each product family.

Product Family Name	Discovery Status	Administration Server Host	Port	JMX Protocol		Username	Password	Agent
Oracle Fusion Applications Technology, Oracle Fusion Common, Oracle Fusion Setup, Oracle Fusion Governance, Risk, and Compliance	Newly Discovered	fa9host.paramlabs.com	7001	t3	▼	FAADMIN	••••••	fa9host.param
Oracle Fusion Customer Relationship Management	Newly Discovered	fa9host.paramlabs.com	9001	t3	▼	FAADMIN	••••••	fa9host.param
Oracle Fusion Financials, Oracle Fusion Financials and Supply Chain Management	Newly Discovered	fa9host.paramlabs.com	7401	t3	▼	FAADMIN	••••••	fa9host.param
Oracle Fusion Human Capital Management	Newly Discovered	fa9host.paramlabs.com	9401	t3	▼	FAADMIN	••••••	fa9host.param

Figure 14-33. Newly discovered Fusion Applications product families

Ideally you will not need to make any changes in this screen unless the port details of the product family domain administration servers are not correct or the agent port information has changed. Review the details and click Next to start the target discovery process. It will display a pop-up screen with the target discovery status. Once the targets for each product family domain are discovered, review the generated list and click Next to save the details in Cloud Control. The final screen will show you a summary of all added targets for each product family, as shown in Figure 14-34.

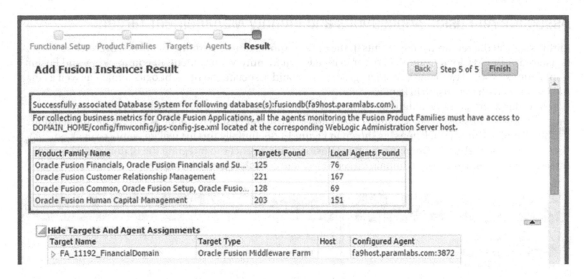

Figure 14-34. *Add Fusion instance completion summary*

Add Business Intelligence Components

Note that adding Fusion Applications instance discovers all product family domains except the Oracle Business Intelligence domain. Hence we must manually discover and add the BI domain in Cloud Control. The procedure to add the BI domain is similar to what we followed for the IDM domain. Choose Targets ➤ Middleware ➤ Add ➤ Oracle Fusion Middleware/WebLogic Domain to start the BI domain discovery. Make sure to provide the BI domain administration server host and port details, as shown in Figure 14-35, to start the BI domain discovery. Assign a unique identifier to easily locate this domain for future management.

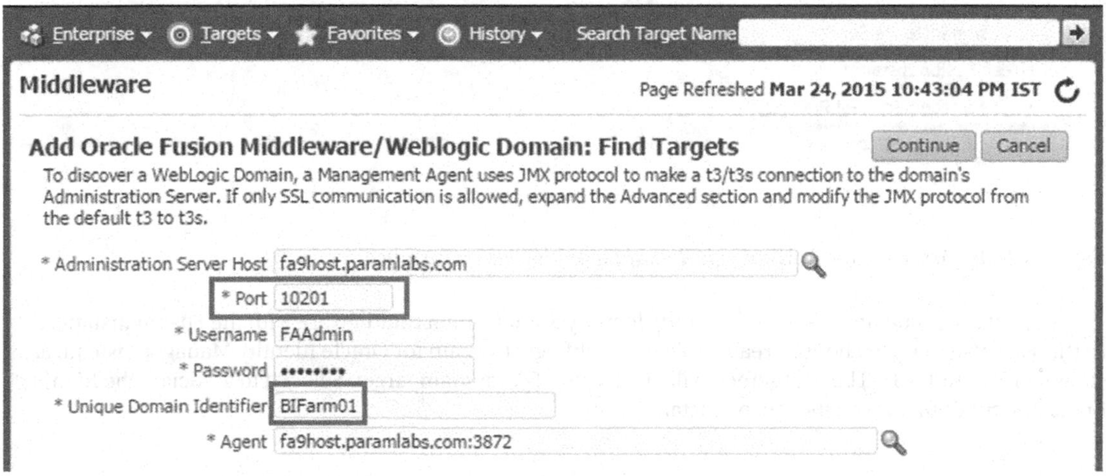

Enterprise ▾ ⊙ **Targets** ▾ ⭐ **Favorites** ▾ ⊙ **History** ▾   Search Target Name ⟶

Middleware

Page Refreshed **Mar 24, 2015 10:43:04 PM IST** ↻

Add Oracle Fusion Middleware/Weblogic Domain: Find Targets

Continue   Cancel

To discover a WebLogic Domain, a Management Agent uses JMX protocol to make a t3/t3s connection to the domain's Administration Server. If only SSL communication is allowed, expand the Advanced section and modify the JMX protocol from the default t3 to t3s.

* Administration Server Host fa9host.paramlabs.com

* Port 10201

* Username FAAdmin

* Password ••••••••

* Unique Domain Identifier BIFarm01

* Agent fa9host.paramlabs.com:3872

Figure 14-35. *Discover BI WebLogic domain*

Associate All Fusion Applications and Identity Management Targets

At this stage all the required components in the Fusion Applications environment are discovered and registered with EM Cloud Control. In order to manage all Identity Management, BI components, and Fusion Applications product domains as a single group, we should associate the BI WebLogic domain as well as the IDM domain with the Fusion instance.

In order to create associations, open the Fusion instance homepage by choosing Targets ➤ Fusion Applications ➤ <Fusion instance name>. Now choose the menu Fusion Instance ➤ Additional Associations to open list of existing associations, as shown in Figure 14-36. Initially this list will be empty so click on Create ➤ Oracle WebLogic Domain for Oracle Business Intelligences to integrate the BI domain. The next screen will show the existing BI domain target. Select it to complete the association.

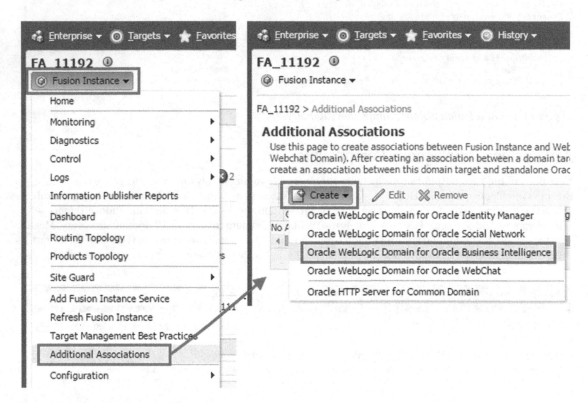

Figure 14-36. *Associate the BI WebLogic domain with the Fusion instance*

Repeat this same process for Associating Identity Management middleware with the Fusion instance. In this case you need to choose Create ➤ Oracle WebLogic Domain for Oracle Identity Manager instead, as shown in Figure 14-37. The next screen will display the IDM domain target. Select it to associate the Identity Management domain with the Fusion instance.

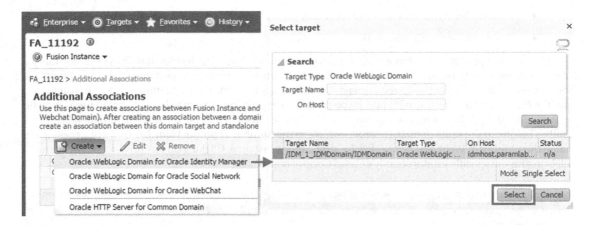

Figure 14-37. *Associate the IDM WebLogic domain with the Fusion instance*

This concludes the configuration of Fusion Applications with Cloud Control and we will move on to monitoring activities.

Monitoring the Fusion Applications Environment

In this section, we will look at monitoring of the complete technology stack and application components of Fusion Applications environment. We will look at the Cloud Control interface only for monitoring activities, which is the recommended method by Oracle. However, most of the monitoring activities can be done through the default management interfaces like Fusion Applications control or Fusion middleware control but it becomes cumbersome to monitor the environment by keeping a number of consoles open at the same time. We will also see how we can navigate to homepages that are very similar to the Fusion Applications Control as well as Fusion middleware control for each product family from Cloud Control.

Oracle's new generation of applications as well as Enterprise Manager work on the principles of management by exception, which means while monitoring you are more interested in knowing the exception conditions instead of those components that are working as expected. So the focus is always on the exception conditions, including unavailability, performance issues, and so on. This also instantaneously allows you to initiate troubleshooting and diagnosing activities right from the monitoring dashboards.

Understanding the Fusion Applications Product Family Homepage

Before we navigate to the monitoring dashboards, let's understand the various homepages in Cloud Control. Each of these represent one aspect of Fusion Applications monitoring. These homepages are enormously useful, especially for troubleshooting application performance issues. Since most of the time troubleshooting is invoked or preceded by monitoring, it remains equally useful while proactively identifying any underlying issues with the environment. The following are the main dimensions of monitoring Fusion Applications environment. The first three homepages are related to Fusion Applications while the remaining ones are related to Fusion middleware.

- Product Family
- Product
- Application Deployment

- Fusion Middleware for the Product Family

- WebLogic Server Cluster or Managed Server

The Fusion Applications Summary screen has two major sections. The top section shows the summary inventory of each component being monitored along with the version-based grouping of the components. The second main section of the screen displays the Fusion Applications product families in a tree structure with the Fusion instance as the root node. If you have more than one instance being monitored then you will see a similar collapsible tree for each instance. As you can see in Figure 14-38, the three highlighted product families belong to the same domain (CommonDomain), so the number of product families may not necessarily match the number of WebLogic servers for the applications instance. Clicking on any product family name will bring up the specific product family's Cloud Control homepage.

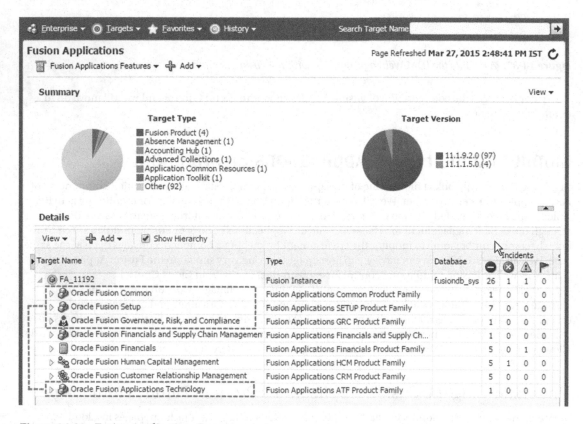

Figure 14-38. *Fusion Applications Summary screen*

Since the product family homepage contains various sections and the layout is customizable as well, let's see a simplified generic view of a product family homepage, which is shown in Figure 14-39.

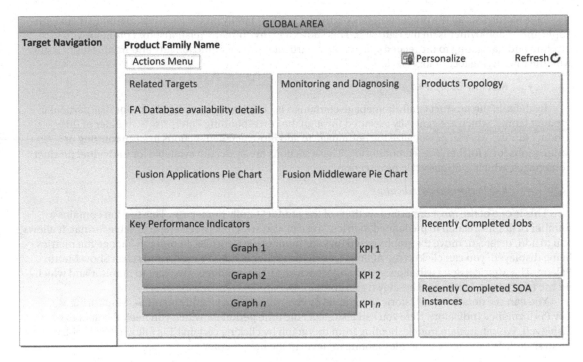

Figure 14-39. Generic view of Fusion Applications product family homepage

The product family homepage looks very similar to the Fusion Applications control homepage, as it is intended to perform the identical function of a product family's EM Fusion Applications control. As you can see in Figure 14-39, this homepage contains a multi-column view that can be personalized to two columns, three columns, or any other layout based on your requirements. We will discuss personalization in the next section. Figure 14-39 shows some of the default regions in this homepage but depending on your personalization you may have more or fewer sections. Let's explore the default sections in this page.

- *Fusion Applications and Middleware Availability Pie Charts*

This is the first region that you will notice in this page. It provides a quick summary of the number of components that are down or having issues at the moment. As you know, Fusion Applications monitoring works on principles of management by exception, so that you always know which components are down or unavailable at any point in time. This region contains two pie charts—Fusion Applications and Fusion middleware charts. The Fusion Applications chart displays the availability of application deployments and the second chart shows the availability of underlying WebLogic servers. Both of these pie charts should show up green, which means all components are up and running. In case you see any red areas in the chart, you may immediately want to navigate to the related homepage and bring those components up or troubleshoot the issues.

- *Monitoring and Diagnosing*

While these pie charts display the availability of components at any given time, the Monitoring and Diagnosing section contains the number of recent critical errors or warnings that are marked as incidents. This gives you an indication that an issue requires your attention. You can drill down to the incidents and troubleshoot if the issue still persists or if it was historical one.

- *Products and Topology*

This region lists all the products in this particular product family on the left while mapping them with applications deployments on the right side. This shows a many-to-many relationship. This helps you in locating and navigating to the related clusters for a particular product functionality and troubleshoot issues with the underlying technology stack.

- *Recently Completed Jobs*

By default, the product family homepage contains a list of recently completed jobs for that particular product family, which are generally executed through the corresponding Enterprise Scheduler of this product family. You can personalize the homepage to add more detailed sections like top running or waiting jobs for a further level of monitoring. These sections are by default available for individual product homepages, which is discussed in next section.

- *Key Performance Indicators*

This is one of the most important sections of the product family homepage. This section contains a number of graphs related to predefined metrics. You can also switch between graph or table format. It allows you to add, delete, or move the graphs based on your monitoring priorities. In order to change the metrics being displayed, you can click on the Actions icon at the corner of the KPI region and select Show Metric Palette. The Metric Palette will allow you to choose which Fusion products you want to monitor and which metric for that product should be shown as a graph.

You can see detailed and historic KPI graphs by choosing Product Family menu ➤. Monitoring ➤ Key Performance Indicators. Here you can also select the time period for which you need the data to be displayed. We can initiate troubleshooting from this graph by clicking certain KPIs followed by Problem Analysis link. We will look at troubleshooting in detail in the next chapter.

- *Related Targets*

This area lists the summary of related targets like the Fusion Applications transaction database along with the database JDBC URL. It also allows you to navigate directly to the database monitoring home.

- *Recently Completed SOA Instances*

This section lists all the related SOA composites along with the number of completed executions of each SOA composite in the last 24 hours along with the response time in milliseconds.

- *Target Navigation*

The Regional area of the Fusion Applications related pages in Cloud Control contains the list of all available targets of the selected Fusion Applications product family. The Target navigation region allows you to navigate between various homepages, including Fusion Applications and middleware components. Figure 14-40 shows the breakup of the target navigation region in Cloud Control.

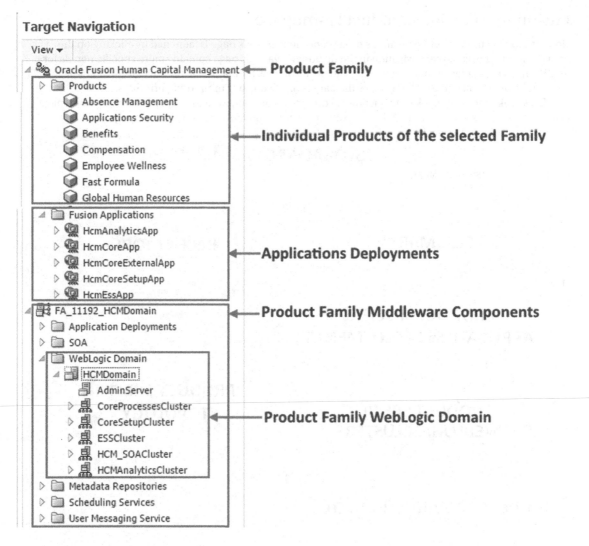

Figure 14-40. Target navigation region

As you can see in Figure 14-40, the Target Navigation panel contains two major sections. Note that these targets correspond to the selected product family only, not to the entire Fusion instance.

- Fusion Applications Targets
  - Products
  - Applications Deployments
- Fusion Middleware Targets

Clicking on a target from any of these sections will lead to the corresponding homepage. For example, clicking on Absence Management Product in the HCM product family will open the homepage for Absence Management Product. Similarly, clicking on the HCM domain middleware target name will launch Fusion Middleware Homepage for HCM. You will notice that the middleware homepage contains the same hierarchy as the classic Fusion middleware control homepage.

Fusion Applications Product Homepage

Now let's look at the Fusion Applications product homepage. This page is launched by clicking on the name of product from target navigation in the Regional area. This page contains more specific panels for monitoring a particular product availability and performance. Similar to the product family homepage, this also can be personalized to add or remove the panels based on your monitoring priorities.

Let's look at some of the key distinctions in this screen as compared to the product family homepage. Figure 14-41 shows the various regions in a generic Fusion Applications product homepage.

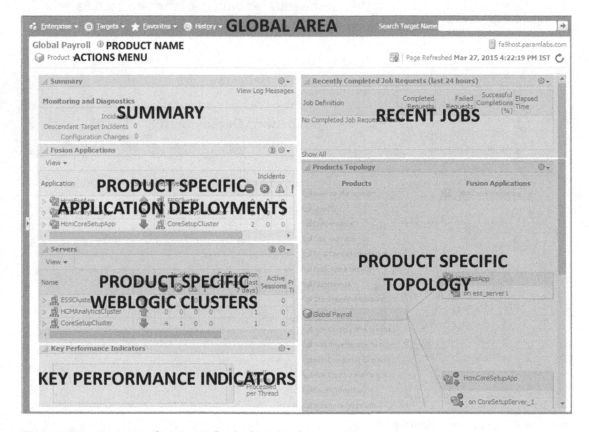

Figure 14-41. Fusion Applications individual product home in EM

You will notice that the topology section now contains a one-to-many relationship since on left side you see only the selected product. On the right side is the list of deployed applications that implement functionalities of the selected product along with the managed server name where the application has been deployed.

The default layout also includes availability and incidents details for each application included in the topology region as well as for each WebLogic cluster that hosts these applications. The benefit of these regions is that if you have issues with a specific functionality of the product, you can easily drill down to the managed server level and reduce the time required to troubleshoot.

Similar to the product family home, you can personalize the page layout for the product home as well. Once you click on the Personalize icon at the top, the page will offer various customization options, including changing the layout to one, two, or three columns. You can add or remove regions by clicking on the Add Content button, which will bring up the screen shown in Figure 14-42. You can select from the list of predefined regions based on your monitoring priority. For example, the default page offers a list of recently completed jobs but you may also want to see the top long running jobs as well.

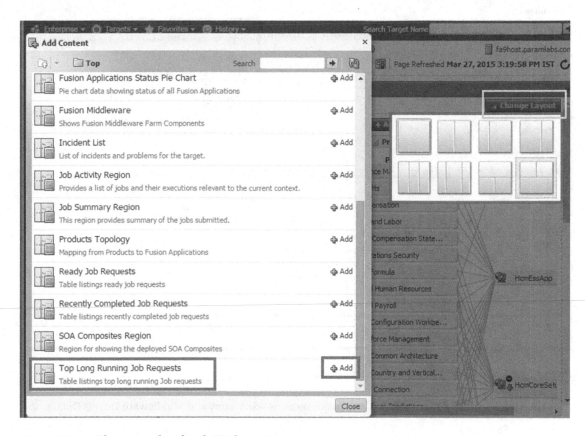

Figure 14-42. *Change product family EM home Layout*

Monitoring Fusion Middleware

In the previous section we looked at product family monitoring as well as product monitoring homepages, both of which are related to Applications monitoring. If you look at the Targets Navigation panel, you will notice the corresponding middleware target name in the lower section of the panel. If you look the targets tree closely from this node onward, then you will notice that this section matches the Fusion middleware control. So we can manage the Fusion middleware components related to this product family domain by navigating through these targets.

We can navigate to the Fusion middleware monitoring home either via any of the Fusion Applications homepages or directly using Cloud Control's middleware dashboard. The benefit of the middleware dashboard in Cloud Control is that you will get a consolidated summary of inventory and availability of all Fusion middleware domains in the environment. Click on Targets ➤ Middleware in any screen to launch the middleware summary page in Cloud Control, as shown in Figure 14-43.

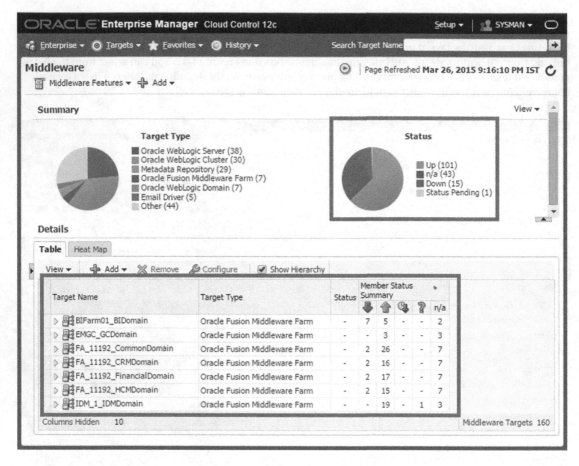

Figure 14-43. *Fusion middleware summary screen*

The Middleware summary page has two major sections—Summary and Middleware Targets Details.

- *Summary*

  - *Target Type*: This section shows a summary inventory of different Fusion middleware components registered with Cloud Control in the form of a pie chart. Clicking on any component name will filter the results in a details section to list only components with the selected type. This allows you to quickly check the status of a particular middleware component in all domains.

  - *Status*: This is very important summary pie chart that provides a quick summary of all middleware components grouped by their availability status. For example, you can click on the Down link to list only those components that are currently down or unavailable in the details section.

- *Middleware Details*: By default this section lists all the Fusion middleware farms, If you click on one, it will open the respective middleware homepage identical to Fusion middleware control. The data in the details section is populated based on the selection in the summary section and mainly used for navigating to other homepages.

Figure 14-44 shows an example of the IDM domain middleware farm homepage. We chose IDM middleware specifically so that you can visually compare the same screen of Identity Management Domain's EM Fusion middleware control homepage. The homepage shows the availability charts of the WebLogic clusters and managed servers along with the availability of application deployments on each of these clusters.

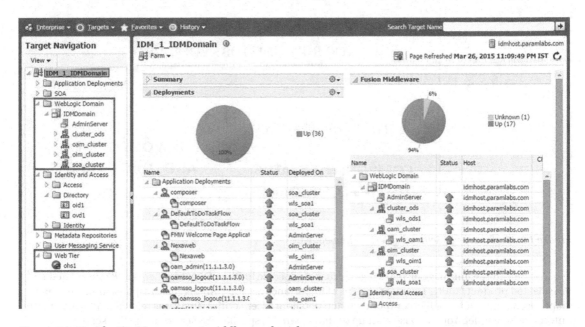

Figure 14-44. *Identity Management middleware farm home screen*

As you can see, you can monitor directory servers and web servers using this interface as they are already registered under the middleware farm. The same applies to Fusion Applications as well where you can monitor the HTTP server using the CommonDomain middleware homepage. You may navigate to any sub-sections of IDM middleware targets tree including WebLogic domain, Identity and Access, and Web Tier to monitor and troubleshoot issues specific to those components. As you saw in Chapter 12, you can start or stop individual managed servers or complete WebLogic domains using the actions menu on the top of each component's homepage.

If you are accessing the Fusion Applications middleware homepage then you may see additional Target group called Scheduling services which will open Oracle Enterprise Scheduler homepage for the product family from where it was invoked. We will look at this in next section. Note that web tier for Fusion Applications is only available through the CommonDomain homepage and not from any other product family homepage.

Monitoring Enterprise Scheduler

Monitoring Enterprise Scheduler is one of the most common tasks for every Fusion Applications Administrator as we constantly need to monitor the performance, pending jobs, and errors related to Scheduler services, which run most of the day-to-day critical reports. As we have seen earlier, Enterprise Scheduler replaces the Concurrent Manager of the Oracle E-Business Suite. If you were managing an EBS instance earlier, all those activities you performed on the Concurrent Manager apply to the Enterprise Scheduler. Each product family domain has a dedicated ESS (Enterprise Scheduler Service) managed server where the ESS application runs. You can launch the Scheduler Service homepage from the respective product family middleware Cloud Control home by expanding Scheduler Services under the middleware farm followed by the ESS cluster name. Figure 14-45 shows an example of Scheduler Service homepage.

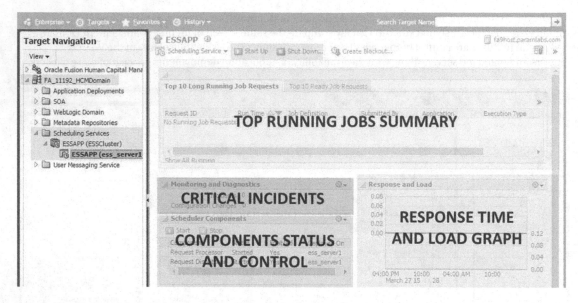

Figure 14-45. *Enterprise Scheduler Service homepage*

As you can see, this page displays regions that are specific for the ESS components and jobs related to the selected product family. The main regions of importance are top running jobs, response time and load graph, availability status of ESS components, and details of recent critical incidents related to this instance of Enterprise Scheduler. You may also start up or shut down this specific ESS service using this screen.

By looking at the response time and load graph you may easily infer if there are any performance issues with ESS. In that case you can launch the more detailed Performance Summary by choosing Scheduling Service ➤ Performance ➤ Service Summary. Figure 14-46 shows example of the Performance Summary page for ESS. Note that this screen is available for each application and middleware component by navigating to Component Menu ➤ Monitoring ➤ Performance Summary so this example applies to all other components as well.

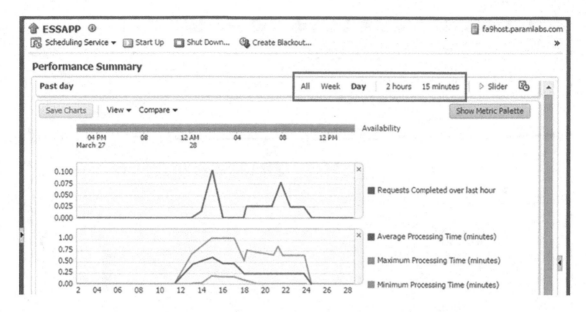

Figure 14-46. *Enterprise Scheduler Performance Summary*

The Performance Summary page for ESS displays default important metrics like the number of running requests, completed requests in the last hour, processing time, and so on. You can choose the time window for which you need the graph to be scaled. You can also choose different metrics by clicking on the Metric Palette.

Since troubleshooting is pretty much dependent on monitoring, we will continue to look at different aspects of Fusion Applications and Fusion Middleware monitoring in the next chapter as well. Let's move on to database monitoring through Cloud Control.

Monitoring a Database

Cloud Control provides all the functionalities provided by the EM database control in addition to a number of personalization options. The Database Administrators or Enterprise Monitoring team can keep the database consoles open to continuously monitor the database as well as database host performance, including currently running SQLs, jobs, and so on, in single dashboard. Since the Enterprise Manager Cloud Control manages all layers of Fusion Applications environment, you can easily navigate between database, application, directory, or web tiers to monitor and troubleshoot any spikes identified during day-to-day monitoring.

In order to view the Databases homepage in Cloud Control, navigate to Targets ➤ Databases. This page will display summary of all databases configured with Cloud Control, including IDM and FA transaction databases. It lists a summary of recent incidents, a database load map based on active sessions, top ADDM findings, recent jobs run status, and availability information of each database. This dashboards list both IDM and FA database status and availability details. You can click on any of these database names in order to manage or monitor them. Clicking on the database will open the Database homepage shown in Figure 14-47. You can relate this page to the EM database control home with enhanced navigation to most important functionalities directly from the menu in the top region.

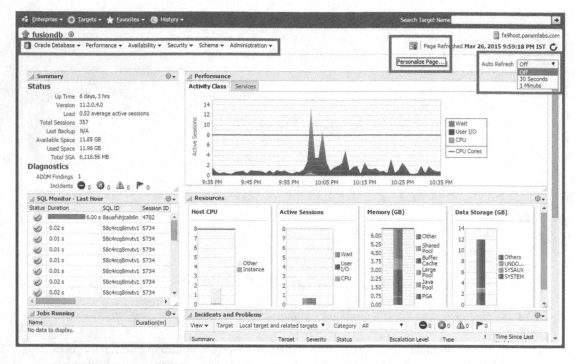

Figure 14-47. *Single Database home screen*

As shown in Figure 14-47, the Database homepage shows all the important regions that an administrator may be interested in, including a performance graph, host resources, active sessions, SQL monitoring, currently running jobs, and more. In addition to this it shows the summary of database including uptime, average number of active sessions, available free space, and so on, which may help you to take proactive steps. If you are keeping this console open for monitoring then it is recommended to turn on Auto Refresh in order to view the latest performance data. Use the Personalize Page icon to add or remove regions, change layout, and so on. This will bring up a similar screen in Figure 14-42 that you saw earlier.

Configuring Common Monitoring Features

In this section we will look at how to use some common features like e-mail notifications and blackouts for monitoring the Fusion Applications environment using Cloud Control. These features apply to Cloud Control in general and are not specifically related to Fusion Applications, so if you have an existing Cloud Control set up then you may already have these properties set.

Setting Up Notifications

In order to receive e-mail alerts you must configure the outgoing mail server for Cloud Control as a primary prerequisite. Make sure that access to the SMTP port of your mail server from Cloud Control Server is allowed through the firewall. In addition to this the mail server itself, allow your Cloud Control server to relay e-mails internally. To set the SMTP server, choose Setup ➤ Notifications ➤ Notification Methods, as shown in Figure 14-48, to open Notification Mail Server Setup screen.

Figure 14-48. Setting up notifications: mail server setup

Provide the details of the outgoing mail server, sender e-mail, SMTP server credentials, and so on and then click Test Mail Servers to make sure that the Details are correct and there is no blocking from the firewall or the mail server side.

Setting Up Administrator E-Mail Preferences

In the previous section, you saw how to set up outgoing e-mails and the sender details. Now you must configure the receiver e-mail address in order to make sure that the administrators can receive e-mail alerts. You can either configure the default administrator's e-mail address or create additional administrators for each target group and assign e-mail addresses to them. Figure 14-49 shows an example of setting up the default administrator's e-mail address for complete Cloud Control. This e-mail could be a generic e-mail account, individual e-mail account, or a group e-mail address (distribution list) for sending notifications to the monitoring team.

Figure 14-49. *Setting up administrator e-mail preferences*

In addition to an e-mail address, you can also select the default E-mail message type from the predefined types—long/short e-mail or pager message. Cloud Control has specific guidelines for these e-mail types and depending on the preference, for example, long e-mail format contains detailed HTML message with URLs, while the short e-mail and pager options limit the e-mail content to short limited characters with short text summary only.

■ **Note**   Enterprise Manager 12c Cloud Control has multiple tiers of configurations in order to receive granular notifications and avoid duplicate alerts. You must set up metric thresholds appropriately as well as create incident rules and rule sets to define when a notification should be sent.

Using EM Blackouts

Enterprise Manager receives target status updates from the EM agent installed on the hosts. So whenever you shut down or bounce any components, the agent will update the Cloud Control about temporary unavailability of targets. This creates inaccuracy in Cloud Control statistics since the scheduled maintenance is actually not an incident and this duration should be excluded from Cloud Control statistics. In order to achieve this you must create a blackout before any scheduled downtime of components. You can create a blackout at any level, including complete Fusion Instance, specific product family, product, or even a specific managed server. You can also schedule agent blackouts in advance for planned maintenance in the future to save time during actual downtime.

Cloud Control provides a large number of predefined blackout reasons for reporting purposes, but you can also create your own custom reasons based on organizational requirements. In order to create a custom reason, choose Monitoring ➤ Blackouts from any target's action menu. Click on the Manage Reasons link at the bottom of the Blackouts homepage. This will bring up Manage Reasons screen, as shown in Figure 14-50. Click Add Another Row followed by New Reason Title and click OK to save the new reason. In the example shown here, we have selected disaster recovery test as a reason since it is not in the predefined list of blackout reasons.

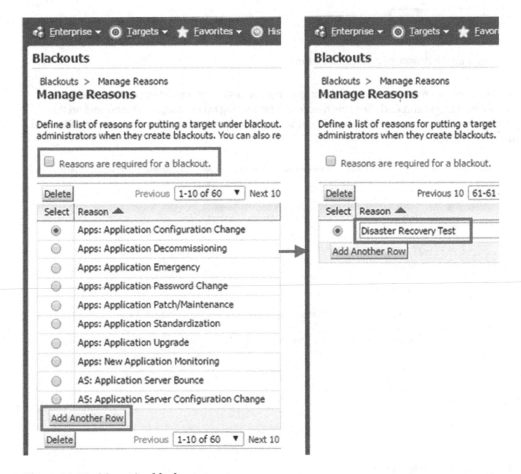

Figure 14-50. *Managing blackout reasons*

At times you may need to take an urgent downtime and may not have time to create an EM blackout or you may have forgotten to create one and then the retroactive blackout feature comes to the rescue. This feature allows you to create a blackout using a past date and duration to ignore the EM statistics for the selected target for the selected duration. By default, this feature is not enabled and we must enable it using the Retroactive Blackout Configuration link on the Blackouts homepage, as shown in Figure 14-51.

Figure 14-51. *Enabling the Retroactive Blackout feature*

Finally let's see how to create a blackout for a target or set of targets. You need to create a blackout before shutting down a target and end the same blackout after starting up the targets. Depending on the target that you are shutting down, choose Target Menu ➤ Control ➤ Create Blackout to start a new Blackout wizard, as shown in Figure 14-52.

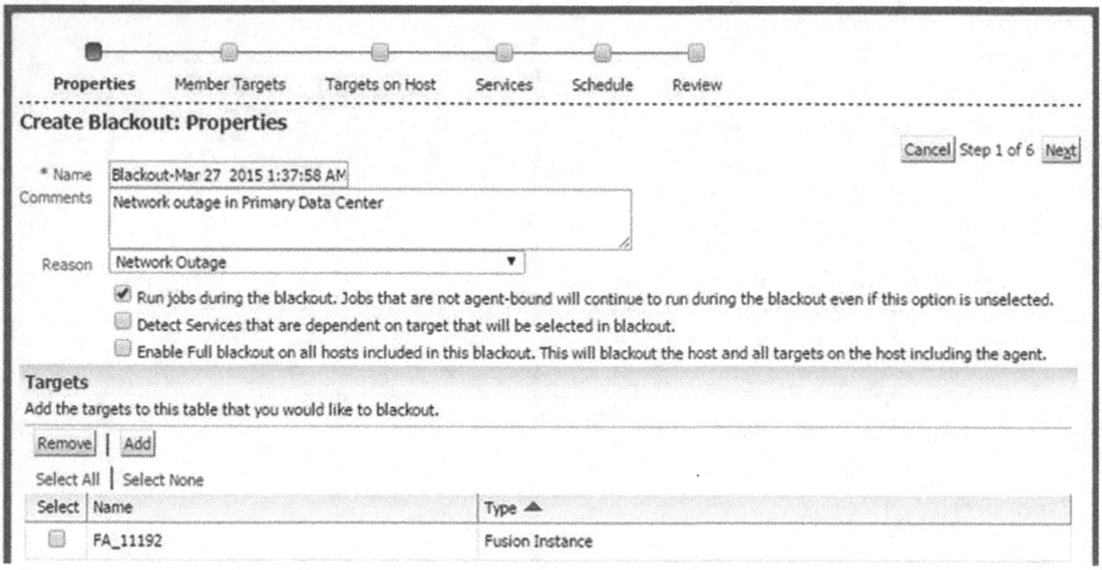

Figure 14-52. *Creating an EM blackout*

If you select the Reasons Are Required for a Blackout option then you must select Reason in this screen. Otherwise, it is recommended that you select an appropriate reason for reporting purposes. Make sure to end this blackout using the Control ➤ End Blackout link to make sure the EM data collection resumes for the selected target.

Summary

In this chapter you saw how to set up Oracle Enterprise Manager Cloud Control in order to effectively monitor and manage the Fusion Applications environment using a single unified interface. Later you saw how to monitor various components of Fusion Applications including Identity Management infrastructure, application components, web tiers, and databases. You also saw how Cloud Control compares to the traditional Enterprise Manager tools available with Fusion Applications and how you can leverage additional features of Cloud Control to replace the default tools with a single monitoring window. It is recommended you learn more about Cloud Control features in order to best utilize its advanced capabilities.

This chapter provided a platform for the upcoming troubleshooting and diagnosing administration activities. In the upcoming chapters, you will learn how to utilize the monitoring outcomes and alerts to troubleshoot issues with every layer of the Fusion Applications environment.

CHAPTER 15

■ ■ ■

Diagnosing and Troubleshooting

Every Enterprise system is prone to performance issues and errors despite best practices being employed. Having looked at Fusion Applications monitoring in the previous chapter, you may have an understanding of what conditions invoke a need for troubleshooting. Since Fusion Applications is a complex enterprise system with large number of components involved, troubleshooting Application-related issues includes a vast variety of techniques and starting points for performance diagnosis. Starting the troubleshooting with the most logical component is the key here. Proficiency in Fusion Applications troubleshooting may be developed over the period of time and once you have worked on a breadth of diagnostic tools, the time taken for effective diagnosis and problem resolution may reduce drastically.

Troubleshooting Tools and Features

In this section we look at some of the common tools and features of Fusion Applications that assist us in diagnosing and troubleshooting the performance issues and error conditions. We will begin with Fusion middleware-related important files and features. Later we move on to Fusion Applications-specific troubleshooting tools and best practices to be followed for agile problem solving.

Important Files Related to the Topology

If you were not involved during the initial provisioning of the Fusion Applications environment, then you may want to review the instance topology of the environment that you are going to administer and troubleshoot.

- *Provisioning Summary File*: The Provisioning wizard would have created an initial environment summary file at the same location as the response file. For example, /app/fusion/provisioning/bin/provisioning-<timestamp>.summary. You can review this summary file to get a quick understanding of the environment, including all domains, URLs, and so on. But if the environment topology had changed after initial installation, this file will no longer be relevant.

- *Domain Registry File*: The Fusion middleware base directory contains a file named domain-registry.xml that contains the list of WebLogic domains configured in the environment along with the location of the home directory for each domain. For example, /app/oracle/fusionapps/domain-registry.xml for Fusion Applications nodes and /app/oracle/products/app/domain-registry.xml for IDM nodes.

© Tushar Thakker 2015
T. Thakker, *Pro Oracle Fusion Applications*, DOI 10.1007/978-1-4842-0983-7_15

- *Domain Configuration File*: Another important file is `config.xml`, which contains the configuration details for each domain. You can see the list of ports, including the Administration server port for the domain in order to log in to the Administration console. This is located at `<Domain_Home>/config/config.xml` for each of the domains.

- *Web Tier Virtual Host Configuration Files*: Depending on whether you have selected name-based, IP-based, or port-based virtual host mode, you need to know the virtual host and port details for each product family in order to access certain URLs. This information is stored in HTTP port mapping and the redirection files located at `<OHS_INST_TOP>/config/OHS/ohs1/moduleconf/FusionVirtualHost_<pf>.conf`, where pf refers to the product family. For example, `/app/oracle/instance/CommonDomain_webtier/config/OHS/ohs1/moduleconf/FusionVirtualHost_hcm.conf`.

Important Fusion Middleware Log Files

You may need to access various log files while troubleshooting and diagnosing various issues, errors, and crashes, including while starting up the environment. The following are some of the important log files that you may access when troubleshooting. We will look at application logging in next sections.

1. *WebLogic server logs and output files*

    - *Domain Log*: The overall domain log file `<DomainName>.log` and the Administration Server log file `AdminServer.log` are created at `<Domain_Home>/servers/AdminServer/logs`.

    - *Managed server log*: The WebLogic server container log file `<ManagedServer_name>.log` for each managed server is created at `<Domain_Home>/servers/<ManagedServer_name>/logs`.

    - *Standard output*: For each managed server, the standard output and errors are redirected to a file named `<ManagedServer_name>.out`, which is located in the same directory as the log file.

    - *Diagnostic log*: Application diagnostics are stored in log file named `<ManagedServer_name>-diagnostic.log` for each WebLogic server and saved along with log and output files at same location.

2. *BI-server related log files*

    - *BI server OPMN log file*: The OPMN related log files for the BI server are located at `<APPLICATIONS_CONFIG>/BIInstance/diagnostics/log/OPMN/opmn`.

    - *BI server components log files*: The log files for the BI server components are located at `<APPLICATIONS_CONFIG>/BIInstance/diagnostics/logs/<process_type>/<Component_name>`. For example, the log files for the BI server component are stored at `/app/oracle/instance/BIInstance/diagnostics/logs/OracleBIServerComponent/coreapplication_obis1`.

3.   *Oracle HTTP server related log files*

- *OHS Server OPMN log files*: The OPMN related log files for Oracle HTTP server are located at `<OHS_INSTANCE_HOME>/diagnostics/logs/OPMN/opmn`. These files can be used to troubleshoot issues specific to the OPMN configuration.

- *OHS server log files*: The OHS server log file is located at `<OHS_INSTANCE_HOME>/diagnostics/logs/`.

- *Access log*: The OHS Server access log file (`access.log`) is created in the same location as the OHS server log file. This helps in troubleshooting the incoming requests to the web server along with source IPs and return code.

- *WebGate process file logger*: The WebGate process logger is located in the same directory and named `oblog.log`. It may help troubleshoot WebGate specific errors.

Problems and Incidents

Fusion Applications diagnostic framework provides automatic problem detection and information collection features, namely problems and incidents. When an application request from a user or an implicit call fails with serious errors without any immediately available resolution, then Fusion Applications creates a Problem record. The Problem record has a unique key with the `[Product Short Code]-[Error Number]` format; for example, BEA-000337. Incidents could be created automatically by Fusion Applications or a support personnel can manually create an incident by manually adding relevant information at the time of problem which may assist in troubleshooting the problem.

An incident directory contains various ZIP files containing important log files and dumps collected at the time to assist during troubleshooting. The following are the contents of automatically created incidents. This can vary depending on the type of incidents and it may create more or fewer logs than the listed here.

- Application Diagnostic Logs including QuickTrace

- JVM Thread Dump

- WebLogic Server Diagnostic Image including JFR (JRockit Flight Recorder)

- DTF (Diagnostic Test Framework) reports

- ADF (Application Development Framework) configuration

- PL/SQL Logs

- A README file for the incident

The WLS diagnostic image ZIP file contains a file named `JRockitFlightRecorder.jfr`, which acts as a black box recorder with detailed information about the activities within JVM. This file can be read by a tool named JRockit Mission Control. We will also look at QuickTrace and the JVM Thread Dump in upcoming sections of this chapter.

Accessing Incidents

If you have managed an 11g database as an administrator then you may have already worked with incidents, which were introduced in the 11g database and later rolled out to other Oracle products. Fusion Applications implements similar mechanisms for storing and viewing each incident. Each incident is stored in a dedicated directory on a file system and contains a number of logs and ZIP files. You must monitor the growth of the incident home directories, especially when moving the incidents that have already been addressed.

Table 15-1 shows typical locations for the incident directory for every type of incidents. Note that the ADR_BASE directory location is <DOMAIN_TOP>/servers/<Server_Name>/adr for WebLogic server domain while for database server the ADR_BASE file is typically the same as the ORACLE_BASE or a directory within it.

Table 15-1. *Incident Directories Location for Each Components*

Incident Component	Incident Directory Location
Fusion Middleware	<ADR_BASE>/diag/ofm/<domain_name>/<server_name>/incident
Java/SOA Composite	<ADR_BASE>/diag/ofm/fusionapps/<application_name>/incident
PL/SQL Code	<ADR_BASE>/diag/ofm/<db_name>/<db_instance>/incident
Oracle Database	<ADR_BASE>/diag/rdbms/<db_name>/<db_instance>/incident

There are various ways of viewing an incident, including the command-line interface. However, Oracle recommends using Support Workbench or Incident Manager only to access and view incidents since it provides a much simpler and more efficient way to working with incidents. The prerequisite for using Support Workbench is to have Enterprise Manager Cloud Control configured in your environment. The following are various ways to access the incidents in Cloud Control.

- Clicking on the incident count in the Monitoring and Diagnostics section of any product or domain page

- Accessing through Product Menu ➤ Diagnostics ➤ Support Workbench

- Accessing through Enterprise Menu ➤ Monitoring ➤ Incident Manager (or using the keyboard shortcut Ctrl+Shift+I) from any page

Figure 15-1 shows the Incident Manager home screen showing a list of all currently open Incidents. You can also access the list of all open problems from the Tasks link in the Regional area. Selecting any of the incidents from the list populates detailed information about the selected incident in the lower region of the screen, as shown in Figure 15-1. You may also collapse this region to view the incident details in a larger window.

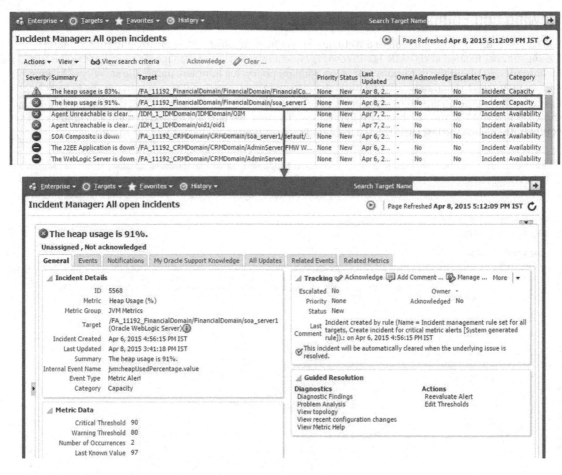

Figure 15-1. *Accessing open incidents*

The advantage of using Support Workbench to access incidents is that it provides immediate access to relevant support knowledge base along with guided diagnostics for the selected incident. It also allows you to view recent configuration changes to see if there was any impact. You can view the collected diagnostics dumps, see the results of automatically triggered diagnostic tests, and use the guided resolution process.

Log Viewer

Fusion Applications log files provide a wealth of information for troubleshooting, including Fusion middleware related logs as well as information gathered through the Application loggers. As you saw in an earlier section, automatically created incidents contain important information from these log files but at times we must access these log files manually in order to diagnose a problem. You can always view the log files directly from the operating system but Fusion Applications control and Cloud Control provide Log Viewer functionality that allows you to search, browse, and look up content in the log files in an easily readable format. The log viewer also detects distinct events, problems, and errors and displays them on the summary page.

Viewing and Editing Log Configuration

You can view the log configuration of a WebLogic server by manually reading the logging configuration file `logger.xml` located at `<DOMAIN_HOME>/config/fmwconfig/servers/<ManagedServer_Name>`. This file includes details about the maximum size of log, rotation policy, log handlers name, the severity of logging, and so on. Instead of manually reading through the logging configuration files, you can use the Logs ➤ Log Configuration menu on any WebLogic server page in Cloud Control to launch the Log Configuration page, as shown in Figure 15-2. You see three tabs in this page. The first two tabs are related to regular diagnostic logs configuration while the last tab is related to QuickTrace configuration that we will see in next section.

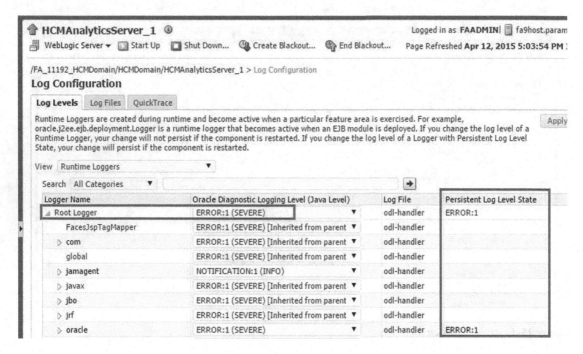

Figure 15-2. *Diagnostic log level configuration screen*

The default level for the root logger and all the other loggers is SEVERE so it only stores a high level of logging when severe errors occur. It is not recommended to keep this level higher for regular operations since it may incur an additional load on the server.

As you can see in Figure 15-2, you can specify two types of logging levels for each logger.

- *Runtime or non-persistent log level*: This is the default setting for all runtime loggers. Any change you make in the Oracle Diagnostic logging level remains applicable only until the component is restarted.

- *Persistent log level*: When you select a log level to be persistent across restarts by selecting the checkbox at the bottom of the screen, this level persists even after a component is restarted.

Let's look at the second tab on the Log Configuration screen, called Log Files Configuration, as shown in Figure 15-3. This page displays the default log files path for each log handler along with the log rotation policy. This helps you quickly locate the log files if you are not sure about the location of required logs. This page should be left unchanged unless there is an absolute need and justification to change it.

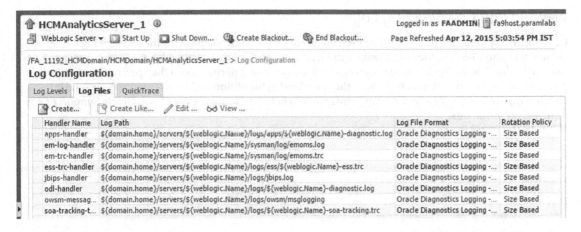

Figure 15-3. Log files configuration screen

Now let's see how you can view the log messages and files manually. Open the Cloud Control page for the WebLogic server for which you want to see the important log messages. Choose Logs ➤ View Log Messages from the WebLogic server menu to access the Log Messages screen, as shown in Figure 15-4.

Figure 15-4. Viewing important log messages

In the Log Messages screen, you can select the type of messages to be searched and displayed or even the messages containing specific text instead of going through the complete contents of log files. The table shows the filtered messages along with the log filename and time of occurrence. You may also save the search query to view the same type of messages again without having to search again.

Viewing and Downloading Logs

Clicking on any of the log filename in this screen will open View Log file page for the selected log file, as shown in Figure 15-5. The messages being displayed are specific to the selected log file. You can set a refresh interval to monitor the log file messages when an activity is being performed at the application level. This page also gives you an option to download the complete log file offline and view it manually or send it to Oracle support. Make sure to remove any sensitive data before sending the log files to Oracle Support or any third-party consultants.

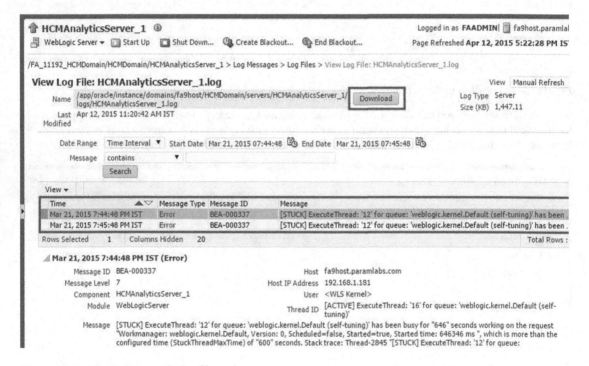

Figure 15-5. Viewing a specific log file

QuickTrace

As you saw earlier, logging can be set at various levels to change the degree of log being collected in order to analyze errors and system performance. However, logging uses the native I/O functionality of the operating system and hardware, which is generally slow and beyond the control of Fusion Applications. This adds up to the resources consumption and may degrade the performance of the application, especially if logging is set to FINE or a similar level. So there is a trade-off here—keeping logging set to SEVERE or another high level of logging will provide limited log information, but setting it to FINE or another low level logging will provide a good amount of data but at a performance cost.

In order to resolve the this dilemma, Oracle has introduced QuickTrace. The difference between QuickTrace and regular logging is that QuickTrace logs the information in memory buffers instead of writing it on disk. This eliminates the I/O drag, hence reducing any performance bottlenecks. QuickTrace is not a replacement of logging, but it can be enabled or disabled in addition to the existing logging and is independent. By default QuickTrace logs at the FINE level and the amount of data contained in it is limited by the size of the buffer specified. It allows you to view the current activities in the WebLogic server while troubleshooting without manually enabling a low level of logging temporarily without affecting the performance of the system.

Setting QuickTrace Related Profile Options

We can set the QuickTrace related parameters using the profile options or the QuickTrace configuration screen, which is similar to the normal application log configuration seen earlier. Let's first look at how to enable/disable QuickTrace and set its important configuration values using profile options. Open the Manage Administrator Profile Options Task using the Task Search work area in the Function Setup Manager. You can search the two most important profile options related to QuickTrace by querying AFLOG_QUICKTRACE_% in the Profile Option Code field, as shown in Figure 15-6.

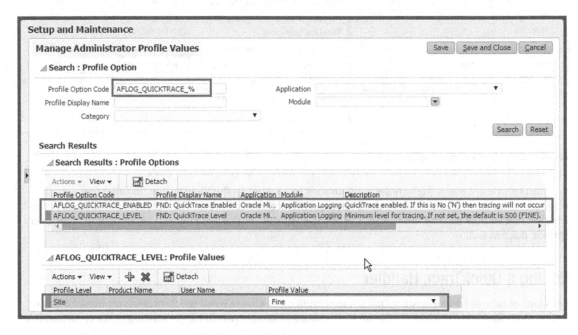

Figure 15-6. *Setting QuickTrace related profile options*

You will see the following two profile options in the results table:

- AFLOG_QUICKTRACE_ENABLED: The value of this profile (FND: QuickTrace Enabled) determines whether QuickTrace is enabled. If the value is set to Yes at the site level, it enables QuickTrace across the application unless it's set at any other level, which may override the site-level value. Set the value to No to disable QuickTrace.

- AFLOG_QUICKTRACE_LEVEL: The value of this profile (FND: QuickTrace Level) determines the level of logging in the memory buffers. The default value is Fine at the site level and this can be overridden by setting it a further level down.

Manually Invoking QuickTrace

By default QuickTrace is created when a critical error occurs and an incident is being created and placed within the incident directory. We can also manually dump QuickTrace if an incident is not created or if its requested specifically by Oracle Support. Let's see how to generate the QuickTrace dump manually.

From the homepage of the WebLogic server for which we need to generate QuickTrace dump, choose the WebLogic Server ➤ Logs ➤ Log Configuration menu option. Once the Log Configuration page is open, click on the QuickTrace tab. This will display the currently configured QuickTrace handlers, including the custom created handlers if there are any, as shown in Figure 15-7.

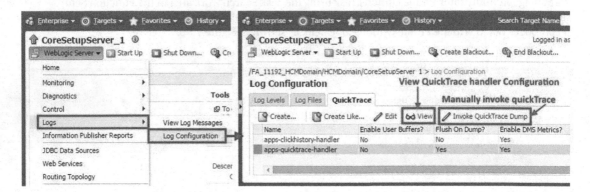

Figure 15-7. *QuickTrace configuration*

You can view the existing handler configuration by clicking on the View button. In order to manually generate QuickTrace dump, click on the Invoke QuickTrace Dump button. The next screen will prompt you whether you want to use the common buffer or a user-specific buffer if the handler is configured to log user specific trace as well.

Editing a QuickTrace Handler

Let's look at how to edit an existing QuickTrace handler. The Create new Handler screen prompts for same input values as seen in this screen. Figure 15-8 shows an example of editing the existing QuickTrace handler.

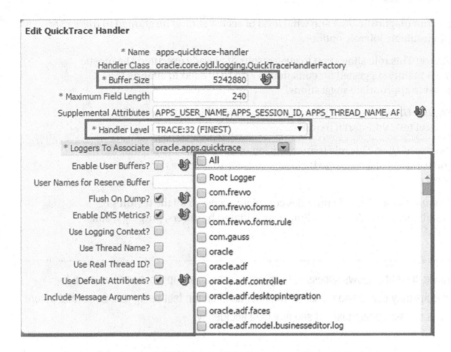

Figure 15-8. *Editing a QuickTrace handler*

The following are the important parameters of interest in this screen:

- *Buffer size*: The default value is 5242880 bytes (5 MB). This value determines how much memory to allocate for this buffer. Ideally, this is enough to log recent issues with the WebLogic server but this can be adjusted in case there are a lot of errors being encountered and if it is not accommodating the required time window.

- *Handler level*: The default value is FINEST, which is same as the one set at site level profile option. It is not recommended to change this since it may defeat the very purpose of QuickTrace.

- *Loggers to associate*: By default, oracle.apps.quicktrace logger is used but if you are troubleshooting a component-specific issue then you may also want to include an additional logger in QuickTrace. The list of values allows you to select multiple loggers at the same time.

- *User buffer-related parameters*: Another important set of parameters in this screen is related to whether you want to trace a specific user to generate a trace for a specific issue. In this case, you can select the Enable User Buffers checkbox. If User Buffer is enabled then you may need to enter the username in the field called User Names for Reserve Buffer.

Diagnostic Dashboard

Fusion Applications provides pre-seeded diagnostic tests to manually check whether an application functionality is working. This tool can be used to either perform a routine health check, diagnose and troubleshoot a problem with a specific application, or collect data to be provided to Oracle Support. In order to access the Diagnostic Dashboard, you must first configure access to it for the selected users. You must decide which users need to run diagnostic tests and what level of access should be granted to these users based on the following four available job role options:

- *Diagnostic Viewer*: This role allows you to view results of already executed Diagnostic tests. This role is mainly suggested for consultants who may need to analyze the results and provide appropriate suggestions.

- *Diagnostic Regular User*: This role allows you to run diagnostic tests, view their results, and cancel tests you start if required.

- *Diagnostic Advanced User*: This role is an extension of the Diagnostic Regular User and allows you to attach test results to incidents in order to prepare data for sending to Oracle Support.

- *Diagnostic Administrator*: This role provides complete access to all the features of Diagnostic Dashboard, including cancelling tests initiated by others, purging results, and so on.

■ **Note**   Fusion Applications currently allows access to diagnostic tests for all applications based on the selected job role and the results may contain some sensitive data based on the test being run. Be careful before assigning diagnostic job roles to users who must not see any data accidently.

Table 15-2 provides a summary comparison of these roles in order to access which user should be granted what role.

Table 15-2. *Comparison of Roles that Provide Access to the Diagnostic Dashboard*

Job Role Name	View Results	Run Tests	Cancel Tests by Others	Attach Results to Incidents	Purge Results
Diagnostic Viewer	Yes	No	No	No	No
Diagnostic Regular User	Yes	Yes	No	No	No
Diagnostic Advanced User	Yes	Yes	No	Yes	No
Diagnostic Administrator	Yes	Yes	Yes	Yes	Yes

There are two types of diagnostic tests available in the Diagnostic Dashboard.

- *Internal Diagnostic Tests*: These tests require the related application to be available since the test or part of the test runs within the application.

- *External Diagnostic Tests*: These tests do not require the related application to be available and can diagnose problems in the application even if it's not running.

Fusion Applications provides two interfaces to run diagnostic tests. The Diagnostic Dashboard that we are going to see now and the command-line utility named `diagctl`. Note that `diagctl` cannot run internal diagnostic tests but the Diagnostic Dashboard can run either type. In fact, the Diagnostic Dashboard can also be used to make sure whether a test is internal or external. We will look at how to check this in next section when you see how to run a diagnostic test.

Accessing the Diagnostic Dashboard

There are multiple ways to access the Diagnostic Dashboard depending on which interface you are currently logged in to. Let's look at each of the ways to navigate to the Diagnostic Dashboard.

- *Accessing through the Fusion Applications interface*: If you are logged in to the Fusion Applications interface using an application user that has been assigned any of the diagnostic roles discussed earlier then you will see a link titled Run Diagnostic Tests from the User menu ➤ Troubleshooting section, as shown in Figure 15-9. Click on this link to launch the Diagnostic Dashboard.

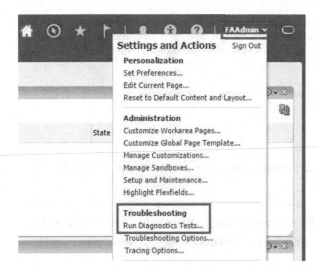

Figure 15-9. *Accessing the Diagnostic Dashboard using the Fusion Applications interface*

- *Accessing through the Cloud Control interface*: You can access the Diagnostic Dashboard from the product family homepage for which you want to run or view the diagnostic tests by choosing Diagnostics ➤ Fusion Applications Diagnostic Dashboard, as shown in Figure 15-10. You can see a small arrow in front of this link that suggests that it points to an external page from Cloud Control. In this case it points to the Diagnostic Dashboard application of the selected product family. You will need to log in using your applications username before you can access the dashboard.

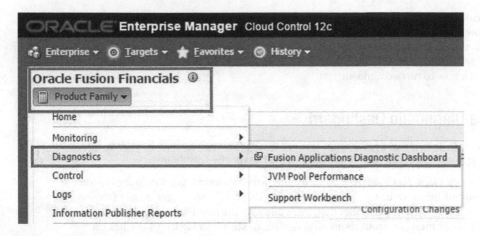

Figure 15-10. *Accessing Diagnostic Dashboard using Cloud Control*

- *Accessing using a direct URL:* If you are not logged in to either interface or you want to access Diagnostic Dashboard as part of your routine job then you can bookmark the following URL. It will prompt you to log in as a Fusion Applications user with appropriate job roles.

  ```
  http(s)://<ProdctDomainHostname>:<WebPort>/diagnosticDashboard/faces/
  DiagnosticDashboard
  ```

  For example:

  ```
  https://fahost.paramlabs.com:10634/diagnosticDashboard/faces/DiagnosticDashboard
  ```

■ **Note** Diagnostic Dashboard is deployed as a J2EE web application in each product domain as part of the `diagnosticDashboard` module of DiagnosticsUI-Assembly Application deployment. This allows you to launch the web application directly using the provided URL.

Running Diagnostic Tests

You may need to run various Fusion Applications diagnostic tests to periodically perform health checks of specific components, check an application's setup, troubleshoot issues, compare the performance with last know good performance, or even generate incident logs for Oracle Support. You can search for specific diagnostic tests or browse through all the available tests on the Diagnostics Dashboard. The following is the list of steps required in order to execute one or more diagnostic tests.

1. Select all the diagnostic tests that need to be run by browsing through the list or by searching them one by one and clicking on Add to Run button. This will add the jobs to the Run queue. As you keep on adding the jobs, the list on the top right pane will continue to populate with these jobs.

2. Next you can select all or specific tests in the Run Queue table to be executed in a single group. You can optionally specify a unique name for the tests execution in the Run Name textbox.

3. If any of the tests require any input parameters before running then you may see an warning or exclamation icon in the Input Status column. You may click on this icon to display the Input Parameters window. Enter the required values to make sure the column now displays the value as Required Input Parameters Validated.

4. You may want to know whether all these tests can be run now or any of the selected test is internal and requires an application to be running. Select all the tests that you want to check and then choose the View ➤ Availability menu item to display the Availability window. Make sure the Availability Column shows check/tick mark for all the selected tests. If you see a warning sign then either any dependent application, Java class, or PL/SQL procedure may be unavailable or the user may not have the required permissions. If the dependent application for the internal diagnostic test is not available then you will see this error message: The following Web Applications were inaccessible. Fix the stated issues before moving on to the next steps.

5. Once the required checks are complete, click Run to execute the selected diagnostic tests. Once the tests are complete, the bottom pane will display diagnostic test results in an expandable list based on job run name. You can now analyze the test results and take appropriate corrective action if required.

Figure 15-11 shows a summary of these steps by highlighting each of the activities.

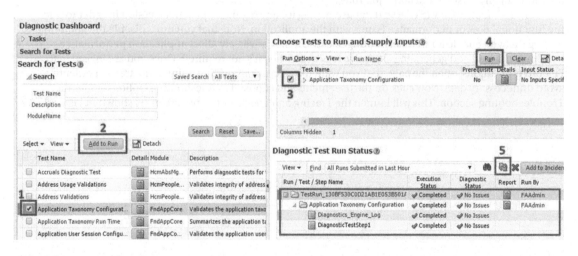

Figure 15-11. *Running diagnostic tests*

Tracing Fusion Applications Issues at Database Level

During the course of troubleshooting you may want to troubleshoot the SQLs running in the database, especially when you have verified that network or application server is not causing the performance bottleneck. There are various ways to check the currently running SQLs in the database, but the most effective option is to enable trace on specific sessions or applications for short durations and then analyze the trace files for further analysis. In this section, we will look at database tracing at the application level as well as at the Enterprise Scheduler level depending on where the performance issue persists.

Tracing Fusion Applications Sessions

Before you look at SQL tracing of Fusion Applications session, you need to know that the Troubleshooting menu is not enabled by default for all users. Table 15-3 lists the duty roles that, if included in the respective job role, enable the troubleshooting option for the user.

Table 15-3. *Duty Role Options for Enabling the Troubleshooting Menu*

Duty Display Name	Product	Duty Internal Name
Supportability Level Management Duty	CRM	FND_SET_SUPPORTABILITY_ LEVEL_DUTY_CRM
Supportability Level Management Duty	FSCM	FND_SUPPORTABILITY_ LEVEL_MANAGEMENT_DUTY_FSCM
Supportability Level Management Duty	HCM	FND_SUPPORTABILITY_ LEVEL_MANAGEMENT_DUTY_HCM

Note that by default no user level job role is seeded with these duty roles except for the following two job roles.

- Application Administrator (FND_APPLICATION_ADMINISTRATOR_JOB)

- Application Diagnostics Administrator (FND_DIAG_ADMINISTRATOR_JOB)

As you can see, these are administrative job roles, so you should not assign these to any non-administrator users just to enable troubleshooting options. Instead, create a new job role or include these duty roles in any existing functional job roles.

Now let's look at how to enable database tracing for any regular application session in order to trace the functional flow or performance issues with the application. Note that you must disable the additional tracing that you enable for troubleshooting because it may adversely affect application performance by additional load and generating excessive logs even when it's not required. Once you are logged in to Fusion Applications, open the page that you want to select as the starting point of the trace in order to avoid unnecessary data. Now click on the user menu and choose Troubleshooting Options under the Troubleshooting section. This will launch the Tracing and Logging options screen, as shown in Figure 15-12.

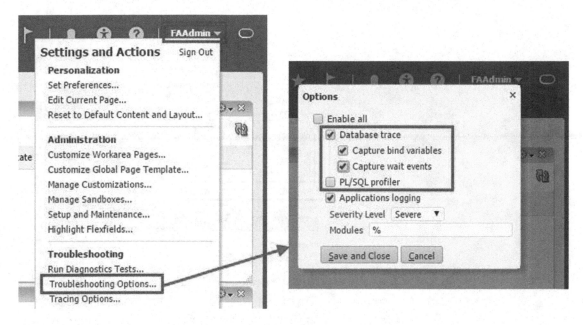

Figure 15-12. *Enabling trace in a Fusion Applications session*

In this screen you can select various combinations of DB trace; for example, DB trace without bind or waits, with bind, with wait, with bind and wait, and same options along with or without PL/SQL profiler, and so on. Once you click Save and Close, any further application navigation creates database trace, which is created in the user session trace dump (user_dump_dest) specified in the database. Since there could be many traces available in this location, it's important to understand how to locate the corresponding trace file for this particular session.

Once trace is enabled in an application, you may need to locate the browser cookie related to this host and session. Note that depending on browser, the procedure to locate cookies will be different. Figure 15-13 shows an example of a cookie for a host named fahost.

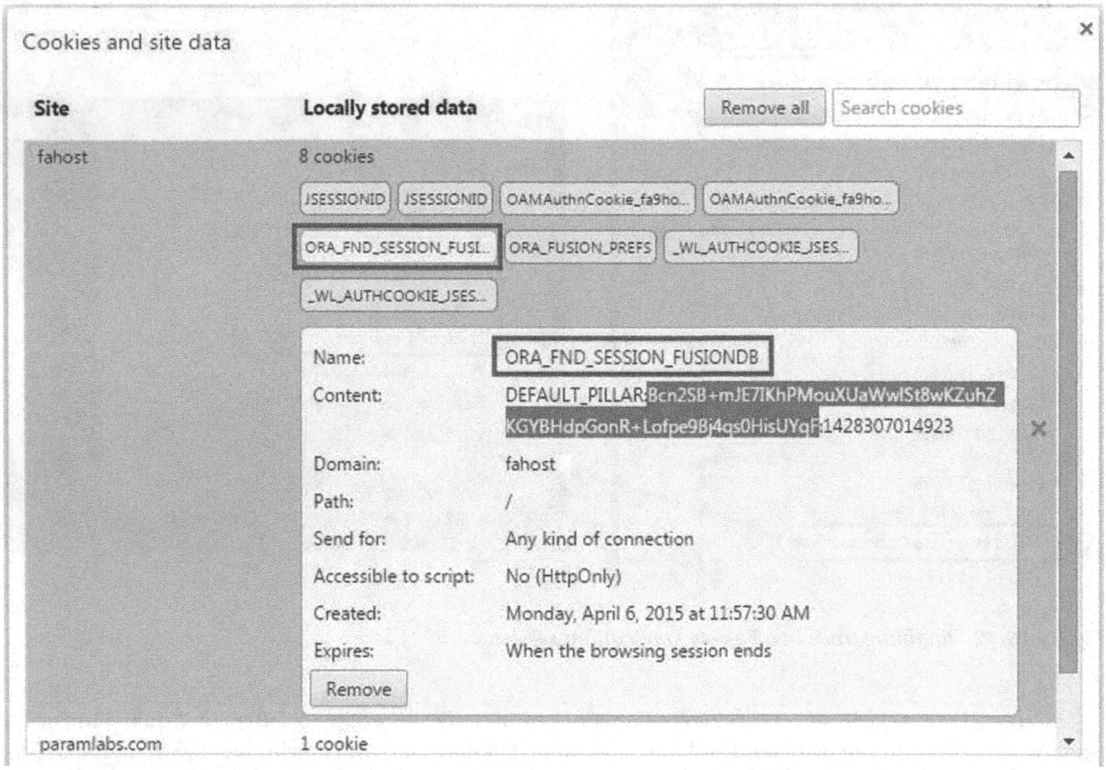

Figure 15-13. *Looking up FND session cookie values*

Once you have located the cookie, you need identify the value for `ORA_FND_SESSION_FUSIONDB`. The value is prefixed by `DEFAULT_PILLAR` and contained between two colons (`:`). In this example, the parameter value in the cookie is `Bcn2SB+mJE7IKhPMouXUaWwlSt8wKZuhZKGYBHdpGonR+Lofpe9Bj4qs0HisUYqF`. Now let's locate the database session ID corresponding to this value by using following query:

```
SQL> select (fnd_session_mgmt.get_session_id_from_
cookie('Bcn2SB+mJE7IKhPMouXUaWwlSt8wKZuhZKGYBHdpGonR+Lofpe9Bj4qs0HisUYqF')) SESSION_ID from dual;

SESSION_ID
--------------------------------------------------------------------------------
130AA3E60F561481E053B501A8C0E0F8
```

Now we can locate the database trace files generated for this application session by using this database session value. We can locate the database trace files with this value as the postfix in the user trace dump location. For example:

```
[fusion@fa9host trace]$ ls -l *130AA3E60F561481E053B501A8C0E0F8*
-rw-r----- 1 fusion dba 237788 Apr  6 13:33
fusiondb_ora_5178_130AA3E60F561481E053B501A8C0E0F8.trc
-rw-r----- 1 fusion dba   1439 Apr  6 13:33
fusiondb_ora_5178_130AA3E60F561481E053B501A8C0E0F8.trm
```

```
-rw-r----- 1 fusion dba  26416 Apr  6 13:33
fusiondb_ora_5247_130AA3E60F561481E053B501A8C0E0F8.trc
-rw-r----- 1 fusion dba    345 Apr  6 13:33
fusiondb_ora_5247_130AA3E60F561481E053B501A8C0E0F8.trm
```

Once the required activity is complete, you should disable the trace using this same method. Now you can go through these traces directly or using the tkprof utility in order to troubleshoot the issue.

Tracing Scheduled Job Sessions

Similar to Fusion Applications tracing, you can trace a scheduled job session as well. In fact in realtime, an administrator may get more frequent requests for scheduled jobs as compared to other elements of Fusion Applications. In order to enable database tracing for an ESS job, you need to enable the tracing option at the job definition level.

In order to edit a scheduled job definition, you must first navigate to the product family's middleware page in Cloud Control or the Fusion Applications Control depending on the product corresponding to the job. Now in the Target Navigation region, open the ESS homepage by choosing the Product Domain ➤ Scheduling Services ➤ ESSCluster ➤ ESS Server (ess_server1) menu option, as shown in Figure 15-14.

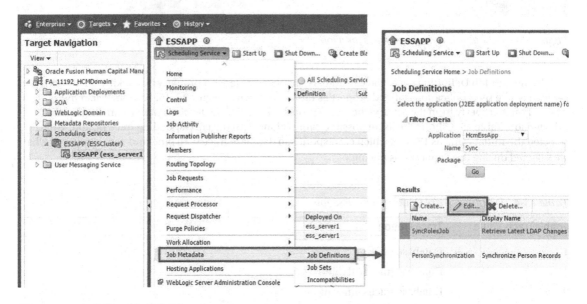

Figure 15-14. *Edit a job definition*

Now you can access the Job Definitions page from the ESSAPP homepage by choosing the Scheduling Service menu ➤ Job Metadata ➤ Job Definitions menu item. Either search for the job or browse through the list of jobs and locate the scheduled job that you want to trace at the database level. We are using the example of same job discussed earlier—Retrieve Latest LDAP Changes (SyncRolesJob). Once the job is located, select it and click the Edit button to open the Edit Job Definition page, as shown in Figure 15-15.

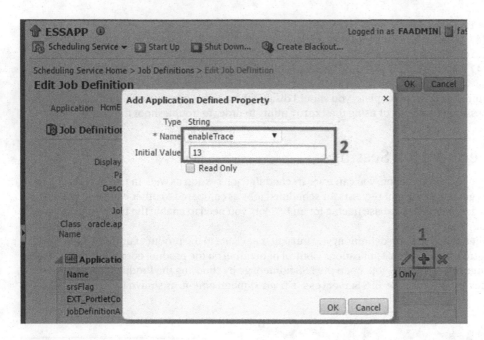

Figure 15-15. *Enabling a database trace for a job*

In the Edit Job Definition page, you can add an Application Defined property by clicking on an Add (+) icon above the Application Defined Properties table, as shown in Figure 15-15. You can select the enableTrace property from the list of values. This property specifies the level of database tracing for the selected job. Table 15-4 shows the list of possible values along with the corresponding trace option. We selected the initial value as 13 here, which corresponds to database trace with bind and wait, similar to what we selected during the applications tracing.

Table 15-4. *Database Trace Options in the ESS Job*

enableTrace Value	Trace Option
1	Database trace
5	Database trace with bind
9	Database trace with wait
13	Database trace with bind and wait
16	PL/SQL profile
17	Database trace and PL/SQL profile
21	Database trace with bind and PL/SQL profile
25	Database trace with wait and PL/SQL profile
29	Database trace with bind, wait, and PL/SQL profile

Once you have enabled tracing at the job level, run the job using the Scheduled Processes work area, as you saw earlier. Once the job starts running, a related database trace file is generated in a user session trace dump location (`user_dump_dest`) specified in the database. In order to locate the correct trace file, you must find the FND session ID similar to the application trace, but the method to look up this value is different here. This information is stored in the REQUEST_CP table of the ESS database schema (FUSION_ORA_ESS).Use the following query to locate the session ID specific to the request ID that was initiated:

```
SQL> select FND_SESSION_ID from fusion_ora_ess.REQUEST_CP where requestid=1404;

FND_SESSION_ID
--------------------------------------------------------------------------------
12DADA70B7051C9FE053B501A8C08F2A
```

This is the same postfix value as the database trace file so we can easily locate the file with this postfix value as follows.

```
[fusion@fa9host trace]$ ls -ltr *12DADA70B7051C9FE053B501A8C08F2A*
-rw-r----- 1 fusion dba   37561 Apr  6 16:24
fusiondb_ora_7327_12DADA70B7051C9FE053B501A8C08F2A.trm
-rw-r----- 1 fusion dba 2428340 Apr  6 16:24
fusiondb_ora_7327_12DADA70B7051C9FE053B501A8C08F2A.trc
```

Once the required tracing is complete, it is recommended that you turn off database tracing for scheduled jobs in order to avoid excessive resource usage.

Troubleshooting Enterprise Scheduler

Troubleshooting issues related to Enterprise Scheduler is one of the most important tasks for a Fusion Applications Administrator because scheduled jobs are some of the most resource-consuming activities performed by business users. As we know now, the function of the Concurrent Manager from the Oracle E-Business Suite is replaced by Enterprise Scheduler in Fusion Applications. If you have worked with Oracle E-Business Suite, you need to spend the same amount of administrative efforts to manage Enterprise Scheduler as you used to do for Concurrent Manager.

Understanding Enterprise Scheduler Jobs execution

Before going into the details of Enterprise Scheduler troubleshooting, let's first understand the basic flow of a scheduled process or scheduled job in Enterprise Scheduler. Figure 15-16 provides a basic understanding of the stages of a scheduled request from submission to completion, but not necessarily covering all conditions.

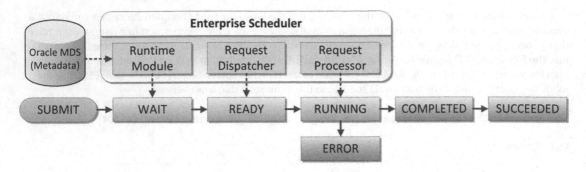

Figure 15-16. *Default execution of a scheduled process*

The execution of scheduled process involves three major components of Enterprise Scheduler—Runtime Module, Request Dispatcher, and Request Processor. You can manually stop or start Request Dispatcher and Request Processor but it is not recommended to manually control them unless there is a specific justification to do so. Even if these components are down, the scheduled jobs will continue to queue up. Once a scheduled request is submitted, the Runtime Module accesses the job's metadata from the Metadata Store in Oracle MDS and puts the job in the WAIT queue. Now the Request Dispatcher processes the WAIT queue and puts the job in the READY queue.

As soon as the Enterprise Manager has a processor available to run the request, the Request Processor changes the job state to RUNNING and sends the job to the relevant application. Once the request completes successfully or with an error, it receives a callback from the application about the completion status. If the request was completed successfully, it changes the status to COMPLETED and starts post-processing. Once post-processing is complete, it changes the status to SUCCEEDED.

Enterprise Scheduler Status Codes

You have seen the basic flow of a scheduled job with WAIT, READY, RUNNING, COMPLETED, ERROR, and SUCCEDED. However, there are few more possible status codes for a job depending on various conditions and events. The job execution details are stored in the REQUEST_HISTORY table of Enterprise Scheduler schema (FUSION_ORA_ESS). The current status code for the scheduled request is stored in a numeric value column named STATE. Some of the statuses are considered terminal since they represent the final status of the request after execution regardless of whether it completes successfully. While remaining codes specify the non-terminal state of a scheduled request, which means they are waiting, running, or not started due to various reasons. The following are the terminal status codes for any scheduled job.

- SUCCEEDED

- WARNING

- ERROR

- CANCELLED

- EXPIRED

- VALIDATION_FAILED

- FINISHED

You can use the following query, which returns the numeric STATE value based on the request ID in order to check the current status of a request directly from the database.

```
SELECT
    STATE
FROM FUSION_ORA_ESS.REQUEST_HISTORY
WHERE REQUESTID = <Request_ID>;
```

Table 15-5 shows a mapping of the STATE column with the corresponding job status. You can use this table to derive the current status based on the returned value.

Table 15-5. *Mapping the STATE value in REQEST_HISTORTY to the Scheduled Process Status*

STATE Value	Corresponding Request Status
1	WAIT
2	READY
3	RUNNING
4	COMPLETED
5	BLOCKED
6	HOLD
7	CANCELLING
8	EXPIRED
9	CANCELLED
10	ERROR
11	WARNING
12	SUCCEEDED
13	PAUSED
14	PENDING_VALIDATION
15	VALIDATION_FAILED
16	SCHEDULE_ENDED
17	FINISHED
18	ERROR_AUTO_RETRY
19	ERROR_MANUAL_RECOVERY

If you notice that certain jobs are in the same status for a long time without doing any activity in the back end, the reason could be associated with the ESS server or due to conflicts with other jobs or resources. Figure 15-17 shows the internal diagnostic codes for scheduled jobs that are in non-terminal state and not executing currently due to various reasons. This figure will help you understand why a request could be in the same status for long time and take further corrective action accordingly if required.

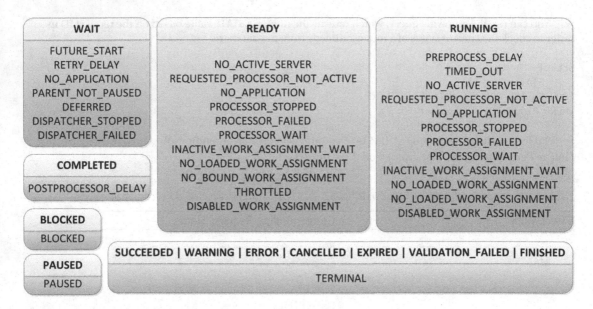

Figure 15-17. *Scheduler jobs status and diagnostic codes*

Important Database Objects of Enterprise Scheduler

Although you can get all relevant information about a scheduled job from the ESS homepage, at times you may want to access backend database for further troubleshooting or sometimes for automatic monitoring purposes. Figure 15-18 lists some of the important database objects that may help you in ESS troubleshooting. Notice that the main ESS schema contains the required tables and packages and you can access those using the FUSION schema through corresponding synonyms. Although some of the queries mentioned here will refer to the ESS schema, you can alternatively use synonyms from the FUSION schema as well.

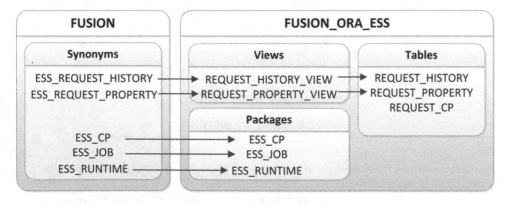

Figure 15-18. *Important database objects related to Enterprise Scheduler*

Execution Flow of BI Jobs Invoked Through Enterprise Scheduler

The Role of Enterprise Scheduler Service (ESS) is to control execution of different types of PL/SQL, C, or Java code based on its job definition. However, the actual execution may be done by the application itself. For example Oracle Business Intelligence runs the reports related jobs invoked via Enterprise Scheduler. Once Scheduler sends the job request to BI, it waits for the callback from BI with an update of final execution status. So at times the status of an ESS and BI job might not be in sync for a short duration. Figure 15-19 explains a general scenario of a BI job execution that's invoked through ESS.

Figure 15-19. *Scheduler job status with corresponding BI job status*

As you can see, once the ESS job enters the RUNNING state, the corresponding BI job may not have been initiated. Once both of the jobs are in the RUNNING state, the ESS job will continue to be in the same state until the BI job completes with a success or failure. Once the BI job is complete, it will send a callback to Enterprise Scheduler, which in turn changes the status of the ESS job for further post-processing.

A similar scenario occurs when you cancel an already running ESS job. You may expect both ESS and BI jobs to end with a CANCELLED status. However, if you look at various scenarios in Figure 15-20, you will understand that this might not always be true. This figure will help you troubleshoot mismatching status between ESS and BI jobs, especially when the BI job was completed successfully and the ESS job was cancelled before reaching the SUCCEEDED status.

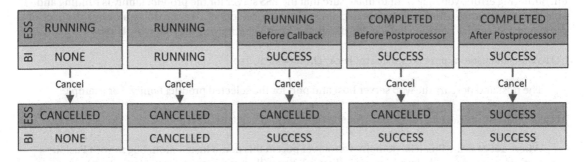

Figure 15-20. *Cancelling the BI publisher-related ESS job*

Troubleshooting Using ESS Job Log Files

If you find some issues with an individual or multiple scheduled jobs through proactive monitoring, alerts, or user complaints, you can look up the scheduled job log and output files. These log files are created temporarily in the respective product family's ESS server log directory. The default location is

APPLICATIONS_CONFIG/domains/<hostname>/<Domain>/servers/ess_sevrer1/logs/ess_requests. Once the job is complete, the Scheduler moves these files to the Universal Content Management (UCM) server. These files can later be accessed through the Scheduled Jobs work area by selecting the request ID. You can see the log and output files as attachments in the Log and Output section of the Job Details pane. We can use the following query to look up the domain, temporary log directory, and output directory.

```
SELECT
    STATE,
    PROCESSGROUP,
    LOGWORKDIRECTORY,
    OUTPUTWORKDIRECTORY
FROM FUSION_ORA_ESS.REQUEST_HISTORY
WHERE REQUESTID = <Request_ID>;
```

For example, this query returns the following values for an example request ID 801.

- STATE: 3 (RUNNING)

- PROCESSGROUP: HCMDomain##ESSCluster

- LOGWORKDIRECTORY: /app/oracle/instance/domains/fa9host/HCMDomain/servers/ess_server1/logs/ess_request//801/log

- OUTPUTWORKDIRECTORY: /app/oracle/instance/domains/fa9host/HCMDomain/servers/ess_server1/logs/ess_request//801/out

You can see that the request is currently running under HCMDomain's ESS cluster. You can view the log file (<request_id>.log) and output file (<request_id>.txt) for further details as to what is currently being processed or where it is stuck. You can further troubleshoot HCM domain's ESS cluster if we see a lot of requests stuck with a particular Scheduler Server.

Enterprise Scheduler Health Check

Once you have identified that multiple requests belonging to same product family are pending or encountering errors, you may want to make sure that the ESS server for the product family is running and able to process requests normally before deciding to bounce the service. We can do a quick health check of a particular ESS service and then launch ESS diagnostic health check using the following URL.

```
https://<hostname>:<port>/EssHealthCheck/checkHealth.jsp
```

The host and port are the web server host and port for the selected product family. For example:

```
https://fahost.paramlabs.com:10624/EssHealthCheck/checkHealth.jsp
```

Where 10624 is the financial domain web server port in this demo installation. Log in with Fusion Applications super user (FAAdmin in our installation). You will see a page similar to Figure 15-21.

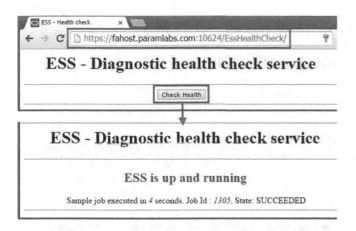

Figure 15-21. *Enterprise Scheduler health check*

Click on Check Health to check the ESS status as well as initiate a sample job run in order to estimate the performance of the ESS Server, as shown in Figure 15-21. This should give you an indication if something is not right with the ESS Service. If you suspect an issue with ESS and want to drill down to the ESS cluster and managed servers level, you can use the following link to further diagnose the problem.

```
https://<hostname>:<port>/EssHealthCheck/diagnoseHealth.jsp
```

For example:

```
https://fahost.paramlabs.com:10624/EssHealthCheck/diagnoseHealth.jsp
```

This will launch ESS Diagnostics page, as shown in Figure15-22. Although it looks same as the previous Health Check page, clicking on the Diagnose Health button does an extensive checkup of ESS and provides details of the corresponding ESS cluster along with the WebLogic managed servers that are part of the cluster, as shown in Figure 15-22.

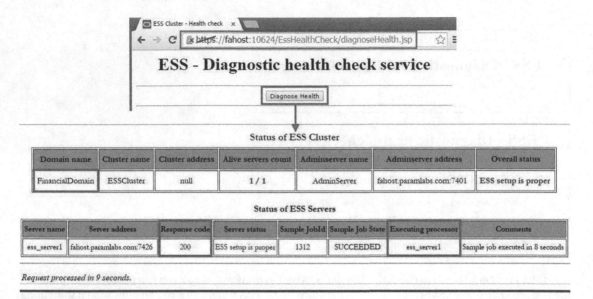

The following are the details shown in the figure:

ESS – Diagnostic health check service

Diagnose Health

Status of ESS Cluster

Domain name	Cluster name	Cluster address	Alive servers count	Adminserver name	Adminserver address	Overall status
FinancialDomain	ESSCluster	null	1 / 1	AdminServer	fahost.paramlabs.com:7401	ESS setup is proper

Status of ESS Servers

Server name	Server address	Response code	Server status	Sample JobId	Sample Job State	Executing processor	Comments
ess_server1	fahost.paramlabs.com:7426	200	ESS setup is proper	1312	SUCCEEDED	ess_server1	Sample job executed in 8 seconds

Request processed in 9 seconds.

Figure 15-22. Enterprise Scheduler diagnostic health check

Note that the response code must be 200 for successful completion of sample jobs. The result page also points out if there are any issues with ESS setup as well as the number of servers alive if more than one server is part of the cluster.

Troubleshooting JVM Performance

Fusion Applications relies on the Oracle Fusion middleware infrastructure, especially Oracle WebLogic Server domains. Troubleshooting application performance issues or hang situations mostly deals with troubleshooting Fusion middleware components. Since Fusion middleware is based on Java Virtual Machines (JVM), troubleshooting JVM plays a paramount role in diagnosing and resolving Fusion middleware-related performance issues. JVM troubleshooting is an extensive and daunting task. It may take quite some time before you completely understand and become adept at troubleshooting JVM-related performance issues. However Enterprise Manager Cloud Control provides excellent JVM diagnostic features to help you succeed and provides quite an edge over manual troubleshooting. This also helps you to continue to troubleshoot JVM issues even if the specific Fusion Applications host, domain, or cluster is not responding in a timely manner. Cloud Control is hosted outside of the Fusion Applications environment and contains the last available data from the hosts. In this section, we will cover some of the JVM troubleshooting tasks that may help you understand how to make better use of the JVM Diagnostics engine to resolve the issues yourself or provide relevant dumps to Oracle for further support and troubleshooting.

Enabling JVM Diagnostics

As you saw in the previous chapter of configuring Fusion Applications with Cloud Control, we deployed the JVM Diagnostics Engine on a Cloud Control Server in order to provide JVM troubleshooting related features for Fusion middleware. Before we can use the features of JVM Diagnostics for the WebLogic server domains of Fusion Applications, we must deploy diagnostic agents to each of the product family WebLogic domains.

As you can see in Figure 15-23, the JVM diagnostics-related items in the Diagnostics menu on the WebLogic domain home are initially grayed out, indicating that the JVM diagnostic agent is not yet deployed on this domain. In order to deploy the agent, click on the Setup Diagnostic Agents option from the Diagnostics menu to launch the Agent Deployment page. Select the Deploy option for the selected WebLogic domain and follow the screens to enter the target credentials to complete the deployment. The last screen will display a link to the deployment job where you can track the deployment status.

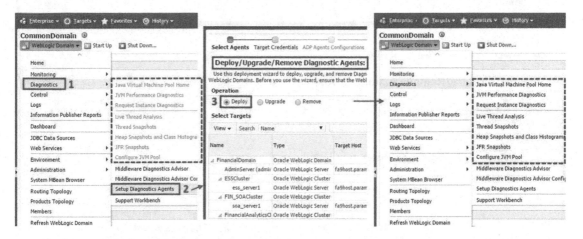

Figure 15-23. *Enable JVM Diagnostics*

As you can see in Figure 15-23, after deployment of the JVM diagnostic agent, the Diagnostics menu on WebLogic domain home now has all the JVM diagnostics related tasks enabled. This will allow you to perform all the required JVM troubleshooting related activities right from this menu.

If you are using this method to deploy JVM agent on multiple domains at the same time then only the job that was invoked first will run and the remaining jobs will show the status as Suspended on Lock until the previous job is complete. The alternate way to deploy diagnostic agents on multiple WebLogic domains is to use the Setup ➤ Middleware Management ➤ Application Performance Management homepage, as shown in Figure 15-24.

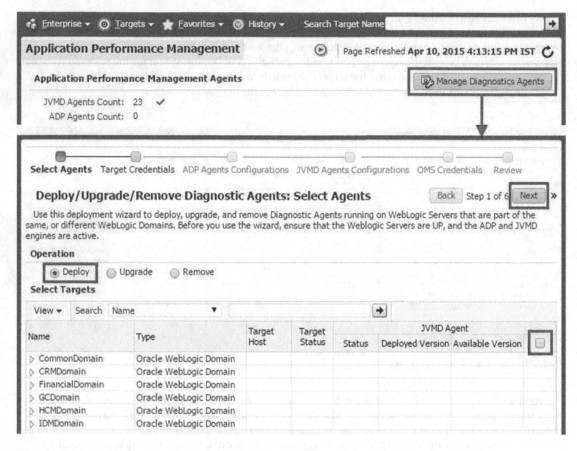

Figure 15-24. Deploy JVM diagnostic agent on multiple WebLogic domains

Once you launch the Application Performance Management homepage, click on the Manage Diagnostic Agents button on the top of the page to launch the Diagnostic Agents deployment screen, as shown in Figure 15-24. This screen is similar to what you saw in Figure 15-23, but here it allows you to select multiple individual WebLogic servers from more than one WebLogic domain and runs the deployments as a single job.

Accessing JVM Diagnostics Homepage

Once you have installed JVM diagnostic (JVMD) agent in one or more WebLogic domains, you can access the JVMD related tasks in Cloud Control. These were not available prior to agent deployment. In order to view the summary of the current status of all JVMs configured for a product family, you can navigate to the Java Virtual Machine Pool home. There are several ways to access the JVM Pool homepage.

- *Using the Middleware Summary page*: You can view all the discovered Java Virtual Machines and JVM Pools by selecting Target Type as JVM in the Middleware Summary screen in Cloud Control, as shown in Figure 15-25. You will notice one JVM pool per WebLogic domain. The JVMs for each managed server will have a _jvm postfix. Clicking on any of these will open the respective JVM pool or JVM homepage.

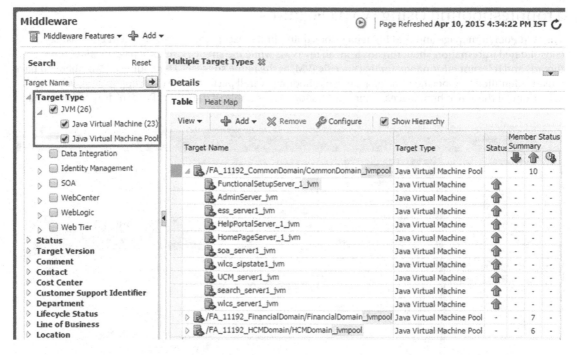

Figure 15-25. *Summary of all monitored JVM targets*

- *Using Target Navigation region*: Once the JVM diagnostics agent has been deployed for the selected product family domain, you will see an additional subtree node called `Java Virtual Machine Pools` in the domain tree in the Target Navigation region as we will soon see in Figure 15-26. Once you expand it, you will see the JVM Pool and JVMs for this domain listed in the subtree. This can be accessed from any product family, product, or WebLogic domain page in Cloud Control.

- *Using Diagnostics menu*: As you saw in Figure 15-23, you can use the Diagnosis menu from any page of WebLogic domain, cluster, or server home in Cloud Control to access various JVM diagnostics-related tasks. These links are disabled until the Diagnostics Agent has been deployed for the selected product family domain.

Troubleshooting Using JVMD Features

The JVM Pool homepage and JVM homepage look quite similar except for the fact that JVM Pool displays consolidated information about threads from all the JVMs while the single JVM homepage displays the threads and relevant information for that specific JVM, as the name suggests. Depending on whether you have already identified the specific JVMs or are troubleshooting overall performance of an application, you may access one of these two homepages. Figure 15-26 shows an example of the CommonDomain_jvmpool homepage.

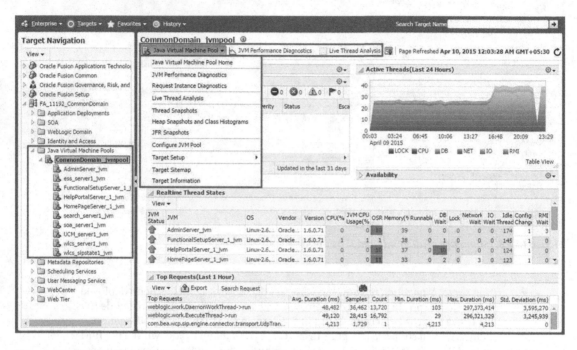

Figure 15-26. *Java Virtual Machine Pool homepage*

As you can see, the JVM or JVM Pool homepage displays threads activity graph along with which layer it is spending most time at, including DB, CPU, Network, I/O, or in situations like Lock. This gives you a quick overview of whether the JVM is acting as a bottleneck or other components in the environment. Any automatically generated incidents are also displayed here so that you can review and access existing issues quickly without manual troubleshooting.

The next section shows availability, resource usage, and important wait events for each of the JVM threads. The default installation configures one JVM per managed server but depending on your custom configuration or tuning you may see multiple JVMs in this section. This section gives a quick overview of which of the JVM is performing badly so that we can focus on those JVMs to troubleshoot further. Clicking on any of the links will open the homepage for the selected JVM.

The last section shows the top requests in the last hour, along with the average duration, count, and the standard deviation, which indicates the amount of variation in the sample data. You may want to customize the screen by adding or removing regions of importance. You can do this by clicking on the Personalization icon at the top.

You can monitor JVM performance by clicking on the JVM Performance Diagnostics link on the JVM homepage or by choosing the Diagnostics ➤ JVM Performance Diagnostics menu option in any product family page in Cloud Control. Figure 15-27 shows an example of a JVM performance diagnostics page for the WebLogic managed server HomePageServer_1.

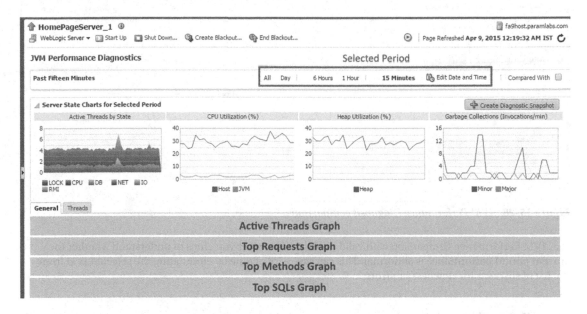

Figure 15-27. Performance diagnostics for the selected JVM

The JVM performance diagnostics page provides a large magnitude of information for running JVM threads, including historical information related to resources utilization, garbage collection, and so on. If users are frequently reporting performance issues with a particular product then you may want to keep this console open to monitor sudden spikes in resources utilization by the selected JVM.

■ **Note** If you have not configured Cloud Control yet, you can monitor JVM performance by choosing the WebLogic Server menu ➤ JVM Performance in Fusion Applications control for a specific WebLogic managed server. The disadvantage here is that by default it shows only the last 15 minutes of performance summary, while Cloud Control stores historical data, which allows you to generate more accurate performance graphs.

An important feature of JVM performance diagnostics is the ability to compare collected data from the current period with historical data and to compare the current period's performance with an earlier good performance period. In order to do this, you need to select the time period for which the performance issue has been reported by either selecting from the default options on the screen or by manually selecting start and end times. Now select the Compare With checkbox. This will prompt you to select another historical time period similar to how you selected current period. Figure 15-28 shows an example of the last 15 minutes server state chart with past day performance charts.

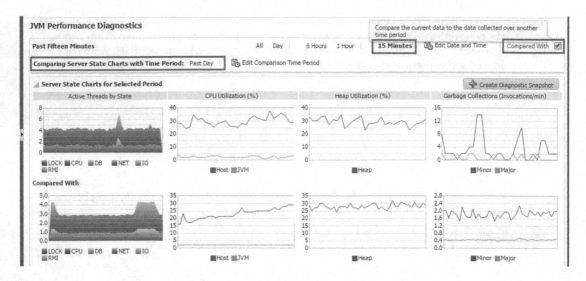

Figure 15-28. *JVM Performance Diagnosis comparison*

JVM Performance comparison with valid historical data gives you clues to understand whether the current period performance is abnormal. This can save a lot of time by eliminating the selected JVM from the list of suspects for slowness or errors.

Live JVM Thread Analysis

Another useful feature of JVM Diagnostics is live thread analysis. Often you may see that once a user has clicked on a page link, it may show a waiting or spinning icon on the page for long time. You can analyze the live JVM threads using Live Thread Analysis page. You can launch this page by clicking on the Live Thread Analysis button from the JVM/JVM Pool homepage or by choosing the Diagnostics ➤ Live Thread Analysis link from any product page menu. The active threads are shown with the [ACTIVE] prefix and the stuck threads are listed with the [STUCK] prefix. You can search for the thread name starting with [STUCK] to filter only those threads. Clicking on any of any of the threads provides detailed information about what the activity was at the thread level and the wait status. This page also provides an option to stop and start the WebLogic server. There could be other dependencies that might be causing the thread to be stuck or not respond, so troubleshoot thoroughly before making a critical decision like service bounce or adding more JVMs.

Figure 15-29 shows an example of Live Thread Analysis for the JVM Pool for the CommonDomain (CommonDomain_jvmpool).

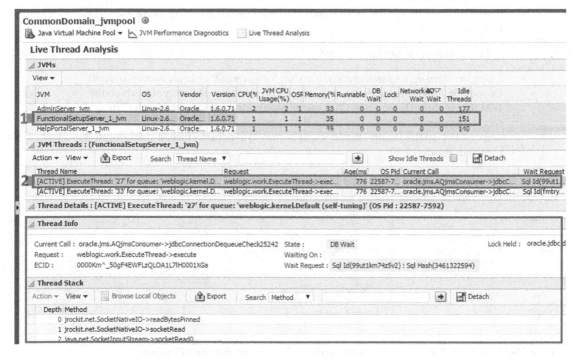

Figure 15-29. *Live Thread Analysis example*

As you can see in Figure 15-29, the Live Thread Analysis of JVM Pool lists all the JVMs included in this pool, each of which corresponds to a WebLogic server. Clicking on any of the JVMs populates the list of JVM threads corresponding to the selected JVM, with a summary of each thread in JVM threads table. Once you select a thread from this table, it populates the Thread Info and Thread Stack subsections under the Thread Details section. You can see what exactly is running on this JVM thread in real time. Unlike other JVM diagnostics pages, this page has an Auto Refresh option that you can select at the top of the page. The default values are 30 seconds and 1 minute, but you can select a custom Auto Refresh interval in seconds.

JVM Thread Dumps

Java Virtual Machine thread dumps are mostly included in the automatically created incidents related to JVM issues. But in many circumstances you may need to obtain JVM thread dumps manually to troubleshoot an issue or to provide to Oracle Support since they contain some of the most critical pieces of information for Oracle Support to diagnose and resolve an issue. There are multiple ways to collect a thread dump. Let's look at some of these methods.

- *Using the Command Line*: In order to generate a thread dump for a WebLogic managed server from the command line, you need to get the OS process ID (pid) for the server JVM process. Use the following command to get the OS pid for the Linux platform.

```
ps -ef | grep <DomainName> | grep <ManagedServer_Name> | awk '{print $2}'
```

Once you have the pid for the JVM, you can generate thread dump using the following command.

```
kill -3 <managed_server_process_ID>
```

- *Using the WebLogic Administration Console*: Navigate to WebLogic Administration Console ➤ Environment ➤ Servers and click on the managed server for which the JVM thread dump is required. Click on the Monitoring tab followed by the Threads tab. Here you will see summary of the JVM thread activity for the selected managed server. Click on the Dump Thread Stacks button to generate a thread stack dump, as shown in Figure 15-30.

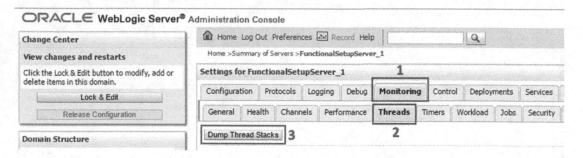

Figure 15-30. *Getting JVM thread stacks dump through the Administration Console*

- *Using Fusion Applications Control*: Alternatively if you are logged in to the Fusion Applications Control interface for the required WebLogic server, you open WebLogic Server ➤ JVM Performance on the WebLogic Server homepage and click on the Thread Dump button on the JVM Performance page to generate the JVM thread stack dump, as shown in Figure 15-31.

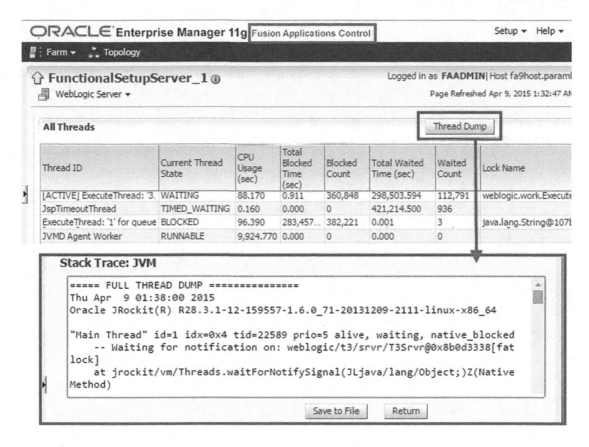

Figure 15-31. JVM thread dump example

Summary

In this chapter you explored some of the important aspects of Fusion Applications diagnostics and troubleshooting. However, troubleshooting all aspects of the Fusion Applications environment is not limited to the activities listed here. Most of the time, it involves teamwork between a support desk team, network-security team, core DBAs, Fusion Middleware and Identity Management experts, and functional specialists. Recent releases of Fusion Applications provide much better diagnostic features and enhancements coupled with Cloud Control features to identify and resolve issues rapidly as compared to earlier releases.

In the beginning of the chapter, you learned about some common troubleshooting features of Fusion Applications followed by various methods of tracing issues at the database level. Since Enterprise Scheduler plays a sizable role in the day-to-day business, you saw Enterprise Scheduler jobs troubleshooting as well. At the end of the chapter, you got a glimpse of JVM troubleshooting features provided by Fusion Applications in conjunction with Cloud Control. This chapter gives you a good starting point in overall troubleshooting and diagnosing of a Fusion Applications environment.

■ ■ ■

## CHAPTER 16

Patching and Ongoing Administration

The discussion of Fusion Applications Administration is incomplete without mentioning *patching* activities. Patching is a mundane but invariably essential task for any Enterprise Application environment. Each shipped application or technology stack could have platform-specific or generic bugs or security vulnerability that's undetected or not exposed at the time of the release. The Oracle Support and Development teams are constantly working on improving the applications or technology components due to issues encountered and reported by customers or as result of sophisticated security scans. Oracle releases fixes for these bugs in the form of patches and patch bundles. Some of these patches are security-related, critical patch updates and are mandatory, whereas others need to be applied on an on-demand basis if the same issue is encountered in your environment.

We will begin this chapter by looking at how to plan, prepare, apply, monitor, and verify patches on your Fusion Applications instance. In the later sections, we will look at how to maintain the applications environment by running a specialized utility called *AD Administration*. At the end of this chapter we will look at another critical administrative activity—backing up and restoring the Fusion Applications environment. In that section, you will see how to plan for the optimal backup strategy for your organization and effectively restore or recover the complete environment or specific components based on requirement.

Understanding Patching Fundamentals

Before we look at the patching procedures, we must first understand the basics of Fusion Applications patches, since there are multiple types of patches applicable to a Fusion Applications environment. Depending on each type of patch we will need to invoke a specific patching method or select the best possible method from multiple possible options, if available. In this section we will first understand different types of patches for Fusion Applications followed by various patching methods. In the later sections we will look at major patching methods in details with the help of example patches. In each section we will explore the directory structure of relevant generic patch and learn how the patching mechanism processes the patch directories.

Types of Patches

In this section we will look at the different types of patches available for overall Fusion Applications environment or its individual components. Some patches address a specific bug while other types of patches include consolidated lists and are released by Oracle at specific times of the year. Fusion Applications patches are mainly classified into two categories—technology and functional patches. Based on the type of patch, you may need to use different patching mechanisms as well. Let's look at types of patches followed by various patching methods in the next section.

© Tushar Thakker 2015
T. Thakker, *Pro Oracle Fusion Applications*, DOI 10.1007/978-1-4842-0983-7_16

Fusion Applications Technology Patches

As we know, Fusion Applications is based on the Oracle Fusion middleware technology so when we talk about Fusion Applications technology patches, we will essentially look at Fusion middleware and database-related patches. Every new release of Fusion Applications also includes essential middleware and database patches. Depending on the specific issue with the Fusion Applications technology stack you may find *one-off patches* for Fusion middleware or database and these patches can be applied on the individual middleware product home.

In addition to one-off patches, Oracle releases *Critical Update Patches (CPU)* for every product every three months. These patches include recommended vulnerability fixes in addition to other mandatory patches. Critical Patch Updates are released on the Tuesday closest to the 17th day of January, April, July, or October. The following are the example dates for CPUs. Since CPUs are cumulative in nature, you can download the latest CPU for any middleware or database product and it will include all the previous fixes for the selected product.

- 14 April 2015

- 14 July 2015

- 20 October 2015

- 19 January 2016

Although Fusion middleware CPUs can be applied on any installation of Fusion middleware, Oracle releases special patches named P4FA (Patches for Fusion Applications) built on the Fusion middleware stack. These patches are released as a bundle that includes cumulative FMW Critical Patch Updates as well as other fixes tested for the Fusion Applications platform. P4FA patch bundles include middleware products like WebLogic, WebCenter, Identity Management, ADF, BI, SOA, and so on, as well as important database-related patches. It is recommended that you apply P4FA patches instead of regular middleware CPUs for Fusion Applications unless they are specifically required to resolve any urgent issue related to the applications technology stack. P4FA patches are released every month and are cumulative in nature, so you can download the latest P4FA patch and skip any previous missed FMW CPU or P4FA patches.

Fusion Applications Functional Patches

Similar to the technology stack patches, you may also need to apply one-off patches for resolving application-specific functional issues. These patches contain application files and/or database scripts for one or more product families or individual products and address a specific issue.

In addition to one-off functional patches, Oracle releases AOO (aggregated one-off) patches on a weekly basis and include existing one-off patches. Apart from aggregate one-offs, Oracle also releases functional patch bundles every month, which include all the AOOs. Unless you have a critical issue and you cannot wait for the patch bundle, you should always apply patch bundles for each product family.

Patches for Oracle Middleware Extensions for Fusion Applications

Since the Fusion Applications functional patches address issues specific to Fusion Applications product families, the middleware extensions for Fusion Applications that are located outside of the Fusion Applications home are not included in these functional patches. The patches for the Oracle middleware extensions include Applications core functional and database artifacts and are released in a similar package as Oracle E-Business Suite patches. They can be applied using the traditional AutoPatch utility. We will look at the patching methods of each of these patch types in the next section.

Note that the P4FA patches also include Applications core patches and soon we will see how the patching utilities are aware of each types of patches included in the bundle and deploy individual utilities for each of the included patches.

Patching Methods

Since Fusion Applications involves a number of components and accordingly various types of patches, the methods to apply each of these patches varies depending on the components impacted by the patch as well as whether the patch is a one-off or a bundle. Although the underlying patching mechanism might be common across multiple patching methods, selecting the appropriate patching method helps you save time and reduce errors. Let's review the various patching methods available for Fusion Applications followed by a detailed discussion of the most frequently used methods.

OPatch

OPatch is the most commonly known patching utility that we have already discussed earlier for database and middleware technology stack patching. *OPatch* is used to apply one-offs, critical patch updates, and bundle patches for database and Fusion middleware patches. You must use the recommended version of the OPatch utility for applying the patch. You must also set the appropriate product home directory before applying OPatch, since the same utility is used by multiple product families.

AutoPatch

If you have worked as an administrator for products like Oracle E-Business Suite then you may already be familiar with the AutoPatch utility, which is used to apply most of the application functional patches. In Fusion Applications, you do not manually use AutoPatch for applying regular functional patches. The next utility that we will discuss will invoke AutoPatch automatically based on the patch requirement. However, when you are applying patches for middleware extensions for Fusion Applications or for the Functional Setup Manager then you may need to run AutoPatch manually to apply those specific patches.

Fusion Applications Patch Manager

The Fusion Applications Patch Manager (`fapmgr`) is a specialized tool that applies Fusion Applications related functional patches. This tool acts as a wrapper for the traditional AutoPatch utility and provides much more advanced control and management functionalities for seamless application of Fusion Applications patches. As discussed earlier, despite the complex architecture of Oracle Fusion Applications, this utility makes it easy to patch and maintain the Applications environment with the help of extensive validation and reporting capabilities.

The FASPOT Utility (Fusion Applications Smart Patch Orchestration Tool)

With the recent release of P4FA bundle patches, Oracle provides a specialized utility named FASPOT *(Fusion Applications Smart Patch Orchestration Tool),* which completely simplifies patching of all Fusion middleware components included in the P4FA bundle. This utility eliminates the need of manually applying CPUs for each middleware component, which is otherwise a highly error-prone activity due to the volume of patches to be applied as well as the number of middleware and database components involved in patching. The FASPOT utility is aware of the Fusion middleware components for Fusion Applications as well as Identity Management tiers. At this moment, FASPOT does not support RDBMS patches, so the included RDBMS patches need to be applied prior to starting the FASPOT utility.

Oracle Identity Management Patch Manager

The *Oracle Identity Management Patch Manager* is another tool to simplify patching of all products within Identity Management. *Identity Management Patch Manager* (idmpatchmgr) and *Identity Management Patch Manager* (idmpatch) are tools included in the Identity Management patching framework and they allow patch application on multiple nodes with capabilities to run pre- and post-patching steps, start and stop of services, and minimizing overall downtime required for Identity Management components patching. This tool is automatically installed while provisioning the Identity Management environment using the Identity Management Provisioning wizard.

Figure 16-1 shows a summary of all the patching methods for each component of a Fusion Applications environment as discussed. Depending on the component type as well as the patch type, you need to decide the appropriate patching method to be selected.

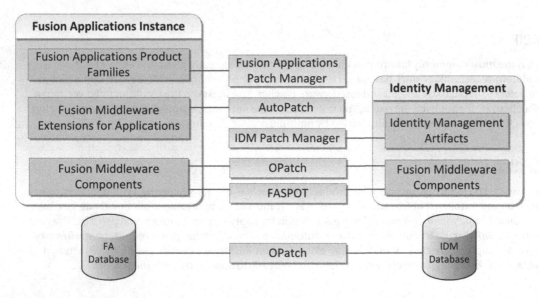

***Figure 16-1.** Patching methods for the Fusion Applications environment components*

Applying Technology Stack Patches

In this section we will look at how to efficiently apply Fusion Applications technology patches that are commonly known as *P4FA (Patches for Fusion Applications)* using FASPOT. Although you can apply the technology stack patches included in the P4FA bundle individually using the OPatch tool, you will see how you can achieve reduced downtime and error-free patch application using this method. In the later sections we will look at patching methods for other types of patches.

P4FA (Patches for Fusion Applications) Directory Structure

Before we start applying a Fusion Applications technology patch bundle (labeled as *P4FA*), let's first understand what a P4FA patch looks like. As we already know, it contains Critical Patch Updates (CPUs) and any additional required patches for Fusion middleware and RDBMS related to a Fusion Applications deployment. Although RDBMS patches should be applied manually before the other patches, all required patches are bundled in the same patch ZIP file. Figure 16-2 shows a typical directory structure for a P4FA patch.

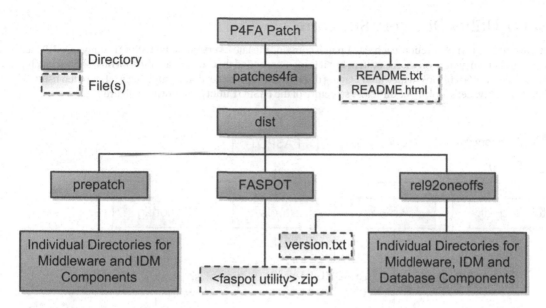

Figure 16-2. P4FA patch directory structure

Most P4FA patches come in multipart ZIP files. Extract the ZIP files labeled 1of4, 2of4, and so on, in a single patch directory. Let's look at the structure of the extracted patch directory.

- *README files*: The README files list the directories and files included in the patch. They might advise you to apply patches individually by reading each patch README files but you may use the FASPOT utility instead.

- *patches4fa*: This is the root directory suggesting that it is a P4FA patch. It contains another top-level directory named dist.

  - FASPOT: This directory contains the latest FASPOT utility in ZIP format. We will look at this directory in the next section.

  - prepatch: Many of the included patches require one or more prepatches. This directory contains these patches for some of the products.

  - rel92oneoffs: This is the main patch directory. It includes one-offs and CPU and PSU patches for middleware products and RDBMS. Each of the product directories includes one or more subdirectories specific to the type of patches included in the P4FA bundle.

■ **Note**   It is recommended that you extract the P4FA patch on a shared file system that's accessible by all Fusion Applications nodes with Fusion middleware components as well as all Identity Management nodes. This allows the utility to apply the related patches on the given host based on the configuration files created during the preparation phase.

FASPOT Utility Directory Structure

As you saw in the previous section, each P4FA patch contains the latest version of the FASPOT utility in a ZIP file. You can extract it anywhere on the file system but it is recommended that you extract the tool on a shared Patch Staging directory. We will look at the Patch Staging directory in the next section of applying a P4FA patch using the FASPOT utility. Let's look at the directory structure of the FASPOT utility, as shown in Figure 16-3.

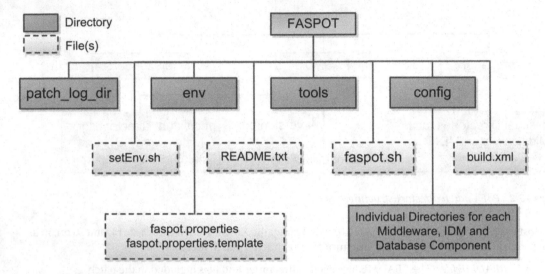

Figure 16-3. *FASPOT directory structure*

Let's take a quick look at the files and subdirectories included with the FASPOT utility.

- env: This directory contains an important property file named faspot.properties, along with a template file with sample values. You need to enter the complete Fusion Applications instance related details in this file so that the faspot.sh utility can correctly identify the components and their locations. We will look at this file during the patching preparation phase in the next section.

- tools: As the name of the FASPOT utility suggests, the patch application is orchestrated by the ANT utility similar to what you saw during the provisioning orchestration process. The tools directory contains important utilities and programs like ANT, JDK, and so on, that are required during the patching process.

- config: This directory contains various sub-directories for the Fusion middleware products. The files are updated once you have created the environment properties file and run the local environment configuration steps using the FASPOT utility. Once these directories are populated, the faspot.properties file is no longer referenced until the environment configuration is manually run again.

- patch_log_dir: By default this directory does not exist in the supplied FASPOT ZIP file. This directory is created during the environment configuration phase. It creates important log files that contain the status of each phase of patch application.

- README.txt: The README.txt file for the FASPOT utility contains a wealth of information on how to apply a P4FA patch using the FASPOT utility.

- `setEnv.sh`: This script contains environment variables to set up the JAVA and ANT environment. However, the `faspot.sh` script also contains the required variables.

- `build.xml`: This is an important Orchestration build file used by ANT to process the tasks required for each phase.

- `faspot.sh`: This is the main FASPOT utility that we will use to apply P4FA patches. Note that at this moment there is no Windows version available for the FASPOT utility.

FASPOT (P4FA) Patching Steps

As you saw earlier, the FASPOT utility is introduced to reduce the hassles of manually applying 100+ patches included in each P4FA patch along with the required post-steps. Prior to introduction of the FASPOT utility, it required lengthy planning and preparation before we could apply the P4FA bundle patches. In this section we will see how quickly we can accomplish this using FASPOT. However, it is not a single step procedure as one may expect from the previous description. Some of the steps that we will follow in the preparation phase may not need to be run every time but are still recommended to review the environment configuration every time you apply a P4FA patch using FASPOT if there have been any changes.

Figure 16-4 shows a summary of tasks required in order to complete a P4FA patch application cycle using the FASPOT utility.

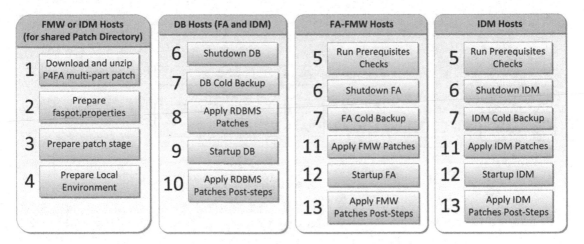

Figure 16-4. Fusion Applications technology patch bundle application

As you can see in Figure 16-4, you can divide the overall patch application in four major stages.

1. *Preparation*: This phase includes downloading and extracting the multipart patch, preparing the property file with the Fusion Applications environment information, creating patch staging and work areas and preparing the local environment, and populating individual properties files related to each middleware product to be patched.

2. *Database Patches Application*: FASPOT does not currently support RDBMS patches due to multiple possible architectures including RAC, non-RAC, minimum or higher versions of database in your environment. However, all the required patches for minimum supported database versions, including `exadata` patches, are included in the patch bundle under the `rdbms` directory. You need to apply database patches along with post-steps at this stage.

565

3. *Identity Management (IDM) Patches Application*: We need to apply the Identity Management related patches followed by the IDM post-steps in this phase. Although IDM and FMW (Fusion middleware) patches for Fusion Applications nodes are separate build targets in the FASPOT patching orchestration process, we can run some phases of both of them in parallel.

4. *Fusion Middleware (FMW) Patches Application on Fusion Applications Nodes*: Next we need to run FMW patches related to the Apply and Post-Apply phases on Fusion Applications nodes, which will patch the Fusion middleware components on each application and web node.

Let's look at each of these steps along with an example P4FA patch.

Downloading P4FA Patches

The first step is to identify, locate, and download the latest P4FA patch. As discussed earlier, each P4FA patch is cumulative in nature and includes all the fixes included in the previous P4FA bundles, so you need to download the latest patch only. In order to download the patches, log in to the Oracle Support portal and navigate to the Patches tab. Figure 16-5 shows the Patch Search screen. Let's explore how to locate a P4FA patch bundle using this screen.

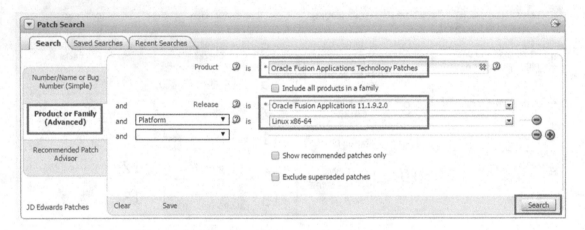

Figure 16-5. *Searching for the Fusion Applications technology patch bundles (P4FA)*

In the Patch Search screen, click on the Product or Family (Advanced) tab to search based on product family, platform, and so on. As shown in Figure 16-5, enter the Fusion Applications Technology Patches as the product, the version of your Fusion Apps instance, the required platform (Linux x84-64 for example), and then click Search. Figure 16-6 shows the search results based on this query. Note that you may get different results based on the latest P4FA patches at the time of search.

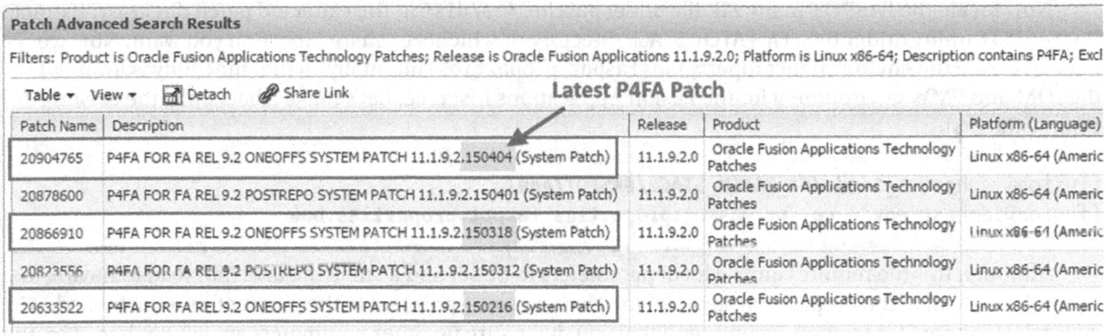

Patch Advanced Search Results

Filters: Product is Oracle Fusion Applications Technology Patches; Release is Oracle Fusion Applications 11.1.9.2.0; Platform is Linux x86-64; Description contains P4FA; Excl

Table ▾   View ▾   ▦ Detach   🔗 Share Link   **Latest P4FA Patch**

Patch Name	Description	Release	Product	Platform (Language)
20904765	P4FA FOR FA REL 9.2 ONEOFFS SYSTEM PATCH 11.1.9.2.150404 (System Patch)	11.1.9.2.0	Oracle Fusion Applications Technology Patches	Linux x86-64 (Americ
20878600	P4FA FOR FA REL 9.2 POSTREPO SYSTEM PATCH 11.1.9.2.150401 (System Patch)	11.1.9.2.0	Oracle Fusion Applications Technology Patches	Linux x86-64 (Americ
20866910	P4FA FOR FA REL 9.2 ONEOFFS SYSTEM PATCH 11.1.9.2.150318 (System Patch)	11.1.9.2.0	Oracle Fusion Applications Technology Patches	Linux x86-64 (Americ
20823556	P4FA FOR FA REL 9.2 POSTREPO SYSTEM PATCH 11.1.9.2.150312 (System Patch)	11.1.9.2.0	Oracle Fusion Applications Technology Patches	Linux x86-64 (Americ
20633522	P4FA FOR FA REL 9.2 ONEOFFS SYSTEM PATCH 11.1.9.2.150216 (System Patch)	11.1.9.2.0	Oracle Fusion Applications Technology Patches	Linux x86-64 (Americ

Figure 16-6. *Selecting the latest P4FA patch*

In the Patch Search Results screen, you may see more than one P4FA patch applicable to your environment. The patch description may be in the following format.

```
P4FA for REL <Release> ONEOFFFS SYSTEM PATCH <version>.<patch_creation_date(YYMMDD)>
```

For example:

```
P4FA for REL 9.2 ONEOFFFS SYSTEM PATCH 11.1.9.2.150404
```

Note that the date shown is the patch creation date, not the release date, so you may see a difference here. As you can see in Figure 16-6, we have P4FA patches released in February, March, and April so we will download the April patch only. The P4FA patches come in multiple parts, so you need to download all the parts and extract them into a single directory.

Setting Up the FASPOT Utility

Since the FASPOT utility needs to be applied on all IDMs as well as on the FA nodes with the Fusion middleware components, you must create the patch staging area on a shared location. This location could temporarily be created and moved later if security is a concern. In this example we have created a shared location at /FA_PATCH_STAGE and all required P4FA patches are going to be created in the rel92_patches directory under the staging directory. Since the P4FA patch bundle includes all required patches in ZIP format in each product directory, we must allocate a patch work area under the shared staging directory where the FASPOT utility can extract the patches before applying to the respective product homes.

```
[root@idmhost ~]# mkdir -p /FA_PATCH_STAGE/rel92_patches
[root@idmhost ~]# mkdir /FA_PATCH_STAGE /WORK
```

Assign ownership of the patch stage directory to the Fusion middleware owner user.

```
[root@idmhost ~]# chown -R fusion:dba /FA_PATCH_STAGE
```

Now locate the FASPOT utility ZIP file under patches4fa/dist in the extracted patch directory. Extract the FASPOT utility under the /FA_PATCH_STAGE directory or whichever shared location you want. Now we need to create the environment property file (faspot.properties) manually so that the utility is aware of the IDM and FMW environment for the Fusion Applications instance. Let's make a backup of the existing sample file first.

```
[fusion@idmhost ~]$ cd /FA_PATCH_STAGE/FASPOT/env/
[fusion@idmhost env]$ cp -pr faspot.properties faspot.properties.bak
```

Although this file requires quite a lot of parameters to be set and a small mistake may lead to having to rerun through all of the preparation steps, let me give you some pointers to the parameters to be looked at in general. However, it is strongly recommend that you make sure no other parameters are left out based on the current version of the FASPOT utility at the time you are applying the patch. Let's first confirm the changes in faspot.properties file related to the patching utility.

```
[fusion@idmhost env]$ grep PATCH faspot.properties
#PATCH_DOWNLOAD_DIR should contain the following folders
PATCH_DOWNLOAD_DIR=/FA_PATCH_STAGE/rel92_patches/11.1.9.2.150404/20904765/patches4fa/dist
PATCH_WORK_DIR=/FA_PATCH_STAGE/WORK
ATGPF_ADPATCH_WORKERS=4
```

Now make sure all URLs are updated and confirm the complete list with the following command.

```
[fusion@idmhost env]$ grep URL faspot.properties
```

Next make sure all the required passwords are set correctly. Look for the PASS string only since some parameters have PASSWD while others have PASSWORD in the parameter names.

```
[fusion@idmhost env]$ grep PASS faspot.properties
```

Next make sure that the hostnames for the IDM and FMW components are set correctly.

```
[fusion@idmhost env]$ grep HOST faspot.properties
```

Make sure the path for each component home directory is set correctly.

```
[fusion@idmhost env]$ grep HOME faspot.properties
```

Make sure all required domains are included since the sample file may not have all the domains as per your provisioned environment.

```
[fusion@idmhost env]$ grep DOMAIN_HOME faspot.properties
```

Next, confirm that the required database-related properties are set correctly. This includes IDM, OID, and FA databases.

```
[fusion@idmhost env]$ grep DB faspot.properties
```

■ **Caution**   Note that even if you have same database for your OID and IDM components (`idmdb`), the IDM provisioning process created the TNS entry named `OIDDB` with the same values as IDMDB. Hence, you should leave the value for `OID_DB` in the `faspot.properties` file to `oiddb` unless you have manually changed the TNS entry in `<OID_INSTANCE>/config/tnsnames.ora`.

Finally, make sure all the required port values for each component is set as per your environment.

```
[fusion@idmhost env]$ grep port faspot.properties
```

Preparing the Patch Stage Directory

The next step is to create the Patch Stage and Work Area directories. Instead of manually unzipping all patches for each product, you can use the `prepare-patch-stage` target of the FASPOT utility to seamlessly prepare the patch as well as the prepatch directories in the work area. Since the FASPOT utility is currently available on the Linux/Unix platform only, all references to FASTPOT effectively refer to the `faspot.sh` script.

Let's invoke the `faspot.sh` script to prepare the patch stage directory first. Note that you may need to change the directory to the location where you extracted the FASPOT utility. You can change the log filename to any desired format. Here we are using `<target-name>.log` for ease of understanding. Since the actual script output may be quite lengthy, we show truncated output that lists only the important messages that need to be noticed.

```
[fusion@idmhost ~]$ cd /FA_PATCH_STAGE/FASPOT/
[fusion@fahost FASPOT]$ ./faspot.sh -Dlogfile=prepare-patch-stage.log prepare-patch-stage
Buildfile: FA_PATCH_STAGE/FASPOT/build.xml

prepare-patch-stage-pre-check:
     [echo] The required files for prepare-patch-stage are present in the /FA_PATCH_STAGE/
     rel92_patches/11.1.9.2.150404/20904765/patches4fa/dist

prepare-patch-stage:
     [move] Moving 1 file to FA_PATCH_STAGE/FASPOT/env
     [move] Moving 1 file to FA_PATCH_STAGE/FASPOT/env
     [echo] **********PATCH_WORK_DIR**** - [/FA_PATCH_STAGE/WORK]

clean-up:
     [echo] Cleaning up DIR - [/FA_PATCH_STAGE/WORK]
   [delete] Deleting directory /FA_PATCH_STAGE/WORK
     [echo] Creating Fresh DIR - [/FA_PATCH_STAGE/WORK]
   [mkdir] Created dir: /FA_PATCH_STAGE/WORK
     [echo]  STARTED : Copying patches to /FA_PATCH_STAGE/WORK

p4fa-copy:
     [echo]  Processing P4FA Patches
     [copy] Copying 158 files to /FA_PATCH_STAGE/WORK

patch-unzip:
   [delete] Deleting: /FA_PATCH_STAGE/WORK/prepatch/atgpf/generic/install_ps6_16928612.zip
```

```
chmod-dir:
    [echo] STARTED : Changing permissions(775) of files and directories under /FA_PATCH_
    STAGE/WORK/prepatch/atgpf/generic
    [echo] COMPLETED : Changing permissions(775) of files and directories under /FA_PATCH_
    STAGE/WORK/prepatch/atgpf/generic
    [echo] One-off Patches are extracted in /FA_PATCH_STAGE/WORK/prepatch/atgpf/generic
...
...
prepare-patch-stage-post-check:
    [echo] The required files for prepare-patch-stage are present in the /FA_PATCH_STAGE/WORK

BUILD SUCCESSFUL
Total time: 40 minutes 18 seconds
```

As you can see from this output, the faspot.sh utility copies the patches from the rel92oneoffs directory to the work area in prepatch as well as individual patches in the work directory. Then it proceeds to unzip the patches and deletes the ZIP files from the work directory (PATCH_WORK_DIR). At the end of this step, the required patches for the FASPOT utility are present in the work directory. The patch download directory (PATCH_DOWNLOAD_DIRECTORY) is no longer referenced.

Preparing the Local Environment Configuration

The next step in the preparation phase is to prepare the local environment configuration that populates product-specific property files for each product's subdirectories in the env directory of the FASPOT utility. Note that the required product subdirectories are present in the FASPOT/config directory even before this step and they include the properties file template. Once you run the prepare-local-env target using the FASPOT utility, it populates the <product>-env.properties file for each of the middleware products using the parameters specified earlier in the faspot.properties file. Note that any changes in the faspot.properties file from this point onward are not reflected in the configuration directory. They are therefore not effective in any further FASPOT patching activities. So if you find any incorrect information in the faspot.properties file, you must rerun this step in order to populate the product-specific properties files.

```
[fusion@fahost FASPOT]$ ./faspot.sh -Dlogfile=prepare-local-env.log prepare-local-env
Buildfile: FA_PATCH_STAGE/FASPOT/build.xml

prepare-local-env-pre-check:
    [echo] The required files for prepare-local-env are present in the /stage/WORK

prepare-local-env:
    [echo]  STARTED : Creating FA_PATCH_STAGE/FASPOT/patch_log_dir

create-patchlogdir:

clean-up:
    [echo] Cleaning up DIR - [FA_PATCH_STAGE/FASPOT/patch_log_dir]
    [echo] Creating Fresh DIR - [FA_PATCH_STAGE/FASPOT/patch_log_dir]
   [mkdir] Created dir: FA_PATCH_STAGE/FASPOT/patch_log_dir
...
...
    [copy] Copying 4128 files to FA_PATCH_STAGE/FASPOT/patch_log_dir
```

```
    [copy] Copied 10169 empty directories to 6825 empty directories under FA_PATCH_STAGE/
    FASPOT/patch_log_dir
    [copy] Copying 27 files to FA_PATCH_STAGE/FASPOT/patch_log_dir
...
...
    [echo] SUCCESS : NO FAILURES FOUND  IN TARGET LOG FILES00
    [touch] Creating FA_PATCH_STAGE/FASPOT/patch_log_dir/audit_status_logs/logs/prepare-
    local-env.log-fahost.suc
prepare-local-env-post-check:
    [echo] The required files for prepare-patch-stage are present in the FA_PATCH_STAGE/
    FASPOT/patch_log_dir

BUILD SUCCESSFUL
Total time: 5 minutes 12 seconds
```

As you may notice, patch_log_dir also gets created at this stage. We have seen this directory while discussing the FASPOT directory structure. By default, this directory is not available in the shipped directory structure but gets created at this stage.

Applying Database Patches

Before proceeding to the IDM or FMW patches application, you must manually apply RDBMS patches using the latest version of OPatch, which is also included in the rdbms directory. You need to apply all the required generic or platform-specific patches, including the one-offs as well as the PSU (Patch Set Update) patches. Since the database patching requires setting the RDBMS Oracle home and applying patches using OPatch in the same way as you saw in Chapter 4 during database preparation for Fusion Applications installation, this does not require any further explanation here.

Running the Prerequisites Check

Before applying patches on the IDM or FMW nodes, you must run a prerequisites check on all the nodes in order to detect any conflicts or incorrect information in the properties file. This gives you an opportunity to fix the faspot.properties file and rerun the local environment step.

Running Identity Management Prerequisites Check

Let's first run the prerequisites check on the Identity Management nodes using the idm-prereq-check build target name. Run the following command on the IDM node from the FASPOT installation directory. Make sure that all previous steps have been completed and the same FASPOT directory was used while creating the local environment files.

```
[fusion@idmhost FASPOT]$ ./faspot.sh -Dlogfile=idm-prereq-check.log idm-prereq-check
Buildfile: /mnt/hgfs/FA_PATCH_STAGE/FASPOT/build.xml

idm-prereq-check:
    [echo] Directory path validations...
```

```
dirpath-check-list:
    [echo] Performing dirpath check for oid
    [echo] Valid Host. Continue Dir Path check execution
...
...
opatchlock-check-list:
    [echo] Performing opatch lock check for oid
    [echo] Valid Host. Continue OPatch Lock Check ...

opatchlock-prereq-check:
    [echo] Performing Opatch Lock Check for /app/oracle/products/dir/oid...
    [echo] SUCCESSFUL : No Opatch Lock found at ORACLE_HOME=/app/oracle/products/dir/oid.
...
...
load-oim:
    [echo] Loading of oim-env.properties
host.check:
    [echo]  Current Hostname is : idmhost.paramlabs.com
    [echo]  Component target Hostname is : idmhost.paramlabs.com
    [echo] Validating host before component target execution
    [echo] Valid Host. Continue executing component target
oim-prereq-check:
    [echo] Opatch lock check for OIF components...
opatchlock-prereq-check:
    [echo] Performing Opatch Lock Check for /app/oracle/products/app/idm...
    [echo] SUCCESSFUL : No Opatch Lock found at ORACLE_HOME=/app/oracle/products/app/idm.
...
...
dbconnection_check:
    [sql] Executing commands
    [sql] 1 of 1 SQL statements executed successfully
    [echo] Checking DB Connections for OIM-mdsDB
dbconnection_check:
    [sql] Executing commands
    [sql] 1 of 1 SQL statements executed successfully

BUILD SUCCESSFUL
Total time: 31 seconds
```

The prerequisites check should be quick. If the status of this check is FAILED, you must fix all mentioned issues before proceeding to the next step. Make sure that the OPatch version for each Identity Management product home matches the same or minimum required OPatch version of the Fusion Applications nodes. If the OPatch version of the IDM nodes is older, you may get false errors related to prerequisite patches existence, as follows.

```
FASPOT-EC-1055 - PREREQ_PATCH_ID - 16178493 NOT found in inventory
```

If you look up the log files you may see following error.

```
Syntax Error... Unrecognized Command or Option: failed to parse arguments "unknown option
'-customLogDir'"
Please use the option 'opatch lsinventory -help' to get correct syntax
OPatch failed with error code 14
```

As you can see, the older versions of OPatch do not recognize arguments like -customLogDir and failures in OPatch commands show false errors related to prerequisite patches. In this case, you can rename the existing OPatch directories on the IDM node and replace them with a higher version OPatch directory from the Fusion Applications nodes. Then you can rerun this step.

Running Fusion Middleware Prerequisites Check

The next step is to run the prerequisites check on the Fusion Applications nodes that have Fusion middleware components using the fmw-prereq-check build target. Run the following command on each FMW node using the same shared location.

```
[fusion@fahost FASPOT]$ ./faspot.sh -Dlogfile=fmw-prereq-check.log fmw-prereq-check
Buildfile: FA_PATCH_STAGE/FASPOT/build.xml

fmw-prereq-check:
    [echo] Directory path validations...

dirpath-check-list:
    [echo] Performing dirpath check for atgpf
    [echo] Valid Host. Continue Dir Path check execution

dirpath-prereq-check:
    [echo] Performing directory path check for /app/oracle/fusionapps/atgpf...
    [echo] SUCCESSFUL : Directory Path DIR_PATH=/app/oracle/fusionapps/atgpf existing for
atgpf component

dirpath-prereq-check:
    [echo] Performing directory path check for /app/oracle/fusionapps/jdk6...
    [echo] SUCCESSFUL : Directory Path DIR_PATH=/app/oracle/fusionapps/jdk6 existing for
atgpf component
...
...
check-string-in-file:
    [copy] Copying 1 file to FA_PATCH_STAGE/FASPOT/patch_log_dir/logs/prereq-check
    [echo] COMPONENT_ID - 11.1.9.2.0 found in inventory
    [echo] COMPONENT_VERSION_ID = true

BUILD SUCCESSFUL
Total time: 1 minute 11 seconds
```

Similar to the IDM prerequisites check, if you encounter any errors or mismatching values, you must fix the issues, update the faspot.properties file, and rerun the prepare-local-env target before rerunning the prerequisites check on the IDM and FMW nodes.

Applying Identity Management Patches

In order to apply Identity Management patches, you must make sure that the application and web tier are shut down while database should have already been started after RDBMS patching. We can also apply IDM and FMW patches in parallel but if the patches are relatively small and sufficient downtime is available, it is better to apply the patches one-by-one in order to make sure each phase completes without any issues. This also leaves enough room for troubleshooting patches on one server instead of focusing on multiple servers at the same time.

Execute the following command to run the idm-patch-apply target on the IDM hosts. The script output is truncated here to display major milestones only.

```
[fusion@fahost FASPOT]$ ./faspot.sh -Dlogfile=idm-patch-apply.log idm-patch-apply
Buildfile: /mnt/hgfs/FA_PATCH_STAGE/FASPOT/build.xml

idm-patch-apply:
    [echo]  STARTED : Performing patch pre-reqcheck  for IDM components
idm-prereq-check:
    [echo] Directory path validations...
dirpath-check-list:
    [echo] Performing dirpath check for oid
    [echo] Valid Host. Continue Dir Path check execution
dirpath-prereq-check:
    [echo] Performing directory path check for /app/oracle/products/dir/oid...
    [echo] SUCCESSFUL : Directory Path DIR_PATH=/app/oracle/products/dir/oid existing for
oid component
...
...
oid-patch-apply:
opatch.check:
    [echo] Opatch exists = true
napply:
    [echo] Applying using napply /app/oracle/products/dir/oid
    [echo] Applying PATCHES in /stage/WORK/label-patches/pltsec/linux64
    [echo] Applying PATCHES in /stage/WORK/label-patches/pltsec/linux64 is completed
    [echo]
    [echo] Checking the APPLY PATCH STATUS in log file
    [echo] APPLY PATCH SUCCESSFUL
    [echo] OID_LINUX64_STATUS - 0
...
...
check-string-in-file:
    [copy] Copying 1 file to /mnt/hgfs/FA_PATCH_STAGE/FASPOT/patch_log_dir/logs/failure
    [echo] SUCCESS : NO FAILURES FOUND  IN TARGET LOG FILES
    [touch] Creating /mnt/hgfs/FA_PATCH_STAGE/FASPOT/patch_log_dir/audit_status_logs/logs/
    idm-patch-apply.log-idmhost.suc

BUILD SUCCESSFUL
Total time: 32 minutes 28 seconds
```

Once the overall IDM patches application is successful, the tool will create a flag file named idm-patch-apply.log-<hostname>.suc to indicate successful completion. You must fix all the issues in patching before moving to the post-steps execution.

Applying Fusion Middleware Patches

The process of applying Fusion middleware patches using the FASPOT utility is identical to the one you saw seen while applying IDM patches. The build target name for applying FMW patches is fmw-patch-apply. Run the following command on the FMW hosts in order to apply patches to the middleware homes on the current host.

```
[fusion@fahost FASPOT]$ ./faspot.sh -Dlogfile=fmw-patch-apply.log fmw-patch-apply
Buildfile: FA_PATCH_STAGE/FASPOT/build.xml

fmw-patch-apply:
smartclone-check:
    [echo] SC_ENABLED_STATE - REGULAR_POD
    [echo] SC_ENABLED_STATE - REGULAR_POD
    [echo]  STARTED : Performing patch pre-reqcheck  for FMW components
fmw-prereq-check:
    [echo] Directory path validations...
dirpath-check-list:
    [echo] Performing dirpath check for atgpf
    [echo] Valid Host. Continue Dir Path check execution
dirpath-prereq-check:
    [echo] Performing directory path check for /app/oracle/fusionapps/atgpf...
    [echo] SUCCESSFUL : Directory Path DIR_PATH=/app/oracle/fusionapps/atgpf existing for
atgpf component
...
...
p4fa-label-apply:
check-string-in-file:
    [copy] Copying 1 file to FA_PATCH_STAGE/FASPOT/patch_log_dir/logs

check-string-in-file:
    [copy] Copying 1 file to FA_PATCH_STAGE/FASPOT/patch_log_dir/logs/failure
load-pfcore:
    [echo] Loading of pfcore-env.properties
    [echo] ORACLE_HOME - /app/oracle/fusionapps/applications
host.check:
    [echo]  Current Hostname is : fahost.paramlabs.com
    [echo]  Component target Hostname is : fahost.paramlabs.com
    [echo] Validating host before component target execution
    [echo] Valid Host. Continue executing component target

fmw-apply-label:
...
...
check-string-in-file:
    [copy] Copying 1 file to FA_PATCH_STAGE/FASPOT/patch_log_dir/logs/failure
    [echo] SUCCESS : NO FAILURES FOUND  IN TARGET LOG FILES
    [touch] Creating FA_PATCH_STAGE/FASPOT/patch_log_dir/audit_status_logs/logs/fmw-patch-
    apply.log-fahost.suc

BUILD SUCCESSFUL
Total time: 7 minutes 31 seconds
```

Move on to the post-steps execution only once the FMW patches are applied successfully and the success flag called fmw-patch-apply.log-<hostname>.suc is created.

Applying Identity Management Patches Post-Steps

If you have applied Fusion middleware patches manually, you would know that the process of identifying and applying manual post steps from a large number of patches is tiresome and error-prone. With the FASPOT utility, you need to run a build target named idm-patch-postinstall in order to apply all required post-install steps for the patches that have been applied on the IDM nodes. Run the following command to apply post-patching steps on the IDM hosts.

■ **Note** Make sure to bring up the IDM components before applying post-patching steps since the steps may require you to communicate with the middleware components.

```
[fusion@idmhost FASPOT]$ ./faspot.sh -Dlogfile=idm-patch-postinstall.log \
idm-patch-postinstall
Buildfile: /mnt/hgfs/FA_PATCH_STAGE/FASPOT/build.xml

idm-patch-postinstall:
     [echo]
     [echo] ######################################################
     [echo]  STARTED : Performing  Post Install redeployment actions for OID Components
load-oid:
     [echo] Loading of oid-env.properties
host.check:
     [echo]  Current Hostname is : idmhost.paramlabs.com
     [echo]  Component target Hostname is : idmhost.paramlabs.com
     [echo] Validating host before component target execution
     [echo] Valid Host. Continue executing component target
...
...
check-string-in-file:
     [copy] Copying 1 file to /mnt/hgfs/FA_PATCH_STAGE/FASPOT/patch_log_dir/logs/failure
     [echo] SUCCESS : NO FAILURES FOUND  IN TARGET LOG FILES
   [delete] Deleting: /mnt/hgfs/FA_PATCH_STAGE/FASPOT/patch_log_dir/audit_status_logs/logs/
   idm-patch-postinstall.log-idmhost.dif
    [touch] Creating /mnt/hgfs/FA_PATCH_STAGE/FASPOT/patch_log_dir/audit_status_logs/logs/
   idm-patch-postinstall.log-idmhost.suc

BUILD SUCCESSFUL
Total time: 1 minute 52 seconds
```

The post-steps may complete fairly quickly. Once the execution status is successful and the completion flag file idm-patch-postinstall.log-<hostname>.suc is created, proceed to the FMW post-patching steps.

Applying Fusion Middleware Patches Post-Steps

The last step in applying the P4FA patch bundle using the FASPOT utility is to apply Fusion middleware post-patching steps. The target name to execute is fmw-patch-postinstall. Run the following command on Fusion Applications nodes to apply the included patches specific to the middleware homes.

```
[fusion@fahost FASPOT]$ ./faspot.sh -Dlogfile=fmw-patch-postinstall.log fmw-patch-
postinstall
Buildfile: FA_PATCH_STAGE/FASPOT/build.xml

fmw-patch-postinstall:
    [echo]
    [echo] #########################################################
    [echo]  STARTED : Performing  Post Install and Redeployment actions for FMW Components
load-pfcore:
    [echo] Loading of pfcore-env.properties
    [echo] ORACLE_HOME - /app/oracle/fusionapps/applications
host.check:
    [echo]  Current Hostname is : fahost.paramlabs.com
    [echo]  Component target Hostname is : fahost.paramlabs.com
    [echo] Validating host before component target execution
    [echo] Valid Host. Continue executing component target
pfcore-patch-postinstall:
smartclone-check:
    [echo] SC_ENABLED_STATE - REGULAR_POD
    [echo] SC_ENABLED_STATE - REGULAR_POD
    [echo] Executing PFCORE Post Patch Steps - Configure
    [echo] Executing PFCORE Post Patch Steps - Bootstrap

    [echo] Execution of PFCORE Post Patch Steps was SUCCESSFUL
...
...
check-string-in-file:
    [copy] Copying 1 file to FA_PATCH_STAGE/FASPOT/patch_log_dir/logs/failure
    [echo] SUCCESS : NO FAILURES FOUND  IN TARGET LOG FILES
    [touch] Creating FA_PATCH_STAGE/FASPOT/patch_log_dir/audit_status_logs/logs/fmw-patch-
    postinstall.log-fahost.suc

BUILD SUCCESSFUL
Total time: 11 minutes 58 seconds
```

Once the Fusion middleware post-patching steps are completed successfully and the success flag fmw-patch-postinstall.log-fahost.suc has been created, the FASPOT patching process is complete. Now you can do a smoke test of application functionality and the issues that are expected to be resolved before releasing the environment to the users.

Applying Applications Patches

Fusion Applications one-off patches, AOOs, or patch bundles may include database or middleware artifacts depending on the included bug fixes. Before you look at how to apply an applications patch, let's explore how a Fusion Applications patch looks. Figure 16-7 explains the generic directory structure of an applications patch.

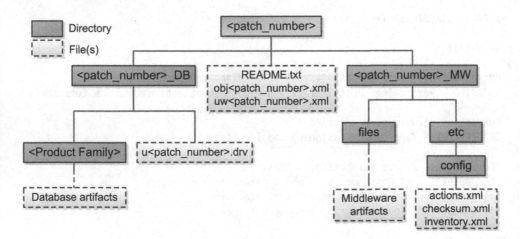

***Figure 16-7.** Directory structure of an applications patch*

As you can see in Figure 16-7, each Fusion Applications patch contains two main sections.

- *Database Artifacts*: The database artifacts directory <patch_number>_DB contains subdirectories and a unified driver file similar to a standalone database artifacts patch that can be applied using the AutoPatch utility.

- *Middleware Artifacts*: The Middleware artifacts directory contains the directory structure in a format that can be accessed and applied by the OPatch utility.

Apart from database and middleware artifacts directories, there are two important XML files in the patch directory.

- uw<patch_number>.xml: This file contains the overall information about the patch, including patch type, translation, language, and platform attributes, bug fixes included, prerequisite patches, and impacted components list.

- obj<patch_number>.xml: This file contains the patch objects manifest, which includes details about each database and middleware artifact included in the patch. The details for each artifact include the artifact name, type, product family, location, version, required action, and so on.

Using Fusion Applications Patch Manager

If you have used Oracle E-Business Suite patching mechanisms then you may already know that Applications patching is a niche domain and involves thorough understanding of the applications suite. Although Fusion Applications patching also involves similar tools such as AutoPatch, applying patches on complex architecture such as Fusion Applications that involves multiple architectural components, products, and artifacts could be generally seen as a complex process. Thanks to the Fusion Applications Patch Manager (fapmgr), the patch application has been quite simplified as well as less error-prone due to the various pre-patching validations and reports. In fact, if you have worked with AutoPatch for the E-Business Suite then you may find it even more comfortable applying Fusion Applications patches with the help of the Fusion Applications Patch Manager tool.

Let's first understand the Fusion Applications patching process using the fapmgr tool. Figure 16-8 lists the high-level steps involved in Fusion Applications patching.

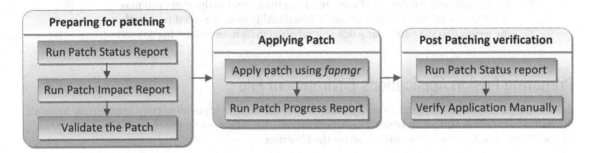

Figure 16-8. *Steps for patching using Fusion applications patch manager*

Let's now have a quick look at the high-level steps of patching using the Fusion Applications Patch Manager (fapmgr) and later we will discuss these steps in detail by applying an example patch.

Preparing for Patching

1. *Run patch status report:* You first need to check whether the patch is applied by running the Patch Status report before proceeding with any of the steps. Only if the patch is not already applied can you download the patch.

2. *Run the Patch Impact Report:* This report provides an excellent overview of the impact of applying this patch on your instance. It suggests if any prerequisites are required to be applied before this patch can be applied. It also lists the product families, servers, and files that will be impacted by this specific patch. It also helps in deciding the downtime length based on the impact report.

3. *Validate the patch:* Patch validation is automatically done as part of the patch application phase, but it is recommended to do a manual validation before actually applying the patch or taking downtime. The validation process does a simulation of actual patch application by checking the required prerequisites, taxonomy, and platform information, as well as any conflicts.

Applying Patches

4. *Apply the patch using the fapmgr tool*: Once the patch is validated, it may ask whether the patch can be applied online or offline. Accordingly you may apply the patch now. We will look at various optional parameters for the Apply phase in the next section.

5. *Monitor the patch progress*: You can monitor the patch progress using the built-in online patch progress report, the diagnostic report feature, or by manually running it depending on the version of Fusion Applications.

Post-Patching Verification

6. *Run the patch status report*: Once the patch is applied, you may want to confirm it by running the Patch Status report again for the same patch number.

7. *Verify application manually*: Before releasing the system to the users you may need to do a smote test for application functionality as well as confirm whether the issues that the particular patch was required to fix have indeed been resolved.

Preparing Fusion Applications Environment File

Before applying Applications patches we must first source the Fusion Applications environment file to set all the required OS environment variables. The default location for the environment file is $APPL_TOP/lcm/ad/bin/APPSORA.env. Let's first determine whether the file exists.

```
[fusion@fahost ~]$ cd /app/oracle/fusionapps/applications/lcm/ad/bin/
[fusion@fahost bin]$ ls -l APPSORA.env
ls: APPSORA.env: No such file or directory
```

If the file does not exist, you can create it manually using the adsetenv.sh script in the same directory so that you can use it in future.

```
[fusion@fahost bin]$ ./adsetenv.sh

Successfully created: APPSORA.env
adsetenv succeeded.
```

Now you can confirm that the file has been created.

```
[fusion@fahost bin]$ ls -l APPSORA.env
-rw-r--r-- 1 fusion dba 4420 Apr 15 22:59 APPSORA.env
```

Let's source this file to set the environment variables. Add the following line to the Fusion user's OS profile (for example, .bash_profile) to source it every time the user logs in.

```
[fusion@fahost bin]$ ./app/oracle/fusionapps/applications/lcm/ad/bin/APPSORA.env
```

We can test whether the variables have been set correctly. For example:

```
[fusion@fahost bin]$ env | grep APPL_TOP
APPL_TOP=/app/oracle/fusionapps/applications
APPL_TOP_NAME=FUSION
```

Running Pre-Patch Reports

Fusion Applications Patch Manager provides a number of reporting features, including listing all applied patches, looking for specific patch, specific components, as well as running Patch Impact Reports. Here we will look at pre-patch reports that are mainly required to understand whether the required patches are already applied and if they are not applied, what the impact is of applying the same.

Running Applied Patches Report

Fusion Applications Patch Manager can be used to list all the patches that have been applied on the Fusion Applications system. This can be used as an inventory of patches if Oracle Support requires it to resolve a particular issue. The following is an example of the running and applied patches report using the listpatches option.

```
[fusion@fahost bin]$ ./fapmgr.sh report -listpatches
...
Report Name: Patches Applied
Report for: FUSION [/app/oracle/fusionapps/applications]

Product Family (OUI Component) :: oracle.fusionapps.atgpf (oracle.fusionapps.atgpf)
Patch No. : 19526766
Language : American English
Patch Type : PATCH-SET
Date Applied (mm-dd-yyyy hh:mm:ss) : 10-28-2014  05:07:18
Bugs Fixed : 19526766

Patch No. : 19526765
Language : American English
Patch Type : PATCH-SET
Date Applied (mm-dd-yyyy hh:mm:ss) : 02-21-2015  04:57:11
Bugs Fixed : 19526765
...
Oracle Fusion Applications Patch Manager completed successfully.
```

List Applied Patches for Specific Components

If you want to run the applied patches report for specific components only, the same command allows you to filter the required components. Let's first see how to get the list of all components using the famgr.sh script. The output of the script will include the internal name of each component along with version, product family name, and so on.

```
[root@fahost bin]# ./fapmgr.sh report -listcomps
...
Report Name: Product Families
Report for: FUSION [/app/oracle/fusionapps/applications]
...
OUI Component : oracle.fusionapps.scm
Version : 11.1.9.2.0
Product Family : Oracle Fusion Supply Chain Management 11.1.9.2.0
Description : Oracle Fusion Supply Chain Management
```

```
OUI Component : oracle.fusionapps.prj
Version : 11.1.9.2.0
Product Family : Oracle Fusion Projects 11.1.9.2.0
Description : Oracle Fusion Projects
...
OUI Component : oracle.fusionapps.fin
Version : 11.1.9.2.0
Product Family : Oracle Fusion Financials 11.1.9.2.0
Description : Oracle Fusion Financials

OUI Component : oracle.fusionapps.crm
Version : 11.1.9.2.0
Product Family : Oracle Fusion Customer Relationship Management 11.1.9.2.0
Description : Oracle Fusion Customer Relationship Management

OUI Component : oracle.fusionapps.com
Version : 11.1.9.2.0
Product Family : Oracle Fusion Common Artifacts 11.1.9.2.0
Description : Oracle Fusion Common Artifacts
...
Oracle Fusion Applications Patch Manager completed successfully.
```

Now since we have the internal name of each component, we can filter the list of patches based on one or more components from this list in a comma-separated format, as follows.

```
[root@fahost bin]# ./fapmgr.sh report -listpatches -comps oracle.fusionapps.com
...
Started validating the OPatch version.
Completed validating the OPatch version.

Started validating the Database connection.
WLS ManagedService is not up running. Fall back to use system properties for configuration.
Completed validating the Database connection.
```

Report Name: Patches Applied
Report for: FUSION [/app/oracle/fusionapps/applications]

Product Family (OUI Component) :: Oracle Fusion Common Artifacts (oracle.fusionapps.com)
```
Patch No. : 19840904
Language : American English
Patch Type : Standard
Date Applied (mm-dd-yyyy hh:mm:ss) : 04-16-2015  01:09:43
Bugs Fixed : 19840904
...
Oracle Fusion Applications Patch Manager completed successfully.
```

List for Specific Patch or Bug Number (Patch Status Report)

In most cases you may need to check whether a particular patch or bug fix is already applied. This is required to make a decision on whether the patch or bug fix needs to be downloaded and applied. Use the following syntax to run the Patch Status report. Note that Language is an optional parameter.

```
./fapmgr.sh report -isapplied -patch <Patch_Number>[ :<Language> ]
```

or

```
./fapmgr.sh report -isapplied -bug <Bug_Fix_Number>[ :<Language> ]
```

Let's use an example patch to see if it is already applied.

```
[fusion@fahost bin]$ ./fapmgr.sh report -isapplied -patch 19898891
Oracle Fusion Applications Patch Manager Version 11.1.9.2.0
Copyright (c) 2009, 2013, Oracle and/or its affiliates. All rights reserved.

Archiving existing log files from [/app/oracle/instance/lcm/logs/11.1.9.2.0/FAPMGR] to
[/app/oracle/instance/lcm/logs/11.1.9.2.0/FAPMGR/logarchive/REPORT-
PATCHIMPACT/20150419201529].

Started validating the OPatch version.
Completed validating the OPatch version.
Started validating the Database connection.

WLS ManagedService is not up running. Fall back to use system properties for configuration.
Completed validating the Database connection.

Report Name: Patch Status
Report for: FUSION [/app/oracle/fusionapps/applications]

Bug No. : 19898891
OUI Component : NA
Status : Not Applied
Patch No. : NA
Date Applied (mm-dd-yyyy hh:mm:ss) :
...
Oracle Fusion Applications Patch Manager completed successfully.
```

The result confirms that the patch has not been applied so we can download and apply it.

Validating Patch List from Database Tables

Since Fusion Applications database records all the applications patches that have been applied in the environment, you can directly query these two tables to check the status of the patch.

- AD_APPLIED_PATCHES: This table lists all the patches that have been applied to the system with one record each patch regardless of whether it is one-off or bundle/maintenance patch. Once you apply a patch, an entry is added to this table along with patch application date.

- AD_BUGS: This table lists all the bug fixes that have been applied on the Fusion Applications instance. For example, if you have applied a bundle patch that included various bug fixes or patches, each of them is listed in this table along with the patch application date. Technically this table includes more details but if you applied a patch manually then both these tables will have an entry.

Let's view the contents of these tables by running example queries against them.

```
SQL> SELECT PATCH_NAME, PATCH_TYPE, LAST_UPDATE_DATE FROM FUSION.AD_APPLIED_PATCHES;
```

PATCH_NAME	PATCH_TYPE	LAST_UPDATE_DATE
19526766	PATCH-SET	28-OCT-14 05.02.46.000000 AM
19526766	PATCH-SET	28-OCT-14 05.07.18.000000 AM
19222260	PATCH-SET	28-OCT-14 05.10.04.000000 AM
19222260	PATCH-SET	28-OCT-14 05.10.54.000000 AM
11410231706	MAINTENANCE-PACK	28-OCT-14 06.19.03.000000 AM
11410231706	MAINTENANCE-PACK	28-OCT-14 08.53.41.000000 AM
20123584	PATCH-SET	17-APR-15 03.55.12.000000 PM
20123584	PATCH-SET	17-APR-15 04.03.45.000000 PM
19898891	SNOWBALL	19-APR-15 08.44.45.000000 PM
19898891	SNOWBALL	19-APR-15 08.45.04.000000 PM
19526765	PATCH-SET	21-FEB-15 04.55.28.000000 AM
18951938	PATCH-SET	21-FEB-15 04.59.03.000000 AM
18951938	PATCH-SET	21-FEB-15 04.59.58.000000 AM
19526765	PATCH-SET	21-FEB-15 04.57.12.000000 AM

```
SQL> SELECT BUG_NUMBER, APPLICATION_SHORT_NAME, LAST_UPDATE_DATE FROM FUSION.AD_BUGS;
```

BUG_NUMBER	APPLICATION_SHORT_NAME	LAST_UPDATE_DATE
19526766	atgpf	28-OCT-14 05.07.18.000000 AM
19222260	fsm	28-OCT-14 05.10.54.000000 AM
11410231706	ofat	28-OCT-14 08.54.03.000000 AM
20123584	atgpf	17-APR-15 04.47.41.000000 PM
19898891	fin	19-APR-15 08.45.05.000000 PM
18951938	fsm	17-APR-15 04.50.42.000000 PM
19526765	atgpf	21-FEB-15 04.57.12.000000 AM

Running a Patch Impact Report

Once the patch has been downloaded from Oracle Support portal, you can extract it to any directory. We will refer to this patch directory as patchtop during the example patch application. The first report that you need to run on the downloaded patch is the Patch Impact Report. This report essentially compares the files included in the patch with the files on your system. It achieves this by comparing the patch files with Current View Snapshot of your system. The Current View Snapshot basically keeps an inventory of your current file system and every change to the file system, especially after the patch application and so on, this snapshot gets updated. However, you can manually update the snapshot as well. We will look at the snapshots in the AD Administration section of this chapter.

Use the following command to run a Patch Impact Report for the downloaded patch.

```
[fusion@fahost bin]$ ./fapmgr.sh report -patchimpact -patchtop /home/fusion/Patches/19898891/
...
Started validating the OPatch version.
Completed validating the OPatch version.

Started validating the Database connection.
WLS ManagedService is not up running. Fall back to use system properties for configuration.
Completed validating the Database connection.

Started running apply pre-reqs.
Please monitor OPatch log file: /app/oracle/instance/lcm/logs/11.1.9.2.0/FAPMGR/opatch/
opatch/19898891_Apr_19_2015_20_34_01/ApplyPrereq2015-04-19_20-34-18PM_1.log
All apply pre-reqs for middleware artifacts have passed.
Patch Impact Report
Patch Number: 19898891
Oracle Fusion Applications Oracle Home: /app/oracle/fusionapps/applications
Language: NA
Platform: Generic

Bug Fixes
Bug No. : 19898891
Bug Description : REL92:BYPASS JERS LOCK VALIDATION FOR EXTRACT OBJECT AND REFERENCE OBJECT
CHANGE
Exists in Oracle Home : No

Oracle Fusion Applications Prerequisite Bug Fixes
No prerequisite bug fixes required.

Prerequisites on other products: Although Patch Manager does not enforce cross-product
prerequisite patches, you should apply them before applying patch #19898891
No prerequisites for other products found.

Product Families Impacted
Product Family : oracle.fusionapps.fin
Product : xla
Lba : FinXlaAmsAcctRules,FinXlaAmsDescriptionRule,FinXlaAmsEventModels,FinXlaAmsJlts,FinXla
AmsMappingSet
```

```
Patch contains the following artifacts that impact the following run-time servers
Artifact Type : DB
Domain(Servers) : fusiondb
```
Expectation/Impact : The database must be running. Artifacts like schema,seed data will be updated.

```
Artifact Type : Flexfields(NameSpace)
Domain(Servers) : NONE
Expectation/Impact : Flexfield namespaces will be merged.
```

```
Artifact Type : Flexfields(FndSetup.ear)
Domain(Servers) : CommonDomain(HelpPortalServer_1)
```
Expectation/Impact : Impacted managed servers will be bounced.
```
...
Files included in the patch
File Name : xla_slam_sddyn.sql
File Type : DB
File Version : /st_fusionapps_11.1.9.2.0fin/1
...
File Name : SvcFinXlaAmsDescriptionRuleModel_MiddleTier.jar
File Type : JEE
File Version : st_fusionapps_11.1.9.2.0fin/20141209170255
...
Oracle Fusion Applications Patch Manager completed successfully.
```

The output of the Patch Impact Report provides a list of bug fixes included in the patch, a list of prerequisite bug fixes required by the patch, files included along with version details, the servers and product families that will be impacted by the patch. This information is crucial to prepare for the downtime for affected product families and servers as well as to know which patches need to be applied before proceeding with the selected patch.

Validating the Patch

Validating a patch manually is an optional but recommended practice while applying patches using Fusion Applications Patch Manager. This saves troubleshooting time during the patch application by manually checking the prerequisites, file versions, validating SOA composites, and database by running a mock pass of the patch application. It can also suggest whether the patch can be run in *online* or *hotpatch* mode if you have passed those arguments while running validation. It also suggests if the patch is being applied online then which managed servers will be bounced at the end of patching activity. This greatly helps you identify downtime requirement for applications. Any conflicting patches or missing prerequisites are also listed here. Validation also checks taxonomy details, which confirm whether the required applicable products have been provisioned.

The command to validate a patch is as follows. You can add the -online and -hotpatch switches if you want to make sure the patch can be applied *online* and if so whether can be applied in *hotpatch* mode.

```
[fusion@fahost bin]$ ./fapmgr.sh validate -online -patchtop /home/fusion/Patches/19898891/
...
Completed validating the OPatch version.
```

Started validating the Database connection.
WLS ManagedService is not up running. Fall back to use system properties for configuration.
Completed validating the Database connection.

Started validating taxonomy URL.
Completed validating taxonomy URL.

Started checking pre-requisite bug fixes for the patch.
Completed checking pre-requisite bug fixes for the patch.
...
Validation successful.
Completed validating the Database components of the patch.

Started checking if the middleware portion of the patch will make any impact to the system.
Completed checking if the middleware portion of the patch will have an impact on the system.

Started running apply pre-reqs.
...
All apply pre-reqs for middleware artifacts have passed.

Started checking for the files that will not be deployed.
Completed checking for the files that will not be deployed.

Completed running apply pre-reqs.
Skipping execution, as the mode is not APPLY.
Submitting tasks for parallel execution.
...
Executing validate task [JEEPatchaction_stopManagedServers] with ID [49]. Monitor the log
file :
/app/oracle/instance/lcm/logs/11.1.9.2.0/FAPMGR/fapcore_validate_jeepatchaction_
stopmanagedservers_49_20150419203455.log
validate Task [Name: JEEPatchaction_stopManagedServers ID: 49] completed with status
[SUCCESS].
...
Tasks [3] completed out of [3].
Successfully completed execution of all tasks.

Started running deployment pre-reqs.
...
All deployment pre-reqs for middleware artifacts have passed.

Completed running deployment pre-reqs.

Validation of patch is SUCCESSFUL.
You can apply the patch either in online or offline mode successfully.

Generating Diagnostic Report
...
Oracle Fusion Applications Patch Manager completed successfully.

Applying the Patch

Once the patch has been validated against your environment, you may need to decide on whether downtime is required and if so for which applications. You might also determine whether the patch can be applied as a *hotpatch*. In order to decide this, you must first understand the difference between various modes available for applying patches using the Fusion Applications Patch Manager.

- **Offline Mode:** Assumes that all the affected managed servers are down and once the patch is complete, you need to manually start all those affected servers. You may either keep them down at the beginning or bounce after the patch application but the users should not be accessing the application during this time. Additionally, any post-steps like deployment of SOA, BI, or other middleware artifacts, or flexfields needs to be done manually after the patch application. You may avoid offline mode unless a validation step confirms that the patch cannot be applied online.

- **Online Mode:** Although the name suggests that application will always be available, this is not true. The difference between *online* and *offline* mode is that during online mode, you need not shut down the affected managed servers manually. Instead, the Patch Manager takes care of bouncing the required servers. It also completes all post-patching steps including deployment of all middleware artifacts. In order to run a patch in online mode, you must first validate the patch for checking whether it can be run online followed by running the Patch Manager Apply phase with the -online option. Additionally you must specify the command-line option -stoponerror so that if there are any errors during patch or post-patching steps, it may stop any further action. You can then fix the problem and restart the patch.

- **Maintenance Mode (Only for Fusion Applications 11g Release 8):** This was introduced in Oracle Fusion Applications version 11.1.8 and was replaced by the hotpatch option in version 11.1.9. So if you are patching Fusion Applications 11.1.8, then you can use the maintenance mode to apply patches in a controlled environment by changing the user application status to read only mode. In this mode, users can access the application and view data but it disables transactions at the application level. Maintenance mode can be enabled by using the profile option FND_MAINTENANCE_MODE, which can be set to ENABLED, DISABLED, or WARNING to display warnings about upcoming maintenance window based on the FND_MAINTENANCE_START_TIME and FND_MAINTENANCE_END_TIME parameters.

- **Hotpatch Mode (for Fusion Applications 11g Release 9 onward):** From Fusion Applications 11g Release 9 (11.1.9.x) onward, you can use the hotpatch mode, which is an extension of maintenance mode and allows you to apply patches even when there are active users and ongoing transactions in the Applications. However, not all patches can be applied in hotpatch mode. You must verify whether the patch can be applied in hotpatch mode by validating the patch by passing the -online and -hotpatch options, as seen earlier. All changes in hotpatch mode are applied and users are automatically directed to new versions after the changes are applied, the affected Enterprise schedulers are paused based on maintenance start and estimated end times.

You may optionally add another parameter called -workers <number> as the command-line argument for the fapmgr.sh script to specify the number of parallel workers if the patch involves any database tasks as well. By default, the workers value is automatically selected based on your system configuration, including operating systems, CPUs, and virtual CPUs. If the number you entered is not within the permissible range for your environment then the script may prompt you to enter another value.

Let's now proceed to apply the same patch that you validated earlier for applying online. As mentioned earlier, since you are using -online option, we will pass the -stoponerror option. Note that from Fusion Applications 11g, Release 9 onward, the Patch Manager (fapmgr) uses parallel processing of any non-dependent tasks, hence improving overall patch application time.

```
[fusion@fahost bin]$ ./fapmgr.sh apply -online -patchtop /home/fusion/Patches/19898891
-stoponerror -workers 4
...
Started validating the OPatch version.
Completed validating the OPatch version.

Started validating the Database connection.
WLS ManagedService is not up running. Fall back to use system properties for configuration.
Completed validating the Database connection.

Started validating taxonomy URL.
Completed validating taxonomy URL.

Started  checking pre-requisite bug fixes for the patch.
Completed checking pre-requisite bug fixes for the patch.

Reference number for the current Oracle Fusion Applications Patch Manager run is 143.

Started validating the Database components of the patch [19898891(US)].
Patch validation is in progress. This might take a while.
Monitor the adpatch log file : /app/oracle/instance/lcm/logs/11.1.9.2.0/FAPMGR/adpatch_
validate_19898891_20150419203607.log.
Validation successful.
Completed validating the Database components of the patch.

Started checking if the middleware portion of the patch will make any impact to the system.
Completed checking if the middleware portion of the patch will have an impact on the system.

Started running apply pre-reqs.
Please monitor OPatch log file: /app/oracle/instance/lcm/logs/11.1.9.2.0/FAPMGR/opatch/
opatch/19898891_Apr_19_2015_20_36_13/ApplyPrereq2015-04-19_20-36-39PM_1.log
All apply pre-reqs for middleware artifacts have passed.

Started checking for the files that will not be deployed.
Completed checking for the files that will not be deployed.

Started identifying Post Apply tasks.
Completed identifying Post Apply tasks.

Submitting tasks for parallel execution.
Diagnostic report is generated at /app/oracle/instance/lcm/logs/11.1.9.2.0/FAPMGR/
FAPMgrDiagnosticsSummary_apply_20150419203607.html. This will be updated every 5 mins.
```

```
Executing apply task [JEEPatchaction_stopManagedServers] with ID [59]. Monitor the log file
:
...
Tasks [1] completed out of [5].
apply Task [ Name: OfflinePatching_applybits ID: 60 ] completed with status [ SUCCESS ].
...
apply Task [ Name: DeployInventoryAction_updateDeployInventory ID: 62 ] completed with
status [ SUCCESS ].
Tasks [5] completed out of [5].
Successfully completed execution of all tasks.

Generating the data fixes XML file.

Generated patch inventory file: /app/oracle/instance/lcm/faPatchInventory/
fusionAppsPatchHistory.xml

Generated patch inventory file: /app/oracle/fusionapps/applications/admin/
fusionAppsPatchHistory.xml
...
Oracle Fusion Applications Patch Manager completed successfully.
```

Monitoring the Patch Application Using Online Patch Progress Report

Until Fusion Applications 11g Release 9, the Online Patch Progress Report had to be run separately using the -patchprogress option in the Fusion Applications Patch Manager script. From version 11.1.9 until now, it is integrated into the Apply phase. As you can see in the Apply phase output shown previously, you may notice he following lines related to the Online Patch Progress Report or diagnostic report.

Diagnostic report is generated at /app/oracle/instance/lcm/logs/11.1.9.2.0/FAPMGR/
FAPMgrDiagnosticsSummary_apply_20150419203607.html. **This will be updated every 5 mins.**

During the current patch application session, the Online Patch Progress Report filename remains the same (FAPMgrDiagnosticsSummary_<Phase>_<Timestamp>.html), but this file is updated every five minutes. You can refresh the report file to see the current status of each task. Once the patch is complete, the same report is referred to as a diagnostic report. Note that these tasks are not same as workers in the AutoPatch tool.

Figure 16-9 shows an example of the Online Patch Progress Report for this example patch.

Module Phase Summary

Mode	Phase	Duration	Start Time	End Time	Task Count	Skipped	Failed	Completed	Percent Complete
Generic	Environment Validation	00:00:21.099	2015-04-16 01:06:13.079 [+05:30]	2015-04-16 01:06:34.178 [+05:30]	3	0	0	3	100.0
Generic	Pre Staging	00:00:00.831	2015-04-16 01:06:34.178 [+05:30]	2015-04-16 01:06:35.009 [+05:30]	1	0	0	1	100.0
Generic	Task Staging	00:00:01.828	2015-04-16 01:06:35.020 [+05:30]	2015-04-16 01:06:36.848 [+05:30]	1	0	0	1	100.0
Middleware	Patch Validation	00:00:11.119	2015-04-16 01:06:37.615 [+05:30]	2015-04-16 01:06:48.734 [+05:30]	2	0	0	2	100.0
Middleware	Patch Application	00:00:03.093	2015-04-16 01:06:48.954 [+05:30]	2015-04-16 01:06:52.047 [+05:30]	3	0	0	2	66.66667

Top

Failures, Errors and Warnings Summary

Mode	Phase	Product Family	Task	Status	Warning/Error Messages	Log File	Line Numbers

Top

Module Task Details

Mode	Phase	Product Family	Task	Status	Duration	Start Time	End Time	Warning/Error Messages	Log File	Line Numbers
Generic	Environment Validation	-	OPatch Version Validation	Success	00:00:00.409	2015-04-16 01:06:13.079 [+05:30]	2015-04-16 01:06:13.488 [+05:30]	-	FAPatchManager_apply_20150416010558.log	19-26
Generic	Environment Validation	-	DB Connection Validation	Success	00:00:18.705	2015-04-16 01:06:13.488 [+05:30]	2015-04-16 01:06:32.193 [+05:30]	-	FAPatchManager_apply_20150416010558.log	27-32
Generic	Environment Validation	-	Taxonomy URL Validation	Success	00:00:01.978	2015-04-16 01:06:32.200 [+05:30]	2015-04-16 01:06:34.178 [+05:30]	-	FAPatchManager_apply_20150416010558.log	33-38
Generic	Pre Staging	-	Prestaging tasks	Success	00:00:00.831	2015-04-16 01:06:34.178 [+05:30]	2015-04-16 01:06:35.009 [+05:30]	-	FAPatchManager_apply_20150416010558.log	41-46
Generic	Task Staging	-	Staging tasks	Success	00:00:01.819	2015-04-16 01:06:35.029 [+05:30]	2015-04-16 01:06:36.848 [+05:30]	-	FAPatchManager_apply_20150416010558.log	49-62
Middleware	Patch Validation	-	MW Validation	Success	00:00:07.961	2015-04-16 01:06:40.676 [+05:30]	2015-04-16 01:06:48.637 [+05:30]	-	FAPatchManager_apply_20150416010558.log	70-419
Middleware	Patch Validation	-	Staging	Success	00:00:02.247	2015-04-16 01:06:49.343 [+05:30]	2015-04-16 01:06:51.590 [+05:30]	-	FAPatchManager_apply_20150416010558.log	424-429
Middleware	Patch Application	-	Stop all Managed Servers	Success	00:02:41.332	2015-04-16 01:06:54.188 [+05:30]	2015-04-16 01:09:35.520 [+05:30]	-	fapcore_apply_jeepatchaction_stopmanagedserver	6-213
Middleware	Patch Application	-	Application of Bits	Success	00:00:15.066	2015-04-16 01:09:36.369 [+05:30]	2015-04-16 01:09:51.435 [+05:30]	-	fapcore_apply_offlinepatching_applybits_30_20	2-544

Top

Tasks Pending

Figure 16-9. *Example of an online patch progress report*

As you can see in Figure 16-9, the Patch Progress report shows a summary of the phase followed by any failures, errors, or warnings encountered during the current patch apply session. This is followed by detailed information on each phase, along with individual tasks within the phase. Next, it displays the list of pending tasks in the wait queue. Note that the diagnostic report that's created at the end of patch's Apply session does not include this last section of pending tasks.

Verifying the Applied Patch Status

Once the patch application is successful, you can run the Patch Status Report again to make sure that the patch has been applied and registered in the database and inventory.

```
[fusion@fahost bin]$ ./fapmgr.sh report -isapplied -patch 19898891
...
Started validating the OPatch version.
Completed validating the OPatch version.

Started validating the Database connection.
WLS ManagedService is not up running. Fall back to use system properties for configuration.
Completed validating the Database connection.

Report Name: Patch Status
Report for: FUSION [/app/oracle/fusionapps/applications]
```

```
Bug No. : 19898891:US
OUI Component : oracle.fusionapps.fin
Status : Applied
Patch No. : 19898891
Date Applied (mm-dd-yyyy hh:mm:ss) : 04-19-2015  20:39:01
...
Oracle Fusion Applications Patch Manager completed successfully.
```

Manually Applying Patches

Although you should use the Patch Automation tools as much as possible, sometimes you might be required to apply a specific patch using the traditional *OPatch* or *AutoPatch* utilities depending on whether the one-off is specific to Fusion Applications in a supported format for these utilities. Let's look at both of these utilities.

Manual Patching Using AutoPatch (adpatch.sh)

If you have managed an Oracle E-Business Suite (EBS) instance then you would already be aware of the AutoPatch (adpatch) utility. The AutoPatch utility is quite similar to Fusion Applications but in the case of Fusion Applications patching, you need to make sure to run adpatch.sh from APPL_TOP depending on the type of patch and impacted component. Each adpatch session can be monitored and partly controlled using a utility called the *AD Controller* (adctrl). First we will look at the directory structure of a generic patch followed by how to apply the same using adpatch utility. Later we will see how to monitor the patch progress using the adctrl utility.

Directory Structure of an Applications Core Patch

Before looking at how to apply a patch manually using AutoPatch, let's understand the structure of an Application core or Functional Setup Manager database artifacts-related patch. Such patches can be applied manually using AutoPatch (adpatch). Figure 16-10 shows an example directory structure of one such patch.

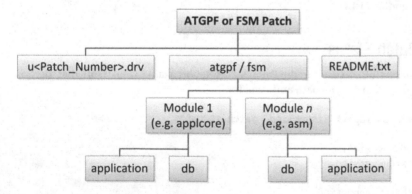

Figure 16-10. Structure of an ATGPF or functional setup manager patch

The Applications core patch looks very similar to an Oracle E-Business Suite patch. It contains a unified driver file named u<Patch_Number>.drv, which contains the list of database execution tasks as well as application artifacts copy and deployment steps. The README.txt file contains important information about prerequisites, installation steps, and whether manual post-patching steps are required.

Applying the Patch Using adpatch

Similar to EBS patches, which no longer have separate copy, database, and generate driver files because they have been replaced by unified driver, Fusion Applications artifacts-related patches also have a unified driver containing all required actions for the patch.

The adpatch utility can read the driver file to first determine any dependencies or pre-requisites for the patch. Next it compares the file versions of existing files with those included in the patch and determines whether the files need to be copied or no action needs to be taken. Before copying the files it makes a back up of the existing files being changed. After the copy portion is complete, it updates the required database objects and executes the included scripts. However, you must make full backup of file system and database before applying the patch since there is no direct rollback available for most patches. It is advisable to update the current view snapshot before applying any patch using adpatch for the first time to save time.

■ **Note** Note that AutoPatch utility is located at APPL_TOP/lcm/ad/bin/adpatch while the wrapper script is located at ATGPF_HOME/lcm/ad/bin/adpatch.sh. You must invoke the wrapper script adpatch.sh from ATGPF_HOME for applying an Applications core patch in order to detect the appropriate APPL_TOP. The same applies to the AD Controller utility, which is discussed next.

Use the following syntax to apply a patch using the adpatch utility interactively.

```
$ATGPF_HOME/lcm/ad/bin/adpatch.sh [patchtop=<Path_to_Patch_Dir] [driver=u<Patch_Number>.drv]
\ [workers=<number>]
```

By running the adpatch.sh script without an argument, AutoPatch will initiate an interactive session by prompting for each required parameter. You can select the patch top, number of workers, name of driver files, and so on, for the other parameter. You can change them at the prompt or leave them set to the default values. Alternatively, you can specify interactive=no at the command line and put all the required parameters in the defaults.txt file located at APPLICATIONS_CONFIG/atgpf/admin/.

Using the AD Controller to Monitor Patch Progress

During an ongoing adpatch session, you can monitor the progress of the patch using a utility named AD Controller (adctrl) from the same location from where the adpatch session was invoked. This utility is same as the one used for E-Business Suite patch monitoring. AD Controller can monitor the status of each worker, the task being performed by each worker, as well as control the status of the worked by restarting failed workers after reviewing the worker log file and resolving the underlying issue with the relevant database task execution. Although you can restart a failed worker using AD Controller, if you want to restart a failed adpatch session then you can run the adpatch.sh script with the restart=yes parameter.

Starting an AD Controller session requires the following. The script will prompt you to confirm or modify the APPL_TOP value. Make sure to enter ATGPF_HOME instead of the default APPL_TOP (FA_ORACLE_HOME).

```
[fusion@fahost bin]$ $ATGPF_HOME/lcm/ad/bin/adctrl.sh
...
Your default directory is '/app/oracle/fusionapps/atgpf'.
Is this the correct APPL_TOP [Yes] ?
...
```

```
Filename [adctrl.log] :
            Start of AD Controller session

AD Controller version: 11.1.9.2.0
...
```

Note that these selections will work only if there is an existing AutoPatch session going on and the FND_INSTALL_PROCESSES table has already been created. The following is the AD Controller menu along with a short description for each of the options.

AD Controller Menu

1. *Show worker status*: Lists the current status of each of the configured workers. The status could be Wait (default), Assigned, Running, Completed, Failed, Fixed, Restart, or Restarted, depending on status of the current task being handled by the worker process.

2. *Tell worker to restart a failed job*: If the assigned task (e.g. a SQL execution) for the worker failed or completed with an error then the worker status shows as FAILED. Review the log file for the specific worker, identify and resolve the underlying issue, and then manually instruct the worker to restart the failed job using this option.

3. *Tell worker to quit*: If the worker process has hung or has encountered some issue or if you want to shut down the workers or complete the manager process then you can use this option to stop one or more of the worker processes.

4. *Tell manager that a worker failed its job*: If you have to terminate a hung database session or any other spawned task manually then you can terminate the spawned process using OS commands first. Then you can inform the manager that a worker has failed its job to manually change the status to FAILED. Now you may proceed to either restart the job or terminate the worker using the next option if the worker process has also hung.

5. *Tell manager that a worker acknowledges quit*: If you have manually killed a worker process due to any specific issue then you must manually update the manager that the worker has quit and acknowledge it.

6. *Restart a worker on the current machine*: Once the worker process and all spawned processes for the specific worker have terminated, you can restart the worker on the machine. Make sure to clean up all the processes related to the worker before restarting the worker to avoid duplicate workers with the same ID.

7. *Exit*: Use this option to exit the AD Controller session. All worker processes continue to run and you can launch AD Controller again any time later if the patching or AD Administration session (to be discussed next) is still going on.

Manual Patching Using OPatch

At times you may need to apply a one-off patch to resolve specific issues related to Fusion middleware before the monthly P4FA patch has been released. In this case you may apply the patch manually using the traditional OPatch utility. The one-off patch might contain middleware artifacts for Fusion Applications Core or Functional Core.

You learned earlier how to apply OPatch so make sure to set the correct ORACLE_HOME and apply one or more patches using OPatch. The version of OPatch should match the OPatch in the Applications home directory. Alternatively you can use the OPatch binaries from FA_ORACLE_HOME/OPatch or APPL_TOP/OPatch and point the inventory from Oracle home to the product being patched.

Performing Maintenance Tasks

Apart from patching, as an administrator you are required to make sure that the application file system and database are in correct shape especially after maintenance activities like patching. Oracle Fusion Applications comes with a specialized utility called *AD Administration* (adadmin) to help you perform some of these maintenance activities effortlessly. Some of the tasks are required to be performed on a regular basis, a few tasks can be invoked by other utilities, and the rest of the tasks are invoked on a demand basis. We will have a quick overview of the features of AD Administration utilities and the major tasks you will need to do often during day-to-day administration of a Fusion Applications environment.

Using AD Administration Utility

Similar to AutoPatch, AD Administration also can help you work with both Applications Core as well as Fusion Applications Homes depending on where the utility has been invoked. You also can do this by manually overriding the APPL_TOP parameter value. You need to use the wrapper script adadmin.sh, which internally calls the adadmin utility from Fusion Applications Oracle home by setting the appropriate parameters and command line-arguments. Selecting the appropriate APPL_TOP helps you maintain the application files snapshot accordingly.

Use the following commands to invoke the AD Administration utility. If you look at the prompts in the truncated output, notice that it first confirms the correct APPL_TOP followed by prompting for the adadmin log filename, batch size, database details, and so on. You may choose to leave the values to the defaults or change as per your environment and logging requirements.

```
[fusion@fahost   ~]$ cd $APPL_TOP/lcm/ad/bin
```

Or

```
[fusion@fahost   ~]$ cd $ATGPF_HOME/lcm/ad/bin
[fusion@fahost bin]$ ./adadmin.sh
...
...
Your default directory is '/app/oracle/fusionapps/applications'.
Is this the correct APPL_TOP [Yes] ?

AD Administration records your AD Administration session in a text file
you specify.  Enter your AD Administration log file name or press [Return]
to accept the default file name shown in brackets.

Filename [adadmin.log] :

            Start of AD Administration session

AD Administration version: 11.1.9.2.0
...
Log level = NOTIFICATION:1.
Please enter the batchsize [1000] :

Applications System Name [FUSION] : FUSION *
```

```
Do you currently have files used for installing or upgrading the database
installed in this APPL_TOP [Yes] ? Yes *

Do you currently have Java and HTML files for HTML-based functionality
installed in this APPL_TOP [Yes] ? Yes *

Do you currently have Oracle Fusion Applications forms files installed
in this APPL_TOP [Yes] ? Yes *

Do you currently have concurrent program files installed
in this APPL_TOP [Yes] ? Yes *

APPL_TOP Name [FUSION] : FUSION *
You are about to use or modify Oracle Fusion Applications product tables
in your ORACLE database 'fusiondb'
using ORACLE executables in '/app/oracle/dbclient'.

Is this the correct database [Yes] ?
...
Reading AD_LANGUAGES to see what is currently installed.
Currently, the following language is installed:

Code    Language                             Status

US      American English                     Base

Your base language will be AMERICAN.
...
```

The following is the AD Administration main menu, which may look familiar to those who have managed Oracle E-Business Suite applications. However, the main tasks in the menu are less than the one in EBS because the standardization of application development interface. There are only a few Administration tasks in AD Administration that you may need to do regularly as compared to the traditional application suite.

```
AD code level : [11.1.1.5.1]

          AD Administration Main Menu
     ---------------------------------------------------

    1.    Maintain snapshot information

    2.    Maintain Applications Database Entities menu

    3.    Exit AD Administration

Enter your choice [3] : 1
```

Let's look at the administrative tasks that can be performed using each of these options in the AD Administration main menu.

Maintaining Snapshot Information

We have seen the important role that snapshots play while applying patches since snapshots contain a virtual image of the complete Applications file system at any given point of time. This includes information about every file that's supplied by Oracle as part of Applications Suite with version headers and does not include C binaries and log files. Although at the database level, Oracle keeps track of every file that was ever introduced at the Fusion Applications file system level, the snapshots only include the list of files present at the time of snapshot. Any new or modified files are not included in that specific snapshot.

We can have two types of snapshots—Current View Snapshot and Named Snapshot. As the names suggest, the Current View Snapshot should be updated every time there is a change in the Oracle provided application files to keep a current inventory of files at any point of time. The Named Snapshots are created at a specific point in time and are never updated. However, these snapshots compare the Oracle homes at different points in time or with different instances. You can create, delete, export, or import snapshots as well.

Let's look at the list of options in the Maintain Snapshot Information menu.

Maintain Snapshot Information

1. *List snapshots*: Use this option to list all the existing snapshots for each Applications file system. For example:

```
List of snapshots :

Snapshot ID  Name           APPL_TOP     Applications System
-----------  -------------  --------     -------------------
    1        CURRENT_VIEW   ATGPF        FUSION
    1001     CURRENT_VIEW   FUSION       FUSION
```

2. *Update current view snapshot*: Use this option to refresh the current view snapshot for the selected APPL_TOP. If you want to update the current view snapshot for a different APPL_TOP then you need to exit and restart adadmin using other APPL_TOP.

3. *Create named snapshot*: Use this option to create a named snapshot for the selected Application home. Once it's complete, this snapshot will be added to the list of snapshots.

4. *Export snapshot to file*: You can specify an output file to export a snapshot from a list of available snapshots for review or future import purpose.

5. *Import snapshot from file*: This option allows you to select a snapshot export file and update relevant snapshot database tables based on the file.

6. *Delete named snapshot(s)*: If you no longer require any old named snapshot then you can delete them using this option.

Database Tables Associated with Snapshots

All the snapshots related information is stored in the relevant database tables and if there are any issues with AD Administration utility, you can manually validate the details at the database level as well. The following are the important tables related to snapshots.

- *Snapshots-related tables*

  - AD_SNAPSHOTS: This table contains the list of all snapshots including current as well as named snapshots.

  - AD_SNAPSHOT_FILES: This table contains the list of every file included in the specific snapshot. Note that the list of files can vary across snapshots if some files were created or removed at any point.

- *Individual files-related tables*

  - AD_FILES: This table includes a record for each application file that was ever part of any snapshot. Even if a file was deleted later, the entry from this table is not removed for historical purposes and mapping with previous named snapshots.

  - AD_FILE_VERSIONS: This table includes every version for each file. Each file can have one or more entries in this table depending on how many times it was changed.

- *Bugs- and patches-related tables*

  - AD_SNAPSHOT_BUGFIXES: This table records the list of patches applied at the time of snapshot creation or update.

  - AD_BUGS: We saw this table earlier during patching and this table gets updated every time the patch has been applied and the current view snapshot is updated.

Maintaining Applications Database Entities

For a proper functioning of Fusion Applications it is essential that the database objects are always valid and appropriate grants, synonyms exist in order to allow required access to business objects. A DBA could manually check such integrity of database but it is always recommended to let the Fusion Applications AD Administration utility validate it based on the expected database structure. Even though you can compile the invalid objects manually, you should use the Compile Invalid Objects menu option in AD Administration since it takes care of compiling prerequisite dependency objects first followed by the dependent objects in order to maintain integrity of the database.

You should regularly do health checks of database objects using AD Administration in addition to your regular database administration activities. Especially if the required grants or synonyms are missing, regular database queries may not be able to determine that if it has not caused any invalids. The AD Administration utility can validate them based on built-in rules.

Let's look at the options available in the Maintain Applications Database Entities menu.

Maintain Applications Database Entities

1. *Compile Invalid Objects*: When you apply large patches or perform migration, a number of objects can become invalid. You can use this option to compile any Fusion Applications related invalid objects. This option first internally executes the $APPL_TOP/lcm/ad/db/sql/adutlrcmp.sql script to compile all invalid objects in database. Then it generates a list of all invalid objects in the FUSION schema and runs the $APPL_TOP/lcm/ad/db/sql/adallinvobj.sql script against the FUSION schema to compile those objects. After compilation is complete, it generates HTML reports for any pending invalid objects that could not be compiled at the following location.

   `<INSTANCE_TOP>/lcm/logs/<verision>/FAPMGR/adadmin_prepatch_invalidobjects.html`

2. *Health Check*: The next important option in the Maintain Applications Database Entities menu is Database Health Check. Ideally this task should precede invalid objects compilation since the report generated by Health Check option lists the invalid objects in a database that may require you to run the previous task Compile Invalid Objects. As you can see in Figure 16-11, the database Health Check report runs the script $APPL_TOP/lcm/ad/db/sql/adhlcheck.sql and generates the report with a list of important deviations in terms of system- or object-level privileges, current list of invalid objects, and so on. This report is generated at **<INSTANCE_TOP>/lcm/logs/<verision>/FAPMGR/ad_health_check_report.html**. Based on this report you may need to run other adadmin tasks, such as Compile Invalid Objects, Re-Create Grants for FUSION Schema, or any manual activities.

Health Check Report of the database as of 23-Apr-2015 13:59:16

FUSION PRIVILEGES REPORT					
Action	Grantee	Privilege		Admin	Reason
GRANT PRIVILEGES	FUSION	EXECUTE ANY PROCEDURE		NO	Privilege needed

DYNAMIC DDL SUPPORT REPORT				
Action	Owner	Object Name	Object Type	Reason

DYNAMIC PRIVILEGES REPORT				
Action	Grantee	Privilege	Admin	Reason

INVALID OBJECTS REPORT				
Action	Owner	Object Type	Count	Reason
DROP	FUSION_DYNAMIC	SYNONYM	17	Synonym(s) invalid or refer to non-existent tables
DROP	SYS	SYNONYM	1	Synonym(s) invalid or refer to non-existent tables

Figure 16-11. *Health check report of Fusion applications database*

3. *Re-create grants for FUSION schema*: This option ensures the required grants for FUSION schema objects and ensures that necessary roles are assigned to the FUSION_RUNTIME schema.

4. *Maintain multi-lingual tables*: Since Oracle Fusion Applications supports multi-lingual tables, for each base table there is a corresponding table with the _TL postfix. Based on the active languages installed on the Fusion Applications environment, there must be a corresponding record in these tables for each record of translation-enabled tables. This procedure prompts for selecting from the list of languages for which you want to synchronize the missing language transaction records to MLS (Multi-Lingual Support) tables. This task should *not* be run on a regular basis since it is executed automatically whenever a new language gets installed. You may run this task manually only when you have a valid justification and confirmation from support team that the data needs synchronization.

■ **Tip**   While you're responding to the prompts during any of the selected tasks and you want to exit AD Administration utility, answer the prompt with the abort value instead of pressing CTRL+C to cleanly exit the utility.

Backup and Restore

Backup is one of the most essential tasks for an administrator regardless of whether you are managing database, applications, middleware, storage, or operating systems. Since Fusion Applications comprises multiple technology stack components and various code artifacts, backing up a Fusion Applications environment includes multiple backup methods and strategies. You must consider the complete list of components and servers in your instance topology, including Identity Management and Fusion Applications database, application, directory, web servers, and file servers, if any. You must have regular online backup strategies as well as ad hoc offline backup strategies. Having well documented backup policies is essential for a Fusion Applications environment. This also helps to reduce time when recovering or restoring specific component or complete environment.

■ **Note** It is recommended to keep copies of the backup on different hosts, devices, or mount points than those where any of the Fusion Applications components are hosted.

When you are planning Fusion Applications backup strategy, you must consider the following components for each online (hot) and offline (cold) backup policies.

- Database components
- Middleware components
- Fusion Applications product directories
- Oracle software inventory specific files

Types of Files to Be Backed Up

Before looking at strategies of backup and restore, it is essential to understand the types of files in the Fusion Applications environment that you need to back up. Depending on the type of the files you may be able to decide whether they require regular backup or ad hoc. This list is generic and applies to both Fusion Applications as well as Identity Management tier nodes. Note that this is generic list and any custom directories, code, or other artifacts created in your environment for third-party integration or any other purpose should be taken care of in addition to this list.

Applications, Web, and Directory Tier

We will begin by looking at the file system of application, web and directory tiers that contain Fusion middleware components-related home directories and configuration files. It is possible that you may include these files from each tier in separate backup groups or policies but the underlying classification remains the same. We can mainly classify these files in two main categories based on the frequency of change, static files, and configuration files. Let's look at which directories are a part of each of these types.

Static Files

Certain files on applications as well as web tier do not change frequently; hence, we call them *static files*. However, the term *static* is only relative since they are not always static in nature. So you need to take backup of these files when we are applying any changes to these files. Let's look at which files are considered static in a Fusion Applications environment.

- *Oracle key common files*
    - *oraInst.loc file*: This file is located at /etc on the Linux Operating System and at /var/opt/oracle for Solaris. The file contains the pointer to current inventory directory location. Oracle Installer refers to this location for identifying the local inventory directory. This file should not change in normal circumstances.
    - *beahomelist file*: This file is located at the $HOME/bea location, where $HOME refers to the middleware owner user's home directory. This file contents the list of Middleware homes on the Application Server nodes.

- *Oracle Software Inventory*: The inventory directory is generally located at the middleware owner user's home directory unless a different directory was specified during installation. For example, /home/fusion/oraInventory. You can verify the location of the correct inventory directory in the oraInst.loc file, as explained. This directory contains list of all Oracle software installed along with the home directories and versions of each installed component.

- *Applications Base*: This is the root directory specified at the time of installation. This directory contains various important subdirectories, including middleware home (for both application and web tiers). For example, /app/oracle.

  - *Middleware Home*: This is the home directory for all Fusion middleware components. It also contains other Oracle homes, including Fusion Applications home, Oracle Common, and so on. It mainly contains the binary files that are generally static in nature unless a patch is applied. For example, /app/oracle/fusionapps.

  - *Fusion Applications Home (on FA nodes only)*: This is the root directory for all Fusion Applications Product Families and standalone products. This includes J2EE code, executables, templates, and so on, related to each product. For example, /app/oracle/fusionapps/applications.

  - *DB Client Home (on FA nodes only)*: This directory contains the Oracle Client to be used by the middleware components. As of Fusion Applications 11g Release 9, it contains the 11gR1 client to connect to the 11gR2 database. For example, /app/oracle/dbclient.

Configuration Files

Configuration files are generally specific to the node or instance and can be edited for various reasons including performance tuning, changing logging levels, adding or removing managed servers in cluster, parameter changes, and many other reasons. Although changing these files might not have affect until you restart, it is best practice to make a backup of these files before and after any such change. The following are some of the examples of directories containing Configuration files.

- *Applications Configuration Directory*: This directory contains topology-specific domains directories and directories for instances of individual middleware components. For example, /app/oracle/instance.

  - *Domains directory*: This directory contains individual sub-directories for each domain containing the configuration files, startup/shutdown related wrapper scripts, admin server, and managed servers configuration, startup parameters, and so on. For example, /app/oracle/instance/domains/<hostname>.

  - *Middleware component instances*: The application configuration directory also contains subdirectories for individual instances of middleware components like BI, ESS, and so on.

Database Tier

There are several ways a database tier backup can be taken, depending on the type of infrastructure, storage, disaster recovery setup, and existing database backup policies. In this section, we will only look at the file system backup for database binaries and configuration files.

Static Files

- *Oracle Key Common Files*

    - oratab: This directory exists on all servers but in recent versions it is mainly used by Oracle Database hosts. This includes information about the list of Oracle databases configured on the host along with home directory and automatic startup flags.

    - oraInst.loc: As discussed in the previous section, this directory contains location pointers for the Oracle Inventory directory.

- *Oracle Software Inventory*: Contains the central inventory directory for all Oracle software on the host.

- *ORACLE_HOME Directory*: This is the Oracle home directory for the database server software and includes required binary files.

- *GRID_HOME directory (for RAC)*: This is the home directory for the Oracle Clusterware software and includes required binary files.

Configuration Files

- *TNS_ADMIN directory*: This directory contains important network configuration files such as tnsnames.ora, listener.ora, sqlnet.ora, and so on.

- *ORACLE_HOME/dbs directory*: This directory contains configuration files like parameter files, password files, optional SPFILEs, and so on. Although any changes in these files are not reflected without restarting, these files could be modified online and must be backed up before changed.

- *Oracle Cluster Registry files (for RAC)*: In case of Oracle RAC, you may need to take backups of important shared files like OCR, voting disks (included in OCR backup from 11gR2), and so on.

Backing Up the Fusion Applications Environment

Let's discussed two main types of strategies for backing up a Fusion Applications environment, namely offline and online backups. Depending on whether your organization uses an Enterprise Backup Management suite, you may configure these backups to run as scheduled or on an on-demand basis. The backup frequency and retention period should match your organization's backup policy, especially if there are any internal or legal requirements for retaining backup for a specific period of time.

■ **Note**   You can also back up and restore the Fusion Applications environment using a simple interface of Enterprise Manager Cloud control, but it requires Oracle Secure Server configuration. Also, all the nodes in the selected topology must be configured as secure backup clients.

Offline Backup

It is recommended to take offline backups before and after performing critical activities, including applying large bundle patches, upgrades, migrations, or OS upgrades that already involve an approved downtime. Offline backups are always consistent and the restoration is quick and generally error-free as compared to online backups. You can use the Enterprise Backup Suites used by your organization or use manual file backup by creating a tar backup at the OS level and moving the files to a secure location.

As the name suggests, while taking offline backups, the application must be offline and not accessible by any users or background processes. All services must be shut down before initiating an offline backup. If you are planning to take a cold backup of your database, shut down the databases as well. Let's look at what files need to be backed up as part of an offline backup.

Application, Web, and Directory Tier

Shut down all application and web servers and take a back up of all the static files, including key Oracle files, middleware-related binary files, and configuration file-related directories. You can create a single tar backup for each top-level directory since the subdirectories will be included. While restoring you can select complete or partial archives to be restored. For example, if you take an Applications base cold backup, you need not take a Fusion Applications Oracle home backup but you can still restore partial backup from the tar file later.

Database Tier

While talking offline backups for your environment, it may require the database also to be offline to make sure that it's not being accessed and that no background jobs are running. However, depending on your organization policy you may want to take a complete cold backup or hot backup by making sure no transactions are happening on the database. Ideally, cold backups are required when you need to perform a complete restore in case of a failure. Restoring an offline database backup is much quicker as compared to online backups since it involves restoring the physical database files and the Oracle home and does not require recreating indexes that otherwise consume a lot of time. The disadvantage of database cold backup is that the restore is always full and you cannot restore specific objects. However, while performing mission-critical activities like upgrade or migration, it is mandatory to take cold or offline backup to revert back to the original state in the shortest possible time.

In order to take a database offline backup, you need to back up the ORACLE_HOME directory as well as the database files (data files, redo logs, and control files), the grid infrastructure home (in the case of RAC), and the cluster registry files (in the case of RAC).

Online Backup

We read that offline backups need to be taken on a demand basis when you are performing critical activities that include changes in static as well as configuration files. But in order to achieve the highest recoverability, you must schedule regular backups of all configuration files that are generally not static. Such online backups must be done at least once daily when you do not expect any configuration related changes, preferably at night or at a time suitable per your organization's policy. In addition to this whenever an administrator is making changes to configuration files or through Enterprise Manager Console, an online backup must be taken before and after the change. The same applies when you are applying patches that do not require offline backups but involve post-steps that affect the application configuration files, so you could take online backup before and/or after the patching activity. Let's look at which files need to be backed up during an online backup.

Application, Web, and Directory Tier

Since online backups are taken only when you are expecting configuration related changes, you need not take backup of static files. You can schedule online backups the of Configuration directory on both Identity Management as well as Fusion Applications nodes. You can either create shell scripts to create tar backups of these files and copy them to secure external locations or use your enterprise backup software to configure backup of the selected directories every night or another scheduled time. Whenever you need to take an on-demand online backup, you can rerun the scripts manually or run online backup through your organization's enterprise backup tool.

Database Tier

Online backup of Oracle Database can be done through RMAN as well as data pump export backup of the entire database. You can either select a full or incremental backup for RMAN. Since the newer versions of Oracle database (12c onward) will support fine-grained recovery, including individual tables or objects, it is advisable to move to catalog-based RMAN backups for online backup instead of export data pump backups for possible partial recovery.

For file system backups on the database tier, you should back up the configuration file-related directories, including TNS_ADMIN, ORACLE_HOME/dbs, Oracle Cluster Registry (OCR) files. If password files and/or SPFILEs are stored in a shared location, those directories also should be backed up as part of an online backup.

Take a consolidated view of all these directories, their backup types, and their mappings in a single diagram. Figure 16-12 shows the static as well as configuration directories for Fusion Applications and Identity Management nodes and classifies the files based on the suggested inclusions in online and offline backup.

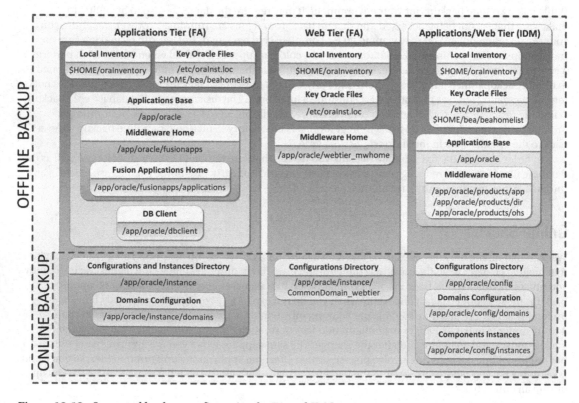

Figure 16-12. *Suggested backup configuration for FA and IDM components*

Restoring Fusion Applications Environment

The purpose of a sound backup strategy is to make sure that you have the required files available if there's an accidental loss or a failed maintenance activity, a business request, or any other justifiable reason. Depending on the situation you may need to recover the file system to as recent state as possible or restore it to a specific point in time backup. With enterprise backup solutions or storage based replication solutions, you can recover until near no loss state but here we will look at how to recover or restore the application from the backups we have discussed here.

Complete Restore

Complete Restore is one of the simplest and straightforward methods of restoring the file system. All you need to do is restore the offline backup and restore the backdated consistent full file system backup. The next step should be to replace the configuration files using the latest online backup to apply the latest changes on the old consistent backup. Another alternative is to restore the static directories from the latest offline backup and then restore the configuration directories from the latest online backup. We will see a partial restore in the next section of partial restore. Figure 16-13 summarizes the complete restore option in a typical scenario.

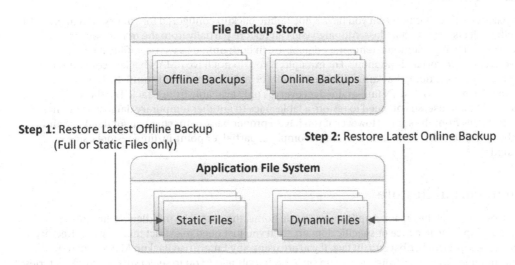

Figure 16-13. *Typical file system full restore scenario*

A typical scenario for a Complete restore is when you are applying major patches to an application or OS level and your go-live decision is based on complete success. If there's a failure you may want to go back to an earlier state with complete restore. Other than that, if there's a storage issue or a disk crash and your file system is lost completely or partially, you may want to perform a complete restore of the static configuration files considering your configuration files are not changed since the last online backup.

■ **Note** You may not need to restore the database in many cases even if you are performing a full restore of the application file systems. For example, if you had file system loss due to a storage issue, you may only want to restore the file system without rolling back any database transactions. If a major patch bundle fails, you might need to do database restore as well. Depending on scenario you might need to take a decision on whether database restore is required.

Partial Restore

Since complete restore is required only in a disaster situation or major activity fail that forces you to completely roll back the changes. In most cases you may need to recover only part of the file system or database depending on the issue or business request. Although you can take a separate backup for individual directories, technically you do not need to do this and the method described previously to take top-level directory backup is sufficient only to restore any subdirectories beneath them.

Database Partial Restore

In case of a partial restore, it is best that you have a hot/online backup configured for your system in order to restore specific objects without data loss. Although you can restore partially from the offline backup (static tables) as well using additional temporary databases, in both online as well as offline backup scenarios, you may have certain limitations. For example, if you do not have RMAN backup configured and you have only daily export dump backup available, you may be able to restore only until the last export dump backup. Also in case of RMAN fine-grained recovery is only available from Oracle Database 12c onward, for 11gR2 database, so you need to restore a tablespace to another temporary database and then export specific tables from the same. However, if you have a proper backup mechanism for database and archive log backups, you should be able to perform complete, partial, or point-in-time restore using on several methods.

File System Partial Restore

If you want to restore only the Fusion Applications Oracle home, the complete middleware home, applications base, specific instance or specific domain, then you just need to extract the relevant directory structure from the top-level tar backup. In fact, if you are using any Enterprise Backup Management tool then you may not need to restore from tar backup since such tools allow you to select specific subdirectories or files from the list of earlier backups on disk or tapes.

Let's take an example of partial restore from a top-level directory tar backup. For example, you need to restore only Fusion Applications Oracle home from the last offline backup. Since you already have backup of an Applications base directory /app/oracle as oracle_<date>.tar, you can simply run the following command by specifying the base directory from where you want to restore the files, which in this case is oracle/fusionapps/applications.

```
[fusion@fahost ~]$ cd /app
[fusion@fahost app]$ tar -xvf oracle_25042015.tar oracle/fusionapps/applications
oracle/fusionapps/applications/
...
oracle/fusionapps/applications/common/
oracle/fusionapps/applications/common/templates/
oracle/fusionapps/applications/common/templates/applications/
```

```
oracle/fusionapps/applications/common/templates/applications/oracle.apps.prc.
SupplierPortalServer_template.jar
...
```

After this partial restore, the rest of the files will remain unaffected. Make sure to shut down all components that may be using the files being restored before starting the restore activity. Once restore is complete, start these components and validate that everything is running as expected and make sure the issue for which restore was initiated has been resolved. After the restore is complete and the application test is successful, you must create another backup as soon as possible in order to prepare a baseline backup.

Summary

Although this concludes the important list of day-to-day administrative tasks being covered in this book, Fusion Applications administration may involve efforts from various other teams. When your role overlaps with other teams like the IT security team, Identity Management consultants, and application development teams, the overall administration may include advanced tasks that not have been discussed here. This chapter gives you an overview of the installation and ongoing administration tasks for managing a Fusion Applications environment.

In this chapter you learned about some of the regular activities in the Fusion Applications administrator's role. The chapter started with understanding the types of patches that exist for the complete Fusion Applications environment, including Fusion middleware as well the applications artifacts. Following that, you saw the types of patching methods available for each of the different types of patches. You saw multiple ways of applying an applications or middleware patch, including manual applications as well as using patch-automation utilities.

Later you saw how to preform regular maintenance tasks related to the Applications file system and database using AD Administration. You should now know that you can maintain the integrity of the Fusion Applications instance using the adadmin utility. You learned how to use the AD Control utility to monitor the progress of various AD utilities.

Finally, you learned about the recommended practices for backup and restore of the complete Fusion Applications environment. You explored the classification of files based on the frequency of change and learned to best prepare a backup strategy according to each file type. You also learned about the relationship between restore and recovery of file systems based on specific scenarios and learned how to perform full or partial restores in the shortest possible time.

Index

Printed in the United States
By Bookmasters